Syed Hussein Alatas and Critical Social Theory

Studies in
Critical Social Sciences

Series Editor
David Fasenfest (*Wayne State University*)

Editorial Board
Eduardo Bonilla-Silva (*Duke University*)
Chris Chase-Dunn (*University of California–Riverside*)
William Carroll (*University of Victoria*)
Raewyn Connell (*University of Sydney*)
Kimberlé W. Crenshaw (*University of California, Los Angeles/
Columbia University*)
Raju Das (*York University*)
Heidi Gottfried (*Wayne State University*)
Karin Gottschall (*University of Bremen*)
Alfredo Saad-Filho (*King's College London*)
Chizuko Ueno (*University of Tokyo*)
Sylvia Walby (*Lancaster University*)

VOLUME 233

The titles published in this series are listed at *brill.com/scss*

Syed Hussein Alatas and Critical Social Theory

Decolonizing the Captive Mind

Edited by

Dustin J. Byrd
Seyed Javad Miri

BRILL

LEIDEN | BOSTON

Cover illustration: Syed Hussein Alatas in his office library at the National University of Singapore in the early 1980s. Courtesy of Syed Farid Alatas.

The Library of Congress Cataloging-in-Publication Data is available online at https://catalog.loc.gov
LC record available at https://lccn.loc.gov/2022043642

Typeface for the Latin, Greek, and Cyrillic scripts: "Brill". See and download: brill.com/brill-typeface.

ISSN 1573-4234
ISBN 978-90-04-52168-1 (hardback)
ISBN 978-90-04-52169-8 (e-book)

Copyright 2023 by Dustin J. Byrd and Seyed Javad Miri. Published by Koninklijke Brill NV, Leiden, The Netherlands.
Koninklijke Brill NV incorporates the imprints Brill, Brill Nijhoff, Brill Hotei, Brill Schöningh, Brill Fink, Brill mentis, Vandenhoeck & Ruprecht, Böhlau, V&R unipress and Wageningen Academic.
Koninklijke Brill NV reserves the right to protect this publication against unauthorized use. Requests for re-use and/or translations must be addressed to Koninklijke Brill NV via brill.com or copyright.com.

This book is printed on acid-free paper and produced in a sustainable manner.

This book is dedicated to the Egyptian sociologist, Mona Abaza, who succumbed to cancer in Berlin in July of 2021. Her indominable spirit lives on in the many books and articles she wrote, but more importantly, it lives in the many lives she shaped through her teaching and through the powerful presence she had wherever she was

∴

Contents

Acknowledgements XI
Notes on Contributors XII

Introduction 1
   Dustin J. Byrd and Seyed Javad Miri

PART 1
Alatas' Work and Legacy

1   Developing a School of Autonomous Knowledge
    Thoughts of the Late Syed Hussein Alatas   9
      Syed Imad Alatas

2   The Midlife of an Idea
    Syed Hussein Alatas' Captive Mind after Fifty Years   22
      Masturah Alatas

PART 2
Theorizing the Captive Mind

3   Alatas on Colonial and Autonomous Knowledge   53
      Syed Farid Alatas

4   The Psychological Dynamics of Mental Captivity
    Subsequent Conceptual Developments   77
      Dustin J. Byrd

5   The Cartography of Reception of 'The Captive Mind' in Iran   94
      Esmaeil Zeiny

6   "The Captive Mind" and Social Sciences in Southeast Asia
    Syed Hussein Alatas   115
      Mona Abaza

7   The Captive Mind Syndrome in Indian Sociology   143
      N. Jayaram

8   Psychological Feudalism
     Malay Political Culture and Responses towards Modernization   168
        Norshahril Saat

9   "Irrational" Beliefs in a "Rational" World
     Religion and Modernization   189
        Hira Amin

PART 3
Mythologizing and Demythologizing the Native

10   Demythologizing Dominant Discourses
     Syed Hussein Alatas' The Myth of the Lazy Native *and the Discourse on Malay Cultural Values and Underdevelopment*   211
        Zawawi Ibrahim

11   Syed Hussein Alatas
     Colonialism and Modernity   246
        Joseph Alagha and Mostafa Soueid

12   The Invention of "Islam"
     How (Lazy) Historians and Social Scientists Created a Fantasy   261
        Carimo Mohomed

PART 4
Alatas and the Socio-political

13   Syed Hussein Alatas and the Question of Intellectuals   309
        Seyed Javad Miri

14   West-Centric Geopolitical Discourse
     Situating Syed Hussein Alatas in International Relations   336
        Sharifah Munirah Alatas

15   Alatas
     Pioneer in the Study of, and the Struggle against, Corruption   357
        Chandra Muzaffar

CONTENTS

16 Syed Hussein Alatas and the Question of Political Thought 376
Teo Lee Ken

17 Contributions of Syed Hussein Alatas towards Global Sociology 395
Habibul Haque Khondker

18 East-West Interactions and Complexities
Syed Hussein Alatas, Willem Wertheim and Edward Said 420
Victor T. King

19 Hidden Connections
Syed Hussein Alatas and Latin American Sociology 455
João Marcelo E. Maia

Index 469

Acknowledgements

First, we would like to acknowledge the many contributors to this edited volume. Without their meticulous and important work on Syed Hussein Alatas, we would be impoverished in terms of our knowledge of his revolutionary intellect and his lasting legacy. Although Syed Hussein Alatas is the repertoire of wisdom from which we have drawn in this work, it is with these scholars, from all parts of the world, that Alatas' work is preserved, elevated, and expanded upon for generations to come. We would like to thank Jamie Groendyk for all her assistance in preparing the manuscript for publication, as well as the editorial and production staff at Brill, who make academic publishing an enjoyable experience. We would especially like to thank Dr. David Fasenfest, the *Studies in Critical Social Sciences* series editor, who has supported our work by publishing this and our previous volumes on Malcolm X, Ali Shariati, and Frantz Fanon. We would also like to thank Olivet College, Michigan (USA) whose support of academic scholarship allows for the time and resources to do such work. Last, but not least, we would like to thank the Institute of Humanities and Cultural Studies in Tehran, Iran, for their continued support of our work on non-Eurocentric critical social theory.

Notes on Contributors

Mona Abaza

was born in Egypt. She obtained her Ph.D. in 1990 in sociology from the University of Bielefeld, Germany. Her last position was Professor of Sociology at the American University in Cairo. In 2009–2011, she was Visiting Professor of Islamology, Department of Theology, Lund University. She was a visiting scholar in Singapore at the Institute for South East Asian Studies (ISEAS 1990–1992), Kuala Lumpur 1995–1996, Paris (EHESS) 1994, Berlin (Fellow at the Wissenschaftskolleg 1996–1997), Leiden (IIAS, 2002–2003), Wassenaar (NIAS, 2006–2007) and Bellagio (Rockefeller Foundation, 2005). Professor Abaza died peacefully in Berlin on 5 July, 2021, after a long battle with cancer.

Joseph Alagha

teaches Political Science, Sociology, and Intercultural Studies at Haigazian University in Beirut, Lebanon. Employing the interdisciplinary social sciences and humanities approach, Alagha published four peer-reviewed university press books, two monographs, three books in Arabic, and more than one-hundred refereed publications in four language: English, Dutch, French, and Arabic. His research focuses on Critical Social Theory, minorities in the Middle East, family law, gender, violence against women, and human rights. He also specializes in Islam and popular culture; humor and the performing arts; philosophy of art and aesthetics; political mobilization; contemporary Islamic movements, as well as democratization and liberalization in the MENA region.

Masturah Alatas

is a Singapore-born Malaysian writer and teacher who has been living in Italy for thirty years. She is the author of the memoir-biography of Syed Hussein Alatas, *The Life in the Writing* (Marshall Cavendish, 2010). She is one of several writers along with Naomi Klein and Amitav Ghosh to be published in the *Will the Flower Slip Through the Asphalt: Writers Respond to Climate Change* (2017) anthology. She teaches English and translation at the University of Macerata in Italy.

Sharifah Munirah Alatas

is Assistant Professor in the Strategic Studies and International Relations Program at the National University of Malaysia. She earned her BA at the University of Oregon and an MA and doctorate from Columbia University. Her specialties are in geopolitics, strategic thought, and foreign policy. Alatas received the Fulbright Malaysian Scholars Fellowship (2021/2022) and is a member of the Executive Committee of the Academic Movement of Malaysia (GERAK). Prior to joining academia in 2003, Alatas' previous appointments include Director of Research and Publications, Institute of Diplomacy and Foreign Relations (IDFR), Malaysia, and Political Analyst/Research Fellow at the Institute of Strategic and International Studies (ISIS), Malaysia. She has published extensively in leading journals such as the *Asian Journal of Social Science*, the *Journal of South Asian Studies, African and Asian Studies Journal, Journal of the Indian Ocean Region, India Quarterly, Global Studies Quarterly*, and *Al Shajarah*. As a scholar and academic activist, Alatas contributes regularly to her op-ed columns in *Free Malaysia Today, Malaysiakini, Asian Defence Insights*, and the *Islamabad Policy Research Institute*. Her opinions on current affairs, politics, and regional higher education developments are regularly sought after by news portals such as *The Malaysian Insight* and *Times Higher Education*. Recurring themes in Alatas' scholarly and popular writings are West-centrism, intellectual imperialism, hegemony, academic dependency, and post- colonialism.

Syed Farid Alatas

is Professor of Sociology at the National University of Singapore (NUS). He is also appointed to the Department of Malay Studies at NUS and headed that department from 2007 to 2013. He lectured at the University of Malaya in the Department of Southeast Asian Studies prior to joining NUS. In the early 1990s, he was a Research Associate at the Women and Human Resources Studies Unit, Science University of Malaysia. Alatas has authored numerous books and articles, including *Ibn Khaldun* (Oxford University Press, 2013); *Applying Ibn Khaldun: The Recovery of a Lost Tradition in Sociology* (Routledge, 2014); and with Vineeta Sinha, *Sociological Theory Beyond the Canon* (Palgrave, 2017). Additionally, he published "The State of Feminist Theory in Malaysia," in *Feminism: Malaysian Reflections and Experience* (special issue of *Kajian Malaysia: Journal of Malaysian Studies*) 12, no. 1–2 (1994): 25–46, edited by Maznah Mohamad and Wong Soak Koon. His areas of interest are the sociology of Islam, social theory, religion and reform, intra- and inter-religious dialogue, and the study of Orientalism.

Syed Imad Alatas

is currently pursuing his Ph.D. in sociology at the University of North Carolina-Chapel Hill. His research interests include the sociology of religion, gender, and youth. His Masters' thesis at the National University of Singapore (NUS) focused on female Muslim NGOs in Malaysia and their discourses on women's roles and gender relations. Prior to commencing his Masters' studies, he worked at the Middle East Institute at NUS, where he oversaw the institute's publications and was in charge of the internship program. He has written on anti-Semitism in Malaysia and Indonesia and adolescent masculinities for the *Asia Pacific Social Science Review* and the *Southeast Asian Social Science Review*, respectively. Alatas also contributed a chapter on interfaith harmony to the book, *Budi Kritik* (Math Paper Press (BooksActually), 2019), a collection of essays on intellectual life, religion, ethnic identity, and the political activity of Malays in Singapore. Outside academia, he has written for Malaysian online publications such as Free Malaysia Today and the Malay Mail.

Hira Amin

is an Associate Professor and Post-doctorate Researcher of Islam and Global Affairs at the College of Islamic Studies, Hamad Bin Khalifa University, Qatar. She completed her Ph.D. in history at the University of Cambridge, focusing on transnational Muslim movements in the British context, and is currently developing this research for publication. As a post-doctorate researcher, she is part of a large, multi-disciplinary cluster project examining Sustainable Development and Global Citizenship education in Qatar.

Dustin J. Byrd

is a Professor of Philosophy and Religion at Olivet College, Michigan, USA. He holds a Ph.D. from Michigan State University, where he specialized in Political and Social Philosophy. He is also a Visiting Professor of Religious Studies at Michigan State University. His expertise is in the Frankfurt School, Critical Theory of Religion, Psychoanalytical Political Theory, and Contemporary Islamic Thought. He is the author of numerous monographs, including *The Frankfurt School and the Dialectics of Religion: Translating Critical Faith into Critical Theory* (Ekpyrosis Press, 2020); *Critical Theory of Religion: From the Frankfurt School to Emancipatory Islamic Thought* (Ekpyrosis Press, 2020); *Islam in a Post-Secular Society: Religion, Secularity, and the Antagonism of Recalcitrant Faith* (Brill, 2017), among others. Along with his longtime collaborator, Seyed Javad Miri, he has co-edited books on Malcolm X, Ali Shariati, and Frantz Fanon, all published with Brill. He is the founder and Editor-in-Chief of Ekpyrosis Press; the Editor-in-Chief of the journal *Islamic Perspective*, and the Founder and Co-Director of the Institute for Critical Social Theory.

Zawawi Ibrahim

is currently a Visiting Professor at Taylor's University, Malaysia. His was most recently Professor of Sociology and Anthropology at Universiti Brunei

Darussalam, Brunei. Working within the field of anthropology broadly understood, his wide-ranging research interests include youth, popular culture, storytelling and narratives, religious diversity, and multiculturalism. He is the author of *The Malay Labourer* (Institute of Southeast Asian Studies, 1995), and co-editor of *Human Insecurities in Southeast Asia* (Springer, 2016) and *Borneo Studies in History, Society and Culture* (Springer, 2017). He is a member of the EU-funded research project 'Radicalisation, Secularism, and the Governance of Religion: Bringing together European and Asian Perspectives' (2019–2021).

N. Jayaram

was born in Bangalore (now Bengaluru), South India. He obtained all his education in Bangalore: BA (1970) in Economics, Political Science, and Sociology from St. Joseph's College; MA (1972) and Ph.D. (1976) in Sociology from the Department of Sociology, Bangalore University. He has taught at Bangalore University, Goa University, and the Tata Institute of Social Sciences in Mumbai. He is presently a Visiting Professor at the National Law School of India University, Bangalore. He specializes in Sociology of Education, and has research interests in trans-disciplinary areas such as Theory and Method, Political Sociology, Urban Studies, and Sociology of Diaspora. He has written, edited, and adapted over twenty books.

Teo Lee Ken

is an independent researcher based in Kuala Lumpur. His research interests include comparative politics, sociology of knowledge and culture, and political history. He holds a Ph.D. in Malay Studies from the National University of Singapore (NUS), as well as an LLM (NUS) and an LLB from the Universiti Kebangsaan Malaysia (UKM). His areas of study now focus on intellectual thought and political narratives, and the influence of social thought and theory on civil action and social policy. Among his publications include "Islamic Feminist Political Narratives, Reformist Thought, and its Discursive Challenges in Contemporary Iran," co-author Afsaneh Tavassoli, in *Inter-Asia Cultural Studies* (2021) and "Usman Awang: Justice, Literature and Society," in *Revisiting Malaya: Uncovering Historical and Political Thoughts in Nusantara*, eds. Show Ying Xin and Ngoi Guat Peng (2020).

Habibul Haque Khondker

is a professor at the Department of Humanities and Social Sciences, Zayed University, Abu Dhabi, UAE. He obtained his Ph.D. from the University of Pittsburgh (1985). Among Khondker's publications are: *The Emergence of Bangladesh: Interdisciplinary Perspectives* (Springer, 2022) co-edited with Olav

Muurlink and Asif Ali. *Covid-19 and Governance* (Routledge 2021) co-edited with Jan Nederveen Pieterse and Harean Lim. *Globalization: East and West* (Sage, 2010) co-authored with Bryan Turner; *21st Century Globalization: Perspectives from the Gulf* (I.B. Tauris, 2010) (co-edited with Jan Nederveen Pieterse) and *Asia and Europe in Globalization* (Brill, 2006) (co-edited with Goran Therborn). He is the co-chair of Research Committee, Social Transformation and Sociology of Development of International Sociological Association.

Victor T. King

is Professor of Borneo Studies, Institute of Asian Studies, Universiti Brunei Darussalam; Emeritus Professor, School of Languages, Cultures and Societies, University of Leeds; Senior Editorial Advisor, Regional Center for Social Science and Sustainable Development, Faculty of Social Sciences, Chiang Mai University; and Visiting Professor, Korea Institute for ASEAN Studies, Busan University of Foreign Studies. He was formerly Executive Director of the East Asia Centre, Universities of Leeds and Sheffield (2006–2012), and Pro-Vice-Chancellor at the University of Hull (1998–2000). His research interests are in the sociology and anthropology of Southeast Asia. Among his recent publications are *UNESCO in Southeast Asia: World Heritage Sites in Comparative Perspective* (NIAS Press, 2016); and co-edited books on *Borneo Studies in History, Society and Culture* (Springer, 2017); *Origins, History and Social Structure in Brunei Darussalam* (Routledge, 2021), *Continuity and Change in Brunei Darussalam* (Routledge, 2021), *Discourses, Agency and Identity in Malaysia: Critical Perspectives* (Springer, 2021), *Fieldwork and the Self: Changing Research Styles in Southeast Asia* (Springer, 2021) and *The Routledge Handbook of Contemporary Brunei* (Routledge, 2021).

João Marcelo E. Maia

is an Associate Professor of Sociology in Fundação Getulio Vargas, Rio de Janeiro, Brazil. He leads the Social Thought Lab (LAPES) in FGV and is a member of the steering committee of the Research Committee on the History of Sociology (RC08) of the International Sociological Association (ISA). Maia's main research interests are history of sociology in the Global South, Brazilian social though and teaching sociology. His latest publication in English is the short text "Remote teaching and sociological reflexivity: a few insights from Brazil," published in ISA's Pedagogy Series (2021) He also co-authored (third author) with Fran Collyer (first author), Raewyn Connel and Robert Morrell the collective book *Knowledge and Global Power: Making New Sciences in the South* (Monash, 2018).

Seyed Javad Miri

is a Swedish-Iranian sociologist and Professor at the Institute for Humanities and Cultural Studies in Tehran, Iran. He is a specialist in Islamic social theory, inter-civilizational discourse, and contemporary Islamic thought. He has publisher numerous books and articles and is the founder of the journal *Islamic Perspective*.

Carimo Mohomed

is an independent researcher, born in 1973 in Mozambique, a Portuguese territory at the time. He graduated in History (1995) and obtained his doctorate in Political Theory and Analysis (2012), both from the Universidade Nova de Lisboa – Nova University of Lisbon. In between, he specialized in Library and Information Sciences (University of Lisbon, 2004), and in Islamic Cultures, Civilizations and Religion (National University of Distance Education, Spain, 2006). Based in Lisbon (Portugal), his main areas of interest have been the relationship between Religion and Politics in different cultural and civilizational contexts, past and present, which led him to the field of Political Theology; and the History of Political Ideas, especially in the Islamic world, with a particular focus on different theories of Justice, Authority, and Community, which led him to the field of Political Philosophy. He sits on the Editorial Board of the *International Journal of Islamic Thought*, the *Journal of Philosophy and Ethics*, the *Journal of Islamic Research*, and the *Annals of Global History*. He also serves as Executive Member of IPSA's Research Committee "RC43-Religion and Politics." Lately, he has also been working as a translator and writing several novels, short stories, and a politico-theosophical treatise on Cosmopolitanism.

Chandra Muzaffar

is the President of the International Movement for a Just World (JUST), an international NGO based in Malaysia, which seeks to critique global injustice and to develop an alternative vision of a just and compassionate civilization guided by universal spiritual and moral values. He has published extensively on civilizational dialogue, international politics, religion, human rights, and Malaysian society. The author and editor of thirty-two books in English and Malay, many of his writings have been translated into other languages. Among Muzaffar's latest publications are, *A World in Crisis: Is there a Cure?* (JUST, 2014) and *Reflections on Malaysian Unity and Other Challenges* (Zubedy Ideahouse, 2017). In 1977, he founded a multi-ethnic social reform group called Aliran Kesedaran Negara (ALIRAN), which he led for fourteen years. Muzaffar was Professor and Director of the Centre for Civilizational Dialogue at the

University of Malaya (1997–1999) and Professor of Global Studies at Universiti Sains Malaysia (2007–2012).

Norshahril Saat

is Senior Fellow at the ISEAS – Yusof Ishak Institute (Institute of Southeast Asian Studies, Singapore). He is Coordinator of the Regional Social and Cultural Studies (RSCS) Program. In June 2015 he was awarded his doctorate in International, Political and Strategic Studies by the Australian National University (ANU). He is the author of *The State, Ulama, and Islam in Malaysia and Indonesia* (Amsterdam University Press, 2017) and *Tradition and Islamic Learning: Singapore Students in the Al-Azhar University* (ISEAS Publishing, 2018); and *Islam in Southeast Asia: Negotiating Modernity* (ISEAS Publishing, 2018). His articles have been published in journals such as the *Hawwa: Journal of Women of the Middle East and the Islamic World, Asian Journal of Social Science, The Commonwealth Journal of International Affairs, Contemporary Islam: Dynamics of Muslim Life, Review of Indonesian and Malaysian Affairs,* and *Studia Islamika.*

Mostafa Soueid

is majoring in psychology at Haigazian University (HU), Beirut, Lebanon. He is an assistant to Dr. Joseph Alagha.

Esmaeil Zeiny

is an Assistant Professor of Literature and Cultural Studies, Xiamen University Malaysia. He was previously a Research Fellow at the Department of English Language and Literature at Kharazmi University, Iran, and the Institute of Malaysia and International Studies at the National University of Malaysia. He received his Ph.D. in Post-Colonial Literature in English from the National University of Malaysia. His areas of specialization include English literature, Sociology of Literature, Cultural Studies, Visual Culture, Diaspora Studies, and Political Theory.

Introduction

Dustin J. Byrd and Seyed Javad Miri

Syed Hussein Alatas was many things in his long life: a young man growing up in the Dutch East Indies, a student at the University of Amsterdam, a sociologist, a theorist of progressive Islam, political analyst, the Vice-Chancellor of the University of Malaya, a politician, and a founding member of the Malaysian People's Movement Party (*Parti Gerakan Rakyat Malaysia*). He is most known for his many books that laid the foundation for much of today's post-colonial thought, including: *The Sociology of Corruption* (1968), *Thomas Stamford Raffles: Schemer or Reformer* (1971), *Intellectuals in Developing Societies* (1977), *The Myth of the Lazy Native* (1977), *The Problem of Corruption* (1986), and *Corruption and the Destiny of Asia* (1999), among others. It is well known that the work of Syed Hussein Alatas influenced the Palestinian-American scholar, Edward Said, whose own famous 1978 book, *Orientalism*, acknowledges the debt Said owed to Alatas' *The Myth of the Lazy Native*. Said was impressed by Alatas' critique of the ideological image of the non-Western "other," which was imposed upon much of the world through European imperialism and colonialism. This wholly negative image of the world outside of Europe – that it was lazy, shiftless, irrational, backwards, and therefore calling out for Western guidance: the "White man's burden" – had to be undermined, as it justified the continual exploitation and abuse of the non-Western world, especially in the global south. Just as Edward Said deconstructed the "orientalist" ideology of the European masters, so too did Syed Hussein Alatas in regard to the Malay, Filipinos, and others who found themselves under the domination of Western empires.

Despite the similarities between Edward Said and Syed Hussein Alatas, Alatas remains little known outside of certain academic and political circles in Southeast Asia. Among Southeast Asian academics, he is an intellectual giant, one that has had an immense influence on philosophy, sociology, cultural studies, religious studies, etc. Yet, although much of his corpus of work has been translated into Western languages, including English, it is hard to find his writings as required reading with Western academia. Whereas Edward Said's work is widely recognized as foundational in post-colonial thought and the "decolonization" movement, Alatas' work remains neglected. Much like so many other brilliant social theorists from the lands of "darker people," he has been relegated to the provinces – seen as someone whose analyses have no bearing on the metropoles and the Western world at large. This volume is an attempt to remedy that myopic opinion.

© DUSTIN J. BYRD AND SEYED JAVAD MIRI, 2023 | DOI:10.1163/9789004521698_002

In this book, we have gathered the works of numerous scholars, many of whom called Syed Hussein Alatas their colleague and friend, and others who called him their father. Some of us only know Syed Hussein Alatas through his work, but nevertheless have learned much from his creative and penetrating analyses. As a critical theorist and someone who has attempted to bridge the ever-deepening chasm between Western socio-political philosophy and contemporary Islamic thought, including post-colonial theory, I found Syed Hussein Alatas' work to be revolutionary, as it demolished the ideological constructs that imperialistic thought/politics relies upon for the continual reproduction of the new imperialist and colonial status quo: neoliberalism. Alatas' work was not irreconcilable with my own theoretical background in German Idealism, Historical Materialism, and the Frankfurt School. Rather, his work is a congruent perspective on much of the same structure of domination that pervades the West, albeit his perspective derived mainly from the perspective of the colonial "wretched" in Southeast Asia and mine from the "wretched" of the traditional Eurosphere. As Alatas was at home in both Western philosophical and sociological thought, rooted in his time as a student in Amsterdam, as well as non-Western and Islamic thought, I felt akin to his thinking, and therefore allowed it to influence my own on a variety of topics. His attempts to formulate and develop the "progressive" and emancipatory elements within the Islamic tradition was not only forward-thinking for his time but helped set the stage for the progressive Islam movement today, which counts within its ranks imminent scholars such as Omid Safi, Farid Esack, Ebrahim Moosa, Sa'diyya Shaikh, Amir Hussein, Ahmad S. Moussalli, Talal Assad, Bassam Tibi, Hamid Dabashi, and Tariq Ramadan. While many of these scholars may remain unaware of Alatas' tremendous influence on their own thinking, his voice is often found within theirs. His critique of colonialism, colonial ideology, the "captive mind," and endemic corruption, echoes in today's social theorists and activists who serve on the frontlines of humanity's struggle to create societies worthy of human dignity. The rediscovery of Islamic and native knowledge, which can be recruited into both an academic and public post-colonial discourse, as well as made into a means by which the colonial ideology is deconstructed, is a rediscovery that was pioneered by Alatas himself. While many other Muslim thinkers in the 20th century, such as Muhammad Iqbal, Muhammad Abduh, Jamal ad-Din al-Afghani, and Ali Shariati, have gain notoriety as progressive modernists, attempting to reconcile modernity with Islam, Alatas emphasized the urgent need to first throw off the shackled of mental captivity – the result of decades of colonial domination – so that one could, from the firm grounds of autonomous knowledge and identity, enter into the modern discourse and formulate a vision of modernity that is both congruent with the modern world,

INTRODUCTION

without leaving behind its critique of modernity, and at the same time respectful of the diversity within humanity.

As we continue to develop techniques and strategies through which humanity's library of knowledge is de-colonized, we must continue to return to those who have laid the groundwork for such labor. As such, the work of Syed Hussein Alatas must be recognized much more widely as being foundational to that task. In other words, in order to gain the *fruits* of such labor, we must also recognize and strengthen the *roots* of that labor. Among those roots is Syed Hussein Alatas.

Dustin J. Byrd
Associate Professor of Philosophy and Religion
Olivet College
Olivet, MI, USA

Social Theory as a field of intellectual activity aims to engage the "big questions" of humanity beyond the boundaries of academic disciplines. Of course, it does not deny the principles of scientific division of labors, but it aspires to take issue with *life* and *being* in its totality. In other words, a social theorist is an intellectual whose field of inquiry is *leben* in all its forms and shapes and in this capacity disciplinary boundaries are not cherished bureaucratically as s/he is of the opinion that the miseries that have enveloped human existence on the planet are related to the very bureaucratization of the human faculty of *curiosity*. Syed Hussein Alatas is one the significant intellectuals of the 20th century who demonstrated this genre of intellectuality, which addressed the ills of human societies in their totality by raising simple but fundamental questions beyond the disciplinary boundaries. There is an interesting phase in Alatas' life where we see him actively engage in politics as one of the six founders of the Gerakan Party in Malaysia in 1968, along with Dr. Tan Chee Khoon, Dr. J.B.A. Peter, Lim Chong Eu, Professor Wang Gungwu, and V. Veerapan. However, Alatas gradually left the active political life and instead wore the mantle of an academic sociologist, focusing on political and social issues from a purely intellectual point of departure. How could this transformation be interpreted? One of the main reasons that we could think of is that Alatas came to realize the fact that political disorders and social problems cannot solely be solved at the political level. On the contrary, political ills have intellectual roots and those who are capable of addressing them are not politicians or administrators, but rather are *intellectuals*. He makes an important distinction between educated elites and intellectuals. In his view, educated elites could have an excellent formal education, but based solely on this formal education one cannot expect them to be able to address serious questions of life and society. In other words, we are faced with elites who are educated but *stupid.* Alatas does not employ this term in an ethical fashion; rather he conceptualizes stupidity as *a form of shortsightedness* regarding society in its totality. As such, Syed Hussein Alatas did not leave politics because he stopped caring about political issues. On the contrary, he distanced himself from day-to-day political activities in order to reflect upon the roots of the political ills that have enveloped human existence at large, which are ironically left to *stupid politicians* to solve. These gigantic problems are of *intellectual nature* and politicians lack the proper outlook to tackle them. In Alatas's view, what is needed is *vision,* which we cannot find in the elites who have been merely "educated," most at prestigious institutions. By getting their elite degrees, they wrongly assume that they are capable of solving social and political problems. They are wrong.

Bebalisma is a concept that encompasses the notions of foolishness, stupidity, brainlessness, unreliability, feeblemindedness, and half-wittedness. By constructing this concept, Syed Hussein Alatas demonstrates that the ills of society cannot be remedied by fools, yet this is how we have organized our societies. They are steered by the hand of fools. Syed Hussein Alatas, lexiconnoisseur par excellence, devoted an entire chapter to bebalisma (Chapter 3) in his masterpiece, *Intellectuals in Developing Societies.* There, he explains how we may find a solution to this dilemma. A society cannot be emancipated through *bebalisma* and fools would surely lead us further down in the dungeon of history. By reading Alatas we are not only faced with a social theorist who engages us with intellectual questions and existential problems, but we also encounter an *alternative mode of analyzing* that is not Eurocentric. In his works, we can discern a distinct mode of looking at the questions of reality, religion, humanity, liberty, justice and social order. Another important subject is Alatas' biography, which put an indelible mark on his worldview and theoretical outlook. He was from a Yemeni and Caucasian (Circassian) background and born in Buitenzorg (now Bogor), Dutch East Indies (now Indonesia) and studied in the Netherlands. He married to a Dutch lady and had a son, only to then moved to Malaysia and marry his second wife, who was of Indian origin. From this marriage he had three children. His first son, Syed Farid Alatas, is now a distinguished professor at National University of Singapore and is married to an Iranian from Tehran. By looking at his multicultural backgrounds, you can see that Syed Hussein Alatas is truly a cosmopolitan social theorist in whose life the different religions of Christianity, Islam, Hinduism and distinct languages of Arabic, Dutch, English, and Bahasa, as well as the different races and ethnicities of Caucasia, Turkish, and Arab, are present in his daily life. Multiculturalism was not only an abstract concept for him, but it was a reality he personified in his being. This gave his intellectual perspective a caliber that is needed for global thinkers. The world of tomorrow is deeply in need of intellectuals who are able to cross over boundaries of religions, ethnicities, nationalities, languages, and denominations, and in Syed Hussein Alatas' social theory we can find a paradigmatic intellectual model where humanity at large is its towering subject of concern. Here we are trying to revisit the intellectual legacy of one of the leading critical social theorists of the southern canon who is *not* only addressing local questions, but rather whose concern is the emancipation of the entire human race.

Seyed Javad Miri
Professor of Sociology and Religious Studies
Institute of Humanities and Cultural Studies
Tehran, Iran

PART 1

Alatas' Work and Legacy

∴

CHAPTER 1

Developing a School of Autonomous Knowledge

Thoughts of the Late Syed Hussein Alatas

Syed Imad Alatas

1 Introduction

The 23rd of January 2007 is the day my grandfather passed on. Fourteen years have passed since then. Four years ago, I wrote an essay on the occasion of the tenth anniversary of his death. The piece was more personal than academic, focusing on the impact he had on me. This time, I would like to share his thoughts on intellectual development in the developing world and what was needed to create a more progressive society. In particular, I will focus on his ideas for what we may today call the School of Autonomous Knowledge. Before proceeding, a few remarks about the background of intellectuals in the developing world will help us appreciate their importance in society today. Intellectuals in the developing world can be said to have emerged during the period of colonialism, where they sought to subject the colonial project and colonial ways of knowing to critique. Filipino nationalist José Rizal is one such example. When Western writers and officials averred that Filipinos were lazy, Rizal accepted the charge but attributed it to historical rather than hereditary factors.[1] He was able to intellectually challenge colonial assumptions about the Filipinos. Nevertheless, intellectuals also rose to prominence in the post-independence period as they observed the oppressive ruling establishment of their countries. In Iran, Ali Shariati is known as the "architect" of the 1979 Islamic revolution due to his criticism of the tyranny of the monarch and forms of Westernization, which he felt damaged Iranian religion and culture and uprooted the Iranian people. He believed that Shi'ite Islam was a force for social justice while acknowledging that it had been misused due to its institutionalization by political leaders. Intellectuals such as Rizal and Shariati embody the spirit of the School of Autonomous Knowledge.

---

1 Syed Hussein Alatas, *Intellectuals in Developing Societies*, London: Frank Cass and Company Limited, 1977, p. 11.

© SYED IMAD ALATAS, 2023 | DOI:10.1163/9789004521698_003

2   The School of Autonomous Knowledge and the Captive Mind

The School of Autonomous Knowledge can be defined as a school of thought where theory building, concept formation, the application of methods, and the recognition of definite phenomena are undertaken in a way that is relevant to a specific society and in contradiction to Eurocentric, androcentric, nationalist, or sectarian interests. Embedded in this school is an autonomous social science tradition. Alatas' ideas for such a social science tradition can be located in his thought as he was observing the backwardness of developing societies at both the political-economic and knowledge production levels. The latter led him to think of the problem of the captive mind in developing societies.

Alatas developed the concept of the captive mind to diagnose the nature of scholarship in the developing world in relation to Western dominance in the social sciences and humanities. His development of the concept should not be confused with that of Polish writer Czeslaw Milosz. "Captive mind" was the title of Milosz' nonfiction work where he discussed the phenomenon of hiding one's true belief under the communist dictatorship. He was talking about domination at the hands of a dictatorship, by which even a creative and great mind was held captive. Alatas was referring to another kind of domination by Eurocentric orientations, and one characterized by a lack of critical thinking. He defined the captive mind as an 'uncritical and imitative mind dominated by an external source, whose thinking is deflected from an independent perspective.'[2] This external source was Western social science and humanities. The captive mind characterized the mindset of scholars in developing societies who uncritically accept Western scholarly literature without being discerning or selective in their reading. When discussing social problems unique to their society, captive minds lack the ability to think critically or on their own and are instead held "captive" by Eurocentric ways of thinking. Alatas' conceptualization of the captive mind was inspired by American economist James Duesenberry's idea of the demonstration effect. According to this effect, higher incomes lead to higher levels of consumption as consumers seek to match the lifestyles of those they wish to imitate.[3] Alatas argued that the thinking of scholars in the developing world could be understood through the

---

2   Syed Hussein Alatas, "The Captive Mind and Creative Development," *International Social Science Journal* 26, no. 4 (1974): 691–700, 692.

3   James S. Duesenberry, *Income, Saving and the Theory of Consumer Behavior* (Cambridge, MA: Harvard University Press, 1949), 26–7.

demonstration effect. Scholars with a captive mind consume social science knowledge from the West believing in its superiority.

The problem of the captive mind is unique to the non-Western world. While captive minds exist in the West as well, social scientists there are hardly trained in non-Western sciences or trained by non-Western scholars in non-Western languages. Hence, a captive mind in the West does not exist in the context of domination by the non-Western world. The problem of the captive mind is apparent today in the form of academic dependency where there is a great deal of prestige attached to a western university education, publishing in European and North American journals, and the use of western textbooks in nonwestern universities, among other indicators.[4] The captive mind also leads to a phenomenon known as "brain drain," where promising scholars in the developing world opt to pursue their studies in Western universities, resulting in a dearth of home-grown intellectual scholarship. The problem of the captive mind does not mean that there are no scholars in the developing world consciously trying to address the needs and problems of their own societies through concepts and methodologies suitable to the societies in question. However, the captive mind is a problem precisely because such a mindset is and continues to be dominant in the developing world. It is this dominance that Alatas hoped would be challenged.

Alatas divided the problems of any community into two categories: the subjective and the objective. While subjective problems concerned the individual, the objective referred to problems that were found beyond the individual. The captive mind was the most pressing subjective problem in Asian societies. On the other hand, corruption was the most pressing objective problem in its many manifestations. For Alatas, solving the subjective problem of the captive mind was a pre-requisite to dealing with objective problems such as economic underdevelopment and the attitude of political leaders towards corruption. Alatas noted that the "backwardness" of Asian and African societies was caused more by subjective factors than objective problems. Objective problems, even if seemingly insurmountable, could be overcome if society could restrict the influence of the captive mind.

Although the captive mind was originally used to talk about academic dependency on Western scholarly literature, it has also manifested itself in more practical areas of life such as development planning, local politics, and religious affairs. A captive mind in the area of development planning adopts

---

4 Syed Farid Alatas, "Academic Dependency and the Global Division of Labour in the Social Sciences," *Current Sociology* 51, no. 6 (2003): 599–613, 604.

the language of "change" and "efficiency" when thinking about economic development, while dehumanizing students and workers as "human capital" useful only as input in accelerating economic growth. Lessons on how to be a good, ethical human being are foregone as countries in the developing world simply ape development models in the First World in the narrow pursuit of economic growth.

Syed Farid Alatas (personal communication, Jan 2021) also expanded the concept of the captive mind by noting its manifestations within political and religious institutions in Malaysia. In the political realm, racial exclusivist mindsets within some segments of the Malay scholarly community constitute a blind imitation of the discourse of ultranationalist Malay parties and politicians. Whatever hatred ultranationalist parties may spout is simply repeated by scholars and others without questioning the origins of such hate speech. In the religious sphere, anti-Shia discrimination and stereotypes prevalent among some Sunni Muslim scholars is the result of an uncritical acceptance of anti-Shia hate speech disseminated by religious authorities. In these examples of local domination, there is no attempt or wherewithal to think critically about race or religion. Instead, the opinions of a few are adopted wholesale. Regardless of where and how the captive mind manifests itself, what is needed to counter it is the creative mind. Only the creative mind can overcome local and international forms of domination and facilitate the emergence of intellectuals and progressive leadership to create a more progressive society.

3 Islam and Socialism

Alatas felt that a progressive society was one guided by socialist ideals due to the latter's emphasis on social justice. Alatas' interactions with Indonesian intellectuals during his studies in the Netherlands sparked his interest and curiosity in socialist ideas. His book *Islam dan Sosialisme* (*Islam and Socialism*) was written during a time when socialism was dismissed as atheistic and un-Islamic by segments of the Islamic resurgence movement during the 1970s. Yet, an equal outrage against the excesses of capitalism did not exist. This section of the Islamic resurgence movement was held "captive" by the capitalist model while disregarding any alternative framework for nation-building. Alatas noted that the group of Muslims who were anti-socialist due to the presence of strands of socialism that were atheistic ignored the fact that capitalism too was atheistic. While he stressed that various strands of socialism were contrary to Islamic beliefs, he viewed Islam and socialism in general as compatible belief systems.[5] Alatas showed that Islam and socialism were not very dissimilar; Islam contained many socialist elements such as treating people equally regardless of gender, religion, or socio-economic background. In his book, he listed ten traits of socialism.[6]

1. Socialism places heavy emphases on the needs of human life and the means of production. These means of production, and efforts to organize them for areas which are important for livelihood, should be controlled and owned by the state or cooperatives, and not by individual capitalists.

2. This ownership and control by the state or cooperatives is to prevent any exploitation of workers and consumers so that the prices of goods are not deliberately raised, and the quality of goods are not deliberately reduced.

3. The state has to actively formulate and implement laws so that the production and distribution of goods is done fairly and equitably.

4. Socialism posits that one's surrounding conditions determine the nature of an individual and the emergence of social problems. If humanity lives in a state of deprivation, it will not progress.

5. Socialism posits that society is influenced by classes with specific interests. The dominant class forces its agenda on the people. The dominant class decides the law and brings to life a belief system that protects their own and not the public interest.

6. Socialism aims to eradicate the injustices that arise from the capitalist system, which is the opposite of socialism. In capitalist countries, logging companies, mining, rice milling, housing, and others, are all privately owned. In socialism, companies that can be maintained by the state and are much needed by the public, are managed by the state or cooperatives.

7. Socialism posits that every member of society who is healthy and of age should work. In society, nobody should be unemployed and rely on funds from the state or other members of society.

8. Socialism posits that all the spheres of society such as the cultural, the social, the religious, the educational and so on should be such that they do not prevent but promote economic growth, scientific knowledge, justice, health, and life satisfaction in general.

---

5 Syed Hussein Alatas, *Islam dan Sosialisme* (Petaling Jaya: Gerakbudaya Enterprise, 2020), 4.
6 Alatas, *Islam and Socialism,* 6.

9. In considering an issue, socialism advocates for the majority and the disadvantaged based on the principles of justice. If a government is driven by the spirit of socialism, it will place emphasis on raising the salaries of the low-income rather than higher-income workers.

10. Socialism employs science as far as possible in the formulation of problems, in the understanding of history and in the construction of a belief system.

Alatas listed these ten traits of socialism as conditions that had to be fulfilled in order to bring about a society based on justice and fairness. However, such a society had to be led by capable leaders who possessed a critical mind. Alatas had just finished writing *Islam dan Sosialisme* before he read Dr Mahathir's *Menghadapi Cabaran (Facing the Challenge)*. He was aware that Mahathir viewed Islam and socialism in oppositional terms. Alatas' criticism of Mahathir is noteworthy as the latter was prime minister of Malaysia at that time. He felt that Mahathir too was not aware that there were different types of socialism. As the chief leader of Malaysia, he could be said to have promoted views that were contrary to ideals of progress.

4 Intellectuals and Capable Leaders

Alatas had emphasized the importance of intellectuals and effective leaders during his lifetime. In his book *Intellectuals in Developing Societies,* he noted that the role of an intellectual was to pose problems and suggest solutions to them. He compared functioning intellectuals with members of the intelligentsia who were not intellectuals. Functioning intellectuals were actively involved in: '(1) the posing of problems; (2) the definition of problems; (3) the analysis of problems; and (4) the solution of problems.'[7] A functioning intellectual did not necessarily have to possess academic qualifications as long as the person had adequate knowledge on the subject matter. By contrast, a member of the intelligentsia may be highly educated in terms of qualifications but accepts what is taught to him uncritically. Such an individual lacks an emotional commitment to the intellectual pursuit and does not strive to think of pressing problems. Lastly, this individual is not capable of articulating an opinion beyond what most people already know.

Alatas also compared the intellectual with the fool. He invented the term *bebalisma* (derived from the Malay word *bebal*) to describe an attitude of mind

---

7 Alatas, *Intellectuals in Developing Societies*, 15.

DEVELOPING A SCHOOL OF AUTONOMOUS KNOWLEDGE

of someone who was *bebal,* or a fool. He attributed the attitude of a fool to several traits whose end manifestation included 'ignorance, persistent stubbornness instead of persistent effort, indolence and indifference.'[8] Although found throughout the world, *bebalisma* is most visible in developing countries. The fool does not use logic, empirical evidence, or rational thought when faced with intellectual and practical challenges. Being a Malaysian sociologist, Alatas illustrated several examples from Malaysia to show the fool at work. One such case was the $50 million construction of the Malaysian national airport in Kuala Lumpur (KLIA). Most of the expenditure was done for the land and building. Even with such an exorbitant amount of spending, KLIA was not the most advanced airport. The volume of air traffic also did not justify such an expenditure. Alatas felt that the money could have been spent on improving the old airport instead. Ultimately, the decision to spend $50 million on the construction of KLIA was not an efficient one. It was a foolish one.

Alatas listed several traits of the fool.[9] (1) He is not able to recognize problems; (2) if told to him he is not able to solve them; (3) he is not able to learn what is required; (4) he is also not able to learn the art of learning; (5) he usually does not admit he is a fool. Alatas' treatment of the fool is important in its nuance. An individual is not a fool simply by being an ordinary simpleton. An individual may or may not have knowledge, experience, or training in a particular field and still be a fool, nonetheless. A fool is not an outcome of these three indicators. Rather, a fool exists due to a particular mindset. For example, a teacher is not a fool just because they fail to achieve stellar grades for all the students in the class. A teacher is a fool, however, if they are not able to recognize pedagogical problems or problems in the style of teaching and do not take steps to overcome them. According to Alatas, the fool is usually exposed in times of crisis. Additionally, a person who is a fool can neither inspire nor be inspired and cannot be guided by ideals of excellence.

5 Ideals of Excellence and Ideals of Destruction

Functioning intellectuals and leaders possess several traits that Alatas described as the ideals of excellence (*cita sempurna*). He elaborated on this term during a workshop entitled, "Asian Youth Council 4th Advanced Youth

---

8 Alatas, *Intellectuals in Developing Societies,* 26.
9 Alatas, *Intellectuals in Developing Societies,* 35.

Leadership Training Workshop."[10] Alatas was delivering a lecture to youth in Singapore on social development in Asia. Instead of discussing the political and social system Asia should have, he suggested that Asian societies needed to have an ideal of excellence in order to achieve the right system, whatever it may be. According to him, an ideal of excellence is 'an all-encompassing view geared towards achieving a society of excellence. These ideals of excellence also inspire great efforts towards achieving such a society.'[11] Alatas went on to explain the concept of the ideals of excellence in greater detail. The ideals of excellence may be defined as a view of life that is decent, just, and dignified for a society. These ideals of excellence, if all-encompassing, create an antipathy towards various kinds of social ills such as corruption, hunger, lack of dignity and so forth. Hence, a person who embodies ideals of excellence has a sense of shame when individuals are not treated justly. During the workshop, Alatas provided an example of a transport service in a Southeast Asian country. The taxi drivers were exploited (working in alternate 24 hours shifts) so that the service could make a profit by not employing additional drivers. Coupled with meagre earnings, these drivers lacked adequate rest. Alatas explained that such exploitation could prevail because there was no sense of shame governing the behavior of the transport service higher management. This lack of shame meant that some Asians were against the ideal of excellence. In fact, Alatas worried that Asians were increasingly viewing corruption as a way of life. This way of life was destructive. On the other hand, leaders who possess ideals of excellence are attentive to the welfare of their people rather than their own needs. Within Islamic history, Alatas included Sayyidina Ali (*karramallah wajhhu*), Khalifah Umar ibn Abdul al-Aziz and Sultan Salahuddin Al-Ayubi as examples of individuals who possessed ideals of excellence.

These ideals of excellence are hindered by what Alatas called the ideals of destruction (*cita bencana*). The ideals of destruction encompass an understanding of life that is immoral, unsatisfactory, unfair, and not ennobling for society. Such ideals, if widespread, will give rise to an attitude of indifference towards corruption, social injustice, hunger, ignorance and so on. In the example on the transport service that Alatas gave, the managers were guided by ideals of destruction in their pursuit for profit at the expense of the well-being of the taxi drivers.

---

10   Asian Youth Council 4th Advanced Youth Leadership Training Workshop, 28 May–9 June 1978.

11   Syed Hussein Alatas, *Cita Sempurna Warisan Sejarah* (Selangor: Penerbit Universiti Kebangsaan Malaysia, 2000), 7.

Related to the discussion of the difference between the ideals of excellence and the ideals of destruction, Alatas proposed five types of new individuals in our society.[12] We may assess five types of leaders based on the following typology of traits. The first type of leaders represents backwardness in terms of thinking, although they strive to portray themselves as progressive. Examples include Maulana Maudoodi and Muhammad Qutb. The four other types of leaders are derived from the influence of modern education. Alatas adopted these four examples from Indonesian history. He listed former president Ahmad Sukarno as an example of an individual influenced by modern education. This kind of individual adhered to Islamic beliefs but was not involved in Islamic movements. Individuals such as Sukarno did not trust those who were in charge of Islamic affairs.

The first prime minister of Indonesia and non-Marxist socialist leader, Sutan Syahrir, was the second example of the new individual. Like Sukarno, although Muslim, he was more influenced by the humanism of the West and did not show any interest in Islamic affairs. The spirit of Islam was nowhere to be found in his writing. The third kind of new individual was Ibrahim Datuk Tan Malaka, the communist thinker. Alatas read his work *Islam in the Perspective of Madilog* (*Islam dalam Tinjauan Madilog*) several times and did not come across any statement that showed he was a Muslim. According to him, Tan Malaka actually left Islam, although he was not antagonistic towards the religion. At the 4th Comintern Congress in Moscow, he stressed that Pan-Islamism and communism could collaborate due to their common revolutionary zeal. He valued the potential that Islam could offer to communist followers. Although he adhered to the philosophy of dialectical materialism, which was atheistic, Tan Malaka was not a radical critic of Islam.

The final kind of new individual influenced by modern education is illustrated by individuals such as Syafruddin Prawiranegara, who briefly served as president of the Republic of Indonesia from 1948 to 1949 due to the capture of fellow revolutionaries Sukarno and Hatta. He also held other posts such as the governor of Bank Indonesia and minister of finance. Among the four kinds of new individuals, Syafruddin was the most devout Muslim. He valued modern education while being rooted in Islamic values. He considered Islam as an important tool that could solve social problems such as corruption, greed, and waste. He also felt that economic planning should be guided by Islamic values.

---

12 · Syed Hussein Alatas, *Kita dengan Islam: Tumbuh tiada Berbuah* (Singapura: Pustaka Nasional Pte Ltd, 1979), 107.

We are able to choose the type of individuals that we want to groom as our future leaders. In Alatas' view, the fourth type, that of individuals like Syafruddin, is one that most adheres to Islamic values. Throughout his life, Alatas regretted that the intellectual awakening among the political leadership and the Malay elite, which would have trickled down to the rest of society, never happened in Malaysia. Unfortunately, *bebalisma* as a style of thinking still persists in society.

6　A Tradition of Nurturing the Mind

Intellectuals in developing societies have a role to play in fostering and encouraging a tradition of cultivating the mind. Harnessing the creative mind, and restricting the influence of the captive mind, should lead to the development of an autonomous social science tradition. Writing in the context of Asian societies, Alatas defined an autonomous Asian social science tradition as the 'linking of social science research and thinking to specifically Asian societies.'[13] This means raising problems, creating concepts, and applying methods in a creative manner where one may be influenced by but is not intellectually dominated by another tradition. Such an endeavor has to consider the specificities of Asian societies.

However, having a creative mind does not mean being antagonistic towards the West. Ideas cannot be rejected based on their national or cultural origins. An antagonistic attitude towards the West constitutes what is known as orientalism in reverse or nativism.[14] Within nativism, 'the native's point of view becomes the criterion by which descriptions and analyses are to be judged.'[15] The call for an autonomous Asian social science is not to suggest that Asia have its own "brand" of social sciences. A creative mind is not someone who goes "native"; a creative mind engages in a process of selective and independent assimilation of knowledge from the West. This selective process of assimilation can be done by separating knowledge on Asia and the West into three groups: (1) general scientific knowledge, which is universally valid, (2) knowledge on Western societies, which is of little or no interest to the developing societies, and (3) knowledge about the past and present of the West, which is

---

13　Syed Hussein Alatas, "The Development of an Autonomous Social Science Tradition in Asia: Problems and Prospects", *Asian Journal of Social Science* 30, no. 1 (2002): 150–157, 151.

14　Syed Farid Alatas, *Alternative Discourses in Asian Social Science: Responses to Eurocentrism* (New Delhi: Sage Publications, 2006), 108.

15　Alatas, *Alternative Discourses*, 110.

of high comparative value to the developing societies.[16] A creative mind also aspires to higher intellectual standards within the local and regional social sciences by engaging with those in the West. Alatas himself rightfully acknowledged the contributions of the West insofar as Western socialism fought for the rights of vulnerable workers, opposed imperialism, and advocated for a more equal distribution of wealth. Alatas also suggested the writings around the French revolution as an example of the relevance of Western scholarship for Asia. The fight against religious intolerance, the implementation of human rights and the humanization of laws are aspects of Western society that developing societies should be familiar with in the hope of effecting social change.

What kind of knowledge will an autonomous social science tradition produce? Alatas divided this knowledge into four kinds: (1) Foundational knowledge, (2) consolidative knowledge, (3) reactive knowledge, and (4) developmental knowledge.[17] The first refers to knowledge of key aspects of Asian social life such as their culture, religion, and economic mode of production. The second refers to knowledge that consolidates and builds upon the foundational knowledge. The third kind of knowledge reacts to ideas that either strengthen or corrode the basis of social life. Finally, developmental knowledge is geared towards attaining peace, justice, welfare, and insight into human living. These four kinds of knowledge point to values necessary for any kind of scientific activity. Without these values, Alatas worried that science would become a nihilistic enterprise. One such trait of this nihilistic trend is the study of topics without any consideration for significance. Suppose we conduct a study on the chemistry of our eyebrows. The study may be scientific but how will it aid in our understanding of the human body? It is not immediately clear.

7 Conclusion: Developing the School of Autonomous Knowledge

Universities in the Malay world, including Malaysia, should encourage and foster the critical tradition in order to produce useful leaders and intellectuals. Building upon his clarion call for an autonomous social science tradition, Alatas' intellectual endeavor included the founding of the Department of Malay Studies at the then University of Singapore in 1967. On one level, the department was meant to be an important platform for scholars to discuss the developments and problems of the Malay world, a region of historical

---

16   Alatas, "The Development of an Autonomous Social Science Tradition," 153.
17   Alatas, "The Development of an Autonomous Social Science Tradition," 154.

and sociological significance. However, more importantly, Alatas sought to encourage the development of alternative and multi-disciplinary approaches to the Malay world in terms of its history, economy, politics, and society. This meant a critical application of concepts, theories, and methods suitable to the region rather than a blind imitation of ideas adopted from Western scholarly literature. We can say that the Malay Studies department was a kickstart to the development of a school of thought that we may today call the School of Autonomous Knowledge.

Although Alatas did not speak of a school of thought, his ideas for an autonomous social science tradition have influenced scholars for two generations. Scholars and activists of the Malay world such as Chandra Muzaffar, Shaharuddin Maaruf, Wan Zawawi Ibrahim, Syed Farid Alatas, Noor Aisha Abdul Rahman, Norshahril Saat, Azhar Ibrahim, Farish Noor, Okky Puspa Madasari, Teo Lee Ken, Mohamed Imran Taib, and Pradana Boy Zulian are all part of this autonomous social science tradition in their various fields and can be said to represent the School of Autonomous Knowledge. Subsequently, young scholars of my generation in Singapore, Malaysia, Indonesia and beyond are incorporating this critical tradition in their scholarship as they embark on dissertations and other projects. Emerging scholars of my generation and the next can only continue this tradition if educational institutions encourage critical discourse. Universities should teach more courses that challenge styles of thinking underpinned by Eurocentric, androcentric, nationalist, or sectarian interests. For example, a history teacher adopting a critical approach towards colonialism in Malaya would not blindly praise the British as a beacon of Western modernity. Neither would this teacher chastise the British through an occidental lens. This teacher would introduce students to archives and oral histories that illustrate how the people of Malaya themselves felt when they were being ruled by the British. This kind of approach to teaching and learning will hopefully cultivate the critical and creative minds in our society.

We should note that the influence of Alatas' thought is not limited to this region. Just as the Frankfurt School and Chicago School have influenced scholars beyond Europe and North America, so too has the School of Autonomous Knowledge influenced scholars beyond the Malay world in regions such as Africa and South Asia. Finally, we can also say that the School of Autonomous Knowledge is likely the only school of thought in the human sciences to have emerged in the Malay world.

Bibliography

Alatas, Syed Farid. *Alternative Discourses in Asian Social Science: Responses to Eurocentrism*. New Delhi: Sage Publications, 2006.

Alatas, Syed Hussein. "The Captive Mind and Creative Development." *International Social Science Journal* 26, no. 4 (1974): 691–700.

Alatas, Syed Hussein. *Intellectuals in Developing Societies*. London: Frank Cass and Company Limited, 1977.

Alatas, Syed Hussein. *Kita dengan Islam: Tumbuh tiada Berbuah*. Singapura: Pustaka Nasional Pte Ltd, 1979.

Alatas, Syed Hussein. *Cita Sempurna Warisan Sejarah*. Selangor: Penerbit Universiti Kebangsaan Malaysia, 2000.

Alatas, Syed Hussein. "The Development of an Autonomous Social Science Tradition in Asia: Problems and Prospects." *Asian Journal of Social Science* 30, no. 1 (2002): 150–157.

Alatas, Syed Farid. "Academic Dependency and the Global Division of Labour in the Social Sciences." *Current Sociology* 51, no. 6 (2003): 599–613.

Alatas, Syed Hussein. *Islam dan Sosialisme*. Petaling Jaya: Gerakbudaya Enterprise, 2020.

Duesenberry, James. S. *Income, Saving and the Theory of Consumer Behavior*. Cambridge, MA: Harvard University Press, 1949.

CHAPTER 2

The Midlife of an Idea

Syed Hussein Alatas' Captive Mind after Fifty Years

Masturah Alatas

1 Genesis of the Captive Mind

In 1969, Malaysian sociologist Syed Hussein Alatas was forty-one years old and Head of Department of Malay studies at the University of Singapore (now National University of Singapore). He was also co-founder and Chairman of a new opposition political party in Malaysia called Gerakan. The party, multiracial in membership and veering towards socialism in ideology, won key seats in the General Elections of May 10 that year.[1] However, joy was cut short when during Gerakan's victory rally on May 12 in downtown Kuala Lumpur, supporters were blamed for offending the sensitivities of the Malay community, members of whom retaliated the next day. Tensions rapidly deteriorated into what became known as the May 13 Racial Riots, which dragged on for months, leaving hundreds of people dead.

Alatas was not present at the rally, nor was he in Kuala Lumpur during the riots. He was in Singapore. It was in the aftermath of the May 13 tragedy that Alatas boarded a Boeing 707 at Singapore's Payar Lebar International airport and departed for New Delhi where The Society for International Development was holding its eleventh World Conference from November 14–17, 1969. There, along with British economist Dudley Seers, who presented his seminal essay "The meaning of development," Alatas delivered a paper that tried to articulate his own meaning of development. It was titled 'The Captive Mind in Development Planning: Some neglected problems in development studies and the need for an autonomous social science tradition in Asia.' A revised version

---

1 For more on Alatas' views on socialism, see Syed Hussein Alatas, *Islam and Socialism,* trans. Sharifah Afra Alatas (Kuala Lumpur: Gerakbudaya, 2021). See also translator's Introduction "From Hurling the Sacred to Relearning Tradition and History" and Foreword by Syed Farid Alatas.

© MASTURAH ALATAS, 2023 | DOI:10.1163/9789004521698_004

THE MIDLIFE OF AN IDEA   23

of this paper was published in 1972 in the International Social Science Journal (ISSJ).[2] It was the first of two essays on the topic.

The 1972 essay did not directly address the May 13 riots as such, nor does the phrase "captive mind" appear anywhere in the essay, other than in the title. However, the essay was already an early appeal to those involved in development planning – from entrepreneurs to the government to those teaching the future experts – to not simply blindly and uncritically accept and apply the scholarship, predominantly Western, on development. Asian scholars, Alatas felt, were "still under intellectual dominance."[3] Even how to recognize and choose what problems to study were conditioned and clouded by this dominance. As a result, some problems were neglected in favor of others. Alatas knew this problem of neglect was real and would have serious consequences for the nation. Already in 1968, Alatas had made a prophetic recommendation at a youth conference in Penang:

> May I make a suggestion that a Malaysian research committee on communal relations be established. As a sociologist involved with this problem, I had suggested research into such a problem, but of no avail. The time has now come to interest the public in this issue. Without research into our problems, we will be doomed in time to come.[4]

The May 13 riots happened a year later.

The 1972 Captive Mind essay was Alatas' first publication in the ISSJ. The editor at the time was Peter Lengyel, an Australian of Hungarian Jewish origin who had occasion to meet Alatas more than once in Singapore. The journal's associate editor was Ali Kazancigil, a Turkish political scientist. Alatas became the journal's Singapore correspondent, starting from 1973 and continuing into the 1980s.

As Peter Lengyel explains in *International Social Science: The UNESCO Experience* (1986), the ISSJ's editorial policy those days was 'precisely *not* to cater to specialists but rather to those who might take an occasional and incidental interest in a certain field and therefore appreciate an international

---

2 Syed Hussein Alatas, "The Captive Mind in Development Studies: Some Neglected Problems and the Need for an Autonomous Social Science Tradition in Asia," *International Social Science Journal*, Vol. XXIV, no. 1 (1972): 9–25.

3 Alatas, "The Captive Mind in Development Studies," 10.

4 Syed Hussein Alatas, "Preliminary Observations On The Study Of Communalism And National Integration In Malaysia," in *Proceedings and Papers: Seminar On Research Programs In Singapore*, ed. Nanyang University Editorial Board (Singapore: Nanyang University, 1970).

coverage of it in essentially non-technical terms.'[5] Lengyel writes: 'We therefore sought material from contributors with broad views writing about what they knew about the background to, and current status of a given subject rather than reports on recent research findings more appropriate for first-publication scientific journals.'[6] It is important to be aware of the ISSJ's editorial policy to know how to critically appraise the Captive Mind essays. Already at their publication genesis they were not to be considered as strict social science scholarship only for social science specialists. Already at its inception the concept of the Captive Mind was intended for other disciplines and a more general public.

2   The Captive Mind Defined

In 1974, Alatas wrote a follow-up to the 1972 essay; this too was published in the ISSJ as "The Captive Mind and Creative Development."[7] It is this essay which is the focus of the present chapter for two reasons: First, it provides a definition of the term with ten non-exhaustive characteristics, and second, a search of databases and citation indexes has revealed that over the past five decades, the 1974 essay has been more frequently cited than the 1972 one.

What the present chapter seeks to do is to draw attention to unexplored areas and add something new to the topic of the Captive Mind. How, for example, has the Captive Mind thesis been appropriated or misunderstood? Is it possible to devise a checklist to detect manifestations of the Captive Mind? And finally, can the critical construct Captive Mind be rescued from the social sciences and other academic disciplines – even though it has by no means been held hostage by them – to make it part of general, critical vocabulary the way Antonio Gramsci's "hegemonic," Edward W. Said's "orientalist" and Jacques Derrida's "deconstruction" are used in descriptive and diagnostic ways across the disciplines, entering even so-called lay discourse? Or even the way Oblomovism, Uncle Tomism, or Catch-22 – terms derived from novels – are now used as critical terms? To answer these questions, we would do well to revisit Alatas' oft quoted definition of the Captive Mind with its ten characteristics.

---

5   Peter Lengyel, *International Social Science: The Unesco Experience* (New Jersey: Transaction, 1986), 74.
6   Ibid.
7   Syed Hussein Alatas, "The Captive Mind and Creative Development," *International Social Science Journal* Vol. XXVI, no. 4 (1974): 691–700.

THE MIDLIFE OF AN IDEA   25

3   What Is a Captive Mind?

Confining ourselves to the Asian context for convenience, a captive mind possesses the following characteristics:

- A captive mind is the product of higher institutions of learning, either at home or abroad, whose way of thinking is dominated by Western thought in an imitative and uncritical manner.
- A captive mind is uncreative and incapable of raising original problems.
- It is incapable of devising an analytical method independent of current stereotypes.
- It is incapable of separating the particular from the universal in science and thereby properly adapting the universally valid corpus of scientific knowledge to the particular local situations.
- It is fragmented in outlook.
- It is alienated from the major issues of society.
- It is alienated from its own national tradition, if it exists, in the field of its intellectual pursuit.
- It is unconscious of its own captivity and the conditioning factors making it what it is.
- It is not amenable to an adequate quantitative analysis, but it can be studied by empirical observation.
- It is a result of the Western dominance over the rest of the world.[8]

Let us annotate these points one by one.[9]

1)   While Alatas recognized that Captive Minds do not all have to have attended institutions of higher learning and need not necessarily be produced by them, he was most interested in the ones that did because it is the educated class that a country's development most depends on.[10] Plus, it is in institutions of higher learning that Western knowledge is most prevalent. To see captivity, one must first acknowledge the involvement of the captor.

2)   The uncreative, unoriginal captive mind produces the kind of work that one would feel has already been done before elsewhere by others. An uncreative, unoriginal mind also overlooks what needs to be studied and

---

8   Alatas, "The Captive Mind and Creative Development," 691.

9   The following annotations are developed from private conversations that the author had with Syed Hussein Alatas in his home in Kuala Lumpur in December 2004 and 2006 respectively.

10   See also Patrick Pillai's "In Conversation with Prof. Syed Hussein Alatas," in *International Sociological Association e-bulletin* 4 (2006): 25–31.

given due attention to, as in the case of the neglected study of race relations in Malaysia mentioned above.

3) As long as an individual remains captive, their analysis will be the analysis of the captor. An example would be to, say, buy into Thomas Jefferson's theory of environmental determinism that people who live in tropical climates are lazy.[11] A captive mind believes that "if Jefferson said it, it must be true."

4) For Alatas, the Oedipus complex 'is a valid, scientific concept but its incidence and manifestation differ in different societies.'[12] For him, the Oedipus complex had to be adapted and understood according to culture, as some cultural mechanisms and conditions of child rearing did not produce an Oedipal situation. It was important to understand science within the context of culture. Likewise, if valid scientific knowledge around the world tells us that lactating women should not eat spicy food because the babies won't like Mamma's milk or it will give them colic, this might be true and good advice for Western women who do not habitually eat spicy food. However, it may not necessarily be true for the millions of women around the world for whom spicy food is a normal part of their diet. It does not mean that millions of nursing women all around the world should give up consuming spicy food on the recommendations of the research of the American Medical Association which may not be corroborated by local findings in other countries.

5) One can be a captive mind about literature or science but not about cuisine. Likewise, one can accept the technology and consumerism of the West and vehemently reject its sexual permissiveness and liberalism.[13] This is what it means for the captive mind to be "fragmented" in outlook.

6) The Asian Captive Mind that is alienated from the major issues of society might be more attracted to, say, writing a thesis about Shakespeare rather

---

11   Thomas Jefferson, "Notes on the State of Virginia," in *Call and Response: Key Debates in African American Studies*, eds. Jennifer Burton and Henry Louis Gates (New York: Norton & Company, 2011), 17–24.

12   Alatas, "The Captive Mind and Creative Development," 697.

13   John Tomlinson makes a similar point and argues that this is why globalisation should not be equated with Westernization. See John Tomlinson, "Cultural Globalisation: Placing and Displacing the West," in *The European Journal of Development Research* 8, no.2 (1996): 22–35. See also Syed Hussein Alatas, *Modernization and Social Change* (Sydney: Angus and Robertson, 1972).

THE MIDLIFE OF AN IDEA

than an author from their own society. It is more interested in trends and movements abroad and draws inspiration from them to apply and adapt them to their own society. It seems not to be able to come up with original responses without external stimulation, in particular Western stimulation.

7) A national tradition "if it exists." Indeed, Malaysia does not have a national tradition of historiography, for example. Evidence of this is the heavy dependence on foreign sources for the reconstruction of its own ancient and modern history. Traditions can always be invented, although this may lead to other problems of mythmaking, obscurantism, and nativism in scholarship.[14]

8) When individuals are unconscious or unaware that they are captive, it means they have implicitly accepted their captivity. One does not even feel it as captivity. Influence and dominance have been internalized, which means they are harder to get rid of. This is why the psychology of colonialism is still an urgent subject of study, as it was for Frantz Fanon in his book, *Black Skin, White Masks*. Regarding how domination has been internalized, others have made important observations. On the topic of the brainwashing power of the media, Malcom X famously said 'the newspapers will have you hating the people who are being oppressed and loving the people who are doing the oppressing.'[15] Similarly, Paulo Freire has said: 'the oppressed, having internalized the image of the oppressor and adopted his guidelines, are fearful of freedom.'[16] Theories of cultural imperialism similarly stress that long after the end of real political and economic imperialism, the legacy and effects of the latter continue to influence postcolonial peoples culturally and in systems of power.[17]

9) Yes, it is difficult to ascertain how many captive minds there actually are; we can only identify one when traits of mental captivity manifest themselves.

10) Alatas confined the study of The Captive Mind to the context of Western global hegemony of the times he lived in and under which we still live

---

14   See Eric Hobsbawm and Terrence Ranger, eds., *The Invention of Tradition* (Cambridge: Cambridge University Press, 1983).

15   Malcolm x, "Speech at the Audibon 13 December 1964," in *Malcolm X Speaks,* ed. George Breitman (New York: Grove Press, 1990), 93.

16   Paolo Freire, *Pedagogy of the Oppressed,* trans. Myra Bergman Ramos (New York: Continuum, 2005), 47.

17   See Edward W. Said, *Culture and Imperialism.* New York: Vintage, 1994.

today. While he acknowledged that mental captivity may have existed during the heyday of the Ottoman or other Empires, it would be difficult to study the phenomenon empirically. Moreover, that is not the kind of captivity that most affects the postcolonial world today.

On this last point, it must be stated that Alatas uses the terms "Western" or "Asian" as monolithic categories. While I agree that we need to use them as referential terms, I am aware that the West, and Asia for that matter, does not have one sense of itself as superior; there are hierarchies of superiority and inferiority within the West and Asia. An Italian may be captive to the United States or Scandinavia or vice versa, a Singaporean may be captive to Japan or vice versa. While Alatas makes a clear argument in the 1974 ISSJ essay for why he thinks the phenomenon of the Captive Mind is not found in the West, I would like to propose that it is.[18] If we are to make a case for Captive Mind theory as a critical theory of imperialism, then it must be universally applicable especially if we agree that different forms of imperialism still exist all over the world today, including within the West.

4 What Is a Captive Work?

Alatas has told us what a Captive Mind *is,* but how do we recognize one through empirical manifestations of it? The following is an orientating, non-exhaustive checklist devised by me. By "work" it is intended any verbal, written, or visual text, or any material expression of human creativity like food, architecture, or science.

- Is the work imitative and of what?
- Is the imitation innovative in that it acquires its own unique identity, distinguishable from what is being imitated and maybe even an improvement of it? Or is the result 'not the impressive intellectual palace but the hut around the corner?'[19]
- Is the work dependent on foreign, in particular Western, knowledge or expertise?
- Is the work addressed to a Western audience, either looking for approval from such an audience or to lambaste it? Does the work make an implicit or

---

18   Alatas' point is that even if captive minds were to be found in the West, their effect would not be as deleterious in Western societies as it would be for captive minds in the developing world.

19   Alatas, "The Captive Mind in Development Studies," 18.

explicit comparison to standards set by the West? Is the work in some way obsessed with the West?[20]
- Does the work transmit a sense of inferiority or self-loathing?[21]

While applying one or more of these criteria to various topics, where might we find manifestations of mental captivity?

Education: Exulting when a student or researcher accomplishes something in reputable, high-ranking universities abroad. The exultation is far less for achievements in local universities. And when there is exultation for local achievements, it is met with suspicion. For example, consider the National

---

20   See Dipesh Chakrabarty's notion of being in the "waiting-room of history," in *Provincialising Europe: Postcolonial Thought and Historical Difference* (Princeton: Princeton University Press, 2000), 9. 'The achievement of political modernity in the third world could only take place through a contradictory relationship to European social and political thought.' The oriental, for so long considered by the European not quite ready yet for modernity, which has happened first in the West, is still in "the waiting-room of history" in which they have been placed by the European colonizer. After Independence, the oriental knows that to get out of the room they are dependent on European knowledge and paradigms of modernity. Captive Mind theory helps us see when people are still trying to get out of the waiting-room. Singapore's first Prime minister, Lee Kuan Yew, often said that Singaporeans were not quite ready for the political and social freedoms of the West (see Barr, 2000), yet Singapore was, and is, very open to liberal forms of economic development. On Chakrabarty's book and the habit of, as Amit Chaudhuri writes "not only invoking Europe but making it the starting point of all discussion" see also Chaudhuri's excellent essay "In the waiting-room of history." Chaudhuri writes: 'Chakrabarty's work suggests, I think, that the word "Eurocentric" is more problematic than we thought; that, if Europe is a universal paradigm for modernity, we are all, European and non-European, to a degree inescapably Eurocentric. Europe is at once a means of intellectual dominance, an obfuscatory trope and a constituent of self-knowledge, in different ways for different peoples and histories.' https://www.lrb.co.uk/the-paper/v26/n12/amit-chaudhuri/in-the -waiting-room-of-history.

21   See A.A. Phillips "On the Cultural Cringe," in *The Cultural Cringe* (Melbourne: Melbourne University Publishing, 2005), 1–9. The cringe, Phillips writes, assumes that 'the domestic cultural product will be worse than the imported article'; there is 'a tendency to make needless comparisons.' Phillips was writing about the "Australian intellectual who is forever sidling up to the cultivated Englishman", the Australian intellectual who is in the habit of 'hurling denigratory criticisms at the Australian community without any attempt to check their accuracy.' While Philips recognises that measuring one's 'cultural achievements by universal standards' is healthy to prevent "parochialism," an obsession with it can prevent writers from being "unconsciously themselves" the way, according to Amit Chaudhuri (see note 20), 'for almost two hundred years, in countries like India, there has been a self-consciousness (and it still exists today) which asks to be judged and understood by "universal" standards. It isn't possible to begin to discuss that self-consciousness, or sense of identity, without discussing in what way that universalism both formed and circumscribed it.'

Council of Professors in Malaysia whose members are described in the media as being "experts" and having "knowledge and wisdom," although no critic has spelt out specifically what these achievements are; whether they, as Alatas would say, match the standards of achievements elsewhere, including developed countries.[22] He may even invite us to think, when some of these professors have been called "thinkers," whether this label is justified according to what the word "thinker" means not just in Malaysia but in the rest of the world.

Publishing: A writer from say, Malaysia or Singapore, is considered to have made it (by other Malaysians and Singaporeans) when they publish with a US or UK publisher or when they win international prizes. There is nothing wrong with celebrating this if not for the fact that publishing with a "local" publisher or in a local context (the word local itself has connotations of being lower in quality) is somehow seen as less of an achievement. Was the late Lloyd Fernando a little unconsciously captive when he said, speaking of an anthology he himself edited, "there are no Chekovs as yet, nor Turgenevs among the prose writers in the present collection."[23]

One does not get the same feeling of exultation for writers writing in the Malay language, publishing with Malaysian publishers, and winning Malaysian literary prizes. Italian writers might also be very happy to have their works translated into English or other languages and receive praise and recognition abroad; the difference being that Italian writers also want to have their works published by the best Italian publishers and to win the most prestigious Italian literary prizes. And the opposite scenario is unlikely, that Italians would exult when one of their writer's publishes in Malaysia.

The Myth of the Lazy Native, too, and its author began to get more recognition after Palestinian-American Columbia University scholar Edward W. Said mentioned it in his book, *Culture and Imperialism*, more than fifteen years after the publication of *Myth*. In much captive writing coming out of Malaysia and Singapore, it is quite common to find references to what Edward Said thought of *Myth* – as if the endorsement of Said is necessary to give value to *Myth* – although the reverse is less common – to find Alatas mentioned in writings about Edward Said.[24]

---

22 Bernama News Agency, "National Professors Council Denies Issuing Statement on Emergency Proclamation," *The Malay Mail*. January 14, 2021.

23 Lloyd Fernando, "Introduction" in *Twenty-Two Malaysian Stories: An anthology of Writing in English* (Singapore: Heinemann Asia, 1968), 3.

24 See Masturah Alatas, "Because Said Said So," in *The Life in the Writing: Syed Hussein Alatas* (Singapore: Marshall Cavendish International, 2010), 44–57.

Architecture: Malaysians are right to be proud of their Mughal and Moorish-inspired British colonial architecture as well as the modern, post-colonial Petronas Twin Towers, iconic symbol of Kuala Lumpur, designed by Argentinian-US architect César Pelli. What makes this captive is that pride in the very identity of Malaysia's capital city is dependent on foreign creativity and know-how. Architecture produced by Malaysian architects is side-lined, they are less iconic to what gives Kuala Lumpur its identity.

Gender studies: Did, for instance, LGBT and MeToo movements catch on in Malaysia and Singapore, which has its own history of transsexuality and misogyny, mainly after such movements gained momentum in the West?

5 Was Alatas an Embodiment of His Own Theories? Did He Practice Non-captive, Creative Social Science?

To the best of my knowledge, Alatas was the first to apply the Weber thesis to Southeast Asia, the first to conduct a major study on laziness in Southeast Asia, the first Southeast Asian to write a non-hagiographic biography of British imperialist Thomas Stamford Raffles, the first to critique the Second Malaysia Plan and the first to describe and conceptualize corruption and its long-term effects on Malaysia. If, for Alatas, the opposite of the captive mind is the creative mind, the following works are examples of Alatas as a practitioner of creative sociology.

The Myth of the Lazy Native is an original study on laziness in Southeast Asia.[25] What makes it original is not just the content or the style, but the argument that it makes, which challenge popular held theories of imperialism of the day. For example, the book argues that colonialism 'was a retarding factor in the assimilation of modern science and technology from the West.'[26] Historians who claim instead that 'no matter what negative effects Western colonialism had on Southeast Asia, it introduced modern science and technology to the area' were captive according to Alatas in that they parroted the dominant idea about the general benefits of colonialism that are hegemonic in Western studies.[27]

Whether one agrees with it or not, Alatas' stance in *The Myth of the Lazy Native* was consistent with his 'don't blindly accept everything you read' critical view, which for him generated original research and publications. In the

---

25   Syed Hussein Alatas, *The Myth of the Lazy Native* (London: Frank Cass,1977).
26   Alatas, "The Captive Mind and Creative Development," 692.
27   Ibid.

book, Alatas argues that just because European colonialists thought Southeast Asian natives were lazy, this does not mean that the natives themselves had to believe they were. Additionally, he set out to demonstrate how they did, citing, among others, two books that were published not long after the 1969 May 13 riots: *The Malay Dilemma* (1970) written by Mahathir Mohamad before he became fourth Prime Minister of Malaysia and *Revolusi Mental* (1971) a publication of the ruling party, the United Malays National Organization (UMNO), containing the contributions of fourteen authors.[28]

Alatas did exactly what he thought a sociologist should do: subject the books to analysis. *Siapa Yang Salah?* (Who is to blame?) and Chapters 10 and 11 in *The Myth of the Lazy Native* are his published critiques of *Revolusi Mental* and *The Malay Dilemma*.[29] The critical lens that Alatas used was captive mind theory. To him the authors sound like 'some American Negroes who believe what the white racialists say about them.'[30] Instead of challenging those perceptions, the authors consider them as a motivational point of reference to better themselves. Mahathir, on the other hand, blames the British for encouraging immigration of the business-minded Chinese to Malaysia, thus making the Malays poor in their own country. But he does not say anything about the role of the Malay ruling class, which likewise benefited from colonialism in that their role and position were safeguarded, in contributing to the exploitation and misfortune of the Malays. And when Mahathir argues right after the May 13 riots that running amok is part of Malay national character, as though warning others to be careful in their dealing with the Malays, 'the suggestion has a colonial ring about it,' Alatas writes.[31]

Why is such captive thinking detrimental according to Alatas? For Alatas both books, as expressions of the philosophy of the ruling class, were a justification for definite provisions to be made for the Malays – what became

---

28   Mahathir bin Mohamad, *The Malay Dilemma*. Singapore: Asia Pacific Press, 1970.; Senu Abdul Rahman, *Revolusi Mental*. Kuala Lumpur: Penerbitan Utusan Melayu, 1971.

29   Syed Hussein Alatas, *Siapa Yang Salah*. Singapore: Pustaka Nasional, 1972.

30   Alatas, *Myth*, 166. While some may accuse Alatas of being captive here – using a term invented by White people and colonialists to categorise people of African origin just because the term was popularly used in the 1960s and 1970s – he is actually using the word with irony, to emphasise that the "Negro" is a construction of white racialist discourse. Alatas would approve of the creative and non-captive movement to abolish the use of the word "Negro" in favour of others that people of African origin prefer to use to define their identity. He would also appreciate the ironic, self-referential use of the word – when people of African origin call themselves Negro or Nigger (James Baldwin, Spike Lee) – as a creative and critical use of the word.

31   Alatas, *Myth*, 177.

THE MIDLIFE OF AN IDEA   33

known as the Second Malaysia Plan – to create a Malay entrepreneurial class
that would own and run a high percentage of the country's trade and industry.

> By stressing the predicament of the Malays, funds are made available for
> projects which are ultimately tied up with the interest of some Malays in
> power. Undoubtedly all these things could have been accomplished with-
> out the element of degradation intruding, but this is due to an accident
> of circumstances. The formulators of the ideology are still under the spell
> of the colonial image of the Malays.[32]

All this could have been achieved without denigrating the Malays and Chinese,
but this was "an accident of circumstances" as the authors were writing "under
the spell of" colonial ideology.[33]

Thomas Stamford Raffles: Schemer of Reformer was another original work by
Alatas. While an independent Singapore was lauding Thomas Stamford Raffles
(1781–1826) as the island's "founder," Alatas chose to sing a different tune.

> Raffles was not the humanitarian reformer his admirers made him out to
> be. A humanitarian reformer usually possesses a broad and tolerant out-
> look on other communities and nations. He does not scorn the religion
> and culture of other people. He does not naively preach the superior-
> ity of his own nation in a manner that requires the degradation of other
> nations. A humanitarian reformer is in the first place concerned with
> the injustice within his own society. He does not direct his criticism only
> towards alien societies. A humanitarian reformer does not consider it his
> mission in life to build an empire at the cost of other nations. A human-
> itarian reformer does not spend the best years of his life scheming and
> intriguing as Raffles did.

> It is hoped that the portrayal of Raffles' thoughts and actions in this book
> will be considered as an attempt to correct the persistent historical can-
> onization of Raffles as a lovable and gentle personality surrounded by
> jealous competitors, as a heroic reformer who wanted to bring peace and
> progress to the people of the area in which he operated. It is the British
> colonial historians more than any other group who have been responsible
> in large for the historical canonization of this man. There is a great need

---

32   Alatas, *Myth*, 155.
33   Ibid., 155.

to review the entire historical writing in this region with a view to accomplish a deeper, more meaningful, and objective portrayal of history.[34]

What is interesting is that this little book, first published in 1971 by Australian publisher Angus and Robertson, did not lead to a "Raffles Must Fall" movement. It took the "Rhodes Must Fall" movement five decades after the independence of Singapore (1965) and the erection of the Raffles commemorative statue in 1972 on Raffles' supposed landing site (today the heart of Singapore's financial district) to inspire the "Raffles Must Fall" idea in a play.[35] It is fine for a movement in one geopolitical context to inspire and influence other creative responses in other contexts. Captive Mind critique does not look to berate those who are not the first to do something. Captive Mind critique sets out to analyze when an action is the direct result of an imitative process, and it seeks to understand the many reasons that drive imitation and why creative opportunities are delayed or missed. Rhodes Must Fall was born in a South African university and ignited similar movements in Oxford and Harvard universities. Captive Mind theory does not ignore the relevance of top institutions of learning in Western metropolitan centers in lending fervor to Rhodes Must Fall debates and movements across the globe, reaching as far as Singapore. Were Rhodes Must Fall confined to just an African context, it may have had less of a global reach.

Finally, Alatas recognized that corruption was a cancerous problem in Southeast Asia that infected all areas of life. By writing the books that he did on corruption, he showed that it was a topic worthy of scholarly attention and investigation. Like investigative journalism to expose corruption, showing what corruption is from a more scholarly perspective – how it works to destroy societies and how it can be avoided – corruption, if taught in institutions of learning would, in theory, produce generations of civil servants, other professionals and just the general citizenry at large who would not practice corruption themselves.

What made Alatas' work on corruption non-captive was that it challenged popular notions that corruption exists everywhere, it is an ingrained cultural practice, a way of life that should be tolerated, a little bit of corruption is good and inevitable to move things along.

---

34   Syed Hussein Alatas, *Thomas Stamford Raffles: Schemer or Reformer?* (Singapore: National University Press, 2020), 101. See also Syed Farid Alatas' Introduction.

35   A. Murad Merican, "Remove Raffles, colonial narrative," *New Straits Times.* March 14, 2020, https://www.nst.com.my/opinion/columnists/2020/03/574671/remove-raffles-colonial-narrative.

THE MIDLIFE OF AN IDEA   35

In political scientist Harold Lasswell's foreword to Alatas' book, *The Sociology of Corruption* (1968), he writes that Alatas has 'challenged the supposed impact of the "gift" as a traditional cultural practice whose predisposing effect has been to further a contemporary sub-culture of corruption.'[36] In arguing that bribery is actually not part of Asian culture, Alatas hoped to break the widespread tolerance and justification of this practice.

6   Alatas the Imitator, or the Imitated? Captive Alatas?

In any discussion on theories of imitation, it is only fitting to make Alatas himself the subject of inquiry. That the words "captive mind" appear only in the title of the first essay and not in the body of the essay tells us that Alatas was employing the term generically. The use of the phrase, although with different intentions and meanings, can be traced back to English translations of the New Testament. For example, in John Wesley's *Explanatory Notes on the New Testament* (1757) based on the King James translation, we find in reference to 2 Corinthians 10:5 'the mind itself, being overcome and taken captive, lays down all authority of its own, and entirely gives itself up to perform, for the time to come, to Christ its conqueror the obedience of faith.'[37] This would explain why some Christian-oriented publications might bear titles like "The Freedom of a Captive Mind."[38]

When Alatas used the term Captive Mind he was not intending to make any intertextual reference to the work by Polish poet and Nobel Laureate, Czesław Milosz, which appeared in English translation as *The Captive Mind* (1952) (the original Polish is more like The Imprisoned Mind and even the Italian translation sticks closer to the Polish, *Il mente prigioniero*). Alatas had said that he was not aware of Milosz's book when he was writing his own Captive Mind essays. Indeed, the two works are very different in style and content.[39] Neither

---

36   Harold D. Lasswell, "Foreword," in *The Sociology of Corruption: The Nature, Function, Causes and Prevention of Corruption* by Syed Hussein Alatas. Singapore: Donald Moore Press, 1968.

37   John Wesley, *Explanatory Notes Upon the New Testament* (1757), 489. https://www.google .it/books/edition/Explanatory_Notes_Upon_the_New_Testament/7BlhAAAAcAAJ?hl= it&gbpv=1&dq=john+wesley+captive+mind+new+testament&pg=PA489&printsec=fro ntcover.

38   https://christianworkingwoman.org/https/christianworkingwomanorg/broadcast/the -freedom-of-a-captive-mind-4/.

39   On the "three unifying ideas" driving Alatas' work see Clive Kessler, "Wise Muslim Rationalist, Culturally Grounded Cosmopolitan," *Akademika* 73 (May 2008): 134–136.

was Alatas aware of Gunnar Myrdal's Cairo Lectures (1955) about the dangers of uncritical transplantation of socials science knowledge and methodology to developing societies when he delivered a paper on the same theme in London that year.[40]

What this shows is that Alatas, who writes critically of imitative scholarship, may have appeared imitative himself, although we know he wasn't; he was writing under convictions of originality. It is possible for scholars who have not read each other's works to come up with similar ideas, and words like "mind" and "captive" are commonly used in psychology and humanities scholarship. The "Captivity Narrative" is itself a literary genre, as "captive" and "captivity" are commonly used words.

To the best of my knowledge, there is no detailed study that compares Milosz's *The Captive Mind* to Alatas' concept of the "captive mind." There is reason to believe that Milosz, despite winning the Nobel Prize for Literature in 1980, is not that well-known among Polish youth. When a teacher mentioned his name in an English language class at the University of Macerata, not one of the five Erasmus students from Poland who were present had heard of him. No one in class (except for the teacher) had heard of Alatas either. But it is reasonable to assume that if the Captive Mind persists as a critical construct and is part of analytical vocabulary, it is probably Alatas' meaning of the term that is used and less so Milosz's one. This may be explained by the fact that the creative intellectual mind in captivity of Milosz's cold war era no longer exists after the fall of communism. But the captive mind of Alatas' postcolonial globalized epoch does since no one has announced the end of post-coloniality and globalization yet.[41]

What about Alatas, the imitated? Former president of Singapore, Devan Nair, wrote an article titled "Neo-colonial Captive Minds," which was hosted in the Educational Council on Indic Traditions section of the Infinity Foundation website.[42] There is no date on the article indicating when exactly it was written. However, bibliographical references to work published in the 1980s and after suggests that Nair's article must have been written after 1974. Alatas is not mentioned in Nair's article, although one cannot help but hear echoes of Alatas

---

40   The paper was published the following year. See Syed Hussein Alatas, "Some Fundamental Problems of Colonialism," *Eastern World* (November 1956).

41   See Arif Dirlik, *The Postcolonial Aura: Third World Criticism in The Age of Global Capitalism* (Boulder: Westview Press, 1998) and Walter Mignolo, "Coloniality Is Far From Over, And So Must Be Decoloniality," *Afterall* 43 (Spring/Summer 2017): 39–45.

42   Devan Nair, "Neo-colonial Captive Minds," in https://www.infinityfoundation.com/mandala/s_es/s_es_nair-d_minds_frameset.htm.

THE MIDLIFE OF AN IDEA

in Nair. Alatas (1974): 'A captive mind is the product of higher institutions of learning at home and abroad whose way of thinking is dominated by Western thought in an imitative and uncritical manner.'[43] Compare this to Nair: 'Their [former colonial territories] tertiary institutions of higher learning hardly ever displayed any compelling urge to free themselves from the restrictive, Eurocentric disciplinary paradigms inherited from Western Universities.'[44]

Alatas was again not acknowledged when Malaysian politician and former Minister of Finance and Minister of International Trade and Industry, Tengku Razaleigh Hamzah, said that "captive minds" continue to support the New Economic Policy, a policy of redistribution of wealth originally intended to help the advancement of the Malays and 'bridge the gap between the have and have-nots.'[45] Tengku Razaleigh claimed that the NEP had created an "incubated class of Malay capitalists" while inequitable distribution of income, wanton corruption, wasteful spending and a spiraling national debt continue to persist. Almost quoting directly from the Captive Mind article he said, 'we have become incapable of devising an analytical method independent of current stereotypes about Malays, Chinese, Indians and others.' Despite many years of the NEP, Malaysia's education system has not encouraged "intellectual inquiry" and an intellectual and moral "reform of the mind," which resulted in 'a lack of debate on major issues such as good governance, corruption and rule of law.'[46]

7   Why We Need Captive Mind Theory

1) Captive Mind Theory *Stimulates Creativity*: With the term "creative development," Alatas intended development in the sense of scientific and economic development that is the result of intellectual activity (reading, writing, thinking, teaching, inventing, building), which is adaptive and not merely imitative. Creative development can be understood as development that is creative, but also the development of creativity in intellectual endeavors, as well as development that is sustainable: planning that is the result of serious thinking and is not hurriedly produced; planning that will have long-term advantages.

---

43   Alatas, "The Captive Mind and Creative Development," 691.

44   Nair, "Neo-colonial Captive Minds."

45   See report by Shannon Teoh, "Only Captive Minds Hang On to the NEP, says UMNO's Ku Li." Originally published in *The Malaysian Insider*, now defunct. Reposted here: https://dinmerican.wordpress.com/2012/04/01/only-captive-minds-hang-on-to-the-nep-says-umnos-ku-li/.

46   Ibid.

Our problem in Malaysia is to preserve what we have and to improve on it seriously. This however cannot be achieved through complacency and wishful thinking. I heard of late that we are striving to create Nobel prize winners. But the important condition is first to create an academic, intellectual research culture which is sadly lacking in our country. To have one Nobel prize winner we must have thousands of serious scholars, research infrastructure, formidable labs and libraries, hundreds of professional journals and sustained funding.[47]

To illustrate creative development Alatas provides the example of a hypothetical new kind of bathtub that can be invented for use in homes in Singapore and Malaysia; not the kind of tub widespread in the West or developed countries that would require a lot of water for immersion, nor the use of the tub as a base for a shower. Instead, he imagined a tub made of "rational and scientific" materials but used as a "pond" to collect water for 'pouring over our bodies with a small bucket or bowl,' which is the Asian way of bathing.[48] This way, Alatas surmises, people in Singapore and Malaysia can bathe more regularly in the traditional way, but with a modern tub and without wasteful consumption of water.

Alatas does not discuss whether Asians themselves may be willing to give up the traditional way of bathing because they find a shower – which likewise allows for the possibility to regulate water consumption – to be more enjoyable or efficient. His point is that an opportunity for engineering and design – what he calls "scientific power" – to create a possible market for an original, adapted bathtub has been missed.[49] Many bathtubs in contemporary Malaysian homes today resemble the Alatas tub. This may be a mere coincidence and it has not been possible to establish whether Alatas can be credited for this. But the point is that Alatas was already imagining a tub suitable for Malaysian bathing habits in the early 1970s.

While Alatas does not delve into detail on the notion of intellectual confidence as the antidote to dominance, dependency, and imitation, I would like to propose "the Confident Mind" as the counterpart to the Captive Mind.

---

47   Syed Hussein Alatas, "A Heartfelt Prayer For Our Country," *New Straits Times*, December 27, 1999.

48   Alatas, "The Captive Mind in Development Studies," 19.

49   On "scientific power," see Syed Hussein Alatas, "Intellectual Captivity and the Developing Societies." (Paper delivered at the 30th International Congress of Human Sciences in Asia and North Africa, Mexico, August 3–8, 1976).

THE MIDLIFE OF AN IDEA   39

Regarding the urgency for cosmopolitan and conservationist confidence, the Indian poet Rabrindanath Tagore put it best:

> Before Asia is in a position to co-operate with the culture of Europe, she must base her own structure on a synthesis of all the different cultures which she has. When, taking her stand on such a culture, she turns toward the West, she will take, with a confident sense of mental freedom, her own view of truth, from her own vantage-ground, and open a new vista of thought to the world. Otherwise, she will allow her priceless inheritance to crumble into dust, and, trying to replace it clumsily with feeble imitations of the West, make herself superfluous, cheap and ludicrous.[50]

2) Captive Mind Theory promotes *non-Eurocentric, non-nationalist, non-nativist, non-fundamentalist, non-obscurantist cosmopolitan methodology* and is therefore *more universally humanist in approach*: By autonomous social science traditions in Asia, Alatas did not mean a tradition in opposition to a Western social science tradition or universal scientific knowledge, just as a European social science tradition does not define itself in relation to an Asian social science tradition. He simply wanted Asian sociology to establish a link to specifically Asian problems. "There already exists an idea of an American or European social science tradition. Though both draw upon a common universal fountain of social science knowledge, yet we do speak of an American or European social science tradition."[51]

3) Captive Mind Theory *is essential for decoloniality and the decolonial project*: Ngugi wa Thiong'o speaks of decolonizing the mind, but what do we call the mind that has to be decolonized?[52] A "colonized mind" is similar to a "captive mind." But a colonised mind could refer to the mind that exists within the context of real colonialism as well as one that continues to be metaphorically colonized long after colonialism has ended. The phrase "captive mind," however, escapes this temporal and historical ambiguity and is more concerned with mental bondage or dependency after political imperialism. It is more concerned with the state of captivity of an individual when no one is actively trying to keep that individual captive under colonialism. The word captive also

---

50 Rabrindanath Tagore, "An Eastern University." https://www.tagoreweb.in/Essays/creat
    ive-unity-218/an-eastern-university-2637.

51 Syed Hussein Alatas, "The Development of an Autonomous Social Science Tradition in
    Asia: Problems and Prospects," *Asian Journal of Social Science* 30, no. 1 (2002): 151.

52 Ngugi wa Thiong'o, *Decolonising the Mind: The Politics of Language in African Literature.*
    Nairobi: Heinemann Kenya, 1986.

has associations of being captivated or enthralled (by the West). This is why, along with wa Thiong'o, Ali Shariati, Jamaica Kincaid and many other thinkers of the colonial mentality problem, Alatas' contribution of conceptual vocabulary to the field is necessary.

8 The Captive Mind Misunderstood

The most misunderstood points of the captive mind thesis are the first and last characteristics: 'a captive mind is the product of higher institutions of learning either at home or abroad whose way of thinking is dominated by Western thought in an imitative and uncritical manner,' and 'a captive mind is the result of Western dominance over the rest of the world.'[53]

Alatas did not like it when his ideas were used to indulge in West-bashing, the constant finger-pointing at colonialism and Westernization for the breakdown in traditional family, religious, moral, and social values; the kind of discourse that blames Western models of political and social development as the sources of moral decline and spiritual malaise to justify certain extremist or fundamentalist positions. It is quite evident in works such as *Modernization and Social Change*, *Kita Dan Islam* and *Kemana Dengan Islam* that Alatas never said or implied that a cure for the captive mind would be to create an Islamic state.[54]

Alatas was critical of irrational, emotional, and fanatical thinking. 'An Asian who is vehemently opposed to colonialism may yet be a captive mind. What defines the captive mind is the state of intellectual bondage and dependence on an external group.'[55] Again: 'a captive mind is not merely an uncritical and imitative mind. It is an uncritical and imitative mind dominated by an external source, whose thinking is deflected from an independent perspective.'[56] So the kind of West-bashing discourse referred to above is captive because the West becomes not only the first point of reference in the vision of reality or history, but the sole source of problems. We get a clearer idea of what Alatas means when we substitute some words in a hypothetical West-bashing sentence and

---

53   Alatas, "The Captive Mind and Creative Development," 691.
54   Syed Hussein Alatas, *Kemana Dengan Islam: 22 Artikel Pilihan.* Utusan, 2002.; Syed Hussein Alatas, *Kita dan Islam: Tumbuh Tiada Berbuah.* Pustaka Nasional, 1979.; Syed Hussein Alatas, *Modernization and Social Change: Studies in Modernization, Religion, Social Change and Development in Southeast Asia.* Sydney: Angus and Robertson, 1972.
55   Alatas, "The Captive Mind and Creative Development," 692.
56   Ibid.

THE MIDLIFE OF AN IDEA   41

ask ourselves if a European would write such a sentence. We may conclude that perhaps not even European sympathizers of the English Defense League or Italy's xenophobic Lega Nord would write: 'Many Europeans blame Eastern models of political and economic development as the sources of moral decline and spiritual malaise,' because they would not ascribe such power to Eastern models. They would most likely blame their own politicians and government for the presence of Muslims and immigrants in Europe, not Eastern models of political and economic development.

For Alatas, the West did not cause captivity just as the West was not always the exclusive cause of the miserable existence and state of affairs in many Muslim nations; corruption and leadership played a significant role as well. The tenth characteristic states that the captive mind is "the result of," not that it is "caused by," Western dominance over the rest of the world. People are the cause of their own captivity when they imitate and accept uncritically what is given or is available to them, when there is an absence of resistance or protest against a kind of thinking that is fashionable in the West, especially in cases where that thinking or scholarship about the East is inadequate or erroneous.[57]

> It is the superficial, distorted, and ill-equipped analysis of developing societies that we should reject and combat, not the other kind of knowledge available in the developed societies. We may be sympathetic to the Western civilization. Yet the duty remains for us to ward off the invasion of superficial generalizations, one-sided analysis or ideas pathogenic to our modernization.[58]

What made Alatas cringe in Philips' sense of the term was flawed Western scholarship that Asians were admiring because it was a Western source, thus showing their inferiority complex, or because they were too naïve to recognize what was wrong with it, thus showing their lack of knowledge. It is mainly these two things that Alatas was trying to awaken people to with his Captive Mind thesis.

For him, the way to recognize inadequate or erroneous scholarship was to know one's 'own national tradition, if it exists, in the field of intellectual

---

57   See Syed Hussein Alatas, "Intellectual Captivity and the Developing Societies." Paper delivered at the 30th International Congress of Human Sciences in Asia and North Africa, Mexico, 3–8 (August, 1976), 8.

58   Syed Hussein Alatas, "Erring Modernization: The Dilemma of Developing Societies." Paper delivered at Symposium on the Developmental Aims and Socio-Cultural Values in Asian Society, Bangkok, (3–7 November, 1975), 32.

pursuit.'[59] However, while it is good to criticize where criticism is due, one must know how to do this properly. 'The most profound critics of the West have been Westerners themselves.'[60] And what one proposes as an alternative to Western scholarship must match certain standards. Alatas does not theorize in detail about how quality is recognized or how standards are established, but one way for him was certainly through criticism and the politics of reception.

> Those who are writing on American history are Americans themselves. Other American scholars will review their work. As a result, the standard of scholarship of their country is high because there are many people really critical of each other's works.[61]

In the case of Southeast Asia, he continues, 'there is more scholarship done abroad, reviewed abroad, assessed abroad,' but consumed locally. As a result, 'there is less scholarly debate locally.'[62] Standards are not established just through intra-national and intra-disciplinary dialogue, however. A 'higher standard of scientific and intellectual consciousness' could be obtained by 'measuring Asian attainments with comparable disciplines in developed countries,' which is not the same as measuring one's worth against a Western standard.[63] The first compares one's own sense of excellence with a recognition of excellence in others, whereas the second has the standard of excellence completely defined by the other and feels inferior when it cannot meet that excellence.[64]

One explanation for why Alatas is misunderstood or misappropriated as a West-hater may be because he is not read carefully, or people have access to only some publications and not others (because they are not easily available) in which Alatas has clearly stated his position regarding the West.

> I have explained several times elsewhere that developing societies should assimilate as much as necessary Western science and technology and

---

59   Alatas, "The Captive Mind and Creative Development," 691.

60   Syed Hussein Alatas, "Cultural Impediments to Scientific Thinking," in *Culture and Industrialization,* eds. Rolf E. Vente and Peter S.J. Chen (Baden-Baden: Nomos Verlagsgesellschaft, 1980), 17.

61   Syed Hussein Alatas, "Intellectual Imperialism: Definition, Traits and Problems," *Southeast Asian Journal of Social Science* 28, no.1(2000): 30.

62   Ibid.

63   Alatas, "The Captive Mind in Development Studies," 21.

64   On Alatas' notion of excellence see "The Ideal of Excellence." Paper delivered at the Asian Youth Council 4th Advanced Youth Leadership Training Workshop, National Youth Training Institute, Singapore, May 28-June 9, 1978.

other positive elements of the Western civilization. But this has to be based on proper criteria of selection and the end result should not be the loss of creativity and originality.[65]

For Alatas, one criteria of assimilation is that whatever is imitated or adapted should 'support existing and sound values' that are 'recognized as valuable by large groups of people.'[66] In some instances what Alatas highlights as collective values may sound anachronistic, conservative, and downright sexist to a contemporary reader. For example, a non-captive unemployment analyst for him should consider the fact that

> upon marriage it is the woman who stays at home to manage the household and care for the children. Hence, the exit of women from the labor force into the home is an important factor in the employment situation: it decreases the number of those urgently needing a job.[67]

It must be stated, however, that Alatas nowhere says these values are fixed and should not change.

We hope all this will dispel the myth that Alatas was somehow anti-West or anti-feminist in toto. Neither was his position that of nativism – an unfounded, unwarranted aggrandizement of one's own tradition and past – as sociologist Habibul Haque Khondker points out.[68] For Alatas, an alternative to colonialism was sound development planning, not 'demagogy, xenophobia, empty glorification of the past, bombastic speeches, an attitude of laxity towards truth and virtue, and neglect of the common welfare.'[69]

So rather than a critique of Western civilization, which is where much of the focus of readers of the Captive Mind thesis has gone, the thesis is an exhortation to creativity, an aspect that has been neglected. Therefore, while a critique of the captive mind thesis is valuable and is best left in the hands of experts to identify contradictions and problem areas, this, unfortunately, has been done at the loss of creativity, which was the point of the captive mind thesis to begin

---

65   Syed Hussein Alatas, "Intellectual Captivity and the Developing Societies." Paper delivered at the 30th International Congress of Human Sciences in Asia and North Africa, Mexico (August 3–8, 1976), 24.

66   Alatas, "The Captive Mind and Creative Development," 692.

67   Ibid, 693.

68   Habibul Haque Khondker, "Sociology of Corruption and 'Corruption of Sociology': Evaluating the Contributions of Syed Hussein Alatas," *Current Sociology* 54, no. 1 (January 2006): 33.

69   Alatas, "Some Fundamental Problems of Colonialism," *Eastern World*, (November 1956).

with. Not enough attention has been paid to point out examples of creative sociology or creative intellectual work.

9   The Captive Mind at Large: From Malaysia to Singapore and the Rest of the World

In the 1980s, when Alatas was already an established professor at Singapore's national university, the works of his doctoral students, such as Shaharuddin Maaruf and Chandra Muzaffar, were among the first in the academic milieu of Singapore and Malaysia to demonstrate non-captive approaches. Over the decades that followed, others such as Farish A. Noor, Sharifah Munirah Alatas, Syed Imad Alatas, and Syed Farid Alatas were to follow.[70]

The Captive Mind essays had also begun to be cited outside of its original Malaysian context. For example, Japan scholar E. Patricia Tsurumi provides a succinct and useful definition of the captive mind:

> Even the relatively few Chinese beneficiaries of Japanese colonialism fell victim to what Syed Hussein Alatas has called 'the captive mind'. They learned so well from their captors that they sometimes forgot who they were, though the former never did.[71]

Two decades after Tsurumi, others who discussed the captive mind thesis, perhaps taking a different tone and position from Alatas' in their own works, have been Indian scholars Ashis Nandy, Claude Alvarez, and Vinay Lal.[72]

In more recent research, captive mind theory has been engaged with by tourism scholars Paolo Mura and Sarah Wijesinghe, and British criminologist

---

70   See Syed Farid Alatas, "Against the Grain: Malay Studies and the School of Autonomous Knowledge," *The Edge Malaysia*, May 30, 2021, https://www.theedgemarkets.com/article/against-grain-malay-studies-and-school-autonomous-knowledge See also Farish A. Noor, *The Other Malaysia* (Kuala Lumpur: Silverfish Books, 2002) and *What Your Teacher Didn't Tell You* (Kuala Lumpur: Matahari Books, 2010). See Sharifah Munirah Alatas, "Applying Syed Hussein Alatas's Ideas in Contemporary Malaysian Society,"*Asian Journal of Social Science* 48 (2020): 319–338. See Syed Imad Alatas. "Thoughts of the Late Syed Hussein Alatas," *Free Malaysia Today*, January 7, 2021.

71   E. Patricia Tsurumi, "Colonizer and Colonized in Taiwan," in *Japan Examined: Perspectives on Modern Japanese History*, eds. Hilary Conroy and Harry Wray (Hawaii: University of Hawaii Press, 1983), 220.

72   See "Redesign of Social Science Curricula International Workshop," organized by Citizens International Multiuniversity, November 19–22, 2004. https://www.youtube.com/watch?v=o5IaptZHGF4.

THE MIDLIFE OF AN IDEA   45

Leon Moosavi.[73] All this just to show that in the fifty years of its existence, the idea of the "Captive Mind" has been a useful critical concept for international scholars coming from all over from Italy to Iran to Malaysia, and from a range of disciplines from Criminology to Tourism to International Relations, and of course the social sciences, where it started.[74]

Two new critical constructs have been built on the Captive Mind concept: they are "double captivity," where the intention to decolonize has to be decolonized itself, and "spaghetti Westernization," where imitation really leads to a new and innovative product, as in the case of the Spaghetti Westerns produced by Italian film directors who were inspired by U.S. Westerns. To stick to the food trope, Italian sushi might be an example of Spaghetti Westernization as the Japanese delicacy made with some Italian ingredients and adapted to Italian tastes retains the quality and aspect of the original.[75]

10   Conclusion

Creative thinking was one of Syed Hussein Alatas' pet tropes; this led him to devise the theory of the Captive Mind. However, this was not his only contribution to decolonial thought. Other forms of his "mind" critique found expression in the invention of such terms as "bebalisma," defined as,

> an attitude composed of several traits and whose end manifestation includes ignorance, persistent stubbornness instead of persistent effort,

---

73   See Leon Moosavi, "Decolonising Criminology: Syed Hussein Alatas on Crimes of the Powerful," *Critical Criminology* 27, no.1 (June, 2019): 229–242; Paolo Mura and Sarah N.R.Wijesinghe, "Behind the Research Beliefs and Practices of Asian Tourism Scholars in Malaysia, Vietnam and Thailand," *Tourism Management Perspectives* 31 (July, 2019): 1–13.

74   See Sivapalan Selvadurai, Er Ah Choy, Marlyna Maros and Kamarulnizam Abdullah, "Shifting Discourses in Social Sciences: Nexus of Knowledge and Power," *Asian Social Science* 9, no.7 (2013): 97–106. For International Relations see Sharifah Munirah Alatas, "A Critique of the Indo-Pacific Construct: Geopolitics of Western-Centrism," in *Asia and Europe in the 21st Century: New Anxieties, New Opportunities*, eds. Rahul Mishra, Azirah Hashim, Anthony Milner (London: Routledge, 2021), 185–198.

75   On "double captivity" see Masturah Alatas, "The Double Captivity of Chinese Privilege," *New Mandala*, April 22, 2015, https://www.newmandala.org/the-double-captivity-of-chin ese-privilege/ On spaghetti Westernization, see Masturah Alatas, "Sergio Leone, Captive Minds and Spaghetti Westernization," in *The Life in the Writing: Syed Hussein Alatas* (Singapore: Marshall Cavendish International, 2010), 118–125.

indolence and indifference. Although worldwide, this phenomenon is most conspicuous in backward countries.[76]

Alatas' entire oeuvre has been an attempt to produce non-captive scholarship. He spent his entire life trying to stimulate creativity.

Yet, to date, there is only one biography on him.[77] No Malaysian has published a comparative study in book form between him and his brother, the Islamic philosopher Syed Muhammad Naquib al-Attas. The first attempt to compare the two has been done by the late Egyptian scholar, Mona Abaza.[78]

It has been the intention of the current paper to show how the Captive Mind was born, how it developed, how it has been misunderstood, and how it has been taken up in scholarship over the past five decades. There is much new ground to cover. And it is a necessary project. As Alatas wrote in 1976, 'the emancipation of the mind should be the major struggle now since it conditions greatly the struggle for other emancipations.'[79] Let us continue this struggle, as the struggle is far from over.

Bibliography

Abaza, Mona. *Debates on Islam and Knowledge in Malaysia and Egypt: Shifting Worlds.* London: RoutledgeCurzon, 2002.

Abdul Rahman, Senu. *Revolusi Mental.* Kuala Lumpur: Penerbitan Utusan Melayu, 1971.

Alatas, Hussein. "Some Fundamental Problems of Colonialism," *Eastern World* (1955): 9–10.

Alatas, Masturah. *The Life in the Writing – Syed Hussein Alatas: Author of* The Myth of the Lazy Native. Shah Alam: Marshall Cavendish, 2010.

Alatas, Masturah. "The Double Captivity of Chinese Privilege," *New Mandala*, April 22, 2015, https://www.newmandala.org/the-double-captivity-of-chinese-privilege/.

---

76   Syed Hussein Alatas, *Intellectuals In Developing Societies* (London: Frank Cass, 1977), 26.

77   Masturah Alatas, *The Life in the Writing: Syed Hussein Alatas* (Singapore: Marshall Cavendish International, 2010).

78   See Mona Abaza, "Syed Hussein Alatas and Sociological Investigation in Southeast Asia," in *Debates On Islam and Knowledge in Malaysia and Egypt: Shifting Worlds* (London: Routledge, 2002), 121–141. See also "S.N.al-Attas: The Beacon On the Crest of a Hill or the Fusion of a Military Ethos With Science?," ibid., 88–106.

79   Alatas, "Intellectual Captivity and the Developing Societies." Paper delivered at the 30th International Congress of Human Sciences in Asia and North Africa, Mexico (August 3–8, 1976), 37.

Alatas, Sharifah Afra. "From Hurling the Sacred to Relearning Tradition and History." In *Islam and Socialism,* translated by Sharifah Afra Alatas. Kuala Lumpur: Gerakbudaya, 2021.

Alatas, Sharifah Munirah. "Applying Syed Hussein Alatas's Ideas in Contemporary Malaysian Society," *Asian Journal of Social Science* 48 (2020): 319–338.

Alatas, Sharifah Munirah. "A Critique of the Indo-Pacific Construct: Geopolitics of Western-Centrism." In *Asia and Europe in the 21st Century: New Anxieties, New Opportunities,* edited by Rahul Mishra, Azirah Hashim, Anthony Milner (London: Routledge, 2021): 185–198.

Alatas, Syed Farid. "Introduction." In *Thomas Stamford Raffles: Schemer or Reformer?* (Singapore: National University Press, 2020).

Alatas, Syed Farid. "Against the Grain: Malay Studies and the School of Autonomous Knowledge," *The Edge Malaysia,* May 30, 2021, https://www.theedgemarkets.com/article/against-grain-malay-studies-and-school-autonomous-knowledge.

Alatas, Syed Farid. "Foreword." In *Islam and Socialism,* translated by Sharifah Afra Alatas. Kuala Lumpur: Gerakbudaya, 2021.

Alatas, Syed Hussein, "Preliminary Observations On The Study Of Communalism And National Integration In Malaysia." In *Proceedings and Papers: Seminar On Research Programs In Singapore*, edited by Nanyang University Editorial Board. Singapore: Nanyang University, 1970.

Alatas, Syed Hussein. *Thomas Stamford Raffles 1781–1826: Schemer or Reformer.* Sydney: Angus & Robertson, 1971.

Alatas, Syed Hussein. *Modernization and Social Change.* Sydney: Angus and Robertson, 1972.

Alatas, Syed Hussein. *Siapa Yang Salah.* Singapore: Pustaka Nasional, 1972.

Alatas, Syed Hussein. "The Captive Mind in Development Studies." *International Social Science Journal* 34, no. 2 (1972): 9–25.

Alatas, Syed Hussein. "The Captive Mind and Creative Development." *International Social Science Journal* 36, no. 4 (1974): 691–9.

Alatas, Syed Hussein. "Erring Modernization: The Dilemma of Developing Societies." Paper delivered at Symposium on the Developmental Aims and Socio-Cultural Values in Asian Society, Bangkok, 3–7 November 1975.

Alatas, Syed Hussein. "Intellectual Captivity and the Developing Societies." Paper delivered at the 30th International Congress of Human Sciences in Asia and North Africa, Mexico, August 3–8, 1976.

Alatas, Syed Hussein. *"Intellectuals in Developing Societies."* London: Frank Cass, 1977.

Alatas, Syed Hussein. *The Myth of the Lazy Native: A study of the image of the Malays, Filipinos and Javanese from the 16th to the 20th century and its function in the ideology of colonial capitalism.* London: Frank Cass, 1977.

Alatas, Syed Hussein. "The Ideal of Excellence." Paper delivered at the Asian Youth Council 4th Advanced Youth Leadership Training Workshop, National Youth Training Institute, Singapore, May 28-June 9, 1978.

Alatas, Syed Hussein. *Kita dan Islam: Tumbuh Tiada Berbuah.* Pustaka Nasional, 1979.

Alatas, Syed Hussein. "Cultural Impediments to Scientific Thinking." In *Culture and Industrialization,* edited by Rolf E. Vente and Peter S.J. Chen. Baden-Baden: Nomos Verlagsgesellschaft, 1980.

Alatas, Syed Hussein. "A Heartfelt Prayer For Our Country." *New Straits Times,* December 27, 1999.

Alatas, Syed Hussein. "Intellectual Imperialism: Definition, Traits, and Problems." *Southeast Asian Journal of Social Science* 28, no. 2 (2000): 23–45.

Alatas, Syed Hussein. *Kemana Dengan Islam: 22 Artikel Pilihan* (Utusan, 2002).

Alatas, Syed Hussein. "The Development of an Autonomous Social Science Tradition in Asia: Problems and Prospects." *Asian Journal of Social Science* 30, 1 (2002): 150–157.

Alatas, Syed Imad. "Thoughts of the Late Syed Hussein Alatas." *Free Malaysia Today,* January 7, 2021.

Barr, Michael D. 2000. "Lee Kuan Yew and the 'Asian Values' Debate." *Asian Studies Review* 24 (3): 309–334.

Bernama News Agency, "National Professors Council Denies Issuing Statement on Emergency Proclamation." *The Malay Mail,* January 14, 2021.

Chakrabarty, Dipesh. *Provincialising Europe: Postcolonial Thought and Historical Difference.* Princeton: Princeton University Press, 2000.

Chaudhuri, Amit. "In the waiting-room of history." https://www.lrb.co.uk/the -paper/v26/n12/amit-chaudhuri/in-the-waiting-room-of-history Dirlik, Arif. *The Postcolonial Aura: Third World Criticism in The Age of Global Capitalism.* Boulder: Westview Press, 1998.

Fernando, Lloyd. "Introduction." In *Twenty-Two Malaysian Stories*: *An anthology of Writing in English.* Singapore: Heinemann Asia, 1968.

Freire, Paolo. *Pedagogy of the Oppressed.* Translated by Myra Bergman Ramos. New York: Continuum, 2005.

Hobsbawm, Eric and Terrence Ranger, eds. *The Invention of Tradition.* Cambridge: Cambridge University Press, 1983.

Jefferson, Thomas. "Notes on the State of Virginia." In *Call and Response: Key Debates in African American Studies.* Edited by Jennifer Burton and Henry Louis Gates. New York: w.w. Norton & Company, 2011.

Kessler, Clive. "Wise Muslim Rationalist, Culturally Grounded Cosmopolitan." *Akademika* 73 (May 2008): 134–136.

Khondker, Habibul Haque. "Sociology of Corruption and 'Corruption of Sociology': Evaluating the Contributions of Syed Hussein Alatas." *Current Sociology* 54, no. 1 (January 2006).

Laswell, Harold D. "Foreword." In *The Sociology of Corruption: The Nature, Function, Causes and Prevention of Corruption*, by Syed Hussein Alatas. Singapore: Donald Moore Press, 1968.

Lengyel, Peter. *International Social Science: The Unesco Experience.* New Jersey: Transaction, 1986.

Malcolm x, "Speech at the Audibon 13 December 1964." In *Malcolm X Speaks.* Edited by George Breitman. New York: Grove Press, 1990.

Merican, A. Murad "Remove Raffles, colonial narrative." *New Straits Times*, March 14, 2020.

Mignolo, Walter. "Coloniality Is Far From Over, And So Must Be Decoloniality." *Afterall* 43 (Spring/Summer 2017): 39–45.

Mohamad, Mahathir bin. *The Malay Dilemma.* Singapore: Asia Pacific Press, 1970.

Moosavi, Leon. "Decolonising Criminology: Syed Hussein Alatas on Crimes of the Powerful." *Critical Criminology* (2018).

Mura, Paolo and N.R. Sarah Wijesinghe. "Behind the Research Beliefs and Practices of Asian Tourism Scholars in Malaysia, Vietnam and Thailand." *Tourism Management Perspectives* 31 (July 2019).

Nair, Devan. "Neo-colonial Captive Minds." In https://www.infinityfoundation.com/mandala/s_es/s_es_nair-d_minds_frameset.htm.

Noor, Farish A. *The Other Malaysia.* Kuala Lumpur: Silverfish Books, 2002.

Noor, Farish A. *What Your Teacher Didn't Tell You.* Kuala Lumpur: Matahari Books, 2010.

Phillips, A.A. "On the Cultural Cringe." In *The Cultural Cringe.* Melbourne: Melbourne University Publishing, 2005.

Pillai, Patrick. "In Conversation with Prof. Syed Hussein Alatas." In *International Sociological Association e-bulletin*, no. 4 (2006).

Said, Edward W. *Culture and Imperialism.* New York: Vintage, 1993.

Selvadurai, Sivapalan, Er Ah Choy, Marlyna Maros, and Kamarulnizam Abdullah, "Shifting Discourses in Social Sciences: Nexus of Knowledge and Power." *Asian Social Science* 9, no.7 (2013): 97–106.

Tagore, Rabrindanath. "An Eastern University," https://www.tagoreweb.in/Essays/creative-unity-218/an-eastern-university-2637.

Teoh, Shannon Teoh. "Only Captive Minds Hang On to the NEP, says UMNO's Ku Li." Originally published in *The Malaysian Insider*, now defunct. Reposted here: https://dinmerican.wordpress.com/2012/04/01/only-captive-minds-hang-on-to-the-nep-says-umnos-ku-li/.

Tomlinson, John. "Cultural Globalisation: Placing and Displacing the West." In *The European Journal of Development Research* 8, no. 2 (1996).

Tsurumi, E. Patricia. "Colonizer and Colonized in Taiwan." In *Japan Examined: Perspectives on Modern Japanese History*. Edited by Hilary Conroy and Harry Wray. Hawaii: University of Hawaii Press, 1983.

wa Thiong'o, Ngugi. *Decolonising the Mind: The Politics of Language in African Literature*. Nairobi: Heinemann Kenya, 1986.

Wesley, John. *Explanatory Notes Upon the New Testament* (1757).

PART 2

Theorizing the Captive Mind

∵

CHAPTER 3

Alatas on Colonial and Autonomous Knowledge

Syed Farid Alatas

1   Introduction

The formative period of Alatas' thought was that of European colonialism, particularly in British Malaya and the Netherlands East Indies.[1] While a postgraduate student at the University of Amsterdam, he wrote what must have been his first piece on the problems of colonialism.[2] Here, he divided the problems created by colonialism into three categories. The first was the physical and material problems, involving, for example, agriculture, communication and housing. The second was the problem of organization, involving issues such as economic relations and industrialization, political administration and education, social welfare, and so on. The third referred to the non-material, that is, to the sociological, psychological and moral problems created by colonialism. Alatas believed that the greatest damage that colonialism brought about was in this third area and it was this problem that hampered the solution to the problems of the first and second type.[3] Already then, Alatas attached a great deal of importance to the nature of the elite in development, noting that the ruling elite which was nurtured in the colonial period lacked a well-integrated system of thought, having been unable to bring about a synthesise between their cultural heritage and Western thought. Alatas also noted the sense of inferiority among them.

> A feeling of inferiority implicit in their behavior is certainly due to the more general historical and social setting, since it is recognized that if one country is dominated by another for a considerable length of time, a section of the populace feel that their weakness is inherent in their way of life, and regard that of the dominating one as the cause of their superiority and strength. To get rid of this feeling of inequality they adopt the way of imitation. The classification of this group is not based on political

---

1   For Alatas' biography see Masturah Alatas, *The Life in the Writing – Syed Hussein Alatas: Author of The Myth of the Lazy Native* (Shah Alam: Marshall Cavendish, 2010).
2   Hussein Alatas, "Some Fundamental Problems of Colonialism," *Eastern World* (1956).
3   Alatas, "Some Fundamental Problems of Colonialism," 9.

© SYED FARID ALATAS, 2023 | DOI:10.1163/9789004521698_005

concepts. They are to be found amongst those who are progressive or reactionary, for or against immediate independence, the high and the low economic classes, officials and civilians alike.[4]

It was later that Alatas turned his attention to the political economic dimensions of colonialism. The nature of colonial society was understood in terms of the concept of colonial capitalism, an idea which was discussed in his demystifying and deconstructing work, *The Myth of the Lazy Native*.[5] In this work, the concern with an imitative local elite which internalized certain aspects of colonial ideology was combined with that of the political economic dimensions of colonial capitalism. Some European ideas about the natives functioned as constituent parts of colonial ideology to advance the interests of colonial capitalism. Above all, Alatas was concerned with the nature and perniciousness of colonial depictions and images of the native and how these images affected the colonised to the point of being internalised and believed in by them.

Alatas is an example of a decolonial scholar, having been born during the colonial period and experienced political independence. He is best known for his *The Myth of the Lazy Native*, which appeared in 1977, but he had earlier also wrote a critique of colonial ideology and practice in the form of a critical assessment of the political philosophy and conduct of the colonial founder of Singapore, Thomas Stamford Raffles.[6] The purpose of this chapter is to describe Alatas' decolonial perspective in terms of his theory, method and context. To this end, I discuss his *Thomas Stamford Raffes: Schemer or Reformer* and *The Myth of the Lazy Native*, their theses and method, and also discuss the context in which Alatas understood colonial knowledge to exist, that is, intellectual imperialism and the captive mind. The chapter concludes with Alatas' call for an autonomous social science tradition and a brief discussion on the School of Autonomous Knowledge.[7]

---

4 Ibid.

5 Syed Hussein Alatas, *The Myth of the Lazy Native: A study of the image of the Malays, Filipinos and Javanese from the 16th to the 20th century and its function in the ideology of colonial capitalism* (London: Frank Cass, 1977).

6 Syed Hussein Alatas, *Thomas Stamford Raffles: Schemer or Reformer* (Sydney: Angus & Robertson, 1971).

7 For other discussions on the thought of Alatas, see Sharifah Munirah Alatas, "Applying Syed Hussein Alatas' Ideas in Contemporary Malaysian Society," *Asian Journal of Social Science* 48 (2020): 319–338.

2   The Critique of Colonial Knowledge

Alatas' *The Myth of the Lazy Native* is an example of what Edward Said referred to as "revisionist" scholarship, that is, works that "set themselves the revisionist, critical task of dealing frontally with the metropolitan culture, using the techniques, discourses, and weapons of scholarship and criticism once reserved exclusively for the European."[8] The other example of Alatas' work that comes under this category is his *Thomas Stamford Raffles*.

In *Thomas Stamford Raffles*, Alatas presents a critique of the philosophy of Raffles at a time in Singapore scholarship when there was hardly any critical assessment of the man. Alatas presented a critical account of the thought and deeds of Raffles, and was decidedly against Eurocentric perspectives. Alatas felt that the silence among scholars about Raffles' questionable political philosophy and disturbing conduct was strange in that even by colonial standards he fell short of the humanitarianism that was attributed to him.[9] Alatas noted that there was the lack of an approach that did not take Raffles' words at face value but which assessed his views and conduct within the context of the total ideology of British imperialism, the interest of which was the capitalist transformation of the colonies, embracing all the major aspects of life.[10] Alatas referred to Raffles as a Western civilization monger with his political philosophy informed by the ideology of imperialism.[11]

Alatas had suggested that British historians and biographers displayed an ethnic bias in their treatment of Raffles.[12] In presenting Raffles as a progressive statesman and humanitarian reformer, they failed to discuss his ethnically prejudiced views of the different Asian communities, and various questionable acts such as his involvement in what came to be known as the Massacre of Palembang and the corruption case known as the Banjarmasin Affair. Alatas sought to understand these in the proper context of British imperialism and the ideology of colonial capitalism.

With respect to the Massacre of Palembang, Alatas leans towards the view that Raffles was complicit in the events that led up to the murders of twenty-four Europeans and sixty-three Javanese from the Dutch fort in Palembang, comprising soldiers and civilians.[13] On the Banjarmasin Affair or Banjarmasin

---

8   Edward Said, *Culture and Imperialism* (New York: Vintage, 1993), 293.
9   Alatas, *Thomas Stamford Raffles*, 50–51.
10   Ibid., 42.
11   Ibid., 43, 47.
12   Ibid., 2.
13   Ibid., 18.

Enormity, Alatas suggested that Raffles engaged in a suspicious acquisition of a territory along the Borneo coast by his friend, Alexander Hare, which involved nepotism and corruption.[14] Raffles had appointed Hare as Commissioner and Resident of Banjarmasin. The provision of labour supply to Hare included the transportation of forced labour from Java,[15] which in today's terms would amount to kidnapping, enslavement and human trafficking.[16]

Another dark aspect of Raffles' conduct was his support of the opium trade. He viewed Singapore as an outlet for the distribution of opium throughout the region, and strove to ensure that the Company's opium trade would be "protected and offered every facility."[17] Opium licenses were introduced, that is, "a certain number of houses may be licensed for the sale of madat or prepared opium."[18] These licenses were to be auctioned and re-auctioned "every three months until further orders." In addition to that, Raffles took for himself a 5 percent commission on each opium licence.[19] On the trade, Raffles said:

> Opium is one of the most profitable articles of eastern commerce: as such it is considered by our merchants … it is impossible to oppose trading in the same. In this sitation of affairs, therefore, we would rather advise that general leave be given to import opium at Malacca, and to allow the expectation from thence to Borneo and all the eastern parts *not* in the possession of the state.[20]

---

14   Ibid., 34–5.

15   Ibid., 36–7.

16   Leon Moosavi, "Decolonising Criminology: Syed Hussein Alatas on Crimes of the Powerful," *Critical Criminology* (2018).

17   Raffles to Mackenzie, 20 December 1819, enclosed in Raffles to Dart, 28 December 1819, vol. 50, Sumatra Factory Records, East India Company, National University of Singapore; India Office Library and Records. London: Recordak Microfilm Service. 1960. Monash University. Cited in Nadia Wright, "Farquhar and Raffles: The Untold Story," *Biblioasia* 14, no. 4 (2019).

18   Raffles to Travers, 20 March 1820, vol. 50, Sumatra Factory Records, East India Company, National University of Singapore; India Office Library and Records. London: Recordak Microfilm Service. 1960. Monash University. Cited in Nadia Wright, "Farquhar and Raffles: The Untold Story," *Biblioasia* 14, no. 4(2019).

19   Jennings to Farquhar, 15 August 1820, L. 4, SSR; Accountant General's office, 8 March 1826, vol. 71, Java Factory Records, East India Company, London, Recordak Microfilm Services, 1956. Microfilm, Monash University. Cited in Nadia Wright, "Farquhar and Raffles: The Untold Story," *Biblioasia* 14, no. 4(2019).

20   *The History of Java*, vol. 1, 104. Cited in Hans Derks, *History of the Opium Problem: The Assault on the East, Ca. 1600 – 1950* (Leiden: Brill, 2012), 290.

The British opium trade out of Singapore that Raffles approved of constituted Singapore's largest single source of revenue from 1824 until 1910.[21] Opium was also a major source of revenue during Raffles' governorship of Java.[22] Alatas had noted that the hypocrisy was lost on Abdullah bin Abdul Kadir Munshi, the Malay writer who was also for a time Raffles' scribe and copyist. While Abdullah counselled the Malays against the evils of opium smoking and praised the reputable Europeans for avoiding it, he seemed blind to the reality that while the Europeans did not consume opium, they traded in it, and even offered it, as Raffles did, to Malay emissaries.[23]

According to Alatas, Raffles' supporters and admirers, had generally remained silent about his problematic views and questionable activities. The purpose of *Thomas Stamford Raffles* was to provide an accurate assessment of his political philosophy and his conduct, and in the course of doing so, expose his faults and hypocrisy as well as his possible involvement in the crimes of the powerful.[24]

Moosavi discussed Alatas' work on Raffles as criminology in the decolonial mode.[25] To the extent that criminology as a field is Eurocentric, its research agenda is such that many topics and themes of great relevance to the South are omitted. Once such theme is colonization. Mainstream criminology does not take into account the role of colonialism in the interplay between past and contemporary globalization, global inequality and insecurity.[26] There is a silencing that goes on in Northern theory for which the colonial and coloniality are often deemed irrelevant. Missing or omitted is empire and the role of European capitalism in state formation, and the development of ideas and institutions, often accompanied by violence and criminal behaviour of the colonial state, but also the ideological criminalization of anti-colonial

---

21 C. Trocki, *Singapore: Wealth, Power and the Culture of Control*, London: Routledge, 2006, p. 20. Cited in Nadia Wright, "Farquhar and Raffles: The Untold Story," *Biblioasia* 14, 4(2019).

22 Derks, *History of the Opium Problem*, Appendix 4.

23 A. H. Hill, "The Hikayat Abdullah," Journal of the Malayan Branch of the Roya Asiatic Society 28, pt. 3 (1955), p. 80. Cited in Alatas, *The Myth of the Lazy Native*, pp. 138–9.

24 On colonial hypocrisy see Aimé Césaire, *Discourse on Colonialism* (New York & London: Monthly Review, 1972), 11.

25 See Moosavi's important contribution to this idea in his "Decolonising Criminology: Syed Hussein Alatas on Crimes of the Powerful."

26 Katja Franko Aas, "Visions of Global Control: Cosmopolitan Aspirations in a World of Friction," in *What is Criminology?*, ed. M. Bosworth and C. Hoyle (Oxford: Oxford University Press, 2011); Katja Franko Aas, "'The Earth is One but the World is Not': Criminological Theory and its Geopolitical Divisions," *Theoretical Criminology* 16, no. 1 (2012): 5–20, pp. 13–14.

resistance.[27] Another tendency of mainstream criminology is to focus on 'low level crime', 'street crime', 'everyday crime', or 'crimes of the powerless', at the expense of 'crimes of the powerful'.[28] The study of Raffles is at one and the same time a study of the crimes of the powerful as well as the criminality of the colonial state.

Turning to *The Myth of the Lazy Native*, its task is to understand the origins and function of the myth from the 16th to the 20th century in the Malay world with the explicit use of the sociology of knowledge approach. While this approach also informed Alatas' study on Raffles, it was implicit. Alatas understood the myth of "native" laziness and other incapacities to be a fundamental part of colonial ideology, that is, the ideology of colonial capitalism. This was a system of belief that sought to justify the political economic order of colonial capitalism.[29] Colonial capitalism was defined by Alatas as a capitalist system in which the control of and access to capital was predominantly by an alien power, which was the main beneficiary of that mode of production.[30] The ideology of colonial capitalism justified Western colonial rule not only by emphasizing their own civilizing superiority but by also denigrating the capacities of the "natives." This denigration covered their physiognomy, culture, society and history.[31] The views of the colonizers about the colonized should be seen as a reflection of colonial capitalist interests. For example, Alatas noted that while both Dutch liberals and conservatives in the nineteenth century agreed on promoting the capitalist interests of the Netherlands, their differences lay in the method of economic exploitation that was to be deployed.[32] The conservatives, who favoured the implementation of the culture system that was founded on forced labour, argued that the Javanese were not suited for free labour. The liberals, on the other hand, wished to promote industrialization and European capital, which required free labour. Thus, they, unlike the conservatives, appealed to the principles of justice.[33]

The ideology of colonial capitalism functioned to justify the workings and interests of colonial capitalism. A central feature of this ideology was the denigration of the natives and their history. They were portrayed as unintelligent,

---

27 Kerry Carrington, Russell Hogg & Maximo Sozzo, "Southern Criminology," *British Journal of Criminology* 56 (2016): 1–20, p. 8.
28 Moosavi, "Decolonising Criminology."
29 Alatas, *The Myth of the Lazy Native*, 1–2.
30 Ibid., 2.
31 Ibid., 7–8.
32 Ibid., 62.
33 Ibid., 64.

lazy, evil and unfit to rule.[34] Interestingly, it was the victims of colonial rule who were blamed rather than the colonial masters, the exploiters. Colonial administrators and scholars, that is, the ideologues of colonial rule, rarely pointed to injustices and atrocities committed by the Europeans against the natives or other non-Europeans. All this was done in the name of dispassionate, objective scholarship.[35]

3 The Method of Argumentation: The Sociology of Knowledge Approach

Alatas' approach can be said to be deductive in that is proceeds from the premise that the beliefs and doctrines of a group are influenced by their social location and, therefore, by the interests that the social location generates.

> The sociology of knowledge has established that different people develop different perspectives depending on their location in the class structure, the intellectual stratum, the cultural milieu, the power hierarchy and the cultural group. These factors operated within the context of time, place and situation. Stereotypes of and prejudices against other groups have been a common occurrence in the history of man. The universal and particulars in the forms of these stereo types and prejudices have to be isolated to arrive at a deeper understanding of the phenomenon.[36]

Alatas approvingly cites the "censure" of Marx and Engels on European historians of the 19th century who failed to make the connection between thought and interests. The relevant passage from Marx and Engels is as follows.

> Whilst in ordinary life every shopkeeper is very well able to distinguish between what somebody professes to be and what he really is, our historians have not yet won even this trivial insight. They take every epoch at its word and believe that everything it says and imagines about itself is true.[37]

---

34 Ibid., 8, 10–11.
35 Ibid., 12.
36 Ibid., 29–30.
37 Karl Marx & Frederick Engels, *The German Ideology* (London: Lawrence & Wisehart, 1970), 67. Cited in Alatas, *The Myth of the Lazy Native*, 10, 29.

The point is that the shopkeeper knew better than the historians the difference between what one claimed to be and what one really was.

The sociology of knowledge approach implied by the deductive premise that thought is a reflection of interests which informed Alatas' study on Raffles was further developed in *The Myth of the Lazy Native*. In the *Manifesto of the Communist Party*, Marx and Engels noted that the bourgeoisie wanted to create a world after its own image:

> The bourgeoisie, by the rapid improvement of all instruments of production, by the immensely facilitated means of communication, draws all, even the most barbarian, nations into civilisation. The cheap prices of commodities are the heavy artillery with which it batters down all Chinese walls, with which it forces the barbarians' intensely obstinate hatred of foreigners to capitulate. It compels all nations, on pain of extinction, to adopt the bourgeois mode of production; it compels them to introduce what it calls civilisation into their midst, i.e., to become bourgeois themselves. In one word, it creates a world after its own image.[38]

People then come to have a view of the world in line with that of the bourgeoisie, thereby providing ideological support for political-economic imperialism and capitalism. The function of ideology can be understood from its traits, as listed by Alatas.

> (a) it seeks to justify a particular political, social and economic order, (b) in this attempt, it distorts that part of the social reality likely to contradict its main presuppositions, (c) it exists primarily in the form of a manifest thought content which is different from its latent content, (d) it is authoritative in nature, (e) it expresses the interests of a distinctive group, (f) when it is dominant it creates a false consciousness among the group it represents as well as the group it dominates, (g) it can draw its ideas from any source, science, religion, culture, economics, history, etc., (h) it arises out of the conflicting interests of separate groups, in a society with a pronounced division of labour and social classes, and (i) its major ideas are eventually to a large extent conditioned by the mode of production in a given time and place.[39]

---

38 Karl Marx and Frederick Engels, *Manifesto of the Communist Party* (Peking: Foreign Languages Press, 1963), 38.

39 Alatas, *The Myth of the Lazy Native*, 1.

Alatas' interest in the sociology of knowledge began during his student days at the University of Amsterdam. In a monthly publication, *Progressive Islam*, founded by Alatas, he published an article on Karl Mannheim, outlining his sociology of knowledge approach.[40] According to this approach, the genesis and nature of thought must be understood in the context of the social situation. Knowledge is not just the outcome of individual efforts, but the collective outcome of the co-operative process of group life.[41] In addition to that thought was also influenced by the collective unconscious, volitional impulses and the irrational element in group life that underlay conscious and rational behavior.[42] In other words, Mannheim looked at the origins and nature of knowledge in terms of the social location as well as the interests and motivations of the group connected to collective unconscious. His method sought to establish the relations between a given set of ideas or system of thought, on the one hand, and the historical, social position of a group, its action, and its collective unconscious motivations, on the other.[43]

It is the recognition of such relations that led Marx and Engles to censure the historians of Europe who took statements and reports at face value.

The interests in question may be particular or total, and ideological or utopian. The particular conception of ideology refers to thought that distorts or conceals reality. There is a conscious or deliberate attempt to do so. It operates at the level of the psychology of interests. An example is the claim of professional propogandists that vaccines are dangerous, an assertion that promotes the anti-vaxx industry. The total conception of ideology refers to an entire system of thought, or total *Weltanschauung*, not just fragmentary assertions, that are tied to their socio-historical location, and which function to justify a particular order. An example would be the thought that governs belief in the inherent superiority of males over females as the basis for the organization of society. In the particular conception of ideology, the reference is to conscious interests, while in the total conception of ideology, the reference is to the correspondence between the social situation and the entire system of thought.[44]

Mannheim also made the distinction between two types of styles of thought, that is, ideology and utopia. Ideologies referred to styles of thought of the dominant or ruling groups that functioned to preserve the current order. The group

---

40 Hussein Alatas, "Karl Mannheim (1894 – 1947)," *Progressive Islam* 1, no. 7–8 (1955).

41 Alatas, "Karl Mannheim," 4; Karl Mannheim, *Ideology and Utopia: An Introduction to the Sociology of Knowledge* (London: Routledge & Kegan Paul, 1936), 2–3.

42 Alatas, "Karl Mannheim," 4; Mannheim, *Ideology and Utopia*, 4, 28.

43 Hans Speier, Review of *Ideology and Utopia*, *American Journal of Sociology* 43, 1 (1937).

44 Alatas, "Karl Mannheim," 4; Mannheim, *Ideology and Utopia*, 50–1.

was so interest-bound to the current order or situation that certain facts or realities that undermined their sense of domination. In this case, the collective unconscious veils the real condition of society, both to itself and to others, thus ppreserving the current order. Utopias, on the other hand, referred to the styles of thought of the dominted. The dominated may be so interest-bound to the destruction of the given order or situation such that they may only perceive those aspects of the situation that negate the current order. As a result, they are unable to correctly diagnose the existing condition of society. Here, the collective unconscious, guided as it is by a wishful representation of the real condition of society, veils certains aspects that are not in line with its vision of the future.[45] In Alatas' application of Mannheim's approach, he limited himself to the concern with ideology, specifically the ideology of colonial capitalism.

4   Intellectual Imperialism and the Captive Mind

Alatas not only drew attention to the function of the myth of the lazy native in colonial ideology but also to its internalization by the loclas. He states that colonial knowledge not only functioned to justify the colonial order, but also influenced the indigenous population, the colonised, and noted that "[a]n ideology is never confined to its originating group. It is also shared by those who are dominated by the system of which the ideology is the rationalization."[46] This point takes us to the topic of the captive mind and intellectual imperialism, the psychological and structural contexts within which colonial knowledge operates.

The adoption of the ideology of the coloniser by the colonised is a reflection of the ubiquity of the captive mind that exists within the structure of intellectual imperialism, both being concepts that emerged in Alatas'thought.

Part of that ideological justification for capitalism lay in cultural production, including the social sciences and humanities. In order for this to happen, there had to be the dismantling of the local and indigenous knowledge systems of the various societies that were to eventually be overrun by colonialism and capitalism. This took place through the process of what Santos and Grosfuegel refer to as epistemicide or the murder of knowledge, that is, the destruction of non-Western knowledge systems and discourses.[47] In his elaboration of this

---

45   Alatas, "Karl Mannheim," 4; Mannheim, *Ideology and Utopia*, 36.

46   Alatas, *The Myth of the Lazy Native*, 132, 168.

47   Boaventura de Sousa Santos, *Epistemologies of the South: Justice against Epistemicide* (Oxford: Routledge, 2014), 92, 153; Ramon Grosfoguel, "The Structure of Knowledge in Westernized Universities: Epistemic Racism/Sexism and the Four Genocides/

concept, Grosfuegel discusses how several historical incidences of epistemicide functioned to erase local and indigenous knowledge, thereby contributing to the creation among the natives of a worldview that was more in line with the interests of colonial capitalism. This epistemicide refers to the destruction of knowledge systems that were dominant in Asia, Africa and Latin America prior to capitalist and colonial expansion,[48] and helped to consolidate the hold of intellectual imperialism and establish the presence of the captive mind.

Among the earlier discussions on the problem of academic imperialism was the 1968 issue of *Seminar*.[49] A year before that Johan Galtung defined scientific colonialism as "that process whereby the centre of gravity for the acquisition of knowledge abouyt the nation is located outside the nation itself."[50]

Intellectual imperialism and the related concept of the captive mind were further conceptualized by Syed Hussein Alatas.[51] Intellectual imperialism is analogous to political and economic imperialism in that it refers to the "domination of one people by another in their world of thinking."[52] Intellectual imperialism was more direct in the colonial period, whereas today it has more to do with the West's control of and influence over the flow of social scientific knowledge rather than its ownership and control of academic institutions. Indeed, this form of hegemony was "not imposed by the West through colonial domination, but accepted willingly with confident enthusiasm, by scholars and planners of the former colonial territories and even in the few countries that remained independent during that period."[53]

Intellectual imperialism refers to both the role of research and scholarship in the service of political and economic imperialism, as well as a structure analogous to political and economic imperialism, that is, the "domination of one people by another in their world of thinking."[54] There are imperialistic

---

Epistemicides of the Long 16th Century," *Human Architecture: Journal of the Sociology of Self-Knowledge* 11, no. 1 (2013).

48   Grosfoguel, "The Structure of Knowledge in Westernized Universities."

49   Academic Colonialism: a symposium on the influences which destroy intellectual independence, *Seminar* 112 (1968).

50   Johan Galtung, "Scientific Colonialism," *Transitions* 30 (1967).

51   Syed Hussein Alatas, "Academic Imperialism," Lecture delivered to the History Society, University of Singapore, 26 September 1969; Syed Hussein Alatas, "The Captive Mind in Development Studies," *International Social Science Journal* 34, no. 2 (1972); Syed Hussein Alatas, "The Captive Mind and Creative Development," *International Social Science Journal* 36, no. 4 (1974); Syed Hussein Alatas, "Intellectual Imperialism: Definition, Traits, and Problems," *Southeast Asian Journal of Social Science* 28, no. 1 (2000).

52   Alatas, "Intellectual Imperialism," 24.

53   Ibid., 7–8, 24.

54   Ibid., 24.

relations in the world of the social sciences and humanities that parallels those in the world of international political economy.

Intellectual imperialism in this sense began in the colonial period with the setting up and direct control of schools, universities and publishing houses by the colonial powers in the colonies. It is for this reason that it is accurate to say that the "political and economic structure of imperialism generated a parallel structure in the way of thinking of the subjugated people." These parallels include the six main traits of exploitation, tutelage, conformity, secondary role of dominated intellectuals and scholars, rationalization of the civilizing mission, and the inferior talent of scholars from the home country specializing in studies of the colony.[55]

Today, intellectual imperialism is more indirect than direct. If, under political economic imperialism the colonial powers had direct control over the political systems, production and marketing of goods of the colonies, today that control is indirect via international law, the power of major commercial banks, the threat of military intervention by the major powers, and covert and clandestine operations by various governments of advanced nations. Similarly, it can be said that in the postcolonial period what we have is intellectual neo-imperialism or intellectual neo-colonialism to the extent there is Western monopolistic control of and influence over the nature and flows of social scientific knowledge, even though political independence has been achieved.

If in the colonial past, academic imperialism was maintained via colonial power, today academic neo-colonialism is maintained via the condition of academic dependency. Academic dependency theory is a dependency theory of the global state of the social sciences. It defines academic dependency as a condition in which the knowledge production of certain scholarly communities is conditioned by the development and growth of knowledge of other scholarly communities to which the former is subjected. Then relations of interdependence between two or more scientific communities, and between these and global transactions in knowledge, assumes the form of dependency when some scientific communities (those located in the knowledge powers) can expand according to certain criteria of development and progress, while other scientific communities (such as those in the developing societies) can only do this as a reflection of that expansion, which generally has negative effects on their development according to the same criteria.[56]

---

55   Ibid., 24–7.

56   For more on the theory of academic dependency, see Philip G. Altbach, "Literary Colonialism: Books in the Third World," *Harvard Educational Review* 45 (1975): 226–236; Philip G. Altbach, "Servitude of the Mind? Education, Dependency, and Neocolonialism,"

The dimensions of academic dependency can be listed as follows: (i) dependence on ideas; (ii) dependence on the media of ideas; (iii) dependence on the technology of education; (iv) dependence on aid for research as well as teaching; (v) dependence on investment in education; (vi) dependence of recognition; (vi) dependence on recognition in the knowledge powers; and (vii) dependence of Third World social scientists on demand in the knowledge powers for their skills.[57]

Academic dependency at the level of ideas should be seen in terms of the domination of social science teaching and research by the captive mind, a phenpmenon conceptualized by Alatas. The captive mind can be said to be the psychological dimension of academic dependency whereby the dependent scholar is more a passive recipient of research agenda, methods and ideas from the social science powers. The psychological dimension to this dependency, captured by the notion of the captive mind, is such that the dependent scholar is more a passive recipient of research agenda, theories and methods from the knowledge powers.[58] Alatas defined the captive mind as an "uncritical and imitative mind dominated by an external source, whose thinking is deflected from an independent perspective."[59] The external source is Western social science and humanities and the uncritical imitation influences all the constituents of scientific activity such as problem-selection, conceptualization, analysis, generalization, description, explanation, and interpretation.[60]

Among the characteristics of the captive mind are the inability to be creative and raise original problems, the inability to devise original analytical methods, and alienation from the main issues of indigenous society. The captive mind is trained almost entirely in the Western sciences, reads the works of Western authors, and is taught predominantly by Western teachers, whether in the West itself or through their works available in local centres of education. Mental captivity is also found in the suggestion of solutions and policies. Furthermore, it is reveals itself at the levels of theoretical as well as empirical work.

Teachers College Record 79, no. 2 (1977); Garreau, "The Multinational Version of Social Science"; Frederick H. Garreau, "Another Type of Third World Dependency: The Social Sciences," *International Sociology* 3, no. 2 (1988); Syed Farid Alatas, "Academic Dependency and the Global Division of Labour in the Social Sciences," *Current Sociology* 51, no. 6 (2003).

57 Alatas, "Academic Dependency"; Syed Farid Alatas, *Alternative Discourses in Asian Social Science: Responses to Eurocentrism* (New Delhi: Sage, 2006).

58 Alatas, "Academic Dependency," 603.

59 Alatas, "The Captive Mind and Creative Development," 692.

60 Alatas, "The Captive Mind in Development Studies," 11.

5   The School of Autonomous Knowledge

Intellectual imperialism may or may not be accompanied by academic dependency and the captive mind. In other words, scholars in the South, subjected as they are to intellectual imperialism, may or may not become captive minds that are academically dependent, especially in terms of dependency on ideas. For Alatas, the prospects for academic dependency reversal would depend on the extent to which autonomous social science traditions in the global South could emerge.

In 1979, Alatas had written on the need for an autonomous social science tradition in Asia, by which he meant "the linking of social science research and thinking to specifically Asian problems."[61] This would require the identification of "criteria of significance distinctive of the region."[62] He did not mean by this the mere attention to local issues with the appropriate methods.[63] An autonomous tradition refers to one which has the following features: (1) the identification and treatment of definite problems, (2) the application of specific methods, (3) the recognition of definite phenomena, (4) the creation of new concepts, and (5) the relation with other branches of knowledge.[64]

Alatas goes on to state that it is necessary to specifiy the kinds of knowledge required for the development of an autonomous social science tradition. These are: (1) foundational knowledge, (2) consolidative knowledge, (3) reactive knowledge, and (4) developmental knowledge. Foundational knowledge refers to knowledge of the foundations of societies, their culture, religion and other defining aspects of social life. Consolidative knowledge refers to knowledge that consolidates and strengthens those foundations. Reactive knowledge, on the other hand, refers to knowledge that is required to react to ideas that tend to undermine the basis of social life. Finally, developmental knowledge is the knowledge required to achieve peace, justice, welfare and insight into the life of humans. These types of knowledge are suggestive of the goals of an autonomous social science tradition.[65] In the development of an autonomous social science tradition, Alatas warned against the influence of nihilism, that is, the neglect of the idea of significance in, for example, the selection of topics.[66]

---

61   Syed Hussein Alatas, "Towards an Asian Social Science Tradition," *New Quest* 17 (1979), 265.

62   Alatas, "Towards an Asian Social Science Tradition," 268.

63   Syed Hussein Alatas, "The Development of an Autonomous Social Science Tradition in Asia: Problems and Prospects," *Asian Journal of Social Science* 30, no. 1 (2002), 150.

64   Alatas, "The Development of an Autonomous Social Science Tradition in Asia," 151.

65   Alatas, "The Development of an Autonomous Social Science Tradition in Asia," 153–4.

66   Ibid., 154.

Elsewhere, Alatas elaborates that an autonomous tradition would emerge only if there was consciousness of the need to be free of domination by a hegemonic external intellectual tradition such as that of a previous colonial power.[67] Alatas had something of a combative spirit. He recognized the combative element in the sciences, which he felt was not sufficiently developed in Asia. He believed in the adversarial role of the social sciences, to oppose imperialism and the captive mind, and to correct the erroneous and fallacious.[68]

About six centuries ago, Ibn Khaldun discovered a new science that he called the science of human society (*ilm al-ijtima al-insani*). On this he said:

> Perhaps some later (scholar), aided by the divine gifts of a sound mind and of solid scholarship, will penetrate into these problems in greater detail than we did here. A person who creates a new discipline does not have the task of enumerating (all) the (individual) problems connected with it. His task is to specify the subject of the discipline and its various branches and the discussions connected with it. His successors, then, may gradually add more problems, until the (discipline) is completely (presented).[69]

Alatas cited this passage from Ibn Khaldun, then continued with this plea:

> May I convey here, this message from Ibn Khaldun to the International Sociological Association, that in the coming World Congress of Sociology a session be created on the autonomous sociological tradition? This would alert sociologists throughout the world to pool their attention on this extremely vital need for the development of sociology.[70]

While this was a call for sociologists to think along the lines of autonomous knowledge, Alatas himself had created such a tradition that began in the field of Malay Studies. The Department of Malay Studies at the National University of Singapore has a tradition of creating alternative discourses to Orientalism and Eurocentrism. The department was founded by Alatas in 1967 and headed by him for almost two decades. During that period, a distinctive approach in

---

67 Syed Hussein Alatas, "The Autonomous, the Universal and the Future of Sociology," *Current Sociology* 54 (2006), 10.

68 Alatas, "The Development of an Autonomous Social Science Tradition in Asia," 155.

69 Ibn Khaldun, *The Muqaddimah*, trans. Franz Rosenthal (London: Routledge and Kegan Paul, 1958), vol. 3, 481.

70 Alatas, "The Autonomous, the Universal and the Future of Sociology," 16–17.

sociology and other social sciences emerged and influenced many of the students he trained who had later joined the department as lecturers.[71] Malay Studies, as a systematic field of inquiry in the social sciences, was developed with a distinctive and original approach by Alatas. Noor Aisha's assessment sums this up very well:

> Unlike the dominant anti-social science approach that had characterised representations of the Malays during the colonial period and thereafter, Malay Studies began to witness the emergence of a critical and systematic body of knowledge that creatively selected and assimilated perspectives, concepts and methodologies from both Western social science and indigenous and Asian intellectual traditions, to raise and diagnose problems of relevance to the Malays. Theses and monographs produced by students and academic staff during this period raised original problems that reflected not the interests of those in power but concerns and challenges of the Malays and Asian societies more generally as they adapt to political, economic, socio-cultural changes and the process of development. Even research and the teaching of language and literature departed from the emphasis on formalism but was conceived and approached as a mirror of social history. Studies were approached and understood using the contributions of relevant social science perspectives and concepts such as sociology of knowledge, social structure, ideology and its function, social change, modernisation, elites, and so on. At the same time, new concepts were created from indigenous sources and traditions to explicate phenomenon.[72]

The approach emerged, first of all, in the writings of Alatas. Examples include the historical, sociological research on colonial ideology with a focus on the political philosophy of Raffles[73] and the myth of Malay, Javanese and Filipino laziness,[74] his critique of intellectual imperialism,[75] and his call for an autonomous social science tradition in Asia.[76]

---

71 Noor Aisha Abdul Rahman, personal communication, July 28, 2018.
72 Ibid.
73 Alatas, *Thomas Stamford Raffles*.
74 Alatas, *Myth of the Lazy Native*. See also Masturah Alatas, "Four decades of a Malay myth," *The New Mandala* January 23, 2017.
75 Alatas, "Academic Imperialism"; Alatas, "Intellectual imperialism."
76 Syed Hussein Alatas, "Towards an Asian social science tradition"; Syed Hussein Alatas, "Social aspects of endogenous intellectual creativity: the problem of obstacles – guidelines

Some of Alatas' students wrote along the lines of an autonomous social science tradition. Examples are Shaharuddin Maaruf's works on the re-examination of the concept of the hero in Malay tradition, his critical study on Malay ideas of development in which he examines the ideological nature of what mainstream scholarship considers to be progressive ideas, and his fresh perspective and theorising of tradition and modernisation in the Malay world,[77] and Sharifah Maznah Syed Omar's critical work that examines the role of myth in maintaining the interests of the feudal elite.[78] A Malay Studies scholar from the third generation, Azhar Ibrahim Alwee, has made many contributions to the critique of Orientalism in the study of the Malay world.[79] Azhar has carefully delineated the main features of Orientalism as they are found in the study of Malay literature, history and society. Another scholar from Malay Studies in Singapore, Tham Seong Chee, wrote on the problem of intellectual colonisation.[80]

This approach, which was established at the Department of Malay Studies in 1967 at the then University of Singapore, and which can be said to be a

---

for research," in *Intellectual creativity in endogenous culture*, eds. A. Abdel-Malek & A. N. Pandeya (Tokyo: United Nations University, 1981).

77   Shaharuddin Maaruf, *The Concept of the Hero in Malay Society* (Singapore: Eastern Universities Press, 1984); Shaharuddin Maaruf, *Malay Ideas on Development: From Feudal Lord to Capitalist* (Singapore: Times Book International, 1989); Shaharuddin Maaruf, "Some theoretical problems concerning tradition and modernization among the Malays of Southeast Asia," in *Asian Tradition and Modernization: Perspectives from Singapore*, ed.Yong Mun Cheong (Singapore: Times Academic Press, 1992).

78   Sharifah Maznah Syed Omar, *Myths and the Malay Ruling Class* (Singapore: Times Academic Press, 1993).

79   Azhar Ibrahim, "Orientalisme dalam pengajian Melayu" ("Orientalism in Malay Studies"). Persidangan Antarabangsa Bahasa, Sastera dan Kebudayaan Melayu ke-2, bertemakan "Ke arah bitara kesarjanaan Melayu," Singapore, September 1–3, 2002; Azhar Ibrahim, "Sociological Readings of Classical Malay Literature: Possible Contribution to the Sociology of Religion of Malays of South-East Asia," in *Kesusasteraan Tradisional Asia Tenggara (Traditional Southeast Asian Literature)*, eds. Zaiton Ajamain & Norazian Ahmad (Kuala Lumpur: Dewan Bahasa & Pustaka, 2005); Azhar Ibrahim, "Contemporary Malay Studies: Diverging Visions, Competing Priorities and its Implications: A Critique," *Asian Journal of Social Science* 35, no. 4–5 (2007); Azhar Ibrahim, "Orientalism, Ethno-Religious Exclusivism and Academicism in Malay Studies: The Challenges for the Emergence of an Autonomous Sociological Discourse." Paper presented at the World Congress of Sociology, RC 35: Concept Formation in Asian Sociology, July 16, 2010, Gothenberg, Sweden; Azhar Ibrahim, *Menyanggah Belenggu Kerancuan Fikiran Masakini* (Kuala Lumpur: SIRD, 2016); Azhar Ibrahim, *Historical Imagination and Cultural Responses to Colonialism and Nationalism: A Critical Malay(sian) Perspective* (Kuala Lumpur: SIRD, 2017) [English version of Azhar Ibrahim, *Menyanggah Belenggu*].

80   Tham Seong Chee, "Intellectual Colonization," *Suara Universiti* 2, no. 2 (1971).

decolonial one, is influenced by Alatas, and informs the writings of the first and second generation of scholars following him. Take, for example, Noor Aisha Abdul Rahman, a student of Alatas and former Head of the Department of Malay Studies. She works in the area of the administration of Muslim law and also has a larger interest in the religious orientation of the Malays. In her approach there is a concern with the colonial image, be it of law, religion, Malay culture and so on.[81] Beyond this, there is the recognition of the continuities between the colonial and post-colonial era in which it is noted that certain colonial orientations about the Malays had been internalised by the Malays themselves and survived into the period after independence. Also distinctive of the Malay Studies approach is the position that it was not only colonialism that played a role in the construction of regressive orientations about the Malays, but also the Malay ruling class which not only internalised those orientations but benefitted from colonial capitalism and was party to the exploitation of the Malays.[82] It is further recognised that the dominant thinking about the Malays and their problems tends to be culturalist, overemphasising the role and influence of Islam in an essentialist and ahistorical manner.[83] Noor Aisha defines the culturalist approach in the following manner:

> The approach is characterised by a style of thought in which perspectives and methodology from the social sciences utilised in understanding culture and society are largely neglected. Although culturalists are not anti-culture and do not ignore it in defining a community, the problem lies in their tendency to shore up an essentialist culture, one perceived as a static, homogeneous set of common identifiers that defines a community, such as language, race or religion, wrapped into a sense of common identity. This identity is deemed more or less stable, permanent and fixed at any given point in time in terms of its meanings and forms.[84]

---

81   See her book, *Colonial Image of Malay Adat Laws: A Critical Appraissal of Studies on Adat Law in the Malay Peninsula during the Colonial Era and Some Continuities* (Leiden: Brill, 2006).

82   Alatas, *The Myth of the Lazy Native*, 159–63.

83   Noor Aisha Abdul Rahman, "Changing Roles, Unchanging Perceptions and Institutions: Traditionalism and its Impact on Women and Globalization in Muslim Societies in Asia," *The Muslim World* 97 (2007), 479.

84   Noor Aisha Abdul Rahman, "Issues on Islam and the Muslims in Singapore Post-9/11: An Analysis of the Dominant Perspective," in *Encountering Islam: The Politics of Religious Identities in Southeast Asia*, ed. Hui Yew-Foong (Singapore: Institute of Southeast Asian Studies, 2013), 337. See also, Noor Aisha Abdul Rahman, "The Dominant Pespective on Terrorism and Its Implicaton for Social Cohesion: The Case of Singapore," *The Copenhagen Journal of Asian Studies* 27, no. 2 (2009), 111.

There is a tendency in the culturalist approach to view communities as static and isolated, immune from the variety of material and ideal influences that are often the subject of social scientific investigations.[85] In fact, Noor Aisha notes that the culturalist approach is held to be a survival of the Orientalist thought style inherited from the colonial period.[86] It is a continuation of the reductionist, essentialist thinking that characterised colonial, Orientalist thought in the past that has survived into the post-colonial period and internalised by the post-colonial state and society actors.[87]

The task of critique and reconstruction is to then examine the dominant orientations or styles of thought in a particular domain of life sociologically and to then assess the impact of this orientation on the actual lives of people.[88] The approach is by way of the sociology of knowledge and draws upon the work of Karl Mannheim, in addition to Alatas.[89]

In my own elaboration of what autonomous knowledge means, I have suggested that there are varying degrees of creativity that would define autonomous knowledge. alternateness. At the simplest level, autonomous social science would insist on a cautious but creative application of Western methods and theories to the local situation. The creative application of a theory that originated in the West to the local situation must be included as part of the creation of autonomous knowledge. In this case, however, we cannot yet speak of autonomous knowledge if the mainstream is not engaged, critiqued and subverted or an alternative set of conceptualizations and theories presented. At a higher level of alternateness and, therefore, universality, both locally-generated and Western methods and theories are applied to the local context. At yet another level of alternateness and universality, local, Western and other indigenous methods and theories (that is, indigenous to other non-Western societies) are applied to the local setting.[90]

---

85   Noor Aisha Abdul Rahman, "Issues on Islam and the Muslims in Singapore Post-9/11," 337–8.

86   Ibid., 339.

87   Noor Aisha Abdul Rahman, personal communication, Singapore, July 18, 2018.

88   Noor Aisha Abdul Rahman, "Traditionalism and its Impact on the Administration of Justice: The Case of the Syariah Court of Singapore," *Inter-Asia Cultural Studies* 5, no. 3 (2004).

89   Mannheim, *Ideology and Utopia*; Karl Mannheim, *Conservatism: A Contribution to the Sociology of Knowledge* (London: Routledge, 1986).

90   For more on this see Syed Farid Alatas, "The Definition and Types of Alternative Discourses," in *De-Westernizing Communication Research: Altering Questions and Changing Frameworks,* ed. Georgette Wang (London: Routledge, 2011).

The late Mona Abaza, in her very important comparative study on knowledge production in Egypt and Malaysia, syggested that Alatas "failed to create his own school of empirical research in either Singapore or Malaysia. He provided no generation of students to undertake sociological studies of Southeast Asian societies."[91] John Nery, on the other hand, refers to the "Alatas tradition," that is,

> the lineage of elite Malaysian scholars begun by that towering pioneer, the late Syed Hussein Alatas ... We can use the appropriation of Rizal as object of study or source of inspiration to trace this living tradition of inquiry, beginning with Hussein Alatas' own influential deconstruction of "the myth of the lazy native," to Chandra Muzaffar's founding of a Malaysian social reform group on Rizal's death anniversary, to Shaharuddin Maaruf's brave but unjustly neglected discussion of "the concept of a hero in Malay society," which posited Rizal as one of three ideal heroes; down to Farish A. Noor's web-based ruminations on Rizal and especially Syed Farid Alatas' important, groundbreaking work on alternative discourses, with Rizal as both precursor and paragon. The Alatas tradition is a living lineage ...[92]

Although Alatas himself did not speak of a school of thought, his ideas for an autonomous social science tradition have influenced scholars for two generations, and a school can be said to have emerged. Scholars and writers of Indonesia, Malaysia and Singapore such as Chandra Muzaffar, Shaharuddin Maaruf, Wan Zawawi Ibrahim, Noor Aisha Abdul Rahman, Syed Farid Alatas, Norshahril Saat, Azhar Ibrahim, Teo Lee Ken, Mohamed Imran Mohamed Taib, Pradana Boy Zulian and Okky Puspa Madasari are all part of this autonomous social science tradition in their various fields and can be said to represent the School of Autonomous Knowledge. Young scholars of the third generation in the Malay world are incorporating this critical tradition in their scholarship as they embark on dissertations and other projects. The School of Autonomous

---

91 Mona Abaza, *Debates on Islam and Knowledge in Malaysia and Egypt: Shifting Worlds* (London: Routledge Curzon, 2002), 138–39.

92 John Nery, "All the Honorable Men of the World," *Philippine Daily Inquirer*, December 17, 2012; John Nery, *Revolutionary Spirit: José Rizal in Southeast Asia* (Singapore: ISEAS, 2011), 202. For more on the Alatas tradition as decolonial, see Walter Mignolo, "Spirit out of Bounds Returns to the East: The Closing of the Social Sciences and the Opening of Independent Thoughts," *Current Sociology* 62, no. 4 (2014): 584–602.

Knowledge is likely the only school of thought in the human sciences to have emerged in the Malay world.[93]

Bibliography

Abaza, Mona. *Debates on Islam and Knowledge in Malaysia and Egypt: Shifting Worlds.* London: RoutledgeCurzon, 2002.

Academic Colonialism: a symposium on the influences which destroy intellectual independence, *Seminar* 112 (1968).

Alatas, Masturah. *The Life in the Writing – Syed Hussein Alatas: Author of The Myth of the Lazy Native.* Shah Alam: Marshall Cavendish, 2010.

Alatas, Masturah. "Four decades of a Malay myth." *The New Mandala* January 23, 2017.

Alatas, Sharifah Munirah. "Applying Syed Hussein Alatas's Ideas in Contemporary Malaysian Society." *Asian Journal of Social Science* 48 (2020): 319–338.

Alatas, Syed Farid. "Academic Dependency and the Global Division of Labour in the Social Sciences." *Current Sociology* 51, no. 6 (2003): 599–613.

Alatas, Syed Farid. *Alternative Discourses in Asian Social Science: Responses to Eurocentrism.* New Delhi: Sage, 2006.

Alatas, Syed Farid. "The Definition and Types of Alternative Discourses," in Georgette Wang, ed., *De-Westernizing Communication Research: Altering Questions and Changing Frameworks* (London: Routledge, 2011), 238–253.

Alatas, Syed Hussein. "Some Fundamental Problems of Colonialism." *Eastern World* (1955): 9–10.

Alatas, Syed Hussein. "Karl Mannheim (1894–1947)." *Progressive Islam* 1, no. 7–8 (1955): 4–5.

Alatas, Syed Hussein. "Academic Imperialism." Lecture delivered to the History Society, University of Singapore, 26 September 1969.

Alatas, Syed Hussein. *Thomas Stamford Raffles 1781–1826: Schemer or Reformer.* Sydney: Angus & Robertson, 1971.

Alatas, Syed Hussein. "The Captive Mind in Development Studies." *International Social Science Journal* 34, no. 2 (1972): 9–25.

Alatas, Syed Hussein. "The Captive Mind and Creative Development." *International Social Science Journal* 36, no. 4 (1974): 691–9.

---

93 Syed Imad Alatas, "Thoughts of the Late Syed Hussein Alatas," *Free Malaysia Today*, January 7, 2021. For another discussion on Alatas and autonomous knowledge see Joao Marcelo Maia. "History of Sociology and the Quest for Intellectual Autonomy in the Global South: The Cases of Alberto Guerreiro Ramos and Syed Hussein Alatas," *Current Sociology* 62, no. 7 (2014): 1097–1115. See also Moosavi, "Decolonising Criminology."

Alatas, Syed Hussein. *The Myth of the Lazy Native: A study of the image of the Malays, Filipinos and Javanese from the 16th to the 20th century and its function in the ideology of colonial capitalism.* London: Frank Cass, 1977.

Alatas, Syed Hussein. "Towards an Asian social science tradition." *New Quest* 17 (1979): 265–269.

Alatas, Syed Hussein. "Social aspects of endogenous intellectual creativity: the problem of obstacles – guidelines for research." In *Intellectual creativity in endogenous culture*, eds. A. Abdel-Malek & A. N. Pandeya (Tokyo: United Nations University, 1981).

Alatas, Syed Hussein. "Intellectual Imperialism: Definition, Traits, and Problems." *Southeast Asian Journal of Social Science* 28, no. 2 (2000): 23–45.

Alatas, Syed Hussein. "The Development of an Autonomous Social Science Tradition in Asia: Problems and Prospects." *Asian Journal of Social Science* 30, no. 1 (2002): 150–157.

Alatas, Syed Hussein. "The Autonomous, the Universal and the Future of Sociology." *Current Sociology* 54 (2006): 7–23.

Alatas, Syed Imad. "Thoughts of the Late Syed Hussein Alatas." *Free Malaysia Today*, January 7, 2021.

Altbach, Philip G. "Literary Colonialism: Books in the Third World." *Harvard Educational Review* 45 (1975): 226–236.

Altbach, Philip G. "Servitude of the Mind? Education, Dependency, and Neocolonialism." *Teachers College Record* 79, no. 2 (1977): 187–204.

Derks, Hans. *History of the Opium Problem: The Assault on the East, Ca. 1600 – 1950.* Leiden: Brill, 2012.

Galtung, Johan. "Scientific Colonialism." *Transitions* 30 (1967): 11–15.

Garreau, Frederick H. "The Multinational Version of Social Science with Emphasis Upon the Discipline of Sociology." *Current Sociology* 33, no. 3 (1985): 1–169.

Garreau, Frederick H. "Another Type of Third World Dependency: The Social Sciences." *International Sociology* 3, no. 2 (1988): 171–178.

Grosfoguel, Ramon. "The Structure of Knowledge in Westernized Universities: Epistemic Racism/Sexism and the Four Genocides/Epistemicides of the Long 16th Century." *Human Architecture: Journal of the Sociology of Self-Knowledge* 11, no. 1 (2013): 73–90.

Ibn, Khaldun, *The Muqaddimah.* Trans., Franz Rosenthal. London: Routledge and Kegan Paul, 1958.

Ibrahim, Azhar. "Orientalisme dalam pengajian Melayu" ("Orientalism in Malay Studies"). Persidangan Antarabangsa Bahasa, Sastera dan Kebudayaan Melayu ke-2, bertemakan "Ke arah bitara kesarjanaan Melayu." Singapore, September 1–3, 2002.

Ibrahim, Azhar. "Sociological Readings of Classical Malay Literature: Possible Contribution to the Sociology of Religion of Malays of South-East Asia." In *Kesusasteraan Tradisional Asia Tenggara (Traditional Southeast Asian Literature),* edited by Zaiton Ajamain & Norazian Ahmad (Kuala Lumpur: Dewan Bahasa & Pustaka, 2005), 416–436.

Ibrahim, Azhar. "Contemporary Malay Studies: Diverging Visions, Competing Priorities and its Implications: A Critique." *Asian Journal of Social Science* 35, no. 4–5 (2007): 657–680.

Ibrahim, Azhar. "Orientalism, Ethno-Religious Exclusivism and Academicism in Malay Studies: The Challenges for the Emergence of an Autonomous Sociological Discourse." Paper presented at the World Congress of Sociology, RC 35: Concept Formation in Asian Sociology, July 16, 2010, Gothenberg, Sweden.

Ibrahim, Azhar. *Menyanggah Belenggu Kerancuan Fikiran Masakini* (Kuala Lumpur: SIRD, 2016).

Ibrahim, Azhar. *Historical Imagination and Cultural Responses to Colonialism and Nationalism: A Critical Malay(sian) Perspective* (Kuala Lumpur: SIRD, 2017) [English version of Azhar Ibrahim, *Menyanggah Belenggu*].

Jennings to Farquhar, 15 August 1820, L. 4, SSR; Accountant General's office, 8 March 1826, vol. 71, Java Factory Records, East India Company, London, Recordak Microfilm Services, 1956. Microfilm, Monash University.

Maaruf, Shaharuddin b. *The Concept of the Hero in Malay Society.* Singapore: Eastern Universities Press, 1984.

Maaruf, Shaharuddin b. *Malay Ideas on Development: From Feudal Lord to Capitalist.* Singapore: Times Book International, 1989.

Maaruf, Shaharuddin b. "Some theoretical problems concerning tradition and modernization among the Malays of Southeast Asia." In *Asian tradition and modernization: perspectives from Singapore*, edited by Yong Mun Cheong. Singapore: Times Academic Press, 1992.

Maia, Joao Marcelo. "History of Sociology and the Quest for Intellectual Autonomy in the Global South: The Cases of Alberto Guerreiro Ramos and Syed Hussein Alatas." *Current Sociology* 62, no. 7 (2014): 1097–1115.

Mannheim, Karl. *Ideology and Utopia: An Introduction to the Sociology of Knowledge.* London: Routledge & Kegan Paul, 1936.

Mannheim, Karl. *Conservatism: A Contribution to the Sociology of Knowledge.* London: Routledge, 1986.

Marx, Karl & Frederick Engels. *Manifesto of the Communist Party.* Peking: Foreign Languages Press, 1963.

Marx, Karl & Frederick Engels. *The German Ideology.* London: Lawrence & Wisehart, 1970.

Mignolo, Walter. "Spirit out of Bounds Returns to the East: The Closing of the Social Sciences and the Opening of Independent Thoughts." *Current Sociology* 62, no. 4 (2014): 584–602.

Moosavi, Leon. "Decolonising Criminology: Syed Hussein Alatas on Crimes of the Powerful." *Critical Criminology* (2018).

Nery, John. "All the Honorable Men of the World." *Philippine Daily Inquirer*, December 17, 2012.

Nery, John. *Revolutionary Spirit: José Rizal in Southeast Asia.* Singapore: ISEAS, 2011.

Omar, Sharifah Maznah Syed., *Myths and the Malay Ruling Class.* Singapore: Times Academic Press, 1993.

Raffles, Thomas Stamford. The *History of Java*, 2 vols. London: Printed for Black, Parbury, and Allen, Booksellers to the Hon. East-India Company and John Murray, 1817.

Raffles to Mackenzie, 20 December 1819, enclosed in Raffles to Dart, 28 December 1819, vol. 50, Sumatra Factory Records, East India Company, National University of Singapore; India Office Library and Records. London: Recordak Microfilm Service. 1960. Monash University.

Raffles to Travers, 20 March 1820, vol. 50, Sumatra Factory Records, East India Company, National University of Singapore; India Office Library and Records. London: Recordak Microfilm Service. 1960. Monash University. Cited in Nadia Wright, "Farquhar and Raffles: The Untold Story." *Biblioasia* 14, no. 4(2019).

Rahman, Noor Aisha Abdul. "Traditionalism and its Impact on the Administration of Justice: The Case of the Syariah Court of Singapore." *Inter-Asia Cultural Studies* 5, no. 3 (2004): 415–432.

Rahman, Noor Aisha Abdul. *Colonial Image of Malay Adat Laws: A Critical Appraissal of Studies on Adat Law in the Malay Peninsula during the Colonial Era and Some Continuities.* Leiden: Brill, 2006.

Rahman, Noor Aisha Abdul. "Changing Roles, Unchanging Perceptions and Institutions: Traditionalism and its Impact on Women and Globalization in Muslim Societies in Asia." *The Muslim World* 97 (2007): 479–507.

Rahman, Noor Aisha Abdul. "The Dominant Pespective on Terrorism and Its Implicaton for Social Cohesion: The Case of Singapore." *The Copenhagen Journal of Asian Studies* 27, no. 2 (2009): 109–128.

Rahman, Noor Aisha Abdul. "Issues on Islam and the Muslims in Singapore Post-9/11: An Analysis of the Dominant Perspective." In *Encountering Islam: The Politics of Religious Identities in Southeast Asia*, ed. Hui Yew-Foong. Singapore: Institute of Southeast Asian Studies, 2013.

Said, Edward. *Culture and Imperialism.* New York: Vintage, 1993.

Santos, Boaventura de Sousa. *Epistemologies of the South: Justice against Epistemicide.* Oxford: Routledge, 2014.

Speier, Hans. Review of *Ideology and Utopia, American Journal of Sociology* 43, no. 1 (1937): 155–166.

Tham, Seong Chee. "Intellectual Colonization." *Suara Universiti* 2, no. 2 (1971): 39–40.

Wright, Nadia. "Farquhar and Raffles: The Untold Story." *Biblioasia* 14, no. 4 (2019).

CHAPTER 4

The Psychological Dynamics of Mental Captivity
Subsequent Conceptual Developments

Dustin J. Byrd

From a socio-historical perspective, the Malaysian theorist, Syed Hussein Alatas developed the concept of the "captive mind" over the course of numerous essays, in order to explain the colonial phenomenon wherein the minds of subjugated peoples take on characteristics that cause them to overvalue the culture, ideals, and histories of their subjugators; diminish the value of their own culture, ideals, and histories; reproduce the power dynamics of the colonizer and colonized, and lay the foundations for perpetual colonization via the colonized themselves, by reifying the colonized mind. Syed Hussein Alatas theorized that mental captivity was a form of mental enslavement, wherein the fate of the colonized can be internally directed through the control of their colonized mind.[1] For the colonizer, hegemony over the colonized would be thoroughly complete once the colonized adopted a form of self-enslavement, a process by which they willfully make themselves dependent upon the colonizer, abandoning their own cultural, spiritual, and intellectual autonomy for colonial heteronomy. For Syed Hussein Alatas, this self-enslavement was especially egregious among non-Western intellectuals, who masochistically privileged the knowledge production and knowledge producers of the West over their own.[2] For the captive mind, that which came from the West had value, not by virtue of its truth-content, or that it addressed the needs or realities of the non-Western world, but rather its value came from the mere fact that it derived from the West. In the colonized condition, Occidental concepts structured the discourse in the non-West; Occidental discourse subjects became the subjects of discourse in the non-West, and Western biases against non-Western peoples became self-evident dogmas among the colonized intellectuals. In other words, the apparatuses of Western ideologies absorbed into the self-consciousness of non-Western intellectuals, causing them to adopt a consciousness that was not only self-effacing, but was self-destructive. The

---

1 Syed Hussein Alatas, "The Captive Mind and Creative Development," *International Social Science Journal* 26, no. 4 (1974): 691–700.
2 Ibid.

© DUSTIN J. BYRD, 2023 | DOI:10.1163/9789004521698_006

colonized mind has absorbed into the subconscious the false-binary that was constitutional within Western ideologies: that which is Western is "superior"; that which is non-Western is "inferior." This false-binary has an even larger export: it not only determines the value of intellectual activity, but also the value of the cultures, civilizations, and people from which the so-called "superior" and "inferior" knowledge is produced.

In this chapter, I seek to further Syed Hussein Alatas' notion of the "captive mind" and formulate subsequent concepts that can illuminate the realities of this cognitive condition. In doing so, I will follow a more constellational approach, typical of the works of the Frankfurt School, especially Walter Benjamin, and Theodor W. Adorno, wherein a long argument is not formulated, but rather insights are set beside each other relationally – as if to look at a constellation in the night's sky. As a critical theorist, I am impelled to analyze the captive mind through a variety of disciplines, as the captive mind itself is not only a psychological condition, explained only through psychoanalytic thought, but is a condition that is itself determined by the contours of history, society, politics, and economics. Nevertheless, the chapter will focus on developing subsequent psychoanalytic concepts as they pertain to the captive mind as a psychological phenomenon.[3]

1 Ideological Conditioning and the Three Consciouses

In order to achieve a thorough saturation of colonial biases within the consciousness of the colonized subject, a comprehensive worldview must be disseminated among that same colonized subject. This worldview, either enforced by systems of terror – both psychological and/or physical – takes the form of an all-pervasive ideology. In the Marxist sense, it is a worldview and/or system of thought that is designed to conceal certain social contradictions that favor the colonizer over the colonized. As such, it is designed to camouflage the true intentions of the colonizer, who does not colonize for the benefit of the colonized, but rather does so for his own benefit. Although many of the colonized think otherwise, the colonizers' ideological claims are meant to undermine the sense-of-self of the colonized, to de-link the native

---

3 It is not my goal in the chapter to designate any particular individual, group, or society as being subject to the condition of the captive mind. Here, I'm working within the realm of theory, as opposed to applied sociology or political science. I will leave such applications of the descriptor "captive mind" to others who are more prepared to enter into that contested arena.

THE PSYCHOLOGICAL DYNAMICS OF MENTAL CAPTIVITY

population from their native worldview, and to stealthily and subconsciously detach value from native thought, culture, and way-of-being-in-the-world. The ultimate purpose of colonial ideology is not to set the colonized against the colonizer in a war of ideas, but rather to reform the consciousness of the colonized so that they will become their own colonizer in the name of those who colonize. Ideology, when skillfully executed via metapolitics, has the ability to translate the needs, values, and biases of the colonizer into the needs, values, and biases of those who are subject to the colonizer, bringing out a masochistic submissiveness – the result of the false-consciousness – from the victims of the colonizer. Internal oppression, wherein the brutality and barbarism of the colonizer is internalized among its victims, becomes the subtle means by which the targeted population is dominated. The internalization of ideological claims forms a sense of "learned helplessness," wherein the colonized population come to depend on their colonial masters not only for their daily physical needs, but also for their sense of identity, sense of worth, and vision for the future. Intellectual and national autonomy has been replaced by intellectual and national heteronomy, as the colonized society has been *infantized*, subjugated to the level of an infant dependent upon the good will and graces of the parent society.

As a result of the attempted ideological indoctrination, three forms of consciousness evolve among those individuals subject to colonization:

(1) *Resistant-consciousness*: Wherein the subject of colonization remains recalcitrant against the attempt to capture their consciousness along the lines of the colonial ideology, one has the "resistant-consciousness." In the words of Malcolm x, the "resistant-consciousness" takes the form of the "field slave," who remains cognizant of who his enemy is and is determined to emancipate himself from their control, both physically and psychologically. He sees through the master's ideological tricks; his dehumanization of his victims does not penetrate the consciousness of the field slave. The field slave knows who he is; he knows he is not what the master says he is; he knows he is not inferior, less-than-human, or merely put on this earth to serve his "superiors." The resistant-conscious evades all attempts to control his mind, even if his body, his land, and his people are subjugated. As such, his mind has developed a cognitive-immune system that does not allow for colonizing pathogens to possess his psychological apparatus. Thus, the resistant-conscious may be physically and psychologically tormented by the master, but he will remain cognitively free within himself. That freedom-within will remain a constant threat to the colonizers, as inner-freedom demands a socio-political condition that is worthy of its state of being. As such, the resistant-consciousness

will be targeted for physical annihilation whenever it proves itself to be an antidote to the colonizers' ideological subjugation of an oppressed people.

(2) *Double-consciousness*: The second consciousness that forms out of the master-slave/colonizer-colonized dialectic is the "double-consciousness," as developed by the African-American/Ghanaian intellectual W.E.B. Du Bois, wherein the object of colonization is divided within himself, judging himself by the standards of his masters, thus creating an individual who recognizes that he cannot be that which has been ideologically ingrained in him as being of value or worth. In his 1903 book, *The Souls of Black Folks,* W.E.B. Du Bois wrote, "it is a peculiar sensation, this double-consciousness, this sense of always looking at one's self through the eyes of Others, of measuring one's soul by the tape of a world that looks on in amused contempt and pity."[4] The double-consciousness is aware that he has been taught that he has the wrong hips, lips, hair, and skin tone, and comes from an "inferior" nation of people who have an "inferior" or "backwards" culture. Yet, he is often cognitively unaware as to why such attributes are inferior. Although he likes certain things about himself and his culture and finds felicity in them, he has internalized much of the colonizer's hatred for the colonized. Thus, he lives in a state of ambivalence toward himself; he both loves and hates himself – a pathology that causes him to live in a constant state of confliction. The torment of knowing *what* he is but also feeling that it is somehow inadequate, wrong, or inferior, leaves him in a paralyzed ontology – rendering him unable to fully love himself or to be the authentic individual he wants to be. Although under constant threat, and thoroughly brutalized by the colonial ideology, the consciousness of his nativeness remains intact, longing to transcend the deep-seated ambivalence that the colonizer's ideology has instill in him.

(3) *Captive Mind*: The last of the three consciousnesses that emerge out of the colonizer/colonized dialectic is the consciousness that is determined by its total submission to the ideology of the colonizer: what Syed Hussein Alatas described as the "captive mind." The individual with the captive mind sees themselves through the ideological illusions of their captors, and is simultaneously repelled by the image of his native community. In this sense, the captive mind reproduces the master/colonizers' own repulsion to his nativeness. He cultivates the colonizers' disdain for his native soil, his native religious practices, his native culture, all within his

---

4 W.E.B. DuBois, *The Souls of Black Folks* (Boston: Bedford Books, 1997), 38.

own mind. Nothing good comes from his soil; all that is good comes from the culture and civilization of the masters and colonizers.[5] Nevertheless, the captive mind cannot fully repress his nativeness; it too, like a specter, haunts him. The continual presence of his native community is a constant reminder to the captive mind that he is not fully what he sees himself to be; he is not the colonizer, the master, the captor, but rather is the most complete victims of the colonizer, so thorough is his submission to the master's ideology. In order to escape the cruel reality of being of the "lesser" peoples in the colonizer/colonized dialectic, the captive mind doubles-down on his sycophancy for the colonizer. He identifies with them and their ideology so completely as to escape the torment of reality: the psychologically painful fact that he is not of them, and cannot truly be of them. In this sense, the captive mind too possesses a "double-consciousness," but not in the same way as W.E.B. Du Bois formulated a consciousness divided against itself. For the captive mind, the consciousness that is thoroughly saturated with the colonizers' ideology attempts to wholly repress the consciousness of his ontological reality: his "nativeness." This consciousness is not a mind at war, struggling to liberate himself from the heteronomic image imposed by colonizer, but rather a mind engaged in *self-menticide* – a systematic attempt to destroy the non-ideological subconscious and cultural identity that continues to undermine the full-embrace of his faux-colonizer identity.[6] In other words, self-menticide is the attempt to complete the ideological indoctrination that the colonizer started and continue to pervade. It is an attempt to psychologically wipe clean the last remaining residue of nativeness in the colonized, as to render him dependent on the colonizer, unable to think for himself, and ultimately unable to resist the colonizers' demands. For the captive mind, as long as such residue of nativeness exists within his consciousness, no matter how compromised, it will be the harbinger of constant doubt, for it is an ever-present reminder of the inability of the captive mind to full transcend that which he no longer values: himself

---

5 In mid-twentieth century Iran, this pathological fascination with all things foreign and the simultaneous devaluation of all things Iranian was deemed *"gharbzadegi,"* ("Occidentosis," or "Westoxification") by the sociologist and social critic, Jalal Al-i Ahmad. To be "intoxicated" with the West, or stricken by the "Western plague," was not simply to be fascinated with all things Western, but was also to hold dismissive views of all things native to Iran, or Islamic. This love/hate dialectic will be discussed later in this chapter. See Jalal Al-i Ahmad, *Occidentosis: A Plague from the West,* ed. Hamid Algar (Berkeley, CA: Mizan Press, 1984).

6 Joost Meerloo, *The Rape of the Mind: The Psychology of Thought Control, Menticide, and Brainwashing.* New York: Grosset & Dunlap, 1956.

as native. Until the self-menticide is complete, a nagging sense of "inauthenticity" (*uneigentlichkeit*) will beguile him – he is not who he says he is; the words he's learned from his captors and parrots with pride are but a façade covering up his still lingering native consciousness. His self-doubt tells him he is "performing" for an audience, a mere expression of the false-self, while the "true self" remains hidden, only to show itself in isolation.[7] This self-doubt will plague him. He does not feel at home with himself. An acute neurosis forms, one that could overcome him and sabotage his attempts to transform himself into the colonial ideal. Self-consciousness of his "otherness" (the sense of otherness imposed by the colonizers), especially within the presence of those he idolizes, will feed the self-loathing he attempts to repress. Thus, the only way to liberate himself from his doubts, and deliver himself to his captors, is to kill the native within – an inner-*totalen krieg* against all that he represses within himself.

However, there is another aspect of self-menticide: the captive mind must not only "kill the native within" himself, but also must adopt the colonizers' contempt for this native community. As such, the captive mind no longer simply disregards the community from where he came; he cannot simply ignore it. Rather, it must become an object of disgust. In his bid to kill the native, the captive mind adopts an outright hostile stance towards his community-of-origin, which mirrors the stance of the colonizers towards the colonized. The colonizers' contempt for native "weakness," "laziness," and "backwardness" becomes his contempt for native "weakness," "laziness," and "backwardness"; their disregard for native culture becomes his disregard for native culture; their dehumanization of natives becomes his dehumanization of natives, and so on.[8] To kill the native within, he must become a mirror image of this captor.

2   Beneficia Captivitatis

By adopting the perceived consciousness of the master/colonizers as his own, the captured mind believes himself to be the recipient of certain benefits

---

7 Donald W. Winnicott, "Ego distortion in terms of the True and False Self," in *The Maturational Process and the Facilitating Environment: Studies in the Theory of Emotional Development.* (New York: Aronson, 1990), 146.

8 Syed Hussein Alatas, *The Myth of the Lazy Native: A Study of the Image of the Malays, Filipinos, and Javanese from the 16th to the 20th Century and its Function in the Ideology of Colonial Capitalism.* London: Routledge, 2013.

(*beneficia captivitatis*). These benefits are the psychological bi-product of the abandonment of nativeness and the adoption of the worldview of the captures.

First, the captured mind understands himself to be a member of a "superior" group, one that derives from a "superior" culture and a "superior" civilization. The fact that they are the masters and colonizers is proof enough that they are superior, for it was his people that they conquered, colonized, and are now masters of. Now that he has adopted their identity, their cultural and social norms, their ideology, he too is of that superior group. Subconsciously, he feels he has transcended his own sense of inferiority, his own sense of shame at being conquered or of being from the conquered people; he feels he has "achieved" his greatness through his "ascent" into their civilization. He has overcome the barriers of his own people's barbarity, his own backwardness, and as such he looks back at those he left behind with disgust – thus augmenting his sense of superiority.

Secondly, as the captive mind thoroughly identifies with the masters and colonizers, this identification fosters a peculiar form of narcissism – a pathological "self-love" of what he has become. This narcissistic pathology functions as a defense mechanism against any attack of the subconscious, which is the storehouse of his repressed nativeness. Even if such repressed thoughts were to percolate into consciousness, it would be met with an ego strengthened by a narcissistic barrier that has become so impenetrable that such repressed material would be neutralized (through aggressive repression) at the moment of its appearance. At times, the narcissistic ego does not recognize the repressed material as being from himself, so thoroughly has he made himself in the image of his master/colonizer. Thus, the repressed nativeness presents itself as alien to his narcissistic ego, and he shows due contempt for the foreign element. This narcissistic image of self, coupled by an accompanying sociopathic element, allows him to dehumanize, debase, and if necessary, destroy those from whom he came just as savagely as he represses his own nativeness.

Third, the sense of superiority that has constructed the captive mind's narcissistic and sociopathic consciousness, also delivers to him a sadomasochistic element. In an image, the captive mind can be imagined as a cyclist: bowing to those above him while kicking at those beneath him. Because the captive mind only sees value in the consciousness, cultures, and ways of his masters, he deifies those whom he emulates. And like the gods, he submits to their prerogatives; he worships at the feet of their achievements; he tailors his life around their sacred time and space, and he becomes a true believer in their ideological claims. As such, the captive mind is the supreme masochist, willing to accept – and cherish – abuse that comes from above, for such abuse is a sign of their affection and preference for him. On the other hand, he becomes sadistic over those he believes is beneath him: those still clinging to their nativeness. Because of their inferiority, they have yet to see what he has seen in the world of the masters/colonizers; they have yet to abandon their backwardness and embrace the superior civilization and its culture, as he has; they have yet to discard their native consciousness and thus remain recalcitrant against him and his benefactors. For this, he despises them, looks dismissively at their cultural practices and folk knowledge, and wishes ill towards them. When given the chance, he exacts his revenge on them with psychological (and sometimes physical abuse), thus proving his superiority over them as well as his loyalty to his masters/colonizers. The colonized situation grants him license to be the brutal hand through which the colonizers torment the colonized. He relishes this august position, as he perceives it to further ingratiate himself in his masters' orbit, as giving him the opportunity to impose violence against the hated natives – who subconsciously represent the residue of his own nativeness in need of constant repression.

This sense of superiority, this pathological narcissism, and the subsequent sadomasochism that develops within the captive mind, can be best summed up as a form *Ideological Stockholm Syndrome*, wherein the victim of the colonizer not only identifies with the colonizer, but becomes an integrated part of their criminal enterprise.[9] Although the colonized mind will always maintain a certain level of "otherness," especially when the colonizer and colonized are of different ethnic backgrounds, they nevertheless become identical with the mission of the colonizer. Colonization through deculturalization, epistemiscide, monopolization of resources, exploitation of labor, etc., become the enterprise that the captive mind seeks to further alongside his masters. Where once he was the victim of the masters' plans, and was aware of that, through the absorption of the masters' ideology he now becomes a conduit for the masters' continual brutalization, exploitation, and domination. As he has submitted to the masters/colonizers, the ideological worldview of the colonizer becomes the animus for the captured mind – the guiding spirit, if you will.

---

9   Stockholm Syndrome is the psychological condition wherein hostages will develop strong bonds with their captors during their captivity. Because of the intimacy of captivity, the closeness of the captor and the captive, intensive emotional bonds are created, so much so that the captive begins to identify with the cause of the captor and abandons their desire to be "free" of the captor. In the case of *Ideological Stockholm Syndrome*, I argue that these strong psychological bonds between colonizer and colonized are not an epiphenomenon of captivity, but rather an intentional result of the ideology disseminated by the captors/colonizers. In other words, the abandonment of the desire to be free of the captors is an intentional goal of the ideology itself, not a random occurrence.

3   *Xenos* and *Ethnos* Pathologized

Most healthy consciouses have a certain level of affection for their ingroup and suspicion for outgroups. This mental dynamic came about through the process of human evolution. Those who privileged their group over others tended to survive and flourish, while those who found themselves over-welcoming of others were often taken advantage of, especially during times of social, economic, political and/or religious strife. Being too open to the foreigner was naïve and dangerous, but being too closed created incestuous relations, closed mindedness, and limited space for culture/material growth. A balance had to be devised as human civilizations developed. When out of balance, civilizations collapsed, died, and disappeared.

When suspicion of others turned pathological, especially through mass hysteria and/or a mass psychosis, healthy levels of suspicion turned not only into an irrational fear of others, but transformed into pathological hatred for all things "other." In the modern period, such *xenophobia*, or "fear of the foreign, fear of the others, or fear of the non-identical," was paired with sophisticated weaponry, techniques of psychological manipulation, and propaganda, which resulted in mass murders and genocide on a scale unknowable before the industrial revolution. Despite being the supreme globalists, European colonization and imperialism was not immune from such xenophobia. Rather, European colonizers capitalized on it, using it to justify and advance their colonial and imperial plans. As central as xenophobia is to systems of domination, there is nevertheless a converse concept that is equally important within the dialectics of the master/colonizer and slave/colonized: *xenophilia*.

If xenophobia is the pathological *fear* or even hatred of the "other," then xenophilia is its reverse: the pathological *love* of the other.[10] However, what makes xenophilia a problem, as opposed to a virtue, is the *pathological* nature of xenophilia. Like xenophobia, there is a healthy level of such in each individual. Curiosity in regard to the other, fascination with the other, and even intimacy with the other is not a negative quality to behold, especially in an ever-shrinking world. Tolerance and acceptance of the other seems to be a

---

10   Here, I use the word "pathology" in much the same way of Freud, wherein he states in his *Civilization and its Discontents,* that the pathological occurs when "the boundary lines between ego and the external world become uncertain or in which they are actually drawn incorrectly." With xenophilia, the boundary lines between the individual ego and the other are extremely weak or have dissolved under the weight of the individual's admiration for the other, so much so that they can only see themselves through the image of the other. Sigmund Freud, *Civilization and its Discontents.* (New York: w.w. Norton & Co., Inc., 1962), 13.

necessary condition for a totally-integrated world. Therefore, xenophilia itself, in its non-pathological form, is a foundational need for modernity, especially in ethnically diverse modern societies, wherein "nations" are formed from a variety of peoples.[11] In its non-pathological form, xenophilia is the healthy ability to see oneself – or one's humanity – within the image of the other without losing oneself within that other, i.e., without losing the ego/object distinction. What makes xenophilia a problem is when it becomes simultaneously pathological and migrates into the realm of social relations. Pathological xenophilia exists within a state of imbalance in regard to the "xenos" (ξένος – "alien," "stranger") and the "ethnos" (ἔθνος – nation) from which the xenophilic individual comes.[12] In its pathological state, xenophilia abandons its libidinal connections to the ethnos-of-origin and becomes *xenocentric,* wherein the "Others," by virtue of being "Others," become the highest virtue and standard by which the ethnos-of-origin is judged. In other words, the ethnos-of-origin fades completely into the background as the ego dissolves all distinctions with "the Other," which is viewed merely as a homogenous abstract construction and never a diverse concrete reality. While the xenos becomes the familiar, the ethnos-of-origin becomes estranged. This is the psychological phenomenon that is commonly called "going native," wherein an individual from one culture abandons the norms of their parent culture and wholeheartedly adopts the culture of the Others.[13] This in itself is not necessarily pathological, for in such a situation the ego has consciously chosen to adopt a new identity and has appropriated the cultural norms that would naturally accompany that newly found identity. However, in a pathological form, this augmentation of the "Others" at the expense of the ethnos-of-origin and the complete dissolution of the ego/object distinction casts a shadow in the form of *ethnomasocism,*

---

11   This is especially true in those nations that can be considered *Willensgemeinschaften,* or "willed communities," as opposed to *Volksgemeinschaften,* or "folkish/ethnic communities," since willed communities are created out of shared political commitments instead of ethnic bonds.

12   By "ethnos" I refer not only to the tightly-knit biological units that form the basis of ethnic nations, but also to their collective memories, shared histories, shared religions/religious practices, shared language, and shared historical destiny (*Schicksalsgemeinschaft*), etc. This is what Jürgen Habermas refers to as "pre-political foundations," i.e., those foundational characteristics that determine "a people" and exist prior to their shared constitutional political commitments. Jürgen Habermas, *Between Facts and Norms: Contributions to a Discourse Theory of Law and Democracy,* trans. William Rehg. (Cambridge, MA: The MIT Press, 1996), 492–496.

13   While "going native" generally refers to Whites/Europeans adopting the culture of non-White/non-Europeans, here I use it interchangeably with non-White/non-Europeans adopting wholesale White/European culture, etc.

wherein the ethnos-of-origin (and those belonging to it) is devalued, becomes the object of disdain, and is rendered an impediment to mankind's progress. In the adopted *weltanschauung* of the xenocentric individual, his ethnos-of-origin becomes the source of all negativity, the sum of all backwardness.[14] In some cases, it is even considered by the captive mind to be the source of all his personal travails. He perceives himself to have been cursed by fate or by god(s) to have been born in such a "backwards" ethnos, and sings the praises of the xenos for rescuing him from his misery and giving him a new identity.

The collapse of the xenophile's ego into the abstract and ideological image of the Other brings about a form of what can be called *sadomasochistic symhedonia*. Symhedonia, which in Greek denotes "vicarious joy," or the joy one experiences through the well-being of Others, takes on a pathological component within the captive mind. Authentic joy is felt not simply by witnessing the well-being and eudaimonia of the xenos, but is masochistically predicated on the misery, suffering, and demise of his ethnos-of-origin. A healthy, non-captive consciousness, in a state of guest-friendship (*xenia*) with the Others, need not predicate his symhedonia on the misery of his own ethnos. But for the captive mind, who thoroughly identifies himself with his captors, such is a zero-sum game; his abandoned ethnos must be kept in a state of misery if the deified xenos he identifies with is to maintain its august status. As such, his pathological xenophilic state manifests itself via sadomasochism: his happiness is experienced vicariously with the happiness of the xenos *and* simultaneously his happiness is experienced vicariously from the suffering of his ethnos. Without both, he feels incomplete – less than eudaimonia has been achieved, for the still existing ethnos is a bitter reminder of his own inauthenticity as a willed-member of his adopted demos. As the ethnos suffers, he feels *schadenfreude*, thus validating his mental migration into the camp of the captors.

4   *Proteophobia*: Fear of the Ambiguous

While the captive mind begins to feel increasingly at home within his adoptive culture, seeing himself more and more as an equal and organic member of

---

14   This dynamic helps explain why those who have adopted the identity of the xenos often have a pathologically negative view about their ethnos-of-origin and/or culture, whereas the "Others," do not share a *pathological* hatred for their cultures, but rather remain ambivalent – not hating not loving the colonial ethnos. It appears that an essential part of adopting the xenos' identity is the adoption of pathological hostility towards the culture and ethnos from which they came, often as a way of demonstrating to their adoptive xenos that they've become fully detached from their colonizing ethnos-of-origin.

the master's/colonizer's society and intellectuality, he does so as he increasingly alienates himself from his own ethnos-of-origin, until the point where the bonds that used to bind him to his ethnos are dissolved entirely psychologically. He walks within his own society as an alien within that society. Nevertheless, as he continues to transform his lifeworld on the basis of the colonizer's worldview, he fails to see that which is obvious to those who are identical with the intellectual/cultural worldview he has adopted: his native "residue" stubbornly remains with him like the specter that cannot be exorcized. Only he has become less aware of it as his narcissism blinds him to the obvious. To the "resistant-conscious" individual, he seems both arrogant and out of touch with the reality of his own ethnotic community, as well as a traitor to his own subjugated people. Likewise, to those from the ethnos he has adopted, he appears sycophantic, inauthentic, and desperate to impress. Among both groups, he invokes *proteophobia* – a fear of (or anxiety in regard to) things that are ambiguous, not distinct, and mixed to the point of not having a category for which to place them. A colonizer's mind in a colonized body provokes disgust, much like a "Black slaver" did in the anti-bellum American south, for the Black slaver adopted the master's cruel practice of race slavery instead of fighting against it. He became as cruel as his own captors; he was a slave master in a slave's body.[15] In Europe, for example, assimilated Jews provoked scorn and suspicion from their Aryan and Slavic European counterparts, for they were not quite European, yet they attempted to present themselves as such. They were accused of being camouflaged "Others," nefariously lurking around in the European ethnosphere and slowly undermining its Christian and ethnic foundations. Such assimilated Jews also provoked scorn and suspicion from non-assimilated Jews, who saw assimilation as an inauthentic appropriation of gentile culture: a desperate attempt to be something they were not. No matter how assimilated they were to become, they could not exorcise the "Jewishness" out of them, and thus they remained a synthetic Other to both Christian Europeans and unassimilated Jews. So too is the captive mind such a creature that provokes proteophobia, for he appears as a disturbing anomaly, just as he appears non-identical with his ethnos-of-origin and non-identical with his adoptive demos. He is a pariah to both, and a threat to their closed identities.

---

15   The most poignant example of a Black slaver was William Ellison Jr. (c. 1790–1861) of South Carolina, who escaped slavery only to become a wealthy cotton plantation owner and the owner of at least 63 slaves. Accordingly, he was the wealthiest of 171 Black slave owners in South Carolina alone during his lifetime. See, Michael P. Johnson and James L. Roark, *Black Masters: A Free Family of Color in the Old South.* New York: w.w. Norton & Co., 1984.

What the 20th century has taught us about the dialectic between the colonizer and the captive mind is that no matter how much the colonized mind attempts to dissolve his ethnotic particularities into his adoptive identity and intellectuality, he will perpetually remain, in some way or another, and outsider banging on the doors of the colonizer's castle. The colonized mind will intellectually and spiritually bend himself backwards to be accepted by his "peers" among the colonizers; he will demonstrate his fidelity to their civilization, their thoughts, and their culture by denigrating and cursing his own; he will show his intellectual superiority over his own people's intellectuals by using the jargon of the colonizer, which to him is out of the reach of what his own people are capable of. While he's doing this, he is unaware of the amusement he creates for the colonizers; they watch gleefully as he tries to impress them, knowing that he's trying to ingratiate himself into their orbit. Nevertheless, for a time it is mere entertainment for them; he is not one of them; he cannot be one of them, for he may ape their appearance and parrot their words, but his voice and his writing go unnoticed by those he deifies. However, when the entertaining quality of the captive mind dissipates among the captors, he becomes a threat in need of neutralization, as Adorno wrote in *Negative Dialectics* whilst discussing Auschwitz: the "philosopheme of pure identity [is] death" to the non-identical.[16]

5 Academic Hypocognition among Western Intellectuals

In his work, Syed Hussein Alatas has thoroughly developed the concept of the "captive mind" as "Restern" intellectuals who suffers from mental colonization, colonized by the European/North American intellectual tradition, which they find superior to what non-Western intellectuals are capable of.[17] Nevertheless, within the dialectic of the captive mind, there is a conceptual interlocutor that needs to be developed further: the Eurocentric *hypocognition* of Western Intellectuals.

If Restern academics suffer from a captive mind, then Western academics tend to have a form of what I call "academic hypocognition" regarding non-Western academia. Developed by the American psychiatrist and

---

16   Theodor W. Adorno, *Negative Dialectics* (New York: Continuum, 1999), 362.

17   The term "Restern" comes from the idea that there exists a binary within global power structures: The West and the "Rest." As such, "Restern" denotes all non-Western peoples, cultures, philosophies, etc. See Esmaeil Zeiny, *The Rest Write Back: Discourse and Decolonization* (Chicago: Haymarket Books, 2020).

anthropologist, Robert Levy, in his 1973 book, *Tahitians: Mind and Experience in the Society Islands*, the term "hypocognition" denotes the inability to communicate to/with others on specific topics because of a lack of linguistic representations (words, concepts) for particular phenomenon, realities, and/or experiences.[18] In other words, thought within a given language does not have the conceptual framework or vocabulary to describe the realities that would otherwise be denoted by conceptual language. This leaves the individual and/or society with no way to communicate about the reality that is at hand. When understood in an Restern/Western academic context, the Western intellectual tends to match the captive mind of the Restern intellectual with a cognitive void – there is no conception of non-Westerners doing thorough and advanced academic work, especially in the fields of Philosophy, the Social Sciences, and Humanities. These fields are not the fields of study for non-Westerners, as it is often assumed. "Philosophy" in the East is "mysticism," not the kind of philosophy that is ontologically rooted in the Greco-Roman world or determined by cold rationality, but is rather devoted to secret knowledge of sages and mystical connections between humanity and the cosmos. Social Sciences in the non-Western world are not really "sciences" at all, since Resterners are not the progenitors of science, but rather the receivers and beneficiaries of it; and non-Western "Humanities" are really just religion, not a disinterested *Religionswissenschaft* typical of the West, but rather are religious apologetics from an "insider's perspective." As such, there is an assumption on the part of a large portion of Western intellectuals that the Restern societies are incapable of authentic and original thought along the lines of Western philosophers, scientists, and theorists. Rather, they are merely consumers of what the superior West produces; they are mere imitators of what the superior West produces; and as societies conditioned by the captive mind, they are not welcome to create the feast of the intellect that the West creates, but they can eat the scraps.[19]

Eurocentric hypocognition allows the Western intellectual to disregard even the most profound thought originating from the Restern world. Because of the

---

18   Robert I. Levy, *Tahitians: Mind and Experience in the Society Islands* (Chicago: University of Chicago Press, 1975).

19   I am fully aware that I am essentializing this point. There are numerous academics in the West that specialize in Restern thought, culture, history, etc. However, I do not see any attempt to integrate the knowledge that is produced in Restern societies into the intellectual milieu of the West in any way comparable to the ways in which Western thought is integrated into Restern academia. This imbalance of influence, and therefore of power, in regards to knowledge production and the synthesis of such knowledge within academic work is the essential point here.

inherent bias against the non-West, Western intellectuals rarely enter meaningful discourses with their non-Western counterparts, especially not on issues that they see are entirely dominated by the Western academic tradition, secular epistemology, and scientific methods. Thus, due to the hegemonic nature of Western academia, the non-Western academic learns the vocabulary and methods of Western academia, but the Western academic fails to consider the conceptual developments, philosophic vocabulary, and methodological means of the Restern academic. While the captive mind abandons the conceptual framework of his non-Western peers in order to appropriate and master the conceptual framework of his captors, the Western academic simply lives within his hypocognition in regard to his Restern academic peers, even when they are working within the same discipline and/or on the same subjects. Academic hypocognition develops out of Eurocentric arrogance and the resulting systematic negligence in regard to Restern academia. In this sense, the Western intellectual is not engaged in *epistemiscide*, or the destruction of existing indigenous knowledge, but rather ignores such indigenous knowledge for it is perceived to have no bearing on *his* subject. Rather, it is the role of the captive mind to engage in epistemiscide of his own culture/people's knowledge as he attempts to break into Western academic discourses. The Western academic is too often blissfully unaware of such a dynamic.

The intellectual ghettoization within Western academia is fought against institutionally by symbolic gestures: diversity hires, diversity training, and departments that specialize in non-Western philosophy, etc. While this is all warranted, it does not ultimately solve the problem that I've identified: that fruitful discourses between Western and Restern intellectuals on shared interests, wherein synthetic analyses are created and developed in a balanced form, is not happening on any meaningful level. The intellectuals remain ghettoized, even within faculty diversity. The captive mind is more likely to break into Western academia precisely because he can adequately reproduce the jargon of the master/colonizer, because he does not introduce indigenous ideas into his analyses of "Western" subjects. As such, Western academia has increasingly become impoverished in its conceptual and cognitive constructs in regard to universal human condition and experiences, for it systematically excludes the majority of humanity in the discourse. That is not because the West is demographically homogenous; that surely isn't the case. Rather, it is because intellectual colonization continues when non-Westerners take root within Western academia; they too must often demonstrate their *bona fides* by demonstrating the dialectic of the captive mind – the apotheosis of homogenized Western thought and denigration and/or systematic neglect of Restern thought.

6   Conclusion

In today's globalized planet, the captive mind would appear to be anachronistic – a figure from the past that no longer appears in the present. However, this is not the reality; the captive mind is a phenomenon that continue to appear in much of the Restern world, especially academia. The work of Syed Hussein Alatas has brought attention to the colonial pathogen that creates this mental condition, a condition that is perpetuated by the academic hypocognition of the Western academic, comfortable in their middle-class existence, and unwilling to change a system that thoroughly minimizes the contributions to human knowledge from outside of the Western world. From those who have been able to bridge the academic/cognitive landscape of Western and Restern knowledge, the potentials for fruitful exchange, as well as a fruit synthesis of knowledge, is boundless. We academics in the West can no longer ignore or neglect the knowledge of the Restern world, and Restern academics can no longer place all-things-Western on pedestals. Indigenous knowledge is being lost as instrumental rationality comes to dominate not only the capitalized, technologized, and commodified West, but branches out like a Lernaean Hydra into the rest of the world. The only way to overcome the captive mind and its sinister twin, academy hypocognition, is to read, listen, and study each other's work inter-subjectively; learn how to go out to each other but also to return to self, and value the human knowledge that is produced via inter-civilizational discourse.

Bibliography

Adorno, Theodor W. *Negative Dialectics.* New York: Continuum, 1999.

Ahmad, Jalal Al-i. *Occidentosis: A Plague from the West.* Edited by Hamid Algar. Berkeley, CA: Mizan Press, 1984.

Alatas, Syed Hussein. "The Captive Mind and Creative Development," *International Social Science Journal* 26, no. 4 (1974).

Alatas, Syed Hussein. *The Myth of the Lazy Native: A Study of the Image of the Malays, Filipinos, and Javanese from the 16th to the 20th Century and its Function in the Ideology of Colonial Capitalism.* London: Routledge, 2013.

DuBois, W.E.B. *The Souls of Black Folks.* Boston: Bedford Books, 1997.

Freud, Sigmund. *Civilization and its Discontents.* New York: w.w. Norton & Co., Inc., 1962.

Habermas, Jürgen. *Between Facts and Norms: Contributions to a Discourse Theory of Law and Democracy.* Translated by William Rehg. Cambridge, MA: The MIT Press, 1996.

Johnson, Michael P., and James L. Roark. *Black Masters: A Free Family of Color in the Old South*. New York: w.w. Norton & Co., 1984.

Levy, Robert I. *Tahitians: Mind and Experience in the Society Islands*. Chicago: University of Chicago Press, 1975.

Meerloo, Joost. *The Rape of the Mind: The Psychology of Thought Control, Menticide, and Brainwashing*. New York: Grosset & Dunlap, 1956.

Winnicott, Donald. W. "Ego distortion in terms of the True and False Self," in *The Maturational Process and the Facilitating Environment: Studies in the Theory of Emotional Development*. New York: Aronson, 1990.

Zeiny, Esmaeil. *The Rest Write Back: Discourse and Decolonization*. Chicago: Haymarket Books, 2020.

CHAPTER 5

The Cartography of Reception of 'The Captive Mind' in Iran

Esmaeil Zeiny

1 Introduction

What probably springs to mind upon hearing the term "the captive mind" is the Nobel laureate Czesław Miłosz's 1953 work of non-fiction of the same term wherein he writes of the dilemma of the Eastern European intellectuals in post-World War II Europe.[1] *The Captive Mind,* is an exploration of how individual minds function and change under a totalitarian regime. It is a masterpiece in comprehending how the human mind is gradually enslaved by the "New Faith" and "New Philosophy," in this case, the dialectical materialism. This enslavement, Milosz argues, is through one's own consciousness, thinking, and being in a certain way. The term "the captive mind" also brings to attention Syed Hussein Alatas' 1972 concept of "the captive mind" developed in his seminal articles: "The Captive Mind in Development Studies" (1972),[2] "The Captive Mind and Creative Development" (1974),[3] and "Education and the Captive Mind" (1974),[4] through which he excoriates the 'uncritical and imitative mind' and condemns the over-reliance on the western intellectual contribution in various fields of knowledge in the context of Southeast Asia. While they both share a similar title and both address intellectuals and enslaving of the mind, the concepts they developed are considerably different from one another. Milosz's captive mind concerns the intellectuals collaborating with totalitarian regimes and masking their true beliefs, and Alatas' concept refers to the lack of creativity, critical mind, and dependency on western paradigms

---

1 Czeslaw Milosz, *The Captive Mind.* New York: Knopf, 1953.
2 Syed Hussein Alatas, "The Captive Mind in Development Studies: Some Neglected Problems and the Need for an Autonomous Social Science Tradition in Asia." *International Social Science Journal* 24, no. 1 (1972): 9–25.
3 Syed Hussein Alatas, "The Captive Mind and Creative Development." *International Social Science Journal* 36 (1974): 691–99.
4 Syed Hussein Alatas, "Education and the Captive Mind," in *Asian Seminar Proceedings,* ed. E.H. Medlin (Adelaide: University of Adelaide, 1974), 39–45.

© ESMAEIL ZEINY, 2023 | DOI:10.1163/9789004521698_007

of education, concepts, theories, and ideas. I have no intention whatsoever to write on Milosz's *The Captive Mind* and compare it with Alatas' concept. I have only mentioned his work in passing since it would spring forth from every educated guess upon hearing the term 'the captive mind.' Rather, this chapter looks at Alatas' concept of captive mind in the context of post-1979 Iran.

It is an extremely arduous task to write on Syed Hussein Alatas' concept of the captive mind since one should be strikingly vigilant and innovative as not to reiterate and imitate what has already been written; otherwise, one would be the epitome of the captive mind, one who has an imitative and uncritical mind. What Syed Hussein Alatas said of the captive mind and the mental captivity of intellectuals more than four decades ago still holds true, as the captive mind is real and pervasive in our society today. In what follows, I will map out the reception of the captive mind in Iran. To map this out, I will discuss how Alatas' concept of "the captive mind" traveled to Iran and then examine how it is received in Iran of post-1979 Revolution. This requires a sense of cross-border meditation as ideas are hybridized, resisted and recontextualized. I begin this by analyzing the ways in which discourses such as Jalal Al-e Ahmad's *Gharbzadegi*[5] and Samad Behrangi's *Amrikazadegi*[6] shape the reception of Alatas' captive mind in Iran. The writings of Jalal Al-e Ahmad, Samad Behrangi, and Syed Hussein Alatas complement each other and together provide an approach towards understanding the persisting phenomenon of captive mind in Iran. Reading the three of them brings us to the themes of academic imperialism and academic corruption in the context of Iranian education. This is followed by a discussion on *Gharbzadeh*[7] individual academics and anti-West prayer-bumped professors who further the academic corruptions. This section discusses how *gharbzadeh*'s infatuation with the West and the prayer-bumped professor's anti-West stances perpetuate academic corruption and further mental captivity. Then, I will use the concept of captive mind

---

5 *Ghrabzadegi* is roughly translated as "Westoxication" or "Occidentosis." Al-e Ahmad uses the term to refer to the infatuation with the West and the poisoning of westernization on an indigenous culture. Al-e Ahmad popularized the term through his book *Gharbzadegi*, published in 1962. See Jalal Ale-Ahmad, *Occidentosis: A Plague from the West*, trans. R. Campbell. Berkeley: Mizan Press, 1984.

6 *Amrikazadegi* is the infatuation with America and the poisoning of Americanization on culture and education. It can be translated as "Americatoxication." Brad Hanson coined this term to refer to Berhangi's critique of American influence in Iranian education and teachers' infatuation with American educational materials. See Brad Hanson, "The "Westoxication" of Iran: Depictions and Reactions of Behrangi, Al-e Ahmas, and Shariati," *International Journal of Middle East Studies* 15 no. 1 (1983): 1–23.

7 *Gharbzadeh* is a person who is infatuated with the West; westoxicated.

as an analytical tool to unpack the causes of academic corruption. The final section presents some thoughts on the implication of Alatas' views regarding the captive mind and details the immediacy and relevancy of his thoughts and concept of the captive mind in Iranian society.

2   *Gharbzadegi* and *Amrikazadegi*

A particular approach to begin to think about the reception of ideas, notions, and texts in such a globalized world is to locate them within the similar local ideas, notions, and texts for, as Henry Giroux argues, meaning is not only within cultural artifacts themselves, but also in the ways such artifacts are 'aligned and shaped by larger institutional and cultural discourses.'[8] Such discourses play an important role in how a particular notion is received; these discourses also form the 'horizon of expectation' of the recipients that they bring to a notion – their prior knowledge and their unconscious assumptions. Therefore, such discourses carry weight in teaching one how to approach a particular notion. Although 'no discourse is total, and the multiple discourses present in a single location may clash, overlap and even crack, providing space for subversion and resistance,' these discourses are important in shaping the reception of a particular notion or idea.[9] The discourses that give shape to the reception of Syed Hussein Alatas' captive mind are *Gharbzadegi* and *Amrikazadegi,* which have been circulating in the Iranian society since the early 1960s as the critique and denunciation of heavy western influence. Before delving into these two discourses, a depiction of Iran's dependence on the West is in order.

Iran has never been colonized in the traditional sense of the term. However, its history corroborates that the colonial ideologies and the western imperial powers' political, economic, and educational influences have been imposed over the nation through different historical eras. Iran's heavy economic dependency on the West, its military dependency on western consultation and instruction, its dependency on Russia and Britain in repressing any uprising and insurgency against the governments and the rulers, and the incompetency of the rulers in protecting the country in the Qajar era, jeopardized the independence of the country and legitimated its semi-colony status. Political and

---

8 Henry Giroux, "What Education Might Mean after Abu Gharib: Revisiting Adornos' Politics of Education," *Comparative Studies of South Asia, Africa and the Middle East* 24, no. 1 (2004): 10.

9 Cathrine Burwell, Hillary E. Davis and Lisa K. Taylor, "Reading Nafisi in the West: Feminist Reading Practices and Ethical Concerns," *TOPIA: Canadian Journal of Cultural Studies* 19 (Spring 2008): 65.

economic exploitations aside, it was during this era, especially Nasser-e-Din Shah's reign that western science, technology, and educational methods were introduced into the country. The establishment of *Dar al-Funun* (Abode of Skills) in 1852 literally imported the western-style education. The institution, which was French in spirit and the medium of instruction, recruited many teachers from France, Austria, Poland, and The Netherlands. Following *Dar al-Funun*, many institutions were set up with the same spirit, up until 1934 during Reza Shah's reign, when they were all merged to form the University of Tehran. Consequently, the university's curriculum, administration, and organization, were massively influenced by the French universities. The American influence superseded the French model in 1950 during Mohammad Reza Shah's monarchy when Iran negotiated with America a series of programs of assistance. In terms of assisting with the educational programs, the Americans' task was to modify and boost the curricula, textbooks, methods of teaching, facilities and administrations. This was the dawn of a profound American engagement in the educational affairs of the country, during which the universities, textbooks, curricula, examinations, pedagogical techniques, and education standards were highly impacted by the American education system.

It was within such context that Al-e Ahmad's *Gharbzadegi* appeared, which aimed to arouse Iranians to the increasing westernization of their society. His text traces a long history of *gharbzadegi* in Iran but is especially devoted to 19th and 20th century Iranian history and the British and American influence on the country. Using the analogy of an infestation of weevils and how they chew their way out from the inside, Al-e Ahmad describes *gharbzadegi* as a bran that is intact externally but infested and hollow from within.[10] What caused this diagnosis is the difference between developed industrialized countries and developing nations with low wages, high mortality rates, and dependence on goods from the West. The developing countries as the importers are consumers who lost their own historicultural character by imitating the West; and through uncritical consumption of western products became an "ass going about in a lion's skin."[11] Besides depicting the economic dependency, Al-e Ahmad's *Gharbzadegi* is mostly known for accentuating the cultural dependency on the West. Of all the cultural institutions, education, in his views, had become the most *gharbzadeh*. He particularly finds fault with the schools' programs and their graduates. He argues that, 'in the schools' programs there is no trace of reliance on tradition, no imprint of the culture of the past, nothing of ethics

---

10   Al-e Ahmad, *Occidentosis*, 27.
11   Ibid., 31.

or philosophy, no notion of literature – no relation between yesterday and tomorrow, between East and West.'[12] Consequently, the graduates are nothing but 'future candidates for all manner of unrest, complexes, crises, and (probably) insurrections, people without faith, without any spark of enthusiasm, the unwitting tools of [west-dependent] governments, all accommodating, timid, and ineffectual.'[13] Al-e Ahmad also attacks Iranian returnees from Europe and America for they have become not only alienated from their own culture and traditions but also, wittingly or unwittingly, become agents to further *gharbzadegi*.[14] The Iranian higher education industry is also criticized for its lack of originality, adoption of western curriculum and western standards of assessment, as well as cultural practices. As to the University of Tehran, he states that:

> For all its vulnerability and importance, for all its lost traditions and crumbled independence, it would seem that it ought to remain the center for the most lively, outstanding, and distinguished research it once was. But is this the case? Those university fields that involve applied science, technology, and the machine (the colleges of applied sciences) in the advanced levels of their programs produce nothing more than good repairmen for Western industrial goods. There is no original research, no discovery, no invention, no solutions, just these repairmen, start-up men, or operators of Western machinery and industrial goods, calculators of the strength of materials, and such absurdities.[15]

Iranian scholars of literature, law, and religion have not escaped his criticism as well, for their imitation of western orientalism, and their lack of creativity and lack of concern for Iran's real problem: the excessive obsession of some influential segments of Iran with 'western' manners and matters, which he considers a major disease that gradually weakens the Iranian national character. Al-e Ahmad's *Gharbzadegi* has become extremely influential in Iran and is considered the most powerful indictment of blind "Westernization," which has a dramatic impact upon an entire generation of activists in Iran.[16] The term *Gharbzadegi* became so deeply etched in the Iranian political psyche of the 1960s and beyond that even Ayatollah Khomeini took it up in his lectures and letters.[17] Al-e Ahmad's *Gharbzadegi* became an immediate success and

---

12   Ibid., 113.
13   Ibid.
14   Ibid., 118.
15   Ibid., 114–115.
16   Hamid Dabashi, *Theology of Discontent* (London and New York: Routledge, 2006), 42.
17   Ibid., 74.

was circulated and discussed in high schools and universities as the 'first bibliographical item on a hidden syllabus with which the Iranian youth of the 1960s came to political self-consciousness.'[18] For these youths, *Gharbzadegi* appeared as a clarion call for regaining national identity and cultural protectionism. Hanson rightly asserts that *Gharbzadegi* is a forerunner of many 1960s and 1970s Third World North-South debates that demanded a new world economic and informational order, with the intent to battle 'cultural imperialism.'[19]

A related discourse that resists cultural imperialism belongs to Al-e Ahmad's friend and contemporary, Samad Behrangi, who shares similar concerns and critiques of Westernization. As a social critic and political activist, Behrangi believes 'one should continually question his environment, oppose injustice, struggle against tyranny, and work actively to change the ills of society.'[20] Behrangi's educational heritage has been subject to negligence. In his 1965 book, *Kand-o-kav dar Massael-e Tarbiati-e Iran,* Behrangi derides the bourgeois culture so imitative of western culture, detests the income gaps in Iranian society, and opposes the prevalent American influence in the educational system of the country.[21] His concept of *Amrikazadegi* addresses and questions the use of wide-ranging American books and materials in the Iranian education system. Regarding the use of textbooks in teacher training colleges and universities, Behrangi notes that ninety percent of education and psychology textbooks are American educators' texts translated into Persian. He argues that these books are written by American educators, and they have written these books about and for use in their own environment and society – a society in which students have good eating habits and the parents of these students are educated and informed.[22] He adds that his major concern as a teacher is whether his 'students that walk through the biting cold from another village had a piece of bread to eat for breakfast'; he further asks 'what good does the book of an American educator do for me and my students.'[23] Behrangi takes the authorities involved in educational policies to task for the blind adoption of American curriculum and the adoption of books that are totally irrelevant to Iranian society and Iranian problems. He believes that heavy dependence

---

18   Ibid., 76.

19   Brad Hanson, "The 'Westoxication' of Iran," 12.

20   Eric Hooglund and Mary Hegland, "Introduction," in *The Little Black Fish and Other Modern Persian Stories.* ed. Samad Behrangi, trans. Eric Hooglund and Mary Hegland (Boulder, CO: Three Continents Press, 1976), xiv.

21   Samad Behrangi, *Kand-o-kav dar Massael-e Tarbiati-e Iran (An Investigation of Educational Problems in Iran).* Tehran: Bamdad, 1965.

22   Ibid., 3–22.

23   Ibid.

on American educators and textbooks may lead Iranians to either remain unaware of their own culture and tradition or ignore and forget their own educational and cultural problems. Anchored within such discourse, Behrangi attacks the Iranian *farhangian* (educators, professors, teachers, and administrators in the education establishment) for their facilitation and promotion of *Amrikazadegi*. This group of *farhangian* who are increasingly alienated, morally lax, and indifferent to social problems, are infatuated with the West and anything western, and they infect the entire society. The 'disease of this class is becoming an epidemic.'[24] As for the solution to the problem of *Amrikazadegi* in education, Behrangi suggests that Iranians with actual teaching experience in the villages and towns – not the *farang rafteh* (those who have gone to the West) and those nonchalant *farhangian* – should write the textbooks and devise the curriculum.[25] Although Behrangi, unlike Al-e Ahmad, did not dedicate an entire work on Westernization, his analysis of the educational problems in Iran and *Amrikazadegi* is a significant contribution to the resistance discourses against cultural and academic imperialism. The wide circulation of *Gharbzadegi* and *Amrikazadegi* inevitably affects the ways in which similar notions such as Syed Hussein Alatas' captive mind from outside Iran are approached. Not only do they pre-delineate the discursive space in which such notions are received, but they also produce particular modes of reception.

3   The Captive Mind and Its Reception

Like Al-e Ahmad and Behrangi, Syed Hussein Alatas introduces ways to resist cultural imperialism, specifically 'intellectual imperialism' in an era when knowledge of the rest of the world is highly impacted by the sheer power of western culture. Intellectual imperialism is, in fact, the "domination of one people by another in their world of thinking."[26] Back in the colonial period, the intellectual imperialism was imposed by colonial domination through setting up schools, educating people, and raising up elites who could help control the colonized. Indoctrination through the colonial education system played a momentous role in this intellectual imperialism. However, intellectual

---

24   Ibid., 124.

25   Brad Hanson, "The 'Westoxication' of Iran," 6.

26   Syed Hussein Alatas, quoted in Syed Farid Alatas, "Social Theory as Alternative Discourse," in *Decolonising the University: The Emerging Quest for Non-Eurocentric Paradigms*, eds. Claude Alvares and Shad Saleem Faruqi. (Pula Pinang, Malaysia: Penerbit Universiti Sains Malaysia, 2012), 209.

imperialism today, argues Syed Hussein Alatas (2006), is a form of hegemony that is 'not imposed by the West through colonial domination, but accepted, willingly with confident enthusiasm, by scholars and planners of the former colonial territories and even in the few countries that remained independent during that period.'[27] Through this, he brings our attention to the less-noticed fact that while other forms of western dominance such as political and economic dominance are almost always resisted, *we welcome intellectual domination*. We are ready to accept anything that originates in the West so much so that we become hesitant in trying to validate ourselves.[28] The predominance of the West through the power structure existing in the production and distribution of knowledge resources has led the non-western scholars to think less of themselves and turn into passive recipients of knowledge. Hence, they develop what Syed Hussein Alatas (1972) calls a "captive mind," which arises from the 'overdependence on the western intellectual contribution in the various fields of knowledge.'[29] His "captive mind" captures our attention about the production of scholarship described as colonial knowledge and its fundamental consequences on the "natives."[30]

Colonial knowledge and the captive mind are the twin concepts that inform each other.[31] Alatas believes that the captive mind is a victim of Orientalism and Eurocentrism, hence the mode of knowing termed as colonial knowledge. The captive mind is defined as "uncritical and imitative mind dominated by an external source, whose thinking is deflected from an independent perspective."[32] It is an "uncritical imitation" that spreads through "almost the whole of scientific intellectual activity" including 'problem-setting, analysis, abstraction, generalization, conceptualization, description, explanation, and interpretation.'[33] Alatas discusses that imitation is a typical activity of the captive mind. He connects it to the way pedagogy and curriculum imitate the western content materials, assessment methods, and cultures and values without

---

27   Syed Hussein Alatas, "The Autonomous, the Universal and the Future of Sociology." *Current Sociology* 54, no. 1 (2006): 7–8.

28   Claude Alvares, "A Critique of Eurocentric Social Sciences and the Question of Alternatives," in *Decolonising the University. The Emerging Quest for Non-Eurocentric Paradigms,* eds. Claude Alvares and Shad Saleem Faruqi. Pula Pinang, Malaysia: Penerbit Universiti Sains Malaysia, 2012.

29   Alatas, "The Autonomous," 8.

30   Alatas, "The Captive Mind in Development Studies."

31   Shanta Nair-Venugopal, *The Gaze of the West and Framings of the East.* Basingstoke, UK: Palgrave Macmillan, 2012.

32   Alatas, "The Captive Mind and Creative Development," 692.

33   Ibid., 11–12.

contextualizing them with local conditions.[34] The captive mind was first expounded by Alatas in 1972 which, in fact, led to the nature of scholarship in the non-western world, especially its dominance in the social sciences and humanities. However, the problem of mental captivity was first put forth in the 1950s when he referred to the 'wholesale importation of ideas from the western world to eastern societies' ignoring their socio-historical context as a primary problem of colonialism.[35] Some of the characteristics of a captive mind include the uncreativity and incapability of 'raising original problems,' incapability of conceiving 'analytical method independent of current stereotypes'; incapability of 'separating the particular from the universal in science and thereby properly adapting the universally valid corpus of scientific knowledge to the particular local situation'; a captive mind is also 'fragmented in outlook'; 'alienated from the major issues of society' and 'its own national tradition, if it exists, in the field of intellectual pursuit'; it is unaware of 'its own captivity and the conditioning factors making it what it is' and it 'is a result of Western dominance over the rest of the world.'[36]

This way, Alatas' concept of captive mind resonates perfectly with the notions of *Gharbzadegi* and *Amrikazadegi*. In fact, these two notions are a less systematic but equally important Iranian version of academic dependency theory propounded by Syed Hussein Alatas. For the Iranian audience, Alatas' concepts of "captive mind" and "intellectual imperialism" bear a striking resemblance to Al-e Ahmad's *Gharbzadegi* and Behrangi's *Amrikazadegi*. Iranian scholars have read in Al-e Ahmad's *Gharbzadegi* that western cultural imperialism marked a fundamental change in the East from competition to the 'spirit of helplessness, the spirit of worshipfulness. We no longer feel ourselves to be in the right and deserving.'[37] Al-e Ahmad's particular concern about the way Iranians view themselves was regarded as a wake-up call for Iranian intellectuals to change. He argues that:

> The occidentotic regards only Western writings as proper sources and criteria. This is how he comes to know himself even in terms of the language of the orientalist. With his own hands he has reduced himself to

---

34   Alatas, "Education and the Captive Mind."

35   Syed Hussein Alatas,1956, quoted in Syed Farid Alatas, "The Meaning of Alternative Discourses: Illustrations from Southeast Asia," in *Asia in Europe, Europe in Asia*, eds. Srilata Ravi, Mario Rutten, and Goh Beng Lan (Leiden: Institute of Southeast Asian Studies, 2004), 60.

36   Alatas, "The Captive Mind and Creative Development," 691.

37   Al-e Ahmad, *Occidentosis*, 43.

the status of an object to be scrutinized under the microscope of the orientalist. Then he relies on the orientalist's observation not on what he himself feels, sees, and experiences.[38]

He reveals that the Iranian education system at all levels sought to "foster Occidentosis."[39] On the function of Iranian universities and western-educated scholars, Al-e Ahmad states that Iranian universities function either as 'storefronts for those occidentotic intellectuals who have returned from Europe and America,' or as refuge for traditionalists who 'have retreated into the cocoons of old texts,' and as a result, 'have had no effect on society.'[40] Behrangi has also developed similar notions and attacked the Iranian *farang rafteh* and *farhangian* for their infatuation and imitation of the West, and considered it as an ill of the society. For the Iranian audience, Behrangi reveals the cultural irrelevancy of the educational textbooks and superficial life of the bourgeois cultural environment whose 'world view is limited to the four walls of their home and embraces wife and children (if they have any) and their route restricted to the route from office and school to home.'[41] He further states that the hobbies of this group of Iranians are for 'amusement and taking up time. Their free time is spent in idleness and diversion. Energies are spent in satisfying the stomach and its appurtenances. The result of all this: superficial and conservative men are produced.'[42] Thus, Behrangi also questions the uncritical and uncreative importation of western, especially American, educational materials and system. It is not unfair to contend that the two discourses of *Gharbzadegi* and *Amrikazadegi* have, indeed, helped Alatas' notion of "captive mind" to find a receptive audience within Iran amongst the concerned and committed intellectuals and academics who have always been looking for innovative ways to offset cultural imperialism.

Alatas' travels to Iran and his series of talks in Iranian universities and academic circles brought his much-needed works, notions, and ideas to Iranian scholars' attention. Since his passing in January 2007, the Iranian Sociological Association has been holding conferences and meetings in his commemoration. One particular example is the 'Universal or Indigenous Science: Possibility or Impossibility' conference which was held in May 2007 and revolved around debates and discussions of Syed Hussein Alatas' notions of captive mind,

---

38   Ibid., 98.
39   Ibid., 112.
40   Ibid., 116–117.
41   Behrangi, Kando-kav, 30.
42   Ibid.

indigenizing social sciences, and Asian autonomous social sciences. Three years later, the conference proceedings were published as a book, a *festschrift* in honor of Syed Hussein Alatas.[43] As recent as April 2017, his book *The Problem of Corruption* has been translated into Farsi and was discussed at the Research Center for Culture, Art, and Communication in Tehran.[44] The familiarity of Iranian scholars and academics with Syed Hussein Alatas and his works can be traced back to the 1980s. However, Alatas traveled to Iran once in 1952 and stayed there for several weeks for the purpose of a postgraduate field study. It was to write a paper on, "The Perception of Social Problems amongst the Leading Elites in Iran and Iraq."[45] His stay in Iran coincided with Mohammad Mosaddegh's short premiership during which he introduced a range of social and political measures such as land reforms, social security, and higher taxes. Mosaddegh was the leading person in ending an almost 50 years of British monopoly over Iran's petroleum, and nationalizing the oil industry in 1951. What probably seemed captivating for the young Alatas was Mosaddegh's resistance to foreign domination, but it was here that the young Alatas developed an interest in the problems of corruption. He states that it was in Tehran in 1952 that 'I first became interested in the impacts of corruption; at the time corruption was rampant in Iran. Government officials and employees had not been paid for months but high-ranking authorities owned beautiful houses and cars and had fun outside the city.'[46] What caused this rampant corruption was the considerable economic turmoil due to the British government's imposition and institution of an embargo on the purchase of Iranian oil as the aftermath of oil nationalization. Alatas also traveled to Iran in the 1970s and 1980s and met with Iranian scholars and academics. Iran of the 1970s witnessed series of events, protests, demonstrations, and campaigns of civil resistance that culminated in the 1979 Revolution and overthrew Mohammad Reza Pahlavi. Iran also witnessed the cultural revolution in the immediate years after the 1979 Revolution, which was meant not only to purge the educational textbooks and

---

43   *Ilm-e Boomi, Ilm-e Jahani: Imkan ye Emtenaa* (*Universal or Indigenous Science: Possibility or Impossibility*). Collected and edited by the Iranian Sociological Association. Tehran: Jahad-e Daneshgahi Press. 2010.

44   Syed Hussein Alatas, *The Problem of Corruption*. Kuala Lumpur: The Other Press Sdn. Bhd. 2018, translated into Farsi by Vahideh Sadeghi and published by the Research Center for Culture, Art, and Communication in Tehran in 2017.

45   I have received this piece of information from his son, Syed Farid Alatas through our email correspondence.

46   Syed Hussein Alatas, quoted by Syed Farid Alatas during a conversation with Mehr News Agency. See "The Sociology of Corruption in Syed Hussein Alatas' View." https://www.mehrnews.com/news/2780597.

THE CARTOGRAPHY OF RECEPTION OF 'THE CAPTIVE MIND' IN IRAN   105

materials of complimentary references to the Shah and his dynasty, but also to reassess, reorganize, and reform universities that were in a state of academic dependency. Al-e Ahmad's *Gharbzadegi* and Behrangi's *Amrikazadegi* were of great popularity and use in understanding this dependency. In his cultural revolution speech on April 26, 1980, Ayatollah Khomeini apparently used these two sources when he stated that:

> It is necessary for me to clarify what our aim is in reforming the universities ... When we speak of the reform of the universities, what we mean is that our universities are at present in a state of dependency ... those whom they educate and train are infatuated with the West ... We have universities in our country for fifty years now ... [yet] we have been unable to obtain self-sufficiency in any of the subjects ... We have had universities but we are still dependent on the West for all that a nation needs ... Our universities lack Islamic morality and fail to impart an Islamic education ... They reflect a lack of Islamic education and a true understanding of Islam. The universities, then, must change fundamentally. They must be reconstructed in such a way that our younger people would receive a correct Islamic education side by side with their acquisition of formal learning, not a Western education ... To Islamize the universities means to make them autonomous, independent of the West ... so that we have an independent country with an independent university system and an independent culture.[47]

It was within such context that Alatas' notions of captive mind and his plea for autonomous social sciences were received. Besides the fact that discourses such as *Gharbzadegi* and *Amrikazadegi* have paved the way for the reception of Alatas' captive mind, Iranian scholars have always been looking forward to meeting with Southeast Asian scholars, as Southeast Asia was an active intellectual center in the second half of the 20th century. The regional conferences and symposiums that were held in Malaysia, Singapore, Indonesia, the Philippines, and Thailand were the center for dialogue amongst Southeast Asian scholars and intellectuals in the 1970s and 1980s. The issues that Southeast Asian scholars and intellectuals were addressing bore resemblance with the issues and problems in Iranian society and Iranian universities. It was in one of these gatherings in Indonesia that the Iranian sociologist, Gholamabbas

---

47   Ayatollah Ruhollah Khomeini, *Islam and Revolution*, trans. Hamid Algar (Berekely: Mizan Press, 1981), 295–299.

Tavasoli met with Alatas and struck a lifelong friendship. When Alatas traveled to Iran in 1987, he was already an established scholar in Southeast Asia and his pioneering works were considered foundational and classic. Upon Tavassoli's invitation, Alatas delivered a talk entitled "On Islam and Social Sciences" in University of Tehran, wherein he spoke about the significance of social sciences in improving Muslims' lives and realizing Islamic values. He was of the view that we cannot invite sciences to Islam, but we can foster the Islamic visions in a society with the help of social sciences. He expressed his strong disapproval on using philosophy, Qur'an, and Hadith, to Islamicize social sciences and considered it a simplistic act and argued that this would not only prevent the growth of social sciences in Muslim countries but also weaken the Islamic society. During the course of his talk, he also spoke about academic dependency, intellectual imperialism, and captive mind. He explained how scholars and intellectuals from developing countries are subject to mental captivity for the dependence on western ideas, concepts, theories, research, and structures of education. To defuse this academic imperialism, he suggested that a group of independent and creative intellectuals should produce an autonomous Asian social science tradition.

4   Academic Corruption

I find it very hard to resist decoupling the discussion of the captive mind from the contemporary academic corruption perpetrated and perpetuated by universities' authorities and professors. What Syed Hussein Alatas said of the mental captivity of intellectuals back then still holds true, as the captive mind is real and pervasive in our universities today. Trained almost entirely in the western sciences, the captive mind enjoys reading the western authors, and is educated primarily by western teachers either in the West or through their available works in local institutions of education.[48] Many of our intellectuals and university/college teachers read the works of western authors and teach them; yet they are not aware of this academic dependency and those who are conscious of it do not bother to make an effort to change this. Our teachers use textbooks that are developed in countries very different than ours. Our university professors as academic elites of Iranian society became nonchalant to our own tradition, seek western education, go by their standards, and never

---

48   Syed Farid Alatas, "Intellectual and Structural Challenges to Academic Dependency." *International Sociological Association, E-Bulletin*, 2008.

question them, and boast of receiving a degree at the proximity of the rulers. This total capitulation, I have argued elsewhere, is a 'sort of self-perpetuating academic imperialism.'[49] Most of the Iranian universities encourage their students and staff to pursue their higher education in the West. A degree received from any western institutions stands head and shoulder above a degree from a non-western top educational institute in Iran. Many of the Iranian universities keep hiring these *farang rafteh* to "foster occidentosis." The authorities of these universities are clearly under the impression that recruiting the *farang rafteh* academic would not only bring Western science but also bring fame and glory for the universities. The authorities pay scant attention to their qualifications and hire them on the basis of their western credentials. This conjures up what Syed Hussein Alatas identifies as one type of corruption in a society: nepotism. In this particular context, nepotism is the hiring of the *farang rafteh* in faculties regardless of their merits and consequences on the academic programs. This discrimination sustains the producer-consumed nexus in knowledge production and will cement the so-called superiority of the West. Concomitant with this discrimination is the existing power structure of the West in the production and distribution of knowledge resources, which leads the non-western scholars to think less of themselves and turn into passive recipients of knowledge; hence, total victims of the captive mind.

On the other hand, these *farang rafteh* would not like to have colleagues who have degrees from the West so they could maintain their superior status. But even in encountering another *farang rafteh* colleague, they would boast of their university world ranking in order to keep the upper hand. Unfortunate are those academics who have pursued their higher education in the East. These academics are usually given cold shoulders, their ideas are disregarded and their arguments are given no values. The *farang rafteh* academics whose obsession with the West infects the entire society are, indeed, spreading the mental captivity. In a recent conversation with one of these *farang rafteh* individual academics in the Department of Education at a state university, I learned of his insatiable thirst for using western educational texts and materials in his classes. He encourages his students to only look for western sources in the field. He addresses a number of western scholars in Education as "Prophet," and encourages his students to read and learn these prophets' concepts, ideas, and arguments developed in their scholarly papers. When I pointed out that this dependence on western contribution is a problem of mental captivity,

---

49 Esmaeil Zeiny, "Academic Imperialism: Towards Decolonisation of English Literature in Iranian Universities." *Asian Journal of Social Science* 47 (2019): 92.

I was greeted by the axiom that 'Let's face it. We are far behind the West and none of us can ever produce a significant contribution.' Resulted from academic imperialism, the captive minds' internalized subjugation repudiates the ability to stand on their own in terms of knowledge production. There is no harm in reading and learning western scholars' contributions but treating them as the sole producers of knowledge is "fostering the occidentosis" and spreading the disease of infatuation with the West, but above all legitimizing the mental captivity.

Another sort of nepotism is at work in Iranian universities. To pursue the traditional Iranian strategy of *Movazeneh* (balance), the universities' authorities make it a point to employ religious and *enghelabi* (those who are committed to the Islamic Revolution and the Iranian regime's policies) people who are usually friends, relatives, and political associates. Many of these *enghelabi* academics are appointed to academic positions including dean, chair, and head of academic programs without having the necessary qualifications. They are promoted to associate professor and then would gain their professorship sooner than others irrespective of their merits and qualifications. They wear *yaghe akhoondi* shirts (shirts with a close-fitting collar like a polo neck) and develop a prayer bump after some time to accentuate the semblance of *enghelabi*. Unlike the *farang rafteh,* who boast of receiving a degree in the West and are proud of their stay in a western country, *enghelabi* academics pretend to abhor the West and anything western. They make it a point to let everyone know that they treasure their visits to Karbala and Mecca, and that they would only visit Qom and Mashhad in Iran. They regard traveling to the West as traveling to the center of corruptions and the source of sexual permissiveness, view Iranian scholars residing in the West as "puppets of imperialism," and consider their contributions as "unworthy." Yet, they do not produce such contributions. They encourage their students to be critical of the West and ask them not to measure their success by the western standard. Yet, they uncritically accept and use western educational texts, and prefer to have their papers published in western journals.[50]

Let me cite my own personal encounter with one of these *enghelabi* professors that best illustrate their personality traits and qualifications. I was in touch with a prayer-bumped dyed-in-the-wool anti-western professor who happened to be the head of the English Literature program at one of the leading state

---

50   I have no intention of reducing the *enghelabi* individuals to traits in physique and appearance, and to those who own anti-west mentality. The *enghlabi* individuals that I am referring to are what I call "phony *enghelabi*" who sham to be *enghelabi* through their outward traits.

universities in Tehran where I have secured a Postdoctoral Fellowship. He was supposedly the host professor who agreed to mentor my project. During the course of our very first talk, he spoke of cultural imperialism, he cited Edward Said and Frantz Fanon, and he praised Ngugi wa Thiong'o for his decision to stop writing in English. And then, I spoke of mental captivity, academic dependency and the intellectuals' task in introducing ways to confront cultural imperialism. He seemed to know just enough about mental captivity and told me that he would always encourage his students not to imitate the West. And finally, we talked about my research project and the expected outcome. Much to my chagrin, he asked me to put his name as the first author for the papers that I would produce during my term with the university. I knew that it became an accepted practice for the students to write and teachers take credit for it, but I was not his student. I was a researcher, and he was my host professor. Later, when he found out that I had no intention of giving him the credit for the work that I produced, I was intimidated by the threat that my contract would be terminated. I have approached the university authorities with the complaint, but I was advised not to make a big deal out of it and just put his name as the first author. It was pointed out to me that since he is a Professor and a Senior Fellow, it is difficult to go against his wishes. This is corruption and it is a crime; it should be treated as such, but since he had a prayer bump, no one dared to warn him. He had the sources, forces, courses, and the means (prayer-bump and the anti-western stand) to escape punishment if any. My term with the university ended and my contract for renewal was rejected because the prayer-bumped dyed-in-the-wool anti-western professor has failed to manipulate me to add my paper to his list of publications. On the one hand, he speaks of cultural imperialism, and he is aware of academic dependency and captive mind. And on the other hand, he spreads uncreativity and furthers mental captivity. His anti-western stand should also be denounced too. Neither Alatas, nor Al-e Ahmad and Behrangi, fail to question western technology, materials, and contributions. Al-e Ahmad criticizes *gharbzadegi* and the West's colonial policies; Behrangi questions the irrelevance of western educational materials in the Iranian context; and Alatas criticizes the wholesale importation and blind imitation of western ideas, concepts, and materials. It should be noted that Alatas is not against a "constructive imitation," which may lead to emulation. He argues that 'no society can develop by inventing everything on its own. When something is found effective and useful, it is desirable that it should be adopted and assimilated, whether it be an artifact or an attitude of mind.'[51] He

---

51   Alatas, "The Captive Mind and Creative Development," 692.

believes that the dominance of western science has both positive and negative effects. While the former should be maintained and used, the latter should be avoided. He criticizes those who reject the West wholeheartedly as he believes 'ignoring a valuable contribution from the West is as negative as uncritically accepting whatever is served on the academic platter.'[52] He is cognizant of the urgency not to reject the western social science in toto but rather he selectively adapts it to local needs with caution.

Both *farang rafteh* and *enghelabi* professors further the academic corruption. As I have noted earlier, it is now an accepted practice for the university professors to take credit for the publications that they have not contributed. This is one of the most common types of corruption wherein students are forced to write articles and put professor's name as the first author. The captive mind explains this corruption very well. The individual academics' success is now measured by the number of publications and citations. Rather than focusing on the standard of good research practice, the individual academics outdo each other by publishing more papers and obtaining more citations. Obviously, forcing students to write an article for publication is an easy way to increase their number of publications. Other ways of easy publications to increase the number include submitting an article that has flaws known to the author but concealed from the reviewers; and approaching friends and colleagues for a positive and favorable review. Plagiarism also helps, either from others' papers or a big chunk of one's own prior publications. Submitting work to low-quality journals and publishers is also another easy way for a captive mind to gain more publications. None of these traits teach creativity and develop critical mind. Instead, they bolster uncreativity and uncritical mind. Quality and output are replaced by the number of publications and citations. The rife perpetuation of this academic dishonesty is indicative of the lack of the fear of punishment.[53] Besides, these corrupted behaviors of the academics occur in response to the universities' priorities – manifesting in direct incentives through job requirements, promotion, and remuneration criteria. These incentives are, in fact, bribery, which creates and encourages more corruption. As Syed Hussein Alatas argues, 'corruption stimulates further development of greater corruption, and this further degree in turn causes an even greater increase in corruption ... [corruption] is usually the effect of previous corruption at a higher level.'[54] Bribery is another form of corruption identified

---

52 Syed Hussein Alatas, "The Development of an Autonomous Social Science Tradition in Asia: Problems and Prospects." *Asian Journal of Social Science* 30, no. 1 (2002): 150.

53 Alatas, *The Problem of Corruption.*

54 Ibid., 41–42.

by Alatas in his work *The Problem of Corruption*. The universities bribe the individual academics with incentives to promote university ranking, and the academics perpetrate corruption in enhancing their list of publications. The universities need publications and citations for the institutional ranking. The ranking organizations usually assess research productivity and reputation. For instance, QS (Quacquarelli Symonds) allocates 70% to research and 50% to reputation. THE (Times Higher Education) allocates 90% to research and 33% to reputation.[55] The Iranian national ranking organization, ISC (Islamic World Science Citation Center) also devotes most of its attention to number of publications and citations. This suggests that quantity is valued over quality. A lower number of publications and citations means a lower university ranking and consequently lower allocation of funding and facilities and lower chance of marketability. Ranking brings visibility, and market forces have already made it clear that 'steep competition in the education sector determines the sustainability of the business of education. Hence, the compulsion to be ranked in order to be marketable.'[56] This example is another representation of Syed Hussein Alatas' notion of the captive mind suggesting that Iranian education is 'imitating the global language of market-driven forces.'[57] The over-indulgence with climbing up the ranking ladder sidetracks the quality of education and publication. It is considered a mental captivity to blindly adhere to the ranking standard sacrificing quality over quantity.

5   Conclusion

As noted earlier, Alatas proposes that an autonomous Asian social science tradition should be produced to defuse the academic imperialism and mental captivity. Amongst the significant elements to include in forming a particular tradition are: 1) 'The raising and treatment of definite problems,' 2) 'the application of definite methodologies,' 3) 'the recognition of definite phenomena,' 4) 'the creation of definite concepts,' and 5) 'the relation with other branches of knowledge.'[58] The very first prerequisite in generating an autonomous tradition is a group of creative and independent intellectuals. However, Alatas admits

---

55   Philip G Altbach and Ellen Hazelkorn, "Why Most Universities Should Quit the Rankings Game." *University World News* (2017) 8 January.

56   Sharifah Monirah Alatas, "Applying Syed Hussein Alatas's Ideas in Contemporary Malaysian Society." *Asian Journal of Social Science* 48 (2020): 328.

57   Ibid.

58   Alatas, "The Development of an Autonomous Social Science in Asia," 151.

that 'there is only a small minority among Asian social scientists who feel the need to develop an autonomous a creative social science tradition relevant to Asia as well as to the general development of social sciences.'[59] He further continues that the great majority of social scientists are simply 'extending the use of social sciences current in Europe and America without the necessary adaptation.'[60] This shows that there is a cultural lag in the domain of intellectual consciousness; it also indicates that 'in the world of learning the Asian scholars are still under intellectual domination.'[61] This still holds true in the Iranian context. Alatas' anti-colonial writings, including his notion of captive mind and his plea for an autonomous social tradition as a response to academic imperialism and mental captivity, should have been taken more seriously in Iran. They have been received well, as Iranian sociologists still continue debating, discussing, and evaluating them, but they have not been applied. Alatas' like-minded friend, Tavasoli, who shared his views regarding mental captivity and the need for independent social sciences, changed his position and labeled Alatas' notion of captive mind and his plea for an autonomous social science tradition as outdated but profound.[62] He contends that Alatas' ideas and notions, and those of his contemporary Muslim intellectuals, which belong to the period after the World War II, emanated from 'internal weakness, a reaction to technological advancement of the West and an inefficiency of traditional cultural system and political dependence of these countries.'[63] He opines that these trends of thoughts might foster extremism due to the misunderstanding and reactionary behavior. I wonder how Alatas' ideas are misunderstood. He made it very clear that he is not against the West, but he is against being mere consumers of the imported packages from the West. He admits that the desirable and useful western ideas should not be discarded, and he encourages "constructive imitation," which may lead to emulation. He warns that the rise of western dominance can impoverish non-westerners and suggests forming an autonomous Asian social science to resist this dominance. This resistance does not amount to confrontation but rather it is a dialogical process. His notion of captive mind and his anti-captive mind stand do not hint at any sorts of

---

59   Alatas, "The Captive Mind in Development Studies," 9.

60   Ibid., 9–10.

61   Ibid., 10.

62   For a study of Iranian sociologists' reactions to Syed Hussein Alatas' plea for autonomous social sciences, see Amin Ghaneirad, "Critical Review of the Iranian Attempts toward the Development of Alternative Sociologies." *International Journal of Social Sciences* 1, no. 2 (2011).

63   Gholamabbas Tavasoli 2006–2007, quoted in Ghaneirad, "Critical Review," 131.

extremism as well, and they are not outdated as the captive mind is real and pervasive in our society today. The two instances of individual academics and the discussion on university ranking above point to the continuing presence of captive mind and the phenomenon of mental captivity in Iran.

Bibliography

Alatas, Sharifah Monirah. "Applying Syed Hussein Alatas's Ideas in Contemporary Malaysian Society." *Asian Journal of Social Science*, 48 (2020): 319–338.

Alatas, Syed Farid. "The Meaning of Alternative Discourses: Illustrations from Southeast Asia." In *Asia in Europe, Europe in Asia*, edited by Srilata Ravi, Mario Rutten, and Goh Beng Lan. Leiden: Institute of Southeast Asian Studies, 2004.

Alatas, Syed Farid. "Intellectual and Structural Challenges to Academic Dependency." *International Sociological Association, E-Bulletin*, (2008): 3–26.

Alatas, Syed Farid. "Social Theory as Alternative Discourse." In *Decolonising the University: The Emerging Quest for Non-Eurocentric Paradigms*, edited by Claude Alvares and Shad Saleem Faruqi. Pula Pinang, Malaysia: Penerbit Universiti Sains Malaysia, 2012.

Alatas, Syed Hussein. "The Captive Mind in Development Studies: Some Neglected Problems and the Need for an Autonomous Social Science Tradition in Asia." *International Social Science Journal* XXIV, no. 1 (1972): 9–25.

Alatas, Syed Hussein. "The Captive Mind and Creative Development." *International Social Science Journal*, 36 (1974): 691–99.

Alatas, Syed Hussein. "Education and the Captive Mind." In *Asian Seminar Proceedings*, edited by E.H. Medlin, (39–45). Adelaide: University of Adelaide, 1974.

Alatas, Syed Hussein. "The Development of an Autonomous Social Science Tradition in Asia: Problems and Prospects." *Asian Journal of Social Science* 30, no. 1 (2002): 150–157.

Alatas, Syed Hussein. "The Autonomous, the Universal and the Future of Sociology." *Current Sociology* 54, no. 1 (2006): 7–23.

Alatas, Syed Hussein. *The Problem of Corruption*. Kuala Lumpur: The Other Press Sdn. Bhd., 2018.

Al-e Ahmad, Jalal. *Occidentosis: A Plague from the West*, (R. Campbell, Trans.). Berkeley: Mizan Press, 1984.

Altbach, Philip G. and Ellen Hazelkorn. "Why Most Universities Should Quit the Rankings Game." *University World News*, 8 January, 2017.

Alvares, Claude. "A Critique of Eurocentric Social Sciences and the Question of Alternatives." In *Decolonising the University. The Emerging Quest for Non-Eurocentric Paradigms*, edited by Claude Alvares and Shad Saleem Faruqi. Pula Pinang, Malaysia: Penerbit Universiti Sains Malaysia, 2012.

Behrangi, Samad. *Kand-o-kav dar Massael-e Tarbiati-e Iran* (An Investigation of Educational Problems in Iran). Tehran: Bamdad, 1965.

Burwell, Cathrine; E. Davis, Hillary and Taylor, Lisa K. "Reading Nafisi in the West: Feminist Reading Practices and Ethical Concerns." *TOPIA: Canadian Journal of Cultural Studies*, 19 (spring 2008): 63–84.

Dabashi, Hamid. *Theology of Discontent*. London and New York: Routledge, 2006.

Ghaneirad, Mohammad Amin. "Critical Review of the Iranian Attempts toward the Development of Alternative Sociologies." *International Journal of Social Sciences* 1, no. 2 (2011): 125–144.

Giroux, Henry. "What Education Might Mean after Abu Gharib: Revisiting Adornos' Politics of Education." *Comparative Studies of South Asia, Africa and the Middle East* 24, no.1 (2004): 5–24.

Hanson, Brad. "The "Westoxication" of Iran: Depictions and Reactions of Behrangi, Al-e Ahmas, and Shariati," *International Journal of Middle East Studies* 15, no. 1 (1983): 1–23.

Hooglund, Eric and Hegland, Mary. "Introduction." in *The Little Black Fish and Other Modern Persian Stories*, edited by Samad Behrangi, (Eric Hooglund and Mary Hegland, Trans.). Boulder, CO: Three Continents Press, 1976.

Ilm-e Boomi, Ilm-e Jahani: Imkan ye Emtenaa (Universal or Indigenous Science: Possibility or Impossibility). Collected and edited by the Iranian Sociological Association. Tehran: Jahad-e Daneshgahi Press, 2010.

Khomeini, Ruhollah. *Islam and Revolution*, (Hamid Algar, Trans.). Berekely: Mizan Press. 1981.

Milosz, Czeslaw. *The Captive Mind*. New York: Knopf, 1953.

Nair-Venugopal, Shanta. *The Gaze of the West and Framings of the East*. Basingstoke, UK: Palgrave Macmillan, 2012.

Zeiny, Esmaeil. "Academic Imperialism: Towards Decolonisation of English Literature in Iranian Universities." *Asian Journal of Social Science* 47 (2019): 88–109.

CHAPTER 6

"The Captive Mind" and Social Sciences in Southeast Asia

Syed Hussein Alatas

Mona Abaza

The late Syed Hussein Alatas was not only considered the main founder of sociological investigation in Southeast Asia, but more importantly, he was a unique public intellectual who fought on a number of fronts. He was celebrated for his prolific and timely publications, but he was also an active and engaged politician, a critical mind, and a builder of institutions and organisations in Malaysia and Singapore. He is still remembered for his cosmopolitan upbringing and for his service as Vice Chancellor of the University of Malaya in the 1980s, as well as for having founded the *Parti Gerakan Rakyat Malaysia*. His writings and political stance against corruption, imperialism, and the engagement that Third World intellectuals would have to undertake, and his emphasis on the post-colonial "mental captivity," were pioneering works in sociological investigation in Southeast Asia. His sharp reading and critique of Max Weber's thesis *The Protestant Ethic and the Spirit of Capitalism* in the Southeast Asian context remains timely and inspiring. While acknowledging the crucial significance of learning and borrowing from European sociological theory and its methods – for example, by pointing in his early writings to the value of Karl Manheim's *Wissenssoziologie* (sociology of knowledge)[1] – and equally acknowledging the impact of the late philosopher-anthropologist Ernest Gellner, who encouraged him to publish *Intellectuals in Developing Societies*, Alatas relentlessly continued intellectual excavations in the direction of rethinking the field of indigenous forms of knowledge. His struggles for social justice against racial discrimination in Malysia, and his insistence on calling attention to the increasing privileges that were granted in post-colonial times to the *Bumi Putras* (the "people of the soil," meaning the Malays who were given special privileges at the expense of other minorities), remain vital texts that address a number of challenges that contemporary Malaysian and Singaporean societies

---

1 Syed Hussein Alatas, "Karl Manheim (1894–1947)," *Progressive Islam* 1, no. 7–8 (February–March 1955).

continue to face today. To the end of his life, he remained a sharp critic of both colonial and post-colonial practices, as he traced the clear continuities in the history of mentalities.

Those who personally knew Syed Hussein Alatas will remember him as someone who was most pleasantly approachable. His house was always open to guests, and he was known to be extremely generous to students, colleagues, and friends, prompted by the warm hospitality of his late wife Zahara. He created a circle (a *halaqa*, the Islamic term for a circle of followers and students) who visited him regularly. No need to go through secretaries or assistants to meet Syed Hussein Alatas. He was a nocturnal person, and discussions at his house could last until three o'clock in the morning.

Syed Hussein Alatas was born in Bogor, Indonesia, in 1928, into a family of scholars and well-known religious figures of Hadhrami (Southern Yemeni) origin. The Arab-origin Hadhrami community in Indonesia has often been metaphorically called the Jews of Southeast Asia. They were not only prominent as religious scholars, and transmitters of knowledge from the Middle East, but they also made fortunes in business through the pilgrimage industry, as they maintained close relations with the Middle East. They also managed to obtain prominent positions in the colonial administration.

Alatas studied at the Univesity of Amsterdam, where he obtained his doctorate in 1963 at the Faculty of Political and Social Sciences. He later joined the Department of Malay Studies at the University of Malaya at Kuala Lumpur. During the early years of his academic career, he fused his academic activities with politics.[2] Thus, 'between 1969 and 1971, he served as a member of the National Consultative Council of Malaysia and, in 1971, he became a member of the Malaysian Parliament as a senator.'[3]

Alatas drew attention to the inherent relationship between the Third Worldist sociological discourse and the reconstruction of Islam as a progressive sociological perspective in the political Malaysian scene. More specifically, the present chapter focuses on his life and ideas and contextualises his thought within the Malaysian political scene. In his later years, he seemed to have directed critiques against the advocates of the trend of "Islamizing knowledge" and, more specifically, Islamizing sociology in Malaysia. The journal he founded during his student days in the 1950s, *Progressive Islam*, seems to be the focal point of a culturalist Third Worldist discourse that could be indirectly

---

2   Riaz Hassan, "Introduction," in *Local and Global: Social Transformation in Southeast Asia: Essays in Honour of Professor Syed Hussein Alatas*, ed. Riaz Hassan (Leiden: Brill, 2005), viii.

3   Ibid.

related to the "Islamization of Knowledge" debate, which has become a dominant intellectual discourse in Malaysia. This chapter attempts to highlight the competing trends within the field of sociological production.

It is possible to view the advocates of the Islamization of knowledge as representing one competing force among others in the Malaysian field of institutional academic life. Let us take a close look at the existing field of social sciences, in particular the impact of the older generation of Third Worldist intellectuals. Although the protagonists of the Islamization project seem to attack the West and Western rationalism ruthlessly, a point they might superficially share with Occidental critical theorists, they nonetheless discard the previous debates about decolonisation of history and anthropology. The discursive continuities between the "secular" culturalist stand of the 1950s and the 1960s is, therefore, difficult to trace. Islamists today seldom mention the previous indigenous Third Worldist critiques of Western social sciences. In Malaysia, they seemed to discard the writings of Syed Hussein Alatas, who might be considered an invisible protagonist in shaping the discourse of intellectuals and their role in developing societies. One could interpret the suppression of the writings of Alatas as a generational struggle between this scholar, who is a product of the post-colonial Malaysia/Singapore era and whose orientation was secular, and Anwar Ibrahim, the younger former student leader (who served under Mahathir Mohamed as deputy prime minister and minister of finance, but was later sentenced to jail) and who combined Islam with socialist rhetoric, influenced by the mood of the 1970s. Alatas often expressed strong criticism of the Islamization protagonists as merely fighting for a space in the job market.

A comparison of Syed Naquib al-Attas, the philologist and specialist in Malay Sufism, and his antagonism against "social sciences" as expressed in his book *Islam and Secularism*,[4] with his brother Syed Hussein Alatas, the sociologist, might provide a clue about the power struggle involving Syed Naquib al-Attas' close connection with Anwar Ibrahim and government circles, while Hussein Alatas' policies cost him the the vice chancellorship. It is possible to define Syed Hussein Alatas as a secular intellectual because he drew a clear distinction between religion and state. Although he was influenced in his youth by the Egyptian movement of the Muslim Brothers, he later shifted to a liberal position, insisting that his early vision of the Islamic state was cultural rather than political.

---

4 S.M.N. al-Attas, *Islam and Secularism*. Kuala Lumpur: Muslim Youth Movement of Malaysia, 1978.

Perhaps the events surrounding Alatas's resignation from his position of Vice Chancellor of the University of Malaya in 1990 can be viewed as symbolizing the struggle between two different generations. He headed the Department of Malay Studies at the National University of Singapore for many years. When he was appointed Vice Chancellor at the University of Malaya, he insisted that merit should supersede race.[5] He appointed non-Malay academicians on the basis of merit (Alatas suggested Indian and Chinese deans), which stirred the anger of the Malays. Anwar Ibrahim's Bumiputrist policy (which gave advantages to the "people of the soil," i.e., the Malays) clashed with such claims. This fight apparently forced Alatas to resign from the Vice Chancellor's position. A different interpretation of this incident could be a question of personality clash, since Alatas seemed to have created many enemies even before he started appointing academicians on the basis of merit. On the other hand, one can interpret the incident as a generational power struggle. Bumiputrism and Islamization are embraced to represent new class interests of the rising Malay bourgeoisie. The Singapore daily, *The Straits Times*, portrayed the controversy as being potentially harmful to the interests of Anwar Ibrahim, the then Minister of Education.

For many Singaporeans and Malaysians, the name Syed Hussein Alatas is still associated with the founding and building up of the Department of Malay Studies at the National University of Singapore and, in the late 1980s, with his work as Vice Chancellor at the University of Malaya in Malaysia.[6] Alatas started his academic career as a student of the sociology of religion at the University of Amsterdam in the Netherlands, where he spent over ten years. During this period of intensive academic formation and encounters with the West, Alatas developed a strong network of communication with Indonesian, Malay, and other Muslim intellectuals from Southeast Asia and the Middle East. In 1948, together with other students, he formed the "Association of Islamic Students" in Holland. This Association later merged with the Islamic Council in Holland. He was affiliated with the Indonesian intellectual and politician Mohammad Natsir, who became Prime Minister of Indonesia under Sukarno. They met during Alatas's short stay in Indonesia in 1953 and quickly established a friendship. As a result of this relationship, Alatas launched the magazine *Progressive Islam* (1954–55), which will be looked at more closely at the end of this chapter.

Alatas the Malaysian, like the Paris-based Egyptian intellectual Anouar Abdel Malek who belonged to the same generation, both proposed the notion

---

5   *The Straits Times*, 10 March 1990.
6   Alatas founded the Department of Malay Studies in 1968. *The Straits Times*, 10 March 1990.

of "cultural specificity." The circle of specificity would include the sphere of Islam and "Islamic socialism." In essence, cultural specificity has affinities with the movement of the return to "authenticity" as a movement of social emancipation and cultural recognition. Perhaps a closer look at Alatas and Abdel Malek might provide us with a clue about the link in ideas between these two intellectuals who are the spokesmen of decolonisation and identity construction, and their relationship later to the generation of Islamizers.

1 Syed Hussein Alatas and Anouar Abdel Malek

For anyone interested in the contemporary sociology of Southeast Asia, the works of Syed Hussein Alatas would undoubtedly be considered among the most significant. He is appreciated not merely for being one of the founders of sociological investigation in that part of the world, but also because he is representative of the generation of the post-independence, critical Third World intellectuals who stirred debates about decolonising mentalities, the dilemma of the "captive mind" and the re-thinking of development.[7] The endeavour of decolonizing anthropology saw the light as a result of the crisis in Western social sciences due to the struggle for nationalism. The post-colonial era witnessed the perpetuation of what Alatas called new forms of "academic colonialism" originating in the United States and the Soviet Union.[8] Abdel Malek and Alatas used the term "endogenous creativity" to describe ideas that stemmed from within the national and regional community. It was nevertheless understood as a fusion between Western and non-Western cultures. In anthropology, as a result of the debate on Orientalism, the idea of the "indigenization of social sciences" and "indigenous" solutions versus Western social science, as an ideological stand where the political overtook the ideological, saw the light in the 1970s. It was meant to raise criticism against the "implantation of social sciences" and was, broadly speaking, against American and capitalist social sciences. The debate about the "indigenization" of social sciences, which differs

---

7 Anouar Abdel Malek's article on his relationship to Che Guevara, written in a nostalgic tone in the Egyptian newspaper *al-Ahram Weekly*, reminds us of the vanished Third Worldist revolutionary period. See Anouar Abdel Malek, "A Rose for the 'Che,'" *al-Ahram Weekly* (16–22 October 1997).

8 See Yogesh Atal, "Indigenization: The Case of Indian Sociology," paper presented at The International Workshop on *Alternative Discourses in the Social Sciences and Humanities: Beyond Orientalism and Occidentalism*, Singapore, 30 May–1 June 1998.

from the term "endogenous," seems to take a more dramatic view of the break between East and West.

Alatas pointed to the problem of shaping an "endogenous" culture with the expanding modernization of Southeast Asian societies. Endogenous creativity meant that it should arise from the national culture, and yet, 'It means here that the assimilation of ideas from exogenous sources which are deemed necessary for the intellectual effort should be considered as part of the endogenous activity.'[9] It is no coincidence that Alatas's investigations extended to the struggle of Indian intellectuals in the turmoil of the post-colonial era.[10] His writings found a sensitive reception in Japan, and the volume edited by Anouar Abdel Malek testifies to the *Zeitgeist* and the debates that occupied the minds of the Egyptian, Indian, and Malaysian intellectuals who were struggling for recognition and "space" within the broader international intellectual field of sociological production.[11] Certainly, Japan provided a fascinating model of modernization for many Third World intellectuals. Abdel Malek and Alatas both developed an admiration and a desire to study Japanese society. Both were often invited there, and both often refer to the Japanese experience in their works. However, Abdel Malek's intellectualism owes a great deal to the Marxist heritage, while Alatas' earlier ideological orientations constituted a blend of socialism with the Egyptian Muslim Brothers' ideology. For this generation, "cultural specificity" seemed to swing towards nationalism rather than Islamism. Nevertheless, later in time, Abdel Malek's "specificity" ended up being apologetic for contemporary Islamism. Abdel Malek advanced the idea of a civilisational approach to the issue of political Islam. In an article published in 1982, three years after the success of the Iranian revolution, Abdel Malek altered his jargon to include Islam. He talked of the "progressive sector of popular masses."[12] He linked what he called the "civilizational approach of Islam" with political Islam, arguing that it includes the whole heritage of Egyptian civilisation.[13]

---

9   Syed Hussein Alatas, "Social Aspects of Endogenous Intellectual Creativity: The Problem of Obstacles—Guidelines for Research," in *Intellectual Creativity in Endogenous Culture*, ed. Anouar Abdel Malek (Tokyo: The United Nations University, 1981): 462–70, 462.

10   Syed Hussein Alatas, "India and the Intellectual Awakening of Asia," in *India and Southeast Asia*, ed. B. Sarkar (New Delhi: Indian Council for Cultural Relations, 1968). Alatas's interest also extended to nineteenth-century Russian intellectuals.

11   Syed Hussein Alatas, "Social Aspects of Endogenous Intellectual Creativity."

12   Anouar Abdel Malek, "L'Islam dans la pensée nationale progressiste," *Revue Tiers Monde* 23, no. 92 (Octobre–Décembre 1982): 845–849.

13   Anouar Abdel Malek's stand, his exaggeration of Eastern spirituality, "Eastern specificity" and magical spirituality were criticised by Sadiq Jalal al-Azm in his celebrated article on

In fact, both Alatas and Abdel Malek shared the issue of specificity raised in the 1970s. Alatas, in fact, refers to "endogenous" intellectual creativity. Although Abdel Malek is an "occasional Christian," as Nazih Ayubi qualifies him, his position during his later years became increasingly inclined towards the issue of the specificity of Islam.[14] For Abdel Malek, the cross-cultural civilisational exchange takes a rather confrontational form. His understanding of civilizations, particularly after the success of the Iranian revolution, tended to be reduced to religious essence, a point that he paradoxically criticised in his writings in the early 1960s on Orientalism:

> Le christianisme est la philosophie dominante de l'Occident; le boud-dhisme, essentiellement celle de l'Asie; seul l'Islam recoupe les civilisations et les cultures de notre temps; d'ou vient l'efficacité de son action comme nous l'avons vu au cours des deux derniers siècles.[15]

It was Sadiq Jalal al-Azm who first noted the "orientalism in reverse" in Anouar Abdel Malek's stand. This was an irony of fate, since it was Abdel Malek who, in 1963, first spoke of the essentialisms and biases of Western Orientalism in the much-celebrated article "Orientalism in Crisis," published in *Diogenes*, an article that became one of the major sources of inspiration of Edward Said's *Orientalism*. Abdel Malek's overemphasis of Eastern spirituality, "Eastern specificity" and magical spirituality is what the Islamizers of the 1980s appropriated. It is possible to view the "Islamization project" as a distorted, extended vision of "cultural specificity," a continuation of the same discourse, transposed into a language of the 1990s.

On the other hand, "endogenous" intellectual creativity in the 1970s meant that Marxism, Buddhism, and the Asiatic mode of production could be used as conceptual tools of analysis for the underdevelopment of Asian societies.[16] "Endogenous" was interpreted as (self-reliant) creativity, a creativity that would oppose Orientalism and exoticism.[17]

Abdel Malek refers to different civilizations entailing their own "specificities."[18] Indian, Japanese, and Chinese traditions, scientific heritages and

---

Orientalism in reverse. See Sadiq Jalal al-Azm, "Orientalism and Orientalism in Reverse," *Khamsin* 8 (1981): 5–26.

14   This is according to Nazih Ayubi, *Political Islam, Religion and Politics in the Arab World* (London: Routledge, 1991), 237.

15   Anouar Abdel Malek, "L'Islam dans la pensée nationale progressiste," 849.

16   Syed Hussein Alatas, "Social Aspects of Endogenous Intellectual Creativity," 462–470.

17   Ibid., 3.

18   Ibid., 26.

varieties of philosophical thinking were highlighted in the volume of Abdel Malek and Amar Nath Pandeya. The dynamic of specificity-universality was addressed as follows:

> A work through all scientific problem areas of our project is the problem, and concept, of specificity. It would, therefore, be proper to develop a universally valid theory of specificity, from and bearing upon major civilizational and national-cultural areas of the world.[19]

For students interested in the study of "globalization," it is possible to propose that this notion already operated on the level of South-South intellectual interaction during the period of the 1950s and 1960s. In other words, the language and concerns of this generation of intellectuals revealed similar affinities and worries. Alatas was concerned with how to create a synthesis between "cultural specificities" and, in the case of India, it implied that the "Asian tradition" is to be blended with socialism, as the Indian Marxist Jayaprakash Narayan attempted to undertake. While maintaining a universalist discourse about methodological tools of social inquiry and revealing an intuitive understanding of the significance of Western sociology, Alatas was struggling against the West's monopoly of knowledge. He argued that:

> The effort to construct new concepts for the study of Southeast Asian societies is in keeping with a genuine application of the social sciences. The general universal and abstract concept of the modern social sciences which developed in the West should not automatically be applied to non-western societies.[20]

2   The Weber Thesis and Southeast Asia

Alatas provided a genuine reading of Max Weber and the applicability of his thesis in a Southeast Asian context. In the article "The Weber Thesis and South East Asia," Alatas first analysed the points of view of the various Western scholars who discussed Weber's causal analysis of the emergence of capitalism, in which religion and inner-worldly asceticism led to the birth of a specific personality type. He criticised Robert Bellah's application of the Weber thesis to

---

19   Ibid., 5.
20   Syed Hussein Alatas, *The Myth of the Lazy Native* (London: Frank Cass, 1977), 7.

Japan and is also said to have signalled out the critics of Weber. The Weber thesis was discussed in the light of Asian history, in particular in China and India. Weber said that capitalism could not develop independently in these two civilisations due to the influence of religion. Alatas challenged this point of view through his attempt 'at establishing the proposition that the spirit of modern capitalism can rise in Asia from within itself.'[21] Alatas advanced examples from the coming of Islam in Southeast Asia by pointing to the "mutual alliance between Islam and trade."[22] He noted that the role of the Arab traders and small industrialists before the Second World War, in manifesting a capitalist spirit, was accompanied by inner-worldly religious asceticism.[23] Alatas provided examples of how Asian scholars such as Daniel Marcellus George Koch applied Weber's causality of religion and economic activities in the case of the Indonesian party Sarekat Islam.[24] He also discussed the works of Schrieke and Van Leur, who borrowed from Max Weber and applied some of his observations to Southeast Asia. He concluded his study by arguing that:

> If the capitalist spirit is so closely tied up with the religious attitude, we can expect a uniform pattern of expression among Muslims of common schools and mystical interest. Apparently, what is decisive here is not religion but other factors. The factors which released the capitalist spirit among Arab Muslims, Indian Muslims, Minangkabau, Acheh, and Bugis Muslims, and also the Chinese, must clearly be of non-religious origin.[25]

In *Intellectuals in Developing Societies*, Alatas developed the notion of Bebalisma, from "*bebal*," which is Malay for "stupid," which also implies ignorance and stubbornness, but also seems to be a way of reasoning in developing societies.[26] His critiques of the unconcerned attitude of the scientific worldview were bitter. Alatas poses the problem of "decolonizing" knowledge, and questioning the biases and prejudices promoted by colonial culture against

---

21 Syed Hussein Alatas, "The Weber Thesis and South East Asia," in *Modernization and Social Change* (Sydney: Angus and Robertson, 1972), 3; first appeared in *Extrait des Archives de Sociologie des Religions* 15 (1963).

22 Ibid., 17. Concerning the contextualisation of Alatas' work on the Weber thesis in Asia, see Andreas Buss, "Max Weber's Heritage and Modern Southeast Asian Thinking on Development," in *Religion, Values and Development in Southeast Asia*, ed. Bruce Matthews and Judith Nagata (Singapore: Institute of Southeast Asian Studies, 1986), 4–22.

23 Syed Hussein Alatas, "The Weber Thesis and South East Asia."

24 Ibid., 13.

25 Ibid., 20.

26 Syed Hussein Alatas, *Intellectuals in Developing Societies* (London: Frank Cass, 1977).

the local populations. Obviously, what is at stake is the undermining of the ideology of imperialism. By deconstructing the figure of Raffles, the founder of modern Singapore, Alatas reveals that Raffles was far from a humanitarian colonial administrator. He demonstrates that through sociological devices:

> He (Raffles) was ahead of his Dutch contemporaries in the sense that he conceived Western imperialism as a comprehensive effort of the European to transform the societies of others for their own benefit. He had what *Wissenssoziologie* (the sociology of knowledge, a term which he borrows from Mannheim) calls the "total ideology" concept of imperialism.[27]

3   Islam and Democracy

Alatas' writings on Islam and the democracy of Islam, on Islam and social-ism,[28] on colonialism and corruption,[29] and on the problem of occupational prestige among the Malays and their over-admiration of civil service, deserve attention. I quote him:

> It has been suggested that the present value system of Malay society is a continuity of the past. Though this is the case it does not mean that there has not been any change in the system. Certain occupations have gone down in prestige, and some have completely disappeared. The slaves, the individual warriors attached to the ruler or individual princes, and the court entertainers have disappeared as social classes. The modern-ization of Malaya was the direct cause. The shamans and the medicine men have been reduced in prestige, also because of modernization. In the place of the warrior class, we have now the civil servants and the professionals.[30]

---

27   Syed Hussein Alatas, *Thomas Stamford Raffles: Schemer or Reformer, 1781–1826* (Sydney: Angus and Robertson, 1971), 42.

28   Syed Hussein Alatas, "Islam e Socialismo," *Ulisse* 14, no. 83 (June 1977): 103–13. In this arti-cle Alatas refers to the works of Maxime Rodinson and Sayyed Qutb, and Mustafa al-Seba'i's *Socialism of Islam*.

29   Syed Hussein Alatas, *The Problem of Corruption.* Singapore: Times Books International, 1986.

30   Syed Hussein Alatas, "The Grading of Occupational Prestige Amongst the Malays in Malaysia," *JMBRAS* 41, part 1, no. 213 (1968): 146–56.

Alatas' detailed observations extend to the phenomenon of the perpetuation of *bomoh* (witchcraft) culture among the upper echelons of the royalty in Malaysia. They deserve astute attention as empirical observations.[31]

In attempting to theorise corruption, Alatas was very keen to demonstrate its universality despite the disparity of the specific details in the various individual countries. Alatas argues against relativism in social sciences as follows:

> There are different conceptions of the abnormal personality cherished by different peoples and cultures. Here a certain degree of relativistic explanation is justified. However, we are not justified in eliminating altogether the objective universal criteria of abnormality employed by psychology. A paranoiac is a paranoiac whether he is the president of a modern state or the chief of a primitive tribe.[32]

Furthermore, Alatas provides us with lively examples of corruption in Latin America, Asia, and India. Here again, it is crucial for the sociologist to note that Alatas links the phenomenon with Marcel Mauss's notion of the *gift*, and how it is shrewdly practised under the table in various Third World countries. For those interested in how Islam treated corruption throughout history, Alatas brings examples of later periods of Islam when the office of the qadi (judge) was strongly abhorred by the scholars who wanted to maintain their integrity.[33] He also mentions the case of the African Uthman dan Fodio, who attacked corrupt practices and the habit of giving presents.[34]

> In a society totally gripped by corruption, everything that is possible to corrupt is seized for the purpose. The forms and manifestations of corruption are beyond description. New ideas are continually added. Corruption becomes an industry. Like an industry it seeks to create a public demand. Hence new rules and legislations are added to existing ones for the purpose of corruption.[35]

Before Edward Said's *Orientalism* appeared, Alatas, like Anouar Abdel Malek but later, tackled the question of Orientalism and Western biases in studying

---

31 Syed Hussein Alatas, *Modernization and Social Change* (Sydney: Angus and Robertson, 1972), iii.

32 Alatas, *The Problem of Corruption*, 21.

33 Ibid., 45–48.

34 Ibid., 48.

35 Ibid., 75.

Asian and Muslim societies.[36] Edward Said, in fact, points to the intimate ideological similarity in raising issues between Alatas and other Third World intellectuals, like *A Rule of Property for Bengal: An Essay on the Idea of Permanent Settlement* (1963) by Ranajit Guha, a Bengali political economist. *The Myth of the Lazy Native* is analyzed by Said as a post-colonial critique of Orientalism in which the lazy native is an invention of colonialism.[37]

In *The Myth of the Lazy Native*, Alatas revealed how biased racial views equally affected the Malay indigenous perceptions.[38] This work challenged the views of Mahathir's social Darwinism, which linked backwardness with race, particularly in the case of the Malays.[39] Mahathir Mohammed developed the idea that the Malays are, by heredity, inferior to the Chinese. Alatas challenged Mahathir's view that Malay economic backwardness is related to the myth of the lazy native.[40] Alatas discusses ideas such as that the Malays are fatalistic and ignore time. In his critique of the writings of the United Malay National Organization (UMNO), the book *Revolusi Mental* (*Mental Revolution*), Alatas reveals how the Malays reproduce in themselves stereotyped and colonized ideas about the backwardness of the Malays. Alatas revealed how harsh and biased the Malay indigenous vision of backwardness could be, being even more biased than any British analysis of the colonial society.[41] His merit was to demonstrate the inner contradictions of Malay society and the government's refusal of all responsibility to improve conditions in the Malay community. His critique extends to the fact that no thorough analysis of the mechanism of the capitalist system has been undertaken.

Alatas questioned the Western understanding of "objectivity" in research. It seems that specialists in Asia constructed an affinity between objectivity and

---

36   Edward Said, *Orientalism*. New York: Vintage Books, 1978; Syed Hussein Alatas, "Modernization and National Consciousness in Singapore," in *Modernization and Social Change*, 65–119; Anouar Abdel Malek, "L'orientalisme en crise," *Diogène* 44 (1963): 109–42. Nevertheless, Alatas published, at a much later time than Abdel Malek, "Some Problems of Asian Studies" in *Modernization and Social Change*, 65–119. In fact, it is no coincidence that in *Culture and Imperialism*, Edward Said refers extensively to Alatas' writings, in particular to *The Myth of the Lazy Native*. See Edward W. Said, *Culture and Imperialism* (London: Chatto and Windus, 1993), 296–307.

37   Ibid., 296.

38   Alatas, *The Myth of the Lazy Native*, Chapter 10, "Mental Revolution and Indolence of the Malays."

39   Khoo Boo Teik, *Paradoxes of Mahathirism: An Intellectual Biography of Mahathir Mohamad* (Oxford: Oxford University Press, 1995), 11.

40   Khoo Boo Teik also discusses the significance of Alatas' writings in the Malaysian context. See *Paradoxes of Mahathirism*.

41   Alatas, *The Myth of the Lazy Native*, 150.

"THE CAPTIVE MIND" AND SOCIAL SCIENCES IN SOUTHEAST ASIA 127

being an "outsider" to the field, in order to discredit the position of the "native" studying his own society.[42]

Alatas' understanding of science is positivistic. Although science and technology developed in the West, for Alatas they are universal. Science was borrowed and spread all over the world. In other words, while science belongs to everybody, it is impossible to "modernize" some cultural traits, such as magic. On the other hand, Alatas expressed reservations about the advocates of the Islamization trend.[43] He rejects the scientific validity of Islamizing any field of knowledge (be it science or sociology) and attributes the debate to a political fight instigated by a younger generation of university academics who are attempting to create a space in the academic marketplace.[44]

Alatas is also just as critical of the USA-based Iranian scholar Seyyed Hossein Nasr as he is of ideological manipulation and the failure of Third World intellectuals to develop an "analytical method independent of current stereotypes."[45] Here Alatas' criticism of Nasr is quite revealing:

> The confusion, inconsistency, and credulity in the several writings of Seyyed Hossein Nasr require a separate treatment which shall not be attempted here. One of his views which demands a tremendous amount of credulity on my part is that kingship is not a secular institution but has always been associated with divine authority. I presume the Shah of Iran is considered by Seyyed Hossein Nasr as the embodiment of Divine authority. I find it also difficult to count the number of prophets God sent to mankind. Seyyed Hossein Nasr suggested the figure of 124,000. How he arrived at this figure, we are not told, but it is certainly not from the Qur'an.[46]

Alatas' critique of Nasr derives from the fact that Nasr was closely related to the Shah's politics, rather than from his writings on the Islamization of knowledge.

---

42   Alatas, "Modernization and National Consciousness in Singapore," 182.

43   Personal communication with Professor Alatas, December 1995.

44   Personal communication with Professor Alatas during the conference "Globality, Modernity, Non-Western Civilizations," Bielefeld, May 1993.

45   Syed Hussein Alatas, "The Captive Mind and Creative Development," in *Asian Values and Modernization*, ed. Seah Chee-Meow (Singapore: Singapore University Press, 1977), 77.

46   Syed Hussein Alatas, "Cultural Impediments to Scientific Thinking," in *Culture and Industrialization: An Asian Dilemma*, ed. Rolf E. Vente and Peter S.J. Chen, Verbund Stiftung Deutsches Übersee Institut (Foundation German Overseas Institute) (Singapore: McGraw Hill International Book Company, 1980), 17.

4　Syed Hussein Alatas and Progressive Islam

For those interested in a comparison between the post-colonial culture of the Middle East and Southeast Asia, Syed Hussein Alatas' work is certainly most significant. I will attempt here to combine an analysis of the early writings of Alatas, in particular the monthly publication of *Progressive Islam,* which appeared in Holland during Alatas' time as a student, with his later writings. In fact, *Progressive Islam* still remains unnoticed. The fact that it was published in the Netherlands explains, perhaps, why English was the language of communication.

5　Progressive Islam

"Progressive Islam" is, in fact, the expression of the early Islamic commitments of young Alatas in the period of his studies in Holland.[47] It is of interest to us because these were the formative, interactive years of a young man who was striving for knowledge in the West and yet maintaining his Islamicity. It reflects the concern of a generation of young Indonesians at that time; they perceived the struggle for independence and social justice as being associated with the re-affirmation of religious identity. We have to recall that these were the times when the federation of Malaya was negotiating independence from British rule, while Sukarno's Indonesia was involved in the post-independence struggle in building a modern nation state that would strengthen his Islamic constituency, and the idea of an Islamic state was strongly present in the debates about the charter. The advocates of Islam were competing with ideologies then threatening the West, namely, nationalism and communism. The strong influence of the communist parties in various Southeast Asian nations should not be forgotten. For some observers, Islam was perceived to be a possible card that the West would play against communism. Americans and Russian communists

---

47　*Progressive Islam* appeared while Alatas was completing his Ph.D. in the Netherlands. Meanwhile, in 1957, Alatas went to Bandung. He returned to Malaysia to work in Dewan Bahasa in 1958. In 1961, he returned to Amsterdam to complete his dissertation, and in 1963 he joined the University of Malaya. In Indonesia, Alatas met Natsir, who was very keen to help him. Alatas completed his thesis in 1963; it was titled, "Reflections on the Theories of Religion" (Drukkerij Pasmans, 1963). The thesis was written from the perspective of an 'Asian Muslim who is a student of Western science' (p. 10). It attempts to analyze theories of religion of the following thinkers: Tylor, Frazer, Marret, James, Durkheim, Freud, Jung, Soderblom, Otto, Malinowski, and Radcliffe-Brown. Among Alatas' supervisors were Professor G.F. Pijper and Professor W.F. Wertheim.

were competing to extend their influence on Muslim leaders and intellectuals from the Third World.[48] For example, Haji Omar Tjokroaminoto, the leader of Sarekat Islam of Indonesia, had written a book on Islam and socialism in 1924 in order to counteract communist influences that were infiltrating the Islamic movement.[49] The generation of intellectuals like Natsir and Alatas kept in touch with communists for the sake of friendship, but grew increasingly antagonistic towards them. In fact, Alatas became increasingly anti-communist over time.

Progressive Islam appeared as a monthly publication. It was "dedicated to the promotion of knowledge concerning Islam and Modern thought." The editorial announcement expressed the following:

> This monthly, which we have called *Progressive Islam*, is the realization of an attempt to formulate a serious view concerning the nature of Islam and its relation to modern thought. The condition of the Muslim people, the nature of the Islamic religion and the impact of Western thought upon the societies of the East shall be the primary concern of this monthly.

Ibn Khaldun is also mentioned in the same article as the founder of modern sociology and scientific history. So why was it called *Progressive Islam*?

> The name *Progressive Islam* does not imply any dissection whatsoever as to the nature of the Islamic faith. The idea which we intend to convey is not a kind of abstraction from the totality of the Islamic religion. By calling this paper *Progressive Islam* we do not mean that we have extracted one part of Islam which is progressive and left the other part of Islam which is not progressive. Rather, the name *Progressive Islam* should be regarded as another way of saying that Islam is progressive.

The first issue appeared in August 1954, and the last issue in December 1955. The editorial articles were written by Syed Hussein Alatas. *Progressive Islam* survived with the support of the former prime minister of Indonesia, Mohammed Natsir. Alatas continued to collaborate with Natsir, in particular in 1957 in Bandung, where they had many ideas in common.[50] *Progressive Islam*

---

48   G.E. Von Grunebaum, "Rueckblick auf drei internationale islamische Tagungen," *Der Islam* 34 (1959): 134–49.

49   Syed Hussein Alatas, "Islam e Socialismo," *Ulisse*, Vol. XIV Fasc. LXXXIII- Giugno (1977), 105.

50   Mohammad Natsir (1908–93) was a Muslim intellectual during the Sukarno period. In 1940, he became the head of the Bandung branch of Partai Islam Indonesia ('PII', the Indonesian Islamic Party). Natsir is perhaps best known for his affiliation with the

also received funds from supporters and contributors from different parts of the Muslim world. The short existence of the journal was due to a lack of financial support.

Progressive Islam says a lot about the cross-cultural East-West perceptions. The articles could be read on different levels. On the one hand, many of them attempt to explore Western culture and civilization and its interactive aspects. On another level, *Progressive Islam* portrays the type of Islamic internationalism that existed in Europe in the 1950s. It is an English-language imitation of the Egyptian *al-Manar* magazine, which was launched in 1898 by Mohammed 'Abduh and Rashid Rida and published until 1936. *Al-Manar* intended to disseminate news from all over the Muslim world. *Progressive Islam*, like *al-Manar*, contained many articles about inter-Islamic relations and news from all of the Muslim world.

Natsir's review of Henri Pirenne's book *Muhammad and Charlemagne* (although it might appear outdated today) is a revealing example of Natsir's curiosity during the early, fresh post-colonial period in highlighting the interaction between the West and the Muslim world. Particularly interesting is how he uses Pirenne's thesis about the Arabs' spiritual conquest of Rome versus the Germans' conquest by sword in order to attack C. Snouck Hurgronje, the famous scholar of Islam, regarding Indonesia:

> With a bit of humor, we could express ourselves in the same way as Professor Snouck Hurgronje did towards us in his book *The Netherlands and Islam*. We shall say to them: Christianity has the slogan "Preach the faith to all the nations," but that alone was not enough for them. What they really hoped for was that after the teaching had been spread, the real domination would come. It is not necessary for us to look at Rome.

Indonesian Masjumi Party. He was also Prime Minister of Indonesia for a short period of seven months in 1950–51. In contrast to Sukarno, Natsir advocated the unity of religion and the state. Nevertheless, he differed from the Pakistani Mawdudi in that he did not propose a fixed model of an Islamic state. He strongly distanced himself from communism. Although he maintained friendships with some communists, he faced strong antagonism from the Indonesian communist party. Natsir criticised the activities of the Christian missionaries in Indonesia. For further details about his life and thought, see Yusril Ihza, "Combining Activism and Intellectualism: The Biography of Mohammad Natsir (1908–1993)," *Studia Islamika* 2, no. 1 (1995): 111–47. It is interesting to note that the financing of *Progressive Islam* by Natsir in the early 1950s coincides with his growing interest in Islamic internationalism and in supporting Muslims in different parts of the world. We are told that he travelled to the Middle East, Pakistan, Turkey, and Burma in 1952.

Look at what happened at central Sulawesi. Amongst the missionaries (Protestant) the name of Mrs. Hofman-Stolk is well known; she is regarded as a very active worker, together with her husband, in spreading the Christian faith and not less for pacification of these areas.

In fact, various articles discussed misunderstandings of the interaction between the East and the West. Two other short articles by Natsir, one on Ibn Maskawaih (the philosopher and historian of fifth-century Islamic history, who is compared with Schopenhauer) and another on the life of Imam al-Ghazali, reveal Natsir's general interest in Islamic heritage. Al-Ghazali is compared to David Hume (1711–1776). Both philosophers, according to Natsir, reacted against mainstream philosophical trends. Both of them suggested that beliefs and convictions rested on emotions and passion. However, Natsir, went on to explain the differences as well as the similarities between these two philosophers.

Other prominent Indonesian politicians, such as Mohammed Hatta and Mohammad Roem, are a good illustration of the voices addressing Islam in a post-colonial Indonesia struggling with democracy and "Pancasila" as a state ideology. According to Alatas, Hatta, Natsir and Roem all represent the Muslim viewpoint and radically differ from the Egyptian Muslim Brothers, in that they carry on dialogue with Christians and are more tolerant and democratic.[51] Natsir, in a later period of his life and because of the ban of the Masjumi Party in Indonesia, became increasingly inclined towards expanding contact with Saudi Arabia through the Muslim World League and *Da'ah* activities.

The sociologist might find it curious that Alatas' early work emphasizes the life and work of Karl Mannheim, as well as that of Ibn Khaldun. The attempt to merge the ideas of the eminent Arab historian with Western social theory is worth attention. Alatas provides us with a summary of the major works of Mannheim, namely, *Man and Society in an Age of Reconstruction, Diagnosis of our Time*, and *Ideology and Utopia*. Much has been written in recent years about Ibn Khaldun as the founder of the science of sociology and history.[52] Since the 1930s, thanks to the pioneering studies of Kamil Ayad and Franz Rosenthal, as demonstrated earlier among Egyptian sociologists, there has been a revival

---

51   There is a tendency to draw analogies and resemblances between the Indonesian Masjumi Party and the Egyptian Muslim Brothers organisation. For example, the Indonesian intellectual and leader of the Mohammadiyyah organisation, Arnin Rais, wrote a doctoral dissertation comparing these two movements.

52   For a comprehensive overview of the impact of Ibn Khaldun on contemporary scholarship, see Aziz al-Azmeh, *Ibn Khaldun in Modern Scholarship: A Study in Orientalism*. London: Third World Centre for Research and Publishing, 1981.

of sociological interest in the works of Ibn Khaldun.[53] It is nonetheless interesting to note that an Indonesian student of Arab origin in Holland, Syed Hussein Alatas, was already considering the sociological importance of Ibn Khaldun in the 1950s. Alatas visited Cairo twice.[54] In 1952, he recalled his visit to the house of Taha Hussain.[55] Alatas wanted to question Taha Hussain about the possibility of viewing Ibn Khaldun as the founder of modern sociology. Alatas thought that Hussain was rather inclined to emphasize his qualities as a great historian. The young Alatas initially thought that Taha Hussain was quite Westernized, an idea that quickly vanished after he read Taha Hussain's *al-Fitna al-kubra*. Alatas wrote an article entitled "Objectivity and the Writing of History" about the conception of history of al-Ghazali, Ibn Khaldun, Iqbal and other historians. He suggests that Ibn Khaldun was the first to propose the idea of a universal and objective writing of history and further theories about objectivity in writing. One can see how Alatas fuses Western knowledge by drawing comparisons with other historians such as Arnold Toynbee, Karl Marx, and Mohammed Iqbal.

The wide choice of topics and differing views of Islam – ranging from the poets of Persia, to religious parties in western Europe (written by a religious Dutchman), to education in Islamic society, the reconstruction of Islamic law, information on Islam in Burma and Pakistan, *Sarikat Buruh Islam Indonesia*, the Muslim Labour Union of Indonesia, the Russian Revolution,[56] and the rich and stimulating information presented on the exile of Arabi ('Urabi') Pasha in Ceylon (the leader of the Egyptian revolt in 1882 against the British troops colonising Egypt) – are a good illustration of the type of Islamic internationalism that existed in the 1950s.

I quote at length some of the passages written by Senator A. M. Azeez. It is in the context of struggles of national liberation that examples from other Third World countries are borrowed. The article starts as follows:

---

53   Kamil Ayad, *Die Geschichts-und Gesellschaftslehre Ibn Halduns*, (diss., Berlin 1930); Franz Rosenthal, *Ibn Khalduns Gedanken ueber den Staat* (Munich and Berlin, 1932); and H.A.R. Gibb, "The Islamic Background of Ibn Khaldoun's Political Theory," *Bulletin of the School of Oriental Studies* 7 (1933): 23–31.

54   Alatas visited Cairo in 1952. In 1963 he was invited by the Islamic Congress to give lectures at Cairo and Alexandria Universities.

55   It is important to note here that Taha Hussain (Hussein) wrote his doctoral thesis on Ibn Khaldun. See Taha Hussain, *Etudes analytiques et critiques de la philosophie sociale d'Ibn Khaldoun* (doctoral thesis, Paris, 1917).

56   The article on the Bolshevik Revolution by Rozemond describes the social circumstances and descriptions of landscapes that prepared the revolution.

It was ordained that the national hero of Egypt, Ahmad Arabi Pasha, should spend the best part of his life, a period of nearly nineteen years, from January 11, 1883 to September 18, 1901, in Ceylon—the land of his exile. In his time, he attempted, though unsuccessfully, to purify the civil and military administration of his country and do away with the domination of the foreigners and wrest Egypt for the Egyptians.

Viewing him as a venerated Muslim leader, the Muslims of Ceylon gave Arabi Pasha an impressive welcome. We are told that he enjoyed great success in Candy and that the indigenous people adopted the red fez, or *tarboosh*, as a symbolic act. In Candy, modern education, following the advice of Arabi Pasha, was greatly encouraged:

> Arabi Pasha had known the effects of the educational reforms that were undertaken in Egypt during the early years of the nineteenth century and had later felt the exhortations of Jamaludin Afghani, who during his comparatively short stay in Egypt between the years 1871 and 1879 'preached freedom not only from foreign rule, but also and even more from the obstructive force of rigid worn-out beliefs and practices.'

The article stresses Arabi Pasha's influence in Candy in reforming education, in particular English education and religious practices. Siddi Lebbe created Al-Madrasatuz Zahira in 1892 under the auspices of Arabi Pasha, who chose its name. It received strong support from the Muslims of Colombo. It later became the Zahira College.

> Arabi Pasha came to Ceylon as a forlorn refugee branded as a "heavy fellah" and a disloyal rebel. History has since pronounced its verdict and Egypt will for ever hail him her Hero, who farsightedly foresaw the power for evil wielded against Egypt by the combination of the feudal and foreign elements in the country.

Senator Azeez's article on the *Sarikat Buruh Islam Indonesia* reveals that this labour movement was created in 1947, as a section of the Masjumi Party, but separated from the party a year later. It is interesting that mass action, but not revolution, as a form of social change was advocated:

> 'Mass action as we preach it does not necessarily mean a social revolution or violence to kill each other. Actions are taken through legal ways

in opposing parliament to enact laws relating to social and job security, industrial peace, etc.'

Not all the writers followed a homogeneous line of thought. The general concern about history and religion is illustrated in the summary of the talk by Arnold Toynbee. Indeed, the article, "The Political System of Islam," by Syed Abul Ala Maududi, differs from Natsir's perspective on Islam. Mohammed Roem of the Masjumi Party argued at that time against the separation of state and religion.[57] One possible reading of some articles of *Progressive Islam* is as an attempt to substitute Western modernity with an Islamic framework for national formation and state-building.

The question of the "scientification" of Islam, the initial rejection of the theory of evolution, and then its appropriation for the purpose of giving the *Qur'an* a new scientific explanation, dates back to al-Afghani and Mohammed Abduh, who were both concerned about reviving intellectualism and creating a new class of 'ulama.'[58] Thus, the topic of religion and science,[59] Charles Darwin and the theory of evolution,[60] can be seen as a continuation of such concerns.

In the editorial "Some Problems of Leadership in Islamic Society" (vol. J, no. 6, Jumadal-Ula 1374 A.H., January 1955), Alatas draws a dichotomy between differing and contradictory forms of knowledge that would lead to a clash between the orthodox 'ulama' and the modernist Muslims. He seems to criticise both camps. The 'ulama' lacked the knowledge of modern science and Western languages, while the modernist Muslims preferred to regard religion as a private matter.

When speaking about the 'ulama', one cannot overlook the two inspiring articles on Mohammad Abduh's humanism by the eminent Egyptian philosopher Osman Amin.[61] "Al-Ustaz al-Imam" (The Master and Guide) was the title

---

57   See Mohammed Roem, *Religion and Politics* 1, no. 12 (July 1955, Dhul Qa'dah).
58   Concerning the rejection and then the appropriation of the theory of evolution by early Muslim reformists, see Najm A. Bezirgan, "The Islamic World," in *The Comparative Reception of Darwinism*, ed. Thomas F. Glick (Chicago and London: University of Chicago Press, 1974), 375–387.
59   See vol. 1, no. 1 (Safar 1373 A.H., August 1954).
60   Vol. 1, no. 3 (Safar 1374 A.H., October 1954).
61   Osman Amin (1905–78) was a distinguished philosopher teaching at Cairo University. He held the position of Dean at the Faculty of Literature, Cairo University. Amin studied in France. He made significant contributions in the Academy of Arabic Language. Amin wrote extensively on Mohammad Abduh (see *Muhammad Abduh, Essai sur ses idées philosophiques et religieuses* [Cairo: Ministère de l'instruction publique, Imprimerie Misr], 1944), Islamic philosophy, the philosophy of Arabic language, Heidegger and Jaspers, and

of Mohammad Abduh's article. The first article highlights the life and work of Mohammad Abduh. Amin describes Abduh's inner crisis during his study at al-Azhar and his ascetic exercises. Abduh's biography, his relationship to al-Afghani, his exile in Syria and his sojourn in Paris are beautifully described. Amin stressed Abduh's interest in logic, which he borrowed from Aristotle, as explained by Ibn Rushd. Amin portrays Mohammad Abduh as an 'alim cultivating a scientific spirit with a "highly moral character". An 'alim who by his courage advocated "that man liberates himself from the slavery of Taklid, of all blind submission to whatever authority." An 'alim critical of Muslim society, a reformer, a humanist comparable to Rousseau, and a universalist. These early articles on Abduh gain significance today because they were written in the 1950s, well before Albert Hourani's prominent work on the Egyptian liberal age[62] and Ahmed's *Intellectual Origins of Egyptian Nationalism*[63] appeared and were widely read. Alatas knew Osman Amin personally, and had corresponded with him. Alatas had several encounters with Osman Amin, once in Holland and another time in Egypt, when Alatas gave lectures at various Egyptian universities.

Alatas always maintained relations with the Middle East. As early as 1952, he lived for four months in Baghdad and Tehran to undertake a post-graduate field study for the University of Amsterdam on 'the perception of social problems amongst the leading elites in Iran and Iraq.' Alatas attempted to look at perceptions of governing among three groups: labour, religious leaders, and political leaders. In 1950, he undertook a short trip from the Netherlands to Algeria, contacting (in Algier) Sheikh Bashir Ibrahimi, the leader who created the association of 'ulama', and Messali Hajj during the time he was under house arrest. Perhaps what induced Alatas to travel to Algeria was that he had already met Ben Bellah in Jakarta in the late 1940s and was much impressed by his personality.

The article on the Islamic state, which Alatas wrote at that time, reveals the concerns of the young generation of Indonesians who wanted to merge Islam with nationalism. Islam went hand in hand with independence. Alatas writes the following:

---

      edited works of Averroes and al-Farabi. For a general bibliography of Amin's works see "In Memoriam Osmane Amine," *MIDEO: Mélanges Institut Dominicain d'Etudes Orientales du Caire* 14 (1980): 398–404; London: Oxford University Press.

62   Albert H. Hourani, *Arabic Thought in the Liberal Age 1798–1939*. London: Oxford University Press, 1962.

63   Jamal M. Ahmed, *The Intellectual: Origins of Egyptian Nationalism*. Oxford: Oxford University Press, 1960.

Everywhere in the world of Islam we find intense political fermentation which is getting momentum by the day. In Morocco, Tunisia and Algeria, the people of Islam are pressing for their independence, we know, as a means to attain an ideal. For the areas predominantly inhabited by Muslims, to attain independence without endeavouring to establish an Islamic state would be not only meaningless but also injurious to the welfare of Islam and the community in general, non-Muslims included. This is the reason that all the Islamic organizations in Indonesia are striving with all the might at their disposal for the establishment of an Islamic State.[64]

However, the Islamic state that was proposed was supposed to be devoid of chauvinism and radicalism:

The Islamic state shall be a deadly enemy of both racialism and chauvinism. Professor Toynbee had recommended this Islamic spirit to Western society as a force to diminish the influence of racialism. We might agree with Professor Snouck Hurgronje that the 'The ideal of a league of human races has indeed been approached by the Moslem community more nearly than by any other.'[65]

Alatas was acquainted with the writings of the Egyptian Muslim Brothers, among other Islamic writings. He knew the Egyptian Muslim Brother, Said Ramadan. Nevertheless, Alatas' references in *The Democracy of Islam*, from which he derives his comparative analyses of different civilizations, are strongly influenced by both Muslim and Western thinkers.[66] Here are some of the works and thinkers he refers to: Von Grunebaum, *Medieval Islam*; N.A. Faris, *The Arab Heritage*; Thomas Carlyle, A.J. Arberry and Bertrand Russell, *Scientific Outlook*; Edward Gibbon, *Decline and Fall of the Roman Empire*; Arnold Toynbee, Gerth and Mills *Essays on the Sociology of Max Weber*; H.A.R. Gibb, *Mohammedanism*; P.K. Hitti, *History of the Arabs*; T.W. Arnold, *The Preaching of Islam*; Karl Mannheim, M. Iqbal and Gustav Diercks, *The Arabs of the Middle Ages*; and C. Snouck Hurgronje and Charles Issawi, *An Arab Philosophy of History*.

---

64   Editorial, *The Islamic State* 1, no. 3 (Safar 1374 A.H., October 1954 A.D.).

65   Ibid.

66   Syed Hussein Alatas, *The Democracy of Islam: A Concise Exposition with Comparative Reference to Western Political Thought*. The Hague and Bandung: W. Van Hoeve, Eastern Universities Press, 1956.

In retrospect, it is possible to argue that the ideals of an Islamic state, such as Alatas expresses in the editorial of vol. 1, no. 3, Safar 1374, could be viewed as imprecise. This is perhaps because no real example of an Islamic state was available at that time. In fact, several articles dealing with the ideals of an Islamic state insist upon the non-separation of state and religion. The second point is their emphasis on how Islam would be different from the Western political and cultural system. Alatas has confessed that his early understanding of the Islamic state differed radically from examples such as Sudan, Pakistan, or Iran. Today, Alatas argues that what he meant was rather a form of an Islamic philosophy of the state instead of the political instrumentalisation of the Islamic Shari'a. Although radically different from Maududi's opinions that appeared in *Progressive Islam,* the then-young Alatas underestimated the role that fundamentalists would play in politics in the 1970s and 1980s. His previous worldview had little in common with the practical, instrumental politics of contemporary fundamentalists. Alatas imagined an Islamic state rather as a philosophical base whose organization could be Western. Later, he confessed that he overlooked the "fundamentalist" impact of Maududi's late politics and acknowledged the limits of applying Islamic Shari'a in a punitive manner. In fact, in his later writings, Alatas criticised the Islamists and their simplistic attack of the "materialistic" West.[67] He foresaw that the social sciences could be endangered by further Islamization:

> There is a noticeable growth in social science research on economic and related social problems, but it can hardly be Islamic in thematic orientation. Developing Islamic social science research is a hopeful prospect, but the obstacles are great if cooperation is not forthcoming from authority. For example, in a society attempting to implement the traditional shari'ah law (*hudud*), sociological study of its impact would only be possible with the cooperation of the ruling power and with access to data in official files.[68]

In fact, Alatas' subsequent writings testify that one cannot, as a Third World intellectual, write about religion without tackling the issues related to

---

67   Syed Hussein Alatas, "Über Vermittlung und Vermittler, Erfolg und Misserfolg wissenschaftlicher Modernisierung: eine asiatische Perspektive," *Zwischen den Kulturen? Die Sozialwissenschaften vor dem Problem des Kulturvergleichs,* in *Soziale Welt,* ed. Joachim Matthes, Sonderband 8 (1992): 198–219.

68   Syed Hussein Alatas, "Social Sciences," in *The Oxford Encyclopedia of the Modern Islamic World,* ed. John L. Esposito (New York: Oxford University Press, 1995), vol. 4, 89.

modernization, the elites, and development. It is possible to argue that later, and perhaps through his Singaporean experience, the mature Alatas opted for the nationalist, secular perspective. The trend of "Islamizing knowledge" of the 1970s seeks to create a sociology of faith by stretching the argument to the question of the separation of state from religion which, according to the Islamizers, only occurred in the West.[69]

The Islamizers seem to confuse and transpose various discourses in their arguments. One point they share with Muslim resurgents is the refusal to see the complexity of the West and to link this view with the question of secularism.[70] By doing so, they misinterpret the current political and social processes that most of the Third World countries have been undergoing. The Islamizers borrow the critiques of Western ecologists and pessimists who criticize industrialization in the West to fight for an alternative Islamic epistemology. They ignore the fact that Muslim societies, although invaded by mass culture and integrated into the capitalist system, face a distorted process of industrialization. In fact, the problem might not be that "we" suffer from a mere imitation of the West, as Anwar Ibrahim argues, but rather that what "we" pick from the West are the most negative aspects, such as consumerism, but without proper institutions and democracy. Perhaps Western democracy is not alien to indigenous values, but the problem is merely that it has never been properly applied. Thus, as Alatas puts it:

> Our problem in the developing societies is different. We are not suffering from an overdose of science and technology but from a deficiency in science and technology.[71]

Any text needs to be contextualized. If some of these articles appear in the 1990s to be self-evident and perhaps naive, nevertheless, concepts such as colonialism were still fervently discussed in the 1950s.

For anyone interested today in the question of Islam, modernity, and the state, reading *Progressive Islam* certainly offers insights into the post-colonial epoch, which tends to be forgotten in favour of the discourse on post-modernity and Islamic resurgence.

---

69 Although in *Progressive Islam,* Alatas' "Islamic state" implied a union between religion and state. This shift in political orientation is nevertheless interesting to note.

70 For this point, see Chandra Muzaffar, *Islamic Resurgence in Malaysia* (Selangor, Oarul Ehsan: Penerbit Fajar Bakti, 1987), 73–74.

71 Alatas, "The Cultural Impediments to Scientific Thinking," 17.

6 Conclusion

For many intellectuals, the Iranian Revolution was a trigger to revise ideas about the ambivalent role of religion in resisting despotic regimes. The notion of "theology of liberation" and terms like "leftist Islam," 'al-yasar al-islami,' promoted by the Sorbonne-trained Egyptian philosopher Hasan Hanafi, became popular in the 1980s. Whether one agrees with Hanafi or not, whether his project would indeed lead to a revolutionary ideology, and whether such an ideology would, in practice, be devoured by totalitarian Islamic governments, is still an open issue that needs its own research. Nevertheless, *Progressive Islam* reveals that those debates attempting to establish the link between Islam and progress already existed in the 1950s, although the context and aims were different. Indeed, one could say that the debates on Islam in the 1950s were concerned with the issue of nation-state building and the dilemma of how to adjust in Islam. Both Indonesia's Sukarno and Egypt's Nasser used religious symbols, while opting for the secular solution. Both later undertook antagonistic actions against the religious political parties. *Progressive Islam* represents one of the earliest attempts to create a decolonized Islamic scholarly discourse. In the 1970s, the voice of resurgent Islam rose as communism and nationalism collapsed, abandoning the field to ethnic and separatist conflicts.

This chapter has attempted to trace a continuity in the discourse about Islam between the earlier generation of social scientists like Alatas and the more recent advocates of Islamizing Knowledge. The claim of "cultural specificity" entails affinities with the "return to authenticity" movement and the Islamizers. The notion of endogenous creativity, proposed by post-colonial intellectuals like Alatas and Abdel Malek, seems to be more open to cross-cultural dialogue, in contrast to the claims of indigenizing knowledge, departing from the principle of the inadequacy of Western social sciences in analyzing non-Western societies.

Bibliography

Abaza, Mona. *Debates on Islam and Knowledge in Malaysia and Egypt, Shifting Worlds.* London: Routledge Curzon Press, 2002.

Ahmed, Jamal M. *The Intellectual: Origins of Egyptian Nationalism.* Oxford: Oxford University Press, 1960.

Al-Ameh, Aziz. *Ibn Khaldun in Modern Scholarship: A Study in Orientalism.* London: Third World Centre for Research and Publishing, 1981.

Al-Attas, S.M.N. *Islam and Secularism.* Kuala Lumpur: Muslim Youth Movement of Malaysia, 1978.

Al-Azm, Sadiq Jalal. "Orientalism and Orientalism in Reverse." *Khamsin* 8 (1981): 5–26.

Alatas, Syed Hussein. "The Captive Mind and Creative Development." In *Asian Values and Modernization*, edited by Seah Chee-Meow. Singapore: Singapore University Press, 1977.

Alatas, Syed Hussein. "Cultural Impediments to Scientific Thinking." In *Culture and Industrialization: An Asian Dilemma*, edited by Rolf E. Vente and Peter S.J. Chen (Verbund Stiftung Deutsches Übersee Institut (Foundation German Overseas Institute)) Singapore: McGraw Hill International Book Company, 1980.

Alatas, Syed Hussein. *The Democracy of Islam: A Concise Exposition with Comparative Reference to Western Political Thought.* The Hague and Bandung: W. Van Hoeve, Eastern Universities Press, 1956.

Alatas, Syed Hussein. "The Grading of Occupational Prestige Amongst the Malays in Malaysia." *JMBRAS* 41, part 1, no. 213 (1968): 146–56.

Alatas, Syed Hussein. "India and the Intellectual Awakening of Asia." In *India and Southeast Asia*, edited by B. Sarkar. New Delhi: Indian Council for Cultural Relations, 1968.

Alatas, Syed Hussein. *Intellectuals in Developing Societies.* London: Frank Cass, 1977.

Alatas, Syed Hussein. "Islam e Socialismo." *Ulisse* 14, no. 83 (June 1977): 103–13.

Alatas, Syed Hussein. "Karl Manheim (1894–1947)." *Progressive Islam* 1, no. 7–8 (February–March 1955).

Alatas, Syed Hussein. *Modernization and Social Change.* Sydney: Angus and Robertson, 1972.

Alatas, Syed Hussein. *The Myth of the Lazy Native.* London: Frank Cass, 1977.

Alatas, Syed Hussein. *The Problem of Corruption.* Singapore: Times Books International, 1986.

Alatas, Syed Hussein. "Social Aspects of Endogenous Intellectual Creativity: The Problem of Obstacles—Guidelines for Research." In *Intellectual Creativity in Endogenous Culture*, edited by Anouar Abdel Malek. Tokyo: The United Nations University, 1981.

Alatas, Syed Hussein. "Social Sciences." In *The Oxford Encyclopedia of the Modern Islamic World Vol. 4*, edited by John L. Esposito. New York: Oxford University Press, 1995.

Alatas, Syed Hussein. *Thomas Stamford Raffles: Schemer or Reformer, 1781–1826.* Sydney: Angus and Robertson, 1971.

Alatas, Syed Hussein. "Über Vermittlung und Vermittler, Erfolg und Misserfolg wissenschaftlicher Modernisierung: eine asiatische Perspektive." In *Zwischen den Kulturen? Die Sozialwissenschaften vor dem Problem des Kulturvergleichs*, in *Soziale Welt*, edited by Joachim Matthes, Sonderband 8 (1992): 198–219.

Alatas, Syed Hussein. "The Weber Thesis and South East Asia." In *Modernization and Social Change.* Sydney: Angus and Robertson, 1972.

Amin, Osman. *Muhammad Abduh, Essai sur ses idées philosophiques et religieuses.* Cairo: Ministère de l'instruction publique, Imprimerie Misr, 1944.

Atal, Yogesh. "Indigenization: The Case of Indian Sociology," paper presented at The International Workshop on *Alternative Discourses in the Social Sciences and Humanities: Beyond Orientalism and Occidentalism.* Singapore, 30 May–1 June 1998.

Ayad, Kamil. *Die Geschichts-und Gesellschaftslehre Ibn Halduns.* PhD diss., Berlin 1930.

Ayubi, Nazih. *Political Islam, Religion and Politics in the Arab World.* London: Routledge, 1991.

Bezirgan, Najm A. "The Islamic World." In *The Comparative Reception of Darwinism,* edited by Thomas F. Glick, 375–387. Chicago and London: University of Chicago Press, 1974.

Buss, Andreas. "Max Weber's Heritage and Modern Southeast Asian Thinking on Development." In *Religion, Values and Development in Southeast Asia,* edited by Bruce Matthews and Judith Nagata. Singapore: Institute of Southeast Asian Studies, 1986.

Editorial, *The Islamic State* 1, no. 3 (Safar 1374 A.H., October 1954 A.D.).

Gibb, H.A.R. "The Islamic Background of Ibn Khaldoun's Political Theory." *Bulletin of the School of Oriental Studies* 7 (1933): 23–31.

Hassan, Riaz. "Introduction." In *Local and Global: Social Transformation in Southeast Asia: Essays in Honour of Professor Syed Hussein Alatas,* edited by Riaz Hassan. Leiden: Brill, 2005.

Hourani, Albert H. *Arabic Thought in the Liberal Age 1798–1939.* London: Oxford University Press, 1962.

Hussain, Taha. *Etudes analytiques et critiques de la philosophie sociale d'Ibn Khaldoun* Ph.D. diss., Paris, 1917.

Ihza, Tusril. "Combining Activism and Intellectualism: The Biography of Mohammad Natsir (1908–1993)." *Studia Islamika* 2, no. 1 (1995): 111–47.

"In Memoriam Osmane Amine." *MIDEO: Mélanges Institut Dominicain d'Etudes Orientales du Caire* 14 (1980): 398–404.

Malek, Anouar Abdel. "L'Islam dans la pensée nationale progressiste." *Revue Tiers Monde* 23, no. 92 (Octobre–Décembre 1982): 845–849.

Malek, Anouar Abdel. "L'orientalisme en crise." *Diogène* 44 (1963): 109–42.

Malek, Anouar Abdel. "A Rose for the 'Che.'" *al-Ahram Weekly* (16–22 October 1997).

Muzaffar, Chandra. *Islamic Resurgence in Malaysia.* Selangor, Oarul Ehsan: Penerbit Fajar Bakti, 1987.

Roem, Mohammed. *Religion and Politics* 1, no. 12 (July 1955, Dhul Qa'dah).

Rosenthal, Franz. *Ibn Khalduns Gedanken ueber den Staat.* Munich and Berlin, 1932.

Said, Edward W. *Culture and Imperialism.* London: Chatto and Windus, 1993.

Said, Edward. *Orientalism.* New York: Vintage Books, 1978.

Von Grunebaum, G.E. "Rueckblick auf drei internationale islamische Tagungen." *Der Islam* 34 (1959): 134–49.

CHAPTER 7

The Captive Mind Syndrome in Indian Sociology

N. Jayaram

How does an intellectual class come to accommodate a particular *Weltanschauung*, a particular philosophy or view of life, which affects its understanding of reality and its response to it? The Nobel Prize winning poet and author of Polish-Lithuanian heritage, Czesław Miłosz provides an insightful answer to this question in his celebrated book, *The Captive Mind*.[1] Having lived under two successive totalitarian regimes – Nazism and Soviet communism – in Poland, Miłosz insightfully analyzes the accommodation of many a Polish intellectual to the ideology of Stalinist communism. Besides discussing life in the Eastern European countries during Stalinism generally, he portrays the capitulation of four gifted Polish men to the demands of the communist state. They are identified only as Alpha, the moralist; Beta, the disappointed lover; Gamma, the slave of history; and Delta, the troubadour. He examines the kind of adjustment each made to be a writer under the regime, an adjustment that stifled their creativity. He observes, "these men are, more or less consciously, victims of a historic situation. Consciousness does not help them to shed their bonds; on the contrary, it forges them."[2] He calls this "enslavement through consciousness."[3] The book is an excellent elucidation of "the stages by which the mind gives way to compulsion from without," and becomes "the captive mind," as suggested pithily by the title of Miłosz's book.[4]

However, it is not only under totalitarian regimes that a captive mind is groomed. The experience of countries that came to be colonized under European powers are cases in point. Although most of them have become politically independent since World War II, they have not been able to liberate themselves from the captive mind syndrome. Rather, in many cases, their captive mind has been reinforced by new forms of intellectual imperialism, which,

---

1   Czesław Miłosz, *The Captive Mind* (London: Penguin Books, 2001). The book was first published in 1953 as a collection of essays in Polish titled *Zniewolony umysł*. Miłosz first defected to France and then chose to exile himself in the United States of America. He was awarded the 1980 Nobel Prize in Literature.
2   Ibid, 191.
3   Ibid.
4   Ibid, XVI.

© N. JAYARAM, 2023 | DOI:10.1163/9789004521698_009

interestingly, could achieve what physical occupation could not. The captive mind is most pervasive in the academic and intellectual spheres in these countries, and it has serious implications for their development as a nation in the present times.

In his path-breaking paper entitled, "The Captive Mind and Creative Development," published in 1974, Malaysian sociologist Syed Hussein Alatas described a captive mind as "the product of higher institutions of learning, either at home or abroad, whose way of thinking is dominated by Western thought in an imitative and uncritical manner."[5] His thesis, for convenience, had as its point of reference the Asian context. Nowhere in Asia is this concept more apposite in elucidating the intellectual situation than in India, with its more than two-century-long subjection to British colonial rule and its implanted university system. The captive mind syndrome is most visible in the way social sciences are taught and practiced in the country.

This chapter examines this syndrome with reference to one particular social science, namely, sociology – a subject which has been formally in existence in the country for a century now.[6] It is divided into five sections. *Section One*, elucidates the concept of "the captive mind." It locates the development of a captive mind in the project "colonial modernity" and the introduction of the English system of education, especially the implantation of the university system modelled after the University of London, with its emphasis on the liberal sciences. *Section Two* traces the origin and development of sociology as a "uncertain transplant" in India during British colonial rule and the simultaneous incubation of the captive mind syndrome in the discipline.[7] Despite some early resistance, the syndrome persisted even after India became independent in August 1947 with the discipline coming under the indelible influence of North American sociology. *Section Three* analyzes the critique of the syndrome from within Indian sociology since independence. *Section Four* reviews the efforts made by some sociologists to overcome the captive mind syndrome in

---

5　Syed Hussein Alatas, "The Captive Mind and Creative Development," *International Social Science Journal* 26 (1974): 691.

6　This chapter has its origin in the presentation that I made at the international symposium on "Sociology and the Question of Indigenization," organized by Ibn Khaldon Centre for Humanities and Social Sciences at Qatar University, Doha on 26 October 2019. The revised version of my presentation has been since published. See N. Jayaram, "Towards Indigenization of an Uncertain Transplant: Hundred Years of Sociology in India," *Tajseer* 1 (2020), 99–122, doi.org/10.29117/tis.2020.0026. I have here reproduced appropriate portions from this paper.

7　Satish Saberwal, "Uncertain Transplants: Anthropology and Sociology in India," in *Indian Sociology: Reflections and Introspections*, ed. T. K. Oommen and Partha N. Mukherji (Bombay: Popular Prakashan, 1986), 217.

THE CAPTIVE MIND SYNDROME IN INDIAN SOCIOLOGY 145

which their discipline has been mired. And *Section Five* explains the problems and prospects in engaging with the captive mind syndrome in sociology and indigenizing the discipline.

1   Colonial Modernity, English Education, and the Shaping of a Captive Mind

According to Alatas, a captive mind possesses the following characteristics:
- [It] is the product of higher institutions of learning, either at home or abroad, whose way of thinking is dominated by Western thought in an imitative and uncritical manner.
- [It] is uncreative and incapable of raising original problems.
- It is incapable of devising an analytical method independent of current stereotypes.
- It is incapable of separating the particular from the universal in science and thereby properly adapting the universally valid corpus of scientific knowledge to the particular local situations.
- It is fragmented in outlook.
- It is alienated from the major issues of society.
- It is alienated from its own national tradition, if it exists, in the field of its intellectual pursuit.
- It is unconscious of its own captivity and the conditioning factors making it what it is.
- It is not amenable to an adequate quantitative analysis but it can be studied by empirical observation.
- It is a result of the Western dominance over the rest of the world.[8]

This list, Alatas clarifies, is not exhaustive, but only indicative. Also, the captive mind is essentially an "oriental" phenomenon, and its parallel does not exist in the West.[9] It is found in all fields of knowledge but manifests most vividly in the humanities and social sciences. 'What defines the captive mind,' especially in these disciplines, according to Alatas, is 'the state of intellectual bondage and dependence on an external group through the operation of media such as books, institutions, the radio, the press, television, conferences and meetings.'[10] In South Asia, the development of the captive mind among the academics in general, and the social scientists in particular, is traceable to the

---

8   Alatas, "The Captive Mind and Creative Development," 691.
9   The counterpart of the captive mind is "the captor mind," Ibid, 698.
10   Ibid, 692.

modernity project that European colonialists embarked upon in the region. In what follows, I shall explain this by reference to India, the country that has the largest number of social scientists in the region.

1.1   *Colonialism and Project Modernity: The White Man's Burden*

Colonialism, as Nicholas B. Dirks explains, was itself "a cultural project of control": it 'was made possible, and then sustained and strengthened, as much by cultural technologies of rule as it was by the more obvious and brutal modes of conquest that first established power on foreign shores.'[11] In this project, the European colonizer arrogated to himself the responsibility for civilizing the "uncivilized" people of the lands he had come to possess. Called the "white man's burden," the conceitful condescension underlying this mission was poetically expressed by the English litterateur Joseph Rudyard Kipling[12] in 1899.[13] In the case of India, it was founded on the utter ignorance on the part of the colonial masters of her accomplishments in such diverse areas as grammar, literature, philosophy, mathematics, astronomy, medicine, etc., and an exaggerated sense of superiority of their own attainments in these areas. This is well illustrated in Thomas Babington Macaulay's repulsively arrogant declaration 'a single shelf of a good European library was worth the whole native literature of India and Arabia.'[14]

Of the various facets of this colonial cultural project, education was perhaps the most important, as it has had far-reaching implications for India.[15] The earliest attempt to impart English education in India can be traced to the Christian missionaries and the East India Company and the measures adopted by Warren Hastings, the first de facto Governor-General of Bengal (1772–85), as early as 1772. The efforts generated a protracted controversy between the "Anglicists"

---

11   Nicholas B. Dirks, *Castes of Mind: Colonialism and the Making of Modern India* (Delhi: Permanent Black, 2003), 9.

12   Ironically, Kipling was born in Malabar Hill, Bombay (now Mumbai), India. For his contribution to literature, which included his racially repugnant views and opinions, he was awarded the Nobel Prize in 1907.

13   Rudyard Kipling, "The White Man's Burden: The United States & The Philippine Islands, 1899," in *Rudyard Kipling's Verse: Definitive Edition* (Garden City, New York: Doubleday, 1929). Merriam-Webster dictionary records 1865 as year of the first known use of this expression. See https://www.merriam-webster.com/dictionary/white%20man%27s%20 burden (accessed 26 March 2021).

14   In Henry Sharp, *Selections from Educational Records, Part I, 1781–1839* (New Delhi: Published for the National Archives of India by the Manager of Publications, Government of India), 109.

15   The following analysis of the history of education in India is drawn from N. Jayaram, *Sociology of Education* (Jaipur: Rawat Publications, 2015), 64–78.

recommending a Western approach and the "orientalists" favoring an indigenous direction. William Henry Cavendish-Bentinck, the Governor-General of India (1828–35), finally resolved this controversy in favor of the Anglicist orientation, barely a month after Macaulay had penned his (in)famous *Minute* (on 2 February 1835).[16] Charles Wood's Dispatch (of 19 July 1854) reaffirmed this policy. Upon the recommendation of the committee appointed on 26 January 1955, the first three universities were established in Bombay (now Mumbai), Calcutta (now Kolkata), and Madras (now Chennai) in 1857.

The spreading of English education, however, was not an act of disinterested magnanimity. On the contrary, it was the outcome of a complex combination of motives: religious – proselytizing urge; moral – to inculcate new values in the spirit of Western liberal Christian concepts; administrative – to staff the vast and elaborate bureaucracy; economic – to familiarize the Indians with the modalities and values of the capitalist economic system, and also to develop in them a taste for British products; and, not the least, political – to consolidate and maintain their dominance in the country.

The British, however, did not embark on a program of mass education.[17] What they were concerned with was evolving a small class of English-educated Indians, who may act, in Macaulay's words, as 'interpreters between us and millions whom we govern – a class of persons Indian in blood and color, but English in tastes, in opinions, in morals and in intellect.'[18] This class was expected to filter down to the masses the knowledge and values it had acquired and internalized. This, it was hoped, would eventually stabilize the British Raj.

The system of education that the British introduced was modelled after the system prevalent in Britain. This was particularly so as regards higher education. The striking feature of this educational transplantation was English, which was not only taught as a language, but also became the medium of instruction. Moreover, the content of this education was biased in favor of languages and the humanities, called "the liberal arts," and against science and technology as well as vocational training. For the Indians aspiring for official positions, professional status, or leadership roles, knowledge of English became indispensable. In the long run, the English-educated Indians, dubbed "brown sahibs," oriented themselves to the West and became alienated from the masses.

Although in the short run English education did contribute to the political stability of the British Raj, in the long run it proved to be the undoing of

---

16   Macaulay's *Minute* is reproduced in Sharp, *Selections from Educational Records*, 107–17.
17   In fact, the colonial rule destroyed the indigenous educational system. See Jayaram, *Sociology of Education*, 66–67.
18   In Sharp, *Selections from Educational Records*, 116.

the British stranglehold on India. The English-educated class became more and more vocal in its criticism of British rule. The Sedition Committee, which investigated the revolutionary conspiracies in India, reported in 1918 that most of the conspirators were educated young men. As it turned out, almost all the leaders in the forefront of the nationalist movement belonged to the English-educated elite.[19] About this, Shashi Tharoor has clarified,

> That Indians seized the English language and turned it into an instrument for our own liberation – using it to express nationalist sentiments against the British, as R. C. Dutt, Dinshaw Wacha and Dadabhai Naoroji did in the late nineteenth century and Jawaharlal Nehru in the twentieth – was to their credit, not by British design.[20]

This, however, does not diminish the role of the colonial cultural hegemony via English education in shaping the captive mind among the Indian intelligentsia. The apogee of the captive mind was the Anglophile Bengali intellectual Nirad Chandra Chaudhuri. His *Autobiography of an Unknown Indian*, published in 1951, just four years after independence, is dedicated to the British empire in India:

> To the memory of the British Empire in India which conferred subjecthood on us but withheld citizenship; to which yet every one of us threw out the challenge: *"Civis Britannicus sum"* because all that was good and living within us was made, shaped, and quickened by the same British rule.[21]

'This unedifying spectacle of a brown man with his nose up the colonial fundament,' according to Tharoor, 'made Chaudhuri a poster child for scholarly studies of how Empire creates "native informants," alienated from and even abhorring their own cultures and societies.'[22] Unsurprisingly, Chaudhuri

---

19   Anil Seal, *Emergence of Indian Nationalism: Competition and Collaboration in the Late Nineteenth Century* (Cambridge: Cambridge University Press, 1968).

20   Shashi Tharoor, *An Era of Darkness: The British Empire in India* (New Delhi: Aleph, 2016), 219. To Tharoor's list, we must add the name of Mohandas Karamchand Gandhi, later to become Mahatma Gandhi, who was at the forefront of India's freedom movement. Mahatma Gandhi was educated at the University College London and became a barrister before spending some time in South Africa and returning to India.

21   Nirad C. Chaudhuri, *The Autobiography of an Unknown Indian* (Bombay: Jaico Publishing House, 1964), v.

22   Tharoor, *An Era of Darkness*, 224–25.

THE CAPTIVE MIND SYNDROME IN INDIAN SOCIOLOGY   149

moved to England in the 1970s; in 1990, Oxford University awarded him, by then a long-time resident of the city of Oxford, an honorary degree in letters; in 1992 he was made an honorary Commander of the Order of the British Empire.[23]

Chaudhuri's xenolatry was, no doubt, an extreme manifestation of the captive mind. But the bearing of the captive mind is discernible in the Indian intelligentsia, even if they do not share his xenolatry. This is particularly characteristic of academics, who in their language, reflections, theoretical frameworks, and methodology of analysis as also in their craving for recognition and endorsement beyond the national boundaries, are victims of the captive mind, even if unwittingly.[24] While it would be worth examining how this syndrome has worked itself through in different social sciences in India, the limitations of space and knowledge constrain me to confine my discussion to sociology, a discipline in which I am trained and which I have taught and practiced for nearly five decades now.

2   Sociology and the Captive Mind Syndrome in India

Sociology as a formal academic discipline was transplanted in India during the British colonial era.[25] The first full department of sociology (and civics) was set up in 1919 in the University of Bombay and that of anthropology in 1921 in the University of Calcutta. However, attempts at obtaining sociological knowledge about the country goes back to the late 18th century. Three broad motivations for seeking such knowledge can be identified: (1) the scholarly interest of the *Orientalists* to understand Indian civilization; (2) the evangelical enthusiasm of the *Christian missionaries*; and (3) the administrative needs of the *British officials*.[26] By the beginning of the 20th century, two distinct lines for

---

23   Chaudhuri could not, however, accept the transformation that the English had undergone since the decline of the empire. His disillusionment is reflected in the final volume of his autobiography, *Thy Hand, Great Anarch! India, 1921–1952*, (Reading, PA: Addison Wesley, 1988), which he produced at the age 90.

24   It is ironical that my critique of the captive mind syndrome is written in English, a language medium in which I have had my higher education. The fact that I am conscious of this irony is itself empowering and I am sure that the other contributors to the volume too are similarly conscious.

25   For details on the development of sociology till the early 1970s, see M. N. Srinivas and M. N. Panini, "The Development of Sociology and Social Anthropology in India," *Sociological Bulletin* 22 (1973).

26   Bernard S. Cohn, "Notes on the History of the Study of Indian Society and Culture," in *Structure and Change in Indian Society*, ed. Milton Singer and Bernard

the sociological understanding of society and culture in India were discernible: the Indological – 'which relied heavily on the early literary sources, and in particular, the scriptures, epics and law books'[27] – and studies based on empirical investigation and census and other official reports.[28] Both these traditions have had a lasting imprint on the practice of sociology in India.

Indians who early on took up sociology as a vocation were strongly influenced by Indology, or what came to be called by Srinivas as the "book view" (textual perspective) of society in India, as different from the "field view" (derived from empirical investigation). Govind Sadashiv Ghurye, a Sanskritist, who later became the head of the sociology department at the University of Bombay, was an ardent follower of the Indological approach. He encouraged his students who were well versed in Sanskrit – K. M. Kapadia, Irawati Karve, and S. V. Karandikar – to extend his approach in analyzing the sacred texts and other literature available in that language.[29] Other eminent sociologists who were strongly influenced by Indology included Radhakamal Mukerjee, who headed the sociology department at the University of Lucknow, and Bhimrao Ramji Ambedkar, the architect of independent India's constitution and a leader of the downtrodden caste groups. Of course, Radhakamal Mukerjee (as also Brajendra Nath Seal and Benoy Kumar Sarkar) was critical of western Indologists' interpretation of Indian reality through the evolutionary reductionist matrix.[30] As regards the early fieldwork-based sociological studies conducted in India by English-trained Indian sociologists as well as the British administrator-cum-sociologists, these were heavily influenced by theoretical propositions and methodological strategies then in vogue in the discipline in the West.

S. Cohn, (Chicago: Aldine Publishing Co., 1968), 3–28. See also Yogendra Singh, *Indian Sociology: Social Conditioning and Emerging Concerns* (New Delhi: Vistaar, 1986), xi–x.

27   India has an old tradition of reflection and writing on human beings and society, a tradition that encompasses metaphysical as well as materialist contents. Manu's *Dharmashastra*, Kautilya's *Arthashastra*, Ajit Kesamkambalan's Indian materialism (*Lokāyata* or *Cārvāka*), and the epics *Ramayana* and *Mahabharata* are but a few examples of such works.

28   See Srinivas and Panini, "The Development of Sociology and Social Anthropology in India," 185; see also Bela Dutta Gupta, *Sociology in India: An Enquiry into Sociological Thinking and Empirical Social Research in the Nineteenth Century – with Special Reference to Bengal* (Calcutta: Centre for Sociological Research, 1972).

29   It must be clarified that, Ghurye, though himself was "an armchair scholar," encouraged his students to do intensive fieldwork; he was "catholic in his interests as well as methods," too. See Srinivas and Panini, "The Development of Sociology and Social Anthropology in India," 188.

30   Singh, *Indian Sociology*, 7.

An important factor in the reinforcement of the captive mind syndrome among Indian sociologists was the fact that almost all the pioneers of sociology in the country were trained in the West or strongly influenced by the Western sociologists or social anthropologists or both. For example, Patrick Geddes had a lasting influence on his students, Ghurye and N. A. Toothi; the latter, in fact, extended Geddes' line of research. Radhakamal Mukerjee, too, was influenced by Geddes through his association in the latter's urban surveys. More importantly, the early generation of Indian sociologists were mostly trained in England. Ghurye was a student of Hobhouse at the London School of Economics (LSE) for a year before he went to Cambridge for training under W. H. R. Rivers. Toothi obtained his doctorate from Oxford. After his early training with Ghurye, Srinivas was trained at Oxford; he was greatly influenced by Alfred Reginald Radcliffe-Brown and obtained his doctorate under Evans-Pritchard. D. N. Mazumdar of the Lucknow department went to Cambridge and obtained his doctorate in cultural anthropology under Thomas Callan Hodson. Ambedkar obtained doctorates from both Columbia University (New York, USA) and LSE. C. Parvathamma, the first Dalit (a member of the lowest caste) woman sociologist and head of the department at the University of Mysore, was trained in the University of Manchester under Ian George Cunnison and, later, Victor Witter Turner.

After independence in 1947, the point of reference for sociology in India gradually shifted from England to the United States, consequent upon the changes that took place in 'the worldview of sociology in the West,' following World War II, and shifting of 'the center of gravity in sociology' from Europe to America.[31] Douglas Ensminger, director of the Ford Foundation in India (1951–70) and a trained rural sociologist himself, was hugely successful in making 'sociology popular with the Indian government and with Jawaharlal Nehru [the first prime minister of independent India].'[32] American cultural anthropologists and sociologists began taking a keen interest in the study of South Asian countries and their work found political support in India. Under the "Fulbright Program" of the United States Cultural Exchange Program, many American sociologists found placements in sociology departments in Indian universities and several Indian sociologists have gone to the USA for visits of varying duration. Among the Indian sociologists who went to the USA for doctoral or post-doctoral training, mention may be made of Pratap C. Agarwal, A. Bopagamage, Yashwant Bhaskar Damle, Madhav Sadashiv Gore, Ravindra

---

31   Ibid, 9.

32   Srinivas and Panini, "The Development of Sociology and Social Anthropology in India," 198.

S. Khare, Narmadeshwar Prasad, Satish Saberwal, B. V. Shah, Surajit Chandra Sinha, and Lalita Prasad Vidyarthi.

More importantly, with the expansion of sociology in the 1960s and the persistence of English as the medium of higher education, there came a great demand for sociology textbooks in English. Both Britain and USA provided financial aid for the production of textbooks in India. It is noteworthy that the Indo-American Textbook Program, started in 1961, involved mainly the reprint of American textbooks at a subsidized (and absurdly low) cost under the 'PL [Public Law] 480' funds. Hans Raj Dua notes that "by the end of 1984–85, 1,620 titles were published in India and about four million copies were sold to college and university students."[33] Similarly, under an agreement signed between India and Britain in 1962, the English Language Book Society (ELBS) brought out inexpensive university-level British books. 'An average of a million copies of ELBS editions were printed in England each year [and] ... about 60 per cent of the total books were sold in India.'[34] These books determined the curriculum of what was taught as sociology to students in India. Satish Saberwal views the American interest in the development of sociology and social sciences in general, as '... the cognitive edge to post-war American political expansion in the wake of Europe's colonial withdrawals.'[35]

Although the sociological study of village, caste, and tribe acquired rigor and sophistication since the 1960s, they were all guided by Western theoretical frameworks and methodological strategies. As will be discussed in the next section, those sociologists seeking 'a path cautious of western ethnocentric bias' could not influence the course that sociology took.[36] As Singh rightly observes:

> The emphasis on methodology, research techniques and operationalization of research tools became, under the influence of American sociology, the pre-eminent concern in sociological studies. This generated, on the one hand, rich data, but on the other, took sociology towards a narrowly instrumental and a-historical path of development.[37]

---

33 Hans Raj Dua, "The Spread of English in India: Politics of Language Conflict and Language Power," in *Post-Imperial English: Status Change in Former British and American Colonies, 1940–1990*, ed. Joshua A. Fishman et al. (Berlin and New York: Mouton de Gruyter, 1996), 582.

34 Ibid.

35 Saberwal, "Uncertain Transplants," 217.

36 Partha N. Mukherji, "Sociology in South Asia: Indigenisation as Universalising Social Science," *Sociological Bulletin*, 54 (2005): 313.

37 Singh, *Indian Sociology*, x. No wonder, in India, sociology and other social sciences not only lagged behind in responding to the challenge of colonialism, or the advent of freedom,

Nevertheless, since the 1950s, the transplanted Western sociology expanded considerably as part of a larger boom in the number of colleges and universities and of enrolments therein. Sociology is now taught widely in universities and colleges, and a large amount of sociological research is carried out in universities and institutes. The Indian Council of Social Science Research (ICSSR) and the University Grants Commission, as some academic foundations, sponsor and fund research projects in sociology. There is a large professional body of sociologists – Indian Sociological Society (established in 1951) – with a life-membership exceeding 4,500; it has to date held forty-five gatherings under the banner of the All-India Sociological Conference. In 1986, it even hosted, the XI World Congress of Sociology in New Delhi. Its flagship journal, *Sociological Bulletin*, has been published uninterruptedly since 1952, and is archived by JSTOR.[38] *Contributions to Indian Sociology* is another journal of international repute published in India.[39] Indian sociologists have also been routinely publishing their work in *Economic and Political Weekly* (earlier *Economic Weekly* [1949–1965]), a social science weekly published from Mumbai by Sameeksha Trust; *Social Scientist*, a Marxist monthly published by the Indian School of Social Sciences and Tulika Books, New Delhi; and *Social Action*, a quarterly from the (Roman Catholic) Indian Social Institute, New Delhi.

However, even as academic sociology celebrates its centenary in India, it has not been able to overcome the tendency to imitate the West and continues to adhere to the standards of a social science peddled as universal. If in pre-independence times, sociology was subject to academic colonialism, it has been a willing acquiescent to academic neo-colonialism in the post-independence period. As T. K. Oommen notes, 'the knowledge industry operates in a free-market situation. The academic entrepreneur of the West ... would want to sell his products wherever he can. However, the transaction can take place only if

---

but, in fact, evaded it for long. See Dube, "Indian Sociology at the Turning Point," 10; Yogendra Singh, *Image of Man: Ideology and Theory in Indian Sociology* (Delhi: Chanakya Publications, 1984), 64–65. The two sociologists, who critically engaged with colonialism, namely, Akshay Ramanlal Desai and Ramkrishna Mukherjee, approached it from the Marxian political economy perspective.

38 Two other journals – *The Indian Journal of Sociology* started in Baroda (now Vadodara) in 1929 by Albert Widgery, and *The Indian Sociological Review* started in 1934 under the auspices of Lucknow University with Radhakamal Mukerjee as editor – were short-lived. See Srinivas and Panini, "The Development of Sociology and Social Anthropology in India," 194.

39 *Contributions to Indian Sociology* was founded by Louis Dumont and David Pocock in Paris in 1957 but ceased publication in 1966. A new series commenced publication in 1967 at the initiative of T. N. Madan from the Institute of Economic Growth, Delhi, with the support of Louis Dumont, Adrian C. Mayer, Milton Singer and M. N. Srinivas.

there are willing buyers.'[40] These "willing buyers" have sought endorsement of their work from their western counterparts. This is not to deny the significant contributions that some Indian sociologists have made on their own terms.

It can hardly be denied that there is a growing sense of cynicism among those doing sociology in India, as they seldom see in it any purpose beyond career advancement. This is matched by misgivings among both the policy-makers and the general public about the practical use of sociology. Not surprisingly, the number of students taking up sociology has been dwindling, even as the gross enrolment ratio in higher education is increasing; and, even for most of those taking up sociology, the subject is not their first preference. In the Indian academia, there is a growing concern about the decline in the quality of the products of the discipline, both human and knowledge. This has been a long-term consequence of the captive mind syndrome in Indian sociology.

3 The Critique from Within

Sociology, being the child of the European Enlightenment, carried within it the critical spirit of the age. Interestingly, this transplanted academic discipline not only fostered a captive mind among those who took up its study and practice in India, but also provoked a criticism of its transplantation among some of them. This criticism, which had to wait for India to become independent, mainly had to do with the lack of an ontological and epistemological fit between a universalizing (read, westernizing) social science and a historically conditioned socio-cultural reality of diverse India.

3.1 *The Early Critics: D P and His Disciples*
In the very first presidential address of the newly born Indian Sociological Society in 1955, Dhurjatiprasada Mukhopadhyaya (1894–1961) (known by his anglicized name as D. P. Mukerji and popularly as D P) castigated the sociological knowledge of his times: 'As an Indian,' he said, 'I find it impossible to discover any life-meaning in the jungle of the so-called empirical social research monographs.'[41] He frankly admitted that, 'I am not a sociologist as sociologists would like me to be.'[42]

---

40 T. K. Oommen, "Sociology in India: A Plea for Contextualization," *Sociological Bulletin* 32 (1983): 119.

41 D. P. Mukerji, "Indian Tradition and Social Change," in *Indian Sociology: Reflections and Introspections*, ed. T. K. Oommen and Partha N. Mukherji (Bombay: Popular Prakashan, 1986), 4.

42 Ibid.

DP argued that our first task is 'to study the social traditions [*parampara*] to which we have been born and in which we have had our being ... [as] traditions have great powers of resistance and absorption.'[43] This task, he clarified, 'includes the study of changes in traditions by internal and external pressures,'[44] and 'the thing changing is more real and objective than change per se.'[45] According to him, 'unless sociological training in India is grounded on Sanskrit, or any such language in which the traditions have been embodied as symbols, social research in India will be a pale imitation of what others are doing.'[46] He declared, 'it is not enough for the Indian sociologist to be a sociologist. He must be an Indian first.'[47]

It pained him 'to observe how our Indian scholars succumb to the lure of modern "scientific" techniques imported from outside as a part of technical aid and "know-how" without resistance and dignity.'[48] Therefore, 'in the intellectual transactions which are taking place, it seems that we have no terms to offer, no ground to stand upon.'[49]

DP emphasized that, unlike for the westerner:

> Action for the Indian is not individualistic ... it is "inherently structured on a normative, teleological" *but* not on a "voluntaristic system of coordinates or axes" with the result that the failure to attain it does not lead to "frustration" ... the common "individual's" pattern of desires is more or less rigidly fixed by his socio-cultural group-pattern, and he hardly deviates from it except under severe economic duress.[50]

Therefore, according to DP, 'the Indian sociologist will have to accept the group as his unit and reject the individual.'[51]

DP influenced a few young scholars at Lucknow to question the positivist approach to sociology and to work out an indigenous sociology based on India's traditional social thought. The most notable among these young scholars were Awadh Kishore Saran (1922–2003) and R. N. Saksena.[52] Saran took the

---

43   Ibid, 5.
44   Ibid.
45   Ibid, 15.
46   Ibid, 6.
47   Ibid.
48   Ibid.
49   Ibid.
50   Ibid., 7.
51   Ibid., 9.
52   See Awadh Kishore Saran, "Sociology in India," in *Contemporary Sociology*, ed. Joseph S. Roucek. London: Peter Owen Limited, 1959; R. N. Saksena, *Sociology in India*. Agra: Institute of Social Sciences, 1965.

extreme view that 'sociological cognition and the world-view is fundamentally alien to the Indian tradition, hence any attempt towards its indigenization or adaptation into an *Indian* cognitive system is bound either to fail or to turn imitative.'[53] As Yogesh Atal summarizes, DP and his disciples believed that Indian social reality cannot be interpreted through 'an evolutionary perspective that puts societies of the West on a higher pedestal'; they found the western sociological categories 'to be too parochial to be applicable to the Indian situation'; and that the western theories are not universally applicable.[54]

3.2   *Later Reflections and Introspections: Muted Response*

Although the views of DP and his disciples on western sociology in the Indian context attracted the attention of many, given the captive mind syndrome among Indian sociologists, they hardly found any takers. It was only in the 1970s, that 'introspection and reflections started appearing with determined persistence.'[55] Most contributors to the volume titled *Indian Sociology: Reflections and Introspections,* edited by T. K. Oommen and Partha Nath Mukherji, invariably referred to the concerns articulated by DP, but they had their own interpretations about sociology in India.[56] We may briefly refer to some of the reflections in this regard.

Ramkrishna Mukherjee blindly dismissed the view that the approach of the Indian sociologist towards the appraisal of social reality was imitative in any way.[57] Evaluating 'the content, methodology and value premises in the sociological writings of 1920–1948,' Singh found 'their concern with western sociology or social science' to be 'dialectical and interactive rather than imitative.'[58]

P. C. Joshi finds sociology sharing the predicament with other social sciences. In his opinion, 'What appears as intellectual dominance of western world from one point of view should also be seen as the lack of adequate intellectual independence among the social scientists of the underdeveloped world.'[59] He

---

53   Singh, *Indian Sociology,* 6.

54   Yogesh Atal, *Indian Sociology from Where to Where: Footnotes to the History of the Discipline* (Jaipur: Rawat Publications, 2003), 131, 19.

55   T. K. Oommen and Partha N. Mukherji, "Editorial Introduction," in *Indian Sociology: Reflections and Introspections*, ed. T. K. Oommen and Partha N. Mukherji (Bombay: Popular Prakashan, 1986), ix.

56   T. K. Oommen and Partha N. Mukherji (eds.), *Indian Sociology: Reflections and Introspections.* Bombay: Popular Prakashan, 1986.

57   Ramkrishna Mukherjee, *Sociology of Indian Sociology*, (Bombay: Allied Publishers, 1979), 29.

58   Singh, *Indian Sociology*, 6.

59   P. C. Joshi, "Reflections on Social Science Research in India," in *Indian Sociology: Reflections and Introspections,* eds. T. K. Oommen and Partha N. Mukherji (Bombay: Popular Prakashan, 1986), 139–40.

finds social scientists often grappling with problems considered important in the West and 'not with issues agitating their own national community.'[60] *'This inadequate responsiveness to the challenges of their society,'* according to him, *'is at the root of insufficient release of the creative spirit among the social scientist in India.'*[61] Thus, agenda setting appears to Joshi as the primary problem.[62] Joshi is critical of the work of Indian sociologists in that it does not adequately reflect *'the processes of the emergence of a new India through social conflicts and movements and through the release of creative energies of the Indian people after independence.'*[63] He also bemoans that *'they have not so far even evolved a language of the discipline which is their own.'*[64]

S. C. Dube castigates the sociologists in India for 'imitating the western pattern under the guise of cultivating "international science" without any sense of guilt or even qualms of conscience.'[65] Writing three decades after independence, he finds 'both teaching and research in sociology' in India continuing 'to be cast in the colonial mold': 'Ours was (and to an extent continues to be) largely a sociology of borrowed concepts and methods.'[66] This has led 'to distortions in the perspectives of Indian sociology and also to its stunted growth.'[67] As a consequence of 'the oppressive influence of foreign models, native categories of thought [e.g., *varna* and *jati*] have had to undergo transfers of meaning and, in the process, they now represent something [e.g., caste] which is far removed from their original intent.'[68]

Dube also finds our research priorities distorted and that 'a significant part of our work [is] addressed not to the people or even professional colleagues in India but to peers and mentors abroad.'[69] One continuing problem about the teaching of and research in sociology, that Dube draws our attention to, is the use of English, a language which hardly 10% of the country's population can speak[70] and the percentage of those with proficiency for doing sociology in

---

60   Ibid., 140.

61   Ibid. (italics original).

62   As early as 1973, an ICSSR Committee had observed: 'Much of the current research effort has no relevance to the contemporary social and national problems ... It is not yet emancipated to develop research tools, designs and models of its own appropriate to the Indian situation.' Cited in Oommen, "Sociology in India," 113.

63   Joshi, "Reflections on Social Science Research in India," 142 (italics original).

64   Ibid. (italics original).

65   S. C. Dube, "Indian Sociology at the Turning Point," *Sociological Bulletin* 26 (1977), 10.

66   Ibid.

67   Ibid.

68   Ibid., 10–11.

69   Ibid., 11.

70   This makes India the world's second-largest English-speaking country, next only to USA. See Zareer Masani, "English or Hinglish: Which will India Choose?" BBC News Magazine,

that language being still less.[71] No doubt, in most regional universities, there is a gradual shift to the vernacular as the medium of instruction in higher education, but the availability of good quality reading materials in that language remains a problem.[72] No wonder, there is 'a visible unease within Indian sociology about its direction and purpose'[73] and the subject is 'yet to establish its credibility with the people and the policy makers.'[74]

While recognizing the dominance of Western theory and methodology in sociology since it was implanted in India, Oommen argues why sociology in India cannot 'develop mainly based on analysis of texts, ancient or contemporary.'[75] To the extent, the texts to be studied are Hindu texts, what one would get is in effect "Hindu sociology." Even as Hindus constitute an overwhelming majority, India is home to the second largest Muslim community in the world, and other small minorities – Buddhists, Christians, Jains, Parsees, and Sikhs. Of course, it would be a worthwhile exercise to see where the texts of different religions meet and how they differ. However, it would be wrong to conflate India with Hinduism. Moreover, we cannot mistake the ideal portrayed in the texts as real, as ignoring the phenomenal oral traditions would be perilous to Indian sociology.

In conclusion, Oommen argues that academic nationalism is not the answer to academic colonialism. Academic nationalism, he cautions, 'contains within it seeds of academic communalism and academic feudalism' and academic parochialism.[76] To get out of the impasse, he makes a plea for contextualization of sociology in India. This involves (a) 'recognition of the fact that tradition/past contains both assets and liabilities viewed in terms of the present needs and aspirations'; (b) 'adopting appropriate values and institutions from other societies and cultures' and 'judiciously craft[ing] them on to our own society'; (c) taking into consideration 'gradual adaptation and reconciliation' as the central tendency in our society; and (d) "social engineering" in India – involving 'the selective retention of our tradition, informed borrowing from

---

27 November 2012, accessed 22 October 2019, at: https://www.bbc.com/news/magazine -20500312.

71   See N. Jayaram, "Challenges to Indian Sociology," *Sociological Bulletin* 47 (1998).

72   Atal, *Indian Sociology from Where to Where*, 106–09.

73   Dube, "Indian Sociology at the Turning Point," 1.

74   Ibid., 12.

75   Oommen, "Sociology in India," 115. This comment of Oommen is in reaction to Louis Dumont's claim that 'a sociology of India lies at the point of confluence of sociology and Indology.' See Louis Dumont, "For a Sociology of India," *Contributions to Indian Sociology* 1 (1957): 7.

76   Oommen, "Sociology in India," 123.

other cultures and the judicious mutation of the two' – will have to be 'a process peculiar to India.'[77] He rightly emphasizes that, 'if sociology is to be relevant for India ... it should endorse and its practitioners should internalize the value-package contained in the Indian constitution, the differing interpretations of these values notwithstanding.'[78]

4   Beyond Critique: The Alternatives?

A prerequisite for addressing the captive mind syndrome and coming out of it is recognizing its existence and pervasive influence. Viewed in this context, since independence, there has been a growing sensitivity among Indian sociologists to the challenges of sociology as a western discipline transplanted in their academic system. This sensitivity has been mainly reactive in nature, though some proactive initiatives have been made. Singh's review of the presidential addresses delivered at the successive sessions of the All-India Sociological Conference from 1970 to 1983 reveal the deep concern with the issue of the relevance of sociology in the context of a changing India and an acute sense of national self-consciousness.[79] A clear indication of this is revealed in the debate on "sociology *for* India" initiated by Indophile sociologists like Louis Dumont and David Pocock in the very first issue of the first series of *Contributions to Indian Sociology*.[80] This debate has been continued, though intermittently, in the New Series of the journal published since 1967. The preposition "for" in the caption of the debate clearly indicates the perceived need for postulating a set of concepts and theories suitable to study social reality in India.[81] Singh provides a succinct summary of the key highlights of this debate.[82] In addition to this debate, a notable contribution addressing this theme is Ramkrishna Mukherjee's *Sociology of Indian Sociology*.[83]

---

77   Ibid., 130–31.
78   Ibid., 130.
79   Singh, *Indian Sociology*, 17–22.
80   Dumont, "For a Sociology of India."
81   This is often contrasted from such captions as "sociology *in* India," which focuses on the state of the craft in India and the professional activities of Indian sociologists, and "sociology *of* India," which concerns itself with approaches to the study of society in India as a "space-time chunk." See Oommen, "Sociology in India," 111.
82   Singh, *Indian Sociology*, 23–25.
83   See Mukherjee, *Sociology of Indian Sociology*.

4.1   *Marxism as an Alternative*

One alternative for addressing the quest of the fit between sociology and its existential subject matter was the Marxian approach. In India, this approach in sociology is chiefly associated with DP, Akshay Ramanlal Desai, and Ramkrishna Mukherjee. Of course, Marxism is also an alien theoretical/methodological framework, although India had its own brand of materialism in *Lokāyata* or *Cārvāka* philosophy. Atal remarks that it is interesting that 'the advocates of indigenization somehow spared the Marxist approach from their criticism; the campaign for indigenization appeared as a campaign against capitalist social science.'[84] After all, DP himself was a critique of colonial implantation of sociology, but he invoked Marxian dialectics and called his approach "Marxology."

Desai puts forward a robust case for the Marxist approach to the study of Indian society. He reminds us of a significant observation made by Don Martindale about the origin and function of sociology as a discipline:

> Sociology was born as a conservative answer to socialism ... Only conservative ideology was able to establish the discipline. The linkage between science and reformist social attitudes (e.g., Scientific Socialism) was served. In renouncing political activism, sociology became respectable in the ivy-covered halls of universities. It was received as a scientific justification of existing social order ... as an area of study for stable young men (rather than as a breeding ground for wild-eyed radicals).[85]

Desai advocates 'the Marxist paradigm [as] the most relevant framework that can help in comprehending properly the transformation that is taking place in the Indian society and its various sub-systems. ... [it] can help one to locate the central tendencies of transformation with its major implications.'[86] His analysis of Indian nationalism from a Marxist perspective is regarded as novel and

---

84   Atal, *Indian Sociology from Where to Where*, 117–18.

85   Martindale cited in: Akshay Ramanlal Desai, "Relevance of the Marxist Approach to the Study of Indian Society," *Sociological Bulletin* 30 (1981): 19. There were, however, scholars like Thomas Burton Bottomore in England and C. Wright Mills in USA who viewed sociology as "social criticism" and assigned "sociological imagination" a radical function. See Thomas Burton Bottomore, *Sociology as Social Criticism*. London: George Allen and Unwin, 1975; Charles Wright Mills, *The Sociological Imagination*. New York: Oxford University Press, 1959.

86   Desai, "Relevance of the Marxist Approach to the Study of Indian Society," 10–11.

insightful.[87] Ramkrishna Mukherjee applied the same perspective in analyzing the rise and fall of the East India Company, a classic episode in the history of capitalism and British colonialism in India.[88] That these contributions were quite contrary to sociology in the heyday of its pioneers is remarkable, indeed.

Approaching Indian society through Marxian methodology has yielded rich insights, but this methodology has not taken deep roots in Indian sociology, as one would have expected it to.[89] Ramkrishna Mukherjee, who was an earlier proponent of this methodology, later shifted to survey analysis and quantitative approach to social reality, at the cost of consistent contribution to Marxian sociology. Towards the end of his career, he became a staunch advocate of "unitary social science" and a strident critic of qualitative anthropological research.[90]

Inspired by the Italian Marxist Antonio Gramsci, Ranajit Guha, an Indian, set in motion in the University of Sussex in 1979–80 what has come to be known as "Subaltern Studies."[91] These are postcolonial studies and they approach history from below, focusing more on what happens among the masses than among the elite. Although some Indian scholars have contributed to this genre of studies, it has not taken roots in Indian academia. Internationally, too, its influence is on the wane. Other important developments have been "Feminist Sociology"[92] and "Dalit Sociology,"[93] two alternative approaches to sociology from the standpoint of women and of the lowest caste groups in Indian society respectively.

4.2 Towards Indigenization of Sociology

As a way out of the captive mind syndrome, some sociologists have advocated the indigenization of sociology in India; Atal (2003), Partha Mukherji (2005),

---

87   See Akshay Ramanlal Desai, *Social Background of Indian Nationalism*. Bombay: Oxford University Press, 1949; Akshay Ramanlal Desai, *Recent Trends in Indian Nationalism*. Bombay: Popular Prakashan, 1960.

88   Ramkrishna Mukherjee, *The Rise and Fall of East India Company: A Sociological Appraisal*. New York: Monthly Review Press, 1955.

89   Singh, *Indian Sociology*, 51–62.

90   See Ramkrishna Mukherjee, *Why Unitary Social Science?* Newcastle-upon-Tyne: Cambridge Scholars Publishing, 2009.

91   David Ludden, "Introduction: A Brief History of Subalternity," in *Reading Subaltern Studies: Critical History, Contested Meaning and the Globalization of South Asia*, ed. David Ludden. London: Anthem Press, 2002.

92   See Sujata Patel, "Feminist Challenges to Sociology in India: An Essay in Disciplinary History," *Contributions to Indian Sociology* 50 (2016) and Gita Chadha and M. T. Joseph, *Re-Imagining Sociology in India: Feminist Perspectives*. Abingdon, Oxon: Routledge, 2018.

93   Vivek Kumar, "Situating Dalits in Indian Sociology," *Sociological Bulletin* 54 (2005).

and Singh (1984) being prominent among them. To Singh, the main issue in this regard is that of 'integrating the conceptual and methodological structure with the Indian worldview ... and existential conditions' and of 'operational adaptation of tools and techniques of social research, which cannot be simply borrowed from other cultures.'[94] His well-known book, *Modernization of Indian Tradition: A Systemic Study of Social Change* contains many insights into the indigenization of Indian sociology.[95] But in Ramkrishna Mukherjee's assessment, this and such efforts of Indian sociologists to "Indianize" were doomed to be failures as they commit some major fallacies regarding the "why" question of social reality.[96]

As discussed earlier, Oommen sees in the call for indigenization of sociology the danger of academic nationalism or even academic communalism; he, therefore, recommends contextualization of sociology wherever it is practiced.[97] Partha Mukherji, thinks that we need to go beyond contextualization. He, in principle, does not see a contradiction between "indigeneity" and "universality," and argues that 'when concepts and theories originating elsewhere pass the indigeneity–generalizability test, that is, if the general explained the particular, efficiently,' the 'indigenization of concepts and theories developed elsewhere' will have 'a universal import.'[98] He also advocates "disciplined eclecticism" in social research.[99]

5 Conclusion: Engaging with the Captive Mind Syndrome in Sociology

The captive mind syndrome is so well entrenched among the Indian intelligentsia that it cannot be wished away. Being integral to the system of education, it is a systemic ailment. A prerequisite for engaging with it is to be aware of its existence and possible consequences. Awareness of the syndrome should guide us in responding to it appropriately in whatever we do. Opportunely, sociology, from its inception, has been a self-reflecting discipline. In countries

---

94   Singh, *Image of Man*, 19.

95   Yogendra Singh, *Modernization of Indian Tradition: A Systemic Study of Social Change.* Delhi: Thomson Press [India], 1973.

96   Mukherjee, *Sociology of Indian Sociology*, 97.

97   Oommen, "Sociology in India," 123.

98   Mukherji, "Sociology in South Asia," 319–20.

99   Partha N. Mukherji, "Disciplined Eclecticism," in *Indian Sociology: Reflections and Introspections*, ed. T. K. Oommen and Partha N. Mukherji (Bombay: Popular Prakashan, 1986), 179–92.

that were formerly colonies of European powers there was no indigenous tradition of sociology, though they may have their own traditions of social philosophy. As such, wherever it has been transplanted from Europe or America, its practitioners have, eventually, reflected on the ontological and epistemological fit, or lack of it, between what is transplanted and the social reality of the host country.[100] This has invariably led to a discussion on indigenizing sociology in those countries; some sociologists in these countries have even practiced what they thought was a sociology relevant for understanding their social realities.

With reference to India, the efforts at indigenizing sociology have not been entirely successful. 'The lead given by the pioneers [has been] overtaken by the paradigmatic power of social science crafted in the West.'[101] Hence, sociology in India largely remains a mirror image (distorted though, as all mirror images are) of its primary counterparts in Europe and America, it is a mimic social science even after its hundredth year of formal existence. The habits of the captive mind do die-hard.

What then are the prospects for the indigenization of sociology in India, and what are the problems in its way? First, the problems. With the initial efforts of the pioneers not resulting in a sustained indigenized sociology, over the last fifty years or so, sociology has been on a drift. The theoretical concerns and methodological orientations of western sociology are incorporated into the sociological agenda sooner rather than later. The revolution in information and communication technology has made surfing for ideas on the internet an easier option than serious cogitation and discussion, and one finds more of western sociology than Indian sociology on the internet. The Indian academic administration also lays premium on intellectual endorsement by western universities, journals, and scholars. This engenders an inferiority complex among Indian sociologists.

Moreover, the great diversity of India would make it extremely difficult to define the Indian*ness* of sociology in India. Independent India inherited many institutions – parliamentary democracy, legal system and penal code, education system, etc. – as colonial legacy. In the absence of any revolutionary

---

100 Atal provides details of meetings where the need for indigenization was discussed, not only in sociology, but also in other social sciences. See Atal, *Indian Sociology from Where to Where*, 96–10, 117–19. With reference to sociology in South Asia, this was discussed at the South Asia Workshop on "The State of Sociology: Issues of Relevance and Rigour" at Surajkund, Haryana, India on 23–25 February 2005. See N. Jayaram, Ravinder Kaur and Partha N. Mukherji (eds.), *The State of Sociology: Issues of Relevance and Rigour* (Special Issue on South Asia), *Sociological Bulletin*, 54 (2005).

101 Mukherji, "Sociology in South Asia," 316.

agenda following independence, these institutions have been undergoing evolutionary adaptive changes since then. Sociology, too, will have to undergo gradual adaptive indigenization. This would entail many questions. How to ensure indigenization does not result in parochialism or dominance of the majoritarian view, marginalizing the different minority views? How to ensure that the academic agenda of indigenization is different from its political counterpart? From whose point of view is the relevance of sociology to be established or judged? There are no easy and categorical answers to these questions.

Krishna Kumar has identified three aspects of indigenization: structural, substantive and theoretic.[102] "Structural indigenization" refers to the country's institutional and organizational capabilities for the production and diffusion of sociological knowledge. "Substantive indigenization" refers to the content of sociology being focused on the country's people, society, and institutions. In addition, "theoretic indigenization" refers to the development of distinctive conceptual frameworks and metatheories which reflect the country's worldviews, social and cultural experience, and perceived goals. Sociology in India seems to be well placed with reference to the first two but has a long way to go as regards the third one.

Obviously, sociology in India cannot shut its door to advancements in western sociology. It is neither possible nor desirable. What we need to develop, as Oommen points out, is 'a critical capacity to discern what is good and relevant for us.'[103] In fact, 'to produce knowledge that is rooted in the indigenous,' Partha Mukherji observes, 'it is important that we engage seriously with knowledge emanating from the West and elsewhere in a comparative frame.'[104] Saberwal puts this pithily:

> The sociologist in India has to approach [the] Western tradition seriously – not with apprehension, for it is more than merely a source of our historic difficulties, but as a foil, a particular historical experience, which we may hold to ourselves as a mirror much as Max Weber, Louis Dumont, and others have tried to recognize the West for themselves in the Indian mirror.[105]

---

102   Cited in Atal, *Indian Sociology from Where to Where*, 104–05.
103   Oommen, "Sociology in India," 119.
104   Mukherji, "Sociology in South Asia," 320.
105   Saberwal, "Uncertain Transplants," 228.

Bibliography

Alatas, Syed Hussein. "The Captive Mind and Creative Development." *International Social Science Journal* 26 (1974): 691–700.

Atal, Yogesh. *Indian Sociology from Where to Where: Footnotes to the History of the Discipline*. Jaipur: Rawat Publications, 2003.

Bottomore, Thomas Burton. *Sociology as Social Criticism*. London: George Allen and Unwin 1975.

Chadha, Gita and M. T. Joseph, eds. *Re-Imagining Sociology in India: Feminist Perspectives*. Abingdon, Oxon: Routledge, 2018.

Chaudhuri, Nirad C. *The Autobiography of an Unknown Indian*. Bombay: Jaico Publishing House, 1964.

Chaudhuri, Nirad C. *Thy Hand, Great Anarch! India, 1921–1952*. Reading, PA: Addison Wesley, 1988.

Cohn, Bernard S. "Notes on the History of the Study of Indian Society and Culture." In *Structure and Change in Indian Society*, edited by Milton Singer and Bernard S. Cohn, 3–28. Chicago: Aldine Publishing Co., 1968.

Desai, Akshay Ramanlal. *Recent Trends in Indian Nationalism*. Bombay: Popular Prakashan, 1960.

Desai, Akshay Ramanlal. "Relevance of the Marxist Approach to the Study of Indian Society." *Sociological Bulletin* 30 (1981): 1–20.

Desai, Akshay Ramanlal. *Social Background of Indian Nationalism*. Bombay: Oxford University Press, 1949.

Dirks, Nicholas B. *Castes of Mind: Colonialism and the Making of Modern India*. Delhi: Permanent Black, 2003.

Dua, Hans Raj. "The Spread of English in India: Politics of Language Conflict and Language Power." In *Post-Imperial English: Status Change in Former British and American Colonies, 1940–1990*, edited by Joshua A. Fishman, Andrew W. Conrad, and Alma Rubal-Lopez, 557–88. Berlin and New York: Mouton de Gruyter, 1996.

Dube, S. C. "Indian Sociology at the Turning Point." *Sociological Bulletin* 26 (1977): 1–13.

Dumont, Louis. "For a Sociology of India." *Contributions to Indian Sociology,* edited by Louis Dumont and David Pocock. 1 (1957): 7–22.

Gupta, Bela Dutta. *Sociology in India: An Enquiry into Sociological Thinking and Empirical Social Research in the Nineteenth Century – with Special Reference to Bengal*. Calcutta: Centre for Sociological Research, 1972.

Jayaram, N. "Challenges to Indian Sociology." *Sociological Bulletin* 47 (1998): 237–41.

Jayaram, N. *Sociology of Education in India* (second edition). Jaipur: Rawat Publications, 2015.

Jayaram, N. "Towards Indigenization of an Uncertain Transplant: Hundred Years of Sociology in India." *Tajseer* 1 (2020): 99–122.

Jayaram, N., Ravinder Kaur and Partha N. Mukherji, eds. "The State of Sociology: Issues of Relevance and Rigour." *Sociological Bulletin* 54, no. 3 (2005).

Joshi, P. C. "Reflections on Social Science Research in India." In *Indian Sociology: Reflections and Introspections*, edited by T. K. Oommen and Partha N. Mukherji, 138–61. Bombay: Popular Prakashan, 1986.

Kipling, Rudyard. "The White Man's Burden: The United States and The Philippine Islands, 1899" In *Rudyard Kipling's Verse: Definitive Edition*. Garden City, New York: Doubleday, 1929.

Kumar, Vivek. "Situating Dalits in Indian Sociology." *Sociological Bulletin* 54 (2005): 514–32.

Ludden, David. "Introduction: A Brief History of Subalternity." In *Reading Subaltern Studies: Critical History, Contested Meaning and the Globalization of South Asia*, edited by David Ludden, 1–33. London: Anthem Press, 2002.

Mills, Charles Wright. *The Sociological Imagination*. New York: Oxford University Press, 1959.

Miłosz, Czesław. *The Captive Mind*. Translated by Jane Zielonko. London: Penguin Books, 2001.

Mukerji, D. P. "Indian Tradition and Social Change." In *Indian Sociology: Reflections and Introspections*, edited by T. K. Oommen and Partha N. Mukherji, 1–15. Bombay: Popular Prakashan, 1986.

Mukherjee, Ramkrishna. *Sociology of Indian Sociology*. Bombay: Allied Publishers, 1979.

Mukherjee, Ramkrishna. *The Rise and Fall of East India Company: A Sociological Appraisal*. New York: Monthly Review Press, 1955.

Mukherjee, Ramkrishna. *Why Unitary Social Science?* (Newcastle-upon-Tyne: Cambridge Scholars Publishing, 2009).

Mukherji, Partha N. "Disciplined Eclecticism." In *Indian Sociology: Reflections and Introspections*, edited by T. K. Oommen and Partha N. Mukherji, 179–92. Bombay: Popular Prakashan, 1986.

Mukherji, Partha N. "Sociology in South Asia: Indigenisation as Universalising Social Science." *Sociological Bulletin* 54 (2005): 311–24.

Oommen, T. K. "Sociology in *India*: A Plea for Contextualization." *Sociological Bulletin* 32 (1983): 111–36.

Oommen, T. K. and Partha N. Mukherji. "Editorial Introduction." In *Indian Sociology: Reflections and Introspections*. Edited by T. K. Oommen and Partha N. Mukherji, VII–IX. Bombay: Popular Prakashan, 1986.

Oommen, T. K. and Partha N. Mukherji, eds. *Indian Sociology: Reflections and Introspections*. Bombay: Popular Prakashan, 1986.

Patel, Sujata. "Feminist Challenges to Sociology in India: An Essay in Disciplinary History." *Contributions to Indian Sociology* 50 (2016): 320–42.

Saberwal, Satish. "Uncertain Transplants: Anthropology and Sociology in India." In *Indian Sociology: Reflections and Introspections*, edited by T. K. Oommen and Partha N. Mukherji, 214–32. Bombay: Popular Prakashan, 1986.

Saksena, R. N. *Sociology in India*. Agra: Institute of Social Sciences, 1965.

Saran, Awadh Kishore. "Sociology in India." In *Contemporary Sociology*, edited by Joseph S. Roucek, 1013–34. London: Peter Owen Limited, 1959.

Seal, Anil. *Emergence of Indian Nationalism: Competition and Collaboration in the Late Nineteenth Century*. Cambridge: Cambridge University Press, 1968.

Sharp, H. *Selections from Educational Records, Part 1, 1781–1839*. New Delhi: Published for the National Archives of India by the Manager of Publications, Government of India.

Singh, Yogendra. *Image of Man: Ideology and Theory in Indian Sociology*. Delhi: Chanakya Publications, 1984.

Singh, Yogendra. *Indian Sociology: Social Conditioning and Emerging Concerns*, New Delhi: Vistaar, 1986.

Singh, Yogendra. *Modernization of Indian Tradition: A Systemic Study of Social Change*. Delhi: Thomson Press (India), 1973.

Srinivas, M. N. and M. N. Panini. "The Development of Sociology and Social Anthropology in India." *Sociological Bulletin* 22 (1973): 179–215.

Tharoor, Shashi. *An Era of Darkness: The British Empire in India*. New Delhi: Aleph, 2016.

CHAPTER 8

Psychological Feudalism

Malay Political Culture and Responses towards Modernization

Norshahril Saat

1 Introduction

Syed Hussein Alatas spent more than two decades of his academic career in Singapore and taught at the National University of Singapore (NUS). He was the founding head of the Malay Studies Department at the university in 1967, before stepping down in 1987. Before setting foot in Singapore, Alatas had established a public profile: as a founding member of the Malaysian Gerakan party (Parti Gerakan Rakyat Malaysia) in 1968, a vocal social critic, as well as a progressive Muslim public intellectual. Throughout his career, he has published books, articles in academic journals, and newspaper opinion-editorial pieces, touching on *inter alia* the sociology of corruption, orientalism, Islam, and Malay politics and culture. He made his name through the unpacking of colonial capitalism, Western domination in scholarship or Eurocentrism, and the ideology of the Malay ruling class. Towards the latter part of his academic career, his works focused on the impact of the captive mind, which in essence, demonstrated the inability of academics (particularly in Asian societies) to discuss problems of their societies, but were merely guided by orientalist academic agenda.

This chapter examines Alatas' lesser-known aspiration to reform Malay political culture and behavior, through his coining of the concept of "psychological feudalism." Unlike the concepts of colonial capitalism and captive mind, psychological feudalism was not expanded in his other writings, or developed by other scholars, despite its significance. The lack of application of – or interest in – the concept is by no means a demonstration of its weaknesses; there could be other reasons including the political sensitivity surrounding it. The concept is deliberated in a chapter entitled "Feudalism in Malaysian society: A Study in Historical Continuity," found in his book *Modernization and Social Change: Studies in Modernization, Religion, Social Change and Development in Southeast Asia.* Even though the discussion of the concept only makes up one chapter of the entire book, it ties in with the book's objective calling for social

© NORSHAHRIL SAAT, 2023 | DOI:10.1163/9789004521698_010

reforms and modernization. It is also clear that his target audience is mainly those living in post-colonial societies, especially the Malays in Malaysia.

Through psychological feudalism, Alatas critiques the political culture of the Malays and their responses towards modernization. Some will argue that his approach is developmental, modernist, and positivist by upholding a normative position, but this is consistent with his goal to refashion Malay studies from mainly descriptive research without discussion of problems and forwarding proposals for social reform. It is not the intention of this chapter to discuss the merits and demerits of the developmental approach, but the fact that Alatas' works continue to be read today demonstrates their relevance to contemporary social, religious and political life. This chapter analyzes the main arguments of psychological feudalism, highlighting some of its traits. According to Alatas, even though the Malays are living in the modern era, the political culture and behavior of the elites reflect feudal continuities. Arguably, two traits of psychological feudalism – loyalty to the ruler, and the big gulf between the rich and the poor – remain important to understand the politics of Malaysian society. Plus, he contends that the manifestation of feudal psychology today is coupled with materialism and capitalism. The additional materialist component to feudal thinking is displayed by what the Malay elites promote as ideals in society. The chapter will make references to contemporary examples.

To expand Alatas' discussion of the concept, this chapter also highlights the works of the students he supervised when he was a professor at NUS. To begin, he produced less than ten graduate students throughout his academic career, considered low for a man of his intellectual stature. The works published by his students demonstrate the intellectual continuity of the man. Moreover, the thesis topics of his students are telling; they revolve around feudalism, the political culture of the Malays, corruption, human rights, and orientalism. In this vein, the works of Shaharuddin Maaruf and Chandra Muzaffar – two public intellectuals who obtained their doctoral degree under his supervision – will be discussed.

This chapter first discusses Alatas' role in inculcating critical thinking amongst his students when he was a professor at NUS. Here, his contributions in shaping the intellectual direction of the Department of Malay Studies in NUS, embodied by Shaharuddin's and Chandra's writings, will be discussed. The chapter will then deliberate Alatas' concept of psychological feudalism and compare the Malay political culture during the Malaccan sultanate as demonstrated in the classical text called *Sejarah Melayu* and the contemporary context. It will then explicate the impact of psychological feudalism on the Malay community's response towards modernization, attitude towards scientific knowledge, and politics and governance, and how Islam, being the religion of the Malays, is understood. The chapter will conclude by deliberating the impact of psychological feudalism on Malay society today.

2 Alatas and the Singapore Malay Studies Tradition

Alatas made no pretensions about academic objectivity, which may not meet the standards propounded by some within the academic circles. To him, the value of objectivity can only be found in searching for the progress of society. In many ways, Alatas has built on the sociological tradition that is developmental or modernist. His contribution to Malay studies can be felt to this day. His works are republished decades after they were in circulation, demonstrating their relevance in meeting contemporary needs. By contrast, works that claim to be objective may end up being descriptive scholarship, coupled with the fascination with "thick descriptions." Even so, such scholarship can never be free from biases or ethnocentrism, as Alatas unpacks in his writings that touch on colonialism.

Alatas' works are rich with philosophy. Far from being Occidentalist, his scholarship refers to the Western tradition, as much as he cites Asian and Islamic traditions. From the Western tradition, his ideas were unequivocally influenced by Hungarian-German philosopher Karl Mannheim (1893–1947), especially his seminal work, *Ideology and Utopia: An Introduction to the Sociology of Knowledge.*[1] Mannheim's work forms the crux of Alatas' seminal work, *The Myth of the Lazy Native.* Similarly, his progressive views are reflected in his books, *Islam dan Sosialisma* (Islam and Socialism)[2] and *Kita Dengan Islam: Tumbuh Tiada Berbuah (We and Islam: A Tree Bearing No Fruits).*[3] To be sure, Alatas does not differentiate Western-secular traditions and Islamic traditions when evaluating the progress of his community, but what he saw as good traditions to better understand the origins, nature, and functions of their problems.

---

1   Karl Mannheim, *Ideology and Utopia: Introduction to the Sociology of Knowledge.* (London: Routledge & Kegan Paul, 1936).

2   Syed Hussein Alatas, *Islam dan Sosialisma* (Penang: Seruan Masa, 1976); Syed Hussein Alatas, *Modernization and Social Change: Studies in Modernization, Religion, Social Change and Development in South-East Asia* (Sydney: Angus and Robertson, 1972).

3   Syed Hussein Alatas, *Kita Dengan Islam: Tumbuh Tiada Berbuah* (Singapore: Pustaka Nasional, 1979).

His academic works while heading the Department of the Malay Studies at the National University of Singapore also provided the depth of his thinking towards the Malays. He was also responding and reflecting on the feudal continuity in Malaysia. Writing from Singapore enabled him to have more freedom to reflect and be critical of the political and social culture in his country of origin. But these should not be regarded as him being an external critique of his own country, for he continues to have ties with the Malaysians. Alatas never ran into any problems with the law enforcement agencies in Malaysia for committing *lèse-majesté*; he never received any defamation suits from politicians, for his works are academically sound and backed by references and sources.

Alatas' writings also looked at aspects of Islam and its significance in the construction of the Malay identity. He represents Islam as embodying ideal values crucial for modernizing the Malays. Here, he makes a distinction between Islam as practice – which he refers to as Islamic orientations – to Islam as ideals, traditions, and values. For example, the book *Islam and Sosialisme* (Islam and Socialism) demonstrates the important values found in socialist thinking that highlight the community and aspects of religion that indirectly criticizes the way Islam is practiced in Malay society, which contained feudal elements. He also published several writings in the Malay language – such as a compilation of lectures in *Kita Dengan Islam: Tumbuh Tiada Berbuah* – which demonstrated his reforms and progressive thinking in opposition to what he described as feudal continuities in the practice of Islam in Malaysian society. In these two works, Alatas was mainly interested in tackling the root causes of underdevelopment and move society away from its feudal elements.

Alatas' academic writings have been widely analyzed by scholars. Some are more developed compared to others. For example, Alatas' *The Myth of the Lazy Native* is better circulated among post-colonial scholars, and even Edward Said, the author of *Orientalism*, acknowledged Alatas' contributions in the field. To be sure, his works on feudalism did not receive as much attention among scholars for reasons cited earlier. In the eyes of post-modern scholars, it appeared to be too developmental and lacked objectivity. Even though no one has indicated this explicitly, the direction adopted by social science schools explains why his works on modernization and social change are neglected, along with Western scholars who also adopt a similar school of thought. For example, the works of Karl Mannheim, Ortega Gasset, and Franz Fanon that touch on ideology are rarely discussed in the Malay world and are considered less "fashionable" compared to the likes of Michel Foucault. In the same vein, Asian scholars championing reforms also face the same neglect: including Ibn Khaldun, Jose Rizal, and Tjokroaminoto. Among the Malays, Alatas' critique of the Malay ruling class does not have a wide audience. The reasons for this intellectual neglect may have resulted from the Malays' political and religious orientation and the behavior of the current political elites who seek to retain the status quo.

The lack of interest among international academic circles in his works on modernization and social change does not discount their significance. His ideas resonate among his students at the National University of Singapore, especially cohorts from the 1970s to the 1990s. The seriousness of his engagements on the problems of the Malays is reflected in the thinking of his students, many of whom became community leaders in Singapore and Malaysia, and serve as policymakers, journalists, and teachers. He did not supervise many students because he was not interested in the numbers of students but rather the quality of their works, yet the students who later ventured into academia continued Alatas' intellectual legacy. It is worth highlighting two of his students' works that reflected the continuity of his critical and sharp thinking towards the Malay society, particularly on the aspects discussed above. These prominent students are Shaharuddin Maaruf and Chandra Muzaffar. The works of these two scholars are highlighted because they expanded Alatas' formulation of psychological feudalism, citing numerous examples from Malay historical texts as well as reflections of recent examples.

Shaharuddin Maaruf was Alatas' MA and Ph.D. student at the Malay Studies Department, National University of Singapore in the 1980s. He wrote two theses that were later published: they are *The Concept of a Hero in Malay Society* and *Malay Ideas on Development: From Feudal Lord to Capitalist*.[4] Like his mentor, Shaharuddin later taught at the Department and served as the Head of Malay Studies. He also became a renowned social observer in Singapore and has mentored students carrying on the same intellectual tradition, such as Noor Aisha Abdul Rahman and Azhar Ibrahim, both currently lecturing at the same department that Alatas once headed. Shaharuddin's books trace the genealogy of ideas from the feudal era to contemporary times and highlight how certain political episodes entrenched the Malay feudal culture in society. Shaharuddin critically appraised how and why the warrior class in the feudal era was glorified and regarded as heroes, even though some of their behavior failed to meet the ideals of Islam, the religion of the Malays. Harsh treatment towards the common people, especially the peasants, the lack of private property, and the behavior of the ruling class, which demonstrated the dominant traits of the era, were not problematized.

---

4   Shaharuddin Maaruf, *Concept of A Hero in Malay Society* (Selangor: SIRD, 2014); Shaharuddin Maaruf, *Malay Ideas on Development: From Feudal Lord to Capitalist* (Selangor: SIRD, 2014).

In the *Concept of a Hero in Malay Society*, Shaharuddin traces the groups the Malays regard as elites. He traces the thinking and values of two feudal heroes, Hang Tuah and Hang Jebat, and what the Malay consider ideals, as well as their transition towards a materialistic concept of a hero. In *Malay Ideas on Development*, Shaharuddin examines the Malay feudal values through Malay classical texts and the writings of the voyager Abdullah Munsyi, who was critical of feudalism. He then examined the exploits of colonial capitalism and how capitalism, in general, was internalized by Malay elites, professionals, and writers, which had merged with religion and nationalism. He concluded by demonstrating how in contemporary Malay society the pursuit of capitalistic ethos remains dominant.[5] In *Malay Ideas on Development*, Shaharuddin dedicated a sizeable portion to the discussion of Malaysia's founding prime minister, Tunku Abdul Rahman, and his leadership styles, which reflected feudal continuities. Tunku was a Malay nationalist with royal blood. Shaharuddin concluded that Tunku 'consciously sought legitimacy for his political struggle within the feudal tradition ... He sought to maintain the traditional ties between the Malays and their rulers.'[6] The themes of Shaharuddin's writings in these two seminal works reflect the continuities of Alatas' writings and concerns. The quality of these works, which have been republished and redistributed due to recent demand, demonstrates high-level of thinking, a product of Alatas' supervision.

Shaharuddin observes another development in contemporary Malay politics and society: the coupling of feudalism and the materialist conception of life. Materialism here is demonstrated by the behavior of the political elites to acquire as much wealth as possible, even if it means through unethical and immoral ways. Wealth can be accumulated through power, which itself becomes the goal; religious values and ethics can be compromised to attain this goal. Shaharuddin observes how United Malays National Organization (UMNO) politicians apply this concept of materialism in his book. In the same manner, Alatas uncovered the colonial capitalist ideology in his famous book, *The Myth of The Lazy Native*.[7] Shaharuddin's criticism of UMNO's publication *Mental Revolution*, which demonstrates the feudal and materialist conception of ideals, is mainly an extension of Alatas' criticism of the same book in *The Myth of the Lazy Native*. According to Shaharuddin, 'The ruling class, besides promoting feudal heroes to protect and further its interests, also promotes

---

5 Maaruf, *Concept of A Hero in Malay Society*.
6 Maaruf, *Malay Ideas on Development*, 133.
7 Syed Hussein Alatas. *The Myth of the Lazy Native* (London and New York: Frank Cass and Company Ltd, 1977).

174   SAAT

great capitalists as heroes to seek justification and rationalization for its mate-
rialists outlook.'[8]

Shaharuddin also continued Alatas' efforts in analyzing the values of the
Malay ruling class during the feudal period. While Shaharuddin cautions that
Sejarah Melayu was never intended to be a history textbook, it can lead to valuable insights into the socio-historical conditions of Malay society. He argues
that modern-day historians often dismiss Malay texts as myths and being short
of meeting the standards of historiography; yet a good understanding of the
beliefs, ethics, and morals, particularly that of the ruling class. According to
Shaharuddin,

> On its terms, however, *Sejarah Melayu* remains a valuable socio-historical
> or socio-cultural document if appropriate scholarly demands and expec-
> tation are placed on it. As social history documenting cultural forms, the
> virtues of *Sejarah Melayu* far outstripped its alleged shortfalls from the
> standards of modern historiography. In this regard, the virtues of Sejarah
> Melayu lie precisely in its careful portrayal of beliefs, ethics, and morals,
> blending reality and myths, ignoring the division between the spiritual
> and the temporal, flouting our basic notion of modern history.[9]

Another prominent student of Syed Hussein Alatas is political scientists and
human rights activist Chandra Muzaffar, who is currently heading an NGO
called JUST (International Movement for a JUST World). Chandra wrote his
Ph.D. dissertation that was later published as a book entitled, *Protector? An
analysis of the concept and practice of loyalty in leader-led relationships within
Malay society*.[10] Chandra develops the concept of unquestioning loyalty to the
ruler, tracing the origins during the Malacca period. According to Muzaffar,
'since it is the ruler or the ruling class that expects unquestioning loyalty it is
primarily an attitude that resides in the psychological processes of the ruler
or the ruling class.'[11] But his tracing of the political psychology of the ruling
class does not only stop at the feudal era five centuries ago, but rather in post-
Malaya independence in 1957. He adds that 'the rulers still equal the Sultans

---

8   Maaruf, *Malay Ideas on Development*, 79.

9   Shaharuddin, Maaruf, *To Err is Inhuman and to Punish Divine: A Study on the Religious
     Orientation of the Malays* (Singapore: Department of Malay Studies, National University
     of Singapore, 2002).

10   Chandra Muzaffar, *Protector? An Analysis of the Concept and Practice of Loyalty in Leader-
     Led Relationships within Malay Society* (Pulau Pinang: Aliran, 1979).

11   Muzaffar, *Protector*, 2.

in the post-Merdeka period, but the ruling class incorporates both the Sultans and the political elites of the United Malays National Organization (UMNO), the mainstay of the government and the party that commands most support among the Malays.'[12] By unquestioning loyalty, Muzaffar refers to obeying the ruler's wishes, but not questioning the reasons behind them, even though the requests by the elites 'transgresses moral values and ethical conduct.'[13] Resulting from this ideology of unquestioned loyalty, society abandoned the option to resist and rebel against the rulers' excesses, choosing to remain committed to the status quo.[14] The outcome of this ideology impedes development, and also explains the non-existent social revolution in Malay society as espoused by Alatas, which perpetuates the "oppressive ruling class" and "submissive subject class."[15]

As Alatas' former student, Muzaffar remains a prominent social critic in Malaysia today, and most of his views are carried by social media. Like his mentor, he had a brief experience in politics during the 1998 *reformasi* period and became the co-founder of the Justice Party (Parti Keadilan) after Anwar Ibrahim was sacked by Mahathir Mohamad from UMNO and from his position as deputy prime minister. In 2001, Muzaffar later resigned from the party, but he has become a leading voice against corruption and an internationally renowned human rights activist. In a way, both Chandra and Shaharuddin continued Alatas' legacy, as reflected in their writings. Chandra continues Alatas' reformist voice in the Islamic world, by also pointing out the trends and impact of Islamic revivalism in the 1970s.

The Alatas critical Malay Studies tradition in Singapore did not end with Shaharuddin and Muzaffar, for the two intellectual giants further developed the tradition by mentoring other graduate students. Among Shaharuddin's emerging students is Azhar Ibrahim, who continues Alatas' intellectual legacy by focusing on literary texts. But Azhar is not only a literary scholar, for he has also published on history, culture and heritage, and religion. In one of his publications, Azhar applies Alatas' psychological feudalism. In his article, Azhar reminds us

> what is emphasized here is the conflicting value system in Malaysia society, where many authoritarian and regressive values of Malay feudalism conflict with the universal religious and humanistic values of Malay

---

12   Ibid., 3.
13   Ibid., 7.
14   Ibid., 11.
15   Ibid., 14.

society. The feudal structure which was dominant before the advent of colonialism was very repressive. Its ideological and coercive apparatuses inhibited the development of Malay society in various realms of life and had a lasting effect on Malay society as a whole.[16]

Calling psychological feudalism neo-feudalism, Azhar further updates Alatas' discussion of the term by adding the following traits: authoritarian political outlook, hierarchical social relationships, acquiring power through inheriting and by association and less of merit, inequality between the privileged and less privileged, preference for pomposity rather than substance, and celebrating the feudal past as ideal, which he calls feudal romanticism.[17]

3   Psychological Feudalism

Alatas underlines eight traits of psychological feudalism. The three key ones are as follows: (1) the presence of a big gulf between the poor (usually peasants) and the rich (usually noblemen and chiefs), in the economic, social, political, and judicial field; (2) the political order is dominated by hereditary groups having large estates at their disposal; (3) at the head of the manorial hierarchy was the feudal lord, immune from the supervision of higher authorities, yet possessing judicial, economic, fiscal, and administrative rights.[18] He points out some similarities of the social, cultural, and political situation of the Malays during the feudal period and contemporary ones. However, he also makes a caveat that feudalism did not only refer to a Malay political or social structure but was also present in other communities, although there are similarities and differences.

The crux of Alatas' reflection of feudal continuities in contemporary Malay social life derived from his approach to classical Malay texts. He urges readers to critically examine classical Malay texts beyond how many scholars approached them in their works: mainly for literary and historical subjects. By contrast, he requests scholars look deeper into these texts and ascertain the values promoted by the Malay ruling class, which he defines as their ideology. Alatas argues that the notion of unquestioned loyalty to the ruler or noblemen has been promoted as an essential value in Malay social and political life. The

---

16   Azhar Ibrahim, *Historical Imagination and Cultural Responses To Colonialism and Nationalism* (Selangor: SIRD, 2017), 102.

17   Ibrahim, *Historical Imagination*,104.

18   Alatas, *Modernization and Social Change*, 101.

examples he highlights also demonstrate that the concept of equality espoused by Islam was not practiced in Malay feudal society. There were instances where individuals championing for rights were deemed by the ruling class as akin to committing treason. Through his examination of the Malay classical texts, he argues that two value systems existed side-by-side during the Malay feudal era. He was not referring to values in the ideal sense but aspects that shaped the behaviors of Malay society. On the one hand, the Malays followed the values underlined by Islamic principles. On the other hand, they tend to follow feudal culture, which lacked the ideal principles such as democracy, human rights, integrity, equality, and justice.

In his article, "Feudalism in Malaysian society: A Study in Historical Continuity," Alatas highlights some continuities of feudal values in post-independence Malaysian society. The article draws examples from the 1950s to the point when the book was published in the 1970s. He argues that even though the political system has evolved significantly from the absolute monarchy of the Malaccan sultanate to mere figureheads during the British colonial period (19th century to the early 20th century), to constitutional monarchy in 1957, attitudes and values from the pre-colonial and feudal period have been preserved.[19] What explains this continuity? Alatas contends that Malay society did not experience any major mass uprising but only infighting among chiefs and warlords, and skirmishes with their colonial masters. The colonial masters too had a role in preserving the feudal order. While assuming the role of "advisors" to the Malay rulers, they were running the colonial administration, relegating the rulers as custodians of Malay culture and religion, namely Islam. This preservation of the Malay ruling class was deemed by the colonials to be less disruptive to their colonial capitalist endeavors, for the Malay rulers could still command loyalty from the masses. The British strategy is what scholars have termed as an indirect colonial rule. The purpose of practicing colonialism in this way was to prevent social upheaval.

In *Modernization and Social Change*, Alatas explains how feudal psychology was still in operation in the 1970s, highlighting the factors that led to the continuity of Malay feudal culture. Alatas notes that the absence of mass uprising in Malay history to be one factor; and the other being colonial rule, which preserved the Malay feudal customs and social hierarchy. Colonialism did not bring any substantive change to the Malays political and social life. He also discusses some traits of psychological feudalism in contemporary Malaysian society. One aspect that deserves attention is the lack of differentiation

---

19   Ibid., 100.

between what constitutes private property and public property. Alatas points out that there is also very little differentiation between private life and "official" public life.[20] To illustrate, he cites how members of the state legislative assemblies made travel claims for events that were not official, such as attending the opening of Qur'an reading events, the opening of mosques, funerals of other assemblymen, and election work. Ideally, such claims only apply to attendance at legislative assemblies or parliament sittings. He also cites the example of telephone bills where there was a high number of unofficial telephone calls. The behavior of the Malay political elites during the post-colonial era demonstrates that they were unable to distinguish the two. But the more fundamental critique was the political culture of unquestioned loyalty to the leader. According to Alatas:

> The important conditions to obtain protection from feudal rulers and chiefs were unflinching loyalty and subservience towards the master. In return for these, protection was granted irrespective of the nature and degree of the crime. The modern version of this relationship is found in the political party. If the individual is loyal and subservient to the leader, he can rely on his protection in the hour of need. His misdemeanors and excesses may be tolerated, but never a challenge or defiance to the leader.[21]

Furthermore, other aspects of feudal culture include the accumulation of wealth by the ruling class and their obsession with grandeur and celebration. Alatas points out that resources dedicated towards festivities and celebrations were huge, despite the problems underlying Malay society in the immediate post-colonial society. Much was also invested in recreational activities and entertainment at the expense of other pertinent aspects, such as tackling poverty. He also provides details of the money spent on purchasing medals, and stars, ribbons, and badges for celebratory purposes, as well as chastising the amount of money spent on building golf courses.[22]

Another aspect of feudal continuities in contemporary Malay social and political life is the promotion of magic and superstition. The rulers themselves patronized magicians and shamans. He cited an example of how a magician was invited to the palace to prevent rain so that a royal wedding could proceed. The shaman was invited because he successfully prevented rain in Sabah for

---

20   Ibid., 106.

21   Ibid., 108.

22   Ibid., 109–111.

PSYCHOLOGICAL FEUDALISM

three days when the ruler visited the state. In *Modernization and Social Change*, he dedicated a separate chapter tackling the Malays obsession with magic and superstition, which impeded the community's quest towards modernization and progress. He described the phenomenon as collective representation.

4 Psychological Feudalism Today

The following discusses empirical examples of psychological feudalism in Malay society today. Case studies since the turn of the millennium (after 2000), the period that Alatas and his students did not cover in their writings, will be examined. Examples from this contemporary period proves that despite all the discussion that the Malays have attained economic and social progress through the industrialization of the 1980s and 1990s, the definition of progress is tied to feudal conceptions of power, wealth, and culture. The persistence of feudal psychology has already been explained by Alatas. First, there was never a social revolution that disrupts the political order in Malaysia, unlike in Indonesia, where the majority of the Javanese traditional rulers were over-thrown, although there are contemporary instances where groups are seeking to revive the feudal authority in contemporary political life.

Second, in Malaysia, the traditional Malay rulers continue to be symbols of power in the context of constitutional monarchy. Fragmentation among the political elites has provided more opportunities for the Malay rulers to step up their authority, as the politically neutral guardians of the Malays. Lately, they have stepped out from their roles as custodians of Malay culture and Islam to become the symbol of unity. For example, since 2008, UMNO no longer attains the political dominance it used to have, by obtaining two-thirds major-ity control of parliament. Very briefly, between May 2018 and February 2020, it lost power, only to regain it through defections from the Pakatan Harapan (PH) government. In March 2020, the King appointed the prime minister after it became unclear who would become the leader in a divisive political circumstanced.

Third, as Alatas notes, psychological feudalism does not only refer to the behavior of traditional Malay rulers, Sultans, Raja, or Kings, akin to the illus-trations in the Malay classical texts *Sulalatus Salatin* and *Tajul Salatin*, but the behavior of the political elites, who include politicians from UMNO, PAS (Islamic Party of Malaysia), Bersatu (Parti Pribumi Bersatu Malaysia) and others. Here, we are not limiting feudal psychology only to the Malays, but to non-Malay politicians as well, as we can extend psychological feudalism to encompass the ideology of the ruling class in the country.

Many traits of feudal psychology can be discussed, but this chapter shall be limited to three aspects that touch on socio-economy, religious orientation, and political discourse. First, the gulf between the rich and the poor, which also translates into the choice of lifestyles, such as house ownership, the scale of celebrations or events held, hobbies, and habits. Another trait is the behavior of the elites, who ignore Islamic traditions that emphasize equality, justice, and humility. Second, the model of religious ideas still resembles feudal thinking, which emphasizes magic, ritualism, and dualism. There is a lack of scientific thinking, prioritizes prayers over social justice and values, emphasis on the hereafter and not wordily affairs. Third, the political culture still emphasizes values such as unquestioned loyalty to the elite. Feudal titles also remain a feature in contemporary politics. While it is common in constitutional monarchies for honorary titles to remain, the ideas associated with those titles remain associated with feudal values.

In the *Sejarah Melayu*, the gulf between the rich and poor, between the ruling class and the masses, is huge, the latter being mainly peasants. In the text, there was a narration of how Bendahara Seri Maharaja offered the young children in his household a fiat of gold to play with, demonstrating the amount of wealth he had, compared to stories of ordinary peasants who mainly lived their lives based on their daily earnings.[23] Wealth is also associated with the power and status of the person. For example, it was deemed to be rude for someone to approach a dignitary in a public place; the appropriate place is to meet such a person is the person's home. The ruling class also organized grand celebrations and parties for weddings, which require mobilization of the masses to make them happen, which also meant mass wastage of resources that could be distributed to the poor and needy. Yet, such grand celebrations manifested the person's status and social class in society.

Such mass celebrations for the dignitaries and ruling class remain a common feature in contemporary Malay society, even though there are reports of homeless and underclass Malays. The elites travel for functions using private jets and helicopters, demonstrating the gulf between the rich and the poor. The elites also spent money on fancy cars – which are no longer deemed for travel purposes, but collection – and luxury goods worth millions of dollars. Far from treating these as private preferences, public demonstration of personal wealth and elitist habits is now common through postings on social media, without being sensitive to the needs of the under-class Malays. Rarely are Islamic traditions, including the Prophet Muhammad's lifestyle of humility, and helping

---

23   Maaruf, *Malay Ideas of Development*, 19.

PSYCHOLOGICAL FEUDALISM

the needy, invoked by the elites and the religious scholars to correct the imbalance of power. Values such as exercising restrain are not commonly discussed.

The second trait of the continuation of feudal psychology happens in the realm of religion. Islam is an important marker for Malay identity. It has contributed significantly to the progress of the Malays and led to social transformation in many aspects. Islam has contributed significantly to the Malays' vocabulary, language, architecture, social and political life, and the arts. In the Malaysian constitution, Islam is one of the three elements that defines the Malays, apart from the speaking of the Malay language and the practice of Malay culture. However, what remains in contention here is not Islam as a religion, which encompasses universal values, but the religious orientation of the Malays, namely how Islam is understood, emphasized, and practiced. On this aspect, we observe continuities in terms of ritualist, dualistic, orientations of religion. The religious discourse emphasizes the practice of rituals such as prayers, fasting, tithe, etc., rather than values such as human rights, justice, equality, and humility. As mentioned, the insensitivity towards the plight of the underclass demonstrates how the value of humility remains wanting. A person's morality is judged by the number of rituals conducted.

Another orientation that continues from the feudal period is the magic orientation, which Alatas describes as collective representation. In classical Malay feudal texts, how Islam came to the Malay world was associated with magic and superstition. The magical orientation exists side by side with religious practices, but in more recent times, the two orientations merge. The sultans of the past believed that they had the magical prowess to curse their followers. Moreover, religious leaders also function as medicine men against evil spirits and ghosts. Today, there are reports of the ruling elites patronizing shamans or religious teachers to cure sorcery. In many ways, Islam has been reduced to magic rather than values and principles.

Psychological feudalism is evident in the political culture of the Malays. Here, we are not referring to the constitutional right for Malaysians to express loyalty to the state and the Yang di-pertuan Agong (Malaysian King), who is the head of state. What needs to be deliberated here is how loyalty is manifested in everyday life. The constitution also emphasizes the rule of law and that no one, including the Malay rulers, should be above it. In 1983 and 1993, Malaysia witnessed two constitutional crises that checked the authority of the Malay rulers. In 1983, prime minister Mahathir Mohamed engineered a constitutional amendment that raised the powers of the legislative assembly and executive vis-à-vis the rulers. The King must assent to a bill passed in parliament within 30 days, and if he disagreed with the bill, it would be sent back to parliament again. Parliament may then vote again, but if it feels the bill should stand, then it becomes law automatically after 30 days. In 1993, the government removed judicial immunity from the rulers committing crimes in a private capacity and indicated that rulers can be tried in a special court, which was non-existent previously.[24] These amendments directed at the Malay rulers were meant to demonstrate that nobody is above the law, but still, the rulers' status is many notches higher than the common man regarding privileges.

Recent political developments in March 2020 reiterates that it is the King's exclusive right to appoint the prime minister without having to test the prime minister's majority in a parliament sitting through a vote of no confidence. On 1 March 2020, Muhyiddin Yassin was sworn in as prime minister by the King, even though Dr. Mahathir Mohamad, the fourth and seventh prime minister, claimed he had majority support to form the government. The Malaysian parliament has 222-seats, and to form the government the prime minister must obtain support from at least 112 members. On the eve of Muhyiddin Yassin's swearing-in ceremony, Mahathir claimed he had the support of 114 MPs, and obtained statutory declarations to demonstrate the level of support.[25]

There are precedents to showcase the ruler's prerogative in naming the political leader. In 2014, the Selangor Chief Minister resigned from his post after an internal struggle within his own parky PKR (People's Justice Party). The Selangor Palace asked for three candidates to be forwarded, but the ruling party only submitted one, Wan Azizah Wan Ismail, who is Anwar Ibrahim's wife. The Selangor ruler rejected the candidate forwarded. The Ruler chose Azmin Ali, a candidate who was not the ruling party's first choice. The ruler assumed the right to reject nominations for the position of the chief minister and name the candidate of his choice even though the person may not be agreed to by the party with the majority in the legislative assembly. Thus, the rulers no longer act on the advice of political elites, as other constitutional monarchs do, but have the prerogative to have a say on political matters as well.

Unquestioned loyalty is also exemplified by the behavior of the political elites. The expectation for loyalty to the leader is demonstrated in their speeches. In 1987, the ruling party UMNO (United Malays National Organization), was split into two factions, between the so-called Team A and Team B. Team A was led by the prime minister and deputy prime minister Mahathir Mohamad and Ghafar Baba, and Team B by Tengku Razaleigh Hamzah and Musa Hitam.

---

24 Barry Wain, *Malaysian Maverick: Mahathir Mohamad in Turbulent Times* (London: Palgrave McMillan, 2009), 205–210.

25 *Today,* "Mahathir says has majority with 114 MPs' backing to be PM, will inform King," 29 February 2020, https://www.todayonline.com/world/coalition-backing-mahathir-pm -has-parliamentary-majority-says-anwar.

Musa was previously the deputy prime minister to Mahathir but resigned after being accused of disloyalty.[26] Team A won the internal party elections by a meager 43 votes out of 1497 votes cast by party delegates, but the implication of the divisive election was even greater. Mahathir removed Team B supporters from cabinet positions, nine in total, including Abdullah Badawi, who won a position as the party's vice president and was regarded as senior in the party.[27] Not excluded from this price of disloyalty were civil servants found to have not supported him.

Any form of challenges, criticisms or even differences of opinion is deemed inappropriate and seen as challenging authority. For many years that followed, the leadership positions of the UMNO presidency and deputy presidency were not challenged, in the name of promoting party unity, although in truth, there was the expectation of loyalty from members to the leader, and not the party's ideology or struggle. This culture of loyalty to the leader continued for many years including under Mahathir's successors. For example, in the 2015 UMNO general assembly, at the height of accusations of the 1MDB (1 Malaysian Development Bank) saga, which hit UMNO leaders, especially the then prime minister, and UMNO president Najib Razak, UMNO members were constantly reminded to be loyal to their leaders to play down any criticisms.[28] In 2016, for being critical of the UMNO leader, and asking questions publicly about 1MDB, the party's deputy president Muhyiddin Yassin, and several top leaders were removed from the party. The 2016 episode is not the only instance where loyalty is upheld as an important value in politics.

The opposite of loyalty is *khianat* (treachery) or betrayal. In 2020, a group of leaders from the ruling Pakatan Harapan (PH) coalition quit the coalition, which led to the fall of the two-year-old government. The so-called "Sheraton move" coup was led by Muhyiddin Yassin and some of his loyal followers. Terms *khianat* and betrayal are used many times by PH leaders to describe the coup leaders, and those terms are considered disvalue in Malay society. On the one hand, the *khianat* trend is growing in the Malaysian political scene and is not only a trend among Malay politicians. Several politicians broke ranks from their parties crossing over to the other parties. The Perikatan Nasional government, which came to power in March 2020, did not have a convincing majority; it has only one or two seats more than the opposition. Thus, party hopping

---

26   Wain, *Malaysian Maverick*, 62.

27   Abdullah Badawi later became Malaysia's prime minister between 2003 and 2009. See Wain, *Malaysian Maverick*, 64.

28   Saat Norshahril, "UMNO General Assembly 2015: Najib's Call for Unity and Loyalty is Hardly Enough," *ISEAS Perspective* 72 (December 29, 2015).

from the opposition was what kept the government in power whenever any of the MPs from the government bench quit.

The prevalence of *khianat* does not mean unquestioned loyalty has been replaced by a new political culture of rational politicking, or politics that are based on principles and values. Normally, the justification for crossing over to the other side of the political divide is shallow. At times, the only reason for moving is to keep the country stable, with very little discussion of policies or party ideology. Moreover, the forging of political alliances is based on the call to preserve Islam's supremacy and Malay unity. Thus, the prevalence of *khianat* is justified through a bigger feudal conception of Malay unity, and this unity can only be achieved if loyalty is expressed towards the prime minister of the day, who has always been a Malay and Muslim. This means that politicians must priorities identity politics over morals and ethics. This was deemed to be the point of departure between Mahathir and Muhyiddin on whether to form an alliance with UMNO after the breakup of Pakatan Harapan government. Mahathir insisted that he could not work with UMNO leaders tainted with corruption or still having their cases heard in the court, while Muhyiddin seems to be more pragmatic in this regard.

In his article on Malay Feudalism, Alatas deliberates extensively on social inequality in Malay society.[29] What he discusses does not only touch on class or income disparity, which exists in all societies, but also on cultural norms and habits. Alatas speaks about the wastages of the ruling class and their attitude in prioritizing grand celebrations. One often hears of elites' grand wedding celebrations for their children, and the invitees are exclusively the elites themselves. Millions of dollars of flowers decorated the ceremony, and the number of invitees making up thousands that are akin to the standards of the royalty.[30] We also hear reports of elites engaging in high culture – buying branded handbags and jewelry – and spending time golfing. All these happened when reports of increasing income inequality in the country. In a report in 2020, income inequality has widened between urban and rural residents, and across all ethnic groups.[31]

The gulf between the rich and the poor, as well privileges rendered to the elites, is exemplified throughout the politicians' handling of the Covid-19

---

29   Alatas, *Modernization and Social Change.*

30   Today, "Dr Mahathir critiques Najib daughter's lavish wedding," 25 April 2015.

31   Ida Lim, "Income inequality in Malaysia widened even while median household income rose to RM5,873 in 2019, according to latest statistics," Malay mail, 10 July 2020. https://www.malaymail.com/news/malaysia/2020/07/10/income-inequality-in-malaysia-widened-even-while-median-household-income-ro/1883232.

pandic. Numerous control movement orders were implemented throughout the country, restricting not only international travel but also domestic, inter-state ones. In January 2021, further curbs were imposed after the Malaysian King, at the advice of the prime minister, declared the state of emergency, which further curbs traveling. Throughout these restrictions, there were complaints of a disjuncture between what ministers and parliamentarians can do versus what commoners can. There was an instance where a minister under the Perikatan Nasional government did not abide by the government's quarantine order after returning from an overseas trip. Netizens were unhappy to see other ordinary citizens were slapped with heavy fines and jailed.[32] He was slapped with a fine of RM 1000. In another instance, a deputy minister could travel to New Zealand to be with his wife and child when travel restrictions were imposed on ordinary citizens. The minister claimed that his 55-day leave was approved by the prime minister, and he was mainly doing his duties as a responsible father. He shortened his trip after complaints from the opposition but could serve home quarantine rather than serving it in an isolation center like the rest.[33] During the Covid-19 pandemic and emergency ruling, several ministers conducted official overseas visits. While they did not break any regulations, and the purpose of these visits were diplomatic, overpublicizing them through mainstream media could be deemed as insensitive given that the majority of ordinary citizens could not travel out of the country.

5 Conclusion: Impact on Modernization

Psychological feudalism is a conceptual tool to understand political thought and behavior. In line with Alatas' scholarship, it is useful to examine the impact on society's modernization and progress. The feudal mentality that existed five to six centuries ago is an antithesis to development in today's context. Psychological feudalism persists in contemporary Malay society albeit in new manifestations. Alatas coined the concept based on his observations in the 1970s, and his students have also applied the concept to describe the political and social conditions in the 1980s and 1990s. This chapter applies the concept and reflects contemporary politics and society. Ultimately, psychological feudalism is not only witnessed in the behavior of the elites, but

---

32   *The Straits Times*, "Malaysian minister in hot water for flouting quarantine apologizes, donates 4 months of his salary," 22 August 2020.

33   *The Straits Times*, "Malaysia's deputy minister back home after controversial New Zealand trip," 24 March 2021.

also in the masses. In the age of social media, vocal groups have spoken up against the elites' abuse of power. While this reflects political maturity, some try to protect these behaviors in the name of loyalty, religion, and Malay culture. Conversely, in Islamic history, speaking up against tyranny and abuses of power is the ideal promoted by Islam. Psychological feudalism is also experienced in the lingo of the elites, mainly to protect their interests, consciously or subconsciously. Their calls for loyalty and their demonstration of piety through the practice of rituals are in line with feudal orientations of Islam. Ironically, they accept the promotion of unlimited wealth and grandeur, which are disvalued in Islam.

Feudal psychology today is also impacted by the Islamic revivalism that hit Southeast Asia since the 1970s. While the movement that began in the urban centers and was promoted by educated middle-class Malays forced Malays to rethink the role of religion in public and private life, it also brought about more conservative ideas in society. For instance, there was a movement to provide an Islamic perspective on governance, laws, politics, education, economic system. The movement has many positive elements. Malays became more committed to their faith, and in some increased piety. Still, this does not eradicate feudal elements that are detrimental to society. The promotion of magic, a common feature of Malay feudal psychology, continues to impede the community's quest towards the embrace of rational and scientific inquiry. Worse, such irrational beliefs are considered part of the Islamic faith. During the feudal period, families seek help from shamans rather than medical doctors to treat sickness, and often they resort to non-scientific methods, including the belief in spirits and ghosts as causing the illness. While Malays have now accepted Western medicine, the belief in spirits and ghosts remains common in society. Islamic revivalism, which promotes Islamic perspectives of life, cements the belief that the religious elites too can provide cures to illness, even though they may not be trained in medicine or psychology. Today, *rawatan* Islam (Islamic healing) and holy water is being popularized in Malay society, which indicates that the Malays have yet to move from their feudal past, which promoted Islamic rituals and symbolism.

All in all, while the Malay feudal political structure no longer exists today, ideas, concepts, and discourses continue to apply in a contemporary setting. Alatas' writing in the 1970s is relevant to this day to understand issues touching on Malay politics, society, and behavior. For as long as the community does not recalibrate their understanding of religion and traditions in the form of values and principles, psychological feudalism will continue to stay. This is not to say that economic and technological progress will be stunted; nonetheless, the prevalence of such feudal psychology will stunt the community from reaching greater heights, especially when pertinent issues dealing with good governance, corruption, checks and balances, among other, are swept under the rug in the name of religion, loyalty, and unity.

Bibliography

Alatas, Syed Hussein. *Islam dan Sosialisma.* Penang: Seruan Masa, 1976.

Alatas, Syed Hussein. *Kita Dengan Islam: Tumbuh Tiada Berbuah.* Singapore: Pustaka Nasional, 1979.

Alatas, Syed Hussein. *Modernization and Social Change: Studies in Modernization, Religion, Social Change and Development in Southeast Asia.* Sydney: Angus & Robertson, 1972.

Alatas, Syed Hussein. *The Myth of the Lazy Native.* London and New York: Frank Cass and Company Ltd., 1977.

Azhar, Ibrahim. *Historical Imagination and Cultural Responses To Colonialism and Nationalism.* Selangor: SIRD, 2017.

Chandra, Muzaffar. *Protector? An Analysis of the Concept and Practice of Lloyalty in Leader-led Relationships within Malay society.* Pulau Pinang: Aliran, 1979.

Ida, Lim. "Income inequality in Malaysia widened even while median household income rose to RM5,873 in 2019, according to latest statistics," Malay mail, 10 July 2020, https://www.malaymail.com/news/malaysia/2020/07/10/income-inequality -in-malaysia-widened-even-while-median-household-income-ro/1883232.

Mannheim, Karl. *Ideology and Utopia: Introduction to the Sociology of Knowledge.* London: Routledge & Kegan Paul, 1936.

Norshahril, Saat. "UMNO General Assembly 2015: Najib's Call for Unity and Loyalty is Hardly Enough." *ISEAS Perspective 72*, December 29, 2015.

Shaharuddin, Maaruf. *Concept of A Hero in Malay Society.* Selangor: SIRD, 2014.

Shaharuddin, Maaruf. *To Err is Inhuman and to Punish Divine: A Study on the Religious Orientation of the Malays.* Singapore: Department of Malay Studies, National University of Singapore, 2002.

Shaharuddin, Maaruf. *Malay Ideas on Development: From Feudal Lord to Capitalist.* Selangor: SIRD, 2014.

Shaharuddin, Maaruf. *The Straits Times*, "Malaysian minister in hot water for flouting quarantine apologizes, donates 4 months of his salary," 22 August 2020.

Shaharuddin, Maaruf. "Malaysia's deputy minister back home after controversial New Zealand trip," 24 March 2021.

Today. "Mahathir says has majority with 114 MPs' backing to be PM, will inform King," 29 February 2020, https://www.todayonline.com/world/coalition-backing-mahathir-pm-has-parliamentary-majority-says-anwar.

Today. "Dr. Mahathir critiques Najib daughter's lavish wedding," 25 April 2015.

Wain, Barry. *Malaysian Maverick: Mahathir Mohamad in Turbulent Times*. London: Palgrave McMillan, 2009.

CHAPTER 9

"Irrational" Beliefs in a "Rational" World

Religion and Modernization

Hira Amin

1   Introduction

As many have pointed out, Syed Hussain Alatas' scholarship focused on one primary goal:

> to deconstruct and demystify the dominant ideas and myths which have allowed the exploitations of the people and societies of Southeast Asia, and which are still used to perpetuate their exploitations by the new national elites in many countries of the developing world.[1]

Alatas was a prolific writer. One of his articles published in the prestigious European Journal of Sociology was entitled, *Religion and Modernization in Southeast Asia*. In this article, Alatas challenges the dominant ideas associated with religion, modernity, secularity, and rationality using the rich case study of Southeast Asia, home to multiple faiths, ethnicities, and traditions. Although written in 1970, Alatas' ideas are still very highly pertinent to today's discussions on contemporary understandings and mechanisms of religion in the modern world.

This chapter outlines and discusses his key arguments in this article bringing it in conversation with current research. It begins with a brief overview of the development of the sociology of religion to allow us to place his ideas in context. It then proceeds to discuss two of Alatas' key arguments: first, the multiplicity paths and effects of modernization and the delinking of modernization with Westernization; second, the complex relationship between religion, rationality, and economic development.

---

1   Riaz Hassan, ed. *Local and Global: Social Transformation in Southeast Asia* (Leiden: Brill, 2005), viii.

© HIRA AMIN, 2023 | DOI:10.1163/9789004521698_011

2 Development of the Sociology of Religion

It is now widely accepted that the modernization-secularization thesis has been empirically disproven, and the world is currently experiencing a vibrant surge in religious belief or "re-enchantment."[2] In simple terms, the thesis posits that religion will eventually fade away from the public sphere and will either cease to exist or be relegated to privatized individual practices and beliefs. Central to this thesis is the juxtaposition between "superstitious" religious beliefs against rational, empirical science or, to put it differently, the strict demarcation between the sacred and the profane. According to the hypothesis, this will happen with the advancement of modernity, which can be briefly characterized economically with the industrial revolution; politically with depersonalized bureaucratic structures and the nation state; and ideologically with the valorization of human reason, progress, and liberation. Emphasizing the latter, Webb Keane describes the overarching narrative as a 'story of human liberation from a host of false beliefs and fetishisms that undermine freedom.'[3] In other words, modernity is emancipation of the human mind; it is removing the dark clouds of religious dogma, its institutions and power structures, allowing the human being and societies to finally rise, flourish, and develop.

From the late 1940s, the academic intelligentsia were strong advocates of this thesis. Some of the influential texts published in this period were: Kingsley Davis' book, *Human Society,* published in 1948, where he described religion as leaves before a fire; Peter Berger's 1967, *The Sacred Canopy*, one of the canonical texts in the sociology of religion that described his account of the slow development of secularization through the historical transformations within Christianity; and Bryan Wilson's *Religion in Secular Society* in 1966, illustrating the declining role and significance of the Church in contemporary society.[4]

These interpretations of society and religion were developed against the backdrop of modernization theories that described the stages of civilization where religion was relegated to the first few primitive periods. While each of these theories have their own subtleties and differences, they all hypothesize a future decline in religion, perceive religion as an early and premature stage of societal development, and provide a sharp distinction between religion and

---

2 Peter Berger, "Further Thoughts on Religion and Modernity." *Society* 49, no. 4 (2012): 313–316.

3 Webb Keane, *Christian Moderns: Freedom and Fetish in The Mission Encounter* (Berkeley: University of California Press, 2007), 5.

4 Kingsley Davis, *Human Society.* New York: MacMillan Co., 1948; Peter Berger, *The Sacred Canopy*. New York: Doubleday & Co., 1990; Bryan R. Wilson, *Religion in A Secular Society*. Harmondsworth: Penguin, 1966.

rationality, which was squarely mapped onto being "traditional" and "modern." Modernist theorists include the 19th century French philosopher, Auguste Comte, who posited that all societies pass through three stages: first is theological, where the world and human experiences were given meaning through gods, spirits and magic; second is metaphysical, where life was understood through teleological philosophy, such as the concepts of abstract essences, observable forces of nature and final causes or, in other words, a depersonalized theology; and lastly is scientific, where explanations came from rational, empirical science.[5] The 19th century German philosopher, Karl Marx took a functional approach to religion, arguing that it was a form of protest for the working classes and thus societies free from the shackles of class will not need religion, which, as he famously stated, was merely "the opium of the masses."[6] The 20th century German sociologist Max Weber also espoused the rationalization and, his most-cited term, "disenchantment" of the world as societies transition into modernity.[7] The American sociologist, Talcott Parsons, developed these ideas further in the 1950s, focusing on the evolution of societies from "traditional" to "modern" forms. His work is often regarded as the most important sociological writings of the 20th century.[8]

Yet, these centrifugal ideas were soon to be challenged. The end of the 20th century witnessed many events that puzzled the Western, liberal, and secular imagination: the Iranian Revolution in 1979, the rise of Solidarity and the Polish Revolution in 1980, the spread of Liberation Theology in Latin America, the rapid rise of Evangelical and Pentecostalism, and, of course, the beginning of the 21st century was marked with the Twin Tower Attacks, to name a few. All were social-political upheavals entangled with religious spirit. Meanwhile, the de-regulation of labor markets led to the rise of minority communities in the West, many of whom came from regions where spirituality and faith symbols were ubiquitous. The religious and social pluralism caused instability, particularly for those who were left out of the economic growth spurred by rapid and relentless globalization. Western governments had to reconceptualize multiculturalism in the management of cosmopolitanism societies against the rise of populist, anti-immigrant, and Far Right parties. This has recently reached its

---

5   Auguste Comte and Harriet Martineau, *The Positive Philosophy of Auguste Comte*. London: J. Chapman, 1853.

6   John Raines, *Marx on Religion*, Philadelphia: Temple University Press, 2011.

7   Robert Yelle and Lorenz Trein, *Narratives of Disenchantment and Secularization*. London: Bloomsbury Academic, 2020.

8   Laurence S Moss and Andrew Savchenko, eds. *Talcott Parsons: Economic Sociologist of the 20th Century*. Hoboken, NJ: John Wiley & Sons, 2006.

apex in the refugee crisis in 2015, which culminated in the division of Europe. Some have called this period, from the 1960s onwards, "liquid modernity,"[9] or "late modernity," characterized by fragmentation, fluidity, and mobility.[10]

In this context, many began to adapt, rethink, and eventually reject the triumphant and linear modernization-secularization paradigms that were becoming increasingly untenable. David Martin, in his 1978 book, *A General Theory of Secularization*, began to paint a more nuanced picture that not all European countries are following the same modernization path, owing to their historical trajectories.[11] But it was not until the 1990s where many wholly reversed the paradigm. In 1994, Jose Casanova published his influential, *Public Religions in the Modern World*; Berger published, *The Desecularisation of the World* in 1999, and Roland Robertson published *Globalization* in 1992, in which he highlighted the role of religion and culture.[12] However, the persistence of Christian movements in North America, such as the Moral Majority – an American, political, Far Right Christian association established in 1979 – and Pentecostalism – originating in many places around the world, including Los Angeles, California – originally led many to state America was an exception to the classical modernization thesis. Yet, by this time even this idea was crumbling. Grace Davie's 2002 book, *Europe: The Exceptional Case*, argued instead that Europe was the exception in following a secular path, not the rest of the world.[13] Dipesh Chakrabarty's path-breaking book, *Provincializing Europe* in 2000, also deftly challenged the universalization of Western modernity, including secularism.[14] Many others followed suit highlighting the need to provincialize Western epistemology and cultural assumptions.[15] This was bolstered theoretically with the

---

9   Zygmunt Bauman, *Liquid Modernity*. New York: Polity Press, 2000.

10   Ulrich Beck, *Risk Society: Towards a New Modernity*. Thousand Oaks, CA: Sage Publications, 1992; Anthony Giddens, *The Consequences of Modernity*. Stanford: Stanford University Press, 1991.

11   David A. Martin, *A General Theory of Secularization*. Oxford: Basil Blackwell, 1978.

12   José Casanova, *Public Religions in The Modern World*. Chicago: University of Chicago Press, 1994; Peter Berger, ed. *The Desecularization of the World*. Grand Rapid, MI: William B. Eerdmans Publishing Company, 1999; Roland Robertson, *Globalization*. London: Sage, 1992.

13   Davie, Grace. *Europe, The Exceptional Case*. London: Darton, Longman & Todd, 2002.

14   Dipesh Chakrabarty, *Provincializing Europe: Postcolonial Thought and Historical Difference*. Princeton, NJ: Princeton University Press, 2000.

15   Raewyn Connell, *Southern Theory: The Global Dynamics of Knowledge in Social Science*. Cambridge: Polity Press, 2007; Sujata Patel, ed. *The ISA Handbook of Diverse Sociological Traditions*. London: Sage, 2010; Robbie Shilliam, ed. *International Relations and Non-Western Thought: Imperialism, Colonialism and Investigations of Global Modernity*. London: Routledge, 2011.

conceptualization of modernity in the plural, such as "entangled modernities," "multiple modernities" and "varieties of modernities."[16] All decoupled modernization from Westernization as well as its superior status. By this time, prominent European philosophers, who had hitherto side-lined religion, were forced to enter the debate, for example, Jürgen Habermas, who published *Religion in the Public Sphere* in 2006.[17] More sophisticated understandings of secularism and religion arose, particularly in the works of Talal Asad, Charles Taylor, and Tomoko Masuzawa, with the former and the latter paying particular attention to the role of European imperialism in the shaping and re-making of ideas and concepts.[18]

As researchers increasingly witnessed the rise of religious fervor in the Global South, Europe and its secularization journey became the anomaly. The question switched from why is the non-European world still religious to why is Europe devoid of religious vitality? However, some still argue that this is simply a slow transition period and that with increasing rates of literacy and education, secularization will eventually occur in the Global South. Some call this the "last gasp" thesis but anyone familiar with the religious movements around the world can see that this is not going to end any time soon. Religious movements have proven to be surprisingly resilient, refashioning, altering, and even attracting more religious adherents in the face of a myriad of challenges and rapid social change.

In the last decade, this has been the subject of many publications, namely the transformations, adaptions, and contestations of religion in modernity in the face of growing migration, diasporas, transnational religions, post-colonial politics, development, and globalization. All of which is increasingly complicating the picture of contemporary religion, further illustrating the weakness of the classical and linear modernization-secularization paradigms. In every stage, indeed there were, and still are, dissenters to the overall trends. Publishing in the 1970s ideas that have become more mainstream from the 1990s onwards, Alatas was most-definitely among them.

---

16   Göran Therborn, "Entangled Modernities," *European Journal of Social Theory* 6 no. 3 (2003): 293–305; Shmuel N. Eisenstadt, "Multiple Modernities," *Daedalus* 129, No. 1 (Winter, 2000): 1–29; Volker H. Schmidt, "Multiple Modernities or Varieties of Modernity?" *Current Sociology* 54, no. 1 (2006): 77–97.

17   Jürgen Habermas, "Religion in the Public Sphere," *European Journal of Philosophy* 14, no. 1 (2006): 1–25.

18   Talal Asad, *Formations of the Secular: Christianity, Islam, Modernity*. Stanford: Stanford University Press, 2003; Charles Taylor, *A Secular Age*. Cambridge, MA: Harvard University Press, 2007; Tomoko Masuzawa, *The Invention of World Religions*. Chicago: University of Chicago Press, 2005.

3 Pluralizing Modernity

Alatas began his article *Religion and Modernization in Southeast Asia* with a critical look at modernity, criticizing the field that uses the term without careful consideration. Alatas argued that the problem is two-fold. First, scholars narrowly conflate modernization with Westernization and only categorize as "modern" very particular forms of governance and economic orders that follow Western European-style democracy, institutions, and industrial capitalism. Second, he states that there is confusion between modernization and the *effects* of modernization. He cites the example of the weakening of cultural and religious dogma as not part of modernization, but one possible *side-effect* of modernization that is relative to time and place.[19] He argues that one should consider modernization as:

> autonomous cultural elements which are subject to diffusion *without* necessarily being accompanied by Western culture ...

Looking back at history, he states that this a general pattern:

> We are compelled by the nature of cultural diffusion to make this distinction. In the case of the history of Europe this distinction has never been questioned. When Europe adopted many technological, scientific, philosophical, and material elements of the Islamic civilization during the Middle Ages, this adoption has never been characterized as Islamization or Arabicization, and rightly so. The adoption of those elements were not accompanied by wholesale introduction of Islamic customs, morals, philosophy, rituals, rites of passage, values, habits, etc.[20]

While Alatas did not use the term "multiple modernities" or the "pluralization of modernity," the central tenets are the same. He is essentially arguing that there are multiple forms, pathways, and modes of modernity that are deeply contingent on historical trajectories and social, cultural, and religious traditions. As described above, this concept was popularized and theorized in more depth after a few decades. It proved to be a useful tool in understanding the social phenomena in different societies, particularly in the resilience

---

19 Syed Hussein Alatas, "Religion and Modernization in Southeast Asia," *European Journal of Sociology* 11, no. 2 (1970): 265.

20 Ibid., 268–269.

of religious traditions and their continuous place in the contemporary world. Casanova summarizes this point:

> Traditions are forced to respond and adjust to modern conditions, but in the process of reformulating their traditions for modern contexts, they also help to shape the particular forms of modernity.[21]

The acknowledgement and delinking of modernization with narrow Western experiences was a milestone and positive step forward in the social sciences. Yet, paradoxically, just as religion did not disappear but transformed, so did the modernization-secularization narrative. The thesis stubbornly persists both in academia and in the wider political and public imagination in various guises. In general, religion and people of faith are accepted and celebrated if they resemble or are moving towards "liberal," "Western," "secular" values or else they are branded as "traditional," "irrational," or in need of reform or a reformation. In other words, there is "good" religion and "bad" religion, which maps the original "modern" and "Western" vs. "traditional" and "non-Western" dichotomy. Negative characteristics or actions of people with faith are seen through the prism of unrelenting traditional beliefs and the inability to modernize, rather than the wider political power dynamics usually linked to colonialism.

This is perhaps most conspicuously seen in discussions related to religion and violence, particularly when it involves Muslim subjects. Speaking about sectarian violence in the Middle East, Hashemi and Postel describe a "new orientalism" where instability in this region is framed primarily as a predisposition of violence in Islam. Long-standing religious conflict is due to 'putatively primordial hatred and antagonisms between Sunnis and Shi'a ... since the dawn of Islam.'[22] They illustrate how this view is shared widely from senior politicians, such as Barak Obama, to both liberal and far-right media pundits, as well as established academics and policy makers.[23] They introduce the term, "sectarinization," which, as opposed to "sectarianism," has a heavy emphasis on doctrinal debates, includes politics and how it is shaped by popular mobilization with religious identity markers, class dynamics, fragile states, and geopolitical rivalries.

---

21   José Casanova, "Rethinking Secularization: A Global Comparative Perspective," *The Hedgehog Review* 8 (2006): 14.

22   Nader Hashemi and Danny Postel, *Sectarianization* (New York: Oxford University Press, 2017), 2.

23   Ibid., 3.

Arguably one of the best studies on this topic is William Cavanaugh's, *The Myth of Religious Violence.*[24] Cavanaugh deftly challenges the idea that religion has an innate penchant for erratic behavior and violence. Secular power is not inherently more or less violent than religion – this is not his concern – but he illustrates how certain acts of violence are rationalized and even praised while others are deemed fanatical and savage, legitimizing the use of further violence to curtail it. This stems from the:

> broader Enlightenment narrative that has invented a dichotomy between the religious and the secular and constructed the former as an irrational and dangerous impulse that must give way in public to rational, secular forms of power.[25]

Besides violence, another subtler guise is the focus on how religions are moving either towards or away from Western, secular values including privatization, individualization and rationalization of faith, and liberal values such as gender equality. This is particularly the case in the growing study of Muslims in Europe where successful integration in society is premised on their compatibility with European values.[26] If they are not compatible then they are framed as having unstable identities, caught between tradition and modernity and even prone to violent outbursts. A common way this is portrayed is through a supposed "generational clash," where young Muslims are caught between "traditional" parents and religious leaders and the "modern" wider society. One striking example is Robert Leiken's, *Europe's Angry Muslims: The Revolt of the Second Generation.*[27] The title alone is telling; the text is even more blunt:

> [t]he second-generation British Muslim, lodged between traditional and modern, tribal and urban, was an acute case of a "marginal man," to use the term of Robert Park, a founder of the Chicago school of sociology and a pioneer in the study of immigrant assimilation. Park wrote that one consequence of immigration has been to create "the marginal man," one whom fate has condemned to live in two societies and in two different but

---

24   William T. Cavanaugh, *The Myth of Religious Violence.* New York: Oxford University Press, 2009.

25   Ibid., 4.

26   Frank Peter, "Individualization and Religious Authority in Western European Islam," *Islam and Christian–Muslim Relations* 17, no. 1 (2006).

27   Robert Leiken, *Europe's Angry Muslims: The Revolt of the Second Generation.* New York: Oxford University Press, 2015.

antagonistic cultures. The result can be "an unstable character" in whose mind "conflicting cultures meet and fuse." In Muslim Europe, fusion does not take place without fail. Defiant sons avail themselves of justifications they learn from radical recruiters.[28]

This is not only specific to Muslims. Alexander notes how British Asians in general are framed as being "caught between two cultures" since the 1970s, which purportedly leads them to gang-related violence, fundamentalism, or criminal behavior.[29] Foner and Dreby find that this battleground framework is common for most immigrants in the West.[30] Rather than focusing on negotiation and cooperation, they, as well as others, such as Cooke and Waite, assert that conflicts within the immigrant family are seen as inevitable.[31] It seems as though this idea of the inherently "traditional" and hence "irrational" and potentially dangerous primitive subject has persisted. Not only is modernization still only an act Europeans can do and have done successfully but this leads to securitization and the constant policing non-European bodies, with any means necessary.

The rise of more critical interventions is slowly correcting this narrative. However, yet another subtle way these ideas have persisted is through giving far more attention and praise to "modern" or "modernizing" Muslims, where modern is strikingly Western. This is not to say that Muslims in the West are not moving towards this direction; some definitely are and this is a trend worth studying. Lewis and Hamid's otherwise brilliant and lucid overview of new directions amongst British Muslims, for example, at times implicitly juxtaposes reformist and traditional educational institutions, where the former are moving towards critical thinking, philosophy, and world history and the latter are still ossified in the past.[32] There is research to suggest alternative, more nuanced narratives of these "traditional" institutions.[33]

---

28   Ibid., 154.

29   Claire Alexander, "Imagining the Politics of BrAsian Youth," in *A Postcolonial People: South Asians in Britain*, ed. N. Ali, Virinder S. Kalra, and S. Sayyid (London: Hurst & Company, 2006), 258–271.

30   Nancy Foner and Joanna Dreby, "Relations Between the Generations in Immigrant Families." *Annual Review of Sociology* 37 (2011): 545–64.

31   Ibid; Joanne Cook and Louise Waite, "'I think I'm more free with them' – Conflict, Negotiation and Change in Intergenerational Relations in African Families Living in Britain.' *Journal of Ethnic and Migration Studies* 42, no. 8 (2015).

32   Philip Lewis and Sadek Hamid. *British Muslims: New Directions in Islamic Thought, Creativity and Activism.* Edinburgh: Edinburgh University Press, 2018.

33   Ron Geaves, "An exploration of the viability of partnership between dar al-ulum and Higher Education Institutions in North West England focusing upon pedagogy and

The problem is twofold. First, there is a definite imperative to at least neutralize the negative stereotypes of Muslims that are pervasive in politics, academia, media, and entertainment. These academic accounts are definitely welcome in a hostile atmosphere of growing Islamophobia and populist politics where European Muslims are targeted to increase votes.[34] But second, and perhaps more important, is that the language and paradigms do not exist in secular social sciences to accurately describe these complex phenomena. We still have not moved from the binary categories of "religion" and "secular" or "tradition" and "modern." There is very little space, positive language, or frameworks for institutions that are modern yet not Western without awkward terminology. For instance, Peter Van Der Veer, in his fascinating comparison of religion and spirituality in China and India describes it as a 'syntagmatic chain of religion-magic-secularity-spirituality.'[35] He defines these terms as interconnected, which do not have 'stable meanings independently from one another,' and crucially this chain is an integral part of their modernity.[36] Van der Veer's work is not merely localizing these experiences but illustrating how the "imperial encounter" shaped and help shape the religious-spiritual-secular dynamic.

Therefore, the modernization-secularization thesis persists in multiple guises. While the acknowledgement and theorization of the plurality of modernity has pushed the debate forward, there is still a long way to go to dig out the deeply rooted premises and assumptions associated with the classical thesis. But this raises serious questions. How do we account for a multi-polar world with various, even opposing, epistemological premises in one discipline? How do we account for complex and uncomfortable histories, especially when they play an underlying yet significant role in our current politics and policies?

Reflecting on the current state of sociology, Bhambra and Santos offer two orientations: connected sociologies epistemologies of the South.[37] Bhambra explains connected sociologies as:

---

relevance." *Advance HE Report*, 2012; Haroon Sidat, "Between Tradition and Transition: An Islamic Seminary, or *Dar al-Uloom* in Modern Britain," *Religions* 9, no. 10 (2018).

34   H. A. Hellyer, "Europe's identity crisis: Muslims are collateral damage in the continent's culture wars." In *The Globe and Mail*. (March 2021). https://www.theglobeandmail.com/opinion/article-europes-identity-crisis-muslims-are-collateral-damage-in-the/.

35   Peter van der Veer, *The Modern Spirit of Asia: The Spiritual and the Secular in China and India* (Princeton, NJ: Princeton University Press, 2014), 8.

36   Ibid., 9–10.

37   Gurminder Bhambra and Boaventura de Sousa Santos, "Introduction: Global Challenges for Sociology," *Sociology* 51, no. 1 (2017): 3–10.

recognition of the historical connections generated by processes of colonialism, enslavement, dispossession, and appropriation, that were previously elided in mainstream sociology.[38]

Santos describes epistemologies of the South as allowing:

> Oppressed social groups to represent the world as their own and in their own terms, for only thus will they be able to change it according to their own aspirations.[39]

There are a growing number of voices along these lines, particularly those calling for decolonization. It remains to be seen whether they can dismantle the modernization-secularization thesis or if it will transform into yet another ominous guise.

4   Religion, Rationality, and Economic Development

One of the most influential texts regarding the relationship between religion and economic development was Weber's, *The Protestant Ethic and the Spirit of Capitalism,* published in 1905 (translated in English by Parsons in 1930). In it he argued that Protestantism, specifically the Calvinist strand, imbued people with a particular set of values that was the foundation of modern capitalism in the West.[40] Critical of other faith doctrines, he argued that other regions had equal access to the resources needed for modern capitalism to flourish, the difference is they did not have the Protestant concept of linking worldly success as a sign of God's acceptance and eternal salvation, and to make efficient use of God's resources in the world. Many, including his contemporaries, discredited his ideas through either highlighting other reasons for the rise of modern capitalism or proving other groups such as the Catholics enjoyed similar economic success.[41]

Alatas was another key dissenting voice using Southeast Asia an ideal example, as it was a mixture of different traditions and ethnicities, each with their

---

38   Ibid., 6.

39   Ibid., 5.

40   Max Weber, *The Protestant Ethic and the Spirit of Capitalism*, Trans. Talcott Parsons. Dover Publications, 1930.

41   Mehmet Karacuka, "Religion and Economic Development in History: Institutions and the Role of Religious Networks," *Journal of Economic Issues* 2, no. 1 March (2018): 58.

own rich history related to the region. Using data and a sophisticated understanding of the different religions and social contexts, Alatas main argument in his 1970 article, "Religion and Modernization in Southeast Asia," is that religion never impedes modernization and development; it is either neutral or encourages it.[42] Those who argue otherwise, he says, do so because of three things: lack of understanding of the faith, lack of considering the relationship with other social and cultural factors or the absence of empirical data. He was particularly critical of Weber and his statements against the rationality of Islam and Chinese animism and their subsequent hindrance to modernization.[43]

With Islam, Alatas initially points out some basic facts. First, out of all the founders and Prophets of religion, Muhammad was the only trader. Second, Islam was spread to Southeast Asia through traders and many of the spiritual leaders of the Muslim world are traders. Third, Islamic doctrine clearly favors the one who earns his livelihood through honest and lawful means. Alatas then goes on to illustrate how Muslims of different ethnicities in the region have experienced different outcomes and express various outlooks towards modern economic action depending on many factors such as which industry they dominated. For example, while the Malay Muslims were concentrated in government services and agriculture, South Indian Muslims were centered around tobacco, currency exchange, and worked alongside the Chinese in other industries such as restaurants. Other Muslims such as the Minangkabau, Bugis, and Acehnese Muslims in Indonesia were also economically active. However, some non-Muslim ethnic groups shared similar economic traits and approaches with the Malay. Alatas attributes these values as a 'hangover from the feudal past and consolidated by colonial influence that forms the greatest obstacle to modernization in contemporary Southeast Asia.'[44] Therefore, he cogently argues with empirical data that one cannot conclude that Islam, *per se,* is helping or hindering modern economic development; other complex factors are involved.

How various social, political, religious, geopolitical, and economic factors integrate to generate unique circumstances is described in the article best in relation to the Chinese in Malaysia. Weber was particularly critical of Chinese animism – a belief that spirits inhabit and are embedded in the natural, material world. This went against one of the core principles and pre-conditions of the modernization process, an objectification of nature. Alatas challenges Weber's argument that Chinese animism prevented the rise of modern capitalism by

---

42   Alatas, "Religion and Modernization."
43   Ibid.
44   Ibid., 274.

illustrating how the same belief system yet in a different historical, social, and economic background setting actively supported the Chinese in Malaya to succeed. He gives many reasons why the Chinese were economically more successful in Malaya than in mainland China. One of which was their perceived "irrational" belief in honoring their dead ancestors by building temples, special family graveyards and burning paper money as a way of sending remittances to the dead. These rituals meant that wealth accumulation was important in order to fund these religious practices. This was bolstered in Malaya with the high status that was given to businessmen and successful entrepreneurs. In mainland China, intellectuals, government officials, and teachers had the highest occupation status followed by the businessmen. In Malaysia, the ranking was the opposite. When a person of high-status dies, their deification raises their prestige further, encouraging others to follow their path. Temples based on deceased successful Chinese entrepreneurs in Malaysia became famous centers of worship stimulating even more business and entrepreneurship.

Overall, Alatas' main argument is that religious ideas, concepts, and rituals can either be in line with the modernization process directly or indirectly. Even when it is not congruent, those beliefs could be neutralized by other factors. In other words, he views religion as a complex factor inextricably intertwined and in constant conversation with other surrounding variables that are also in constant motion. He argues that Islam directly promotes trade, commercial exchange, and a strong work ethic. Chinese animism indirectly does this through many means, one primary way is through rituals commemorating and appeasing the dead that require the acquisition of large amounts of wealth. Nevertheless, success lies not just in these doctrinal beliefs but how they interact with the wider ecosystem of social, political, and historical dimensions, which either bolsters them further or suppresses them. This explains the different outcomes for Muslims in Malaya and the Chinese in Malaya who believe in animism.

Since the 1970s, there has been a large body of quantitative studies that seek to examine and quantify the relationship between economic development and religious belief. Despite this, the conclusions are far from conclusive. There are four key problematic issues. First, what precisely counts as religious doctrine; each religion has trends and sub-trends and localized versions of the faith. Hinduism, for example, does not have a defined Divine text that is accessible to all. Pentecostalism, like many global religious movements, has various currents that interact with local indigenous traditions and beliefs. Some argue that all religions to a certain degree promote prosperity, hard-work, diligence, and self-reliance and the trope of the secluded ascetic is inaccurate. Second, being part of a religious group has several indirect and nebulous outcomes that can significantly impact economic development, such as mental health, physical health, social capital, networks, and rituals that require accumulation of wealth, as seen above in the case of Chinese animism and venerating the deceased. Measuring these indirect factors and how they interconnect is no easy task. For example, Campante and Yanagizawa-Drott argue that fasting in Ramadan for Muslims has the potential to limit economic activity.[45] However, one could counter-argue that fasting has a positive impact on mental and physical health as well as increase in social capital as generally people gather in places of worship, and many donate large amounts of money inside and outside their country. These indirect consequences could take time to bear fruit or could be impeded by other external factors. Third, is the interaction of religion with social, historical, and political factors all of that adapt and change with time. Alatas describes this best in his article about the impact of feudalism and the ruling elites' practices that stifled economic growth in segments of the Muslim Malay population.[46] Fourth, is the major debates inside the field of economic development. The factors that impede or promote development and the extent of which each factor is required, and the context is another divisive issue. In short, religion is inextricably bound together with many complex and constantly changing variables, making it almost impossible to draw positive or negative correlations with economic development, however defined. This results in multiple studies without conclusive results or that are not generalizable outside that specific time period and context about the overall impact of religion on economic development.

However, there have also been many qualitative and ethnographic studies that give us a more nuanced picture and common trends. One theme is how many of the rising middle classes and increasingly economically successful communities around the world are also deeply religious, even following strands of faith that are seemingly antithetical to modern, rational principles of nature and science. Once again, this goes against the notion that religions are merely "superstitious" beliefs for the lower stratus of society that will eventually disappear with mass education and rising literacy rates. Even with targeted campaigns against certain religious rituals and beliefs, what is perceived as "superstition" remained. Examining China and India, two rapidly developing nations, Van der Veer discusses and compares modern rationalizing movements

---

45 Filipe Campante and David Yanagizawa-Drott, "Does religion affect economic growth and happiness? Evidence from Ramadan." *The Quarterly Journal of Economics* 130, no. 2 (2015): 615–658.

46 Alatas, "Religion and Modernization."

such as the Brahmanical reform movements and Confucianism both of which attempted to cull "irrational" beliefs and practices.[47] But, he argues that:

> The campaigns against magical superstition definitely had effects, but their insertion in local contexts did not lead to the victory of positivist rationality, but rather to complex transformations of local understandings of historical change and supernatural agency.[48]

In other words, complete "disenchantment" never took place neither through economic development nor through rationalizing movements.

One main example is the spectacular rise of Pentecostalism, dubbed as the fastest growing religious movement in the contemporary world, changing the face of global Christianity from the late 19th century onwards. Pentecostalism includes many indigenous and localized rituals and beliefs, yet scholars loosely define it as having three core characteristics: personal relationship with Jesus Christ; rituals that include invoking the power of the Holy Spirit; experiencing "gifts" of the Holy Spirit, such as speaking in tongues, miraculous healing, and prophecy.[49] What is striking is that Pentecostalism, also known as charismatic Christianity, has multiple birth places from the Global North to the Global South. It is not a continuation or the persistence of an archaic form of Christianity, it is a form that was developed in the midst of modernity, in the late 19th and early 20th century. This is the time that modernization, in terms of capitalist development, urbanization, and migration was in full swing. In short, rather than diminishing religion, the conditions of modernity enabled a vibrant, mystical, and supernatural form of Christianity to spread and flourish.[50]

One specific example is that of the El Shaddai in the Philippines with an estimated 10–15 million members. It is a form of Southeast Asian Pentecostalism, also known as a Catholic Charismatic movement, famous for their members' self-crucifixion and self-flagellation rituals. Peter J. Braunlein states how these practices were born in the 1960s – an intense period of post-colonial modernization for the region.[51] On a recent research trip, he notes that neither the

---

47 Van der Veer, *The Modern Spirit of Asia.*
48 Ibid., 130.
49 Robert W. Hefner, *Global Pentecostalism in the 21st Century.* Bloomington: Indiana University Press, 2013.
50 Ibid.
51 Peter J. Braunlein, "Spirits in Southeast Asia's Modernity: An Overview," *Dorisea Working Paper* 1, (2013).

performers nor the spectators were exclusively from the lower uneducated classes of society; many were university educated and middle class.

Another example of a specific form of Pentecostalism is in Wenzhou, an industrial city in China's Zheijang province. Nanlai Cao describes the strong revival of Christianity throughout China in the last few decades corresponding to the period of rapid economic reform and urbanization.[52] Strikingly, this has not resulted in a sharp divide between the urban and rural. Taking the case of Wenzhou, she describes how there is 'a new synthesis of the charismatic, experiential and the rational, theological forms of Christianity.'[53] She particularly notes how elite businessmen rely on "prayer-calling mothers," usually illiterate, rural women who claim healing powers and spiritual capital, to pray for the business success. She concludes that Pentecostal forms of supernaturalism has 'survived socioeconomic mobility in the reform era.'[54]

Social mobility and rising middle classes are adapting these strands of faith, some of which are associated with miracles, charismatic leaders with supernatural abilities, and vivacity. But crucially, they are not "disenchanting" nor rationalizing them entirely. There are many other examples, such as from Buddhism, Hinduism, and Sufism. Berger also notes a rising number of self-confident Pentecostals and Evangelicals in academia, an elite space.[55] The same trend can be seen amongst religious Muslims, entering academia, and making their mark in conferences and publications.

5   Conclusion

It is predicted that by the middle of the 21st century with very few exceptions all the world's major religions will grow both in absolute numbers and as a percentage of the world's population (Pew Research Centre 2015). Although it is estimated that people with no faith – agnostics and atheists – will also grow in absolute numbers, they will shrink in terms of the world's population from 16% in 2010 to 13% by 2050. This rise is mainly down to fertility and mortality rates; conversion is difficult to measure as in some countries it is illegal or

---

52   Nanlai Cao, "Gender, modernity and Pentecostal Christianity in China," in *Global Pentecostalism in the 21st Century*, ed. Robert Hefner (Bloomington: Indiana University Press. 2013), 149–175.

53   Ibid., 151.

54   Ibid., 171.

55   Peter Berger, "Further Thoughts on Religion and Modernity," *Society* 49, no. 4 (2012): 313–316.

socially unacceptable. Whatever the case, one conclusion we can comfortably state is that religion, with all its sparkle and vitality, is here to stay.

The relationship with modernity and religion is a highly complex one owing to the malleability of religious beliefs and practices as well as constantly changing socio-cultural and political variables, which in turn constitute religiosity. Alatas' article began to unpack this. This chapter only discussed his two core ideas: modernization as not equal to Westernization and the relationship between rationality, religion, and economic development. Both are still highly relevant for today's discussions. While many now concede that there are multiple forms of modernity, the superiority of the Western enterprise still keeps a tight rein on prevailing frameworks. Although broad studies on religion and economic development cannot provide conclusive results, ethnographic and smaller qualitative studies reveal how social mobility does not lead to jettisoning religion and how faith becomes integrated into the economy.

What remains to be seen is if sociology as a discipline can take these concepts and adapt and integrate them on an equal footing, moving past Western-centric paradigms. But what is imperative, is to take theorists from the Global South seriously who have much to offer and have become the rule, rather than the exception.

Bibliography

Alatas, Syed Hussein. "Religion and Modernization in Southeast Asia." *European Journal of Sociology* 11, no. 2 (1970): 265–296.

Alexander, Claire. "Imagining the Politics of BrAsian Youth." In *A Postcolonial People: South Asians in Britain*, edited by N. Ali, Virinder S. Kalra, and S. Sayyid, 258–271. London: Hurst & Company, 2006.

Asad, Talal. *Formations of the Secular: Christianity, Islam, Modernity*. Stanford, CA: Stanford University Press, 2003.

Bauman, Zygmunt. *Liquid Modernity*. New York: Polity Press, 2000.

Beck, Ulrich. *Risk Society: Towards a New Modernity*. Thousand Oaks, CA: Sage Publications, 1992.

Berger, Peter. *The Sacred Canopy*. New York: Doubleday & Co, 1990.

Berger, Peter. "Further Thoughts on Religion and Modernity." *Society* 49, no. 4 (2012): 313–316.

Berger, Peter, ed. *The Desecularization of the World*. Grand Rapids, MI: William B. Eerdmans Publishing Company, 1999.

Bhambra, Gurminder and Boaventura de Sousa Santos. "Introduction: Global Challenges for Sociology." *Sociology* 51, no. 1 (2017): 3–10.

Braunlein, Peter. J. "Spirits in Southeast Asia's Modernity: An Overview." *Dorisea Working Paper* 1, 2013.

Campante, Filipe and David Yanagizawa-Drott. "Does Religion Affect Economic Growth and Happiness? Evidence from Ramadan." *The Quarterly Journal of Economics* 130, no. 2 (2015): 615–658.

Cao, Nanlai. "Gender, Modernity and Pentecostal Christianity in China." In *Global Pentecostalism in the 21st Century,* edited by Robert Hefner, 149–175. Bloomington: Indiana University Press, 2013.

Casanova, José. "Rethinking Secularization: A Global Comparative Perspective." *The Hedgehog Review* 8 (2006): 7–22.

Casanova, José. *Public Religions in The Modern World.* Chicago: University of Chicago Press, 1994.

Cavanaugh, William T. *The Myth of Religious Violence.* New York: Oxford University Press, 2009.

Chakrabarty, Dipesh. *Provincializing Europe: Postcolonial Thought and Historical Difference.* Princeton, NJ: Princeton University Press, 2000.

Comte, Auguste, and Harriet Martineau. *The Positive Philosophy of Auguste Comte.* London: J. Chapman, 1853.

Connell, Raewyn. *Southern Theory: The Global Dynamics of Knowledge in Social Science.* Cambridge, UK: Polity Press, 2007.

Cook, Joanne and Louise Waite. "'I Think I'm More Free with Them" – Conflict, Negotiation and Change in Intergenerational Relations in African Families Living in Britain.' *Journal of Ethnic and Migration Studies* 42, no. 8 (2015).

Davie, Grace. *Europe: The Exceptional Case.* London: Darton, Longman & Todd, 2002.

Davis, Kingsley. *Human Society.* New York: MacMillan Co., 1948.

Eisenstadt, Shmuel N. "Multiple Modernities" *Daedalus* 129, No. 1 (Winter, 2000): 1–29.

Foner, Nancy, and Joanna Dreby. "Relations Between the Generations in Immigrant Families." *Annual Review of Sociology* 37 (2011): 545–64.

Geaves, Ron. "An Exploration of the Viability of Partnership between Dar al-Ulum and Higher Education Institutions in North West England focusing upon Pedagogy and Relevance." *Advance HE Report,* 2012. https://www.advance-he.ac.uk/knowle dge-hub/exploration-viability-partnership-between-dar-al-ulum-and-higher-edu cation.

Giddens, Anthony. *The Consequences of Modernity.* Stanford, CA: Stanford University Press, 1991.

Habermas, Jurgen. "Religion In the Public Sphere." *European Journal of Philosophy* 14, no. 1 (2006): 1–25.

Hashemi, Nader, and Danny Postel. *Sectarianization.* New York: Oxford University Press, 2017.

Hassan, Riaz, ed. *Local and Global: Social Transformation in Southeast Asia*. Leiden: Brill, 2005.

Hefner, Robert W. *Global Pentecostalism in the 21St Century*. Bloomington, IN: Indiana University Press, 2013.

Hellyer, H. A. "Europe's Identity Crisis: Muslims are Collateral Damage in the Continent's Culture Wars." In *The Globe and Mail*. (March 2021). https://www.theg lobeandmail.com/opinion/article-europes-identity-crisis-muslims-are-collateral -damage-in-the/.

Karacuka, Mehmet. "Religion and Economic Development in History: Institutions and the Role of Religious Networks." *Journal of Economic Issues* 2, no. 1 (March 2018).

Keane, Webb. *Christian Moderns: Freedom and Fetish in The Mission Encounter*. Berkeley: University of California Press, 2007.

Kingsley, David. *Human Society*. New York: MacMillan, 1948.

Leiken, Robert. *Europe's Angry Muslims: The Revolt of the Second Generation*. New York: Oxford University Press, 2015.

Lewis, Philip, and Sadek Hamid. *British Muslims: New Directions in Islamic Thought, Creativity and Activism*. Edinburgh: Edinburgh University Press, 2018.

Martin, David A. *A General Theory of Secularization*. Oxford: Basil Blackwell, 1978.

Masuzawa, Tomoko. *The Invention of World Religions*. Chicago: University of Chicago Press, 2005.

Moss, Laurence S., and Andrew Savchenko, eds. *Talcott Parsons: Economic Sociologist of The 20Th Century*. Hoboken, NJ: John Wiley & Sons, 2006.

Patel, Sujata, ed. *The ISA Handbook of Diverse Sociological Traditions*. London: Sage, 2010.

Peter, Frank. "Individualization and Religious Authority in Western European Islam." *Islam and Christian–Muslim Relations* 17, no. 1 (2006).

Pew Research Centre. "The Future of World Religions: Population Growth Projections 2010–2050." (April 2015). https://www.pewforum.org/2015/04/02/religious-projecti ons-2010-2050/.

Raines, John. *Marx on Religion*. Philadelphia: Temple University Press, 2011.

Robertson, Roland. *Globalization*. London: SAGE, 1992.

Schmidt, Volker H. "Multiple Modernities or Varieties of Modernity?" *Current Sociology* 54, no. 1 (2006): 77–97.

Shilliam, Robbie, ed. *International Relations and Non-Western Thought: Imperialism, Colonialism and Investigations of Global Modernity*. London: Routledge, 2011.

Sidat, Haroon. "Between Tradition and Transition: An Islamic Seminary, or *Dar al-Uloom* in Modern Britain." *Religions* 9, no. 10 (2018).

Taylor, Charles. *A Secular Age*. Cambridge, MA: Harvard University Press, 2007.

Therborn, Göran. "Entangled Modernities." *European Journal of Social Theory* 6 no. 3 (2003): 293–305.

Veer, Peter van der. *The Modern Spirit of Asia: The Spiritual and the Secular in China and India*. Princeton, NJ: Princeton University Press, 2014.

Weber, Max. *The Protestant Ethic and the Spirit of Capitalism*. Translated by Talcott Parsons. Dover Publications, 1930.

Wilson, Bryan R. *Religion in A Secular Society*. New York: Harmondsworth/Penguin, 1966.

Yelle, Robert, and Lorenz Trein. *Narratives Of Disenchantment and Secularization*. London: Bloomsbury Academic, 2020.

PART 3

Mythologizing and Demythologizing the Native

∵

CHAPTER 10

Demythologizing Dominant Discourses

Syed Hussein Alatas' The Myth of the Lazy Native *and the Discourse on Malay Cultural Values and Underdevelopment*

Zawawi Ibrahim

1 Introduction

A critical epistemological question in the sociology of knowledge revolves around the imperative for Asian scholarship to decolonize itself from Orientalist and Eurocentric forms of knowledge.[1] As is well known, the Western discourse of Orientalism was eloquently critiqued in the influential writings of Edward Said, which in turn spawned an enormous literature of its own, both critical and complementary.[2] Emerging from a critical sociology of knowledge, Syed Hussein Alatas' *The Myth of the Lazy Native* actually preceded and, in some senses, anticipated Said's pathbreaking argument.[3] Alatas' innovative analysis, harnessed to various disciplines within the social sciences and humanities more generally, has played a vital role in advancing new understandings of

---

1 In writing this chapter, I have drawn upon a number of my earlier publications that reflect on the seminal contribution of Syed Hussein Alatas, notably: Zawawi Ibrahim, "Return of the Lazy Native: Explaining Malay/Immigrant Labour Transition in Terengganu Plantation Society," in *Local and Global: Social Transformation in Southeast Asia: Essays in Honour of Professor Syed Hussein Alatas*, ed. Riaz Hassan (Leiden: Brill, 2005), 45–70; Zawawi Ibrahim and NoorShah M.S. "Indigenising Knowledge and Social Science Discourse in the Periphery: Decolonising Malayness and Malay Underdevelopment," in *Social Science and Knowledge in a Globalising World*, ed. Zawawi Ibrahim (Bangi: Malaysian Social Science Association and Petaling Jaya: Strategic Information and Research Development Centre, 2012), 165–200; and Zawawi Ibrahim, "Indigenising the Discourse on Malayness and Malay Underdevelopment," *International Journal of Trend in Research and Development* 5, no. 4 (2018): 169–81.

2 Edward W. Said, *Orientalism* (London: Routledge and Kegan Paul, 1978). For an insightful engagement with Said's ideas, see Daniel Martin Varisco, *Reading Orientalism: Said and the Unsaid* (Seattle: University of Washington Press, 2017).

3 Syed Hussein Alatas, *The Myth of the Lazy Native: A Study of the Image of the Malays, Filipinos and Javanese from the 16th to the 20th century and Its Function in the Ideology of Colonial Capitalism* (London: Frank Cass, 1977).

© ZAWAWI IBRAHIM, 2023 | DOI:10.1163/9789004521698_012

how and why knowledge is produced and reproduced. It is a book that retains its salience today, more than 40 years after its publication.

Two clear instances of how Alatas' analysis has found purchase in critical social science lie in efforts to create epistemologies of the Global South – in an effort to resist Eurocentric exclusion – and in a sustained engagement with indigenous knowledge. One of the most trenchant statements of the first position comes from Boaventura de Sousa Santos who explores the idea of "cognitive injustice," by which he means the failure to recognize the different ways of knowing through which people across the Global South provide meaning to their lives.[4] In a related manner, and from the perspective of postcolonial anthropology, Linda Tuhiwai Smith has pioneered new imaginings of indigenous anthropology, and launched a vehement critique of colonial modes of epistemology and methodology that had rendered indigenous Māori as mere objects of research. The call by Smith is to move the indigenous as agency and as subjects in their own right, and to foreground indigenous sovereignty and epistemologies, thereby determining a radical research agenda by "decolonizing methodologies."[5] Among Asian social scientists, this call to decolonize and indigenize social science knowledge has been part of the discourse initiated by Syed Hussein Alatas and has been taken up more recently by Syed Farid Alatas and others.[6]

Against this brief background, the main objective of this chapter is to position Syed Hussein Alatas' *The Myth of the Lazy Native* in relation to the discourse on Malay cultural values and underdevelopment. Alatas forensically interrogates what can be understood as a dominant discourse and Foucauldian "regime of truth" constructed by the British colonial state and its ideologues as a means to justify the policy of utilizing imported migrant labor – Indians in rubber and other cash crop plantations and Chinese in tin mines – in the capitalist export sector. As a counterpoint to this policy, the British deployed a

---

4 Boaventura de Sousa Santos, *Epistemologies of the South: Justice Against Epistemicide* (London: Routledge, 2014).

5 Linda Tuhiwai Smith, *Decolonizing Methodologies: Research and Indigenous Peoples* (London: Zed Books, 1999). See also Norman K. Denzin, Yvonna S. Lincoln, and Linda Tuhiwai Smith, eds., *Handbook of Critical and Indigenous Methodologies* (London: Sage, 2008); Brendan Hokowhitu, Aileen Moreton-Robinson, Linda Tuhiwai-Smith, Chris Andersen, and Steve Larkin, eds., *Routledge Handbook of Critical Indigenous Studies* (London: Routledge, 2021).

6 Syed Farid Alatas, *Alternative Discourses in Asian Social Science: Responses to Eurocentrism* (New Delhi: Sage, 2006); Syed Farid Alatas and Vineeta Sinha, *Sociological Theory beyond the Canon* (London: Palgrave Macmillan, 2017). For a more general introduction to creating alternative frameworks in social science, see Georgette Wang, ed., *De-Westernizing Communication Research: Altering Questions and Changing Frameworks* (London: Routledge, 2011).

"colonial capitalist ideology" that deliberately both marginalized Malay peasant farmers and destroyed the indigenous merchant class.[7] It was in this specific context that the trope of the "lazy native" came to be rendered as the "lazy Malay." In order to decolonize this discourse, we follow the arguments laid down by Alatas as well as examine the relevant scholarship on Malay cultural values and underdevelopment. A key objective is to advance an alternative discourse to the one dominated by Orientalism, colonial knowledge, and its regime of truth, with a view to elucidating a sense of indigenous agency and cognitive justice.

The Malay values under consideration refer to those cultural attributes – including religion – of being Malay or Malayness, as documented and represented in both colonial and postcolonial narrations, and how these same attributes have been extended to explain the state of Malay "backwardness" and underdevelopment. Colonial knowledge – in the sense articulated by Bernard Cohn as a key underpinning of the project of control and command – can be regarded as one of the earliest discourses on Malayness.[8] It has since taken its own journey, engaged with by other arguments and contested knowledges, incorporating different indigenous and non-indigenous scholarly viewpoints (including the social sciences), from both within and beyond the Malay world. The discussion here represents an attempt to follow this epistemic journey and to give a holistic and inclusive synthesis to this hybridized discourse on Malay cultural values and underdevelopment.

2 Colonial Knowledge on Malayness and Its Postcolonial Variants

As a colonized subject, the Malays did not escape colonial representations. In this context, the writings of British colonial administrators such as Hugh Clifford and Frank Swettenham on Malay culture and lifeworlds are well known.[9] In the course of their administrative duties, they found time to extend their imperial gaze to write and hypothesize about the sociocultural traits of the Malay character. Perceiving themselves as the bearers of civilization and progress, their views of the independent Malay capacity to develop

---

7 Alatas, *The Myth of the Lazy Native*, 1–7.

8 Bernard Cohn, *Colonialism and Its Forms of Knowledge: The British in India* (Princeton, NJ: Princeton University Press, 1996).

9 Hugh Clifford, *In Court and Kampong: Being Tales and Sketches of Native Life in the Malay Peninsula* (London: Grant Richards, 1903); Frank Swettenham, *British Malaya: An Account of the Origin and Progress of British Influence in Malaya* (London: George Allen & Unwin, 1948).

were negative, paternalistic, and condescending. In their search to denounce the Malay character in the context of colonial capitalism and its broader economic imperatives, an essentialized view of the Other – Malays as the "lazy native" – was constructed. As Alatas argues, a core trait emphasized again and again by colonial observers was 'the alleged dislike of the Malay for hard work and continuous work either of the brains or the hands, and his lack of initiative.'[10] These views had long antecedents. In the words of Stamford Raffles, perhaps the key architect of British imperialism in the Malay world in the early nineteenth century, the Malay "is so indolent, that when he has rice, nothing will induce him to work."[11] More than a century later, at the zenith of colonial rule, Swettenham claimed that 'the leading characteristic of the Malay of every class is a disinclination to work.'[12] He continued, 'whatever the cause ... the Malay of the Peninsula was, and is unquestionably opposed to steady continuous work.'[13] Again, on Malay attitudes to labor, Clifford further reinforced the dominant British image: 'he never works if he can help it, and often will not suffer himself to be induced or tempted into doing so by offers of the most extravagant wages.'[14] There were, however, mildly dissenting points of view. R.O. Winstedt, whose *A History of Malaya* was considered definitive at the time, remarked that 'because he is an independent farmer with no need to work for hire, the Malay has got an undeserved reputation for idleness, which his Asiatic competitors take care to foster.'[15] What should be noted here, however, is the sly way Winstedt blames other Asians for the "undeserved reputation for idleness" rather than colonial stereotypes and ideology. Nonetheless, Winstedt's insights would be taken up in Alatas' counter-narrations against the colonial imagining of the "lazy native."

For our purpose, it is pertinent to note that these Orientalist views of Malays expressed by individual British administrators often found official endorsement. For example, a statement in the Perak Handbook and Civil Service List of 1892 testifies that

> they [the Malays] are an indolent, contented, thriftless, unambitious, polite and peaceful race ... It seems to be doubtful whether the Malays as

---

10 Alatas, *The Myth of the Lazy Native*, 44.

11 Quoted in Alatas, *The Myth of the Lazy Native*, 177.

12 Swettenham, *British Malaya*, 136.

13 Ibid., 139.

14 Clifford, *In Court and Kampong*, 19.

15 R.O. Winstedt, *A History of Malaya* (Singapore: Malayan Branch of the Royal Asiatic Society, 1935), 17.

a race are susceptible of much improvement in their country ... The lower classes are content with a bare subsistence, while the well-born Malay is too proud and often, it must be confessed, too indolent to work.[16]

More often than not, these aspects of Malay behavior were seen as "racial" inadequacies, though they were sometimes counterbalanced by British admiration for certain other qualities such as loyalty, courteousness, honor and generosity, which were said to render the Malays "an extraordinarily attractive people" and which appear to "have aroused the paternalistic sentiments of the British." However, 'juxtaposed against their own strongly-held view of the superiority of the white man, they provided the ultimate racist justification for British rule and domination.'[17]

This kind of knowledge did not disappear with the departure of the colonial rulers from the Malay world. It is pertinent to note how even in the postcolonial period variants of colonial knowledge and its representations of Malayness still persisted in the writings of some scholars and intellectuals, both Western and local, in their attempt to explain Malay underdevelopment under conditions of modernity. These became a central focus of Alatas' later critique. For example, the economist Brien K. Parkinson sees underdevelopment residing in the "fatalism" supposedly inherent in Islam, the religion professed by Malays. As he elaborates the point:

> The Islamic belief that all things are emanations from God is another force affecting the Malay's economic behaviour, for it tends to make them fatalistic in their approach to life ... Such an attitude constitutes a significant drag on economic development. For, if the Malays subscribe to this fatalistic view and believe that any individual efforts to improve living standards are not likely to be successful, then they are not likely to attempt to master nature, or to strive for their own economic advancement by initiating the changes necessary for it. And all this forms part of their impotence in the face of the more powerful influence which shape their destiny.[18]

---

16 Quoted in Lim Teck Ghee, "British Colonial Administration and the 'Ethnic Division of Labour' in Malaya," *Kajian Malaysia* 1, no. 2 (1984): 60.

17 Ibid., 61.

18 Brien K. Parkinson, "Non-economic Factors in the Economic Retardation of the Rural Malays," *Modern Asian Studies* 1, no. 1 (1967): 40.

Parkinson goes on to conclude that Malays are tradition bound and 'reluctant to give up the past,' and they also 'fear or dislike the unfamiliar.' As a result, so his argument goes, changes could only be accepted if they are not too dramatically in conflict with what had gone before. Malays are therefore represented as clinging unflinchingly to custom and traditional law or *adat*, this apparently being the way through which they understand their world and satisfy their desire for security. Hierarchy, according to Parkinson, further imposes an unquestioning respect for authority – hence unquestioning values. When complemented at the level of religion with a fatalistic approach to life, an attitude of resignation rather than innovation, the causes for Malay backwardness become complete and all-encompassing.[19]

In postcolonial Malaysia it is Senu Abdul Rahman's edited volume, *Revolusi Mental* [Mental Revolution], which appears to have been the Malay ruling elites' answer to the perceived woes of Malay underdevelopment.[20] The book, a compendium of articles written by selective Malay intellectuals and ideologues "inside the circle" and edited by a government minister, contains every imaginable negative cultural and psychological trait deemed to be antithetical to Malay economic progress and development. In his coruscating review of *Revolusi Mental*, Alatas succinctly summarizes its contents in the following terms:

> The Malay society, according to the book, is generally characterized by the following attitudes: the Malays are not honest to themselves, and they do not see their own faults ... The Malays on the whole lack the courage to fight for the truth ... The Malays emphasize the general welfare but they are fatalists, and this is a major cause of their general backwardness.... On the whole Malays do not think rationally. They are more often led by sentiment. In the past Malays did not exhibit discipline and punctuality .... Malays show no spirit of perseverance in the midst of adversity.... They are not frugal and like to waste in unnecessary expenditure such as feasts, celebrations, and furniture far beyond their means. Many Malays do not think of their future. They do not save for the future .... The acquisitive instinct is not commonly recognized in Malay society. The Malays also lack originality in thought, imagination, and the spirit of enquiry. They lack a realistic attitude, and are not capable of effort (kurang usaha). They do not find the life of this world sufficiently important; they do not

---

19   Ibid.

20   Senu Abdul Rahman, *Revolusi Mental* (Kuala Lumpur: Penerbitan Utusan Melayu, 1970).

value time, and dare not be serious. They have no courage to take risks, and it is the poverty of their soul (kemiskinan jiwa), not of money, that causes them to be backward. As a nation they are not frank and forthright. They conceal their feeling in order not to hurt others.[21]

With every damning and negative human trait embedded in the character and personality, *Revolusi Mental* represents the ultimate in the Orientalizing of the Malays, albeit by their own political elites. This prospectus represents more than just an extension of colonial knowledge constructed by British administrators. Though the book does suggest in passing that colonialism, exploitation or the capitalist system are also causes of Malay backwardness, the cure for these ills is not sought in the transformation of the system as such but focuses purely on "a change in the attitude, and social philosophy of a given society" which is how a "mental revolution" has been defined.[22] For *Revolusi Mental*, and by implication for the second generation of Malay postcolonial leaders, the way forward in solving Malay underdevelopment is not therefore through structural change. The core focus is in the realm of cultural values. But most tragically, *Revolusi Mental* is also a condemnation of all the existing cultural values associated with Malayness – it homogenizes Malay cultural values as incapable of generating any internal dynamics of development. In essence, the book continues with the same (if not worse) negative image of the Malays as painted by British colonialists.

Many of these negative traits also became the subject matter of Mahathir Mohamad's well-known book, *The Malay Dilemma*.[23] In his treatise, Mahathir gives a new twist to the culturalist emphasis of "mental revolution" by combining both environmental determinism (and its social Darwinist "survival of the fittest" argument) and genetic (hereditary) explanations into the discourse on Malay underdevelopment. His fundamental position is that the Malays are hereditarily inferior to the Chinese. This thesis is argued by invoking the environment and certain types of marriage patterns in order to explain the genesis and continuous transmission of the hereditary racial traits for both the Chinese and the Malay case. As Mahathir states:

---

21 Alatas, *The Myth of the Lazy Native*, 147–48.

22 Ibid., 147.

23 Mahathir Mohamad, *The Malay Dilemma* (Singapore: D. Moore for Asia Pacific Press, 1970). Mahathir was prime minister of Malaysia for two separate terms: 1981–2003 and 2018–2020.

The history of China is littered with disasters, both natural and man-made [such that for] the Chinese people life was one continuous struggle for survival. In the process the weak in mind and body lost out to the strong and the resourceful. For generation after generation, through four thousand years or more, this weeding out of the unfit went on, aided and abetted by the consequent limitation of survival to the fit only. But, as if this was not enough to produce a hardy race, Chinese custom decreed that marriage should not be within the same clan. This resulted in more cross-breeding than in-breeding, in direct contrast to the Malay partiality towards in-breeding. The result of this Chinese custom was to reproduce the best strains and characteristics which facilitated survival and accentuated the influence of environment on the Chinese.[24]

Mahathir goes on to suggest that, unlike China, the lush tropical environment and land resources were more than enough to support the small population of Malays of the time, and early Malaya was blessed with no hunger or starvation.

Under these conditions, according to Mahathir, everyone survived. Even the weakest and the least diligent were able to live in comparative comfort, to marry, and procreate. The observation that only the fittest would survive did not apply, for the abundance of food supported even the weakest. These flaws were explained away by the long-term patterns of Malay marriage.

The absence of inter-racial marriages in the rural areas resulted in purebred Malays. This was further aggravated by the habit of family in-breeding. Malays, especially rural Malays, prefer to marry relatives. First cousin marriages were and still are frequent, and the result is the propagation of the poorer characteristics, whether dominant or recessive, originally found in the brothers or sisters who were parents of the married couple.[25]

Ultimately, when the Chinese and the Malays finally met in Malaya, '[t]he Malays whose own hereditary and environmental influence had been so debilitating, could do nothing but retreat before the onslaught of the Chinese immigrants. Whatever the Malays do, the Chinese could do better and more cheaply.'[26]

---

24   Ibid., 24.
25   Ibid., 29.
26   Ibid., 25.

3 Indigenous Writings and Indigenous Knowledge from within the Malay World

It is crucial to add to the above discourse the contributions and ideas coming from within the colonial Malay world itself. The focus here is on two organic intellectuals, predecessors to Alatas, who, in the process of their society's transition from "feudalism" to British colonial rule, became acute observers of the changes that were taking place and expressed these ideas in their writings. Unlike colonial administrators, these indigenous writers projected alternative views about Malayness and the causes of Malay underdevelopment.

The first was Abdullah Abdul Kadir, better known as Munshi Abdullah, who was among the earliest indigenous writers to analyze the roots of Malay backwardness by focusing on the nature of "feudal" society and its attendant exploitative relations. As an astute observer of the transitional period of the 1830s and 1840s – in his journey to the east coast states of Malaya narrated through his *Hikayat*, or narrative – Munshi Abdullah dwells upon and chides the indolent among a section of the male population. But reflecting upon the poverty and desolation of these Malay states, he takes a different turn from the Orientalism and homogenizing orientation of later colonial administrators. He moves instead toward a proto-class analysis of Malay feudalism, albeit without the sophistication of later more theoretically informed accounts. He argues:

> Nor was it [Malay backwardness] due merely to the laziness of the inhabitants, for there was never yet a country anywhere in the world in which all the inhabitants were lazy; if any man who is willing to exert himself to seek fortune, knows that his enjoyment of such fortune will be undisturbed, even if only half the population do work for their living with energy and loyalty, their country cannot fail to become great and prosperous. No, in my opinion, the reason for the poverty of Pahang is to be found in the fact that its inhabitants lived in continual fear of the oppression and cruelty of the Rajas and other notables. Naturally they feel that it is useless to be energetic when it is certain that any profits they make will be grabbed by those higher up, and so they remain poor and miserable all their lives.[27]

---

27   Abdullah Abdul Kadir, *The Voyage of Abdullah*, trans. A.E. Coope (Singapore: Malaya Publishing House, 1949), 15.

For Munshi Abdullah, the reasons for the backwardness of the Malays have to be sought in the class relations and exploitation embedded within the existing precolonial system itself: the ravages of the ruling class toward any form of visible wealth accumulation on the part of the subject class; the forced involvement of the latter (their manpower and time under the feudal corvée labor or *kerah* system) to underwrite the lifestyle of the overlords; the private affairs of the rulers (such as wars); and, in general, the abuse of power by members of the ruling class. According to Alatas, even when Munshi Abdullah discussed indolence, '[u]nlike his British contemporary he did not generalize. He was very conscious of the fact that the phenomenon of indolence he described was part of a pathological social system. It did not characterize the entire Malay community. He was conscious of the Malay Islamic system of values condemning indolence and injustice.'[28]

In one of his reflections appended to the first volume of the *Hikayat*, Munshi Abdullah further reinforces his earlier views of the causes of Malay state of underdevelopment associated with the feudal conditions:

> I viewed with particular disfavour the lives led by the Malays and the circumstances of those with whom I had been acquainted. I had observed their conduct, behaviour and habits from my youth up to the present time and had found that, as time went on, so far from being more intelligent, they became more and more stupid. I considered the matter carefully in my mind and came to the conclusion that there were several reasons for this state of affairs, but that the main one was the inhumanity and the repressive tyranny of the Malay rulers, especially towards their own subjects. The point had been reached at which their hearts had become like soil which no longer receives its nourishment, and wherein therefore nothing at all can grow. Industry, intelligence and learning cannot flourish among them and they are simply like trees in the jungle falling whichever way the wind blows.[29]

Munshi Abdullah's views of the Malay dominant classes remain just as critical:

> Under Malay rule ordinary folk cannot lift up their heads and enjoy themselves, and dare not show any originality for it is forbidden by the ruler. Wishing possibly to build themselves finely decorated houses of stone

---

28   Alatas, *The Myth of the Lazy Native*, 138.

29   A.H. Hill, ed., "The Hikayat Abdullah," *Journal of the Malaysian Branch of the Royal Asiatic Society* 28, no. 3 (1955): 269.

they are afraid to do so. They are afraid to wear fine clothing, shoes and umbrellas in case these are taboo. They are afraid to keep fine clothing in their houses because it is said that such things are the pre-requisites only of royalty. Rich men especially live in perpetual fear and are fortunate if their only losses are their belongings. For indeed their very lives are in danger.... If a man is reluctant to lend any of his most cherished possessions, it is accounted as serious offence. And once he has given them up they are lost forever; he will never see them again. A beautiful young girl in his home is like a raging poison, for it is quite certain that the ruler will take her as one of his wives with or without the guardian's permission. This practice more than any other arouses the hatred of the servants of Allah. I heard of one courageous man who refused to part with his daughter, the ruler ordered him to be murdered on some pretext, and then took the child away. All such acts as these are forbidden by Allah and His Prophet and incur the censure of mankind throughout the world.[30]

More than a century later, Zainal Abidin Ahmad (better known as Zaa'ba), regarded as the foremost Malay philosopher (*pendita*) of his time, represented yet another strand of indigenous intellectual scholarship emerging from the Malay world in its transition from the feudal world. Though chiding some characteristics of the Malays which he regarded as unprogressive, for example the dependent mentality or inability to be independent (*tiada mempunyai sifat keperangaian bergantung pada diri sendiri*), Zaa'ba recognized that a lot of these characteristics which are associated with a state of poverty are not inborn or innate (*bukanlah pula kejadian mereka memang termentri dengan tabiat kemiskinan otak dari semulajadi*) and in his mind, it does not mean that the Malays are not capable of "higher forms of social behaviour" (*sifat-sifat keperangaian yang tinggi*).[31] Zaa'ba noted that many of these habits and values were a legacy of the conditions of a past feudal society, which was full of "repression, human misery, and intolerable abuses" (*kesempitan, azab sengsara, dan kebuasan yang tiada terderitakan*).[32] For Zaa'ba, however, time (*masa*) is a healer, and "a long time" (*lama juga masanya*) will have to be put aside in order to resocialize and "train" the Malays through the education process. This was necessary so as to wipe out all the negative habits and values that had become ingrained into their cultural system as a result of past societal conditions and

---

30 Ibid., 271.

31 Ungku A. Aziz, *Jejak-Jejak di Pantai Zaman* (Kuala Lumpur: Universiti Malaya Press, 1975), 44, 53.

32 Ibid., 47.

lack of experience or opportunities, in order to catch up economically with "people from other races" (*orang-orang bangsa lain*) who have been trained for "thousands of years."[33] It is clear that while Zaa'ba links certain habits and values with the influence of the social environment, his correlations are not deterministic, nor does he fall into the trappings of Mahathir's genetic arguments to explain Malay backwardness and state of underdevelopment.

Apart from the writings of Munshi Abdullah and Zaa'ba, indigenous knowledge is also a crucial template and a source of reference to gauge and represent the wisdom and intellectual ideas emanating from within the traditional Malay world itself. In contrast to the British Orientalizing of the Malays and the Malay political elite's equally egregious tropes in *Revolusi Mental* and *The Malay Dilemma*, it is also salient to present an alternative discourse of Malay cultural and value systems. To do this, we return to the insights provided by Alatas' *The Myth of the Lazy Native*. In countering the negative arguments and generalizations expressed in hegemonic treatises on the Malays, Alatas goes to great lengths to illustrate the positive elements of Malay cultural values toward development and economic achievement.

In contrast to the argument that Malays are fatalists, Alatas cites several Malay sayings that emphasize agency, suggesting in doing so that these reflect real-life norms and behavior: that Malays "believe human action can influence man's fate ... stressing the value of human effort"; "if we plant wild grass we shall not get a rice crop" (*tanam ladang tidak akan tumboh padi*); "ashamed of rowing, the boat drifts" (*malu berdayong perahu hanyut*); "too shy to enquire, the way is lost" (*segan bertanya, sesat jalan*). All these indicate, Alatas proposes, the Malay belief in "man as a free agent."[34] Against *Revolusi Mental*'s charge that the words "initiative," "self-reliance," "punctuality," and "discipline" did not exist in the Malay lexicon, Alatas argues that "[n]o vocabulary of a people entirely expresses the conscious thoughts and feelings of that people. An idea or a concept which is not formulated in a word, like initiative, can nevertheless exist and find expression in different forms." As an example, the Malay word "*chergas*" denotes initiative while "*patoh*" indicates discipline.[35]

Alatas further defends a Malay conception of rationality, even though this rationality exists side by side with magic and superstition, and this is reflected in the following Malay sayings: "follow the heart you die, follow the feeling you are ruined" (*ikut hati mati, ikut rasa binasa*) and "scratch an itch till the bone

---

33   Ibid., 51–52.

34   Alatas, *The Myth of the Lazy Native*, 169–70.

35   Ibid., 170.

is reached" (*turut gatal sampai ketulang*).[36] The first shows the folly of taking one's wishes and feelings as the sole guide to action, irrespective of the law and social obligations, while the second saying indicates the folly of giving way to passion to the bitter end, leading inevitably to disaster. According to Alatas:

> If rationality meant justifying the ends by the means then the Malays did possess such a quality. Their handicraft, farming, fishing, trade and commerce during the 17th century, all indicated the presence of a rational outlook. If however the term rationality implied modern business practices, industrial ventures and commerce, this, it is true, was lacking. But one can hardly blame the Malay society of the past for lacking an institution created only in the 19th and 20th century in Southeast Asia by the colonial powers.[37]

As part of his exposition of indigenous knowledge, Alatas also cites historical records in the Malay world that stress the value of labor and industriousness. In contrast to the colonial mythologizing, he argues that indolence had never been felt or perceived as a problem in precolonial indigenous societies. In defense of his contention, he cites *Undang-Undang of Sungai Ujong*, a digest summary of customary law of Sungai Ujong, an area in the modern state of Negeri Sembilan, whose inhabitants were originally immigrants from Minangkabau, Sumatra. On the content of this particular digest Alatas notes its detailed features:

> Out of 113 articles of the Digest, 7 stressed the value of labour and industriousness. Article 99 classified the roots of evil into: cock-fighting and gambling, drinking, smoking opium, and slothfulness, the avoidance of work. The philosophical basis of this Digest, a synthesis between Islam and *adat*, customary law, goes back at least to the 16th century if not earlier. The text as is written probably dates back to the 18th century. What is beyond doubt is that the text was formulated in pre-colonial times. It expresses the indigenous philosophy of values and social life in the pre-colonial society. The basis conditions for clearing land cultivation were: great effort and care, strength, intense planting, keen watch, great economizing, careful purchasing, knowing what to consume, intelligence, knowing prices and values, and generosity to friends. The

36   Ibid.
37   Ibid., 171.

basic conditions for a successful trader were similar: knowing how to fix prices, and to evaluate properly: intelligence, economy, knowing how to fix dress, a capacity for great effort, being able to wait for a favourable wind, being able to remember negotiations, looking after profits and losses, selling when prices were high and buying when prices were low. Industriousness was further stressed in acquiring knowledge, in practising a craft, in breeding animals and poultry. The conditions for becoming a chief in the land were: refinement in speech, saying pleasant things to his friends, a willingness to spend, showing a greater industry, profundity of thought, and a great alertness. Basically, the values upheld by the Digest were those common to the Malay world. The Malays strongly disapprove of indolence (malas). In the Malay society it is a disgrace to be called a *pemalas*, one who is indolent.[38]

In countering views that Islamic values are not conducive to economic development and achievement, Alatas cites the content of a brochure entitled *Semangat Kehidupan* (The Spirit of Living), composed by Haji Wan Mohammed bin Haji Wan Daud Patani. Apparently the Majlis Ugama dan Istiadat Melayu Kelantan (Council of Islam and Malay Custom of Kelantan) approved its contents in 1918, the brochure being intended for the religious schools under the council's administration. As Alatas' reading of the contents of the brochure highlights:

> There was a great deal of emphasis on labour, on hard work, on the proper use of time and energy. Inaction was condemned. A man who did no work was considered a stone pillar. "Man's duty to work is because work is the best means of purifying him from weak and evil habits. Is not work the cause of bringing man towards a situation of trial and effort leading to true existence?"
>
> Laziness, wasting time and unpunctuality were condemned. Patience and frugality were stressed in the execution of work, and the attainment of knowledge, together with careful scrutiny and investigation. Play and exercise were recommended as alternatives to labour. When man was not working, he was advised to keep himself busy with either play or exercise, to ensure good health. The whole 46 page booklet, is an all round philosophy of labour, written in simple language. It was an attempt to establish the value of work and the evils of indolence ... The content and spirit of

---

38   Ibid., 136.

the philosophy in the booklet were indigenous. It was an assertion of the Malay Islamic attitude towards labour.[39]

What this summation of the writings of Munshi Abdullah, Zaa'ba and finally Alatas demonstrates is the existence of a long intellectual trajectory of critical discourse drawing on indigenous forms of knowledge. Each of them also innovated in the *forms* of writing they mastered. Munshi Abdullah took the classical Malay chronicle associated with royal dynasties, the *hikayat*, and fashioned a highly distinctive and personalized critical narrative of what he observed. For his part, Zaa'ba was a product of the print revolution in the Malay world, using journalism as a forum for his social criticism. And Alatas, as we have seen, was a major figure in the academic discipline of the sociology of knowledge and an advocate of indigenous knowledge at a time when his approach was barely visible with academe.

4 Social Science Perspectives: Feudalism and Malay Political Culture: Loyalty (*Setia*) versus Agency (*Durhaka*)

The issue of the Malay feudal structure giving rise to certain types of cultural values (as in the earlier arguments of Munshi Abdullah and Zaa'ba) has also been elevated to another level of discourse on the political culture of Malays, which contains its own scholarly contestations and contrasting viewpoints. Two strands of Malay political culture run concurrently and are in contestation with one another in the context of the traditional Malay political system's evolution into a modern parliamentary democracy. This transition comprises one in which the institution of its feudal monarchy is preserved and incorporated into the constitutional governance embodied in the Malaysian nation-state.

The first strand of Malay political culture emphasizes loyalty, *setia*, while the other highlights agency, *durhaka*, which literally means "to rebel." In Malay legends and popular culture, the former is symbolized by the loyal warrior, Hang Tuah, while the latter is represented in the person of Hang Jebat, a comrade in arms, both being touted as heroes during the heyday of the historic Melaka empire. Yet as fate would have it, the story of these two "brothers" ends in tragedy, with Hang Tuah having to kill Hang Jebat for rising in *durhaka* against the sultan even though Jebat did so in order to avenge the "death" of Tuah, a punishment that was ordered by the sultan himself after succumbing to the

---

39   Ibid., 141.

false rumors (*fitnah*) spread by those in the Melakan court who were envious of Tuah's favored position at court. The wise minister, the *bendahara*, despite the instruction by the sultan to have Tuah killed, sent Tuah into exile instead. When Jebat's *amok* to avenge Tuah's "death" became unstoppable, it was much to the sultan's relief to have Tuah recalled for duty after learning that he was still alive.

⸱ This legend has been told and retold to affirm the axiom, "Malays will never rebel" (*pantang Melayu mendurhaka*) and validate the principle of *setia* as underlying the subordination of the Malays to their feudal overlords in the traditional polity. This perspective has, however, been contested by another alternative discourse which sees Jebat's *durhaka* as a manifestation of agency, in representing the real democratic variant of Malay nationalism, rather than its government-led aristocratic variant which was endorsed by the British when granting independence to the country in 1957. According to Kassim Ahmad, Hang Jebat 'is thus a rebel of the nationalist turn of mind ... a prophet and hero of Malay nationalism. His tragedy then, serves to demonstrate artistically and concretely that nationalist ideals and aspirations are non-realisable within the feudal social scheme.'[40] Chandra Muzaffar argues that the Malay feudal system has given rise to a conception of loyalty among the subject class. In his book *Protector?* he relies heavily on elucidating the concept of unquestioning loyalty (*setia*) as an attitude which resides in the psychological processes of both the ruling and ruled classes in Malay society.[41] It is obvious that Chandra faces certain methodological problems in attempting to acknowledge the principle of unquestioning loyalty as an independent variable. Thus, he is aware that there may be individuals and groups in both categories who do not evince the same attitude toward loyalty. Yet he is adamant that 'this should not in any way affect the validity of the overall analysis.'[42] But later Chandra also admits that 'it would be wrong to ascribe every instance of submissiveness to the influence of this idea of loyalty.'[43] In the traditional polity, he grants the fact that submissiveness to the ruler is 'a product of the structure of Malay society,' it being a hierarchical system, with a ruling class and a subject class and

---

40   Kassim Ahmad, *Characterisation in Hikayat Hang Tuah: A General Survey of Methods of Character-portrayal and Analysis and Interpretation of the Characters of Hang Tuah and Hang Jebat* (Kuala Lumpur: Dewan Bahasa dan Pustaka, 1966), 33.

41   Chandra Muzaffar, *Protector? An Analysis of the Concept and Practice of Loyalty in Leader-led Relationships within Malay Society* (Penang: Aliran, 1979).

42   Ibid., 3.

43   Ibid., 20.

hence 'generating its own consciousness among its participants.'[44] In modern Malaysian politics, Chandra argues that it is the persistence of the "unquestioning loyalty" principle that has led to the success of elite manipulation which is built upon the creation of the "false consciousness" among the Malays that "a protector is simply imperative." 'The protector would then be able to perpetuate himself *ad infinitum* – a protector to protect the poor Malay from the rich non-Malay.'[45]

This discourse goes back to the core of *"kerajaan"* in the traditional conception of Malay culture, usually translated as "state," but which Anthony Milner suggests is more accurately rendered as "the condition of having a Raja."[46] In terms of the "social charter" which is considered to be the original source of kingship, and the consequent social exchanges between the raja and the *rakyat* (people or subjects) in the Malay world, reference is normally made to *Sejarah Melayu* (Malay Annals), the epic historical narrative of the Melaka court. The social contract is represented in the form of a covenant (*wa'ad*) between Sri Tri Buana (elsewhere known as Sang Sapurba), an overlord and the ancestor of Malay rulers, with Demang Lebar Daun, a local chief, who entered into an alliance via the marriage of his daughter, Wan Sendari, to Sri Tri Buana. The covenant symbolically represents a social exchange between the ruler and the *rakyat* in the Malay polity: loyalty and respect in exchange for prosperity and social welfare.[47] While conventional wisdom in interpreting this account has been dominated by views leaning toward royal absolutism or the absolute loyalty of the people, some scholars have evolved an alternative interpretation which suggests that the spirit of the social charter is more 'reciprocal, with conditions that do not acknowledge the royal absolutism nor of absolute loyalty of the people to the king.'[48]

---

44 Ibid.

45 Ibid., 92.

46 Anthony Milner, *Kerajaan: Malay Political Culture on the Eve of Colonial Rule* (Petaling Jaya: Strategic Information and Research Development Centre, 2016).

47 Abdul Rahman Ismail, "Kewibawaan Mutlak Raja dan Kesetiaan Mutlak Rakyat kepada Raja: Satu Penilaian Semula Tentang Lunas Perhubungan Raja-Rakyat Masyarakat Melayu seperti yang Terdapat di dalam Kitab-kitab Sastera Sejarah Melayu," *Kajian Malaysia* 3, no. 1 (1985): 32–57; Sharifah Zaleha Syed Hassan, "Gift-giving and Overlordship: The Ideological Basis of Social Exchange in Traditional Malay Society," *Kajian Malaysia* 1, no. 1 (1985): 29–39.

48 Abdul Rahman Ismail, "Sejarah Melayu: Antara Sejarah dan Dakyah," *Kajian Malaysia* 3, no. 1 (1985): 32–57.

Such a "democratic" vision of the covenant is also proposed by Ulrich Kratz who writes:

> Here, as in other Malay texts, we find that the ruler, important as he may be, is nothing without a people, and that it is the people and their traditional leader(s) who choose their ruler, and who decide freely to whom they want to offer their total obedience. In the *Sejarah Melayu* it becomes quite clear that it is the representative of the people, Demang Lebar Daun, and his successors as *Bendahara* who ... set out the rules governing their relationship. The most fundamental customs and traditions of the Malay realm are initiated by the *Bendahara*. Only at a second stage is it the ruler who refines the institutions ... It is very clear ... that loyalty and respect are qualities which have to work in both directions, to and from the ruler, in order to affect positively the well-being of state and society. Thus, while the ruler's role and place appear paramount – he is the symbol of the state and its well-being as well as its ultimate earthly arbiter and guarantor of harmony and welfare – this does not absolve him from taking due note and showing consideration for the views and reputations of those who serve him.[49]

In support of Kratz's analysis (and in opposition to Chandra Muzaffar's take of unquestioning loyalty) Abdul Rahman argues that,

> the *Sejarah Melayu* is a political document – a testament of the political attitudes and values of the ruling class of the Malacca sultanate. The proverbial saying, "Malays have never rebelled against their ruler" is taken to mean a statement of hopes and expectations as well as an instrument of the ruling class to indoctrinate the people to remain subservient ... There is no evidence in the *Sejarah Melayu* to show that the people even uttered such a statement or denied themselves the right to rise in rebellion, except those statements which have issued forth from the lips of the royal classes to commit people to subservience.[50]

Supported by examples from *Hikayat Hang Tuah*, *Hikayat Raja-Raja Pasai*, and other classical Malay texts, which all show examples of resistance and defiance

---

49 Ulrich Kratz, "Durhaka: The Concept of Treason in the *Hikayat Hang Tuah*," *South East Asia Research* 1, no. 1 (1993): 88–90.

50 Abdul Rahman, "Kewibawaan Mutlak Raja," 32.

to royal authority, Abdul Rahman presents an alternative discourse to the conventional interpretation which upholds the saying "Malays will never rebel" as a truism in the world of the Melakan sultanate as well as the traditional Malay polity in general. Indeed, he not only challenges this general view but also shows that "the *Sejarah Melayu* is not consistent in illustrating the political ideology of the Malay ruling class; in fact, it is most ambivalent in its presentation of "royal absolutism" and "absolute loyalty" of the people."[51]

These arguments are important. They show that apart from *durhaka*, at one end of the continuum, there are also possibilities of alternative modes of agency in Malay feudal society. These include its more collective reciprocal and reconciliationary (*mesyuarah*) traditions rather than its dominant authoritarian or autocratic orientations, and that dissent and even resistance could also constitute an alternative (subaltern) aspect of Malay political culture of past.[52] Such a view also has contemporary political culture and what Albert Hirschman called "a bias for hope" for the future,[53] that is to debunk any attempts toward the mythologizing of Malay political culture as one which condones absolutism of any form of political authority.

In a similar vein, among scholars of Malay political culture, it is equally pertinent to examine the plurality of their discourse on Malayness, specifically regarding its political cultural nuances, of *setia* and *durhaka*, or their variants, and the social space which may actualize their possibilities in society. This argument by no means invalidates both the political and socioeconomic realities faced by the Malay masses under the conditions of its feudalism, as documented by Munshi Abdullah, or his correlations of such conditions with the state of Malay backwardness. Apart from Chandra Muzaffar's exposition, an interesting extension of the feudal factor in explaining modern Malay political culture is also identified by Shaharuddin Maaruf who argues that the general state of Malay underdevelopment in contemporary society lies not so much with the values of the masses as such but rather with the perpetuation of "underdeveloped elites" (after Fanon) and their values, which have roots in Malay feudal society.[54]

---

51   Ibid.

52   For a case study of peasant resistance, see Shaharil Talib, "Voices from the Kelantan Desa 1900–1940," *Modern Asian Studies* 17, no. 2 (1983): 177–95.

53   Albert O. Hirschman, *A Bias for Hope: Essays on Development and Latin America* (New Haven, CT: Yale University Press, 1971).

54   Shaharuddin Maaruf, *Malay Ideas on Development: From Feudal Lord to Capitalist* (Petaling Jaya: Strategic Information and Research Development Centre, 2014); Shaharuddin Maaruf, *Concept of a Hero in Malay Society* (Petaling Jaya: Strategic Information and Research Development Centre, 2014).

5 Divine Lot (*Rezeki*), Fate (*Nasib*), and Agency (*Ikhtiar/Usaha*) in the Context of Malay Development

Michael Swift, one of the pioneers of modern research on the early phase of the Malay peasantry under colonial economic and political rule, was perhaps the first anthropologist to analyze the concept of *rezeki* (a person's divinely determined economic lot) in an empirical context and its place in Malay society. According to Swift, a

> marked fatalism, presented in religious form, is also conspicuous among Malay economic attitudes. The Malay is very prone after receiving a setback, to give up striving, and say that he has no luck or that it is the will of God. In economic affairs this is most clearly seen in the concept of 'rezeki,' a person's divinely determined economic lot.[55]

Swift does observe that while such a preference may not in itself be "uneconomic or irrational," it does weaken the Malays in their economic competition with other groups or individuals who have a long-term orientation. According to him, the Chinese economic view is "essentially long term," in contrast to the Malay "who is interested in the short run." For the Chinese, 'wealth is desired not only for consumption but for accumulation, to build up a fortune which can be handed on to future generations.' In the case of the Malays "wealth is strongly desired but for consumption."[56]

The arguments on *rezeki* and fatalism raised by Swift are further elaborated and finessed by Syed Husin Ali, a pioneering indigenous rural sociologist, who suggests that 'at the same time Islam also teaches its believers to use their faculty and effort in order to overcome difficulties and determine their own positions and future; and this is referred to as *ikhtiar*. To say that all Malays – or all Malay peasants – are fatalistic is mere indulgence in stereotypes.'[57] Syed Husin argues that to believe that "fate" (*nasib*) and "divine lot" (*rezeki*) among the Malays have caused their backwardness and lack of response to change is to deny a number of realities: first, that there have been Malays who have responded successfully to economic and educational changes; and second, that there are others who are poor in the country, yet their state of poverty may have little to do at all with their beliefs in fate or divine lot. As an alternative

---

55   M.G. Swift, *Malay Peasant Society in Jelebu* (London: Athlone Press, 1965), 29.
56   Ibid.
57   Syed Husin Ali, "Land Concentration and Poverty among the Rural Malays," *Nusantara* 1 (1972): 111.

explanation, Syed Husin provides an interesting and persuasive elaboration on the place of *rezeki* and *nasib* in Malay society.

> Among the Malays, the concept of *nasib* and *rezeki* can be used and applied in the positive and negative sense. A person can have a good or bad fate, as expressed in *nasib baik* (lit. good luck) or *nasib tak baik* (lit. bad luck), and he can have a blessed or unblessed divine lot, as expressed in *murah rezeki* (lit. cheap lot) or *mahal rezeki* (lit. expensive lot). A person may describe his deprived and poor condition in terms of bad "fate" or "luck." What he has actually done is to explain things in a way that helps to relieve himself from what can otherwise be mental and psychological strain caused by his depressed state. He can take his "fate" philosophically, or even joke about it. On the other hand, a successful landlord or middleman may explain his success as being mainly due to good "fate" or "luck." He thanks God for it. In this way, the means by which he has gained wealth, however unfair, tend to be underplayed. So the belief in "fate" and "divine lot" may explain why the poor are often resigned, but it cannot be elevated as being the cause of poverty or "economic retardation." The concepts of "fate" and "divine lot" need to be relegated to their proper places in trying to explain Malay economic behaviour.[58]

In a similar vein, Parkinson's notions of Malay fatalism outlined earlier have also been contested by William D. Wilder who, in a scathing rebuke, asserts that,

> too much of Parkinson's argument presents us with a stereotype, a caricature of the Malay without consideration of the evidence upon which the picture is based ... His argument must be termed "reprehensible." He has pictured the Malay as a blind, irrational slave of history and custom ... The argument contains palpable errors of fact and subversion of method.[59]

Another scholar, G. Sivalingam, advances an empirical refutation of Parkinson's charges on the basis of his findings from research conducted among Malays in three agricultural development schemes. Sivalingam elaborates the internal dynamics of agency as being very much part and parcel of Malay cultural values. He concludes:

---

58   Ibid.

59   William D. Wilder, "Islam, Other Factors and Malay Backwardness: Comments on an Argument," in *Readings on Malaysian Economic Development*, ed. David Lim (Kuala Lumpur: Oxford University Press, 1975), 344.

the Malays like most other races do allow their personality and behaviour to be influenced by the social environment. Their responses ... suggest that they are undergoing a process of change, that is, they want to do something about their environment; they are interested in social mobility through education; they are interested and responsive to new methods of production that save time; they are more achievement oriented than ascriptive oriented and value scientific findings; they are motivated towards realising the value of smaller families ... Furthermore ... it is possible for a person to be responsive to changes and at the same time be religious. He [Parkinson] gives the impression that Malay peasant society is static and not changing and is not in the process of questioning the validity of traditional values and attitudes.[60]

In my own study of Malay fishermen in the process of being transformed into settler tobacco farmers in Terengganu, I expand on Swift's and Syed Husin Ali's arguments on *rezeki* and elaborate the Malay notion of agency, embodied in the term *usaha*, which in many respects is akin to the Islamic notion of *ikhtiar* mentioned by Syed Husin. Based on evidence from the lives of the tobacco farmers, I argue that,

an important ideological basis of their social existence is defined by a strong belief in *usaha* (literally "to make an effort" or "to strive"). It is through *usaha* that they can face the uncertainties of the new environment. It motivates them to learn the new ways, to innovate, to improve, or sometimes even to question and resist. But that is only half the story. There are things beyond their control, as when they faced with the sudden "death" of their tobacco ... Such misfortune does not mean that they have not made an effort in the past; it is still based on *usaha*, meaning that "even if there is disease (*penyakit*), we must *usaha*, then if they happen to die, it's *nasib* (fate); if it's good, its *nasib*." Their resort to *nasib* thus complements delicately with their belief in *usaha*. "*Usaha* first, if you can't overcome it, then surrender to *nasib*. *Rezeki* does not come by itself." The resort to *nasib* is a crucial stabilising factor in the context of the Malay settlers' battle with the elements. At the subjective level of the individual such a balancing act is still necessary. It attenuates his disappointment and frustration. It calms him down and goads him to face the

---

60   G. Sivalingam, "Non-economic Factors in the Economic Retardation of the Malays: An Empirical Refutation," *Development Forum* 5, no. 1 (1975): 8.

world of routine and work again after a setback. It absolves him of blame. It gives him a sense of reason rather than creating a sense of anger or aggression against his neighbours who do not face the same misfortune; it serves to tone down the competition between them. In the end the whole notion of work, *usaha*, *nasib* and *rezeki* are all intertwined into a single religious cosmology.[61]

Norazit Selat, another anthropologist who studied a Malay urban community – the working class of Lorong Sembilang, Johor – pinpoints the structural context of the totalizing impact of capitalist social relations in which Malay men and women involved in wage labor have been "subjected to a capitalist economic rationality." Under such conditions, he argues that,

> not only their work, but also their mode of expressing themselves, confirms and gives reality to this position. The people's relationships and mode of consciousness manifest in many ways the major governing institutions of the capitalist society: monetization and commoditization.[62]

In an interesting variant on the discourse on *rezeki*, Norazit suggests that *rezeki*, *ikhtiar*, money, and savings, including the belief in spirits (*hantu*), have been redefined as "working for capital," that is in a "quest for money, the commodity of all commodities."[63] This new logic is played out in the emerging consciousness of Malay wage laborers as they justify new modes of behavior. Hence,

> the concepts of *ikhtiar* and *rezeki* go hand in hand with the attempts of urban Malays to improve their lot. Gambling and the search for easy money are *ikhtiar* because one must go after them. Most of the men who engage in these acts agree that they are forbidden in Islam, but argue that they are not *dosa besar* (great sins) as are adultery, murder or culumny (*fitnah*). Yet through ideologically assimilating these morally questionable activities into an acceptable phenomenon, namely work, the people have taken the first step towards the acceptance of bourgeois values.[64]

---

61   Zawawi Ibrahim, "Rural Malays and Tobacco: A Study of Organisation, Response and Changing Values," in *Issues and Challenges for National Development: Selected Papers Presented during the 21st Anniversary Conference, December 1987* (Kuala Lumpur: Faculty of Economics and Administration, University of Malaya, 1990), 176–79.

62   Norazit Selat, *Urban Survival: The Malays of Muar* (Kuala Lumpur: Yayasan Penataran Ilmu, 1996), 180.

63   Ibid.

64   Ibid., 179.

6 Colonial and Postcolonial Capitalism's Construction of the "Lazy Native"

Before the emergence of a critical perspective that correlates power and meaning/knowledge, Syed Hussein Alatas' sociology of knowledge approach was already one in which he sought to link the genesis or social construction of a particular ideological form (the "lazy native") or knowledge (colonial knowledge) to the emergence of a specific type of social formation (and power structure) in the Malay world, namely colonial capitalism. It is on the basis of this sociological method of analysis that he launched his attack against the ideas of British Orientalists as well as their Malay mimics in *Revolusi Mental* and *The Malay Dilemma*. His fundamental thesis in *The Myth of the Lazy Native* suggests that

> the image of the indolent native was the product of colonial domination generally in the 19th century when the domination of the colonies reached a high peak and when colonial capitalist exploitation required extensive control of the area. The image of the native had a function in the exploitation complex of colonial times. This was the time when the capitalist conception of labour gained supremacy. Any type of labour which did not conform to this conception was rejected as a deviation. A community which did not enthusiastically and willingly adopt this conception of labour was regarded as indolent.[65]

Taking a clue from Winstedt's commentary cited earlier, Alatas goes on to argue that 'it was this unwillingness to become a tool in the production system of colonial capitalism which earned the Malays a reputation of being indolent. This was one factor in the creation of the image of the indolent Malay.'[66] Alatas notes Winstedt's insight that the Malay "is diligent where his interest is roused." And he asks the obvious questions:

> Is this not the same for all people? If the Malays preferred to be independent cultivators, did this make them indolent? Did not the Europeans in the colonies avoid manual labor? Did they not avoid coolie labor? Why were they not called indolent? It is clear that through available records

---

65   Alatas, *The Myth of the Lazy Native*, 70.
66   Ibid., 72.

DEMYTHOLOGIZING DOMINANT DISCOURSES

that industriousness meant working at sub-human level in colonial capitalist setting.[67]

Alatas' views are also supported by the economic historian Lim Teck Ghee who, in his review of the Malay peasantry under British economic policy, maintains that

> [i]n dealing with the local people it was also necessary for the British to make use of the social, cultural and economic differences that existed among them, to ascribe these differences to pre-determined and immutable biological and environmental factors, and to manipulate the "racial" difference to suit their own ends. Since the Malays were largely a settled peasant class and less easily attracted to work as labourers in the mines and plantations, the ideas that the Malays were lazy, thriftless, unambitious and unable to develop the natural resources of the country offered a perfect pretext for British intervention in the Malay states. It also justified subsequent policies that brought in cheap immigrant labour and compelled the Malay to grow *padi*, stay on the land and be provided with the most rudimentary education.[68]

The ideological manipulation that Lim highlights to create a "perfect pretext" for colonial capitalist policies echoes Alatas' own insights:

> The conceptual association between industrious-ness and oppressive capitalist labour is thus clear. One would look in vain for any operational proof of Malay indolence. Nothing concrete and empirical has been brought forward to illustrate the concept of Malay indolence.[69]

In dismissing this "vulgar distortion," Alatas points to many examples where the opposite was true, that Malays were just as capable as anyone else of prolonged, sustained labor. Rather, in a penetrating insight, he suggests that the reputation for "laziness" was not so much an "ethnic shortcoming" than a form of passive resistance – as assertion of constrained agency – in the face of the depredations of the colonial capitalist labor regime, and not work as such.

---

67   Ibid., 77.
68   Lim, "British Colonial Administration," 60.
69   Alatas, *The Myth of the Lazy Native*, 76.

They were only incapable, or to be more accurate, *unwilling* to work in the plantations owned by others ... They avoided permanent routine work of the exploitative type in other peoples' mines and plantations. Any observer could see how easily the paddy fields were tended. So was the orchard at home. All these required sustained and permanent labour. The fact that Malays took to other routine employment outside the plantation and estates was ignored.[70]

In Alatas' terms, then, it is evident that origin of the myth of the lazy Malays 'was based on their refusal to supply plantation labour and their non-involvement in the colonially-controlled urban capitalist economic activity.'[71]

In fact, other scholars suggest that even in relation to the plantation economy Malay attitudes were both more pragmatic and rational, especially in times of extreme economic stress. As Halim Salleh notes, the Depression of the 1930s created enormous difficulties for Malay peasants and compelled some to seek employment in British-run estates. This was part of a process of strategic decision-making that arose out of two considerations: the shortfall of migrant Indian plantation labor and the foreclosure of other choices for household production and reproduction.[72] Elsewhere, Michael Stenson also observes that in times of a limited supply of Indian labor, such as in 1946 and 1957, 'there was an influx of Malay labour, which in contrast to pre-war times had shown a greater willingness to accept the disciplines of industrial organizations, even though most of them did not reside in the estates and were only temporary industrial employees, returning to the village or *kampong* during harvesting or when work is short.'[73]

In my own research on postcolonial oil palm plantation society in Terengganu, in Kemaman and Ketengah estates, I was confronted by a postcolonial discourse on labor shortages in the plantation industry, which saw the return of "lazy native" mythologizing. In the plantations, various stakeholders, including the state, the plantocracy, and plantation officials put the blame on Malays *tout court* for "being choosy" (*memilih*) or simply "refusing" to work. These arguments were put forward to justify the intake of foreign labor (mainly Indonesians) in the harvesting of oil palm, through contract labor, and mediated by local Malay contractors. It is interesting to note that during the early

---

70   Ibid., 78–89 (my emphasis).

71   Ibid., 80.

72   Halim Salleh, "Changing Forms of Labour Mobilisation in Malaysian Agriculture" (PhD diss., University of Sussex, 1987), 103–7.

73   Michael Stenson, *Industrial Conflict in Malaya: Prelude to Communist Revolt* (Oxford: Oxford University Press, 1970), 188.

phase of these plantations, from the 1960s to the end of the 1970s, it was Malays and not migrants who were the backbone of this early example of "frontier capitalism." However, after the discovery of oil off the coast of Terengganu in 1975, the coastal strip began to evolve into an industrial zone, which became more attractive to local jobseekers. The new plantations of Ketengah were also preferred by local Malays as the palms were shorter. Local Malay laborers, being citizens, were also more mobile in the search for better wages and working conditions, while many migrant workers, who were often undocumented, had fewer options and hence were forced to accept "totalizing" social control, poor living arrangements and low pay. But the most significant factor that drove many local Malays out of the plantation was the introduction of the contract system for oil palm harvesters. Malay contractors resorted to various elusive strategies to ensure their preference for the employment of Indonesian migrants over local Malays, as the profit margins were bigger. Malay workers were clearly aware of their rights to bonuses, social security benefits, and the like. In addition, labor control of "illegal" migrants was easier, and they could also be forced to work for longer hours than local workers.

Hence the return of the "lazy native" in postcolonial Malaysia is essentially about capital, caught in a labor shortage crisis, and deliberating on familiar ground, that is on the virtues of two fragments of labor. One fragment is local, while the other is the cheap and expendable immigrant labor coming in large numbers from across the Straits of Malacca and the surrounding low-wage sectors of Southeast Asia. In the colonial period, the fragment of local labor about which the "lazy native" discourse was constructed was the indigenous peasantry (as opposed to Indian plantation workers who were recruited through the colonial indentured labor system from India). In the colonial representation of the "lazy native," the traditional Indian plantation workers escaped the Orientalist mythologizing since they had little choice but to accommodate to the exploitative conditions of plantation work and life. In the colonial era, it was Malay relative autonomy as independent cultivators that made them reluctant to embrace wage labor as defined by colonial capitalism, though, as we have seen, there were exceptional periods during which they chose to do so. In the postcolonial period, it was the same reluctance to surrender themselves fully, as their immigrant counterparts have done, to the totalizing demands of capital that has rekindled the same wrath of capital, the state, and the plantocracy. And in the end, this has sustained the projection of the Other – the Orientalized, essentialized "lazy Malay" – even in an independent polity dominated by Malay elites.[74]

---

74   For more detailed discussion, see Zawawi Ibrahim, "Return of the Lazy Native."

Alatas himself was more than aware of this apparent paradox in the reproduction of colonial-era manipulated ideology in the postcolonial era. Some of
his most pressing criticisms in *The Myth of the Lazy Native* are reserved not for
biased colonial administrators but for the Malay ruling elite that emerged in
the 1960s and 1970s. In general terms, as we have seen, Alatas questions the
essentializing of so-called "racial" categories that simply builds on very limited data and a questionable methodology. In deconstructing *Revolusi Mental*
he highlights the crass "distortion" that result from "fallacious" reasoning.
According to Alatas, the negative traits that are alleged to have molded the
Malay character are 'conclusions derived from false premises. They are neither
based on research nor on sensible observations.'[75] For him, *Revolusi Mental,* in
particular, is an even more egregious example of racialized duplicity, mimicking colonial stereotypes and betraying the "class affiliation of the authors." In
a series of persuasive polemical statements, Alatas highlights the ideological
and intellectual continuity of the postcolonial ruling class with its British predecessors. This is nothing less than

> a confirmation of the ideology of colonial capitalism as far as the Malays
> are concerned. It draws on an image of the Malays which is *even more
> negative* in scope than that of colonial capitalism ... It analyses the past
> by means of categories of colonial capitalist thought ... The Malay ruling
> party inherited the rule from the British without a struggle for indepen-
> dence ... As such there was no ideological struggle. There was no intellec-
> tual break with British ideological thinking at the deeper layer of thought
> ... The existing ruling class in Malaysia forms an unbroken link with the
> colonial past. They operated with colonial categories of thought despite
> their anti-colonial pronouncements.[76]

For Alatas, Mahathir's *The Malay Dilemma* followed precisely the same trend
of thinking as *Revolusi Mental,* and for the same reason, in its representation
of the so-called Malay character. According to Alatas, Mahathir's 'views on the
Malays ... are dominated by colonial capitalism.'[77] In other words, the tenden-
tious weakness of both *Revolusi Mental* and Mahathir's analysis is that they put
the blame for the economic underdevelopment of the Malays on their (inherited) character and on supposedly unchanging cultural values. What escapes
their attention is the Malay ruling class that profited directly and indirectly

---

75   Alatas, *The Myth of the Lazy Native,* 153.
76   Ibid., 150–54 (my emphasis).
77   Ibid., 162.

from colonialism. Alatas concludes: 'In this respect, their silence on the contribution of the Malay ruling class to the deterioration of the conditions of the Malays, is an illustration of their hypocrisy.'[78]

7   The Sociology of Development and Beyond

Although Alatas' sustained critique in *The Myth of the Lazy Native* is rightly lauded as a granular exposition of the fallacies of colonial and postcolonial ideology and mythmaking, his analysis did not emerge in a vacuum, either in terms of Malay studies or the broader current of radical sociology of development and underdevelopment. For example, one early doyen in the sociology of development was the rural economist Ungku Aziz, who, in pre-echoes of Alatas, attempted to dispel the myths of the "conservative," "happy," and "lazy" rural Malays by emphasizing instead economic exploitation as the major cause of their poverty. In a pioneering study, he comments that

> [l]ow productivity has been extensively discussed by many of our visiting experts ... They fail to understand that apart from health and education, low productivity is closely tied to the problem of exploitation. It is exploitation which fossilizes the rural economy and inhibits incentives from operating in the interests of progress.[79]

While aware of examples of non-Malay domination over Malay farmers and fishermen in rural society as traders, landlords, and moneylenders, Ungku Aziz's argument moves decisively away from ethnicity as the key explanatory variable, asserting instead that:

> replacing these non-Malay capitalists will not solve the economic problems of the Malays because the exploitation and poverty will be the same ... The key to the eradication of Malay poverty was to be found in the eradication of exploitation.[80]

---

78   Ibid., 163.

79   Ungku A. Aziz, "Poverty and Rural Development in Malaysia," *Kajian Ekonomi Malaysia* 1, no. 1 (1964): 83.

80   Quoted in Kamal Salih, "Unbalanced Growth and Persistent Poverty: The Consequences of Unequal Access in Urban and Rural Development," in *Some Case Studies on Poverty in Malaysia: Essays Presented to Professor Ungku A. Aziz*, ed. B.A.R. Mokhzani and Khoo Siew Mun (Kuala Lumpur: Persatuan Ekonomi Malaysia, 1977), 26.

Although Ungku Aziz's conception of exploitation has been criticized for being too narrowly focused, his views have brought to light a different approach to the understanding of peasant underdevelopment under capitalist domination, one which fed directly to pressing areas of inquiry in the sociology of development.

In the aftermath of Ungku Aziz's contribution to the discourse, the focus on the structural perspectives of underdevelopment has been enriched tremendously. At the theoretical level, the conception of exploitation incorporates not just internal agrarian class relations but also those economic relations at a global level generated by the emergence of the world-system, giving prominence to the dynamics of capital–labor relations at different levels of both the national and global domains. This thrust was enriched by emerging perspectives from various disciplines such as the new economic anthropology or Marxist anthropology which superseded the traditional descriptive anthropology of peasant studies.[81] From a political economy perspective, the sociology of development and underdevelopment pioneered by Andre Gunder Frank became an initial template for a paradigm shift, leading to its own discourse under the rubric of neo-Marxism propagated by Ernesto Laclau, Immanuel Wallerstein, Samir Amin, and others.[82] The intellectual journey of this theoretical trajectory is now already well documented, with the debate taking on its own momentum, embracing different contestations and reformulations. On home ground, different scholars also began to engage with the new paradigm

---

81 See, in particular, the contribution of Henry Bernstein in reformulating approaches to agrarian change over a period of more than four decades. Henry Bernstein, "Notes on Capital and Peasantry," *Review of African Political Economy* 4, no. 10 (1977): 60–73; Henry Bernstein, "African Peasantries: A Theoretical Framework," *Journal of Peasant Studies* 6, no. 4 (1979): 421–43; Henry Bernstein, "Agrarian Questions from Transition to Globalization," in *Peasants and Globalization: Political Economy, Rural Transformation and the Agrarian Question*, ed. A. Haroon Akram-Lodhi and Cristóbal Kay (London: Routledge, 2008), 239–61; Henry Bernstein, *Class Dynamics of Agrarian Change: Agrarian Change and Peasant Studies* (Winnipeg: Fernwood, 2010). See also John Clammer, "Economic Anthropology and the Sociology of Development," in *Beyond the Sociology of Development*, ed. Ivar Oxall, Tony Barnett, and David Booth (London: Routledge and Kegan Paul, 1975), 208–28; John Clammer, ed., *Beyond the New Economic Anthropology* (New York: St Martin's Press, 1987).

82 Andre Gunder Frank, *Capitalism and Underdevelopment in Latin America: Historical Studies of Chile and Brazil* (New York: Monthly Review Press, 1969); John G. Taylor, *From Modernization to Modes of Production: A Critique of the Sociologies of Development and Underdevelopment* (London: Macmillan, 1979); Aidan Foster-Carter, "Neo-Marxist Approaches to Development and Underdevelopment," in *Sociology and Development*, ed. Emanuel de Kadt and Gavin Williams (London: Tavistock, 1974), 67–95; Aidan Foster-Carter, "The Modes of Production Controversy," *New Left Review* 107 (1978): 47–77; Ray Kiely, *Sociology and Development: The Impasse and Beyond* (London: Routledge, 1995).

shift in development economics and the social sciences more generally, especially anthropology, in their research and theoretical reflections.[83]

8 Conclusion

Taking a lead from Smith's landmark anthropological interrogation, and current efforts to advance critical indigenous studies, the most important epistemological objective of our project is to decolonize knowledge and its attendant methodologies. This requires, as we have attempted in this chapter, a rigorous enquiry into and synthesis of a concrete dominant colonial discourse – the "lazy native" mythology – in order to examine its constitutive assumptions, arguments, and ideational implications. Alatas' *The Myth of the Lazy Native* provides an excellent template by which we engage his demythologizing of the colonial dominant discourse and his deconstructionist views on Malay cultural values and underdevelopment. This interrogation is both inclusive and critical. Inclusiveness requires engagements with both colonial and indigenous sources of knowledge and scholarship, with the latter constituting an approach that is decolonizing in its epistemology (for example, in the writings of Munshi Abdullah's and Alatas' exposition of indigenous knowledge), as well as those that operate through (neo)colonial Orientalizing categories (such as *Revolusi Mental* and *The Malay Dilemma*). But in the final analysis, critical social science is our ultimate tool. This means a critical engagement with both Western and indigenous scholarship and an equally critical review of existing corpus of social science research and empirical studies, together with their attendant perspectives, that are relevant to the discourse of Malay cultural values and underdevelopment. It is critical because it does not share colonial and Eurocentric representations of Malayness. Nor is it particularly "nativistic" as it does not necessarily endorse all views that are expressed by local interlocutors. Following a similar rigor to the methodology and critical analysis undertaken by Alatas, the discussion in this chapter refutes not only the colonial allegation of the "lazy native" but also seeks to discover the articulation of agency in both Malay cultural values and Islam with regard to economic development and underdevelopment. The broad sociology of development perspective enlightens us further as to the positioning and limits of such agency and values in

---

83   For a summary see Jomo K.S. *A Question of Class: Capital, the State and Uneven Development in Malaysia* (Singapore: Oxford University Press, 1996); Zawawi Ibrahim, "The Anthropology of the Malay Peasantry: Critical Reflections on Colonial and Indigenous Scholarship," *Asian Journal of Social Science* 38, no. 1 (2010): 5–36.

development when they are confronted by the oncoming structural forces of capitalism. But underlying this deconstructionist project in the non-Western periphery, our objective is to evolve nothing less than a social science discourse that is universal, critical, and liberating, to be shared with other practitioners of social science in a global epistemic community.

Bibliography

Abdul Rahman Ismail. "Kewibawaan Mutlak Raja dan Kesetiaan Mutlak Rakyat kepada Raja: Satu Penilaian Semula Tentang Lunas Perhubungan Raja-Rakyat Masyarakat Melayu seperti yang Terdapat di dalam Kitab-kitab Sastera Sejarah Melayu." *Kajian Malaysia* 3, no. 1 (1985): 32–57.

Abdul Rahman Ismail. "Sejarah Melayu: Antara Sejarah dan Dakyah." *Kajian Malaysia* 3, no. 1 (1985): 32–57.

Abdullah Abdul Kadir. *The Voyage of Abdullah*. Translated by A.E. Coope. Singapore: Malaya Publishing House, 1949.

Alatas, Syed Farid. *Alternative Discourses in Asian Social Science: Responses to Eurocentrism*. New Delhi: Sage, 2006.

Alatas, Syed Farid, and Vineeta Sinha. *Sociological Theory beyond the Canon*. London: Palgrave Macmillan, 2017.

Alatas, Syed Hussein. *The Myth of the Lazy Native: A Study of the Image of the Malays, Filipinos and Javanese from the 16th to the 20th century and Its Function in the Ideology of Colonial Capitalism*. London: Frank Cass, 1977.

Bernstein, Henry. "Notes on Capital and Peasantry." *Review of African Political Economy* 4, no. 10 (1977): 60–73.

Bernstein, Henry. "African Peasantries: A Theoretical Framework." *Journal of Peasant Studies* 6, no. 4 (1979): 421–43.

Bernstein, Henry. "Agrarian Questions from Transition to Globalization." In *Peasants and Globalization: Political Economy, Rural Transformation and the Agrarian Question*, edited by A. Haroon Akram-Lodhi and Cristóbal Kay, 239–61. London: Routledge, 2008.

Bernstein, Henry. *Class Dynamics of Agrarian Change: Agrarian Change and Peasant Studies*. Winnipeg: Fernwood, 2010.

Chandra Muzaffar. *Protector? An Analysis of the Concept and Practice of Loyalty in Leader-led Relationships within Malay Society*. Penang: Aliran, 1979.

Clammer, John. "Economic Anthropology and the Sociology of Development." In *Beyond the Sociology of Development*, edited by Ivar Oxall, Tony Barnett, and David Booth, 208–28. London: Routledge and Kegan Paul, 1975.

Clammer, John, ed. *Beyond the New Economic Anthropology*. New York: St Martin's Press, 1987.

Clifford, Hugh. *In Court and Kampong: Being Tales and Sketches of Native Life in the Malay Peninsula*. London: Grant Richards, 1903.

Cohn, Bernard. *Colonialism and Its Forms of Knowledge: The British in India*. Princeton, NJ: Princeton University Press, 1996.

Denzin, Norman K., Yvonna S. Lincoln, and Linda Tuhiwai Smith, eds. *Handbook of Critical and Indigenous Methodologies*. London: Sage, 2008.

Foster-Carter, Aidan. "Neo-Marxist Approaches to Development and Under-development." In *Sociology and Development*, edited by Emanuel de Kadt and Gavin Williams, 67–95. London: Tavistock, 1974.

Foster-Carter, Aidan. "The Modes of Production Controversy." *New Left Review* 107 (1978): 47–77.

Frank, Andre Gunder. *Capitalism and Underdevelopment in Latin America: Historical Studies of Chile and Brazil*. New York: Monthly Review Press, 1969.

Gardner, Katy, and David Lewis. *Anthropology, Development and the Post-modern Challenge*. London: Pluto Press, 1996.

Halim Salleh. "Changing Forms of Labour Mobilisation in Malaysian Agriculture." PhD diss., University of Sussex, 1987.

Hill, A.H., ed. "The Hikayat Abdullah." *Journal of the Malaysian Branch of the Royal Asiatic Society* 28, no. 3 (1955): 5–354.

Hirschman, Albert O. *A Bias for Hope: Essays on Development and Latin America*. New Haven, CT: Yale University Press.

Hokowhitu, Brendan, Aileen Moreton-Robinson, Linda Tuhiwai-Smith, Chris Andersen, and Steve Larkin, eds. *Routledge Handbook of Critical Indigenous Studies*. London: Routledge, 2021.

Jomo K.S. *A Question of Class: Capital, the State and Uneven Development in Malaysia*. Singapore: Oxford University Press, 1996.

Kamal Salih. "Unbalanced Growth and Persistent Poverty: The Consequences of Unequal Access in Urban and Rural Development." In *Some Case Studies on Poverty in Malaysia: Essays Presented to Professor Ungku A. Aziz*, edited by B.A.R. Mokhzani and Khoo Siew Mun, 22–40. Kuala Lumpur: Persatuan Ekonomi Malaysia, 1977.

Kassim Ahmad. *Characterisation in Hikayat Hang Tuah: A General Survey of Methods of Character-portrayal and Analysis and Interpretation of the Characters of Hang Tuah and Hang Jebat*. Kuala Lumpur: Dewan Bahasa dan Pustaka, 1966.

Kiely, Ray. *Sociology and Development: The Impasse and Beyond*. London: Routledge, 1995.

Kratz, Ulrich. "Durhaka: The Concept of Treason in the *Hikayat Hang Tuah*." *South East Asia Research* 1, no. 1 (1993): 68–97.

Lim Teck Ghee. "British Colonial Administration and the 'Ethnic Division of Labour' in Malaya." *Kajian Malaysia* 1, no. 2 (1984): 28–66.

Mahathir Mohamad. *The Malay Dilemma*. Singapore: D. Moore for Asia Pacific Press, 1970.

Milner, Anthony. *Kerajaan: Malay Political Culture on the Eve of Colonial Rule*. Petaling Jaya: Strategic Information and Research Development Centre, 2016.

Norazit Selat. *Urban Survival: The Malays of Muar*. Kuala Lumpur: Yayasan Penataran Ilmu, 1996.

Parkinson, Brien K. "Non-economic Factors in the Economic Retardation of the Rural Malays." *Modern Asian Studies* 1, no. 1 (1967): 31–46.

Said, Edward W. *Orientalism*. London: Routledge and Kegan Paul, 1978.

Santos, Boaventura de Sousa. *Epistemologies of the South: Justice Against Epistemicide*. London: Routledge, 2014.

Senu Abdul Rahman. *Revolusi Mental*. Kuala Lumpur: Penerbitan Utusan Melayu, 1970.

Shaharil Talib. "Voices from the Kelantan Desa 1900–1940." *Modern Asian Studies* 17, no. 2 (1983): 177–95.

Shaharuddin Maaruf. *Concept of a Hero in Malay Society*. Petaling Jaya: Strategic Information and Research Development Centre, 2014.

Shaharuddin Maaruf. *Malay Ideas on Development: From Feudal Lord to Capitalist*. Petaling Jaya: Strategic Information and Research Development Centre, 2014.

Sharifah Zaleha, Syed Hassan. "Gift-giving and Overlordship: The Ideological Basis of Social Exchange in Traditional Malay Society." *Kajian Malaysia* 1, no. 1 (1985): 29–39.

Sivalingam, G. "Non-economic Factors in the Economic Retardation of the Malays: An Empirical Refutation." *Development Forum* 5, no. 1 (1975): 1–13.

Smith, Linda Tuhiwai. *Decolonizing Methodologies: Research and Indigenous Peoples*. London: Zed Books, 1999.

Stenson, Michael. *Industrial Conflict in Malaya: Prelude to Communist Revolt*. Oxford: Oxford University Press, 1970.

Swettenham, Frank. *British Malaya: An Account of the Origin and Progress of British Influence in Malaya*. London: George Allen & Unwin, 1948.

Swift, M.G. *Malay Peasant Society in Jelebu*. London: Athlone Press, 1965.

Syed Husin, Ali. "Land Concentration and Poverty among the Rural Malays." *Nusantara* 1 (1972): 100–13.

Taylor, John G. *From Modernization to Modes of Production: A Critique of the Sociologies of Development and Underdevelopment*. London: Macmillan, 1979.

Ungku A. Aziz. "Poverty and Rural Development in Malaysia." *Kajian Ekonomi Malaysia* 1, no. 1 (1964): 70–105.

Ungku A. Aziz. *Jejak-Jejak di Pantai Zaman*. Kuala Lumpur: Universiti Malaya Press, 1975.

Varisco, Daniel Martin. *Reading Orientalism: Said and the Unsaid*. Seattle: University of Washington Press, 2017.

Wang, Georgette, ed. *De-Westernizing Communication Research: Altering Questions and Changing Frameworks*. London: Routledge, 2011.

Wilder, William D. "Islam, Other Factors and Malay Backwardness: Comments on an Argument." In *Readings on Malaysian Economic Development*, edited by David Lim, 341–46. Kuala Lumpur: Oxford University Press, 1975.

Winstedt, R.O. *A History of Malaya*. Singapore: Malayan Branch of the Royal Asiatic Society, 1935.

Zawawi Ibrahim. "Rural Malays and Tobacco: A Study of Organisation, Response and Changing Values." In *Issues and Challenges for National Development: Selected Papers Presented during the 21st Anniversary Conference, December 1987*, 166–83. Kuala Lumpur: Faculty of Economics and Administration, University of Malaya, 1990.

Zawawi Ibrahim. "Return of the Lazy Native: Explaining Malay/Immigrant Labour Transition in Terengganu Plantation Society." In *Local and Global: Social Transformation in Southeast Asia: Essays in Honour of Professor Syed Hussein Alatas*, edited by Riaz Hassan, 45–70. Leiden: Brill, 2005.

Zawawi Ibrahim. "The Anthropology of the Malay Peasantry: Critical Reflections on Colonial and Indigenous Scholarship." *Asian Journal of Social Science* 38, no. 1 (2010): 5–36.

Zawawi Ibrahim. "Indigenising the Discourse on Malayness and Malay Underdevelopment." *International Journal of Trend in Research and Development* 5, no. 4 (2018): 169–81.

Zawawi Ibrahim, and NoorShah M.S. "Indigenising Knowledge and Social Science Discourse in the Periphery: Decolonising Malayness and Malay underdevelopment." In *Social Science and Knowledge in a Globalising World*, edited by Zawawi Ibrahim, 165–200. Bangi: Malaysian Social Science Association and Petaling Jaya: Strategic Information and Research Development Centre, 2012.

CHAPTER 11

Syed Hussein Alatas

Colonialism and Modernity

Joseph Alagha and Mostafa Soueid

Western colonialism was an unprecedented project in human history. Its novelty lays in its vast outreach, its enduring length, and the new structure of power that would ensue from it. This latter restructuring of power and articulations is the focus of decolonial as well as post-colonial thinkers. What they share is the recognition of colonialism as the point of departure of the modern world. However, each "school" shares their respective point of departure and proposes different ways forward. What is at stake for both frames of thought is the legacy of colonialism, and what it means to live in a "post-colonial" world; or what is the route towards "decolonization" and delinking.

The decolonial framework has its point of departure in the colonization of the "Americas," whence a small European minority colonized and exploited a vast array of peoples and lands and shifted the balance of power in their favor for centuries to come.[1] Under this view, modernity evolved as the European colonizers restructured "Native American" categories and systems, in order to create a global hierarchy to facilitate colonial expansion and capitalist exploitation. The idea, for example, of race, gender, and similar identities, were all imposed onto the various ethno-linguistic groups that once made up the Americas and were used to situate them into global hierarchies that have Europe at its center.[2] This process allowed Europe to hold sway over a vast number of resources and speed up the industrialization process using serfs and African slaves, and eventually, bred what is known today as "modernity." Consequently, modernity cannot be separated from coloniality, as coloniality was constitutive of modernity.

On the other hand, post-colonial theorists' point of departure is in the 20th century with the advent of Orientalism. Under this view, the modern is a category that was "invented" after the Orientalist discourse that originated in Europe. Following Edward Said's *Orientalism*, European hegemony came

---

1 Aníbal Quijano, "Coloniality and Modernity/Rationality," *Cultural Studies* 21, no. 2–3 (2007): 168.
2 Ibid., 534.

© JOSEPH ALAGHA AND MOSTAFA SOUEID, 2023 | DOI:10.1163/9789004521698_013

into being as the orientalists classified and subjectively described the oriental and portrayed them as docile and backwards people who cannot represent themselves. Consequently, having established Europe's "other," Europe encompassed all that which is the opposite of the Oriental: modern, progressive, free, rational, democratic, and all else. Modernity then, began after the European binaries that dominated knowledge, and was solidified through Imperial conquests and colonization. For the post-colonial school, the question is not how to delink – as is with the decolonial frame of thought – but, rather how to reframe and articulate new positions in the modern debate. As Mignolo says: 'The de-colonial shift, in other words, is a project of de-linking while post-colonial criticism and theory is a project of scholarly transformation within the academy.'[3]

Having summarily touched upon the differences between the two frames of thought, this paper seeks to situate Syed Hussein Alatas in the discourse on colonialism and modernity. Alatas was highly engaged with the consequences of colonialism and made important contributions to the modern debate. The colonial carries with its discussions about "othering," Eurocentrism, imperialism, modernization, religion, and all other modern categories. Considering this, this paper seeks to situate Alatas within the debate regarding the post-colonial and decolonial frameworks and uncover his position in relation to the two, all the while giving new insights into the nature of the "modern" and modernity.

The first section of this chapter seeks to locate Alatas' engagement with orientalism and uncover how the modern came to be constituted in relation to the creation of "others." This section draws mainly upon Alatas' *The Myth of the Lazy Native,* as it begins the contemporary history of interactions between the West and "Orientals" in his works and allows for the location of modern categories onto indigenous peoples and sets the stage for post-colonial dialogues. The second section aims to locate the discourse of colonialism within Alatas' works and compare his conceptions of "colonial ideologies/colonial capitalism" with Quijano's modernity/coloniality. This section's main interest lies in unearthing the relationship between coloniality and modernity in Alatas' works, as opposed to the relationship between the construction of Europe itself in comparison with Oriental others, as the previous section attempts to do. Finally, before concluding, the perpetuation of Western intellectual exceptionality via Eurocentrism will be explored in Alatas' works in reference to

---

3   Walter Mignolo, "Delinking: The rhetoric of modernity, the logic of coloniality and the grammar of de-coloniality," *Cultural Studies* 21, no. 2–3 (2007): 452.

his conceptions of "intellectual captivity," and further compared to the way Eurocentrism operates in the works of Salman Sayyid, Walter Mignolo, and others. Having established all this, what this chapter seeks to advance is a conversation between Alatas and the various thinkers and intellectuals who have dealt with the nature of colonialism and coloniality, as well as endeavors to situate Alatas within the decolonial or post-colonial school.

1   Alatas and the Making of the "Other"

The process of "othering" is a critical process in the formation of the modern world. It set up the possibilities of a global hegemon at the expense of another. From the post-colonial perspective, as argued Said (1978) the initial other for Europe was found through the discourse of Orientalists, and their documentations from their visit to the "Orient." On the other hand, the decolonial "school" stresses the process of Occidentalism, and considers it the *sine qua non* to modernity, and later Orientalism.[4] However, the process of othering inevitably has different points of origination depending on the geo-politics of knowledge of the author. That is to say, scholars from North America share a different history of interactions with the West than do those living in the "Orient." The topic of interest for our present discussion is not where "othering" began as a process, which is undoubtably an important question, but rather, the ramifications, consequences, and shape of this othering.

Having said this, for Alatas, the main interest in his well renowned *The Myth of the Lazy Native* is the Western interaction with the "Malays, Filipinos, and Javanese" in particular. Alatas (1977) showed how the idea of the "the indolent, dull, backward and treacherous native" was used by colonial powers to justify their policies and civilizing mission. It of course was, above all else, a myth, a colonial ideology that was spread throughout South-East Asia, and indeed accepted by many of its constituents because of its material effects after the onset of colonialism. This colonial ideology served the purpose of justifying exploitation, free labor, raw materials, and consequently "conquest and domination."[5]

On the other hand, for Said, Orientalism served not only to dominate, but more importantly, it served to create a Western/Eastern divide, a way to define

---

4   Walter Mignolo, *The Darker Side of Western Modernity* (Durham, NC: Duke University Press, 2011), 97.

5   Syed Hussein Alatas, *The Myth of the Lazy Native* (London: Frank Cass and Co., Ltd, 1977), 117.

oneself at the expense of another.[6] In this sense, whereas othering for Alatas functions to rationalize and provide excuses for domination and colonialism, for Said, colonialism could be considered an after-effect of othering. As Said argues: 'To say simply that Orientalism was a rationalization of colonial rule is to ignore the extent to which colonial rule was justified in advance by Orientalism, rather than after the fact.'[7] The main line of differentiation then, could be in regard to Foucault's discourse on power/knowledge. Said incorporated Foucault's idea of knowledge as power into the history of Orientalism and attempted to show the ways in which the inability of the "Orientals" to define themselves – whereas an entire corpus and encyclopedia of knowledge was to be found in Europe on their behalf – allowed for this system of imperialism and colonialism to take place. This is not to say that Alatas' engagement with Orientalism doesn't have similar connotations, as the myth of the lazy native did after all become a myth entangled in complex power structures and was perpetuated among the elites.[8] However, this power structure for Alatas followed Marxist ideological patterns, wherein knowledge reflects the colonial elites, as opposed to power being intricated into the discourse of knowledge and discursivity as it does in the works of Said and Foucault. As such, Alatas is 'not attempting to evaluate colonialism as a historical phenomenon or the contribution of colonial scholarship to knowledge.'[9] Whereas this is precisely the process in which Said was interested in, specifically the latter. The effects of colonial scholarship on knowledge, and subsequently power, is the focus of interest for Said, while Alatas is interested in the "colonial ideology" that is remnant in post-colonial societies as a consequence of colonial capitalism and these myths. The two books then, complement each other nicely, as one is interested in the discursive power of orientalism (Orientalism), on creating the Orient and its "other," while *The Myth of the Lazy Native* is interested in the specific colonial after-effects and justifications of this project of othering.

Overall, if post-colonialism is an attempt to dispel myths of the "other," what Alatas calls a colonial ideology, then certainly *The Myth of the Lazy Native* allows for just an approach. Whereas Edward Said's main focus was on the effects of such a discourse on the making of modern Europe itself, Alatas shifted the focus onto the indigenous peoples of the Malay region, and the colonial project that was intrinsic to the project of global capitalism. Both works, in the

---

6   Edward Said, *Orientalism: Western Concepts of the Orient* (New York: Pantheon, 1978), 1.

7   Ibid., 39.

8   Alatas, *Myth of the Lazy Native,* 142.

9   Ibid., 218.

2 Alatas and Modernization

Having established that the initial contact between the "West" and the "non-West" came through a process of othering and a colonial ideology, modernity needs to be further explored in the works of Alatas, as this initial contact is what sets the stage for modernity in both post-colonial and decolonial schools. The decolonial frame of thought regards modernity as a non-universal category, one that was constituted by coloniality, and that brought about with it European categories and imposed them on the colonized, and eventually the world at large.[10] In this sense, modernity is a European myth, and there are no pre-modern societies, but rather non-modern societies. In other words, modernity presupposes the idea of progress, and of the transition from tradition/backwardness into modernity.[11]

On the other hand, Alatas' engagement with modernity considers modernity to belong to the realm of the universal, and consequently not a European product, as have argued other decolonial thinkers. Alatas defines modernity – modernization to be more specific – as:

> the process by which modern scientific knowledge covering all aspects of human life is introduced at varying degree, first in the Western civilization, and later diffused to the non-Western world, by different methods and groups with the ultimate purpose of achieving a better and more satisfactory life in the broadest sense of the term, as accepted by the society concerned.[12]

Although this definition locates modernity as beginning in Europe, and states that it was diffused to the non-West – most likely through colonial processes – Alatas' conception of modernity is markedly different from Quijano's conception of modernity/coloniality. Modernity, although originating in Europe, is

---

10   Mignolo, *The Darker Side*, 2.
11   Aníbal Quijano, "Coloniality of Power and Eurocentrism in Latin America," *International Sociology* 15 no. 2 (2000): 542.
12   Syed Hussein Alatas, "Religion and Modernization in Southeast Asia," *European Journal of Sociology/Archives Européennes de Sociologie/Europäisches Archiv für Soziologie* 11 no. 2 (1970): 266.

for Alatas something to be applied by all societies for the betterment of said society. If the above quote defines modernization, then "the modern" seems to be limited to scientific knowledge. Accordingly, Alatas is not at odds with the modern project; as for him, it is but the mere application of scientific knowledge, something that should in fact be – and often is – encouraged by religion itself.[13] This also means that although modernization is a project that began in the West, modernization is not equivalent to Westernization, since as we shall soon see, scientific knowledge in the works of Alatas belongs in the Universal realm.

Nevertheless, this conception of modernity might be considered problematic by some since it regards the nature of modernity as a specific epistemological category. Alatas recognized that modernization is characterized by the "objectification of nature" and "rationality" in dealing with the natural world.[14] The objectification of nature cannot be considered a universal and objective aspect of scientific knowledge, as Alatas seems to imply. This is because the objectification of nature could be seen as a product of Cartesian dualism. As others have argued, there may be some different articulations among different cultures as to the nature of the body and non-body. Cartesian dualism presented a novel split between the two in ways unprecedented. More importantly, it played an integral part in colonialism and the global hegemony of the West. Following Quijano, the split between the body and non-body in the works of Descartes had several consequences. Notably, it laid down the formula suggesting that only that which has reason is capable of "being"; consequently, that without reason is rendered an object by the holder of reason – as so there arises the split between subject – he who is capable of reason – and object – that which is not capable of reason.[15] Accordingly, nature becomes and object capable of being dominated by the subject. This is precisely the type of discourse that arose during colonialism when justifying the exploitation and inferiority of different "civilizations"—they were objects of knowledge.[16]

Similarly, the subject/object relation could be applied to anything that belongs to the non-body, in this case, to nature. The exploitation of nature and the utilization of "natural resources" vis-à-vis disregard to the planet requires a specific epistemology that separates any sense of value from the natural. Consequently, this challenges the proposition that the objectification of nature is a universal characteristic of modernization.

---

13 Ibid., 284.
14 Ibid., 266.
15 Quijano, "Coloniality of Power," 555.
16 Ibid.

Similarly, the categories of modern and modernization presuppose a period of tradition and backwardness. While modernity, like the colonial ideology, could be considered an epistemological category, rather than a mere scientific or technological one. Modernization in the decolonial framework might not be separated from coloniality, which itself is constitutive of modernity. Other scholars might find problematic the usages of "pre-modern" and "traditional" in Alatas' works, which might place it at odds with the decolonial conception of modernity. Alatas shares with decolonial thinkers the provincialization of modernity as a European category, although it is one that uses universal tools, while he also recognizes the colonial effects of the establishment of modernity on "non-modern" societies. These colonial effects, and the call for indigenous societies to modernize, could be considered a call – and a recognition – of Hommi K. Bhabha's conception of hybridity. That is to say, Alatas' separation between colonial ideology on the one hand, and the modern project on the other, and the recognition that they do not necessarily follow from each other – as he argues that the colonial ideology impedes the modernization project.[17] Rather, this allows for the understanding of modernity as a hybrid structure fashioned by the colonized after their encounter with Western colonizers. According to Alatas, hybridity is what was impeded with the colonial process since it disallowed for a cultural synthesis between Western modernity and autonomous cultural products.[18] Modernity then, according to Alatas, lacks Bhabha's notion of hybridity, which he defines as:

> the revaluation of the assumption of colonial identity through the repetition of discriminatory identity effects. It displays the necessary deformation and displacement of all sites of discrimination and domination. It unsettles the mimetic or narcissistic demands of colonial power but reimplicates its identifications in strategies of subversion that turn the gaze of the discriminated back upon the eye of power.[19]

Thus, Modernity is not exclusively a Western product, but rather, following Bhabha, in the works of Alatas modernity is a cultural product that is formed through cultural synthesis and hybridity, a sort of dialectic. However, whereas Bhabha takes as a rule of thumb that hybridity, as an automatic process, takes

---

17 Syed Hussein Alatas, *Intellectual Captivity and Developing Societies* (Ciudad de Mexico: Colegio de Mexico, 1981), 49.

18 Syed Hussein Alatas, "Intellectual Imperialism: Definition, Traits, and Problems," *Asian Journal of Social Science* 28 no. 1 (2000): 32.

19 Hommi K. Bhabha, *The Location of Culture* (London: Routledge, 2012), 112.

place under colonial conditions, which define modernity itself, Alatas seems to imply instead that there is a lack of hybridity, and that hybridity ought to be the way forward for post-colonial societies.

3   Alatas and Eurocentrism

What both decolonial and post-colonial thinkers share is the recognition of the need to dispel Eurocentric narratives and the ideas of Western exceptionality that are perpetuated in academic discourses. This section analyzes the way Alatas' notions of intellectual captivity and the captive mindset interact with decolonial/post-colonial conceptions of Eurocentrism. It is our contention that Alatas' engagement with "intellectual imperialism" provides a case in point into how Eurocentrism operates in everyday life.

For this purpose, we will draw upon Salman Sayyid's conception and definition of Eurocentrism, which he defines as:

> the discourse that emerges in the context of the decentring of the West; that is, a context in which the relationship between the western enterprise and universalism is open to disarticulation and re-articulation. The discourse of eurocentrism is an attempt to suture the interval between the West and the idea of a centre (that is, a universal template). Eurocentrism is a project to recentre the West, a project that is only possible when the West and the centre are no longer considered to be synonymous. It is an attempt to sustain the universality of the western project, in conditions in which its universality can no longer be taken for granted.[20]

In this sense, Eurocentrism is a process that emerges once the universal "modern" categories are appropriated by West as exclusive to them. This might raise a paradox, namely, for how could that which is universal belong to a particularity? Alatas is highly critical of this paradox, as a large amount of his works are interested in dispelling particular applications of the universal onto the world at large. For him, the unquestioning of Eurocentrism is:

> Uncreative and incapable of raising original problems, and it is incapable of devising an analytical method independent of current stereotypes, of

---

20   Bobby S. Sayyid, *A Fundamental Fear: Eurocentrism and the Emergence of Islamism* (London: Zed Books, 1998), 128.

separating the particular from the universal in science and thereby properly adapting the universally valid corpus of scientific knowledge to particular local situations.[21]

Eurocentrism for Alatas is the consequence of what he refers to as "imitation" and "the captive mind." These two concepts refer to the unquestioning application of Western sciences and institutions onto indigenous locations, which of course, is the result of colonial domination and colonial ideology. More specifically, it is caused by

> the more general historical setting, since it is recognized that if one country is dominated by another for a considerable length of time, a section of the populace feel that their weakness is inherent in their way of life, and regard that of the dominating one as the cause of their superiority and strength.[22]

The captive mindset is an idea that is highly explored and engaged with in the vast array of literature dealing with colonialism. It could be seen, for instance, in Fanon's notion of colonial inferiority complex,[23] or in Bhabha's notion of mimicryFor Fanon, this inferiority complex is a result of economic domination on the one hand, and the loss of culture due to colonialism on the other; and is above all a reflection of the colonizers perceived superiority, it is 'the correlative to the European's feeling of superiority.'[24] Similarly, Bhabha introduces mimicry as the process that arises out of "othering," he focuses on the psychoanalytical aspects of mimicry, and relies on Lacan's contributions for this purpose, and shows how mimicry was used as a tool by the colonizers to solidify the authors and subjugate them. What Alatas shares with all these contentions is that he believes that mental captivity arises from economic effects, colonial success, and a will, on the part of the colonizers, have the colonizers "mimic."[25] It is worth pointing out here that such an idea long predates these authors in the works of a thinker that Alatas is highly familiar with, and who he even calls for bringing back into the academic field. Consequently, it would have been interesting to see Alatas incorporate this thinker into his works on intellectual captivity, as this would have been an even more novel approach, and would

---

21   Alatas, *Intellectual Captivity*, 22.

22   Syed Hussein Alatas, "Intellectual Imperialism," 32.

23   Franz Fanon, *Black Skin, White Mask* (New York: Grove Press, 2008), 69.

24   Fanon, *Black Skin, White Mask*, 69.

25   Alatas, *Intellectual Captivity*, 45–49.

further highlight the relevancy of the said thinker. This thinker is Ibn Khaldun, and this form of imitation was explored by him in his *Muqaddimah*, through which he says:

> The vanquished always want to imitate the victor in his distinctive characteristics, his dress, his occupation, and all his other conditions and customs. The reason for this is that the soul always sees perfection in the person who is superior to it and to whom it is subservient. It considers him perfect, either because it is impressed by the respect it has for him, or because it erroneously assumes that its own subservience to him is not due to the nature of defeat but to the perfection of the victor.[26]

Nevertheless, the form of imitation highlighted by Alatas follows the Eurocentric logic that was later developed by decolonial thinkers; namely, the idea that Eurocentrism is a form of domination, or, at the very least, that it is used to perpetuate modernity/coloniality.[27] It is no surprise then that the captive mind 'is the result of the Western dominance over the rest of the world.'[28] In other words, if the captive mindset leads to mere unquestioning imitation of the West, then Eurocentrism – the recentering of the West – inevitably follows from such a situation. This "intellectual imperialism," as Alatas has called it before (2000), seems bears a striking similarity to Mignolo's definition of Eurocentrism, namely, 'imperial knowledge whose point of origination was Europe.'[29] Eurocentrism then, as is the case in the decolonial and post-colonial schools, is an imperial project in the works of Alatas, a direct consequence of colonialism.

Similarly, Alatas challenges Eurocentrism by re-articulation, an approach similar to that highlighted by Sayyid (1998) when discussing the role of Islamism in dispelling Eurocentrism. That is to say, for Alatas, what is required to dispel the captive mindset, and by implication Eurocentrism, is for autonomous – 'the particular social phenomenon valid only in one particular area or shared among certain societies' – applications of the universal – 'that which is valid throughout human society.'[30] Accordingly, for Salman, re-articulation

---

26   Ibn Khaldun, *The Muqaddimah: An Introduction to History*, trans. Franz Rosenthal, ed. Dawood, N. J. (London: Routledge, 1978), 116.

27   Quijano, "Coloniality of Power," 542; Sayyid, *A Fundamental Fear,* 128.

28   Alatas, *Intellectual Captivity,* 22.

29   Mignolo, *The Darker Side,* 19.

30   Syed Hussein Alatas, "The autonomous, the Universal and the Future of Sociology," *Current Sociology* 54 no. 1 (2006): 8.

of names and concepts in new particular circumstances, without reference to Eurocentrism and the West, breaks the Western "copyright" that is appropriated through the discourse of Eurocentrism.[31] That is to say, Eurocentrism for Salman exists only insofar as concepts and categories are linked to the West through articulation, similar to the process of intellectual captivity presented by Alatas, while new articulations, what we might call "autonomous applications of the universal," following Alatas, break the chain of signification and the link to the West.

In this sense, intellectual captivity and Eurocentrism go hand in hand. They could even be considered "inversely proportionate," as they feed off of each other, and one diminishes at the expense of the other; thus, they are inversely proportional. Consequently, Alatas' called for autonomous and particular applications of universal categories outside of a process of mere imitation is his program for delinking from Eurocentrism. As such, Alatas' ideas have been applied as instances dispelling Eurocentrism in various domains, as did Moosavi (2009) in his call for including Alatas' works on criminology in academic discourse; or as did Maia and Marcelo (2014) in discussing Alatas' contribution in imagining a non-Eurocentric sociology.[32]

4 Alatas and Alternatives

The question of alternatives is perhaps a misleading one. Mignolo argues that speaking of alternatives implies the acceptance of a point of reference, in this case, to Western modernity.[33] Instead, decolonial thinkers call for "options" outside of the rhetoric of modernity. On the other hand, the prefix "post" implies a form of continuity or acceptance, a moving within and throughout, all the while of course recognizing and rejecting the Eurocentric biases of the "pre." Hybridity is a case-and-point of such a project of bringing to the forefront new indigenous knowledge production to academia. The latter is what is most often found in Alatas' works.

This becomes clearer once we consider the "alternatives" or "options" proposed by Alatas, and compare them to decolonial approaches, namely, that

---

31 Sayyid, *A Fundamental Fear,* 148.

32 Leon Moosavi, "Decolonising criminology: Syed Hussein Alatas on crimes of the powerful," *Critical Criminology* 27 no. 2 (2019): 229–242; Joao Marcelo Maia, "History of Sociology and the Quest for Intellectual Autonomy in the Global South," *Current Sociology* 62 no.7 (2014): 1097–1115.

33 Mignolo, *The Darker Side,* xxviii.

of Mignolo. Because of Alatas' conception of the universal and his belief in the need to autonomously apply the universal, he is opposed to the idea of "indigenization" of knowledge, as that for him is impossible since one cannot indigenize a universal abstract category.[34] In contrast, Mignolo calls for the importance of indigenizing sciences, as this is essential in his conception of appropriating the "geo-politics of knowledge."[35] For Mignolo, decolonization entails a process of border thinking, and the recognition of oneself as outside of the logic of modernity and the ego-politics of knowledge. Quoting Grosfoguel, border thinking is:

> a critique of modernity from the geopolitical experiences and memories of coloniality. According to Mignolo (2000), this is a new space that deserves further exploration both as a new critical dimension to modernity/coloniality and, at the same time, as a space where new utopias can be devised.[36]

Consequently, the geo-politics of knowledge entails recognizing oneself at the border of modernity, and of making use of one's place as a subaltern (cf. Gramsci) to criticize modernity. Indigenization, then, is critical as it allows for one to theorize from the border and question "modern" logic from his place in the global hierarchy. Nevertheless, Alatas undermines one's spatial location in forming and criticizing epistemologies. As such, the autonomous application gives room for the voices of the subaltern to be heard and allows for societies to free themselves from the binds of intellectual captivity. Although this is important in decolonial literature, it only solves one part of the problem, namely that of "appropriating" certain academic discourses, as Mignolo argues: 'In order to be decolonized, sociology and the social sciences must be submitted to the double movement of appropriation and radical criticism from the perspective of the indigenous to the point of revealing the colonial difference in the social sciences.'[37] Decolonizing then, is not only about autonomous application, but might also be about criticizing the ways in which certain sciences established global hierarchies and constituted modernity. That is to say, it is not merely about being included in modern academic discourse, as Alatas seems to argue

---

34   Alatas, "The Autonomous," 10.

35   Walter Mignolo, "The Geopolitics of Knowledge and The Colonial Difference," *The South Atlantic Quarterly* 101 no.1 (2002): 74.

36   Ramon Grosfoguel, *Colonial Subjects: Puerto Ricans in a Global Perspective* (Berkeley, CA: University of California Press, 2003), 21.

37   Mignolo, "The Geopolitics of Knowledge," 74.

for, but rather, to criticize the academic discourse itself, since it was built upon a specific enunciation of Western supremacy and coloniality.

Considering this, Alatas' approach falls more in line with the post-colonial paradigm, which seeks to form a sort of hybridity and engagement with colonialism, that in turn, seeks to undermine and reject its premises while theorizing new ways of being and belonging. Autonomous applications of the universal and the abandonment of imitation and a captive mindset are the foremost tools utilized by Alatas in this post-colonial project.

5   Conclusion

Perhaps the weakness in our argument is that the question of the belonging to the post-colonial or the decolonial is not as intricate as it appears. That is to say, both "schools" do not form a set of opposing theories, or even theories in general. Rather, they could be regarded as ways of thinking, articulating, and imagining the end of the mandated colonial era. The insistence on classifying someone in one of these two respective frameworks could be contested, as there are no set criteria for this taxonomy, viz. to the belonging in either realm, when both are mainly predicated on praxis. Most likely, Syed Hussein Alatas seems to fit into this latter formula of praxis, as he established a political movement, although he might have been theorizing at the academic level per se.

Nevertheless, the purpose was to put him into an imagined conversation with two differing approaches that dealing with the modern and the colonial. It seems that Alatas resonates more with the post-colonial framework. His insistence on a universal nature and the essence of sciences allows him to attempt and maintain an objective approach; grounded in a call to dispel imitation and autonomously, and thus to apply an already existing universally valid corpus of knowledge for the betterment of society. Nevertheless, this universality seems to not be in conformity with the decolonial framework, as decolonization's main aim is to reject claims to universality, and rather aims at establishing a "pluriverse." The objectification of nature is an example of the call for rejecting universality, as science, and the scientific method, carries with it epistemological grounds that are specific, and thus, cannot with ease be introduced as universal categories. Similarly, anthropology or sociology is not considered by them as a universal science, as they are contextually sensitive. This means that the sciences were contextual, viz. they were used in particular circumstances, by specific people in the discourse on colonialism in order to build on global hierarchies and study people as objects of knowledge. This is perhaps the fundamental difference between Alatas' writings and the decolonial school.

Nevertheless, it might be erroneous to entirely claim that Alatas does not seem to resonate with the decolonial framework of thought altogether, as his notions of "intellectual captivity," and the ways in which such captivity propel and perpetuate Eurocentrism, are fundamental aspects of decolonial thought. Similarly, his discourse on the "othering" and the creation of the myth of the lazy native predates Quijano's concept of coloniality-modernity dichotomy. Alatas labelled this as a "colonial ideology" seemingly without thoroughly exploring the nuances of such a terminology, as it might be argued that a "colonial ideology" might be the first and foremost offspring that the decolonial school is endeavoring to delink from and take distance of.

On the other hand, Alatas' rejection of the universalization of the particular, and his call for native people to merge and utilize their culture in the face of Western modernity seems to resonate with the following: Bhabha's notion of hybridity; the general post-colonial program of further inclusion within the academic field at large; and the presentation of non-Western alternatives to certain academic discourses.

Nevertheless, this chapter is far from doing justice to Alatas' numerous works; rather, it is a humble attempt to gauge the thought of a prolific and erudite thinker who left his imprints via the enormous legacy and diversity of his works, which has become reference works to the future generations. Alatas' lasting impact goes beyond Southeast Asia to the Globe at large, as he not only made significant contributions to understanding the nature of colonialism and its ramifications, but also offered an outstanding framework vis-à-vis critical social theory, which ought to be included in academic curricula world-wide.

Bibliography

Alatas, Syed Hussein. *The Myth of the Lazy Native: A Study of the Image of the Malays, Filipinos and Javanese from the 16th to the 20th Century and Its Function in the Ideology of Colonial Capitalism.* London: Frank Cass and Co., Ltd., 1977.

Alatas, Syed Hussein. "Religion and Modernization in Southeast Asia," *European Journal of Sociology/Archives Européennes de Sociologie/Europäisches Archiv für Soziologie* 11 no.2 (1970): 265–296.

Alatas, Syed Hussein. *Intellectual Captivity and Developing Societies.* Ciudad de Mexico: Colegio de Mexico, 1981.

Alatas, Syed Hussein. "Intellectual Imperialism: Definition, Traits, and Problems." *Southeast Asian Journal of Social Science* 28 no. 1 (2000): 23–45.

Alatas, Syed Hussein. "The autonomous, the universal and the future of sociology." *Current Sociology* 54 no. 1 (2006): 7–23.

Bhabha, Hommi K. *The Location of Culture*. London: Routledge, 2012.

Fanon, Frantz. *Black Skin, White Masks*. New York: Grove Press, 2008.

Grosfoguel, Ramon. *Colonial Subjects: Puerto Ricans in a Global Perspective*. Berkeley, CA: University of California Press, 2003.

Khaldun, Ibn *The Muqaddimah: An Introduction to History*. Translated by Franz Rosenthal. Edited by N.J. Dawood. London: Routledge, 1978.

Maia, Joao Marcelo. "History of Sociology and the Quest for Intellectual Autonomy in the Global South," *Current Sociology* 62 no. 7 (2014): 1097–1115.

Mignolo, Walter. "The Geopolitics of Knowledge and the Colonial Difference." *The South Atlantic Quarterly* 101 no. 1 (2002): 57–96.

Mignolo, Walter. "Delinking: The Rhetoric of Modernity, the Logic of Coloniality and the Grammar of De-coloniality." *Cultural Studies* 21 no. 2–3 (2007): 449–514.

Mignolo, Walter. *The Darker Side of Western Modernity*. Durham, NC: Duke University Press, 2011.

Moosavi, Leon. "Decolonising Criminology: Syed Hussein Alatas on Crimes of the Powerful." *Critical Criminology* 27 no. 2 (2019): 229–242.

Quijano, Aníbal. "Coloniality of Power and Eurocentrism in Latin America." *International Sociology* 15 no. 2 (2000): 215–232.

Quijano, Aníbal. "Coloniality and Modernity/Rationality." *Cultural Studies* 21 no. 2–3 (2007): 168–178.

Said, Edward. *Orientalism: Western Concepts of the Orient*. New York: Pantheon, 1978.

Sayyid, Bobby S. *A Fundamental Fear: Eurocentrism and the Emergence of Islamism*. London: Zed Books, 1998.

CHAPTER 12

The Invention of "Islam"

How (Lazy) Historians and Social Scientists Created a Fantasy

Carimo Mohomed

1   Introduction

> Although there is no historical proof of this happening, it was an
> event that changed the world.

The reader might think that these words refer to the crossing of the Red Sea
by Moses, or to the Resurrection of Jesus, or the Ascension into Heaven by
Muhammad because, as Sanjay Seth reminds us, it was/is believed that only
the (modern) West had/has historiography, i.e., rational historiography, while
everyone else, with few exceptions that confirm the rule, had/have myths and
religious epics.[1]

However, the above words are a quotation from the website of the German
National Tourist Board and refer to an act that is considered as the moment
when one of the crucial foundations of modern Western civilization was
laid: the nailing of Martin Luther's (1483–1546) *Ninety-Five Theses* to the door
of the Castle Church in Wittenberg.[2] In doing so, the myth goes that he not

---

1   Sanjay Seth, "Reason or Reasoning? Clio or Siva?," *Social Text* 78, no. 22, 1 (Durham: Duke
     University Press, March 2004), 85.
2   All the dates in this chapter are C.E., and when I say C.E. I mean Christian Era and not
     Common Era. For reasons that resemble George Orwell's *Newspeak*, some scholars have
     transformed the abbreviation C.E. from Christian Era into Common Era, the argument
     being that it describes a universal chronology that is not exclusively based on a Christian
     perspective, avoiding the theological expressions "before Christ era" and "Christ era," since
     it is used by non-Christians as well as Christians – this is a fallacy: the so-called "Common
     Era" *is* the Gregorian calendar, which starts with a foundational moment, in this case the
     birth of Jesus, and this calendar was imposed to the rest of the World in the 19th and the 20th
     centuries. For more on "foundational moments," see Martin Heidegger, "Der Zeitbegriff in
     der Geschichtswissenschaft" ["The Concept of Time in the Science of History"], in *Zeitschrift
     für Philosophie und Philosophie Kritik* 161 (1916), 173–188. For further details on Martin
     Heidegger's conceptions, and concepts, of Time, see Martin Heidegger, *History of the Concept
     of Time: Prolegomena*, translated by Theodore Kisiel (Bloomington: Indiana University Press,
     1985), and François Raffoul, "Heidegger and the Aporia of History," in *Poligrafi: Natural
     History*, 16, 61–62 (2011), 91–118. For further details on how the Western concept of Time was

---

© CARIMO MOHOMED, 2023 | DOI:10.1163/9789004521698_014

only called into question the theology and authority of the Roman Catholic Church but also struck a blow for liberty and individual conscience. Despite all the talk about "Rationalism" and "Enlightenment," the supposed fact that gave birth to it, the Protestant Reformation, is itself shrouded in *irrational* and *obscurantist myths*: it seems that the "West" is irrational as well.[3]

As Mark Konnert refers, it is now almost sixty years since Erwin Iserloh (1915–1996) challenged the historicity of the *Thesenanschlag* (the actual physical act of posting of the *Ninety-Five Theses*). It was in 1961 that Iserloh first declared that the *Thesenanschlag* was a legend, prompting a significant controversy and debate in Germany, heightened by the fact that Iserloh was also a Roman Catholic priest, whom German Protestants accused of attempting to rob them of a cornerstone of their cultural identity. What emerged as equally certain was that contrary to the widely perceived myth, there was nothing at all revolutionary or daring about the theses. Not only did Luther not question the validity of indulgences or the authority of the pope, but the great hallmark of Luther's Reformation – salvation by faith alone – also does not appear in them.[4] As Paul Otto and Jaap Jacobs assert, '[t]he writing of history comes with many challenges – dealing with an overabundance or a paucity of sources, reading through bias in the sources, facing disagreements among historians, and the need to communicate historical findings effectively.'[5] Or, as Kenneth Baxter Wolf argues, despite aspiring to scientific rigor, the modern historian knows s/he has not "proved" anything until s/he has "convinced" his/her reader that his/her particular explanation makes the most sense out of the data. Despite the many advances made in the study of history, its practice is still predicated

---

imposed to the rest of the World, see Chris Lorenz and Berber Bevernage (ed.), *Breaking up Time: Negotiating the Borders between Present, Past and Future* (Göttingen: Vandenhoeck & Ruprecht GmbH & Co. KG, 2013), especially 199–215, 216–235, and 252–273.

3 For a recent analysis on how the West has failed its own promises, please see Ben Ryan, *How the West Was Lost: The Decline of a Myth and the Search for New Stories* (London: Hurst, 2019).

4 More recently, Peter Marshall used the details surrounding the alleged *Thesenanschlag* and the reception of the *Ninety-Five Theses* to elucidate the cultural history of an imagined event, and how it ended up becoming a defining episode of European history: Peter Marshall, *1517: Martin Luther and the Invention of the Reformation* (Oxford: Oxford University Press, 2017), and the review by Mark Konnert at http://www.h-net.org/reviews/showrev.php?id=51781. Accessed 23 November 2019.

For another German example of how "the past is always changing," see Christopher Clark, *Time and Power: Visions of History in German Politics, from the Thirty Years' War to the Third Reich* (Princeton: Princeton University Press, 2019).

5 Paul Otto and Jaap Jacobs, "Introduction: Historians and the Public Debate about the Past," *Journal of Early American History* 3 (2013), 1.

THE INVENTION OF "ISLAM" 263

on heavy doses of "convincing." Every historical interpretation should come with a *caveat emptor*: very few conclusions are in fact conclusive.[6]

Jason Ānanda Josephson-Storm, in his new book, *The Myth of Disenchantment: Magic, Modernity, and the Birth of the Human Sciences,* describes the continued vitality of esoteric, magical, and occult ideas in our allegedly disenchanted world.[7] The notion of "disenchantment," supposedly first articulated into a master-narrative by Max Weber (1864–1920), is the view that the road to modernity (capitalism) came through a conscious rejection of magical, numinous, and supernatural beliefs in favor of scientific explanations, thus transforming modern existence into an iron cage of reason. Josephson-Storm, however, rejects this narrative, and argues that the human sciences were founded by scholars in the 19th century who not only were interested in the esoteric but also participated in spiritual séances, theosophical meetings, occult practice, and magic. In providing a "philosophical archaeology" of the idea of disenchantment, Josephson-Storm argues that the theorists who formulated the "disenchantment myth" were surrounded by an enchanted world and maintains that the human sciences emerged as an academic discipline in the 19th century alongside flourishing theosophical and spiritualist movements. Those early social theorists who proclaimed the end of myth were themselves profoundly enmeshed in the occult milieu. In other words, Josephson-Storm argues that one "myth" has merely replaced another.

Even Max Weber, who conceived of modernization as *die Entzauberung der Welt,* the "de-magic-ing" of the world, did not escape from the influence of the Hermetic Brotherhood of Light, a fraternity devoted to practical magic, clairvoyance, and astral projection. Weber, of Protestant background, believed that the disenchantment of the world was carried out to its full conclusion in Protestantism. For him, religion was a robust reality and an effective force in history, and his *The Protestant Ethic and the Spirit of Capitalism* (1905) was one of three volumes in his sociology of religion – the latter two being, *The Religion of China* (1915) and *The Religion of India* (1916) – which, together, attempted to show how Protestantism shaped the world. Weber, a man who, to the best of my knowledge, had never set foot on Asian soil, who had never seen an Indian or Chinese village, never met and spoken to a single Indian or Chinese in his life, was the paradigm of the (modern) Western scholar: "scientific" work based

---

6   Kenneth Baxter Wolf, "Negating Negationism," *Pomona Faculty Publications and Research.* Paper 394 (2014), 9, available at http://scholarship.claremont.edu/pomona_fac_pub/394. Accessed 23 November 2019.

7   Jason Ānanda Josephson-Storm, *The Myth of Disenchantment: Magic, Modernity, and the Birth of the Human Sciences* (Chicago: University of Chicago Press, 2017).

on hearsay (in this case, *readsay* or *readwrite* with the respective footnotes) and selective in choosing what to use to make his point, not to mention his ignorance about the *Bible* (by reading Matthew 6:28, one hardly is exhorted to work hard to attain future prosperity and wealth), and the thesis on the separation of religion and politics in Christianity is based on a false axiom, a delusion bordering on magical thinking ("Christianity is apolitical" – if that is the case, how to explain the fact that the Catholic Church is a political institution, or that several Protestant European countries have state religion?). Indeed, Weber's narrative of disenchantment was infused with theology.[8] Josephson-Storm asserts that those theorists of disenchantment were themselves entangled in enchantment, and, accordingly, both "modernity" and "postmodernity" are myths. Since we have never been modern, since "reason" has never ruled us, there has never been a postmodern age. Both are stories we tell ourselves and are therefore less descriptive than prescriptive.[9]

It should be clear by now that this chapter, inspired by Syed Hussein Alatas' *The Myth of the Lazy Native*, will try to explore how "Islam" was a myth created in the 19th century.[10] To use Irfan Ahmad's words, history is considered as an

---

8   It is always useful to recall Carl Schmitt (1888–1985): "all significant concepts of the modern theory of the state are secularized theological concepts not only because of their historical development – in which they were transferred from theology to the theory of the state, whereby, for example, the omnipotent God becomes the omnipotent lawgiver – but also because of their systematic structure ..." Carl Schmitt, *Political Theology: Four Chapters on the Concept of Sovereignty* (Chicago: University of Chicago Press, 2005), 36. One could paraphrase Schmitt, or Harold Laski (1893–1950) ["What the Absolute is to metaphysics, that is the state to political theory'"], for other examples: the calendar (Christian is replaced with Common); education and knowledge (men of Church are replaced with experts and professors); economics (God is replaced with "the invisible hand of the Market"); astronomy ("Let there be light" with the "Big Bang theory," a theory which, ironically, can be traced back to Georges Lemaître (1894–1966), a Belgian Catholic priest and astronomer); and so on.

9   For further details on how the brain works, when it comes to tell stories to others and to ourselves, see Michael S. Gazzaniga, *The Mind's Past* (Berkeley, CA: University of California Press, 2000).

10   Syed Hussein Alatas, *The Myth of the Lazy Native: A study of the image of the Malays, Filipinos and Javanese from the 16th to the 20th century and its function in the ideology of colonial capitalism* (London: Frank Cass, 1977). Other sources of inspiration were Eric Hobsbawm and Terence Ranger (Eds.), *The Invention of Tradition* (Cambridge: Cambridge University Press, 2012) and Jason Ānanda Josephson, *The Invention of Religion in Japan* (Chicago: University of Chicago Press, 2012). For further details and a re-examination of the triumphalist narrative about how religious freedom was first introduced in Japan by the United States after World War II, please see Jolyon Baraka Thomas, *Faking Liberties: Religious Freedom in American-Occupied Japan* (Chicago: University of Chicago Press, 2019). In this book, the author critically examines the claim that "true" religious freedom and secularism were first introduced in Japan during the Allied occupation,

THE INVENTION OF "ISLAM" 265

ideographic discipline in that it aims to record and describe "the particular facts of past." In contrast, anthropology is regarded as a nomothetic discipline because its goal is "to arrive at general propositions or theoretical statements."[11] Sociology too is considered as a nomothetic discipline.[12] The ubiquity of dichotomized categories in writings on the histories of Islam across regions and times, however, points toward the nomothetic orientation of history vis-à-vis the research and writings on Muslims.[13]

In the "Introduction" to his book, Alatas explains that his work attempts to analyze the origins and functions of the "myth of the lazy native" from the 16th to the 20th century in Malaysia, the Philippines and Indonesia. The methodological approach is by way of the sociology of knowledge. The function of myth as a significant element in colonial ideology is illustrated by recourse to historical and sociological examples. Two concepts that had been consistently used needed clarification, i.e., ideology and colonial capitalism. Relying heavily on Karl Mannheim's (1893–1947) concept of ideology, it reflects that segment of the thought world that has characterized the political philosophy of colonialism in the Asian setting.[14] It reflects an objective reality – the ideology of colonialism. An ideology, accordingly, is a system of belief characterized by several traits:

- it seeks to justify a particular political, social and economic order.
- in this attempt, it distorts that part of the social reality likely to contradict its main presuppositions.
- it exists primarily in the form of a manifest thought content that is different from its latent content.
- it is authoritative in nature.
- it expresses the interests of a distinctive group.

---

and that religion had previously only been nominally free, noting that State Shinto was essentially an invention of the occupiers so that they could eradicate a state religion and replace it with religious freedom. Since the constitutionally secular Imperial Japan did not have a national religion, the Americans essentially had to create State Shinto in order for it to be destroyed.

11   Tim Ingold, "Anthropology is *Not* Ethnography," *Proceedings of the British Academy* 154 (2008), 69–92.

12   John H. Goldthorpe, *On Sociology: Numbers, Narratives, and the Integration of Research and Theory* (Oxford, New York: Oxford University Press, 2000).

13   Irfan Ahmad, "Foreword: On Writing History," in Tauseef Ahmad Parray, *Mediating Islam and Modernity: Sir Sayyid, Iqbal and Azad* (New Delhi: Viva Books, 2019), XI–XII.

14   Karl Mannheim, *Ideology and Utopia: An Introduction to the Sociology of Knowledge* (New York: Harcourt, Brace and Company, 1936).

- when it is dominant it creates a false consciousness among the group it represents as well as the group it dominates.
- it can draw its ideas from any source, science, religion, culture, economics, history, etc.
- it arises out of the conflicting interests of separate groups, in a society with a pronounced division of labor and social classes; and
- its major ideas are eventually to a large extent conditioned by the mode of production in a given time and place.

There are the ideologies of the ruling class and there are the ideologies of the subjugated classes, what Mannheim called "total ideologies" and "particular ideologies." The colonial ideology utilized the idea of the lazy native to justify compulsion and unjust practices in the mobilization of labor in the colonies.[15] It portrayed a negative image of the natives and their society to justify and rationalize European conquest and domination of the area.[16] It distorted elements of social and human reality to ensure a comfortable construction of the ideology.[17] As to colonial capitalism, it was characterized by the following traits:

- predominant control of and access to capital by an alien economic power.
- the control of the colony by a government run by members of the alien power, acting on its behalf.
- the highest level of business, trade and industry, held by the alien dominating community.
- direction of the country's export and import trade to suit the interest of the alien ruling power.
- a bias towards the agrarian mode of production as opposed to that of industry.
- the minimal expansion of technological and scientific skill.

---

15 For an example of this practice in the Portuguese empire, see Eric Allina, *Slavery by Any Other Name: African Life under Company Rule in Colonial Mozambique.* Charlottesville, VA: The University of Virginia Press, 2012.

16 During a trip in 2007 to Switzerland and Luxembourg, I passed by Arlon, a Belgian town near the border, and I had the opportunity to see a statue of Leopold II (1835–1909, r. 1865–1909) with the following inscription: "J'ai entrepris l'oeuvre du Congo dans l'intérêt de la civilisation et pour le bien de la Belgique" ["I have undertaken the opus of the Congo for the sake of civilization and for the benefit of Belgium"] – yes, let's civilize other people through violence, if necessary, at the same time that barking at them on Human Rights ...

17 Robert Clive's (1725–1774) justification for the conquest of Bengal was to take over a region, "whose talented and active population" had created considerable wealth, because its lazy people "did not deserve the wealth that their talent had created" – Bonnie G. Smith, *Modern Empires: A Reader* (New York and London: Oxford University Press, 2017), 147.

THE INVENTION OF "ISLAM"   267

- the organization of production around semi-free labor.
- the absence of guilds or trade unions as a counterweight to exploitation.
- the non-involvement of large sections of the population in direct capitalist enterprise; and
- the presence of a set of antitheses in the colonized society described by the term dualism.

The ideology of colonial capitalism sought a justification of Western rule in its alleged aim of modernizing and civilizing, not to say to "normalize," the societies that had succumbed to Western powers.[18] One of the most outspoken ideologists in this region was Thomas Stamford Raffles (1781–1826).[19]

---

18   A recent book, *Normality: A Critical Genealogy* (Chicago: The University of Chicago Press, 2017), by Peter Cryle and Elizabeth Stephens, aims to broaden current understandings of the concept of normality that go beyond the generally accepted binary of the normal versus the abnormal, which is fine, but the authors argue against the discourse of normality, which rests on its normative function in producing conformity – this is nonsense. And this nonsense is even greater considering that the authors draw from a series of extensive case studies from Europe and the United States that range from criminal anthropology to craniometry, anthropometrics, sociology, and eugenics, arguing that contemporary notions of normality emerged in the first half of the 20th century as a result of the rise of consumer culture within democratic capitalist societies, which centered on self-management and individual improvement. The nonsense of the argument is even more blatant considering that the authors are fully aware that it was used within medical discourse to denote good general and physiological health, tracing the development of the concept of what is "normal" from 1820 up to 1950. The research is based on a diverse range of mostly medical disciplines, such as psychiatry, psychology, sexology, psychoanalysis, and public health. Anyone who is acquainted with the early days of psychiatry and psychology is fully aware that one of the objectives was to normalize people according to a pre-established framework and to make them more "productive" using, if necessary, repressive means. Even nowadays, one just needs to browse the shelves of bookshops and of libraries under the subject of "self-help" or "personal growth" and find books that help you to be more productive in your lives. The case of the athlete Caster Semenya is a very good example of "be normal according to our 'scientific' standards or else be punished." For an example of "normality" in a colonial context, please refer to David Kloos, "A Crazy State: Violence, Psychiatry, and Colonialism in Aceh, Indonesia, ca. 1910–1942," *Bijdragen tot de Taal-, Land- en Volkenkunde* 170 (2014), 25–65.

19   In 1971, with his *Thomas Stamford Raffles, 1781–1826, schemer or reformer?* (Singapore: Angus and Robertson, 1971), Syed Hussein Alatas problematized the untainted image of Raffles and brought to light some aspects of his character, questioning the works written by some historians and biographers. The book did also focus on his political philosophy, and we get a glimpse into how he viewed Southeast Asia, its people, and how he intended to bring "progress" to the region. More recently, in 2011, Syed Hussain's brother Muhammad Naquib, in his *Historical Fact and Fiction* (Kuala Lumpur: UTM Press, 2011), aimed to shed new light on written events dismissed as fiction by European historians, and attempted to provide a new interpretation of the primary sources from over 1,000 years ago.

For example, this was manifested in his discourse in various forms. The first was by way of portraying Hinduism/Buddhism as practiced by the Malays as a binary opposite of Islam. In doing this, Raffles devoted a considerable part of his argument to showing how Hinduism/Buddhism had brought forth an ideal social order – the caste system – and many other achievements in the arts and sciences. Such achievements were manifested in classical texts and monuments of which Islam had obliterated. This is followed by demonstrating how certain aspects of Hinduism/Buddhism were comparable, albeit to a limited extent, to European traditions and religions. To augment it all, Raffles stressed that the Hindu/Buddhist legacy was in a state of decline. The island of Bali was the only "living museum" of the lost Hindu societies with elements of Hinduism/Buddhism perfectly in place. He thus saw it as his duty to be the first and most dedicated proponent of the description, protection, and presentation of the island of Bali. Having read and stayed in the Malay Archipelago since 1805, Raffles was aware that a majority of the Malays were Muslims and saw Islam as one of the vital elements of Malayness. This social fact was further reinforced by the works of his contemporaries, who argued that the Malays often regarded non-Muslim tribes as un-Malay and that one of the prerequisites of *Masuk Melayu* (Becoming Malay), aside from customs and costumes, was the conversion to Islam. Yet, Raffles argued that Hinduism/Buddhism was the first and "real" religion of the Malays, specifically the Javanese. This "real" religion, which had brought forth many positive effects upon the Malays, was eroded by the advent of Islam causing a grave loss to the Malays. In his effort to propound Hinduism/Buddhism as a binary opposite to Islam and thus needing to be recovered, Raffles stressed three features that he posited as absent in the latter: an "ideal" social order, texts, and monuments. Raffles argued that unlike the Muslim societies he had encountered, Hinduism/Buddhism had brought about an ideal social order in line with British interests. Embedded within this social order was the caste system, which was often seen by British Orientalists in the 19th century as a pillar of all Hindu societies. Such a way of life, although perceived as oppressive, needed to be promoted to ensure an ordered, hierarchical society similar to that at home. Also, such structured society was necessary to maintain a self-policing system, which would ensure a degree of peace and harmony for the pursuit of the East India Company's economic ambitions. Raffles subscribed almost fully to such a paradigm. He thus propounded that an established caste system was still in place amongst the Malays who were Hindus/Buddhists. Although he acknowledged that the system was not as rigid as that was practiced in India and that the Malays at all levels "mingle indiscriminately," partly due to the incorporation of Hindu/Buddhist ideas with that of the egalitarianism of Islam, he argued that the revival of such a rigid

THE INVENTION OF "ISLAM"

caste system was necessary for the promotion of agricultural development in Malay societies. Such organization was, to Raffles, a desirable and beneficial feature both for the natives and British economic aspirations that Islam had displaced. Following the importance of the caste system was the recognition of private property. To Raffles, the coming of Islam brought about the subsequent removal of this aspect in Malay societies. The oppressive rule of Muslim rulers had brought about state monopoly of the lands, which eliminated any independent property. Such inequitable social structure was, to him, absent in other Hindu/Buddhist societies in the Malay World where individuals' ownership of land was recognized and protected. Finally, Raffles believed that unlike their Muslim counterparts who were constantly at war, the Hindus/Buddhists lived in a state of peace and harmony. Furthermore, unlike the Muslims, they were never attracted to the evil vices of gambling and opium-smoking. Hence, Hinduism/Buddhism was to Raffles a great religion and civilization, unlike Islam. One essential step to revive this lost civilization was the reinstitution of what was called the "village system," in contrast to the decadent Islamic system. Raffles perceived that such a system was necessary to regain the past greatness of the Malay peoples, whose Hindu/Buddhist cultural matrix was still present behind the veneer of Islamic consciousness. The Malays should also be compelled to revive the idea of the different titles and gradations of rank and revert to what they were supposed to be in the days of *Majapahit* and previously, when Hindu faith and institutions exclusively prevailed. Only then could peace and stability be restored, and British interests pursued.[20]

Whether it was in Malaysia, the Philippines or Indonesia, or whether it was the British, the Spaniards or the Dutch, the same type of arguments prevailed. The historical forms of the civilizing process differed; Catholicism in Malaysia and Indonesia, for example, was not considered as necessary to the civilizing process as it was in the Philippines. But all three powers were agreed that Western rule and Western culture were superior; that Western people should lead the world; that they were most suited to exploit the natural wealth of the East; and that they were the best administrators.[21] Consequently, the ideology

---

20 For a detailed analysis, see Syed Muhd Khairudin Aljunied, "Sir Thomas Stamford Raffles' Discourse on the Malay World: A Revisionist Perspective," *Sojourn* 20, no. 1 (2005), 6–8.
　　At the time that these lines are being written, the Indian government of Narendra Modi is pursuing a policy of defining and identifying who is a true Indian – it seems that albeit more than seventy years of independence the colonial mindset and practice is very alive and kicking.

21 I do not know if Syed Hussein Alatas would be amused or amazed to learn that in 2013 of the Christian era, a "scholarly" paper was published defending that the Dutch colonial containment of Islam in Manggarai (West-Flores), in favor of Catholicism, during 1907

of colonial capitalism played down the capacities of Southeast Asian societies, and every conceivable item was invoked to denigrate the Southeast Asian, including his size and physiognomy. Alatas gives the example of Geoffrey Gorer (1905–1985), an anthropologist specializing in the study of national character, a discipline intended to correct prejudices and arrive at true understanding, who early in his career observed of the Javanese that he did not personally find the Javanese very sympathetic:

> despite their fertility they give somehow the impression of being a race of old and exhausted people, only half alive. This impression may I think be due partly to their religion, and to the abysmal poverty of the greater number. Poverty, especially uncomplaining and involuntary poverty, is numbing and repulsive anywhere; and Mohammedanism is the most deadening of all creeds.[22] A purely personal point which prevented me enjoying their company was the question of size; I do not like being among people who appear smaller and weaker than I am, unless they have corresponding superiority elsewhere; I dislike the company of those I feel to be my inferiors.[23]

and 1942 *was in line with the colonial strategy of creating a prosperous Flores* ... Yes, the paper was published in 2013 and not in 1913 or 1963 ... Karel Steenbrink, "Dutch Colonial Containment of Islam in Manggarai, West-Flores, in Favour of Catholicism, 1907–1942," *Bijdragen tot de Taal-, Land- en Volkenkunde* 169 (2013), 104–128.

22 I wonder if, had he had known the American punk rock band Dead Kennedys, Gorer would have *kill[ed] the poor* to solve the problem of poverty ...

23 Syed Hussein Alatas, *The Myth of the Lazy Native*, 7–8. Even before European colonialism established its superiority over the Ottoman Empire and other Muslim regions, European authors took a regal and superior attitude toward the nations of the Orient, as shown by this declaration from an early 18th century collection of pictures from the Near East: "The reader imagines himself inspecting the other inhabitants of the Earth, and exercising over them a kind of sovereignty, he examines them with attention, approves or condemns their choice of customs, amuses himself and often laughs at the oddness of some, sometimes admires the beauty and majesty of others, always preferring the customs of the country where he was born." Jean-Baptiste Vanmour (1671–1737), *One Hundred Prints Representing Different Nations of the Levant* (Paris, 1712–13), quoted by Lisa Small, "Western Eyes, Eastern Visions," in *A Distant Muse: An Orientalist Works from the Dahesh Museum of Art* (New York: Dahesh Museum of Art, 2000), 9, and in Carl W. Ernst, *Following Muhammad: Rethinking Islam in the Contemporary World* (Chapel Hill & London: The University of North Carolina Press, 2003), 191. For examples of how Anthropology was politically used to "define and rule," and the ways in which was a bedfellow of Colonialism, please refer to Gérard Leclerc, *Anthropologie et colonialisme: essai sur l'histoire de l'africanisme* (Paris: Fayard, 1972); Talal Asad (ed.), *Anthropology and the Colonial Encounter* (London: Ithaca, 1973); Bernard S. Cohn, *An Anthropologist Among the Historians and Other Essays* (New York: Oxford University Press, 1988); Bernard

As Mohammad R. Salama clearly asserts, anthropology was a famous academic discipline involved in that particular field of colonial cultural production, which was perhaps the most productive rubric under which the native "Other" was imported and exported from Europe.[24] From the real differences of non-European peoples, 19th century anthropologists constructed another being of a different nature; differential cultural and physical traits were constructed as the essence of the African, the Arab, the Aboriginal, and so forth. When colonial expansion was at its peak, while the European powers were engaged in a scramble for Africa, anthropology and the study of non-European peoples became not only a scholarly endeavor, but also a broad field of public instruction.[25] The so-called "Other" was imported to Europe – in natural history museums, public exhibitions of primitive peoples (the (in)famous *Volkerschau* or *human zoos*), in sociological and archaeological research – and thus made increasingly available for the popular imagination. Nineteenth-century anthropology presented the Islamic world, as well as many non-European peoples and cultures, as underdeveloped versions of Europeans and their civilizations, namely, as signs of primitiveness that represented stages on a very long road of European civilizations. The anthropological presentation of non-European others within the evolutionary theory of civilizations served to confirm and validate the eminent position of Europeans and thereby legitimate the colonialist project as a whole.[26]

As Alatas asserted, the ideological denigration of the native and of his history and society ranged from vulgar fantasy and untruth to refined scholarship. Ideology intrudes upon scholarship not only in the formation of concepts but also in the selection of problems. As Mannheim pointed out, an observer could

---

S. Cohn, *Colonialism and its Forms of Knowledge: the British in India* (Princeton: Princeton University Press, 1997); Mahmood Mamdani, *Define and Rule: Native as Political Identity* (Cambridge, MA: Harvard University Press, 2012); and C. J. Fuller, "Colonial Anthropology and the Decline of the Raj: Caste, Religion and Political Change in India in the Early Twentieth Century," *Journal of the Royal Asiatic Society* 26, no. 3 (2016), 463–486.

24   Mohammad R. Salama, *Islam, Orientalism and Intellectual History* (London: I. B. Tauris, 2011), 240, footnote 65.

25   For an example of the perpetuation of the myth of the "civilizing" of Africa, see Thomas Pakenham, *The Scramble for Africa: The White Man's Conquest of the Dark Continent from 1876 to 1912* (New York: Random House, 1991), and the review of this book by A. G. Hopkins, "'Blundering and Plundering': The Scramble for Africa Relived," *The Journal of African History* 34, no. 3 (1993), 489–494.

26   For further details, see Nicholaus Thomas, *Colonialism's Culture: Anthropology, Travel, and Government* (Princeton, N.J.: Princeton University Press, 1994); Michel de Certeau, *The Writing of History* (New York: Columbia University Press, 1992); and Michael Hardt and Antonio Negri, *Empire* (Cambridge, MA: Harvard University Press, 2000).

escape the distorting influence of ideology provided he became conscious of the social roots of his ideas and general attitudes. Thus, the statement that scholarship is conditioned by ideology should not be taken in the absolute sense that each and every scholar is necessarily and unconsciously influenced by his/her ideology. What Alatas was saying is that during the colonial period, and to a large extent thereafter, the study of the Malays, Javanese, and Filipinos had been overwhelmingly dominated by ideological forces of the uncritical and superficial kind. A scholar who is mature and objective may allow ideological considerations in his/her choice of subject but his/her study on the subject itself will have to follow normal scientific procedures and seek objectivity.[27]

Alatas acknowledges that his own ideological considerations in the book affected the choice of subject. It was an effort to correct a one-sided colonial view of the Asian native and his/her society. He believed in the primarily negative influence of colonialism, and in the need to unmask the colonial ideology, for its influence was/is still very strong, but an attempt to correct this should not be considered automatically as a reversal of the coin. It is the facts adduced, the evidence marshalled, the themes introduced, the analyses accomplished, and the attitudes of the scholar that should finally decide whether the attempt is merely a reversal of the coin or a real extension and supplementation of existing knowledge. That objectivity in scholarship is possible despite the influence of ideology on the choice of theme – but not on the reasoning and analysis. In a total and fundamental sense, no scholarship is free from the influence of ideology. The influence of ideology can be vulgar, and it can be refined. Whatever decision a researcher takes is based on a certain system of values which are in turn related to his/her ideology. The influence of ideology

---

27   It should be stressed that even in the "hard" sciences objectivity is not a given. For example, according to Lorraine Daston and Peter Galison, objectivity means different things at different times and its history did not begin in the 17th century. According to them, mechanical objectivity emerged as a scientific ideal in the mid-nineteenth century, and it did so in tandem with subjectivity – Lorraine Daston and Peter Galison, *Objectivity* (New York: Zone Books, 2007). For further details on how science is done/made/created and validated, please see Pierre Bourdieu, *Science de la science et refléxivité. Cours au Collège de France, 2000–2001* (Paris: Éditions Raisons d'Agir, 2001) [English translation, *Science of Science and Reflexivity* (London: Polity, 2004)] – In this work, Bourdieu (1930–2002) declares that science is in danger of becoming a handmaiden to biotechnology, medicine, genetic engineering, and military research; that it risks falling under the control of industrial corporations that seek to exploit it for monopolies and profit. Science thus endangered can become detrimental to mankind. The line between pure and applied science, therefore, must be subjected to intense theoretical scrutiny, and his goals are to identify the social conditions in which science develops in order to reclaim its objectivity and to rescue it from relativism and the forces that might exploit it.

THE INVENTION OF "ISLAM" 273

at this level is unavoidable but once the scholar is aware of it and if s/he is sincerely devoted to an ideal of objectivity s/he can proceed without allowing his/her initial ideological commitment to distort their analysis and conclusions. It should be possible for a native scholar committed to the ideal of independence to recognize the merits of colonialism without distorting them, Similarly, the converse should be true. What he was concerned with was the negative influence of ideology, the distorting, uncritical, inconsistent streak in a scholar's reasoning that arises from an unconscious attachment to their ideology.[28]

Drawing on several works, I will explore how historians and social scientists, having as starting points assumptions and truisms, platitudes, and canards, particularly in "scientific" fields such as Political Science or International Relations, create myths about "Islam," myths that were used for the advancement of the Western Colonial project, and are still used for maintaining a discursive hegemony. In fact, many formerly colonized people still accept the "knowledge" that is produced, and the (hi)stories told by others, regarding themselves.[29]

2   History at the Service of Ignorance, Social Sciences at the Service of Barbarity

One does not need to be uneducated or a member of a far-right group to think that there is a country called "Islam." It was possible for Immanuel Wallerstein

---

28   For Sanjay Seth, Eurocentrism can be challenged through two strategies, *i.e.*, Historical Sociology and Postcolonial Theory. As a practitioner of the latter, Seth prefers that strategy. I personally think that combined are more valuable. Sanjay Seth, "Historical Sociology and Postcolonial Theory: Two Strategies for Challenging Eurocentrism," *International Political Sociology* 3, no. 3 (September 2009), 334–338. For a nice analysis of the pitfalls of Postcolonial Theory, see Frederick Cooper, *Colonialism in Question: Theory, Knowledge, History* (Berkeley: University of California Press, 2005), especially 3–32. For more on Postcolonial Theory, please see *Leela Gandhi, Postcolonial Theory: A Critical Introduction: Second Edition* (New York: Columbia University Press, 2019).

29   In what follows, I have relied on, and developed further, previous writings of mine: Carimo Mohomed, "Ideology by Any Other Name: Social Sciences and the Humanities as Western Catechism," in Dustin J. Byrd and Seyed Javad Miri (eds.), *Ali Shariati and the Future of Social Theory* (Boston and Leiden: Brill, 2017), 21–63; Carimo Mohomed, "'The Parting of the Ways': A Qutbian Approach to International Relations," in *Islam and International Relations*, ed. Deina Abdelkader, Nassef Manabilang Adiong, and Raffaele Mauriello (London: Palgrave Macmillan UK, 2016), 165–183; Carimo Mohomed, "Rethinking the 'Middle East' as an Object of Study," *Annals of Japan Association for Middle East Studies* 31, no. 2 (2015), 265–301; Carimo Mohomed, "Reconsidering 'Middle East and Islamic Studies' for a changing world," *International Critical Thought* 2, no. 2 (2012), 197–208.

(1930–2019) to write in his article "Islam, the West, and the World",[30] originally delivered as a lecture at the Oxford Centre for Islamic Studies on 21 October 1998, that the title had two geographic terms in it, so he thought it was best to start by taking a look at the geography.[31] And all the problems of the Social Sciences start here, with the method employed. In any scientific endeavor, or considered as such, methodology and epistemology are paramount, not to mention ontology: what is the nature of the reality that we are studying? What is the nature of the knowledge that is being produced and its rationality?[32] What are the methods applied to the field of study?[33]

It is commonplace today for pundits, government officials, and journalists to couch discussion of Muslim majority societies in terms of a global "Muslim World" – an analytical term employed by both Muslims and non-Muslims alike

---

30   Immanuel Wallerstein, "Islam, the West, and the World," *Journal of Islamic Studies* 10, 2 (1999), 109–125.

31   More than a century ago, the French Orientalist Bernard Carra de Vaux (1867–1953) warned his readers not to confuse "Islam" and "Orient," since the former was a religion and the latter a region. Furthermore, he considered that it was doubtful to explain everything solely based on religion or geography – Baron Carra de Vaux, *Les penseurs de l'islam* (Paris: Paul Geuthner, 1921–1926), vol. 5, 420–421.

32   For a personal account on the perils of studying "Islam," see Carl W. Ernst, *Following Muhammad: Rethinking Islam in the Contemporary World* (Chapel Hill & London: The University of North Carolina Press, 2003), especially the "Preface" on pages XIII–XXV.

33   Personally, I think that novels teach us more about a certain age or period than many history books. Fiction can sometimes be more illuminating about certain periods and societies, its social conditions, mores, mentality, than many historiographical studies dealing with that period. In fact, there are several works of fiction which could be better used as introductions to history and to the historian's fundamental problems than many books on epistemology or methodology: what is the Past? How do we know it? What is knowledge and, in this case, the knowledge of the past? Current and future historians would learn more about their own craft, and be more entertained, with some works of fiction than with many books on historiography, epistemological theory or methodology. For further details, see Carimo Mohomed, "The abolition of the Past: History in George Orwell's *1984*," *2011 2nd International Conference on Humanities, Historical and Social Sciences IPEDR* vol.17 (Singapore: IACSIT Press, 2011), 71–76. Here it is a personal list of some books that I found very entertaining and useful: A. S. Byatt, *Possession: A Romance* (London: Chatto & Windus, 1990); Ray Bradbury, *Fahrenheit 451* (London: Harper Collins Publishers, 1996 [1954]); Gustave Flaubert, *Bouvard et Pécuchet* (Paris: Lgf, 1999 [1881]); George Orwell, *Nineteen Eighty-Four* (New York: Harcourt, Brace and Company, 1949); Iain Pears, *An Instance of the Fingerpost* (London: Jonathan Cape, 1997); Kim Stanley Robinson, *Icehenge* (London: Voyager, 1997 [1984]); Jules Verne, *Les Enfants du capitaine Grant* [*The Children of Captain Grant*], translated as *In Search of the Castaways* (Paris: Pierre-Jules Hetzel, 1867–1868). Agnes Heller (1929–2019), in her *A Theory of History* (London: Routledge & Kegan Paul, 1982), has a very nice analysis of this work by Jules Verne.

THE INVENTION OF "ISLAM" 275

evoking a trans-historical geo-political unity among vastly diverse and disparate Muslim majority societies.

As Cemil Aydin explains in his *The Idea of the Muslim World*, it is a misconception to think that the world's 1.5 billion Muslims constitute a single religiopolitical entity, and he tries to answer to questions such as how did this belief arise, and why a mistaken notion is so widespread. Conceived as the antithesis of Western Christian civilization, the idea of the Muslim world emerged in the late 19th century, when European empires ruled the majority of Muslims. It was inflected from the start by theories of white supremacy, but Muslims had a hand in shaping the idea as well.

3 Political Science

As Jessica Blatt shows, race was crucial in the formation and development of American political science.[34] In her book, rather than suggesting that race lay outside of mainstream political science, the author argues that it was at its core. Starting from John William Burgess (1844–1931) in the late 19th century to Charles Edward Merriam (1874–1953) in the early 20th century, Blatt shows how ideas and conceptions concerning racial difference shaped the expansion of political science as a field of study in the academy to the articulation of different methodologies within the field. Let us not forget that the book *Essay on the Inequality of the Human Races* by Joseph Arthur de Gobineau (1816–1882)[35] was translated into English and published in America in 1856 soon after the first volume appeared [an abridgement, *The Moral and Intellectual Diversity of Races, with Particular Reference to Their Respective Influence in the Civil and Political History of Mankind* (Philadelphia: J. B. Lippincott, 1856)].

Gobineau's two-thousand-page book, although it did not invent race thinking, it raised it to the dignity of a theory of world history, promising to account for the rise, and especially the fall, of civilizations, and to make history into a science. Gobineau recognized ten civilizations in world history, and imagined unchanging qualities of race, more especially of the special virtues of the white race, which were causes of the rise of the world's ten civilizations, and the

---

34 Jessica Blatt, *Race and the Making of American Political Science* (Philadelphia: University of Pennsylvania Press, 2018), and the review by Vanessa E. Quince, available at http://www.h-net.org/reviews/showrev.php?id=53055. Accessed 23 November 2019.

35 Joseph Arthur, Comte de Gobineau, *Essai sur l'inégalité des races humaines* (Paris: Firmin Didot, 1853–1855), 4 vols.

racial mixture that empire inevitably brings was the cause of the fall of nine of them, Europe being the lone remaining exception, and only for the time being. For him, it was essential to keep in mind that race is not skin color, an observable phenomenon, but an invisible, inferred, unseen entity of which skin color and other bodily attributes are taken to be the signs. Gobineau asserts that the nature of this unseen entity, race, is that it is the unmoved mover of all history, itself a trans-historical object that never changes.[36]

One of the most compelling aspects of Blatt's discussion is the role of racial difference both within and outside of the United States, whose racism had long fascinated Europeans. For example, David Ciarlo,[37] with his *Advertising Empire*, shows how the construction of a racial, and ultimately racist, imagery of colonialism in Germany flowed from the United States. Blatt's text forces us to question the ways in which political scientists have used race as an explanatory variable to understand political phenomena. One of the most pressing questions that political scientists have tried to address since the field's founding in the 19th century to today is: why do ethnic minorities have different political behavior from their white counterparts, all else equal?[38] The answers have both theoretical and empirical implications. From the onset and throughout many parts of the book, Blatt centers the role of Burgess in making political science a field of social inquiry, giving special attention to his theory of Teutonism, where the state was the natural unit of analysis, and the racial homogeneity of the state was crucial to its development. For Burgess, the implications of this ideology were that the Aryan race was highly political while Asia and Africa were composed of unpolitical nations. Burgess's understanding of political science was to argue that there was a natural order of things and, according to Blatt, he made these arguments to justify how and why political science was a field uniquely different from those who philosophized about an ideal world.

---

36 Thomas R. Trautmann, "Does India Have History? Does History Have India?," *Comparative Studies in Society and History* 54, no. 1 (2012), 186–187.

37 David Ciarlo, *Advertising Empire: Race and Visual Culture in Imperial Germany* (Cambridge: Harvard University Press, 2011).

38 Usually, in the Social Sciences, in this kind of research, the "expert" already has the answer that it is trying to "discover." Of course, that other problems are not discussed or researched: why do "white counterparts," and not "ethnic minorities," have invented concentration camps and the gas chambers, all else equal?

THE INVENTION OF "ISLAM" 277

4 International Relations

In what refers to International Relations, Jennifer Pitts, in her study *The Boundaries of the International*, calls that the idea that conceives of the global society of nations as a European system of states writ large is a categorical fallacy, a "parochial universalism," and shows that it has deep roots in European thought: The world is not Europe; it never has been and never will be; neither does the world follow Europe's model; not even Europe follows its own purported model.[39]

Nevertheless, this "Parochial universalism" still has a tenacious hold on the present imagination, even if it is nowadays stripped of its 19th century racialized grandstanding. Pitts sees the English school of international relations theory in this tradition,[40] finding fault, first, with the historical presumption that the global society of nations evolved from the European society of nations and, second, with the systemic view that it resulted from the diffusion of the key principle of the European system, the equality of sovereign states. She rejects this as a "flat-earth" design for global politics, and while she puts too much trust in the equality of nations in Europe, her study shows that inequality and hierarchy had always been key features of the European system in its relations with the rest of the world.

Contemporary political theory about the society of nations has not gone very far beyond what was thought in Europe in the 18th and early 19th centuries. The "English school" is only one of the examples she offers that all build on the presumption that what once was right for Europe is still right for the world. We can observe, by reading Pitts's book that past legal and political thinkers debated how to grasp reality in international relations and how to recognize struggles over differences in approach and worldview. Drawing on the work of C. H. Alexandrowicz (1902–75), who had forcefully argued that the shift from the 18th to the 19th century was one from (enlightened)

---

39   Jennifer Pitts, *Boundaries of the International: Law and Empire* (Cambridge: Harvard University Press, 2018), and the review by Michael Geyer, available at http://www.h-net.org/reviews/showrev.php?id=51932. Accessed 23 November 2019. For international law, see Antony Anghie, *Imperialism, Sovereignty, and the Making of International Law* (Cambridge: Cambridge University Press, 2005).

40   The starting point is Hedley Bull, *The Anarchical Society: A Study of Order in World Politics* (New York: Columbia University Press, 1977). For a more recent work, see Adam Watson, *The Evolution of International Society: A Comparative Historical Analysis* (New York: Routledge, 1992).

cosmopolitanism to (imperial) Eurocentrism,[41] Pitts reworks this argument and takes as a historical fact what Alexandrowicz famously argued, namely, that British international and imperial politics were (and are) articulated in the language of international law, which as a result is a biased and flawed language, showing the fusion of international law and international and imperial politics: International law became the language of (the British) empire. Jeremy Bentham (1748–1832) coined the term "international law" to distinguish it from the older Christian and European *ius gentium* and to create a new understanding and, indeed, constitute a new type of law. Before Bentham, Emer (Emmerich) de Vattel (1714–67), whose *Droit de gens ou principes de la loi naturelle* (1758) remains a founding text of international law,[42] had radicalized the notion of reciprocity and recognition, eliminating hierarchy and deference, by insisting on the principled equality of nations as the main dictate of the law of nations. Vattel presumed this equality of nations to be "universal" and meant to say "worldwide," but the legal norms undergirding his universalism were thoroughly continental European and Christian;[43] Muslim states were excluded on suspicion of being incurably violent; and empire as a territorially amorphous regime of direct and indirect forms of dominion did not exist in Vattel's "Swiss" world of nations as moral persons.[44] In short, Vattel's universalism of equality among nations was predicated on the acceptance of the standards and norms of a European world. He was the quintessential "parochial universalist." Bentham's concept of "international law [jurisprudence]" emerged from these discussions, although his own views on the matter changed drastically over the course of the Revolutionary and Napoleonic Wars.

In the tradition of Vattel, he started out with a plan for "international law," whose main features were mutual recognition of states, non-intervention, and "mutual good offices" – in other words, a program for the self-restraint

---

41   C. H. Alexandrowicz, *The Law of Nations in Global History*, ed. David Armitage and Jennifer Pitts (Oxford: Oxford University Press, 2017).

42   Emer de Vattel, *The Law of Nations, or, Principles of the Law of Nature, Applied to the Conduct and Affairs of Nations and Sovereigns, with Three Early Essays on the Origin and Nature of Natural Law and on Luxury*, ed. Bela Kapossy and Richard Whatmore (Indianapolis: Liberty Fund, 2008); Vincent Chetail and Peter Haggenmacher (eds.), *Vattel's International Law from a XXIst Century Perspective / Le Droit International de Vattel vu du XXIe Siècle* (Boston: Brill – Nijhoff, 2011).

43   See Tetsuya Toyoda, *Theory and Politics of the Law of Nations: Political Bias in International Law Discourse of Seven German Court Councilors in the Seventeenth and Eighteenth Centuries* (Leiden: Martinus Nijhoff Publishers, 2011). Vattel was councilor at the Saxon Court.

44   See André Holenstein, *Mitten in Europa: Verflechtung und Abgrenzung in der Schweizer Geschichte* (Baden: Hier und Jetzt, 2014).

THE INVENTION OF "ISLAM"

of empire(s) as a prerequisite for peace. He subsequently shrank these far-flung "universal" ideas to apply to Christian nations only and interpreted non-intervention as freedom from international law in the internal affairs of colonies. Colonials thus lost their rights as sovereign actors, which in principle they had possessed within the *ius gentium*. Henry Wheaton's (1785–1848) *Elements of International Law: With a Sketch of the History of the Science* (1836) provided the definite articulation of this Benthamite line of argument. Wheaton was an American, but his arguments became the new normal,[45] racializing and rebaptizing the law of nations, declaring that the teachings of justice were a uniquely European (Christian) heritage and, hence, the law of nations could not possibly be universal. Therefore, the international community was an exclusively European, in fact "Western," club. The only way for non-Europeans to join was to adopt European law and presumably Christianity wholesale. It was left to British thinkers, such as John Stuart Mill (1806–1873), to develop it further. Teaching (civil) law to colonials became imperial pedagogy, and Pitts points to a tenacious opposition both against exclusions and against unequal integration, which is to say against the imperial encroachment on an existing worldwide society of nations.

This heritage, nevertheless, left vexing traces, presuppositions about the nature of humanity and of the society of nations that were remolded and reshaped, but proved to be difficult and indeed impossible to remove in their entirety. Old prejudices were powerfully reloaded. Thus, the idea of the universality of the *ius gentium* implied that all human societies and certainly the great imperial civilizations of Eurasia demanded respect and recognition. They were urban, literate, and commercial societies with well-defined state and legal institutions. This understanding of the universality of empire and, hence, of the law of nations had already caused terrific problems as a consequence of Spanish imperial expansion. It had also been a notorious bone of contention in relations with the Ottoman Empire, not simply as a Muslim power but as a Muslim empire on the European continent. In the 19th century it was rehashed on a much grander canvas. The British stepped into a centuries-old lively debate when they began to make the law of nations their own. Strict adherence to the universalism of the law of nations predicated that relations between major Eurasian polities, despite their diverse religious, political, and legal backgrounds, were "naturally" based on mutually binding, reciprocal legal arrangements. That is to say, they were full members of the

---

45   Anne Orford (ed.), *International Law and Its Others* (Cambridge: Cambridge University Press, 2006).

society of nations, much like the various political entities in Europe, irrespective of their religion or size. But with the advance of the notion of "oriental despotism," the balance of argument shifted decisively against equal recognition. Because Asian empires did not know or were incapable of adhering to the (European/universal) "rules of the game," so it was argued, they could not possibly be members of the society of nations. Counterarguments were presented vociferously by, for example, Abraham Hyacinthe Anquetil-Duperron (1731–1805), who in 1778 published at Amsterdam his *Legislation Orientale*, in which he endeavored to prove that the nature of oriental despotism had been greatly misrepresented; or Edmund Burke (1729–1797), who pursued impeachment efforts against Warren Hastings (1732–1818), formerly Governor-General of Bengal, and condemned the damage to India by the East India Company, holding that the advent of British dominion had destroyed much that was good in Indian traditions.

But the thought-architecture had shifted: the British debate on international law started with the presumption of non-reciprocity in imperial encounters, but instead of negating international law altogether, British thought worked up an international law that incorporated the imperial reality of unequal relations.[46]

The main thrust in remodeling the older *ius gentium* into "modern" imperial international law came with the seemingly ever more unlimited ability to order the world.[47] It involves some of the more perplexing developments in 19th century international law: the rise of a hard-nosed positivism intersecting with historicism. Pitts discusses this imperative of world ordering under the dual heading of legal positivism and historicism, which on the surface of it looks like a contradiction. International lawyers in Britain came to insist on the "positive" (written, codified) record of governments (sovereigns) in

---

46 As Syed Hussein Alatas underlines (Alatas, pp. 231–239), to show the strength of Eurocentrism, the sense of ethnic and cultural superiority, it is best to refer to the group from whom one could least expect it, the socialist and radical revolutionary thinkers of Europe: the Russians Vissarion Grigoryevich Belinsky (1811–1848) and Alexander Herzen (1812–1870), or the Germans Eduard Bernstein (1850–1932) and, obviously, the Dynamic Duo – Karl Marx (1818–1883) and Friedrich Engels (1820–1895), whose condescending attitude, carelessness about facts, misinterpretation of Asian institutions, and ethnic pride, were clearly revealed in their writings. No wonder that for thinkers such as Sayyid Qutb (1906–1966) or Ali Shariati (1933–1977) the "West" was all the same, either in its Euro-American form or in its Russian disguise: their views were of the same kind as those of the civilizing mission with the only difference that the mission was to be socialistic.

47 Lauren A. Benton and Lisa Ford, *Rage for Order: The British Empire and the Origins of International Law, 1800–1850* (Cambridge, MA: Harvard University Press, 2016).

THE INVENTION OF "ISLAM"   281

their interaction with each other, supplemented by earlier "codifications" of the law of nations. They positivized law by "historicizing" the written record, which also meant that they shunned older fictions of (unwritten, uncodified) natural law. Legal pluralism moved into the realm of imperial ethnography. International lawyers historicized by demonstrating the progression of (written) law, mowing backward to the written record to Greek and Roman times and forward to a global world of European international law.

Pitts's discussion of Henry Maine (1822–88) is highly instructive in this context. In his thinking, positive international law shrank to the binding, statutory writ of states-writ, moreover, that followed European conventions and was practiced in recognizable juridical institutions, underwriting the right to adjudicate international legal norms and deploy violence in an administrative (rather than either political or legal) mode over those societies Europeans deemed not yet candidates for legal inclusion. The *ius gentium* had always been parochial in its universal ambitions. But at the apex of British expansion it was transformed, against opposition from within, into a pliable international law that gave legal language to inequality and thus could become the unilateral instrument of a globalizing sovereign.

5 Islam and Muslims

As Martin Kramer asserted, debate over terminology has always surrounded the West's relations with Islam, and its outcome has been as much a barometer of the West's needs as a description of the actual state of Islam.[48] According to Carl W. Ernst, in some ways, the recent prominence of the word "Islam" indicates a momentous shift in religious thought, dating from the early 19th century. In the scale of values found in traditional theology, the Arabic term *islam* (اَلْإِسْلَام) was of secondary importance. Meaning "submission (to God)," *islam* effectively denoted performing the minimum actions required in the community (generally defined as profession of faith, prayer, fasting during Ramadan, giving alms, and performing pilgrimage to Mecca). Much more important for religious identity was "faith" (*iman*, إِيمَان), described as believing in God and everything revealed through the prophets, and all the debates of theologians revolved around how to define the faithful believer (*mu'min*, مؤمن). But the term "Muslim," meaning "one who has submitted (to God)," always had a

---

48   Martin Kramer, "Coming to Terms: Fundamentalists or Islamists?," *Middle East Quarterly* 10, no. 2 (Spring 2003), 65–77, available at http://www.meforum.org/541/coming-to -terms-fundamentalists-or-islamists. Accessed 23 November 2019.

corporate and social significance, indicating membership in a religious community. "Islam" therefore became practically useful as a political boundary term, both to outsiders and to insiders who wished to draw lines around themselves. Historically, Europeans had used the term "Muhammadan" to refer to the religion of followers of the Prophet Muhammad, although Muslims regard that as an inappropriate label. The term "Islam" was introduced into European languages in the early 19th century by Orientalists such as Edward William Lane (1801–1876), as an explicit analogy with the modern Christian concept of religion; in this respect, "Islam" was just as much a newly invented European term as "Hinduism" and "Buddhism" were. The use of the term "Islam" by non-Muslim scholars coincides with its increasing frequency in the religious discourse of those who are now called Muslims. That is, the term "Islam" became more prominent in reformist and proto-fundamentalist circles at approximately the same time, or shortly after, it was popularized by European Orientalists. So, in a sense, the concept of Islam in opposition to the West is just as much a product of European colonialism as it is a Muslim response to that European expansionism. Despite appeals to medieval history, it is really the past two centuries that set up the conditions for today's debates regarding Islam.[49]

Cemil Aydin, with his *The Idea of the Muslim World: A Global Intellectual History*,[50] traced the rise and development of this geopolitical idea, locating its enduring power from the late 19th century until today.[51] As Sahar Bazzaz

---

49   Carl W. Ernst, *Following Muhammad: Rethinking Islam in the Contemporary World* (Chapel Hill & London: The University of North Carolina Press, 2003), especially the "Preface" on pp. 10–11.

50   Cemil Aydin, *The Idea of the Muslim World: A Global Intellectual History* (Cambridge MA: Harvard University Press, 2017).

51   Some years ago, Aziz Al-Azmeh had already tried a similar endeavor with his *The Times of History: Universal Topics in Islamic Historiography* (Budapest and New York: Central European University Press, 2007). For two thought provoking analyses on the interactions between "Islam" and "West," please refer to Ali Mirsepassi, "Mistaken Antimodernity: Fardid After Fardid," *Working Paper Series of the HCAS "Multiple Secularities – Beyond the West, Beyond Modernities"* 6 (Leipzig: Universität Leipzig, February 2019), for an Iranian context, and to Seema Alavi, *Muslim Cosmopolitanism in the Age of Empire* (Cambridge, MA: Harvard University Press, 2015). By showing that some Muslim networks depended on European empires and that their sensibility was shaped by the West in many subtle ways, and by engaging equally with the South Asian and Ottoman worlds, and by telling a non-Eurocentric story of global modernity without overlooking the importance of the British Empire, Alavi challenges the idea that all pan-Islamic configurations are anti-Western or pro-Caliphate. Indeed, Western imperial hegemony empowered the very inter-Asian Muslim connections that went on to outlive European empires. Diverging from the medieval idea of the *umma*, this new cosmopolitan community

THE INVENTION OF "ISLAM" 283

asserts in the review of the book,[52] rather than locate the persistence of the idea of the "Muslim World" in a shared history of immutable ideology within Muslim societies, Aydin shows how it was a function of the civilizational and geopolitical narratives concocted in the encounters of Muslim societies with European empires, reconfigured according to the exigencies of the Cold War. Aydin examines historical developments across Asia, Africa, and the Middle East to argue that, despite assertions that Muslims are part of a global political unity, Muslims did not embrace such a notion until the late 19th century when a process of "racialization" of Muslims occurred in tandem with increased European imperial hegemony. As Aydin puts it, the Muslim world arrived with imperial globalization and its concomitant ordering of humanity by race. Over the course of the 20th century, the ideology of Muslim unity evolved and served disparate political agendas.[53] At the center of such arguments are two historically inaccurate yet politically expedient assumptions. The first is that the notion of the "Muslim World" derives from the concept of "*umma*," an age-old notion associated with the beginnings of Islam, which refers to the de-territorialized Muslim religious community. The second is that until European colonialism and the ideology of nationalism emerged, Muslims were united. As Aydin shows, these notions do not stand up to scrutiny. Aydin reminds us that those clashes between warring Muslim states during the early modern period were often far greater than those between Muslims and Christians. Furthermore, gestures made by Muslim rulers in the name of Muslim solidarity often failed to materialize.

From the 7th to the early 19th century, Muslim political experience tells a story of multiplicity, contestation, and change, leaving the idea of the Muslim

---

stressed consensus in matters of belief, ritual, and devotion and found inspiration in the liberal reforms then gaining traction in the Ottoman world.

52   Sahar Bazzaz in *Hespéris-Tamuda* 52, no. 2 (2017), 431–4.

53   Aydin had already shown with his Ph. D. thesis how the idea of "Islam" had been constructed in certain imperial Japanese circles as an alternative to the "West" and as a possible ally against it, exploring the links between Pan-Asianism and Islamic Studies – for example, Okawa Shumei (1886–1957), a radical nationalist and pan-Asianist, was a pioneer of Islamic Studies in Japan. Cemil Aydin. *The politics of civilizational identities: Asia, west and Islam in the pan-Asianist thought of Ōkawa Shūmei*. Ph. D. Committee on History and Middle Eastern Studies Harvard University (2002); Cemil Aydin. *The Politics of Anti-Westernism in Asia: Visions of World Order in Pan-Islamic and Pan-Asian thought* (New York: Columbia University Press, 2007). For more details, see Komatsu Hisao, "Muslim Intellectuals and Japan: A Pan-Islamist mediator, Abdurreshid Ibrahim," in *Intellectuals in the Modern Islamic World: Transmission, transformation, communication*. Edited by Stephane A. Dudoignon, Komatsu Hisao, and Kosugi Yasushi (London and New York: Routledge, 2006), 273–288.

world to emerge later, alongside the later civilizational narrative of the West. Until the mid-nineteenth century, relations between Muslims and Christians cannot be said to have been uniform; in some cases, Muslims ruled Christians, as in the Ottoman Empire, and in others Muslims were ruled by Christians (as in India and Russia). Russian and Indian Muslims did not call for geopolitical unity, nor did Ottoman Christians make similar claims. The emergence of the idea of the Muslim world occurred during the 19th century and crystallized after the 1870s, when geopolitical debate among imperial powers – including the Ottomans – began to center on nationality and race instead of upon imperial strategy. Aydin traces this process arguing that even as new discourses of pan-Islamic unity were ascendant and could circulate more quickly as a result of advances in communications technologies, Muslim thinkers such as Mirza Asadullah Ghalib (1797–1869) and Sayyid Ahmad Khan (1817–1898),[54] could weigh the merits of the British and Mughal empires without allowing religious sympathy to dictate their preferences. Indeed, Indian Muslims imagined their political future under Queen Victoria (1819–1901), and many Balkan Christians accepted the rule of a reformist Muslim sultan in Istanbul. But as the century proceeded, European support for breakaway Christian movements in the Ottoman Balkans and their concomitant conquests in Ottoman domains worked to undermine the imperial system, which in the earlier part of the century had focused on prioritizing strategic alliances above ethnic and religious solidarity. Ironically, it was European support for Serbian, Greek, Bulgarian independence that is, their claim to serve as protectors of Christian populations in the Ottoman Empire that fueled the flames of pan-Islamist discourse among Muslim intellectuals from across Muslim majority societies. This was especially true during the reign of Abdulhamid II (1842–1918, r. 1876–1909), who promoted the Ottoman state as a spiritual caliphate for Muslims worldwide thereby fusing the imagined Muslim community with Ottoman geo-strategic interests at the time namely, securing an alliance with Great Britain against Russia. Just as Europeans used Christian solidarity to intervene in Ottoman domestic politics, so too did Abdulhamid attempt to extend Ottoman reach farther afield among Muslim populations in India and elsewhere. Such a strategy made sense given that Great Britain ruled a vast percentage of the world's Muslim population. Yet as Aydin emphasizes, Abdulhamid's pan-Islamism was meant to secure *not to undermine* empire. Sultan Abdulhamid's promotion of Ottoman spiritual sovereignty solidified the imagination of a geopolitical

---

54   Carimo Mohomed, "Indian Muslims are the Most Loyal Subjects of the British Raj: Sir Sayyid Ahmad Khan and the Caliphate," in *The Cambridge Companion to Sayyid Ahmad Khan* (Cambridge: Cambridge University Press, 2018), 38–54.

THE INVENTION OF "ISLAM"

Muslim world in the age of high imperialism. This version of pan-Islamism was no *jihad* against the European empires. On the contrary, it aimed to guarantee Ottoman sovereignty by leveraging foreign Muslims' dual loyalty to empire – particularly the Crown – and caliph.

The implications of Aydin's work are significant. First, the author shows how the term "Muslim World" – an analytical term employed by both Muslims and non-Muslims alike evoking a trans-historical geo-political unity among vastly diverse and disparate Muslim majority societies – has a specific historical trajectory whose emergence as a concept arose in the late 19th century as a result of specific political and ideological contingencies. By arguing for historical contingency, Aydin fundamentally challenges the (utterly absurd and ignorant) "Clash of Civilizations" arguments, which portray the relationship between the West and Muslim majority societies in terms of perpetual conflict and struggle.[55] On the positive side, one can always argue that "scholars" such as Samuel Huntington (1927–2008), Bernard Lewis (1916–2018), and their intellectual lackeys, were, and are, very eco-friendly since they recycle, reuse and reheat stale, and molded (thus toxic), ideas: what once was "religion," and then "race," now is "culture" or "civilisation."[56]

Second, Aydin shows how the concept serves specific political interests including those of Islamophobes and Islamists alike, who readily embrace as a given the notion of a territorially grounded and politically unified "Muslim World."[57]

---

55 As far as I know, no one has been able to explain, under this "theory," the alliance between the United States of America and Saudi Arabia, on the one hand, and, via Uncle Sam, the alliance between Israel and Saudi Arabia on the other hand. One can always argue, as I have heard frequently, that the United States are not representative of the "West." However, for the German Protestant historian cum politician Heinrich August Winkler, the West is composed by the United States of America, Catholic and Protestant Europe (explicitly excluding Greece), and Israel. One really has to ask if, had he been an adult during the 1930s and 1940s in Germany, Winkler would have considered the people of Israel as being part of the West or would have been sending them to concentration camps and to the gas chambers ... It seems that the only real representatives of the West are Duckburg and Mouseton. For a nice review of Winkler's books, please refer to Dylan Riley, "Metaphysicking the West," *New Left Review* 113 (Sept-Oct 2018), 125–138.

56 One just has to read Hugo Grotius's *On the Truth of the Christian Religion*, first published in Latin in 1627, and then Huntington's *On the Truth of the Western Civilization*, a.k.a. *The Clash of Civilizations*.

57 For a fine assessment on how social scientists use of historical monographs end up in selection bias, please refer to Ian S. Lustick, "History, Historiography, and Political Science: Multiple Historical Records and the Problem of Selection Bias," *The American Political Science Review* 90, no. 3 (September 1996), 605–618. According to this author, social scientists are bound to be more attracted to and convinced by accounts that accord

If it is true that in certain "academic" circles Islam has been considered as an alien, unsettling and intrusive presence in the universal scheme of things, there has also been fascination and reluctant admiration. Furthermore, in its monotheistic essentials, this faith bore a disquieting resemblance to Judaism and Christianity, and thus could hardly be dismissed casually. For example, the historian John Tolan, with his *Faces of Muhammad*,[58] explores, among other things, how in European culture, Muhammad has been vilified as a heretic, an impostor, and a pagan idol at the same time that commentators have also portrayed Muhammad as a visionary reformer and an inspirational leader, statesman, and lawgiver. To Reformation polemicists, the spread of Islam attested to the corruption of the established Church, and prompted them to depict Muhammad as a champion of reform. In revolutionary England, writers on both sides of the conflict drew parallels between Muhammad and Oliver Cromwell (1599–1658), asking whether the prophet was a rebel against legitimate authority or the bringer of a new and just order. Voltaire (1694–1778) first saw Muhammad as an archetypal religious fanatic but later claimed him as an enemy of superstition. To Napoleon (1769–1821), he was simply a role model: a brilliant general, orator, and leader. The book shows that Muhammad wears so many faces in the West because he has always acted as a mirror for its writers, their portrayals revealing more about their own concerns than the historical realities of the prophet.[59]

In 2014, Kecia Ali[60] had already focused on the biographies written in the 19th and 20th centuries although she also briefly mentions the earlier accounts. She aimed to reveal the interconnection between non-Muslim biographers from Britain and North America and Muslim biographers who wrote English responses from Egypt and India, concluding that while pre-modern biographers recount Muhammad's prophethood with his special seal of prophecy

---

with the expectations about events contained in the concepts they deploy and the theories they seek to test. For two illuminating personal accounts on how historians and social scientists work, please refer to, respectively, Keith Thomas, "Diary," *London Review of Books* 32, no. 11 (10 June 2010), 36–37, and Charli Carpenter, "'You Talk of Terrible Things So Matter-of-Factly in This Language of Science': Constructing Human Rights in the Academy," *Perspectives on Politics* 10, no. 2 (2012), 363–383. Carpenter raises several and important issues regarding the ethics of those doing "scientific" work in the Social Sciences.

58 John V. Tolan, *Faces of Muhammad: Western Perceptions of the Prophet of Islam from the Middle Ages to Today* (Princeton: Princeton University Press, 2019).

59 For more on mythologies surrounding the prophet Muhammad, please see Matthew Dimmock, *Mythologies of the Prophet Muhammad in Early Modern English Culture* (Cambridge: Cambridge University Press, 2013).

60 Kecia Ali, *The Lives of Muhammad* (Cambridge, MA: Harvard University Press, 2014).

and his miraculous ascent into heaven, modern biographers reconstruct his life as an ideal statesman or social reformer. The enlightenment critique of the religion, the growth of academic Orientalism and the rise of colonialism led to an increased interplay between Muslim and non-Muslim narratives of Muhammad's life.[61]

In what refers to Sufism, many people wonder what relationship, if any, Sufism has to Islam. This debate is not new; from the time European scholars began to conceptualize these subjects two centuries ago, they viewed Sufism as an attractive form of universal spirituality. In their view, Sufism (an English word with the characteristic "-ism" ending of modern ideologies) could have nothing to do with what they considered the dry and legalistic religion of Islam. Although European scholars assumed that Sufism therefore had to derive from Indian yoga or some other extra-Islamic source, Sufi spiritual circles used a religious vocabulary based almost entirely on Arabic and Islamicate sources. The European concepts of Sufism and Islam were in effect separated at birth when they were naturalized in English and other languages early in the 19th century. Modern Muslim reformists subsequently mirrored the Europeans in regarding Sufism as something apart from Islam; the difference lay in the reformists' negative evaluation of Sufism as an innovation and a foreign intrusion into Islam, while the Orientalists saw Sufism as something positive. Yet this negative attitude of reformist Muslims toward Sufism is relatively recent; for most of Islamic history, this form of spirituality and mystical practice has been a major feature of Muslim societies.[62]

We are now going to turn our attention to two more examples of this attitude: Islamic Spain, or al-Andalus, and women.

6   Al-Andalus

In 2013, Alejandro García Sanjuán published his *La conquista islámica de la Península Ibérica y la tergiversación del pasado: Del catastrofismo al*

---

61   For more on this, see Firoozeh Kashani-Sabet, "Before ISIS: What Early America Thought of Islam," available at https://www.academia.edu/39137309/Before_ISIS_-What_Early_A merica_Thought_of_Islam. Accessed 23 November 2019; Farman Ali and Humaira Ahmad, "Early Christian Sīrah Writings of Subcontinent: A Comparative Study of their Methods, Impact and Cogitating on New Contemporizing Methodology," *Journal of Islamic Thought and Civilization* 8, 1 (2018), 129–143; and Anna Della Subin, "It has burned my heart," *London Review of Books* 37, no. 20 (22 October 2015), 21–24, which is a review of Kecia Ali's book.

62   Carl W. Ernst, 166.

negacionismo[63] with the aim of debunking two myths related with the Islamic conquest of the Iberian Peninsula: catastrophe and negationism. As Kenneth Baxter Wolf[64] asserts in the review of the book, much of the volume is dedicated to a careful and commendable assessment of the sources upon which any understanding of the Islamic conquest of the Iberian Peninsula must be based. But the driving force behind this investigation of the evidence is an impassioned call to arms against the *"tergiversación"* of the past, a "distortion" that the author associates with two modern myths surrounding the conquest of 711. The first myth is the idea that the Muslim presence in the peninsula was a fundamentally alien, even illegitimate, one, the result of a "catastrophic" twist of fate that placed a large part of what was "properly" Christian Spain under Muslim rule. The second myth contends that the Muslim conquest never really happened; that the changes traditionally associated with 711 were in fact part of a long-term transformation of southern Spain that involved the Arabs and Islam only as secondary agents. The problem with both of these interpretations, as García Sanjuán observes, is that they depend less on their fidelity to actual historical data than on their consonance with self-serving collective memories, and so they end up distorting our understanding of what actually happened in 711 and beyond.

The first of García Sanjuán's two *tergiversaciones*, the myth of the "conquest as catastrophy," is by far the more deeply rooted, fueled as it was by 19th and early 20th century handwringing over the sense that Spain had not kept up with its European neighbors as it entered the modern world. This *catastrofista* myth had the advantage of being grounded in a medieval one, which was forged by the earliest Christian chroniclers faced with the unanticipated challenge of describing the displacement of the Catholic regime by a Muslim one. This early medieval "discourse of the vanquished" proved amazingly durable, not only providing a convenient ideological framework for the Castilian monarchy in its medieval struggle against the Muslims of al-Andalus and North Africa, but, with minor alterations, informing the nationalist *españolista* ideology that came to dominate 19th century Spanish historical discourse and ultimately to inspire the National Catholicism of Francisco Franco (1892–1975) and his era. Its central premise was the exclusive and absolute identification of *Catholic* and *Spanish*, which meant that al-Andalus, the antithesis of Christian Spain, could never have been anything but an interloper, a fundamentally illegitimate peninsular presence.

---

63 Alejandro García Sanjuán, *La conquista islámica de la Península Ibérica y la tergiversación del pasado: Del catastrofismo al negacionismo.* (Madrid: Marcial Pons, 2013).

64 Kenneth Baxter Wolf, "Negating Negationism" (2014).

THE INVENTION OF "ISLAM"

Nevertheless, this did not impede the Franco regime from using the myth of Al-Andalus to establish good relations with Arab countries (at the same time that it did not recognize the state of Israel), or to legitimize its presence in North Africa. Eric Calderwood, with his *Colonial al-Andalus: Spain and the Making of Modern Moroccan Culture,*[65] shows that the narrative of interfaith tolerance among Muslims, Christians, and Jews was born out of a far more recent and historiographical obscure past: the Spanish colonization of northern Morocco in the 19th and 20th centuries. The book charts the evolution of what Calderwood calls this "Andalus-centric narrative" from its origins among Spanish proponents of colonization in the Spanish-Moroccan War (1859–60), to its apogee during the Spanish Civil War (1936–39), and ultimately to its adoption by Moroccan nationalist activists in the 1940s and 1950s, or to Franco's assertion that al-Andalus could rival Mecca as a site of Muslim pilgrimage, translating colonial discourse into an Arabic literary idiom and exemplifying the unexpected ties between the Moroccan elite and Spanish fascism. The texts Calderwood analyzes vividly illustrate how this idea of al-Andalus developed between Muslims and Christians, North Africans and Europeans, and past and present.

Calderwood identifies the Spanish-Moroccan War of 1859–60 as the moment when al-Andalus emerged as a powerful image for both Spaniards and Moroccans, and in the 1920s and 1930s the Spanish writer Blas Infante (1885–1936) articulated a vision of Andalusian nationalism (*andalucismo*) based on the conflation, in time, space, and culture, of medieval al-Andalus, the modern region of Andalusia, and Morocco. Infante's *andalucismo*, a "cosmopolitan imperialism," drawing on idealized notions of tolerance and racial mixing in al-Andalus, served as a critique of Catalan nationalism and Spain's connection with the rest of Europe. This idea was taken up by an ally of Franco, Rodolfo Gil Benumeya (1901–1975), who argued that Andalucia – and thus Spain and Morocco – was "neither Orient nor Occident," but rather a combination of both.[66]

A famous traveler to al-Andalus was Muhammad Iqbal (1877–1938). In January 1933, he visited Spain, inspiring several poems, which were later incorporated into a major composition, *Bal-I Jibril (Gabriel's Wing)*. The trip also

---

65 Eric Calderwood, *Colonial al-Andalus: Spain and the Making of Modern Moroccan Culture* (Cambridge, MA: Belknap Press of Harvard University Press, 2018) and the review by Samuel Anderson, available at http://www.h-net.org/reviews/showrev.php?id=53657. Accessed 23 November 2019.

66 Rodolfo Gil Benumeya Grimau, *Ni oriente, ni occidente: el universo visto desde el Albayzín* (Granada: Editorial Universidad de Granada, 1996), originally published in 1930.

provided him an opportunity to experience Spain's Islamic heritage, having the opportunity to see the presence of Muslims in history. Among the various monuments of Islamic Spain, the most intense yearning of his soul was to experience Granada and the Grand Mosque of Cordoba. For Iqbal, just being there was overwhelmingly therapeutic, for there, before his own eyes, was about the most vivid reminders of the Golden Age of Islam, an era that provided the roots of Europe's Enlightenment. At the great mosque of Cordoba, he wrote *Masjid-e-Qurtaba* (*The Mosque of Cordoba*)[67] and offered his prayers, although this ritual had been forbidden by the Government of Spain. The centrality of the mosque of Cordoba to Islamic Spain is compared to the centrality of the Kaaba to Islam generally; while the positive impact of Islam on Spain and Europe are extolled.[68]

The arguments about al-Andalus appealed to both sides in the Spanish Civil War but, as Calderwood shows, had particular power in Franco's fascist regime. Moroccan elites took up the Spanish Andalus-centric narrative during the colonial period and, focusing on a travel narrative, Ahmad al-Rahuni's (1871–1953) *Journey to Mecca* (1941), Calderwood shows how Franco's regime sponsored *hajj* voyages for favored Muslim elites like al-Rahuni, much like other European imperial powers,[69] but it also incorporated visits to Andalusi heritage sites like the Mosque-Cathedral of Cordoba. Al-Rahuni's text uses Qur'anic language to lend credence to Franco's assertion that al-Andalus could rival Mecca as a site of Muslim pilgrimage, translating colonial discourse into an Arabic literary idiom.

Calderwood also pays attention to Shakib Arslan (1869–1946), a prominent advocate for pan-Islamic resistance to European colonialism whose interpretation of al-Andalus as a "lost paradise" deeply influenced Moroccan nationalists from the 1930s to the 1950s. During a 1930 visit to Morocco and Spain, Arslan encountered and mentored many young activists and scholars from both Spanish and French Morocco, including Ahmad Balafrij (1908–1990), M'hammad Binnuna, Muhammad Dawud (1901–1984), and Muhammad al-Fasi (1910–1974).[70] These men actively reinterpreted Arslan's notion of al-Andalus

---

67   Available at http://www.allamaiqbal.com/poetry.php?bookbup=24&orderno=317&lang _code=en&lang=2&conType=en. Accessed 23 November 2019.

68   For further details, please see Annemarie Schimmel, *Gabriel's Wing: A Study into the religious ideas of Sir Muhammad Iqbal* (Leiden: E. J. Brill, 1963); and Yaseen Noorani, "The Lost Garden of Al-Andalus: Islamic Spain and the Poetic Inversion of Colonialism," *International Journal of Middle East Studies* 31, no. 2 (May 1999), 237–254.

69   For the British Empire and the Hajj, please refer to John Slight, *The British Empire and the Hajj: 1865–1956* (Cambridge, MA: Harvard University Press, 2015).

70   For further details on Shakib Arslan, please refer to Raja Adal, "Constructing transnational Islam: the East-West network of Shakib Arslan," in *Intellectuals in the Modern Islamic*

THE INVENTION OF "ISLAM" 291

both to insert their specific activism into the broader anticolonial struggle across the Muslim world and to assert a direct, genealogical connection
between medieval Andalusis and contemporary Moroccans, who deployed the
same language Spanish fascists used to justify colonialism when making their
claims of a distinct Moroccan national identity.

7 The Women

In the 19th century, French Orientalist painters created luxuriant depictions
of seductive harem life, using European prostitutes as nude models. The conservative clothing worn by many Near Eastern women (including Eastern
Christians and Jews through the 19th century) and the segregation of unre-
lated men and women in public spaces also encouraged male European travelers with overactive imaginations. Another form of European appropriation
of Islamicate culture came to the fore in the mid-nineteenth century in the
school of realistic painting known as Orientalist art. Born at roughly the same
time as the new technique of photography,[71] Orientalist painting was the creation of artists (especially but not exclusively in France) who had travelled at
least once to North Africa or the Near East. For Europe, at that time, Oriental
defined the immediate East, which was primarily the Ottoman Empire, viewed
as a stand-in for Muslim countries in general. With the growth of printing and
the immense popularity of travel literature, pictorial representations of exotic
cultures had become a staple of visual illustration. Yet neither the travel books
nor the illustrations of faraway countries provided genuine encounters with
other cultures. Travelers tended to take with them deeply ingrained prejudices frequently based on the reading of earlier travel books rather than their
own observation. Illustrations were often commissioned by publishers, who
frequently recycled stock images on the basis of well-established stereotypes.
Ironically, works of fantasy were often more eagerly accepted as authentic
representations of remote lands. This tendency had been seen in medieval
times, when the realistic travel narrative of Marco Polo (1254–1324) was generally considered far inferior to the outrageous adventures of John Mandeville
(1300–1371), which are filled with tales of encounters with fabulous beasts and

---

World: Transmission, transformation, communication. Edited by Stephane A. Dudoignon,
Komatsu Hisao, and Kosugi Yasushi (London and New York: Routledge, 2006), 176–210.

71 For an example of photography and Orientalism, Ali Behdad and Luke Gartian (eds.),
Photography's Orientalisms: New Essays on Colonial Representation (Los Angeles: Getty
Research Institute, 2013).

monsters. The imagined Orient was a counter image against which Europe defined itself.[72]

One of the most remarkable aspects of Orientalist art was the erotic fantasy that permeated many paintings. The travelers, usually males, who visited the territories of the Ottoman emperors, of course had no access to the women's quarters, which are generally known as the harem or private residence. This was no obstacle to their imagination, however, and there are countless harem scenes filled with dozens of naked women in the bath. Far from being realistic portrayals of Turkish society, these voyeuristic paintings (using nude European models) confused the living quarters with the Turkish bath, and they reduced the Muslim woman to the status of a plaything of unseen Eastern males.[73] Other favorite locations in paintings of Oriental women depicted them for sale in the slave market like so much horseflesh or as dancers performing in front of a male audience; in either case, they were seen as oppressed. The erotic image is the reversal of the stereotype of the veil; the only difference is that the veil has been removed by the imagination. Oriental (*i.e.*, Muslim) men, in the alternate stereotype, were frequently depicted as warriors, whether engaged in fierce battle or in indolent relaxation. These images reinforced the notion of violent Islam while suggesting that these behind-the-times soldiers could be easily conquered.[74]

---

72 Carl W. Ernst, 26 and 190–191.

73 For a recent not so veiled apology of Western lechery, as long as the target are non-Western women, please see Richard Bernstein, *The East, the West, and Sex: a history of erotic encounters* (New York: Alfred A. Knopf, 2009). At the same time that he admits its hypocrisy, the author considers Christian monogamy, and the heritage of chivalry to which it is (supposedly) related, a higher standard that holds women in far higher regard than the cultures of the harem, which are spread throughout the East, widely understood as northern Africa, the Middle East, Asia, the Pacific Islands (Mars is not included) – a fine exercise in hypocrisy indeed, not to mention that it is a piece of bad scholarship (Islam did not come to India with the Mughals), and it is ludicrous to say that the strict and puritanical Wahhabism from Saudi Arabia dominates much of Islamic discourse today.

74 Carl W. Ernst, 192–193. Here is a list of some paintings which can be considered as proto-centerfolds: *La Grande Odalisque* (1814), *La Petite Baigneuse* (1826), *L'Odalisque à l'esclave* (1839), *Le bain turc* (1862), all by Jean-Auguste Dominique Ingres (1780–1867); *La mort de Sardanapale* (1827), by Eugène Delacroix (1798–1863); *Odalisque* (c. 1900), by Maurice Bompard (1857–1936); *Parisiennes habillées en Algériennes* (1872), by Pierre-Auguste Renoir (1841–1919); *L'esclave blanche* (1888), by Jean-Jules-Antoine Lecomte du Noüy (1842–1923); *Le marché d'esclaves* (1866), *Bain turc* or *Bain maure* (1870), both by Jean-Léon Gérôme (1824–1904), who was very prolific; *Femme mauresque sortant du bain au sérail* or *Intérieur de harem* (1854), by Théodore Chassériau (1819–1856); and *Juda et Thamar* (1840), by Horace Vernet (1789–1863), which depicts a veiled woman with one of her breasts exposed.

8 Conclusion

Being a woman, Virginia Woolf (1882–1941) knew quite well the importance of letting other people know one's (her/his)story, told with our own words, because, in the end, everything is summed up into *who tells what about whom, and why*.[75] And women in British India have been historian Antoinette Burton's main topic, but she is also widely known for her reflections on imperial historiography, being among the "new imperial" historians who appreciate and utilize insights drawn from cultural, feminist, and postcolonial studies. In the introduction to her book *Empire in Question*,[76] Burton recounts her experience as a graduate student working with faculty who were often utterly unconvinced of either the legitimacy of women's history or the possibility of postcolonial studies. Traditional, usually male historians, Burton contends, often fetishize "hard data" while often also treating the history of the Empire as somehow separate from that of England. The traditionalists behave as though they have a privileged access to reality, while practitioners of newfangled "studies" supposedly spin cobwebs of "theory."

As Burton notes, traditional historians reject theory in favor of empiricism, which can lead to the worship of facts and documents that Edward Hallett Carr (1892–1982) long ago skewered in *What Is History?* (London: Macmillan, 1961). As Carr pointed out, "the facts" do not "speak for themselves." And "facts" are what Syed Hussein Alatas discusses in the "Conclusion" of his book. Using the phenomenon of imperialism and colonialism as a "fact," he asks: What

---

75   In his *The Theft of History* (Cambridge: Cambridge University Press, 2006), Jack Goody, building on his own previous work, extended further his highly influential critique of what he sees as the pervasive Eurocentric or occidentalist biases of so much western historical writing, and the consequent "theft" by the West of the achievements of other cultures in the invention of (notably) democracy, capitalism, individualism and love. Before him, James Morris Blaut (1927–2000) had already criticized Eurocentric theories of a "European miracle" with his *The Colonizer's Model of the World: Geographical Diffusionism and Eurocentric History* (New York: Guilford Press, 1993) and *Eight Eurocentric Historians* (New York: Guilford Press, 2000). In fact, as far as the 18th century, there were many intellectuals, including in Europe, who were against Imperialism or Colonialism, such as Johann Gottfried von Herder (1744–1803). For more on this, J. Noyes, "Herder, Postcolonial Theory and the Antinomy of Universal Reason," *Cambridge Journal of Postcolonial Literary Inquiry* 1, no. 1 (2014), 107–122, or Nicholas Robinette, "The World Laid Waste: Herder, Language Labor, Empire," *New Literary History*, 42, 1 (2011), 193–203.

76   Antoinette Burton, *Empire in Question: Reading, Writing, and Teaching British Imperialism* (Durham: Duke University Press, 2011), and the review by Patrick Brantlinger, available at: http://www.victorianweb.org/history/empire/burton.html. Accessed 23 November 2019.

do we mean by this? Modern Western imperialism marked the expansion of Western rule and dominance over the greater part of the non-Western world. It had profound effects both on the West as well as the non-Western world. This is a "fact." But this is a "fact" only in the general and abstract sense. The moment we go into the concrete our discourse on the "fact" entails a value orientation. We may not use terms such as "good" and "bad" in our discourse but the moment we say that colonialism has generated peace and stability, has introduced modern sanitation, has developed the natural resources, we are proclaiming it to have been good. On the other hand, we may select the negative influence of colonialism and by so doing we are proclaiming it to have been bad.

Michel de Certeau (1925–1986) made a distinction between historical events and historical knowledge. Knowledge about historical events is produced through practices of writing history, or discourses. Although events themselves are independent of discourse, they can only be represented in this form and therefore historical knowledge is necessarily discursive. Discourse organizes historical events along lines of causality, and therefore defines the ways in which we can and cannot conceive of the past; in this sense, discourse is a "mode of intelligibility." Discourse is produced in a kind of power-field generated through the interaction of three factors: a social institution of scholarly knowledge, a discipline or tradition of knowledge within the institution, and a subject, which here has the specific meaning of a dialogical relationship between the scholar as subjective being and his or her subject matter. This relationship engenders "subject" as the third entity, which interacts with "discipline" and "institution" to produce the discourse. Thus a historical discourse expresses identity on the three levels of institution, discipline, and subject, and should consequently also be interpreted in relation to these three levels, beginning with the institution, which de Certeau refers to as the "place" in society where historical writing is practiced. By distinguishing between historical events and historical knowledge, de Certeau rejects the positivistic assumption that there is an objectively existing history, with objective laws of causality, which can be deduced and known through appropriate empirical evidence. De Certeau locates historicity not in "history itself," but in history as a discipline and practice of writing, in the movement which links an interpretive practice to a social praxis. History thus vacillates between two poles. On the one hand, it refers to a practice, hence to a reality; on the other, it is a closed discourse, a text that organizes and concludes a mode of intelligibility. And since the interpretation of a historical discourse is as much a practice as the interpreted discourse, there is an irreducible difference between the interpreter and the

THE INVENTION OF "ISLAM" 295

interpreted, which results from the difference of identities of institution, discipline, and subject, with concomitant difference in praxis.[77]

According to Alatas, it was not the intention of the book *The Myth of the Lazy Native* to evaluate the total effect of colonialism and imperialism. The difficulty was no doubt there, to assess the myriad of events which constituted the phenomenon of imperialism; events which changed in nature and effect in different times. For instance, the British fought malaria in Malaya. But they did this after increasing it on a large scale, with their haste to plant rubber, their massing of physically weak immigrant labor in infested area, and their neglect of medical welfare for the populace. To evaluate this aspect of colonialism we would have to ask the question what would have happened to the population of Malaya if a Western colonial capitalist government had not been there, but since it did exist what could it have done to prevent malaria? Shocking and inhuman conditions were camouflaged by the phrase "labor conditions unsuited to native physique." Native physique was blamed for the high mortality rate. What exactly of this physique which caused the high mortality was not suggested. Here we find another trait of colonial studies, their fondness for generality when it comes to matters outside their interest or which may cause embarrassment. Human relations are discussed in the language of commodities. The image of the native was constructed on the basis of generalities without any operational foundation.[78]

Up to the Second World War it seemed to be the dominant trend in Europe to view the Asian and non-European world as an inferior world not only technologically and scientifically but also morally, culturally and religiously. The great Asian civilizations such as Hinduism, Buddhism and Islam, judged by contemporary European standards did not show any inferiority except in technology and science which eventually caused a less developed system of production and economic organization. The superiority of the West in this field gave rise to the claim that it was also superior in all fields, and this also applied retroactively to history. It was this sense of superiority and righteousness

---

77   Michel de Certeau, *The Writing of History* (New York: Columbia University Press, 1992). For further details, please refer to Ulrika Mårtensson, "Discourse and Historical Analysis: The Case of al-Ṭabarī's History of the Messengers and the Kings," *Journal of Islamic Studies* 16, no. 3 (September 2005), 287–331; Mohammad R. Salama, "Fact or Fiction? How the Writing of History Became a Discourse of Conquest," in *Islam, Orientalism and Intellectual History* (London: I. B. Tauris, 2011), 39–75; and Sanjay Seth, "Reason or Reasoning? Clio or Siva?," *Social Text* 78, no. 22, 1 (Durham: Duke University Press, March 2004), 85–101.

78   Syed Hussein Alatas, 215–221.

which had caused the distortion of history by colonial writers, the hegemony of the principle of misplaced responsibility in the writing of history, the placing of events out of context, and the construction of the distorted image of the native. Attempts from within European society itself to correct this image, to introduce a measure of objectivity in the study of native life and customs, were made from time to time but with little success.

Studies of colonial rule by colonial writers had focused attention on colonialism as an agent of social change but there is also another side to it. Colonialism had impeded social change. It had retained and consolidated feudal elements from traditional society while it transformed the feudal order to suit its purpose. The image of the native constructed by colonialism has been an impediment to a profound and genuine understanding of native life. This image is still influential today. Hence the relevance of a deeper enquiry into the origin and function of the colonial image of the native or non-Western peoples. The exposition of the ideological roots of this image should in no way be regarded as an attempt to establish the opposite image, an image of perfection. The roots of the image of the lazy native was an important element in the ideology of colonial capitalism. It was a major justification for territorial conquest since the degraded image of the native was basic to colonial ideology. Imperialists of different times and nationalities have shared many common ideas. Thus, the American social philosopher Benjamin Kidd (1858–1916), an imperialist, compared the inhabitants of the tropics to a child, in the same manner as some Dutch imperialists considered the Javanese, claiming that there could never be a good native government. Like the Spanish friars who blamed the Filipinos for the moral deterioration of the Spaniards, Kidd blamed the natives for pulling the white man down. This served as the ideological justification for bad colonial government. Kidd went to the extent of saying we had no right to expect a good European colonial government, giving several reasons: climatic conditions which are a burden to the white man; in the midst of races in a different and lower stage of development; divorced from the influences which have produced him, from the moral and political environment from which he sprang.

The colonial ideologists frequently stressed the inability of native governments to exploit the natural wealth of the country. Hence native ability was questioned, and the image of the backward native grew up. They had to be judged incapable, with retroactive application, of developing their resources. Since they were judged incapable they forfeited the right of independence. The other historical alternative was not considered, namely that the indigenous society might develop its own resources, assimilating modern Western science and technology. The colonial ideologists projected the view that the scientific and technological gap between Western society and native society which lasted until the outbreak of the Second World War could be traced back several hundred years but, in reality, the gap was hardly there during the 16th and 17th centuries.

As Alatas had noted earlier, it was colonial bondage which blocked the flow of assimilation from the Western world. Had there been a free intercourse between independent Acheh and the Western world from the 16th century onwards, Acheh and similarly other Indonesian states would have reached an advanced stage of development by then. Instead, the Dutch destroyed Acheh by a prolonged war. The portrayal of the native was part of a total ideological campaign, which was carried out without any deliberate instruction. It was a collective reaction of a group moved by a common outlook and consciousness of interest. The degradation of the native brought in its train a similar phenomenon with reference to native activities.

Giving as an example the economics of native life, Alatas considers that economic studies of the colonies had mostly focused on those items which brought profit to Western capitalists, and that was still the case: economics which were not related to the profit pursuit of colonial capitalism were not paid any attention. What was studied were exports to and imports from the West, the production of commodities required by the West, capital inflow from the West, and profit transfer to the West. The general definition of economics relied heavily on the concept of the satisfaction of wants and the means thereof; the colonial capitalist attitude towards economics was the satisfaction of profit by the colonial interest groups and the means thereof.

Historically speaking, an ideology of an epoch rarely expresses itself bluntly, consciously revealing its entire nature. But it is also not entirely concealed; here and there it reveals itself, as for example in the work of the Dutch professor of economics George Gonggrijp (1885–1969) who defined economic history entirely in terms of Western capitalism: "Economic history presupposes economic change. Villages, towns, and nations that year in and year out and century after century satisfy their wants in the same manner, have no economic history." By this definition, China, Japan and India before the 19th century had no economic history. Gonggrijp was referring to traditional Indonesian society. Villages, he said, existed also in Central and Western Europe but the Indonesian village life missed the individualism present in the European village of earlier centuries. European individualism is here considered as a significant criterion of what constitutes economic history. Here is a cultural imperialism in the realm of scientific conceptualization. Consequently, an economic process which does not conform to such a concept of significance is abandoned by the ethnocentric colonial scholarship. As Alatas had already noted in the "Introduction," the colonial ideology influences scholarship in the selection of themes as well as in analysis and conclusion. Similarly, as regards the image of the natives, these are neglected; hence a distorted and unbalanced picture emerged. Consequently, what was important in the history of the natives was also neglected.

In his book, Alatas was not attempting to evaluate colonialism as a historical phenomenon or the contribution of colonial scholarship to knowledge. His attention had been focused on the colonial image of the native and its function in the colonial ideology. He had also noted the negative influence of ideology on scholarship, which is distortive, one sided, generative of inconsistencies and superficiality. Sometime a point of view is offered, which appears objective and dispassionate, but lurking beneath it is the sympathy with colonialism, or any other ideology. A truly objective, honest, scholar will pronounce his/her sympathy and then argue for it in the most reasonable manner. Camouflaging an attitude by a posture of objectivity and impersonality serves to retard scholarship more than to advance it. An attempt to evaluate colonialism or imperialism, whether it was beneficial or not to the colonized society, cannot be considered scientific. It is a matter of conscience, but imperialism as a "fact" is not a matter of conscience, it is a scientific treatment. To consider the evaluation of colonialism as non-scientific entails a similar judgement on the evaluation of the various aspects of colonialism, in this case the colonial ideology and its negative image of the native. Why can one not be allowed to say that the colonial image of the native did not promote inter-ethnic harmony, that it was a blend of prejudice, that it was an unprovoked insult, that it was a distortion of reality, in short, that it was something which it should not have been? Agreeing to those authors who say that it is not a scientific endeavor means to allow the colonial image to prevail and influence scholarship. Any effort to reject the image is considered outside the purview of scholarship. Either we are unconsciously influenced by values or allow values to intrude into our scholarship. To expose the distortion, the untruth, and the prejudice behind the image, is another way of saying that the image is bad, even if we do not use the word "bad." The treatment of imperialism and colonialism, or any other subject, as a "fact" without involving any value judgement is a delusion that only lazy, and lousy, "scholars" can defend.

Bibliography

Adal, Raja. "Constructing transnational Islam: The East-West network of Shakib Arslan," in *Intellectuals in the Modern Islamic World: Transmission, transformation, communication*. Edited by Stephane A. Dudoignon, Komatsu Hisao, and Kosugi Yasushi, 176–210. London and New York: Routledge, 2006.

Ahmad, Irfan. "Foreword: On Writing History." In Tauseef Ahmad Parray, *Mediating Islam and Modernity: Sir Sayyid, Iqbal and Azad*. New Delhi: Viva Books, 2019, VI–XVI.

Alatas, Muhammad Naquib. *Historical Fact and Fiction*. Kuala Lumpur: UTM Press, 2011.

Alatas, Syed Hussein. *Thomas Stamford Raffles, 1781–1826, schemer or reformer?* Singapore: Angus and Robertson, 1971.

Alatas, Syed Hussein. *The Myth of the Lazy Native: A study of the image of the Malays, Filipinos and Javanese from the 16th to the 20th century and its function in the ideology of colonial capitalism*. London: Frank Cass, 1977.

Alavi, Seema. *Muslim Cosmopolitanism in the Age of Empire*. Cambridge, MA: Harvard University Press, 2015.

Alexandrowicz, C. H. *The Law of Nations in Global History*, edited by David Armitage and Jennifer Pitts. Oxford: Oxford University Press, 2017.

Ali, Farman, and Humaira Ahmad. "Early Christian Sīrah Writings of Subcontinent: A Comparative Study of their Methods, Impact and Cogitating on New Contemporizing Methodology." *Journal of Islamic Thought and Civilization* 8, no. 1 (2018): 129–143.

Ali, Kecia. *The Lives of Muhammad*. Cambridge, MA: Harvard University Press, 2014.

Aljunied, Syed Muhd Khairudin. "Sir Thomas Stamford Raffles' Discourse on the Malay World: A Revisionist Perspective." *Sojourn* 20, no. 1 (2005): 1–22.

Allina, Eric. *Slavery by Any Other Name: African Life under Company Rule in Colonial Mozambique*. Charlottesville, VA: The University of Virginia Press, 2012.

Anghie, Antony. *Imperialism, Sovereignty, and the Making of International Law*. Cambridge: Cambridge University Press, 2005.

Asad, Talal (ed.). *Anthropology and the Colonial Encounter*. London: Ithaca, 1973.

Aydin, Cemil. *The politics of civilizational identities: Asia, west and Islam in the pan-Asianist thought of Ōkawa Shūmei*. Ph. D. Committee on History and Middle Eastern Studies Harvard University, 2002.

Aydin, Cemil. *The Politics of Anti-Westernism in Asia: Visions of World Order in Pan-Islamic and Pan-Asian thought*. New York: Columbia University Press, 2007.

Aydin, Cemil. *The Idea of the Muslim World: A Global Intellectual History*. Cambridge MA: Harvard University Press, 2017.

Al-Azmeh, Aziz. *The Times of History: Universal Topics in Islamic Historiography*. Budapest and New York: Central European University Press, 2007.

Behdad, Ali, and Luke Gartian, eds. *Photography's Orientalisms: New Essays on Colonial Representation*. Los Angeles: Getty Research Institute, 2013.

Benton, Lauren A., and Lisa Ford. *Rage for Order: The British Empire and the Origins of International Law, 1800–1850*. Cambridge, MA: Harvard University Press, 2016.

Benumeya Grimau, Rodolfo Gil. *Ni oriente, ni occidente: el universo visto desde el Albayzín*. Granada: Editorial Universidad de Granada, 1996 [1930].

Bernstein, Richard. *The East, the West, and Sex: A History of Erotic Encounters*. New York: Alfred A. Knopf, 2009.

Blatt, Jessica. *Race and the Making of American Political Science*. Philadelphia: University of Pennsylvania Press, 2018.

Blaut, James Morris. *The Colonizer's Model of the World: Geographical Diffusionism and Eurocentric History*. New York: Guilford Press, 1993.

Blaut, James Morris. *Eight Eurocentric Historians*. New York: Guilford Press, 2000.

Bourdieu, Pierre. *Science de la science et refléxivité. Cours au Collège de France, 2000–2001*. Paris: Éditions Raisons d'Agir, 2001 (English translation, *Science of Science and Reflexivity*. London: Polity, 2004).

Bradbury, Ray. *Fahrenheit 451*. London: Harper Collins Publishers, 1996 [1954].

Bull, Hedley. *The Anarchical Society: A Study of Order in World Politics*. New York: Columbia University Press, 1977.

Burton, Antoinette. *Empire in Question: Reading, Writing, and Teaching British Imperialism*. Durham: Duke University Press, 2011.

Byatt, A. S. *Possession: A Romance*. London: Chatto & Windus, 1990.

Calderwood, Eric. *Colonial al-Andalus: Spain and the Making of Modern Moroccan Culture*. Cambridge, MA: Belknap Press of Harvard University Press, 2018.

Carpenter, Charli. "'You Talk of Terrible Things So Matter-of-Factly in This Language of Science': Constructing Human Rights in the Academy." *Perspectives on Politics* 10, no. 2 (2012): 363–383.

Carr, Edward Hallett. *What Is History?* London: Macmillan, 1961.

Certeau, Michel de. *The Writing of History*. New York: Columbia University Press, 1992.

Chetail, Vincent, and Peter Haggenmacher (eds.). *Vattel's International Law from a XXIst Century Perspective / Le Droit International de Vattel vu du XXIe Siècle*. Boston: Brill – Nijhoff, 2011.

Ciarlo, David. *Advertising Empire: Race and Visual Culture in Imperial Germany*. Cambridge, MA: Harvard University Press, 2011.

Clark, Christopher. *Time and Power: Visions of History in German Politics, from the Thirty Years' War to the Third Reich*. Princeton: Princeton University Press, 2019.

Cohn, Bernard S. *An Anthropologist Among the Historians and Other Essays*. New York: Oxford University Press, 1988.

Cohn, Bernard S. *Colonialism and its Forms of Knowledge: the British in India*. Princeton: Princeton University Press, 1997.

Cooper, Frederick. *Colonialism in Question: Theory, Knowledge, History*. Berkeley: University of California Press, 2005.

Cryle, Peter, and Elizabeth Stephens. *Normality: A Critical Genealogy*. Chicago: The University of Chicago Press, 2017.

Daston, Lorraine, and Peter Galison. *Objectivity*. New York: Zone Books, 2007.

Dimmock, Matthew. *Mythologies of the Prophet Muhammad in Early Modern English Culture*. Cambridge: Cambridge University Press, 2013.

Ernst, Carl W. *Following Muhammad: Rethinking Islam in the Contemporary World*. Chapel Hill & London: The University of North Carolina Press, 2003.

Flaubert, Gustave. *Bouvard et Pécuchet*. Paris: Lgf, 1999 [1881].

Fuller, C. J. "Colonial Anthropology and the Decline of the Raj: Caste, Religion and Political Change in India in the Early Twentieth Century." *Journal of the Royal Asiatic Society* 26, no. 3 (2016): 463–486.

Gandhi, Leela. *Postcolonial Theory: A Critical Introduction: Second Edition*. New York: Columbia University Press, 2019.

García Sanjuán, Alejandro. *La conquista islámica de la Península Ibérica y la tergiversación del pasado: Del catastrofismo al negacionismo*. Madrid: Marcial Pons, 2013.

Gazzaniga, Michael S. *The Mind's Past*. Berkeley, CA: University of California Press, 2000.

Gobineau, Joseph Arthur, Comte de. *Essai sur l'inégalité des races humaines*. 4 vols. Paris: Firmin Didot, 1853–1855.

Goldthorpe, John H. *On Sociology: Numbers, Narratives, and the Integration of Research and Theory*. Oxford, New York: Oxford University Press, 2000.

Goody, Jack. *The Theft of History*. Cambridge: Cambridge University Press, 2006.

Hardt, Michael, and Antonio Negri. *Empire*. Cambridge, MA: Harvard University Press, 2000.

Heidegger, Martin. "Der Zeitbegriff in der Geschichtswissenschaft" ["The Concept of Time in the Science of History"], in *Zeitschrift für Philosophie und Philosophie Kritik* 161 (1916): 173–188.

Heidegger, Martin. *History of the Concept of Time: Prolegomena*, translated by Theodore Kisiel. Bloomington: Indiana University Press, 1985.

Heller, Agnes. *A Theory of History*. London: Routledge & Kegan Paul, 1982.

Hisao, Komatsu. "Muslim Intellectuals and Japan: A Pan-Islamist mediator, Abdurreshid Ibrahim." In *Intellectuals in the Modern Islamic World: Transmission, transformation, communication*. Edited by Stephane A. Dudoignon, Komatsu Hisao, and Kosugi Yasushi, 273–288. London and New York: Routledge, 2006.

Hobsbawm, Eric, and Terence Ranger, eds. *The Invention of Tradition*. Cambridge: Cambridge University Press, 2012.

Holenstein, André. *Mitten in Europa: Verflechtung und Abgrenzung in der Schweizer Geschichte*. Baden: Hier und Jetzt, 2014.

Hopkins, A. G. "'Blundering and Plundering': The Scramble for Africa Relived." *The Journal of African History* 34, no. 3 (1993): 489–494.

Ingold, Tim. "Anthropology is *Not* Ethnography." *Proceedings of the British Academy* 154 (2008): 69–92.

Iqbal, Muhammad. "The Mosque of Cordoba," in *Gabriel's Wing*, available at http://www.allamaiqbal.com/poetry.php?bookbup=24&orderno=317&lang_code=en&lang=2&conType=en. Accessed 23 November 2019.

Josephson, Jason Ānanda. *The Invention of Religion in Japan*. Chicago: University of Chicago Press, 2012.

Josephson-Storm, Jason Ānanda. *The Myth of Disenchantment: Magic, Modernity, and the Birth of the Human Sciences*. Chicago: University of Chicago Press, 2017.

Kashani-Sabet, Firoozeh. "Before ISIS: What Early America Thought of Islam," available at https://www.academia.edu/39137309/Before_ISIS_-What_Early_America_Thought_of_Islam. Accessed 23 November 2019.

Kloos, David. "A Crazy State: Violence, Psychiatry, and Colonialism in Aceh, Indonesia, ca. 1910–1942." *Bijdragen tot de Taal-, Land- en Volkenkunde* 170 (2014): 25–65.

Kramer, Martin. "Coming to Terms: Fundamentalists or Islamists?." *Middle East Quarterly* 10, no. 2 (Spring 2003): 65–77.

Leclerc, Gérard. *Anthropologie et colonialisme: essai sur l'histoire de l'africanisme*. Paris: Fayard, 1972.

Lorenz, Chris, and Berber Bevernage, ed. *Breaking up Time: Negotiating the Borders between Present, Past and Future*. Göttingen: Vandenhoeck & Ruprecht GmbH & Co. KG, 2013.

Lustick, Ian S. "History, Historiography, and Political Science: Multiple Historical Records and the Problem of Selection Bias." *The American Political Science Review* 90, no. 3 (September 1996): 605–618.

Mamdani, Mahmood. *Define and Rule: Native as Political Identity*. Cambridge, MA: Harvard University Press, 2012.

Mannheim, Karl. *Ideology and Utopia: An Introduction to the Sociology of Knowledge*. New York: Harcourt, Brace and Company, 1936.

Marshall, Peter. *1517: Martin Luther and the Invention of the Reformation*. Oxford: Oxford University Press, 2017.

Mårtensson, Ulrika. "Discourse and Historical Analysis: The Case of al-Ṭabarī's History of the Messengers and the Kings." *Journal of Islamic Studies* 16, no. 3 (September 2005): 287–331.

Mirsepassi, Ali. "Mistaken Anti-modernity: Fardid After Fardid." *Working Paper Series of the HCAS "Multiple Secularities – Beyond the West, Beyond Modernities"* 6. Leipzig: Universität Leipzig, February 2019.

Mohomed, Carimo. "The abolition of the Past: History in George Orwell's *1984*." In *2011 2nd International Conference on Humanities, Historical and Social Sciences IPEDR* 17, 71–76. Singapore: IACSIT Press, 2011.

Mohomed, Carimo. "Reconsidering 'Middle East and Islamic Studies' for a changing world." *International Critical Thought* 2, no. 2 (2012): 197–208.

Mohomed, Carimo. "Rethinking the 'Middle East' as an Object of Study." *Annals of Japan Association for Middle East Studies* 31, no. 2 (2015): 265–301.

Mohomed, Carimo. "'The Parting of the Ways': A Qutbian Approach to International Relations." In *Islam and International Relations*, edited by Deina Abdelkader, Nassef Manabilang Adiong, and Raffaele Mauriello, 165–183. London: Palgrave Macmillan UK, 2016.

Mohomed, Carimo. "Ideology by Any Other Name: Social Sciences and the Humanities as Western Catechism." In *Ali Shariati and the Future of Social Theory*, edited by Dustin J. Byrd and Seyed Javad Miri, 21–63. Boston and Leiden: Brill, 2017.

Mohomed, Carimo. "Indian Muslims are the Most Loyal Subjects of the British Raj: Sir Sayyid Ahmad Khan and the Caliphate." In *The Cambridge Companion to Sayyid Ahmad Khan,* 38–54. Cambridge: Cambridge University Press, 2018.

Noorani, Yaseen. "The Lost Garden of Al-Andalus: Islamic Spain and the Poetic Inversion of Colonialism." *International Journal of Middle East Studies* 31, no. 2 (May 1999): 237–254.

Noyes, J. Noyes. "Herder, Postcolonial Theory and the Antinomy of Universal Reason." *Cambridge Journal of Postcolonial Literary Inquiry* 1, no. 1 (2014): 107–122.

Orford, Anne (ed.). *International Law and Its Others*. Cambridge: Cambridge University Press, 2006.

Orwell, George. *Nineteen Eighty-Four*. New York: Harcourt, Brace and Company, 1949.

Otto, Paul, and Jaap Jacobs. "Introduction: Historians and the Public Debate about the Past." *Journal of Early American History* 3 (2013): 1–8.

Pakenham, Thomas. *The Scramble for Africa: The White Man's Conquest of the Dark Continent from 1876 to 1912*. New York: Random House, 1991.

Pears, Iain. *An Instance of the Fingerpost*. London: Jonathan Cape, 1997.

Pitts, Jennifer. *Boundaries of the International: Law and Empire*. Cambridge, MA: Harvard University Press, 2018.

Raffoul, François. "Heidegger and the Aporia of History," in *Poligrafi: Natural History* 16, no. 61–62 (2011): 91–118.

Riley, Dylan. "Metaphysicking the West," *New Left Review* 113 (Sept-Oct 2018): 125–138.

Robinette, Nicholas. "The World Laid Waste: Herder, Language Labor, Empire." *New Literary History* 42, no. 1 (2011): 193–203.

Robinson, Kim Stanley. *Icehenge*. London: Voyager, 1997 [1984].

Ryan, Ben. *How the West Was Lost: The Decline of a Myth and the Search for New Stories*. London: Hurst, 2019.

Salama, Mohammad R. *Islam, Orientalism and Intellectual History*. London: I. B. Tauris, 2011.

Schimmel, Annemarie. *Gabriel's Wing: A Study into the religious ideas of Sir Muhammad Iqbal*. Leiden: E. J. Brill, 1963.

Schmitt, Carl. *Political Theology: Four Chapters on the Concept of Sovereignty*. Chicago: University of Chicago Press, 2005.

Seth, Sanjay. "Reason or Reasoning? Clio or Siva?." *Social Text* 78, no. 22, 1. Durham: Duke University Press, March 2004, 85–101.

Seth, Sanjay. "Historical Sociology and Postcolonial Theory: Two Strategies for Challenging Eurocentrism." *International Political Sociology* 3, no. 3 (September 2009): 334–338.

Slight, John. *The British Empire and the Hajj: 1865–1956*. Cambridge, MA: Harvard University Press, 2015.

Small, Lisa. "Western Eyes, Eastern Visions." In *A Distant Muse: An Orientalist Works from the Dahesh Museum of Art*. New York: Dahesh Museum of Art, 2000.

Smith, Bonnie G. *Modern Empires: A Reader*. New York and London: Oxford University Press, 2017.

Steenbrink, Karel. "Dutch Colonial Containment of Islam in Manggarai, West-Flores, in Favour of Catholicism, 1907–1942." *Bijdragen tot de Taal-, Land- en Volkenkunde* 169 (2013): 104–128.

Subin, Anna Della. "It has burned my heart." *London Review of Books* 37, no. 20 (22 October 2015): 21–24.

Thomas, Jolyon Baraka. *Faking Liberties: Religious Freedom in American-Occupied Japan*. Chicago: University of Chicago Press, 2019.

Thomas, Keith. "Diary." *London Review of Books* 32, no. 11 (10 June 2010): 36–37.

Thomas, Nicholaus. *Colonialism's Culture: Anthropology, Travel, and Government*. Princeton, N.J.: Princeton University Press, 1994.

Tolan, John V. *Faces of Muhammad: Western Perceptions of the Prophet of Islam from the Middle Ages to Today*. Princeton: Princeton University Press, 2019.

Toyoda, Tetsuya. *Theory and Politics of the Law of Nations: Political Bias in International Law Discourse of Seven German Court Councilors in the Seventeenth and Eighteenth Centuries*. Leiden: Martinus Nijhoff Publishers, 2011.

Trautmann, Thomas R. "Does India Have History? Does History Have India?." *Comparative Studies in Society and History* 54, no. 1 (2012): 174–205.

Vattel, Emer de. *The Law of Nations, or, Principles of the Law of Nature, applied to the Conduct and Affairs of Nations and Sovereigns, with Three Early Essays on the Origin and Nature of Natural Law and on Luxury*, edited by Bela Kapossy and Richard Whatmore. Indianapolis: Liberty Fund, 2008.

Vaux, Baron Carra de. *Les penseurs de l'islam*. Paris: Paul Geuthner, 1921–1926, 5 vols.

Verne, Jules. *Les Enfants du capitaine Grant* [*The Children of Captain Grant*], translated as *In Search of the Castaways*. Paris: Pierre-Jules Hetzel, 1867–1868.

Wallerstein, Immanuel. "Islam, the West, and the World." *Journal of Islamic Studies* 10, no. 2 (1999): 109–125.

Watson, Adam. *The Evolution of International Society: A Comparative Historical Analysis.* New York: Routledge, 1992.

Wolf, Kenneth Baxter. "Negating Negationism," *Pomona Faculty Publications and Research.* Paper 394 (2014), available at http://scholarship.claremont.edu/pomona _fac_pub/394. Accessed 23 November 2019.

PART 4

Alatas and the Socio-political

∵

CHAPTER 13

Syed Hussein Alatas and the Question of Intellectuals

Seyed Javad Miri

1 Introduction

At the outset of Intellectuals in Developing Societies, Syed Hussein Alatas refers to Alexander Herzen, where the Russian philosopher says,

> The religion of the revolution, of the great social reformation, is the only religion which I bequeath to you. It has no other paradise or rewards but your sense of right, your own conscience.[1]

The key idea in Herzen's conceptualization is the way in which an intellectual engages with the question of social reformation. This is how Alatas approaches the problem of intellectuals. It may not be an exaggeration to classify Alatas' approach to the problem of intellectuals as a form of Russified reading of intellectual praxis. But it would be a mistake to consider the Russification of intellectual activity in Alatas' frame of reference as a mere duplication of the Russian literary thinkers of the 19th century. Does a country need an intellectual community? This is a question that Alatas puts forward at the outset of his intellectual sojourn in *Intellectuals in Developing Societies,* with its seeds being planted as early as 1968. Alatas believed that in the "intellectual history of mankind problems have often been ignored not because of objective circumstances but because of the limited vision of particular societies."[2] Geography is of great significance in the Alatasian narrative of intellectual praxis and that is why when he conceptualizes the question of awakening of intellectuals in Asia, which he terms as "the Asian awakening," he refers to the year 1905, which is related to the victory of Japan over Russia.[3] Alatas' definition of an intellectual is "a person who is engaged in thinking about ideas and non-material

---

[1] Alexander Herzen, *Selected Philosophical Works.* (Moscow: Foreign Language Publishing House, 1956), 336–337.

[2] Syed Hussein Alatas, *Intellectuals in Developing Societies* (London: Frank Cass, 1977), 4.

[3] Ibid.

© SEYED JAVAD MIRI, 2023 | DOI:10.1163/9789004521698_015

problems using the faculty of reason."[4] Alatas critiques Ignazio Silone's thesis on redundancy of intellectuals by arguing that "Silone's suggestion that intellectuals do not now guide public opinion is a historical judgment on particular groups and places, not a generalization."[5]

When Alatas argues that Silone's thesis is not applicable to all social and historical contexts, this brings up the question of sociohistorical particularities that are not taken seriously by Eurocentric scholars and thinkers. That is why he refers to the concept of "different stages of history" by reflecting upon the intellectual class in non-western contexts. He writes,

> One missing item, and it is the one of most interest to us at this stage of our history, is the emergence of a functioning intellectual group. In Europe and America the group is already there. Hence, what is discussed are problems surrounding this group rather than the question of its creation.[6]

The interesting point that needs to be delved into deeper is Alatas' untiring referential point, as far as intellectual archetype is concerned, i.e., the Russian Model of Intellectuality. Within current literature, there is almost nothing about the connection between Russian intellectual history and the Alatasian perspective on intellectual praxis. Such a connection would be very intriguing research as far as intellectual history of Malaysia is concerned. However, the question that I am interested in is the Alatasian perspective on intellectuals and how this question has been conceptualized by Syed Hussein Alatas and whether his framework could be employed in a more generalized fashion to discuss global condition of intellectual praxis. Of course, to study the "Russian link" could be interesting research, but we just alluded to aspects of this link that could be useful for historians of ideas. Nevertheless, our major concern is the Alatasian reading of the question of intellectuals that has hitherto been less debated in mainstream social sciences and social and philosophical circles around the globe. Now that we have stated clearly which problems we are not going to inquire upon, it is time to move on and focus on aspects that we are planning to discuss in this chapter.

How does Alatas conceptualize the concept of intellectual? The problem of intellectuals in the modern world is one of the most challenging questions in the context of social sciences and humanities. In this chapter, we shall first

---

4 Ibid., 8.
5 Ibid., 14.
6 Ibid., 15.

focus on the definition of the "intellectual" by Alatas and see what he means by this concept. We know that this concept has been constructed, reconstructed, deconstructed, and reinterpreted by many critical social thinkers, philosophers, and social theorists since 18th century onward. Thus, to assume that the meaning of this word is crystal-clear is naïve, as we have diverse opinions on this issue within current global literature. Therefore, the first thing we need to clarify is how Syed Hussein Alatas has defined this concept and then raise the second question, why should we bother with intellectuals in human societies? In other words, do intellectuals have any function in our societies in his view? If they have any kind of function in human societies then what are their functions in Alatas' perspective? The third question that we need to inquire upon is the relevance of his assessment on the role of intellectuals, as he argues that his conceptualization on intellectuals is based on the context of developing societies. Said differently, we are interested in the possibility of universalizing his concept of intellectuals on the global stage. Is this feasible? The fourth section of this chapter is on the future of intellectuals in human history in relation to theories that talk about the redundancy of intellectuals. Does Alatas' view on or his reading of intellectuals falsify these trendy theories or endorse the redundancy theories?

2   Intellectual: A Conceptual Makeup

According to a well-established interpretation, the "intellectual" as a concept dates back to the early 19th century in Europe and applies to an individual who is existentially engaged with critical thinking that is applicable to improving society.[7] In this fashion, intellectuals could be considered a new breed in society and as such they conceptualize, discuss, write about, and concern themselves with ideas. Of course, there are others who may disagree with this form of intellectual historiography, but the question here is on Alatas' definition of this concept.

We are interested in finding out how Alatas conceptualizes the term intellectual? What does he mean by the concept intellectual? In *Intellectuals in Developing Societies,* Alatas argues that intellectuals "perform an essential function in the promotion of society's progress."[8] This is to argue that in Alatas' definition an intellectual is someone who performs a vital role in the progress

---

7   Anthony Grafton, "The History of Ideas: Precept and Practice, 1950–2000 and Beyond," *Journal of the History of Ideas* 67 no. 1 (2006): 1–32.

8   Alatas, *Intellectuals,* xiv.

of society. Of course, one may wonder why he is conceptualizing the intellectual in terms of functionality. In order to understand his position on the question of the intellectual we need to learn about Alatas' philosophical orientation. He urges us to compare an engineer and a social scientist by arguing that an,

> engineer who studies the building of bridges is expected to be in favor of bridges, although he may hesitate over particular types of bridges. It is true that a bridge may not have top priority in the development policy of a particular government at a particular time and place, but the engineer's science nevertheless has as its goal the building of bridges and his whole scientific training is directed to that aim. When he prescribes the construction of a bridge, it is a value-judgment associated with the goal of his science. Similarly, when I express value-judgments on the need for intellectuals ... based on the premise that they perform an essential function ... this expression should be considered as applied social science. Just as applied bacteriology prescribes the elimination of some types of germs, so applied social science prescribes the elimination of certain phenomena which obstruct the development of human society.[9]

Here, we can see that Alatas' view on intellectuals is based on a normative understanding of sociology, and intellectuals are individuals who can think about the germs, so to speak, in society that obstruct the development of human society. In other words, intellectuals are bacteriologists of society's body. If this interpretation of his view on intellectuals is correct, then one can claim that intellectuals have a grandiose position in the philosophical worldview of Alatas. Of course, it should be noted that Alatas distinguishes between the conditions of developing societies and developed societies and based on this distinction he prescribes different strategies as far as intellectuals are concerned. But we should not forget that he worked out his reflections on intellectuals half a century ago and the conditions of human societies around the globe in the context of post-novel epoch has dramatically changed the contours of the human condition. This post-novel transformation allows us to apply his views on intellectuals at a global level instead of reading and interpreting them in a local fashion.

Why is that so? Alatas argues that the existence of certain phenomena obstruct the possibility of growth within human society. However, the question

---

9 Ibid.

is what kind of people are able to understand these obstructing phenomena and yet again who are in a position to have the ability to provide remedies for their eliminations. In *Intellectuals in Developing Societies,* Alatas employs time and again the concept of development, but it is wrong to assume that he reads this concept in a quantitative fashion, as development is not a computable concept in his frame of reference. On the contrary, he considers the concept of development in a qualitative fashion. That is why he chooses the question of intellectuality as a demarcating criterion between the developing and developed societies. In other words, if the concept of development is not solely defined in a quantitative manner, then we could argue that Alatas is concerned with the growth of human society in a general fashion, and as such his thought on intellectuals should not be confined to the local conditions of developing societies. This is to argue that we need to reinterpret his views in a reconstructive fashion that could encompass general conditions of human society in regard to human growth and obstructive phenomena that may hinder the emergence of a good society.

Is my approach violating the primary horizons of the text? I think there are strong indications in Alatas' text that allows us to read his views on intellectuals in a more general fashion rather than confining his views either to Malaysia or to developing societies. It seems there is an organic relation between the emergence of intellectuals and crisis situations. Alatas describes this correlation by stating that "crisis situations ... often exacerbate the need for intellectuals" and "without an intellectual community it is futile to hope for a conscious and intelligent choice of solutions to the problems faced by" any society that aspires to become a good society.[10]

When he was working on his thesis on intellectual communities in developing societies one could see that a vast gap between the developing and developed societies existed. However, the current state of the post-novel world makes such assumptions hard to hold. The post-novel realities allow us to read Alatas' thesis in a more general fashion, which could apply to various societies across the globe as the post-novel crisis situations have encompassed the planetary life of all human societies in a similar (but different in degree) fashion.

Does Alatas have a definition of an 'intellectual'? When we look at his descriptions of intellectuals in relation to the particular context of Malaysia, it seems that he is more concerned with the functional dimensions of intellectuals rather than other dimensions regarding their presence in modern societies. However, this does not mean that he has not defined this concept in an

---

10   Ibid., xv.

academic fashion. Alatas regards intellectuals as "leaders of thought ... [who are able to create awareness] of the fundamental problems ... [which concern] ... man and society."[11] At the same time, Alatas cautions us about another persistent problem in human history: the suppression of the emergence of intellectuals in various societies. He argues that in "the intellectual history of mankind problems have often been ignored not because of objective circumstances but because of the limited vision of [people across human] ... societies."[12] This is to argue that despite the lack of awareness of the need for intellectual effort, "the historical necessity for intellectual life is certainly" present globally across different societies at the planetary level.[13] Alatas tries to confine himself into the Malaysian context, but the problem is evident at the planetary level and we can refer to few of those urgent problems that require the "meddling of intellectuals" (using Sartre's concept), such as populism, systematic racism, planetary war, genocide, homicide, suicide, ecocide, and nihilism.

We have earlier mentioned that Alatas considers intellectuals as thought leaders. However, this is not a working definition as it is too generalized to be a working definition. Let us have a closer look at Alatas' definition of an intellectual by referring to his own words on this subject. In *Intellectuals in Developing Societies*, Alatas defines an intellectual as an individual "who is engaged in thinking about ideas and non-material problems using the faculty of reason."[14] This is to argue that intellectuals are thinkers who have a general view on social issues, and in this fashion we should distinguish between intellectuals and degree-holders, or academic professors. Alatas holds that knowledge,

> of a certain subject or the possession of a degree does not make a person an intellectual although these often coincide; there are many degree-holders and professors who do not engage in developing their field or try to find the solution to specific problems within it. On the other hand, a person with no academic qualifications can be an intellectual if he utilizes his thinking capacity and possesses sufficient knowledge of his subject of interest.[15]

Said differently, Alatas makes a distinction between intellectuals and educated elites as well as academic staff who are, in his view, more specialists rather

---

11 Ibid., 1.
12 Ibid., 4.
13 Ibid.
14 Ibid., 8.
15 Ibid.

than intellectuals who have "social concern," i.e., a certain sense of responsibility towards the well-being for one's own society or community. If there is a distinction between an intellectual and a degree-holder, then the question is how can we characterize the contours of concerns that distinguishes between these two types of social agents?

Syed Hussein Alatas enumerates six major characteristics for an intellectual that could be considered as general qualities applicable to any individual in an abstract fashion. Why do I insist that his enumerated characteristics are applicable to all intellectuals regardless of their social contexts in developed or developing countries? One of the main reasons is that theories of subaltern theorists tend to be underestimated in global sociology and mainstream social theory contexts. The pretext is that these theories are context-bounded while the Eurocentric theories are valid globally and trans-culturally applicable. However, the fact is that these assumptions are false and the cogent arguments against these distorted opinions need to be demonstrated and discussed in detail. This is to argue that subaltern theories are not only locally valid but they can be employed in a more generalized fashion provided we rectify the problems of under-theorization, which many of these theories and theoretical frameworks suffer from. In the 1970s, when Alatas was reflecting upon the question of intellectuals and their social roles, it was hard to display more theoretical guts; the lack of such should not be understood solely in psychological terms, but rather the absence of a more reckless theoretical confrontation with colonial masters was almost historically impossible. Although Alatas was one of the pioneers in the theory of the "captive mind," the historical conditions did not allow post-colonial and de-colonial theorists to dream beyond their own borders. In other words, we can now deconstruct Alatas' take on intellectuals and read them in a more generalized and cosmopolitan fashion, which was not conceivable half a century ago in a marginalized and newly decolonized society such as Malaysia.

Alatas maintains that intellectuals manifest six general social characteristics:

(1) they are recruited from all classes though in differing proportions; (2) they are to be found supporting or opposing various cultural or political movements; (3) their occupations on the whole are non-manual being for the most part writers, lecturers, poets, journalists, etc.; (4) to a certain extent they remain at a distance from the rest of society, mixing in a group of their own; (5) they are not merely interested in the purely technical and mechanistic side of knowledge: ideas about religion, the good life, art, nationalism, planned economy, culture and the like belong to their world of thought. Furthermore, intellectuals in contrast with

specialists, try to see things in a broad perspective in terms of their inner-relation and totality; (6) the intellectual group has always been a small proportion of society.[16]

Here, we can see the general traits of intellectuals that could be employed while conceptualizing the intellectual activities in any human society, regardless of whether such intellectuals belong to the "developed" or "developing" countries. Such categories are even applicable to "underdeveloped" countries. In other words, we can read Alatas' *Intellectuals in Developing Societies* as a discourse on intellectuals in the contemporary world without confining his analyses into a very limited domain of subaltern societies or Southeast Asia.

For instance, Jean-Paul Sartre, Noam Chomsky, Edward Said, Michel Foucault, or Antonio Gramsci have all in different ways reflected upon the role of intellectuals in modern societies and their respective paradigms have become normative paradigms in articulating the problems of intellectualness. However, within current literature, very few academic references exist on Alatas' discourse on intellectuals. Why is this so? Does his conceptualization lack depth? Is his analytical framework useless in comparison to competing global discourses on intellectuality?

I doubt this is the case, as Alatas is a very conceptually-conscious social thinker, who delves into the complexities of social problems and acutely conceptualizes the intricacies of social reality in a profound sociological fashion. Then, if this is the case, why do we not hear from him in mainstream global sociological debates on intellectuals? I think we can mention various reasons for the systematic absence of Alatas in the mainstream sociology and social theory circles, but two of the reasons could be categorized as primary motives in this context: the first one is due to the hegemony of Eurocentrism in academic contexts around the globe. This is not a very new phenomenon as postcolonial critics have written abundantly on this issue. The second reason is of an internal nature and by that I refer to Alatas' mental landscape as far as his debates on the role of intellectuals are concerned. That is to argue that Alatas aimed his attention on intellectuals in developing societies and whenever he referred to the developed societies it seemed that in these Euro-American contexts, we are faced with totally different issues and problems that could not be discussed or compared to the conditions of the developing societies. In other words, it seems there is an internal inhibitor that stops the possibility of generalizing his findings in order to be applied to a more universal context. Here we

---

16   Ibid., 8–9.

shall attempt to focus more on the possibility of Alatas' analyses of intellectuals that could be deconstructed and then reconstructed for broader scenarios.

The six broad characteristics that Alatas classified in his analysis are universal traits that cross over the boundaries of developing and developed societies. One of the main distinctions that could be used among these six traits is the differentiation that he makes between an intellectual and a specialist. Today we are faced with an army of specialists who hold various types of degrees, but Alatas reject their claim to leadership. Why is he refusing to accept specialists as modern leaders of human societies? Are we not living in complex societies where the division of labor has brought the supremacy of specialism/expertism to the core of modernity? In other words, the rule of disciplinary thought necessitates specialism as a virtue that without the modern machinery would soon or later collapse. If this is the case, then why should Alatas rebuke the rule of specialists and degree-holders and instead focus on the role of intellectuals? This is a valid question and as such is not only a problem for the developing societies. On the contrary, specialism and compartmentalization of human activities and knowledge are more rampant in developed societies than in developing societies and as such the critique leveled by Alatas could have a more general validity than what it has been recognized.

Alatas argues that intellectuals possess an ability that he conceptualizes as "broad perspective," which, in his reading, is absent in the hearts and minds of specialists.[17] This is to argue that specialists lack broad perspective, and this shortage demonstrates itself among intelligentsia who holds power in the strict sense of politics. However, it seems this critique is vague as we do not know what he means by the concept of "broad perspective" when he ascribes this quality to intellectuals in contrast to specialists/degree-holders. Does Alatas say anything clear about his key concept in reference to intellectuals? How does he define broadness of perspective in reference to intellectuals? I think if we could determine the scope of his definition then possibilities of theoretical generalizations in terms of his discourse on intellectuals could be enhanced due to the fact that a certain degree of abstractness is needed whenever we think of the concept of general in strict philosophical sense of the term. This is to contend that a level of abstractness should be present in any theory if it is going to be categorized as a general theory, and I think we can discern this level of abstractness in Alatas' conception on intellectuals. Intellectuals are thinking individuals who have broad perspectives, but the soaring question that needs to be delved into is what are the constitutive elements of a broad perspective?

---

17   Ibid., 8.

Alatas mentions two constituents as decisive factors in making up the contours of a broad perspective: the first element is that intellectuals see things in their inter-relationality, and the second factor is that intellectuals are capable of seeing things in terms of their totality.[18] Thus, when Alatas conceptualizes intellectuals as a different kind of social class he identifies two qualities that are the most important, i.e., seeing things in their inter-relationality and conceiving things in their totality. These two abilities are general qualities that could be considered as measuring indices in a global context whenever any sociologist attempt to study an intellectual group in any human society.

3 Interrelation and Totality as Key Features of Intellectuals

What does Alatas mean by arguing that intellectuals see things in their inter-relation and totality? First of all, it could entail that there are others who belong to elite category in human societies such as "politicians, administrators, religious dignitaries, artists, industrialists, businessmen, aristocrats" and specialists but, in spite of being elites of the society, they are unable to conceive social issues in terms of their inter-relation and totality.[19] Secondly it seems that Alatas attempts to make a point that intellectuals belong to a particular group in society that has a particular function, and to understand their function we need to analyze intellectuals in terms of two significant elements: inter-relation and totality. In other words, we cannot deny that all members of aforementioned elites have different kinds of functions in human society, but there seems to be a difference between all these functionalities and the intellectual function in overarching framework. The function of intellectuals is to provide,

> leadership in the realm of thinking. It is the intellectuals who explain the problems of society and attempt to find solutions – the intellectuals produce ideas and spread them to other members of society.[20]

Thus, when Alatas enumerates the two key qualities of intellectuals as inter-relationality and totality, we should understand them in relation to the concept of "leadership." But this notion is a much-contested concept, and many theorists and scholars define it in different fashions. Therefore, we need to find out exactly what he means by this concept. What does the concept of "leadership"

---

18   Ibid., 8–9.
19   Ibid., 9.
20   Ibid.

mean in the Alatasian frame of reference? When Alatas talks about intellectual leadership he refers to the act of leading the masses by increasing their critical faculty, their sense of self-consciousness, their level of sensitivities towards social issues, and assisting them to understand that society is a fact that is interrelated to our acts. This is to argue that social facts are born out of our social acts and if we see dysfunctionalities in various realms of our society, we should rest assured that these are the outcomes of the totality of our acts. Alatas, as mentioned before, considers intellectuals as the leaders in the realm of thinking. Here, the concept of leadership refers to actors "who explain the problems of society and attempt to find solutions [and they do this by producing] ideas and [spreading] them to other members of society."[21]

Alatas defines the contours of intellectual leadership by arguing that intellectuals lead the others due to the fact that they are able to explain social problems in an inter-relational and total fashion. If this is the definition of intellectual leadership then one must pose the following question: what are the characteristic problems and activities that only the intellectuals carry out? Can't other elites or academics and disciplinary professors take the mantle of leadership in the realm of thinking? If we follow the logic of Alatas then the answer is negative, as the particular characteristics that he attaches to intellectuals cannot be found among intelligentsia. By intelligentsia, Alatas refers to,

> those who have gone through higher formal and modern education, the specialists and the professionals, and those who have acquired higher level education by other means.[22]

We can see that Alatas distinguishes between the two concepts of intellectual and intelligentsia and considers the latter unqualified for carrying the task of "leadership in the realm of thinking."[23] However, we still do not know what are the key characteristics that could solely be undertaken by intellectuals and not intelligentsia? Does Alatas reflect upon these characteristics in his works?

We know that intellectuals should be equipped by the two grand qualities of inter-relational vision and holistic outlook, but what are the typical problems and concerns that intelligentsia cannot undertake but intellectuals are able to carry out? This is a pivotal question, which needs to be reflected upon, and so far, scholars in the fields of social sciences have not thought about it adequately as far as Alatas is concerned. There are a few studies on various

---

21 Ibid.
22 Ibid.
23 Ibid.

aspects of his sociology of law and corruption or even his post-colonial and de-colonial ideas, but no considerable attention on the role of intellectuals in the post-globalized world. We do not know what a sociology of intellectuals based on the Alatasian perspective would look like.

It is safe to state that we are at the infancy phase as far as the Alatasian sociology of intellectuals is concerned and more academic works are needed in this field. In the second chapter, "Intellectuals and Their Function," of his *Intellectuals in Developing Societies*, Alatas mentions six characteristic problems and activities that only the intellectuals are able to undertake. They are

> (1) problems which are not and cannot be handled by specialists. (2) The area of intellectual activity cannot follow any demarcation laid down by any particular discipline. (3) The intellectual attitude cannot be created by formal and discipline-oriented training in terms of syllabus and fixed number of years of study. (4) The object of intellectual activity is always related to the wider context of life and thought, penetrating into funda-mental values and commitments. (5) The intellectual pursuit is not a pro-fession and therefore not subject to the sort of factors which determine the emergence and development of professions. (6) The intellectual interest involves the past, the present, and the future.[24]

By analyzing these six issues we can discern certain general traits that could be employed trans-culturally in studying intellectual phenomenon in vari-ous societies. Alatas makes clear that the intellectual is not a specialist, and this means that an intellectual should have a comprehensive outlook on social problems of humanity. The second point that we should deduce from his analysis is that intellectual imagination is not of disciplinary nature, but rather is tantamount to a holistic vision of reality. By saying this, Alatas makes us reflect upon the very nature of intellectuals as a social type, which are not made organizationally but are born existentially. The next issue that is of piv-otal significance is the distinction Alatas makes in terms of subject of study by disciplinary specialists and intellectuals. This is to argue that the subject of intellectuals' study is life in its entirety; they do not approach social/cultural/political problems in compartmentalized fashions as specialists and degree-holders do. It seems Alatas considers intellectuals as a class of thinkers who have holistic approaches to questions of life, and this is deeply rooted in his

---

24   Ibid., 10.

concepts of inter-relationality and totality, which are universal qualities of optimal intellectuals in his narrative.

Now, it is time to ask the following: if a society lacks individuals who have these comprehensive qualities, then what kind of society is it? Does Alatas reflect upon this question? Now that Alatas has laid bare the general features of intellectuals as a social class, then the next question should be on the level of social growth and the presence of intellectuals rather than specialists, because most researchers who focus on modernization, development, and economic prosperity, quickly jump to conclusions by referring to statistical data on the numbers of specialists and degree holders. Based on these calculations, they surmise whether or not a country is on the right path.

While it is true that Alatas takes a keen look at quantitative dimensions of development and modernization, is it wrong to assume that he conceptualizes modernity in a simple statistical fashion? On the contrary, his engagements on the question of intellectual class in Malaysia since 1960 demonstrates clearly that development is not a linear problem for him, which could be copied straightforward from one country to another. In other words, a sustainable modernity is an intellectual task, and this task cannot be managed by specialists or degree holders. On the contrary, we need to have an intellectual class who are able to engage in life's questions in a comprehensive fashion. This class is a rare commodity in many parts of the world. While he was writing on intellectuals in developing societies, he believed that they are few in numbers in Restern societies, but we can find them abundantly in Western societies. This assessment does not hold true today; We know for fact that intellectuals are rare species on this planet wherever we go and it is hard to find individuals who are equipped with a totalized vision of reality and inter-relational approach to life in its entirety. What would happen if a society were deprived of intellectuals? Alatas argues that a "society without a functioning group of intellectuals is deprived of a certain level of consciousness and insight into vital problems."[25]

4 Intellectuals and Essential Issues in Social Life

In order to understand Alatas' view on the relation between intellectuals and society, we need to focus on the role that consciousness plays in an individual's life, and by that analogy get a glimpse of what he had in mind. In other words,

---

25   Ibid.

322   MIRI

if we argue that an individual turns into a complete person when they acquire a certain level of consciousness, then it could be argued that intellectuals play the same role in the body of society, i.e., they are the consciousness of a society, without which a society is at loss. However, if that is what Alatas means, then we should ask about consciousness as he interrelates its presence to vital problems without which life would be barren. To put it differently, Alatas states that when we have functioning intellectuals in a society, then that society is privileged by a·certain level of consciousness. Thus, the absence of intellectuals affects the level of consciousness in human societies as the lack of consciousness drives the human body into a coma, which is tantamount to the loss of consciousness.

Alatas does not discuss the intricacies of consciousness philosophically or conceptually, but it seems he is aware that if a society is deprived of intellectuals, then people in that particular society cannot distinguish between essential and inessential issues in their collective life. Because, in accordance with Alatas' definition of intellectual as the perceptual faculty of social body, it is the mission of intellectuals to generate insights among people so they can differentiate and realize the vital and insignificant dimensions of life. This is to argue that intellectuals are equipped by a type of imagination that could create "a certain level of consciousness and insight into vital problems" in the minds and hearts of ordinary people in human societies.[26] Alatas talks frequently about vital problems and the insights that intellectuals generate for society in order to discern these vital problems, which without the society will fall into "an intellectual desert."[27] But we must ask the following: what are these vital problems? Does he talk about them in a concrete fashion?

Alatas talks about "vital problems," but the scope of his analyses is not global or even general in character. He often attempts to address local issues, but the problems he is referring to are not solely confined to developing societies, but rather are global and endemic to all contemporary societies. For instance, Alatas refers to "intellectual indolence" as one of the vital problems, but he does haste to add that this problem is particularly acute in developing societies. As a case-study he mentions "the indolence of Filipinos" as elaborated by Jose Rizal.[28] To explain, Alatas argues that

> Jose Rizal was a leading intellectual of his time. One of his most interesting works is his study of the indolence of the Filipinos. The whole of Asia

---

26   Ibid.
27   Ibid., 7.
28   Ibid., 11.

has been accused of laziness by successive Western writers and officials, so consistently in fact that many Asians began to believe it. Replying in 1890, Rizal accepted the charge but attributed it to historical and not to hereditary factors. The interesting thing to note is his intellectual reaction to the challenge. In spite of the relevance of Rizal's theme it elicited no response from most of the Asian intelligentsia.[29]

After relating this story, Alatas concludes that the Asian intelligentsia could not develop into a real group of intellectuals due to the lack of a "philosophic spirit"; this is a salient trait of the developing societies. I think what he says about the developing societies is a very interesting critique, but the truth is that this characteristic is not confined to the developing societies. On the contrary, the lack of "philosophic spirit" or "intellectual spirit" is a global phenomenon, and we can employ the Alatasian frame of reference to analyze the intellectual indolence even in Europe, Russia, and American societies. In other words, the intellectual indolence is not an Asian pandemic, but should be studied as a global problem today.

The second vital issue that Alatas mentions in relation to intellectuals is the question of leadership. This is to argue that one of the most vital issues in any human society is the problem of good leadership. This is not a technical question but rather an intellectual problem. What does he mean? Why is the existence of intellectuals a vital question for the growth of society? Alatas states that the emergence of a functioning intellectual group is a prerequisite for social growth and thus the absence of intellectual class could have dire effects on the developmental condition of any human society. He explains this point in the following fashion:

> To lack intellectuals is to lack leadership in the following areas of thinking: (1) the posing of problems; (2) the definition of problems; (3) the analysis of problems; and (4) the solution of problems. Even the posing of problems is in itself an intellectual problem. A society without effective intellectuals will not be in a position to raise problems.[30]

These four dimensions are of great significance in understanding the way in which Alatas conceptualizes the concept of the "intellectual." These questions are not by any standard a local problem, but they are of general nature

---

29   Ibid.
30   Ibid., 15.

and envelope any human society on earth. Imagine the madness (global war, pandemic, famine, ecocide, genocide, suicide, exploitation, injustice, racial attacks, etc.) we are now living in, a condition that is deeply interconnected to the question of leadership on the planetary scale, and then try to re-imagine the concept of intellectuality in relation to leadership in terms set by Alatas. What is the problem?

This may seem a very simple question, but Alatas argues that the very posing of problems is in itself an intellectual problem. In other words, if we look at the "global madness" in an Alatasian fashion then we can argue that the reason we cannot solve problems and sooth the pains inflicted upon humanity is due to the fact that we are incapable of posing the right questions. When you are not in a position to pose the right questions about social problems then you cannot construct effective policies either and all your political solutions are, in fact, counterproductive and inimical.

Alatas defines leadership in terms of intellectual competency and when this merit is lacking then the leadership in any society cannot pose the problems, define the problems, analyze the problems, and even worse, they are unable to solve the problems. For you can master all these four skills when and only when you can think of life in an inter-relational and totality fashion. However, most contemporary leaders in the world lack these qualities as they see life in compartmentalized manners and are unable to connect different dimensions of life in a totality.

For example, ecologists for years have warned societies about ecocide due to greenhouse gas emissions, which enters the atmosphere through the burning of fossil fuels (coal, natural gas, and oil), solid waste, trees and other biological materials. It is also as a result of certain chemical reactions (e.g., manufacture of cement). Nevertheless, the global political establishment is mentally disabled; it cannot see the world in its totality and the interconnectivity of life due to techno-capitalist development. By building on Alatas definition of leadership as an intellectual custodianship, we can then be in a position to critique the current techno-capitalist establishment that is driving the planetary life into an "infernal condition." If we agree that a "functioning intellectual group should be considered as a development need," and also define the concept of development differently than the terms set by the techno-capitalist developmental paradigms, then it could be argued that Alatas' concern with the problem of intellectual leadership is not a local concern of developing societies of Asia.[31]

---

31   Ibid.

On the contrary, we should reinterpret his concern for the emergence of a functioning intellectual group as a global concern wherein the developmental paradigm is not divorced from ideals of fraternity, liberty, equality, and sustainable growth. In order to go beyond the terms set by techno-capitalist developmental classes (and their intellectual cronies), we need, as Alatas emphasizes, intellectuals who are able to take the mantle of leadership in the following areas of thinking: (1) the posing of problems; (2) the definition of problems; (3) the analysis of problems; and (4) the creation of solutions to such problems. These four items that Alatas conceptualized in terms of the local setting of Malaysia should be deconstructed in order to encompass the global context of humanity at the planetary scale.

This is to argue that the concept of "intellectual leadership" is a much-contested concept that should be analyzed in relation to the concept of class conflict. This argument entails that we are faced with different types of intellectuals at the global level who have diverse loyalties to ruling powers and dominant ideals and hegemonic ideologies. In other words, the four issues that Alatas articulates should be understood in terms of different types of intellectuals who problematize each of the four steps in distinct fashions based on their overarching ideological loyalties. Alatas did not develop his conceptual arsenal at a global level, but his concepts and problems have great potentials to be employed in a more general fashion.

Is this really so? Does the Alatasian point of departure on intellectuals have universal significance or general importance? For instance, Jean-Paul Sartre conceptualized an intellectual as someone who meddles in what does not concern them; Noam Chomsky holds that intellectuals are basically political commissars; Edward Said considers intellectuals as individuals who speak courageously the truth to power and stands on the side of the dispossessed, the unrepresented, and the forgotten; and Ali Shariati argues that intellectuals are the heirs of the Prophets and stand on the side of the outcasts. One could ask whether Alatas' definition on intellectuals has these kinds of generalities or is his solely of particular significance in terms of the developing societies.

5   Intellectuals and the Question of Eurocentrism

The key concept in Alatas' narrative is the concept of "intellectual," but the question is how does he articulate it? Is he contextualizing it in a Eurocentric frame of analysis, or does his reading differ from a Eurocentric vision of reality? In Chapter 5 of his *Intellectuals in Developing Societies,* Alatas argues that,

> There are countless instances that demonstrate the effects of the weakness or absence of a functioning intellectual community in a country. The need for a functioning intellectual group is not a modern Western import. We are not reading Western history into [Restern] societies.[32]

The key point here is that Alatas does not consider the European historical patterns as the only valid interpretative model of historical analysis. On the contrary, he clearly states that the need for a functioning intellectual group is not a modern Western import. If this concept is not a "Western import" then how should we reinterpret the need for a functioning intellectual group as a sociological category?

Although Alatas argues that the need for a functioning intellectual group is not a modern Western import, he nevertheless uses this argument in a way that could enhance his position in contextualizing the need for a functioning intellectual group in the context of developing societies. But our concern is not aimed at focusing on the need for intellectuals in the developing countries. On the contrary, we are interested in Alatas' argumentative frame of analysis so we can employ it as a conceptual framework when discussing theoretical issues related to intellectual agency in a universal fashion. Our question would then be different than Alatas' problems. He was trying to make a case for the need "for a functioning intellectual group" in the developing societies, but our point of departure is to deconstruct his language so it could be employed when addressing the quest for intellectual group as a "universal need."[33] This is exactly the position that needs to be reconceptualized and worked out in details through the vector provided by Alatas within social theory discourses at a global level, and not confined to a localized context of Malaysia. He is of the opinion that the need for a functioning intellectual group is a universal need. When he argues that the need for a functioning intellectual group is a universal need then this inadvertently entails that the Alatasian perspective does not fit within a Eurocentric framework, which defines the act of intellectualness in terms of the European Enlightenment Tradition in 17th and 18th century.

How can we assume this conclusion? Is there any textual evidence that would support Alatas' framework for the intellectual beyond the parameters of a Eurocentric vision of history of ideas? In *Intellectuals in Developing Societies,* where he refers to the "intellectual need" as a "universal category," Alatas draws the maps of his philosophy of history by arguing that the birth of intellectual

---

32   Ibid., 53.

33   Ibid.

group is not a Western import, but rather the "intellectual community developed in ancient Greece, in the Islamic Middle Ages, in the Renaissance, in ancient India and ancient China, and in other places."[34]

Here we can see that the notion of progress is not linear in his philosophy of history and the story of thinking about life and social existence is not primarily a Western commodity. On the contrary, the story of human growth is a very complicated historical event that cannot be reduced to modern western historiography, and as such, we should not read "Western history" into Restern societies, as the category of "intellectual community" is of a multifaceted origin that owes for its development to the entire human endeavors across cultures, civilizations, eras, and societies.

However, it is important to note that Alatas does not stop at generalizations as far as the question of intellectual group is concerned. On the contrary, he delves into details by demonstrating on what ground he thinks that a functioning intellectual community is a universal need and not only a Western invention. Alatas looks at this question as a sociologist who is investigating the correlations between complexities and social development. This is to argue that when societies expand, cities grow, trades develop, complex forms of religions emerge, new classes are born, divisions of labour occur, and forms of social relationships increase, then we cannot exclude the need for a functioning of intellectual community. He explains this phenomenon in a sociological fashion by arguing that the intellectual community,

> becomes a necessity as social life becomes more complex, as society develops more problems, as city life grows, as classes are formed, as division of labour takes place – in short, as the human community evolves a complex social system. In such a system, problems emerge and, with the problems, the thinkers are born.[35]

When we look at the history of cities in ancient Iran, China, India, Rome, Greece, and the Islamic Middle Ages, we can readily discern that different social guilds, as well as distinct and complex forms of associations, existed across the empire of Islam in Africa, Europe, and Asia, which necessitated the emergence of intellectual groups. Alatas argues, on the one hand, complex societies develop complicated problems, and, on the other hand, he proposes a thesis that when we have complicated problems, then the very existence of

---

34   Ibid.
35   Ibid.

these multifaceted problems necessitates the emergence of a distinct social class who are able to think through and solve these kinds of complex problems. The sociological genius of Alatas lies in the fact that the emergence of intellectuals is not analyzed subjectively, but rather he attempts to develop an immanent sociological explanation for this problem. What is sociological about the Alatasian perspective? Within current sociological literature on intellectuals, nobody has worked on the Alatasian sociology of intellectuals, and this impels us to start our analysis directly from his own texts.

In *Intellectuals in Developing Societies,* Alatas contends that when a complex social system evolves, the evolution by itself brings about new forms of problems. This emergence of novel problems creates the necessary conditions for the birth of thinkers. Alatas establishes a sociological correlation between social complexities and the birth of thinkers as a universal rule that could be investigated across various cultures and civilizations. Now, the next question that one could ask is that if this emergence were not to happen, what then would be the answer based on an Alatasian perspective?

Yet, if we agree that the evolution of complex social systems generates systemic problems and the pervasiveness of problems would create the necessary conditions for the birth of thinkers, then what would occur if, despite of the necessary conditions, they are not born? How does Alatas explain this phenomenon? He hypothesizes that every complex society needs an intellectual community, and this need is defined as a universal need, thus one is right to ask if this does not materialize in a particular society then how, sociologically, we should explain this lack. Does Alatas have any theoretical answer for this problem? He holds that in complex social systems, specific problems are likely to emerge, and with the problems, the thinkers are born. However, if this "does not occur, something is wrong with that society. [This condition could be described] as a cultural lag."[36]

In *Social Change with Respect to Culture* and *Original Nature,* William Fielding Ogburn offered his theory of social change, which is based on the idea that technology is the primary engine of progress but tempered by social responses to it. Ogburn posited four phases of technical development: invention, accumulation, diffusion, and adjustment.[37] He argued that adjustment is the process by which the non-material dimensions of a culture respond to invention, and any retardation of this adaptation process causes "cultural lag." Alatas employs this Ogburnian concept of cultural lag in understanding why

---

36   Ibid.
37   W.F. Ogburn, *Social Change with Respect to Culture and Original Nature.* New York: B.W. Huebsch, 1922.

an intellectual community does not emerge in many developing societies. He finds,

> two general causes ... colonial rule and the absence of tradition. We are merely describing the situation and its consequences for the development of these societies. To render a complete account of the absence of a functioning intellectual community in many developing societies would take us into historical and sociological explanations. But we can discuss the contemporary impediments to the birth and growth of the intellectual community.[38]

It is obvious that Alatas is concerned with universal questions, but he confines his analyses to developing societies, but this should not deter us from the fact that his concepts and intellectual categories are capable of being deployed as a general theory. Although he himself does not venture into these terrains, his concepts and categories are up to this task. For instance, the absence of tradition as one of the causes of cultural lag in relation to the lack of intellectual community is not solely a problem confined to the developing countries. On the contrary, the absence of a functioning intellectual tradition is a global challenge that has not properly been debated by sociologists and philosophers today. For instance, the problem of cultural lag is not squarely an Eastern/ Southern challenge, but this could be identified in many Western/Northern countries, where their cultural fabrics have not taken time to catch up with technological/scientific innovations and thus have resulted in social problems. We can mention biological studies and DNA research, which have concluded that race as a scientific concept is a redundant notion. As such, we can see that most of these developed societies suffer from cultural lag as far as racial issues are concerned.

In most developed countries, human beings are categorized racially, and this clearly demonstrates the fact that the cultural lag is a universal problem. Thus, this question could be conceptually related to the Alatasian sociological framework, i.e., the absence of a functioning intellectual tradition.

To put it differently, we do not need to confine general concepts of Alatas within the context of the developing societies alone, but we can deconstruct them in a manner so that they could be redeployed in the context of the developed societies as well. This is how we understand his critical insight when he contends that his approach to the concept of intellectual community is not

---

38   Alatas, *Intellectuals*, 53.

based on a Western reading of history. This gives us an opportunity to expand the conceptual parameters of his intellectual categories beyond the Asian societies, as even the western societies have different forms of cultural lags, which could be theorized in terms of the absence of functioning intellectual traditions that Alatas mentioned but did not develop fully.

6 Intellectuals and Social Crisis

Could one assume that the notion of intellectual in the Alatasian discourse is intertwined with the "condition of crisis"? What do we mean that the "condition of crisis" is intertwined with the act of intellectuality? Alatas distinguishes between two types of social time; the first period is conceptualized as "times of crisis" and the second phase is articulated as "periods of routine activity."[39]

He believes that there is an inherent correlation between the "rise of intellectuals" and the "condition of crisis" in any human society. He formulates this axiom in an eloquent fashion by stating that,

> intellectuals linger for a time passively outside the establishment until another social crisis emerges which require their services. In such a manner the process of history repeats itself.[40]

This reemphasizes the idea that intellectuals rise to prominence in times of crisis and this is a rule for understanding the role of intellectuals in the history of human societies in accordance with the Alatasian frame of analysis. However, within the Alatasian paradigm, the role of intellectuals is not solely confined to times of crisis but has a role to play in a period of routine activity.

Of course, the function of intellectuals in these two different conditions differ from each other. As such, one should not mix up these two paradigms when analyzing the contours of intellectual activities in various societies across the globe at any given time. Alatas touches upon another important dimension of intellectuals that bears some similarities to the concept of "organic intellectuals," as developed by Antonio Gramsci. The organic intellectual, in Gramsci's social theory, assumes that intellectuals do not merely illustrate social life in accordance with scientific rules, but rather express, through the language of

---

39   Ibid., 68.
40   Ibid., 64–65.

culture, the feelings and experiences that the masses could not articulate for themselves. It is interesting to note that Alatas defines the role of intellectuals in relation to masses. In other words, the need for intellectuals is an existential need that cannot be modified through political calculations or economic considerations. On the contrary, intellectuals,

> are needed when there is any problem to be explained to the masses. In revolutionary periods this need becomes obvious and urgent for any social movement. Hence the leadership falls into the hands of the intellectuals. During a peaceful routine period, occasions may still arise when problems have to be explained to the masses. The reason why the intellectuals are best suited to do this work is because such problems require a mind that is able to encompass many angles of a problem. Not all intellectuals are inclined to assume such a role but some are and are able to do so. It is this ability which causes the intellectuals to rise to prominence in situations involving mass participation, as in a revolution.[41]

From this excerpt, is clear that the acts of intellectuals are interconnected to the lives of masses in society. This is to emphasize that intellectuals are, so to speak, the tongue of the masses, and in this capacity, they can explain the problems to the masses and. Indeed, intellectuals are the ones who raise our social consciousness about vital problems of human existence.[42]

In the Gramscian perspective, the organic intellectuals are the ones who express through the language of culture, the feelings and experiences of the masses. In the Alatasian paradigm, intellectuals "are needed when there is any problem to be explained to the masses."[43] Although Alatas does not speak about the concept of "organic intellectual," it is clear that this conception of intellectuals is deeply interrelated to the Gramscian notion of masses who cannot articulate their own feelings, aspirations, emotions, and problems to the dominant classes.

One could critique Alatas' conception of society as far as the function of intellectuals is concerned, as he seems to be oblivious to class conflicts and their respective intellectual classes. Is this a fair critique of Alatas? Is his concept of society class-blinded? He argues the following:

---

41   Ibid, 68.
42   Ibid., 10.
43   Ibid., 68.

it is true that intellectuals rise to prominence in times of crisis, it is nevertheless true that in a period of routine activity the intellectuals do have a function provided society recognizes their function.[44]

In this passage it seems Alatas is employing the concept of "society" in an nonsociological fashion, as though "society" as such should recognize or overlook the function of intellectuals. But it is well-known sociological wisdom that society is not a judiciary system; rather, it consists of classes, networks, lobbies, elite clubs, and various forces of different categories and classifications. Thus, it is not society that recognizes or overlooks the function of intellectuals, but we are faced with complex political, religious, economic, cultural, and educational mechanisms that determine the parameters of recognition or nonrecognition in any particular society. Alatas himself is aware of these issues, and as a matter of fact, his research has been dedicated to unearthing these various mechanisms of negligence in regard to the function of intellectuals in the developing societies. However, here it seems he has employed a metaphor that is disputable. In other words, when he states that "intellectuals have a function provided society recognizes their function," here "society" is used as a metaphor to refer to the establishment, but we know (and Alatas knows very well too) that society is not identical to the establishment. However, the slip of the tongue in this context by Alatas demonstrates the residues of colonial mentality, which appears at the metaphoric realm of intellectual rhetoric. As such, this is a question that could be carefully debated.

7   Intellectuals as Superfluous Individuals

Syed Hussein Alatas speaks of superfluousness as a social phenomenon in regard to intellectuals who are (1) ignored by bureaucratic power and (2) left out of public affairs. Although he describes this phenomenon as a salient defect in regard to developing societies, in the global context of the 21st century, it is almost impossible to limit the phenomenon of superfluousness to decolonized nations of the South.

On the contrary, the phenomenon of superfluousness can be detected among the nations of the North too. But Alatas has not applied his theoretical insights on Western societies of Europe and America. What we need to do first is to describe in detail the Alatasian frame of analysis in regard to the

---

44   Ibid.

phenomenon of superfluousness as a social problem in relation to intellectuals, then debate whether this is squarely a Restern social problem. Is this a general problem in post-novel societies around the globe? Alatas did not pose this question as his main concern was to analyze the state of intellectuals in the developing societies. But we do not need to confine our analysis within the parameters of Alatas' research program.

On the contrary, we will employ his general concepts and apply them on global problems. In doing so, we shall reconstruct what we call the Alatasian Sociological Perspective or the Alatasian Research Program. Alatas argued that in,

> countries like Malaysia, India, the Philippines, Indonesia, Ceylon, Singapore, and Lebanon, the sense of superfluousness may yet be overcome by forging one's own public hearing where recourse to publication is still open. Being ignored by the bureaucracy and left out of public affairs may still be compensated for in this way. But only the very few would have the energy and patience to adopt this line of action-to swim against the tide. They must put up with a sense of helplessness to influence events, see mediocrities dominating the scene, and watch the sway of bebalisma on the minds of many. The superfluous individuals in the developing societies are part of the transition to a full-fledged intellectual community. Many members of the academic community in Asia are superfluous individuals. Their talent and energy is in excess of what is used in their profession. They are debarred from public affairs by a monopolistic government. Their intellectual powers are not utilized by the bureaucracy. They are free only to teach, and perhaps engage in research. A certain amount of anxiety surrounds their existence and their consciousness of superfluousness. Only in extreme situations did the problem come into full perspective. It involves repressive state organization or an indirectly repressive social system.[45]

Alatas contextualizes the problem of superfluousness in regard to the countries in the South, but when we look at the characteristics that he enumerated as features of intellectual superfluousness, then it is not hard to see that these traits are not solely confined to the countries of the South, but rather is a global dilemma today.

---

45   Ibid., 73.

Of course, we are not arguing that the degree of repressiveness of the state is similar in all countries around the globe, but it is not deniable that all states are repressive towards intellectual dissent. Another issue is the question of repressiveness of social system, which again, is not only a Restern phenomenon, but it is detectable in Western societies too. For instance, during the first half of the 20th century, when colored immigrants, non-white refuges, *Gastarbeiters*, colonized immigrants, and various minorities accepted (and did not have any syndical power to refuse) repressive policies under the concept of assimilation, it was hard to discern both the repressiveness of various Western states and the repressiveness of their social systems vis-à-vis "others."

However, when these repressed people in these various countries became more conscious about their civil rights, the repressiveness (both at the state level and social level) was more visible to discern and study. Now we have, for instance, a vast Muslim population in many Western countries and their values and worldviews are very different from the host countries and we can see how repressive policies are devised against Muslim citizens in many Western countries by their respective states. At the cultural level as well, we can see the Islamophobic attitudes by segments of these societies against those who have different value-systems or religions. This is to argue that state-repressiveness is a global phenomenon and cannot be confined to Restern societies. What could be debated in detail is the degree, i.e., the subtlety of repressive mechanisms or the intensity of direct violence.

In other words, intellectuals and/or academics that do not share the dominant value-systems of the Enlightenment Tradition and adhere to other forms of worldviews, or attempt to speak on behalf of the repressed groups (e.g., Malcolm X or Tariq Ramadan), are not only ignored by the bureaucracy and left out of public affairs but are also actively murdered by the state or repressed by state apparatus. This is to argue that the Alatasian concept of intellectual superfluousness could be employed and applied generally and sociologically to other contexts other than the one Alatas initially applied, as "repressive state organization or an indirectly repressive social system" is a global phenomenon and "certain amount of anxiety surrounds [intellectual existence] and [the] consciousness of superfluousness [is a worldwide problem]."[46]

---

46   Ibid., 73.

8   Conclusion

I think this study should be treated as a preliminary step towards more extensive research on the question of intellectuals at the global level based on the Alatasian perspective. In this study, I tried to highlight aspects of this sociological perspective, but it would be wrong to assume that the task is complete. On the contrary, what it demonstrated here should be treated as a tentative attempt to bring to light the significance of one of the most creative postcolonial social theorists whose oeuvre has not received the theoretical attention that it deserves. I would not venture into the latent reasons in relation to systematic negligence as far as Syed Hussein Alatas is concerned (dialectic of periphery-core or academic imperialism) but it is undeniable that if we are serious in confronting daunting global crises then we need visionary intellectuals and critical social theorists such as Syed Hussein Alatas. Maybe the next step should be comparative studies on social theorists such as Abraham Maslow, Nikolay Berdayev, Ali Shariati, Allama M. T. Jafari, Walter Benjamin, Malcolm X, Frantz Fanon, Rudolf J. Siebert, Antonio Gramsci, Erich Fromm, and the works and ideas of Syed Hussein Alatas. There is no doubt that the future of humanity lies in inter-civilizational dialogue and the construction of an inter-civilizational social theory that brings humanity closer to each other and finds broad commonalities that can make us humane beings rather than inhumane creatures.

Bibliography

Alatas, S. H. *Intellectuals in Developing Societies*. London: Frank Cass, 1977.

Grafton, Anthony. "The History of Ideas: Precept and Practice, 1950–2000 and Beyond," *Journal of the History of Ideas* 67 no. 1 (2006): 1–32.

Herzen, Alexander. *Selected Philosophical Works*. Moscow: Foreign Language Publishing House, 1956.

Lewis, Bernard. "The Islamic Guilds." *The Economic History Review* 8 no. 1 (November 1937): 20–37.

Ogburn, W. F. *Social Change with Respect to Culture and Original Nature*. New York: B.W. Huebsch, 1922.

CHAPTER 14

West-Centric Geopolitical Discourse

Situating Syed Hussein Alatas in International Relations

Sharifah Munirah Alatas

> And his writings reveal a man who was observant and attentive to life, whose thinking was fair and just without any obvious biases. He was a progressive mindset, battling extremist, irrational thinking, whether it came from the West or East and keen to improve Malaysian paradigms of thinking. He was objective in his assessment of Western influence, knew when it stifled and when it enriched.
>
> CAROL LEON[1]

∴

1 Alternative Discourses in International Relations

In 2006, a year before his passing, Syed Hussein Alatas published an article titled "The Autonomous, the Universal, and the Future of Sociology."[2] It was an urgent call for sociologists (and social scientists in general) to critically reflect on the discipline and the field, due to epistemic problems that had emerged over time. He wrote, 'This problem is the emergence of imitative thinking arising from over-dependence on the western intellectual contribution in the various fields of knowledge, not so much at the practical level of the applied sciences, but at the level of intellectual reflections, planning, conceptualization, and the need to establish a genuine and autonomous scientific tradition.'[3] The discussion in the article is about developing an autonomous social

---

1 Carol Leon, Book Review of Masturah Alatas, *The Life in the Writing: Syed Hussein Alatas,* Kuala Lumpur: Marshall Cavendish, 2010. *Asiatic* 5, no. 1 (2011): 142–143.
2 Syed Hussein Alatas, "The Autonomous, the Universal and the Future of Sociology," *Current Sociology* 54, no. 1 (2006): 7–23.
3 Ibid., 8.

© SHARIFAH MUNIRAH ALATAS, 2023 | DOI:10.1163/9789004521698_016

science tradition and the relation to its universal foundation. The move for autonomy is not a rejection of other traditions but rather a process of linking social science research, thinking, and pedagogy to regional problems, selected by regional scholars.[4]

Alatas saw the need for an autonomous tradition because of the distortions present when conceptualizing universal phenomena and their concrete manifestations in societies of different histories, political structures, social stratifications, classes, cultures, values, and religions. There is validity in universal concepts, but Alatas suggests that they must also be conditioned by their "temporal, spatial, and cultural frameworks."[5] Even though the article focuses on the discipline of sociology, his analysis is relevant to other social sciences disciplines, including International Relations (IR). The development of the field of IR since the end of World War Two (WWII) reveals its Eurocentric (or West-centric) domination, and hence the need to decolonize IR theory. First, a clarification of the terms "West" and "non-West," as it is used in this chapter, is needed. This is followed by a discussion of the terms "Eurocentrism/West-centric" and "decolonization."

The terms West and West-centric are not portrayed as geographical constructs, but rather epistemic ones. As such, even though the history of European colonialism and imperialism are brought into the discourses on IR, the concepts are also about designating Europe and North America as the originators of fundamental thinking in international affairs. Therefore, West and non-West are discussed here within epistemic queries concerning the primacy of the Euro-American processes of knowledge production in IR. In other words, IR theorizing and its dissemination may have originated in the geographic West, but the concepts are conditioned by history, politics, and attitudes, as opposed to geographic position. For example, Australia is not situated in the geographic West. Yet, knowledge production in and about the continent has been epistemically Western in nature.[6] This orientation, together with historical linkages, cultural attitudes, and geopolitical positioning, places Australia as "Western."

West-centrism is a Euro-American style of thought in which the assessment and evaluation of non-Western societies is shaped by one's own cultural assumptions and biases. In IR, this understanding is applied to a Euro-American analysis of geopolitics. Since the beginning of the twentieth century, the trend

---

4 Ibid., 12.
5 Ibid., 8.
6 Zeynep Gülsah Çapan, "Eurocentrism and the Construction of the 'Non-West'," *E-international Relations* (Jun 19, 2018), https://www.e-info/2018/06/19/eurocentrism-and-the-construction-of-the-non-west/.

in the discipline was to build a grand narrative of global events, based on the glory of the nation state, i.e., a history of sovereign nations since the Peace of Westphalia (1648). In this sense, West-centrism or Eurocentrism in IR perpetuates the Westphalian bias. It suggests that the Treaty of Westphalia, which was intended to represent peace in the Holy Roman Empire, is supposed to create an international (global) order, thus solving the problem of anarchy that existed in European history. The Westphalian system set in motion, a history-specific form of contractual evolution among nation states that had not existed before. The Westphalian understanding of the incessant wars prior to 1648, is based on the concept of anarchy and the Hobbesian necessity for a "Leviathan" or body politic. According to Thomas Hobbes, the absence of peace was due to the prolonged religio-political conflict, perpetuated by a lack of a common authority. Without the leviathan, society will be in a constant struggle for power because people only took care of themselves, not each other.[7] The Peace of Westphalia was supposed to end this state of anarchy and establish a civilized order embodied in the sovereign state system. Since the process began in Europe, non-Western states lacking this European "contractual agreement," have supposedly remained in anarchy and in a less-than-civilized state.

At the center of this argument is the emergence of the sovereign system of states, also known as the nation state. The series of agreements leading up to the Peace of Westphalia represents the benchmark against which global stability is measured today. Mainstream IR parlance also refers to this development as the emergence of an international system of world order, premised on peace. Hence, the use of the term "peace" of Westphalia in IR discourse. However, the goal for a universal calm and order among states premised on the structures established after Westphalia must be contextualized within a pre-Westphalian European reality. It was a reality engulfed in a century of endless slaughter over religious and political domination, among entities vying for exclusive hegemonic status. It can be argued that this European reality did not mirror conditions outside Europe during the same period. The events leading up to the Treaty of Westphalia can hardly be considered a global reality warranting an "international" benchmark.[8] It is here that Syed Hussein Alatas' call for an autonomous selection of data applies. It allows us to apply theoretical constructs that are more relevant to regional and local conditions.

---

7   A. Nuri Yurdusev, "Thomas Hobbes and international relations: from realism to rationalism," *Australian Journal of International Affairs* 60, no. 2 (2006): 305–321.

8   Barry Buzan and Richard Little, "Beyond Westphalia? Capitalism after the 'Fall'," *Review of International Studies, Vol. 25, The Interregnum: Controversies in World Politics, 1989–1999* (Dec. 1999): 89.

WEST-CENTRIC GEOPOLITICAL DISCOURSE

While Europe was facing almost a century of anarchy from the mid-16th to 17th centuries, other civilizations were thriving and were hardly less-than-modern. Europe was integrating into a more global economic system, expanding its geographic reach, trading in new commodities, and producing goods from raw materials obtained from newly discovered and colonized lands in Africa, Latin America, and Asia. These beginnings of commerce were also highly unstable, and led to economic, financial, and political crisis among competing European powers. This explains the century of extreme instability and conflict.

Similarly, regions outside Europe were equally engaged in active commerce. There were other densely-populated regions dotted with markets and shops, with streets and towns engaged in active commerce. However, the degree of conflict was considerably low, if not absent, despite the intense economic activities that were prevalent. Also, the emergence of different classes in societies did not seem disruptive to daily social activities. For example, in Latin America general stores sold everything from flour, dried meat, and beans to precious stones, and even traded in slavery.[9] Fernand Braudel writes the following about regions under Muslim control:

> Islam is famous for its crowded markets and streets of narrow shops, grouped according to their specialty and still to be seen today in the celebrated souks of its big cities. Every imaginable kind of market is to be found here; some outside the city walls, spreading over a wide area and forming a gigantic traffic jam at the monumental city gates [....] In short, all the characteristic of the European market are there: the peasant who comes to town, anxious to obtain the money he needs to pay his taxes, and who simply looks in at the market long enough to do so: the energetic salesman with his ready tongue and manner who pre-empts the rural seller's wares, in spirt of prohibition.[10]

In India, the situation was similar. Under the Moghuls, there were villages outside the towns and cities that had bustling markets engrossed in active trading. There was also movement of peoples between villages and towns, in pursuit of merchandise through trading activities. Immanuel Wallerstein provides ample evidence of the rural-urban class relations, as well as the existence of a global

---

9   Fernand Braudel, *The Wheels of Commerce, Civilization and Capitalism 15th-18th Century: Volume II*, (London: William Collins Sons & Co Ltd, 1979), 114.

10 Ibid., 115.

class structure in the sixteenth century.[11] China too, according to Braudel, had an abundance of towns and busy markets.[12]

The question of instability and anarchy in Europe during the same period warrants a discussion on the role of the state in maintaining law and order. When referring to the pre-Westphalian era, we conceptualize the state as a socially constructed identity and organization, devoid of the concept of "nation" state, with its notions of citizenship, national boundaries, and sovereignty. These concepts had not yet emerged. Instead, the pre-Westphalian order was shaped by the role of the Church and the monopoly of power by ruling dynasties through the coercive loyalty of their subjects. Empire and religion functioned in an interactive network of commerce, warfare, socialization, and long-distance communication with colonies in the non-West.

External to Europe, the Ottoman Empire was a formidable power with which these European polities had some form of interaction. It is common to find early modern and contemporary Euro-American writings about the Ottoman Empire, which often referred to the Ottomans as "living for war." These depictions implied that the Ottoman state was relentlessly martial. Another misleading aspect of this analysis is that such militarism was peculiarly foreign and contrary to Western norms.[13] Yet, as we observe European literature between the 15th and 18th centuries, such as the plays of William Shakespeare, many espouse soldierly virtues. For example, King Henry V seemed to become kingly only through the vehicle of war.[14] Francois-Marie Arouet (Voltaire) states that 'the first who was king was a successful soldier. He who serves well his country has no need of ancestors.'[15] His writings are known as crusading works against tyranny, bigotry, and cruelty, convinced that kings were indispensable agents of progress. The environment within which he wrote was one of military conflict and religious persecution, both of which were reflected in his literature. Voltaire ironically referred to Shakespeare's plays are barbaric

---

11   Immanuel Wallerstein, *The Modern World-System I: Capitalist Agriculture and the Origins of the European World-Economy in the Sixteenth Century* (Berkeley: University of California Press, 2011), 85–87.

12   Ibid., 117.

13   Daniel Goffman, *The Ottoman Empire and Early Modern Europe* (Cambridge: Cambridge University Press, 2002), 1.

14   Ibid., 4.

15   Francois Marie Arouet de Voltaire, *Merope, a tragedy*, by Aaron Hill, adapted for theatrical representation, (London, 1795), Act I, sc. 3.

due to the dramatic force of the plots.[16] Both were in fact immersed in a world-view of conflict and violence.

Often, biased interpretations of history inform the discipline of IR. The idea that the Treaty of Westphalia represents a transition from medieval to modern civilization is an accurate interpretation, insofar as European history goes. However, these same events had different or minimal impact on other regions of the world. Here is where the particular selection of data is vital, as Syed Hussein Alatas suggests, in critically evaluating the place of Westphalia in benchmarking state behavior in the non-West.

Data relating to the events leading up to the Treaty of Westphalia should not be automatically and uncritically applied to the study of geopolitics, strategy, anarchy, and other forms of state behavior in non-European traditions. Also, the process of interpreting relevant data is important to avoid, what Alatas observes as 'the emergence of imitative thinking, arising from overdependence on the western intellectual contribution in the various fields of knowledge'.[17] The period-specific economic, cultural, and political patterns, or *zeitgeist* (spirit of the times) varies around the globe, but is fundamentally uniform between regions. For instance, in higher education, universities in both the West and Asia are engaged in the business of recruiting international students, modifying traditional courses in order to participate in the global university ranking exercises as part of a strategy to produce graduates who are relevant for the liberal market economy. Media reports, industry, and official government statements that allude to their respective human resource needs, employ standard vocabulary to describe excellence or decline in education quality. For example, "future-proofing" students is standard global lingo in higher education policy.

The term future-proof refers to the ability of something to continue to be of value into the distant future; that the item does not become obsolete. The concept of future-proofing is the process of anticipating the future, and developing methods of minimizing the effects of shocks and stresses of future events. The term is commonly found in electronics, data storage, and communications systems, industrial design, computers, software, and product design.[18] It has now

---

16   Rene Henry Pomeau, "Voltaire: French philosopher and author," *Encyclopedia Britannica* (Jan. 7, 2021). https://www.britannica.com/biography/Voltaire.

17   Syed Hussein Alatas, "The Autonomous, the Universal and the Future of Sociology," *Current Sociology* 54, no. 1 (2006): 8.

18   Brian Rich, "The Principles of Future-Proofing: A Broader Understanding of Resiliency in the Historic Built Environment," *Journal of Preservation Education and Research* 7 (2014): 32.

infiltrated the political economy of concepts, used worldwide by politicians, particularly when it comes to fiscal allocation in specific areas of government, such as education and health care. However, the use of this term cannot and should not be conceptualized across different societies that exhibit different levels of development, political structures, and geopolitical aspirations, which are conditioned by unique social and cultural dynamics.

West-centrism is a system of knowledge, and therefore an epistemic question in the field of inquiry, rather than a geographic one. It is not just about writing the history of IR from the Euro-American (i.e., Eurocentric) perspective. It is about designating Europe and North America as the originator of all developments that define world order, i.e., what was, is, and should be an established and universal understanding of world order.[19] The phenomenon of Eurocentrism is an offshoot of ethnocentrism, which is the belief that one's own ethnic group or society is superior to others. Other groups are assessed and judged in terms of the categories and standards of evaluation of one's own group, often defined as "othering" in post-colonial discourse.[20] In her essay, "The Rani of Sirmur,"[21] Gayatri Chakravorty Spivak argues that 'the turning of foreign lands and people into an Other for the European, colonial master occurs not just in official documents or high culture but also in everyday interactions between colonialists and the indigenous population[...]during the nineteenth century.'[22]

West-centrism (also Eurocentrism) in IR is reflected in how the category of non-West is articulated, and its assigned place in world order. Over the last two decades or so, discourses on the non-West have been expressed in the following three ways: (1) why the need for such a classification to begin with, (2) how the category functions in the global matrix of hierarchy among states, and (3) how the discourses of state hegemony, material power, anarchy, threat, and peace are represented in the language of diplomacy and in pedagogical literature. Epistemic binaries are present in IR discourses, resulting in hierarchical representations that define the nature of state behavior and how they "fit in" with world order.

---

19 Sharifah Munirah Alatas, "Decolonising International Relations: Theory and Practice" (unpublished research notes, November 18, 2020).

20 Syed Farid Alatas, "Eurocentrism," in George Ritzer (ed.) *The Blackwell Encyclopedia of Sociology*, 2016, John Wiley & Sons, Ltd.

21 Gayatri Chakravorty Spivak, "The Rani of Sirmur: An Essay in Reading the Archives," *History and Theory*.

22 Nasrullah Mombrol, 'The Other, The Big Other, and Othering,' in Dino Franco Felluga (ed.) *Critical Theory: The Key Concepts*. New York: Routledge, 2015.

For example, the nation-state, sovereignty, hegemony, anarchy, human rights, and peace are a few of the concepts on which IR theories (IRT) are based. These are designated as European in origin, and assumes the West introduced these to the non-West. This epistemic binary is articulated through spatio-temporal hierarchies, which in turn constructs and classifies universal standards for state behavior and modes of interaction. The decolonial move against Eurocentrism challenges the notion of universal standards, and argues for, as Alatas suggests, the inclusion of autonomous conceptualization. In an article published in 2006, Alatas wrote that 'autonomous development means the choice of new themes with relevant connection to western affairs as well as conceptual contribution to general and universal theory formation.'[23] He discusses what was lacking in the conceptualization and teaching of sociology in the non-West. After WWII and decolonization, there was a 'great outburst of culture contact and intellectual interaction following the independence of the countries previously colonized by the West.'[24] However, another form of hegemony, according to Alatas, emerged. This was not the kind of domination or coercion imposed by Western colonialists over the colonized. Rather, it was the emergence of 'imitative thinking arising from overdependence on the Western intellectual contribution in the various fields of knowledge, not so much at the practical level of the applied sciences, but at the level of intellectual reflections, planning, conceptualization and the need to establish a genuine and autonomous scientific tradition.'[25]

A similar trend in IR knowledge production exists in the Global South, highlighting the need for more autonomous thinking in IRT. Such a paradigm shift would help to eradicate the hierarchical binary in IR epistemology, which imposes one form of conceptualization over another. In other words, a West-centric concept of power would leave no room for another, which may be tied closely to non-Western cultural or religious practices. Also, the concepts of "world order" and the "path to stability" need to consider temporal and spatial trajectories of different polities, with diverse historical and political backgrounds. Such paradigm shifts have implications on how countries interact, manage conflict, and negotiate at a diplomatic level. Geopolitical reality dictates that diverse cultures with equally diverse historical and political development have different approaches to conflict management, diplomacy, and peace.

---

23 Syed Hussein Alatas, "The Autonomous, the Universal and the Future of Sociology," *Current Sociology* 54, no. 1 (2006): 21.

24 Ibid., 6.

25 Ibid., 7.

2 Western IR's False Universalisms and the Global South

The idea of alternative approaches in IR emerged for two important reasons. First, the discipline needed to "confront itself" amidst debates to legitimize its autonomy as a separate field of enquiry.[26] There was a need to determine whether it is indeed a sub-discipline of Political Science (mainly in the United States) or a legitimate autonomous field of inquiry with its unique concepts, research agendas, methodology, and priorities. The second reason is related to both the tangible and abstract effects of colonialism on the developing world. This reality has defined the imperial structures of material power and the nature of intellectual hegemony in today's geopolitics.[27] Both colonialism and the post-WWII world order have impacted a significant portion of humanity in the Global South in terms of how the core-periphery binary was established, and how it defined state interaction. For example, conversations about IR and the Global South, and about IR and the core countries are epistemically two different phenomena.[28] They were not treated as mutually connecting discourses during the nineteenth century. A significant reason for this is colonialism.

The political economy of colonial capitalism was established in the early modern era between the 15th to 18th centuries, in overseas colonies. It was structured in a core-periphery construct and remained unaltered during the 19th century era of modernism. The revolutions of modernity were unfolding rapidly, increasing the powers of production and technological change among the few core countries, which were the colonial powers. It is here that the notion of "the universal" most appropriately served its economic and geopolitical strategy.

---

26   The theme of IR "confronting" itself was explicitly discussed at an academic session in 2019, at the SOAS University of London Centre for International Studies and Diplomacy. The session convened a discussion between the scholars, Amitav Acharya and Barry Buzan, with Dan Plesch as commentator, about their recently published book *The Making of Global International Relations Theory: The Origins and Evolution of IR at its Centenary* (2019).

27   Syed Hussein Alatas used the term intellectual imperialism. See Syed Hussein Alatas, "Intellectual Imperialism: Definition, Traits, and Problems," *Southeast Asian Journal of Social Science* 28, no. 1 (2000): 23–45.

28   In the early 19th century, the revolutions of modernity reshaped what was known formally in the 20th century, as the discipline of IR. Enlightenment thinking in philosophy, science (including evolution) and the free-market system underwent further transformation. New theoretical approaches in the social and human sciences were concentrated in a small number of modernizing countries which are now known as "the core" in IR parlance. These include Great Britain, Germany, France and to a lesser extent Italy, and the United States and Japan.

WEST-CENTRIC GEOPOLITICAL DISCOURSE

An aspect of a false West-centric universalism is how periodization is used in IR. The world has been in a core-periphery divide, which has framed both the practice and discipline of IR as a twentieth century system of thought. As such, one myth is that the discipline of IR emerged in the early 20th century (1919). The justification for establishing a "new" field of inquiry during this period is premised on three ideas: the "international" system, anarchy, and power. From a European point of view, it makes sense because the core countries see events that culminated in WWI as traumatic.[29]

However, it also stunts knowledge production in IR since the discipline focuses mostly on Euro-American history and policy issues, as opposed to a wider and more expansive view of non-Western history. This also begs the question of what is, in practical terms, an international system, and whether such a notion should invoke a universal characteristic? The ahistorical character of the IR discipline encourages expertise in current events and promotes a positivist/rationalist rather than a reflectivist/interpretive perspective.[30] Critiques suggest that IR's ahistoricism (about its origins and practice) means insufficient thought has been given to the idea of an "international" system.[31] After all, the object of analysis in IR is the nation state and the nature of their interaction over a long spatial and temporal trajectory (the *longue durée*). If a more interpretive perspective can be established, one may be able to conceive of the necessary and sufficient conditions for an international system, inclusive of events that predate 1919. This system would automatically include the periphery, as object and agency of global dynamics, without any question. It would also force IR theorizing to focus on pre-Westphalian history beyond the Euro-American imagination.

If we recognize the need to overcome IR's ahistoricism, there may be more avenues to prevent conflicts or sustain peace. We would be able to observe developments outside Europe, the pervasive nature of colonialism, its unique effects on post-independence states in the periphery and accept a more shared responsibility for conflict that currently exists in the international system. Barry Buzan writes:

---

29   Barry Buzan and Richard Little, "The Idea of 'International System': Theory Meets History," *International Political Science Review* 15, no. 3 (July 1994): 231.

30   Robert W. Murray (Editor), *System, Society, and the World: Exploring the English School of International Relations,* 2nd Edition. Bristol, UK: E-International Relations Publishing, 2015.

31   Buzan and Little, "The Idea of 'International System,'" 233.

The tendency toward a-historicism in international relations blends subtly into a powerful Eurocentrism in the very conception of the international system. On one level this is an understandable ethnocentrism: the discipline of international relations was founded by, and is still dominated by, Europeans and North Americans, and it is only natural that it therefore reflects their perceptions and concerns. But there is more to this Eurocentrism than the cultural biases of most of its writers. There is also the undeniable fact that the European international system emerged from the obscure and backward corner of its feudal period to conquer or dominate the whole planet. During the several centuries of its imperial ascendancy, Europe forcibly and durably transplanted its own forms and principles of political and economic organization worldwide, in the process overrunning not only a host of barbarian tribal peoples, but also all five ancient centres of civilization.[32]

Is WWI a big disjuncture in IR? How much did WWI really change the world? How much did it mean to other parts of the world outside the geographic West? It is worth asking these questions because from the Global South perspective, it hardly changed the world at all. In a sense, the big impact of WWI was on the small group of core countries, not the periphery. For the periphery, the international system set up between the 19th century and 1945, remained unaltered; imperialism and racism continued. This goes against the "disjuncture" paradigm, which highlights 1919 as a turning point in the international system. Despite different historical experiences and the negative effects of colonialism, IR in post-colonial nations continues to be understood through European lenses.

Similarly, Syed Hussein Alatas critically evaluated the discipline of Sociology. He questioned the validity of its concepts and methods for the non-Western world by observing post-colonial societies. For example, Alatas notes that imitative thinking did not exist in the West, when sociologists studied revolutions in specific countries of Europe or the United States. The contents of studies of revolution in general are not automatically and uncritically applied to the study of the French or American Revolution.[33] The concept *ancient régime* used by de Tocqueville was not automatically used in an American historical analysis of the American revolution of 1776. Yet, geopolitical analyses of events in the South China Sea and ASEAN's strategic role are conditioned by concepts

---

32   Ibid., 234.
33   Syed Hussein Alatas, "The Autonomous, the Universal and the Future of Sociology," *Current Sociology* 54, no. 1 (2006): 8.

of anarchy, power, and the international system (or structure), imposed by a theoretical framework based on modern European history.

Refreshing ideas on alternative IR theoretical approaches are discussed in a recent publication co-authored by Barry Buzan and Amitav Acharya. *The Making of Global International Relations Theory: The Origins and Evolution of IR at its Centenary* (2019) argues that Western colonialism is a thing of the past, and that it is time for post-colonial, non-Western voices to attain a higher profile in debates about geopolitics, international relations, and schools of thought. Western IR theory has had the advantage of 'being the first in the field, and has developed many valuable insights, but few would defend the position that it captures everything we need to know about world politics.'[34] After 1945, there was a significant paradigm shift, when IR "came of age" in the United States. Its center of gravity shifted when Stanley Hoffmann, a Harvard professor claimed IR was born and raised in the US.[35] This was deeply offensive to the British. However, other scholars, such as Buzan and Acharya, critiqued the argument further by rejecting the original premise that IR was "founded" in the United Kingdom.

Syed Hussein Alatas partakes in a similar discourse about the beginning of sociology as a field of inquiry or discipline.[36] He credits the West for developing 'a genuine and autonomous tradition in western historical, sociological and other social-scientific disciplines' and that the 'reason why the autonomous tradition in western sociology has been able to flourish so vigorously had to do with developments in European history.'[37] However, Alatas distinguishes the autonomous Western development of sociology as a discipline, from the discovery of sociology as the study of human society. He attributes this to the Muslim historian and sociologist Abd al-Rahman Ibn Khaldun (1332–1406). Therefore, Western autonomy of sociological thinking had developed from its fundamental non-Western origins.

Alternative interpretations about the origins of IR do not credit the West entirely. Rather, they suggest its pre-1919 Euro-American origins, and even its pre-Westphalian, non-Western agency as a more accurate assessment of the

---

34   James Mayall, "Book Review." Amitav Acharya and Barry Buzan (Eds.), *Non-Western International Relations Theory*, London, and New York: Routledge, 2010, *International Relations of the Asia-Pacific* 11 (2011): 331–338.

35   Stanley Hoffmann, "An American Social Science: International Relations," *Daedalus*, 106, no. 1 (1977): 41–60.

36   Syed Hussein Alatas, "The Autonomous, the Universal and the Future of Sociology," *Current Sociology* 54, no. 1 (2006): 9.

37   Ibid., 9.

discipline's genesis, while acknowledging the significance of European historical events. Following Alatas' argument, the year 1919 is assumed to be an autonomous juncture in IR's development as a field of inquiry. Also, Hoffmann's 1945 claim is a similar epistemological juncture for the discipline's paradigm shift in the United States. For the periphery however, these dates do not represent turning points in the international system. Both WWI and WWII make little difference to the colonized world. Their worldview continued as a world of imperialism and racism, colonial capitalism, and intellectual subjugation.[38] For the periphery, this period was still a mainly European, American, and Japanese international system, a colonial international society.

3   Discourses on Geopolitics: Beyond West-Centric Paradigms

The preceding discussion addressed the need to revisit IRT, the international system, and world order because of the false universalisms implied, and their incompatibility for the non-West. Incompatible assumptions about what constitutes order and the international system have important ramifications outside the Euro-American imagination. This is primarily because of how anarchy, threat, and security are assessed to ensure conducive security environments within which nations are supposed to co-exist. However, the assessments are based on a core-periphery binary, whereby this division in IR discourse has proven problematic for current geopolitical realities.

Having said that, mainstream textbooks on IR have made limited concessions to the non-Western world when it comes to dependency theory. Dependency Theory argues that the division of the international economic structure into the core and periphery makes the latter dependent on the former.[39] The work of Fernando Cardoso and Enzo Faletto (1972) highlighted social forces and ideologies that contributed to underdevelopment and dependency.[40] This indicates that there was a move away from a purely materialist and economic argument for dependency, to a more political economy analysis. These ideas were significant for IR when dependency theory shifted to World Systems Theory (WST) and the works of Immanuel Wallerstein. However,

---

38   Syed Hussein Alatas, "Intellectual Imperialism: Definition, Traits, and Problems," *Southeast Asian Journal of Social Science* 28, no. 1 (2000): 23–45.

39   Amitav Acharya and Barry Buzan, *The Making of Global International Relations: Origins and Evolution of IR at its Centenary*, Cambridge University Press (2019): 170.

40   Fernando Cardoso and Enzo Faletto, *Dependency and Development in Latin America*, Berkeley, and Los Angeles: University of California Press, 1972.

the broad theoretical scope of both approaches was essentially structural and materialist. For the non-West, both dependency theory and WST did not address the problems of post-colonialism. The heavy reliance on materialism prevented these approaches from addressing issues of race, ethnicity, gender, and religion. More importantly, these aspects of society play significant roles in the geopolitics of the Global South and are too significant to exclude in the fundamentals of IR as an academic discipline.

Syed Hussein Alatas's writings on intellectual imperialism, and modernization and social change, are relevant here.[41] Alatas felt that the study of imperialism should not only be confined to the political or economic spheres. In the historical process, we have to consider imperialism as a 'cluster, comprising different aspects of human undertakings.'[42] Alatas defined imperialism as 'the subjugation of one people by another for the advantage of the dominant one.'[43] He listed six traits of imperialism, of which three are relevant in our present discussion on geopolitics. These are conformity, domination, and rationalization.

According to Alatas, conformity, domination, and rationalization are social processes imposed by the subjugating power over a dominated people. The intention is for the dominated to conform to certain aspects of life, organization, and rules. If we apply this rationale to the idea of regional constructs in IR, West-centric interpretations of regionalism neglect the active participation and perceptions of non-Western actors, their agency being silenced. The situation is complicated further when subjugated societies self-silence or subconsciously imitate narratives.

Within the social sciences and humanities, silencing as method (active silencing) suggests that non-Western ideas, perspectives, and voices are marginalized. Non-Western knowledge communities are assumed to be consumers of Western theories and policies, as well as methods and research agendas that originate in specific knowledge centers, namely in the United States, Britain, and France. IR scholars, whose research fall under critical approaches, seldom refer to the concepts of intellectual neo-colonialism or ideological discrimination in their writings. However, they conform to mainstream discourse through the use of legalistic language in discourses on regionalism. An example is the

---

41   Syed Hussein Alatas, "Intellectual Imperialism: Definition, Traits, and Problems," *Southeast Asian Journal of Social Science* 28, no. 1 (2000): 23–45; Syed Hussein Alatas, *Modernization and Social Change: Studies in modernization, religion, social change and development in South-East Asia*, Sydney: Angus and Robertson Publishers, 1972.

42   Alatas, "Intellectual Imperialism," 23.

43   Ibid., 23.

Indo-Pacific construct led by the Quadrilateral Security Dialogue (Quad) partners, comprising the US, Japan, India, and Australia.

In 2020, the Quad expanded membership, with the involvement of New Zealand, South Korea, and Vietnam. This conjectural alliance, which is currently referred to as the 'Quad Plus' in international strategic circles, confirms a process of strategic alignments in the Indo-Pacific, but without conforming completely to the 'alliance framework' that the US would like to promote in the region.[44] Since the formation of the Quad in 2007, and later the Quad Plus, the Association of Southeast Asian Nations (ASEAN) persists in officially acknowledging it as a strategy to link both oceans, and nothing more. After 2017, with former US Secretary of State Rex Tillerson's twist to the notion, the Indo-Pacific took on a different meaning, implying it to be more a containment strategy against China's activities in the region.

The Quad Plus process indicates the members' growing embrace of a US worldview that aims to 'defend and strengthen a liberal international order while focusing on building an Indo-Pacific narrative that has been threatened by the rise of a "revisionist" China.'[45] Revised policies for, and new narratives about the South China Sea region invoked specific language such as 'Freedom of navigation' (FON), the 'Free and Open Indo-Pacific,' (FOIP) and 'rules-based order.'[46] Global media, governments, business leaders, and scholarly publications all seem to have latched onto this new vocabulary, which reflects an apparent 'universal outlook on world order.' However, this is far from the reality on the ground. With or without the Quad Plus and its accompanying narratives of world order and security, Southeast Asian nations face new challenges that have less to do with a powerful China or a hegemonic US.

For ASEAN, "threat" and "fear" present a real but myopic view of the region. It is a Eurocentric bias, that ignores indigenous Asian geopolitical traditions that could sustain regional order, despite these challenges. Rather than balancing or band-wagoning, Southeast Asia's response to China's rise is one of engagement. Even though a powerful China is worrisome, the region does not see it as a threat that warrants a posture of security dependency with extra-regional powers. ASEAN's response to the Indo-Pacific construct is openly cautious. It prefers to engage with, rather than isolate China. Given several member

---

44 Jagannath Panda, "India and the 'Quad Plus' Dialogue," *Rusi Commentary*, (2020), https://rusi.org/commentary/india-strategic-quad (accessed April 11, 2021).

45 Ibid.

46 Gurpreet Khurana, "'The Indo-Pacific' Concept: Retrospect and Prospect," *National Maritime Foundation*, (2020), http://www.maritimeindia.org, accessed March 22, 2021: 1–8.

countries' historical experiences with China over several centuries, there is less suspicion of a Chinese hidden agenda. China also engages individual ASEAN members on a bilateral basis, which minimizes suspicion in the region. The history of ASEAN-China relations falls into three phases: hostility, friendship, and uncertainty. Phase three became more challenging, and culminated in 2012, when the issues of the South China Sea began to affect ASEAN-China trust. However, ASEAN's strategic norms of behavior, known as the ASEAN Way, prioritizes consensus and non-confrontational bargaining. The latter depends largely on discrete and informal negotiations, often more successful on a bilateral, rather than a multilateral platform. Therefore, China's accommodation of the ASEAN Way facilitates bilateral engagement with member nations, as an ideal tool for building trust and confidence in the relationship. Furthermore, this mechanism does not contradict China's peaceful co-existence policy.[47]

It is clear that the new narratives have meant different things to different nations.[48] Indonesia and Thailand, for example, do not want the Southeast Asian region to be overlooked in this new geopolitical dynamic, while at the same time asserts the non-aligned posture of ASEAN. Therefore, the "rules-based order" begs the question: "whose rules?" Also, Indonesia, in particular, has expressed its goal to evolve as a primary power in the geostrategic theatre of the Indo-Pacific, which explains Indonesia's lead in drafting the ASEAN Outlook on the Indo-Pacific (AOIP).[49] Despite ASEAN's non-aligned stance, there is an element of subjugation or conformity in official media and scholarly comments about the regional strategic theatre. For one, 'rising' China narratives always invoke the notion of threat and trepidation. Yet, 'powerful' US or Quad Plus seem to invoke protection and security. Secondly, China's policy of peaceful co-existence is often scoffed at, or observed with skepticism. Yet, the Quad Plus's rules-based order' is welcomed as a necessary tool of discipline. These are examples of Syed Hussein Alatas' intellectual imperialism that promote conformity, domination, and rationalization, to condition thinking about phenomena, and in this case, geopolitics.

---

47   Sharifah Munirah Alatas, "ASEAN's Engagement with China: A Pragmatic Alternative to the Quad's Eurocentric Strategy," *Turkish Center for Asia Pacific Studies*, (2020). http://www.asianpacificcenter.org/asean-s-engagement-with-china.html, accessed March 12, 2021.

48   Trent Scott and Andrew Shearer, "Building Allied Interoperability in the Indo-Pacific Region," In *Discussion Paper 1: Command and Control*, Center for Strategic and International Studies (2017).

49   ASEAN Secretariat, "ASEAN Outlook on the Indo-Pacific" (2019): 1–5. https://asean.org/asean-outlook-indo-pacific/.

4   Conclusion

Mainstream IRT has neglected the non-West due to a combination of reasons, such as a lack of interest, the need to intellectually dominate, socio-cultural ignorance, and the belief that Western theories are sufficient to guide and offer explanations for all socio-political phenomena. In a footnote to a chapter on "Theory of World Politics" (1989), Robert O. Keohane claimed the contents of the chapter were limited due to the American-centric nature of his knowledge:

> An unfortunate limitation of this chapter is that its scope is restricted to work published in English, principally in the United States. I recognize that this reflects the Americanocentrism of scholarship in the United States, and I regret it. But I am not sufficiently well-read in works published elsewhere to comment intelligently on them.[50]

Many other scholars claim Western theories should be applied as a standard 'rule of thumb,' to the Asia-Pacific, including the non-West. For example, the edited book by Joseph Grieco, John Ikenberry, and Michael Mastanduno (2014)[51] argues that these regions have adopted Western financial institutions after decolonization, so they should be able to adapt to Western theories as a 'standard of civilization.'[52] While colonial-era language of the kind Alatas mentions in *The Myth of the Lazy Native* (1977) is no longer employed, the narrative clearly implies subordination.[53]

A substantial number of critical or alternative approaches in IRT are produced in the core. For example, many argue that post-modernism and post-structuralism merely replaced a West-centric rationale but do not do much to bring in non-Western concerns and voices. Post-colonial scholars from

---

50   Robert O. Keohane, *International Institutions and State Power: Essays in International Relations Theory*, Boulder: Westview Press (1989): 67, note 1.

51   Joseph Grieco, John Ikenberry, and Michael Mastanduno (Eds.), *Introduction to International Relations: Perspectives, Connections, and Enduring Questions*. London: Red Globe Press, 2014.

52   Amitav Acharya and Barry Buzan, *The Making of Global International Relations: Origins and Evolution of IR at its Centenary*, Washington D.C., and London: Cambridge University Press (2019): 183.

53   Syed Hussein Alatas, *The Myth of the Lazy Native: A Study of the Image of the Malays, Filipinos, and Javanese from the 16th to the 20th Century and its Function in the Ideology of Colonial Capitalism*. Singapore: Times Books International, 1977.

the Global South such as Syed Hussein Alatas embody a profound intellectual development from the periphery. There is creative emphasis on resistance and dissent, but unlike Alatas, there is still a lack of attention to agency. Constructivism in IRT considers cultures and identities as influencing world politics, but their roles as agents in the dynamics of geopolitical transformation continues to be underplayed. Rather, constructivism implies that "global norms" originate in the West but are compatible with the rest of the world. As Syed Hussein Alatas has critiqued, non-Western societies are passive recipients and mere students of West-centric theoretical phenomena.

A serious obstacle to epistemological advancement in societies of the Global South, as highlighted by Alatas is the willingness to import ideas from the Western world to the non-West without due consideration to their socio-historical context. While the problems of Eurocentrism and intellectual subjugation by the core over the periphery are a reality, Alatas' idea of the captive mind also applies. He defined the captive mind as 'an uncritical and imitative mind dominated by an external source, whose thinking is deflected from an independent perspective of raising original problems.'[54] Alatas argued that there is a need to rise above mimicking explanations for socio-political behaviour.[55] This also applies to theorizing in scholarship.

Bibliography

Acharya, Amitav. "Theorising the international relations of Asia: necessity or indulgence?: Some reflections," *The Pacific Review* (2017): 1–13.

Acharya, Amitav. "Studying the Bandung conference from a Global IR perspective," *Australian Journal of International* Affairs 70, no. 4, (2016): 342–357.

Acharya, Amitav and Barry Buzan. "Why Is There No Non-Western International Relations Theory? An Introduction," *International Relations of the Asia Pacific*, 7 no. 3 (2007): 287–312.

Acharya, Amitav and Barry Buzan. *The Making of Global International Relations: Origins and Evolution of IR at its Centenary*, Washington, D.C. and London: Cambridge University Press, 2019.

---

54   Syed Hussein Alatas, "The captive mind in development studies: Some neglected problems and the need for an autonomous social science tradition in Asia", International Social Science Journal 1: 11.

55   Sharifah Munirah Alatas, "Applying Syed Hussein Alatas' Ideas in Contemporary Malaysian Society," *Asian Journal of Social Science* 48 (2020): 319–338.

Alatas, Masturah. *The Life in the Writing Syed Hussein Alatas: Author of the Lazy Native,* Shah Alam, Selangor: Marshall Cavendish, 2010.

Alatas, Sharifah Munirah. "A Critique of the Indo-Pacific Construct: Geopolitics of Western-Centrism," In Rahul Mishra, Azirah Hashim and Anthony Milner (eds). *Asia and Europe in the 21st Century: New Anxieties, New Opportunities,* London and New York: Routledge, 2021. Chapter 15, pp. 185–197.

Alatas, Sharifah Munirah. "Applying Syed Hussein Alatas's Ideas in Contemporary Malaysian Society." *Asian Journal of Social Science* 48 (2020): 319–338.

Alatas, Sharifah Munirah. "ASEAN's Engagement with China: A Pragmatic Alternative to the Quad's Eurocentric Strategy." *Turkish Center for Asia Pacific Studies,* (2020).

Alatas, Sharifah Munirah. "Decolonising International Relations: Theory and Practice," unpublished research notes, November 18, 2020: 1–5.

Alatas, Syed Farid. *Silencing as Method: Leaving Malay Studies Out.* National University of Singapore Working Papers, NUS: Department of Malay Studies (2018).

Alatas, Syed Farid. "Eurocentrism," in *The Blackwell Encyclopedia of Sociology,* ed. George Ritzer (John Wiley & Sons, Ltd., 2016): 1–4.

Alatas, Syed Farid. "Eurocentrism and the Role of the Human Sciences in the Dialogue among Civilizations." *The European Legacy: Toward New Paradigms* 7, issue 6 (2002): 759–770.

Alatas, Syed Farid. "An Introduction to the Idea of Alternative Discourses." *Southeast Asian Journal of Social Science* 28, no. 1, (2000): 1–12.

Alatas, Syed Hussein. "On the Need for an Historical Study of Malaysian Islamization." *Journal of Southeast Asian History,* 4, no. 1 (Mar. 1963): 68–81.

Alatas, Syed Hussein. "The captive mind in development studies: Some neglected problems and the need for an autonomous social science tradition in Asia," *International Social Science Journal* (1972) 1: 9–25.

Alatas, Syed Hussein. *Modernization and Social Change: Studies in modernization, religion, social change and development in South-East Asia.* Sydney: Angus and Robertson Publishers, 1972.

Alatas, Syed Hussein. *The Myth of the Lazy Native: A Study of the Image of the Malays, Filipinos, and Javanese from the 16th to the 20th Century and its Function in the Ideology of Colonial Capitalism.* Singapore: Times Books International, 1977.

Alatas, Syed Hussein. "The Development of an Autonomous Social Science Tradition in Asia: Problems and Prospects," *Asian Journal of Social Science* 30, no. 1 (2002): 150–157.

Alatas, Syed Hussein. "The Autonomous, the Universal and the Future of Sociology." *Current Sociology* 54, no. 1 (2006): 7–23.

Alatas, Syed Hussein. "Intellectual Imperialism: Definition, Traits, and Problems." *Southeast Asian Journal of Social Science* 28, no. 1 (2000): 23–45.

Braudel, Fernand. *The Wheels of Commerce, Civilization and Capitalism 15th-18th Century: Volume II*, London: William Collins Sons & Co Ltd., 1979.

Buzan, Barry and Richard Little. "Beyond Westphalia? Capitalism after the 'Fall'." *Review of International Studies, Vol. 25, The Interregnum: Controversies in World Politics, 1989–1999* (Dec. 1999): 89–104.

Buzan, Barry and Richard Little. "The Idea of 'International System': Theory Meets History." *International Political Science Review,* 15, no. 3 (July 1994): 231–255.

Çapan, Zeynep Gülsah. "Eurocentrism and the Construction of the 'Non-West'." *E-international Relations* (Jun 19, 2018), https://www.e-info/2018/06/19/eurocentrism-and-the-construction-of-the-non-west/.

Cardoso, Fernando and Enzo Faletto. *Dependency and Development in Latin America*. Berkeley and Los Angeles: University of California Press, 1979.

Eun, Yong-Soo. "Beyond 'the West/non-West Divide' in IR: How to Ensure Dialogue as Mutual Learning." *The Chinese Journal of International Politics,* (2018): 435–449.

Goffman, Daniel. *The Ottoman Empire and Early Modern Europe*, Cambridge, UK: Cambridge University Press, 2002.

Goldstone, Jack A. "East and West in the Seventeenth Century: Political Crises in Stuart England, Ottoman Turkey, and Ming China," *Comparative Studies in Society and History*, 30 no. 1 (1988): 103–142.

Grieco, Joseph, John Ikenberry, and Michael Mastanduno (Eds.), *Introduction to International Relations: Perspectives, Connections, and Enduring Questions*. London, Red Globe Press, 2014.

Hoffmann, Stanley. "An American Social Science: International Relations." *Daedalus,* 106, no. 1 (1977): 41–60.

Khurana, Gurpreet. "The 'Indo-Pacific' Concept: Retrospect and Prospect." *National Maritime Foundation*, http://www.maritimeindia.org, accessed August 19, 2020: 1–8.

Pomeau, Rene Henry. "Voltaire: French philosopher and author." *Encyclopedia Britannica* (Jan. 7, 2021), https://www.britannica.com/biography/Voltaire.

Rich, Brian. "The Principles of Future-Proofing: A Broader Understanding of Resiliency in the Historic Built Environment." *Journal of Preservation Education and Research* 7 (2014): 31–49.

Scott, Trent and Andrew Shearer. "Building Allied Interoperability in the Indo-Pacific Region." *Discussion Paper 1: Command and Control*, Washington, D.C.: Center for Strategic and International Studies, 2017.

Tay, Simon and Jessica Wau. "The Indo-Pacific Outlook: a new lens for ASEAN." *East Asia Forum Quarterly*. Volume 12, Number 1 (2020): 3–5.

de Voltaire, Francois Marie Arouet. *Merope, a tragedy*, by Aaron Hill, adapted for theatrical representation, London, 1795, Act I, sc. 3.

Wallerstein, Immanuel. *The Modern World-System 1: Capitalist Agriculture and the Origins of the European World-Economy in the Sixteenth Century*. Berkeley, CA: University of California Press, 1974.

Yurdusev, A Nuri. "Thomas Hobbes and international relations: from realism to rationalism." *Australian Journal of International Affairs* 60, No. 2 (2006): 305–321.

CHAPTER 15

Alatas

Pioneer in the Study of, and the Struggle against, Corruption

Chandra Muzaffar

Professor Syed Hussein Alatas devoted almost his entire life to the study of corruption. He was more than a mere student of this terrible scourge. For much of his adult life he was also actively involved in combating corruption.

Alatas' identification of corruption as a monumental challenge in so many societies, both ancient and contemporary, is one of the five dimensions of his engagement with the scourge that we shall examine in this chapter. We shall also evaluate his thoughts on the causes of corruption; its costs and consequences for society; and the struggle against this vice right through history. What has been the impact of Alatas' scholarship and his activism on corruption as a field of study and as a social malignancy?

1   Identifying Corruption as a Major Problem

As a student in the political and social sciences at the University of Amsterdam in the Netherlands in the early fifties, Alatas was already writing about the ill effects of corruption upon society. He became acutely aware of the devastating impact of corruption as he was growing up in Indonesia in the forties, in the midst of the Second World War. Bribes and inducements were required in almost every sphere of society in order to facilitate life's essentials. In a situation where law and order had broken down, illicit exchanges between giver and taker had become a pervasive culture. It was the real-life experience of a society that he was so familiar with that convinced him of the devastating impact of corruption upon lives and livelihoods and the need to focus upon this evil.

This is an important aspect of Alatas' approach to the study of social problems that we should keep in mind at all times. Problems had to be *real*. A problem was worth exploring not because some scholar or researcher thought that it was vital but because it affected the lives of ordinary women and men. This more than anything else made Alatas a sociologist rooted in the realities that confronted society.

© CHANDRA MUZAFFAR, 2023 | DOI:10.1163/9789004521698_017

Few other young scholars in the Global South or the Global North at that time regarded corruption as an urgent challenge that demanded their attention. In the Global South, the concern was with nation-building, issues of development, and indeed the question of how one could protect one's Independence and sovereignty in the post-colonial era. These were all legitimate concerns but there was seldom any attempt to link the ability to preserve a nation's sovereignty with elite corruption. In the Global North, there were some scholars who were preoccupied with the "Western" – specifically the capitalist model of development and modernization and its relevance to countries in the Global South. Corruption that often colored actual efforts at modernization seldom figured in their writings. Perhaps the exception was the Swedish thinker Gunnar Myrdal.[1]

Seen from this perspective, Alatas was in a sense a pioneer who realized the significance of a phenomenon that many students of society today in both the Global North and the Global South regard as fundamental in explaining the success or failure of nation-building.

With this as the backdrop, let us now analyze three aspects of corruption that Alatas had written about for decades.

2 Causes

The causes of corruption are complex. Alatas adopts both a contextual and a deductive approach in trying to understand why the phenomenon occurs. In the books he had written about corruption, he provides numerous examples of acts of corruption in India, Pakistan, Sri Lanka, Iran, Turkey, Japan, China, the Philippines, and Singapore, apart from Indonesia and Malaysia. He also draws from the experience of Western countries such as the United States of America, Britain, France, and the Netherlands. It is not just the liberal democracies in the West that he covers. Socialist states, such as the Union of Soviet Socialist Republics (USSR), also receive his attention. His time span transcends the post Second World War decades. Alatas digs deep into the past, dynasties of yesteryears from different cultures and civilizations, in order to show how corruption had evolved through the ages.

This huge reservoir of examples and episodes from the past and the present enhances the quality of his writings on the subject. I have not come across

---

1 Gunnar Myrdal, *Asian Drama: An Enquiry into the Poverty of Nations*. New Delhi: Kalyani Publishers, 2018.

other studies of corruption that are so rich in content and context. This is one of the main reasons why his books on corruption are a researcher's delight.[2]

At the same time, however, Alatas was aware of the importance of drawing out some general conclusions about the causes of corruption. He lists the following ten factors as contributory factors based to some extent upon the work of the well-known scholar on bureaucratic corruption, Ralph Braibanti. The factors are, 'a) The absence or weakness of leadership in key positions capable of inspiring and influencing conduct mitigating corruption. As the Chinese and Japanese proverb says, "As the wind blows so bends the reed." b) The weakness of religious and ethical teachings. c) Colonialism. An alien government does not awaken the necessary loyalty and devotion capable of inhibiting corruption. d) Lack of education. e) Poverty. f) Absence of severe punitive measures. g) Absence of environment conducive to anti-corrupt behavior. h) Structure of government. i) Radical change. Whenever a value system is undergoing a radical change, corruption appears as a transitional malaise. j) The state of society. Corruption in a bureaucracy reflects the total society.'[3]

Alatas argues that while "the above factors are the constituent elements in the occurrence of corruption, yet by themselves these factors are not sufficient to explain the phenomenon."[4] He concurs with Braibanti that these elements are part of a 'complicated matrix of causes, each of which are of varying importance depending on special temporal and circumstantial factors.'[5] However, he does emphasize the absence of sacral personalities who are capable of inspiring the masses through their moral conduct as a major cause of the spread of corruption in certain societies. Alatas is of the view that, 'it makes a great deal of difference to the country if a few courageous, efficient, and honest individuals are occupying positions of power. This is particularly so when a country is in a precarious situation bordering on outright corruption, and when a strong, articulate and aggressive public opinion against corruption has not yet crystallized. To form this public opinion the mediation of the sacral personalities is extremely functional.'[6]

---

2   Among Syed Hussein Alatas' leading works on corruption are, *The Sociology of Corruption: The Nature, Function, Causes and Prevention of Corruption.* Singapore: Donald Moore Press, 1968; *The Problem of Corruption.* Kuala Lumpur: The Other Press, 1986; *Corruption and the Destiny of Asia.* Singapore: Simon and Shuster, 1999.
3   Syed Hussein Alatas, *The Problem of Corruption* (Kuala Lumpur: The Other Press, 1986), 37–38.
4   Ibid., 38.
5   Ibid.
6   Ibid., 59.

Recognizing the role of sacral personalities in checking corruption was a unique contribution that Alatas made in his study of the scourge. He should have at the same time shown how another form of activity has become critical in intensifying and expanding corruption in almost every society. Politics, more specifically the pursuit of power, is undoubtedly a major reason why corruption has become endemic in so many different parts of the world. There are at least five dimensions to contemporary politics that encourage the sort of wrongdoings that are easily categorized as acts of corruption.

(1) The competition for power among political parties and individuals through elections that often witness the competitors appealing to the voters for support by promising them all sorts of material and non-material rewards. The promise may be to build a new road, a new housing project, a new school, or a new hospital in return for votes that in many electoral systems would be regarded as an inducement and even a violation of electoral law. Often, the promise may take another form. It may be to advance a community's language or education or religion or economic status. Because such promises are so widespread, prosecution under the law is seldom carried out. There are very few electoral systems where such practices or rather malpractices have been put to an end. Besides, an offending party can always argue that it is merely presenting its manifesto to the voters, or it is doing its duty by telling them what it intends to do based upon its track record.

(2) Electoral competition may also result in direct bribes to local-level leaders or vote mobilisers in a particular constituency. A candidate or some sponsor of the candidate may through direct or indirect means channel money to a grassroots leader with the aim of getting him to mobilize votes on his behalf. Rather than offer cash, the bribe may take the form of an overseas holiday for the local leader and his family. There have been occasions when all expenses connected with the pilgrimage of some Muslim opinion maker in a constituency are taken care of by the candidate or his representative. Even the children of a grassroots leader may sometimes be targeted through a scholarship or some other aid.

(3) Companies are sometimes known to offer lucrative shares to a candidate or his family. This may be executed in a surreptitious manner. In return, the company would expect the candidate after he is elected to make it easier for the former to expand its business or multiply its profits. The company's failure to adhere to certain labor or health standards are often overlooked by the Minister or civil servant in charge partly because of the influence of the candidate who had been given those shares in the first instance.

(4)   Well-heeled companies also have other ways of influencing the electoral process. There have been many cases of companies financing and organizing the campaign of a particular candidate with the hope that the latter would return the favor at some point in the future. Sometimes, it may not even be a company. A well-to-do individual with a political agenda may offer his private jet to a candidate to enable him to campaign more effectively. Or he may place at the disposal of the candidate his staff and machinery.

(5)   Every now and then one hears of direct cash assistance to candidates from businesspeople. This may run into millions in certain settings. Even if there are laws that require candidates to disclose their electoral or political financing, there are ways of circumventing them. In some places, there are businesses that back both the candidate and his electoral rival as a sort of insurance. Financial backing for candidates and political parties has created a situation where some businesses wield enormous influence upon public policies and the decision-making process. Most of the time, this is not known to the populace.

What all this shows is that electoral politics and the political process as a whole has become a massive arena for corrupt acts. It is also among the arenas that are most difficult to reform, partly because the lawmakers who should be at the forefront of such changes are themselves often the beneficiaries of the corrupt system. We shall return to this issue later.

For the time being, let us note that almost all the various dimensions of inter-party electoral competition that cause corruption also occur within a political party. Buying and bribing those who possess the vote; the pledges and promises of those seeking power; and the involvement of businesses are also part and parcel of intra-party politics.

3   Costs and Consequences

In his reflections on the costs and consequences of corruption, Alatas reiterates that 'corruption has inflicted suffering upon human society from time immemorial. From ancient Near East, Greece, Rome, China, and India, we have ample evidence of the prevalence of corruption. Ancient China and the Roman Empire provide striking materials of it. Corruption affected their history in no small way. The frequent wars, the violent overthrows of ruling powers, the disorganization and breakdowns of societies, have always been related to corruption. It became crucial to the break-up of these societies in combination with other causes.'[7]

In order to ensure that the costs and consequences of corruption are properly understood, Alatas then explains what he means by corruption. It is 'essentially the abuse of trust in the interest of personal and private gain. When a public servant violates the norms of his duty in the interest of another party in return for inducement in monetary or other forms, he is said to have committed a corrupt act. It is an intentional violation of duty with the motive of gaining personal advantage by receiving a bribe or other benefits from a party in need of a particular decision affecting interests the public servant can bring about.'[8]

Alatas then provides numerous examples of the abuse of trust from a variety of countries – India, Malaysia, Pakistan, and Indonesia. In the Indian case, he focuses upon a government-initiated report – the Santhanam Report – that sought to unravel massive and widespread corruption in the country at that time. It is significant that among the many causes for the increase in corruption it cites "rapid urbanization," which 'brought about the weakening of rural values. Social controls resulting in the maintenance of frugality and simplicity of life were replaced by those encouraging materialism, impersonalism, status craving, greed for money and power, and an unwillingness to adhere to moral values. In this climate, the business and commercial classes whose ranks were swelled by speculators and adventurers of the war period exerted their corruptive influence. The salaried classes meanwhile experienced a decline in real income. A large part of these classes belonged to government service. All these formed a fertile soil for corruption.'[9]

The Santhanam Report then observes that the scope and incentives for corruption were greatest at the points where important decisions that would substantially affect the fortunes of interested groups or individuals were taken, such as the assessment and collection of taxes, obtaining licenses, contracts, or in orders of supplies. It was suggested that 'the corruption cost was between 7 to 11 percent in undertakings done for the government.'[10] The Report also examines the roles of businesspeople, industrialists," contact men" black marketeers, smugglers and so on. Black marketeers even had,

---

7   Ibid., 63.
8   Ibid.
9   Ibid., 67.
10   Ibid., 68.

their influence in Indian politics. They joined a political party, became office bearers and eventually controlled the party. They donated to the parties that did not have independent sources of income. Once entrenched, the black marketeers would seize any available opportunity: the disposal of goods illegally produced, theft of relief food or other materials, hoarding and the release of selected commodities, and trade in money. Black marketing operations were more significant apparently in iron, steel, cloth, cotton, yarn. man-made fibers, cement, fertilizers, aluminum. sugar, molasses, motor vehicles, coal and paper. Scarcity of goods, coupled with dishonest industrial practices to perpetuate the scarcity, was the main cause of the black-market operation which assumed staggering heights after the mid-1960s.[11]

If black marketing is germane to most corrupt societies, how does one explain theft and deception carried out in houses of worship? "A colossal amount of gold and grain," Alatas notes,

> were donated to these houses of worship. Some, no doubt were used for maintaining the shrines, providing relief for the poor, assistance for pilgrims and money for salaries of temple workers. But a good deal was embezzled, systematically and cynically. The most dumb-founding incident was the disappearance of 40,000 acres of land belonging to the Brihadeswara temple in Thanjavur, Tamil Nadu. Both Hindu and Muslim religious endowments were attacked by corruption.[12]

An even more tragic example of corruption in India is corruption that affects schools and school students. Students are exposed to the scourge at a young age. As a case in point, in Delhi, it is alleged that,

> Principals usually prefer children of parents who can dispense patronage or favors as well as those who can pay. A list of rich children in each class is maintained and they are sought after for the purpose of selling fundraising tickets. In some schools, teachers squeeze out gifts from students. The good-old practice of giving flowers to the teacher has been replaced by giving her a watch, an imported pen, lipstick and even a sari.[13]

---

11 Ibid., 71.

12 Ibid., 70.

13 Ibid., 72.

In such a system one should not be surprised that examination questions are leaked out for the benefit of certain students that the school intends to oblige. Leakages also take place in exchange for cash. 'Admission to the university,' it is said, 'is also a big racket.'[14] Sometimes bogus certificates are issued to boys and girls from influential or well-to-do families to help them gain entrance. It is not just bogus certificates. Examination marks are tampered with, and admission requirements manipulated in order to ensure that students from well-placed families get into university.

After his exhaustive analysis of the Indian situation, Alatas turns his attention to his own country, Malaysia. The Auditor-General's Report prepared annually during those years when Alatas diligently analyzed the document was a major source of information for the scholar.[15] He discovered all sorts of discrepancies and irregularities in those reports that often revealed the extent of corruption and malpractice prevalent in the nation's administration at federal and state levels. A couple of instances highlighted in one of his books will be mentioned here to illustrate the nature of the problem facing Malaysia.

> One concerned instant noodles for the period of January 1977 to December 1978. The contract prices were RM 4.90 and RM 3.90 respectively per packet while the average price in Peninsular Malaysia for that period was only 14 sen. The Ministry of Defense had really been cheated. The government could have saved RM 962,000 had this item been bought in the peninsula and then transported to East Malaysia.[16]

The Auditor-General had also recommended for further investigation "another rather dubious instance" of the

> sale of 11,517 pairs of ankle boots in good condition but no longer used by the army. This was tendered together with twenty-nine types of minor motor vehicles spares. The Ministry of Defense received only one offer for all the items. The Tenders Board met and decided to accept the offer. But before this, the Tenders Opening Committee prepared the papers for consideration by the Tenders Board. The items to be disposed of by the Army were entered into two pages of the tender forms. Twenty-two of the

---

14   Ibid., 73.
15   This role played by Alatas is alluded to in, "Integrity and Malaysia," in my *Reflections on Malaysian Unity and other Challenges* (Kuala Lumpur: Zubedy and Yayasan Perpaduan Malaysia, 2017), 108–110.
16   Alatas, *The Problem of Corruption*, 77.

ALATAS

twenty-nine types of motor vehicles spares were identified in quantities. Seven types of spares were not identified in quantities. The boots were also not identified in quantities. Both these items not identified in quantities appeared in the second page.[17]

Alatas comments,

the amazing thing was that the Tenders Board with incomplete information given by the Tenders Opening Committee decided to accept the offer from the sole bidder. How much was the offer? RM 120! A shock should have followed and caused a mental earthquake amongst members of the Tenders Board. The original cost of the 11,517 pairs of boots alone was about RM 146,000. Forgetting the original cost of the twenty-nine types of motor vehicle spares, just taking the cost of the boots, it meant that the sole bidder paid about 1.04 sen for each pair of boots. If we include the cost of the spares, that genius of a bidder must have paid minus one sen for each of the items.[18]

Leakages of this sort, which as the Auditor-general's reports have exposed, every now and then over the decades would have drained the nation of billions of ringgit. Needless to say, this is money that could have been used for the well-being of the people, for building schools and hospitals, roads and bridges, for enhancing the scientific and technological skills of the people and invigorating our arts and culture. But none of these losses and leakages could match the loans scandal involving Bumiputra Malaysia Finance (BMF), a subsidiary of a state-owned bank, Bank Bumiputra Malaysia Berhad, that shook the Malaysian nation in 1983. This is a scandal in which a few individuals siphoned off RM 2.5 billion (US 1.02 billion) through dubious loans from BMF transmitted via a private company, the Carrian Group in Hong Kong.[19] Their misdeed revealed deceit, fraud, and subterfuge, which led eventually to the murder of a young, conscientious accountant who was investigating the heinous crime.[20] Alatas analyzed the BMF scandal in some detail. As he put it,

---

17   Ibid., 78.
18   Ibid., 78.
19   Ibid., 97–98.
20   This was the brutal murder of Abdul Jalil Ibrahim, the background to which is discussed in my writings on the Bank Bumiputra scandal. See Chapter 4 of *Issues of the Mahathir Years.* Penang: Aliran, 1988.

The BMF scandal is indeed a most alarming and revealing scandal ... It is not only the loss of RM 2.5 billion that is the issue here, but the surrounding phenomena of decadence, indifference, inattentiveness, the absence of communication, and most alarming, the freedom exercised by the corrupt manipulators to operate at such a scale and for so long, a couple of years, with boldness and minimal intelligence. The things they did as revealed by the Report (on the scandal) does not show much intelligence. It is not a highly sophisticated scheme to defraud, nor is it difficult to detect or prove. It is a crude and rapacious manipulation leaving traces all over the place.[21]

The BMF scandal was superseded by yet another scandal that was exposed many years later, in 2015. This is the 1 Malaysia Development Berhad (MDB) scandal, a scandal of global proportions that is now being adjudicated in Malaysian Courts. It involves an investment company established by the Malaysian government in 2009 when Najib Razak was Prime Minister and Finance Minister. The company, 1MDB was implicated in the massive theft of state funds and abuse of state power by Najib and people close to him.[22] Najib has already been convicted by a High Court and is now appealing against his jail sentence and fine. The 1 MDB scandal became public through local and foreign channels, more than 8 years after Alatas had passed away in January 2007. It was undoubtedly the epitome of the elite venality that Alatas was so deeply concerned about all his life.[23]

After Malaysia, we shall now look at Pakistan. Alatas begins his probe by stating unequivocally that,

In Pakistan the situation is much more odious because the corrupt pay lip service to religion. A Pakistani observer appraising the ignominious state of his country sadly stated that Islam in Pakistan is only in theory, in recitation, in prayers but not in the moral behavior of the people. The influence of the leading classes, the hypocritical religious leaders, the scheming professionals, the greedy businessmen, the extortionist bureaucrats, has steadily increased the momentum of corruption.[24]

---

21   Alatas, *The Problem of Corruption*, 113.

22   My criticisms of the 1MDB scandal are contained in the chapter on Integrity, in *Reflections on Malaysian Unity*, 126–164.

23   For a comprehensive analysis of the 1MDB scandal see P. Gunasegaram, *1 MDB: The Scandal that brought down a Government.* Selangor: The Strategic Information and Research Development Centre (SIRD), 2018.

24   Alatas, *The Problem of Corruption*, 82.

In the early stages, bribes were small and confined largely to the lower echelons of the public services. They increased as ties between government officials and businessmen grew stronger. Large-scale transactions occurred as 'The services of touts and brokers came into being.'[25] Initially, 'corruption was done in secrecy – but later it was practiced in broad daylight in government offices.'[26] As in a number of other countries,

> corruption in Pakistan affects all walks of life. The courts, the revenue departments, the police, the health services, the railway, the customs, the telephone service, the postal service, the professional services, were all vigorously dominated by corruption of the most extortive type. Amongst the lawyers, corruption took the form of wrong advice, bribery of court and police officials, at times including judges and magistrates, and also the opponent's advocates. A common device was to entangle the clients into complications that cost them a lot of money.[27]

In the medical profession, corruption assumed a different form. Specialists and surgeons,

> attached to big hospitals prefer the patients to come to their private clinics first, settle their bills, and then they would be helped with admission into the hospitals. For operations, patients making such arrangements would get preferential treatment. Others had to wait days to get their turn.[28]

As one should expect, corruption was also pervasive in the education system. Alatas notes that 'examiners were bribed by students to obtain the required marks. In addition, some teachers forced tuition upon students and extracted loans from them.'[29]

By the mid-fifties, almost a decade after Pakistan was established, corruption had become so ubiquitous that the people had begun to lose faith in the democratic system and in politics as a whole. A religious scholar had even suggested at that point that elections should be abolished and declared unlawful (haram). He argued that since 80 to 90 percent of the people were corrupt,

---

25   Ibid., 82.
26   Ibid., 82.
27   Ibid., 83.
28   Ibid., 83.
29   Ibid., 83.

invariably a candidate that stood for election would be corrupt. Thus, election was for the corrupt, of the corrupt, and by the corrupt. It was because of disgust towards corruption that the people and the army initially welcomed the introduction of martial law in 1958.[30]

For a while there was some attempt to weed out the corrupt. But there was no determined, sustained effort to eliminate the vice. The underlying causes were not addressed. Corruption returned with a vengeance. By the mid-eighties, Alatas was convinced that,

> corruption in Pakistan has now attained devastating magnitude. The misery and human suffering caused by corruption are beyond description. The state which was formed at great cost to human lives and suffering attending the partition tragedy is now being abandoned by tens of thousands of its skilled and unskilled manpower. The brain as well as the brawn drain from Pakistan is truly impressive. This is one of the serious consequences of corruption which greatly affects the pace of development in the developing societies. The great harm corruption is doing to development is as clear as daylight. It does not require ingenuity and scholarship to recognize what is obvious.[31]

This brings us to Indonesia. 'The harm done by corruption towards development in Indonesia was highlighted by the Report of the Commission of four,' by the order of the late Indonesian president Suharto on 31 January 1970.[32] The Commission was given the task of advising the government on how to enhance the effectiveness of the measures adopted to combat corruption. Alatas reflects on the observations made by the Commission 'on the government–owned oil enterprise Pertamina and some injurious activity in the logging industry.'[33]

According to the Commission, Pertamina 'failed to resist foreign manipulation to push down the price of crude oil.' Furthermore,

> it did not observe its obligation to transfer 55 per cent of its net profit to *Dana Pembangunan* (Development Fund). It paid its taxes according to its own assessment in amounts not reflective of its earnings. Contractual agreements entered into with foreign oil companies were not favourable

---

30   Ibid., 84.
31   Ibid., 85.
32   Ibid.
33   Ibid., 86.

to Pertamina. It appeared as though Pertamina was acting purely as a body to offer facilities to the foreign companies. In the clauses of the agreement on profit and production sharing, Pertamina was continuously linked with its obligations. The clauses on rights referred more to the foreign company.[34]

The account books were to be surrendered to the foreign company. The purchase of materials to carry out the contractual exploration was not in the hands of Pertamina. At the time of the report, Pertamina's area of operation was very extensive. It carried out oil production and marketing activities, as well as profit and production sharing with thirty-four other foreign oil companies.[35]

Amongst the irregularities committed by Pertamina was the non-payment of taxes. Between 1958 and 1963, Pertamina did not send in tax returns. In 1964 without submitting tax returns it paid Rp (rupiahs) 35,855,300 tax. The same amount was paid in 1966. By 1967 the tax debt of Pertamina was Rp. 1,344 billion.[36] As noted, the company also failed to meet its obligation to the Development Fund, required by its charter. It made some contribution in 1964 and 1965 but it was estimated that its arrears for 1970 would be about US $17 billion. There were numerous other malpractices that the Commission discovered. For instance, Pertamina's internal auditor became also the contractor for Pertamina's hotels![37]

Apart from Pertamina, the logging industry also exhibited pronounced corrupt tendencies. The way in which logging licenses were farmed out bred corruption. Even more serious were indiscriminate, destructive logging practices. They resulted in great losses to the government through cheating. The higher quality export timber was classified as local so that it could be sold cheaper. The wood was deliberately sawn in such a manner that it fell outside the export specification. The teak was also exported as logs thereby reducing government revenue. In short, despite the logging of high-quality teak, officially the government received lower quality production figure and sale amount. Both the buyer and the seller benefitted from this deception.[38]

As a long-term observer of the Indonesian scene, Alatas was painfully aware of how corruption had worsened over the years. This was also true of the rest of Southeast Asia. The only exception in Alatas' reckoning was Singapore.[39] It

34   Ibid., 86–87.
35   Ibid., 87.
36   Ibid.
37   Ibid.
38   Ibid., 88.
39   Ibid.

is an irrefutable fact that State and society in Singapore has acquired a reputation as a place that is free of corruption. Transparency International's annual assessment of corruption worldwide has shown that for many years Singapore has remained at the apex of societies that are perceived as "clean."[40]

Why has Singapore succeeded to curb and control corruption when others in the region and elsewhere have failed? The main reason appears to be Singapore's leadership. Alatas suggests as much though he did not analyze in depth and detail how the Singapore leadership fought corruption after the island republic attained self-rule in 1959. In none of his writings did he show through empirical evidence how Singapore, which faced serious corruption before 1959, eliminated the scourge in the civil and public services or in the private sector, or in other segments of society. Such reflections from someone like Alatas with his encyclopedic knowledge of the workings of the vice would have been a huge contribution to the battle against this perennial vice. It would have enabled scholars and politicians alike to compare the experiences of various societies in different parts of the world.

The Singapore leadership was decisive in combating corruption from the following perspectives.[41]

(1) The leadership had a strong collective commitment to the eradication of corruption. It is significant that the man at the helm of Singapore society from 1959 to 1990, Lee Kuan Yew, the secretary-General of the ruling party, the People's Action Party, manifested this commitment through his policies and actions for 31 years. His powerful personality had such a massive impact upon state and society that it set the tone and tenor of the young nation for generations. The aversion towards corruption became intrinsic to the governance and management of the state.

(2) If the collective will of the leadership over decades had such a strong impact it was largely because wrongdoings committed by even important leaders were severely punished. There were no double standards. No one was above the law.

(3) This was integral to the determined, concerted attempt by the leadership over a long period of time to set the right example. Ruling by example was not just a slogan to be preached. It was a reality that leaders at different levels of society sought to put into practice.

---

40 See P. Gunasegaram 1 MDB: The Scandal that brought down a Government.
41 See Lee Kuan Yew, The Singapore Story Memoirs of Lee Kuan Yew Vol 1, Times Edition, 1998. Also see Lee Kuan Yew, The Singapore Story Memoirs of Lee Kuan Yew Vol 2: From Third World to First. Times Media Private limited, 2000.

(4)   Laws directed at wiping out corruption, which were sometimes severe, were implemented and enforced without fear or favor. Over time, Singapore citizens understood that wrongs would be punished and there would be no compromise.

(5)   As laws were enforced and leaders were held accountable, the government also ensured that the basic needs of the people were given priority, that economic progress was achieved, and social mobility guaranteed. By and large, the government upheld the people's trust, which made it easier for them to support the drive against corruption.

It is when governments and leaders fail to uphold the people's trust that the costs and consequences of their misdeeds become an overwhelming burden to society. And no misdeed is a greater burden to bear than elite corruption. Alatas' survey of so many societies from the past and the present bears testimony to this.

4   The Struggle against Corruption

In analyzing Alatas' reflections on the struggle against corruption, I begin by looking at what he has to say about institutional attempts to combat the evil. I then turn to his thoughts on raising public consciousness against corruption, which contain some insightful prescriptions.

His reflections on institutional attempts rely heavily on the experiences of the Pakistani State. Using the editorial of a Pakistani weekly in 1985 as his primary source, Alatas offers his ideas on three proposals adopted by the Pakistani government in the fight against corruption. (1) Islamization pushed forward by the religious lobby; (2) decentralization of powers and deregulation of procedures; and (3) the enforcement of simple living among public servants and a system of proper accountability. He appears to concur with the editorial that acknowledges that,

There is nothing wrong with all these ideas except that their efficacy has always been in doubt. The process of Islamization has been tried and tried under martial law and it has had little effect. In fact, it has sometimes been alleged that the machinery of martial law itself has been tainted by it. The proposal of decentralization and deregulation, despite having been discussed for months, is nowhere near materialization. The public servants dealing with contracts, permissions, permits, etc., are not likely to part with their powers without a fight, and if forced to give them up, are not expected to become saints overnight. Other ways to feather their nests are likely to be found. The campaign for simple living, first thought of and promoted during the early Ayub Khan days, soon came to an ignominious end.[42]

Alatas is acutely aware that,

> the attempt to wipe out corruption is not a simple drawing up a program of action. It is a fight against the corrupt, clinging to their positions, subverting measures against corruption. It is a struggle for survival of two contending groups, the corrupt and those against it, in a manner of jungle warfare in the dark, where the enemy is not seen but nevertheless is fighting back with all its might.[43]

That the corrupt constitute a major obstacle in the struggle against the vice is underscored by the difficulties faced in Pakistan in appointing ombudsmen in the provinces. It is because the resistance was so great that the editorial in the weekly that Alatas quoted from concluded that the fight against corruption as a whole 'requires a lot of courage – courage to probe even one's friends and colleagues.'[44]

It was courage that was missing in Pakistan at that time and in much of the Global South. The situation may not have changed very much since then. It is courage that defines and decides whether a leadership has real integrity or not.

My own modest experience as a member of the board of directors of a National Institute of Integrity in Malaysia from 2004 to 2017 reinforced this truth. The Institute Integrity Malaysia (IIM) ostensibly an independent body entrusted with the task of proposing measures aimed at enhancing integrity in all spheres of society was chaired by the Chief Secretary of the government of Malaysia and had in its board of directors the head of the Malaysian Anti-Corruption Commission (MACC), the Auditor-General, the Attorney-General, and the Secretary-General of a couple of Ministries, apart from a handful of independent public figures (I was in this category).[45] The board made a number of recommendations to the Prime Minister and the Federal Cabinet, some of which were accepted and others set aside. One of our accepted

---

42   Alatas, *The Problem of Corruption*, 101.

43   Ibid., 101–102.

44   Ibid., 103.

45   See Lee Kuan Yew, *The Singapore Story Memoirs of Lee Kuan Yew Vol 1*, Times Edition, 1998. Also see Lee Kuan Yew, *The Singapore Story Memoirs of Lee Kuan Yew Vol 2: From Third World to First*. Times Media Private limited, 2000.

recommendations was to promulgate a law that would require all elected legislators at federal and state levels to declare their assets and liabilities to the people through a publicly accessible register. The IIM had also proposed that political financing should be transparent. An important aspect of this was to make public the donations received by political parties and election candidates and to set rules and regulations pertaining to these donations. The ruling coalition at that time, the Barisan Nasional, accepted in principle the idea although the details gave rise to much wrangling that remains unresolved to this day. A couple of the opposition parties, including some that had been most vocal in their condemnation of corruption, were reluctant to endorse various dimensions of the proposal to make political and electoral financing public. My experience with IIM and political financing convinced me of the age-old truism that deeds speak louder than words.

This is also something that Alatas discovered in his wide-ranging study of corruption. There are not many political actors who will actually walk the talk when it comes to combating this vice. This is one of the main reasons why institutional reforms vis-à-vis the scourge of corruption has been rather weak.

In the struggle against corruption, Alatas had much greater faith in the efficacy of popular consciousness. If a significant segment of society expresses its abhorrence towards corruption, the abuse of power and injustices through a multitude of channels in a consistent manner over a long period of time, this sense of outrage would become a force in itself. This is what Alatas called "collective outrage." A well-known Indonesian daily, *Kompass*, commented on his idea, 'and stressed the need for the entire society to develop a sense of shame and outrage with regard to injustice, corruption, negligence, and inefficiency.'[46] If there is 'such a strong public opinion, an indifferent ruling class would be compelled take notice of it and gradually imbibe it itself. At this stage of Asian history, the propagation of collective shame and outrage is crucial.'[47]

In developing this sense of outrage, the media had a critical role to play. Civil society groups, activists, academics, professionals and citizens in general could all contribute to this mass awakening. Today, more than in the decades that Alatas was actively involved in societal challenges, the scope for mass participation is much greater. New media has made this possible. In Southeast Asia alone, there are millions of users of the new media ranging from WhatsApp to Twitter.

---

46   Alatas, *The Problem of Corruption*, 111.
47   Ibid., 111.

In this regard, it is important to recall that Alatas was a committed and engaged intellectual in Malaysia, Singapore, and Indonesia since the fifties. He was even involved in party politics in Malaysia from 1968 to 1971. He founded together with other individuals a party called Gerakan Rakyat Malaysia (Gerakan), which continues to play its role in Malaysian politics to this day. Needless to say, combating corruption has always been a central plank in its platform.

5 Alatas' Impact

One way of evaluating Alatas' impact upon society is to examine those moments when an eruption of moral outrage occurred revolving around corruption as a major issue and assess whether Alatas' staunch opposition to corruption played a role at all in the people's uprising. In Indonesia where his writings were read in some circles at least, the mass movement against Suharto, the nation's president, that resulted in his ouster in 1998, while concerned about elite corruption, appeared to be somewhat oblivious of Alatas' role in nurturing public awareness about that incorrigible vice. An even more stark example would be Malaysia, where Alatas' contribution as an ardent critic of corruption was better known, and yet in the 2018 opposition to prime minister Najib and his alleged involvement in corruption, Alatas' role as one of the earliest sparks that lit the anti-corruption bonfire was not acknowledged at all by any of the major political actors at that time. For all intents and purposes, Alatas' contribution was completely forgotten. It is true that Alatas had left the world 11 years before the 2018 political change. But it also shows that a public intellectual who was such a staunch opponent of corruption for so long in his own country had hardly any impact upon the public imagination.

This has been reinforced by a more recent development. A veteran journalist supported by a few friends in Malaysian public life launched an anti-corruption campaign in 2021, mainly because they were disturbed by what they perceived as the growing threat of corruption in the country.[48] So far there has been no acknowledgement of Alatas' pioneering role in the struggle

---

48 The campaign is known as Rasuah Busters (Rasuah is the Malay word for corruption). Because the initiator of the campaign, Husamuddin Yunus owns a Malay language daily, it has received some coverage in the media, but its impact is limited. So far it appears to have ignored the history and background to the struggle against corruption in Malaysia. The absence of any acknowledgement of the role of Syed Hussein Alatas is a glaring omission.

against corruption. Nor has any campaign leader drawn the people's attention to Alatas' writings on the subject.

Why a public intellectual like Alatas and his ideas do not appear to have struck a chord with the masses is an issue that should be analyzed in another setting. At this point, it is sufficient to note that there are a variety of reasons linked to a nation's history, its cultural and ethnic pattern, its religious disposition and its political characteristics, which explain society's inability to appreciate the role of its leading public intellectuals.[49] Besides, when a society is intellectually mediocre, its mediocrity itself hinders it from grasping the significance of ideas and values that are inherently transformative.

Nonetheless, within a small segment of Malaysian society and within the larger global community, there is better understanding of the role, relevance, and significance of Alatas' writings on corruption and other concerns today than ever before. I am sure his ideas will grow and develop in the future. Their perennial value will guarantee this.

Bibliography

Alatas, Syed Hussein. *Corruption and the Destiny of Asia*. Singapore: Simon and Shuster, 1999.

Alatas, Syed Hussein. *Intellectuals in Developing Societies*. London: Frank Cass, 1977.

Alatas, Syed Hussein. *The Problem of Corruption*. Kuala Lumpur: The Other Press, 1986.

Alatas, Syed Hussein. *The Sociology of Corruption: The Nature, Function, Causes and Prevention of Corruption*. Singapore: Donald Moore Press, 1968.

Gunasegaram, P. *1 MDB: The Scandal that brought down a Government*. Selangor: The Strategic Information and Research Development Centre (SIRD), 2018.

Muzaffar, Chandra. *Issues of the Mahathir Years*. Penang: Aliran, 1988.

Muzaffar, Chandra. *Reflections on Malaysian Unity and other Challenges*. Kuala Lumpur: Zubedy and Yayasan Perpaduan Malaysia, 2017.

Myrdal, Gunner. *Asian Drama: An Enquiry into the Poverty of Nations*. New Delhi: Kalyani Publishers, 2018.

Yew, Lee Kuan. *The Singapore Story Memoirs of Lee Kuan Yew Vol 1*, Times Edition, 1998.

Yew, Lee Kuan. *The Singapore Story Memoirs of Lee Kuan Yew Vol 2: From Third World to First*. Times Media Private limited, 2000.

---

49   In this regard, the role of intellectuals in developing societies has been studied by Alatas himself. See his insightful *Intellectuals in Developing Societies*. London: Frank Cass, 1977.

CHAPTER 16

Syed Hussein Alatas and the Question of Political Thought

Teo Lee Ken

1 Introduction

Building societies and nations are political projects. Benedict Anderson, the esteemed and important scholar of Indonesian studies, suggested that building such projects is rooted simultaneously in the past, and also the future.[1] The question of the future, and thus, the political project of defending societies has emerged as ever more pertinent and fundamental in our time of a global health pandemic, economic uncertainty, and intense engagements of cultural traditions and discourses.

Our concern in this chapter focuses on the social and intellectual thought of Malaysian sociologist and public intellectual, Syed Hussein Alatas, and the political project of building Malaysia. I seek to discuss how the approaches and concepts conceived by Syed Hussein Alatas assist us in assessing discourses of political ideas in Asian societies. They guide us in deriving perspectives on political thought arising from the interactions between the social conditions of a society and its thinkers.

To do so, the chapter examines Alatas' seminal work *Cita Sempurna Warisan Sejarah*.[2] The sociological and historical approaches and concepts found in this work provide a framework for problematizing and critiquing political discourses in society. Next, it focuses on the comparative survey of Malaysian and Iranian political currents to construct the outlines of key perspectives deriving from the political ideas of their articulators in Malaysia and Iran. In this discussion, I concentrate on the committed and reform political discourses and its salient characteristics in both countries. In concluding, I reflect on the significance of Syed Hussein Alatas' intellectual engagement of the problematic in political thought for contemporary developing societies.

---

1 Ben Anderson, "Indonesian Nationalism Today and in the Future," *Indonesia* 67 (April 1999): 2–3.
2 Syed Hussein Alatas, *Cita Sempurna Warisan Sejarah* (Bangi: UKM Press, 2000).

© TEO LEE KEN, 2023 | DOI:10.1163/9789004521698_018

Alatas insightfully noted that 'the rise of a genuine intellectual consciousness directed to sound humanitarian principles is an absolute condition for us to develop a sense of nationhood' and that an intellectual revolution is necessary for the process of building the nation.[3] Eleven years earlier, Alatas wrote and published an essay titled "The Prerequisites of Asian Political Philosophy."[4]

In this essay, Alatas argued for the need for a discourse regarding political philosophy or political thought, one that reflects the social conditions and caters to the problems of Asian societies. He identified four key problems for the student of political thought to focus on: (1) to identify the dominant ideas distinctive of a modern Asian period; (2) to ascertain the ideals and aims for Asian societies; (3) to set the basis and parameters through which to consider what ideas and values (for example from countries in Europe and North America) to adopt and avoid; and (4) to identify and pose new sets of fundamental questions to focus upon.[5]

Both passages from Alatas' 1977 *Intellectuals* and his 1966 essay have always struck me as timelessly profound in their tone and depth and have and still continue to leave an indelible mark on my thoughts and writings. Its essence and spirit build on the movement of Alatas' commitment and legacy, which was to construct an autonomous social science approach and tradition.[6] Alatas advocated throughout his writings the development of a critical method of social sciences, in particularly sociology, that highlighted and examined the social problems of societies and communities in Asia. The identification of concepts such as "stupid" (bebalisme), the "captive mind", "evil, stupid, arrogant" (jahat, bodoh, sombong – jadong), "intellectual imperialism" and defining of terms, including "modernization" and "progressive Islam," among others, are outcomes of his sociological analysis and perspectives.[7]

---

3   Syed Hussein Alatas, *Intellectuals in Developing Societies* (London: Cass, 1977), 2.

4   Syed Hussein Alatas, "The Prerequisites of Asian Political Philosophy," in *Moral Vision and Social Critique: Selected Essays of Syed Hussein Alatas*, ed. Azhar Ibrahim Alwee, Mohamed Imran Mohamed Taib (Singapore: The Reading Group, 2007), 56–62.

5   Ibid, 61–62.

6   Syed Hussein Alatas, "The Autonomous, the Universal and the Future of Sociology," *Current Sociology* 54, no. 1 (2006): 7–23; Syed Farid Alatas, and Vineeta Sinha, *Sociological Theory Beyond the Cannon* (London: Palgrave Macmillan, 2017); Syed Farid Alatas, *Applying Ibn Khaldun: The Recovery of a Lost Tradition in Sociology* (London; New York: Routledge, 2014); Syed Farid Alatas, *Alternative Discourses in Asian Social Science: Responses to Eurocentrism* (Thousand Oaks: Sage Publications, 2006).

7   Syed Hussein Alatas, *Intellectuals in Developing Societies* (London: Cass, 1977); Syed Hussein Alatas, "The Captive Mind and Creative Development," *International Social Science Journal* 26, no. 4 (1974): 691–700; Syed Hussein Alatas, "The Captive Mind in Development Studies: Some Neglected Problems and the Need for An Autonomous Social

Alatas' works and ideas have also led to the formation of the School of Autonomous Knowledge, which has influenced two and reaching three generations of scholars and academics, writers and researchers, spanning various fields of work.[8] The autonomous social science tradition, one Syed Hussein Alatas (2006) defines as 'the linking of social science research and thinking to specifically regional problems,' is the hallmark of this School and its practitioners.[9] In Alatas' 1966 essay, he explained that the objective of political philosophy is to articulate the 'type of political order best suited to attain the goals of human welfare and happiness' and that political philosophy engages 'the conceptions of human welfare and happiness, with the limitations of power, with the sanctioning of power, with the economic order, with social and educational institutions, with the rights and duties of the group and individual, with law enforcement, etc.'[10]

Building on these parameters and his prompting, I identify and discuss how we can attempt to further develop a contemporary perspective and critique of political discourses and thought in society by examining his work, *Cita Sempurna Warisan Sejarah*.[11]

2   *"Cita Sempurna Warisan Sejarah"*: The Ideal of Excellence and the Historical Ideal

What is the locomotive of human civilization and history? And what is the basis of society? These are the fundamental questions that Syed Hussein Alatas sought to address in his 2000 work, *Cita Sempurna Warisan Sejarah* or "The Ideal of Excellence as a Historical Heritage."[12] Alatas defines *cita sempurna* or the ideal of excellence as 'satu pandangan hidup yang menyeluruh bertujuan untuk mencapai masyarakat sempurna' or 'a comprehensive life view which purpose is to attain the ideal society.'[13]

Science Tradition in Asia," *International Social Science Journal* 24, no. 1 (1972): 9–25; Syed Hussein Alatas, *Cita Sempurna Warisan Sejarah* (Bangi: UKM Press, 2000).

8   Syed Farid Alatas, "Against the Grain: Malay Studies and the School of Autonomous Knowledge," *The Edge Weekly*, https://www.theedgemarkets.com/article/against-grain -malay-studies-and-school-autonomous-knowledge (accessed June 7, 2021).

9   Syed Hussein Alatas, supra at 6 (2006); Syed Farid Alatas, ibid.

10   Ibid., 4, 58.

11   Ibid., 2.

12   Ibid, 7.

13   Ibid.

SYED HUSSEIN ALATAS AND THE QUESTION OF POLITICAL THOUGHT   379

Syed Hussein Alatas proffers the following proposition: the absence of the ideal of excellence inhibits a society from progress and its existence and endurance. The vacuum it leaves enables the opposite trait to develop, which is *cita bencana* or the ideal of destruction. Alatas explains that the ideal of excellence is also a historical ideal.[14] It manifests from the history of society and human struggle against its realities and conditions. He highlights the examples of the American and French revolutions, as well as moments in Islamic history that demonstrate the struggle of societies based on and in the pursuit of the ideal of excellence. Alatas discusses at length particularly the values and political principles espoused by Saidina Ali, the fourth caliph to Malik al-Ashtar.[15]

Just as how revolutions and struggles, as well as oppression and violence, have occurred throughout human and world history, the existing historical ideal shapes the emergence and development of the ideal of excellence. Aspects of the historical ideal may encompass and be driven by an epoch, or other aspects of it supported by countries and nations, and still other aspects of it move and drive individuals. Alatas emphasizes the last component where he elaborates on the significant influence of the ideal of the excellence on individuals. In drawing the relation between the ideal of excellence, human agency, and leadership, Alatas identifies four categories of leaders. The first consists of figures such as the Islamic caliphs Abu Bakar al-Sadiq, Umar ibn al-Khattab, and Ali ibn Abu Talib, who emphasized the wellbeing of society and typified its expression though their personal lives.[16] The second includes leaders such as Umar Abdul Aziz and Salahuddin al-Ayubi. These leaders, according to Alatas, care for the poor, the ill, the deprived, those in difficulty, and those who are oppressed in their sufferings. These leaders also remember that they will have to answer for their lives in the hereafter.[17]

The third type of leaders and those who hold power and pursue the ideal of excellence in the governance but are cruel and ruthless in their personal lives and dealings towards enemies and individuals outside their circle of friends.[18] Finally, the fourth category of leaders include those who Alatas calls *jadong*, a term he constructs from the words "evil" (*jahat*), "stupid" (*bodoh*), and "arrogant" (*sombong*). Unlike the previous three archetypes of leaders, these individuals imbibe and pursue *cita bencana,* or the "ideal of destruction." These figures do not possess self-dignity, nor purpose and/or vision for society, and

---

14   Ibid, 15.
15   Ibid, 20.
16   Ibid, 30.
17   Ibid, 30–31.
18   Ibid, 35.

they are also violent and cruel. Further, their rule destroys societies and promotes corruption.[19]

In *Cita Sempurna*, Alatas focused on the fundamental question of good and evil. He posed what I would suggest are ethical and social questions. Ethical, because Alatas believed it is the ethics and moral values of an individual, the ethics that one chooses, which shapes one's perspective of life and vision for society, consequently, determining the basis and social order of society. He disagreed that material and economic conditions are the primary factors that underpin and dictate society's level of progress. Instead, the disposition of those in power affect its development.[20] Moral choice, values, and principles compose and guide the ideal of excellence and its practices.

There is also a social component, for the ideal of excellence is built on social philosophy and social knowledge.[21] In the absence of social knowledge, the ideal of excellence cannot be pursued to define the weaknesses and gaps of the human condition. Encapsulated in the ethical and social question is the principle of social justice. Posing the ethical and social question means to ask the characteristics and purpose of such a principle in society. For Alatas, the aim of *cita sempurna* is thus to implement social justice among all groups of society.[22]

3 Malaysia and Iran: The Political Discourses of Commitment and Change

I sought in the previous sections to highlight how Alatas signaled the need for a tradition of political thought or political philosophy, and in his *Cita Sempurna* provided a framework for the identification and subsequent guidance for the development of political thought in society.

In this section, I demonstrate the way in which such a framework can guide critical analysis of political discourses by using the case studies of Malaysia and Iran. I further discuss how this process or discussion can be used as a starting point for us to begin to conceptualize traditions of political thought, or at least explore currents of political perspectives rooted in the historical and trajectories and social conditions of Asian societies.

In my discussion of the two pivotal political discourses – one in Malaysia and one in Iran – I explain how the pursuance of the ideal of excellence is

---

19   Ibid, 40 and 46.
20   Ibid, 46.
21   Ibid, 20.
22   Ibid, 21.

founded upon a historical basis and memory, grounded on the social realities of society, and deployed social knowledge in the form of social analysis and commentary.

4 The Malaysian 'ASAS 50', Iranian Committed Literary Movement, and Memory

The *Angkatan Sasterawan* 50 (ASAS 50), or the Writers Movement of 1950, was a pivotal cultural and political current in Malaysia that pursued the ideal of excellence. Established on August 6th, 1950, the movement sought to employ art and literature as a vehicle through which to promote social change in society. The ASAS 50 adopted the slogan of *Seni untuk Masyarakat* or "Art for Society." Writers, teachers, and journalists, including Mohammed Ariff Ahmad (Mas), Jymy Asmara, Hamzah Hussein, Masuri S.N. Kamaluddin Muhamad (Keris Mas), and Asraf constituted among its early founders and supporters.[23]

ASAS 50 was influenced by cultural and nationalist movements in Indonesia. The radical nationalists and writers in Indonesia had always believed that culture and language were integral parts of political movements for change and revolutions. One of these groups, the Angkatan 45, or Generation of 45, cultural movement took an active part in supporting the 1945 Indonesian revolution against the Dutch.

The founders of the Malaysian ASAS 50 were inspired by the Angkatan 45. It laid an important historical basis for which it became the reference point for struggle and protest, particularly against the British colonizers. The movement rode on the wave of nationalist sentiments and the idealism behind the liberation of the homeland as well as the building of a new and independent nation. Usage of symbolisms and memory occupied a central position in the writings and ideas of its authors. Such tendency developed and continued even after the *Tanah Melayu* or the Malay Peninsular attained independence on August 31, 1957.

One of its most important figures, the writer-poet Usman Awang, used numerous symbolisms and metaphors in his lyrical verses and critical proses. At the same time, memory in the form of remembrance narratives were also incorporated into these writings. Consider for instance his poem, *Jiwa Hamba,* or "Enslaved Spirit" (1949):

---

23   Keris Mas, *The Memoirs of Keris Mas: Spanning 30 Years of Literary Development*, translated by Shah Rezad Ibrahim, Nor Azizah Abu Bakar (Kuala Lumpur: Dewan Bahasa dan Pustaka, 2004), 109–114.

Termenung seketika sunyi sejenak
Kosong di jiwa tiada penghuni
Hidup terasa diperbudak-budak
Hanya suara melambung tinggi

Berpusing roda beralihlah masa
Pelbagai neka hidup di bumi
Selagi hidup berjiwa hamba
Pasti tetap terjajah abadi

Kalau hidup ingin merdeka
Tiada tercapai hanya berkata
Ke muka maju sekata, maju kita
Melemparkan jauh jiwa hamba

Ingatkan kembali kata sakti
Dari bahang kesedaran berapi
Di atas robohan Kota Melaka
Kita dirikan jiwa merdeka.[24]

For the purposes of our discussion, the last stanza is particularly relevant. Usman writes that 'remember again the sacred words, from the heat of flaming consciousness, on the ruins of Kota Melaka, we inaugurate a free spirit.' The term "Kota Melaka" refers to the site of one of the historical kingdoms in the Malay Peninsula. Melaka was an important center of civilization and trade situated in the Malay Archipelago region.

His reference to Melaka points in part to the rich and prosperous political and cultural capital that represented the height of Malay civilization, which occupies a prominent place in Malay and Malaysian classical and modern history. By invoking the memory of Melaka, Usman seeks to draw a connecting line between the strength and eminence of an ancient kingdom to the pursuit

---

24 Usman Awang, *Koleksi Terpilih Sasterawan Negara* (Kuala Lumpur: Dewan Bahasa dan Pustaka, 1995), 4. "In contemplation there is a moment of silence / Empty in spirit without presence / A life of being humiliated / Only the voice that rises high. As the wheel turn so does time shifts / The diverse life on this earth / As long as we live with our spirits enslaved / Eternal domination is maintained. To live freely / Speak not only words / To the front we step forward, we advance / Hurling afar our enslaved spirit. Remember again the sacred words / From the heat of flaming consciousness / On the ruins of Kota Melaka / We inaugurate a free spirit."

of struggle for an independent nation. Such vision can be attained only with a free spirit not subjected to the slave mentality of submission to a foreign power.

The usage of "on the ruins of Kota Melaka, we inaugurate a free spirit" (di atas robohan Kota Melaka, kita dirikan jiwa merdeka) is also referenced from the nationalist Burhanuddin Helmy, who first uttered this call in a conference of the Parti Kebangsaan Melayu Malaya (PKMM) or Malay Nationalist Part of Malaya.[25] Usman Awang had attended the conference as a police constable of the British regime. It was his experience at this conference and his hearing of Burhanuddin's call that he decided to leave the police force to become a writer and reporter involved in the nationalist and radical cultural movement then emerging in the Malay Peninsula, including Singapore. The use of memory in Usman's aesthetic expressions can also be found in his other writings, including "Paddling with Longing on the Straits of Teberau" (Berkayuh Rindu di Selat Teberau, 1983) and *Boestamam* (1983).[26]

These developments were not confined only to Malaysia and Indonesia; a similar literary movement emerged as well in Iran, preceding the 1979 Iranian Revolution. The cultural current employed rhetorical language and distinct symbolisms and took a revolutionary slant. It was a literary movement socially committed to social and political change.[27]

Some of its prominent figures include Jalal Al-e Ahmad (1923–1969), Samad Behrangi (1939–1967), Gholam-Hoseyn Sa'edi (1936–1985), Forough Farrokhzad (1934–1967), Mehdi Akhavan Sales (1929–1990), and Simin Daneshvar (1921–2012).[28] The writer and intellectual, Jalal-e Ahmad, was one of the earliest and important critics of the Pahlavi regime and the West. He famously used the term *gharbzadegi* or "westoxication" as a critique against the West for its embrace of modernity and modernizing tendencies.[29]

He was also against Iran's imitation of the West.[30] For him, modern ideas developed by the West eroded Iranian values. And in doing so, he also opposed

---

25 Zurinah Hassan, *Sasterawan Negara Usman Awang* (Kuala Lumpur: Dewan Bahasa dan Pustaka, 2006), 19–20.

26 Ibid., 24, 92, 95.

27 Kamran Talattof, "Iranian Women's Literature: From Pre-Revolutionary Social Discourse to Post-Revolutionary Feminism," *International Journal of Middle East Studies* (1997): 534; Hamid Dabashi, "The Poetics of Politics: Commitment in Modern Persian Literature," *Iranian Studies* 18, no. 2/4 (1985): 151 and 176.

28 Dabashi, "The Poetics of Politics," 175–176.

29 Hamid Dabashi, *Theology of Discontent: The Ideological Foundation of the Islamic Revolution in Iran* (New York: Routledge, 2017), 76; Hamid Dabashi, *The Last Muslim Intellectual: The Life and Legacy of Jalal Al-e Ahmad* (Edinburgh: Edinburgh University Press, 2021), 142.

30 Dabashi, *Theology of Discontent*, 53, 73.

the Shah and his government for the importation of Western modernity into Iran that harmed and exploited Iranian identity and society. Notwithstanding these views expressed by or associated to Jalal Al-e Ahmad, and readings by scholars on Al-e Ahmad's works and legacy, recently however, Dabashi has called for a critical reappraisal of Al-e Ahmad's thought and writings, including "Westoxication" (*Gharbzadegi*, 1962) and "On the Services and Treasons of the Intellectuals" (*Dar Khedmat va Khiyanat-e Roshanfekran*, 1964–68).[31]

As Dabashi highlighted, the rise of the social critic and intellectual is a recent phenomenon, caused by structural shifts in the social life and economy of society.[32] The emergence of this class in Iran for instance was shaped by factors such as education and exposure to modern ideas and conflicting ideologies. Al-e Ahmad was one of the figures that arose from this process of change. Observing that more traditional classes, such as the religious class, were excluded or did not keep up with changes, while the developing and progressing intellectual class were becoming estranged from its roots, Al-e Ahmad carved out a kind of third tendency or path. Returning to tradition but not exactly entirely disconnected from modern thought, he produced works of various genres ranging from essays to novels and fiction (Dabashi, 2021: 119), such as "By the Pen" (*Nun wa al-Qalam*, 1961), *Gharbzadegi* (1962), "The Curse of the Land" (*Nefrin-e Zamin*, 1967) and *Dar Khedmat va Khiyanat-e Roshanfekran* (1977).[33]

Jalal Al-e Ahmad's ideas and writings carried embedded historical memories. Al-e Ahmad was aware of events such as the 1890–1891 Tobacco Revolt and the Constitutional Revolution of 1905–1911. He knew the immense power that those moments had in potentially informing and steering political movements and change. Al-e Ahmad also utilized religious symbolisms, turning Shi'ism into political narratives. Opposed to Western culture and values that he felt were depraved, the reference to tradition and Shi'i Islam served as a counter to westoxication.[34] The ideas of Al-e Ahmad were shaped by these memories that were then manifested and articulated in his writings. His expressions therefore had history as its basis.

Another figure of the literary movement and consciousness, the vibrant poet Forough Farrokhzad, displayed similar use of aesthetic flair, social criticism and evoking of memories. Consider the opening stanzas of her poem, *Delam Baroyeh Baghcheh Misoozad* or "I Pity the Garden":

---

31   Dabashi, *The Last Muslim Intellectual*, 168.
32   Ibid., 30, 33.
33   Ibid., 31, 119.
34   Ibid., 30, 14, 42.

No one thinks of flowers,
No one thinks of fishes
No one wishes
To believe that the garden is dying
That the garden's heart is swollen in the sun
That the garden's mind is softly, slowly
Emptying of green memories
And the garden's perception seems to be
An abstract thing rotten in the garden's solitude

Our house is lonely
Our house
Yawns
In anticipation of the rainfall of an unknown cloud
And our pond is empty
Inexperienced little stars
Fall to the ground from lofty trees
And from among the pale windows of fish houses
The sound of coughing can be heard at night
Our house is lonely[35]

In the poem, Farrokhzad reflects on the passing of time that has occurred in the country.[36] The reference to the garden that is something elusive and far away alludes to the cultural and material developments that have taken place, and how society has changed. Writers of this social consciousness movement focused on the consequences of transformation and the loss of traditional values.

5   Writers, Committed Literature, Social Reality

Other than the element of historical basis and memory, the commonality of rootedness in social reality also binds the socially committed Malaysian and

---

35   Forough Farrokhzad, *Another Birth: Selected Poems*, translated Ismail Salami (Tehran: Zabankadeh Publications, 1386), 126–133.

36   Ahmad Karimi-Hakkak, "Revolutionary Posturing: Iranian Writers and the Iranian Revolution of 1979," *International Journal of Middle East Studies* 23, no. 4 (Nov 1991): 507–531; Farzaneh Milani, *Word not Swords: Iranian Women Writers and the Freedom of Movement* (Syracuse, NY: Syracuse University Press, 2011), 133–134.

Iranian literary movements. The "art for society" (*seni untuk masyarakat*) slogan of the ASAS 50 in Malaysia espoused the need for writers to reflect the harshness and sufferings of communities as well as the commoner. In Usman Awang's essays and poems, for instance, he expressed the everyday life of the fisherman and farmer in the rural outskirts, laborers and clerks in the city life, and multiracial and multireligious communities in the Malay Peninsula, as well as Malaysia in general.

Keris Mas, a writer and key figure of the ASAS 50 movement, was a discerning and sharp writer of the "short story" genre (*cerpen*). The writings of Keris Mas possessed, among others, a depiction of the far-reaching political and economic changes taking place in Malaysia from before independence to after independence in 1957. One of the other striking themes articulated by Keris Mas relates also to the critiqued of the political class for its neglect of the needs of society. Some of these works include *Salah Pimpin* (False Leadership) (1960), *Kedai Sederet di Kampung Kami* (A Row of Shops in Our Village) (1956), *Mereka tidak Mengerti* (They Do Not Understand) (1959) and *Korban Masyarakat* (Society's Sacrifice) (1948).[37]

The poems of Usman Awang, *Penjual Air Batu* (Ice Seller) (1955) and *Penjual Pisang di Kaki Lima* (Banana Seller on the Sideway) (1958), are distinctive works of Usman showcasing the everyday life in realist form of the ordinary person such as the banana seller who 'sits on the sideway, with two baskets of bananas between her.' This can be found in "Banana Seller on the Sideway." Consider the following parts of the poem:

> Lalu gadis tionghua cheongsam biru
> Pemuda di belakang bergegas melesetkan hujung sepatu
> Penjual pisang tercatuk di kaki lima
> Dua bakul pisang terletak antaranya
> (Melihat sepatu dan betis yang lalu
> dengan jemu bas kutunggu)

• • •

> Berat-berat langkah pengawal jalan bertapak
> Hati penjual pisang sesak berkocak

---

37 Keris Mas, *Kumpulan Cerpen Sasterawan Negara Keris Mas, 1946–1989* (Kuala Lumpur: Dewan Bahasa dan Pustaka, 1991), 333, 762, 794, 831.

He, mana lesen?
Tutup kaki lima, ha?

Manakah rasa yang dapat merasa
Manusia hidup sesamanya, memburu apa?
Ah, bakul pisang sudah diregang
Ibu tua tionghua berbaju ungu menyerah salah
(Pasti anak-anak menanti di rumah)
dalam lori terkepung pengawal, matanya berlinang![38]

The poem tells of an old Chinese lady, a banana seller who sits at the sideway waiting to sell her fruits to customers. However, before she manages to sell anything more than the sum of ten cents, the enforcement authorities arrived. They questioned her, asking for her license of which she does not possess. She however relents and the authorities confiscate her goods. Teardrops form in her eyes as she thinks of her children who wait for her at home. Usman's works stand out for their realistic ordinariness yet insert profound meanings and portrays them in simple language.

The works of the writers of social commitment in Iran are no different, having similar tone and depictions. Simin Daneshvar's "A Persian Requiem"[39] or *Savushun* (1969) is an example of the narration of political and cultural contestations in Iran. Her work presents the different forces in conflict with one another locally and also those from outside, such as with the British involvement in Iran. The struggle between Iran against foreign powers, and the ideological currents contending in society, take place in the background of the struggles and living conditions of the family of Zari.

We are taken through a journey of inner conflict and humanistic struggle, and vivid reliving of the economic and political turmoil in 1940s Iran, narrated through Zari. Daneshvar's writing is moved by social and socialist realism contributing to and reflecting the influential tendency of the time in

---

38   Ibid., 24, 26: "A Chinese lady in a cheongsam walks over / A youth hurries behind slipping on the end of his shoes / The banana seller sits on the sideway / Two baskets of bananas are placed in between / (Watching shoes and limbs passing by / I await the bus with weariness). The heavy footsteps of guards arrive / The heart of the banana seller shakes uneasily. He, where is your license? / Blocking the sideway, ha? Who can feel what others are feeling / Humans living together, what is to be pursued? / Ah, the pulling of the basket of bananas begin / The old Chinese lady in purple confesses guiltily / (For certain the children are waiting at home) / in a truck surrounded by guard, her eyes are filled with tears!"

39   Simin Daneshvar, *A Persian Requiem: A Novel* (New York: G. Braziller, 1992).

Iran.[40] In the novel, the social realist account intensifies when Zari's husband, Yusof, is killed. Daneshvar's *Savushun* is an influential work for students of history and memory, literature and social realism, and social theory.

6 Social Knowledge and the Pursuance of *Cita Sempurna*

Up to this point, I have discussed how the literary movements in Malaysia and Iran embodying the ethos of a social commitment to society and change, which are built on the foundations of a historical base and memory, as well as rootedness to social reality. My explanation is guided by Alatas' *Cita Sempurna*, wherein it highlights the element of a historical ideal. The latter shapes and determines social idealisms and the pursuit for an "ideal society" (*masyarakat sempurna*). Moving on, I seek to identify the third and last foundational feature, social knowledge, which also informed the Malaysian and Iranian literary movements, particularly the ASAS 50 in Malaysia and the socially committed literary movement in Iran. And from this third aspect, tied to memory and reality, seek to revert back to these aspects of Alatas' elaboration of the "ideal of excellence" (*cita sempurna*).

Social knowledge as a reference and tool was central to the values and struggles of the cultural currents and political discourses both in Malaysia and Iran. By social knowledge, I mean the use of social analysis and commentary in understanding and critiquing society and the world. In the cases of Malaysia and Iran, such critique was directed towards the economic, political, and social injustices that prevailed during the period.

In Iran and Malaysia, the literary movements emerged and developed in tandem with the rise of the intellectual and cultural discourses, and political movements. These discourses provided a lens through which to identify the problems of society and its causes. Iranian and Malaysian intellectuals and writers exchanged ideas and theories with other groups, both domestically and regionally, as well as globally. Hence, the ASAS 50 and committed writers' movements are inseparable from the intellectual class and ideological currents. The field of literature, language and the arts, among others, and its practitioners adopted competing intellectual and ideological discourses. And they further became central vehicles that linked the conversion from ideas to political protest and movements, and consequently, social change.

---

40   Talattof, "Iranian Women's Literature," 535.

SYED HUSSEIN ALATAS AND THE QUESTION OF POLITICAL THOUGHT

One of the proponents of the "art for society" (*seni untuk masyarakat*) approach in writing and literature, the Malaysian writer and literary critic Kassim Ahmad (1933–2017), emphasized the need for social analyses and perspectives regarding the critique of injustices and corruption in society. He noted that a work of literature needed to encompass three fundamental components. These are, firstly, the identification of social realities confronted by society, secondly, the articulation of the causes and those responsible for these realities and problems, and thirdly, the call to change the existing social conditions caused by these problems in accordance with moral and humanitarian values, such as social justice, solidarity, and egalitarianism.

One of Kassim's poem, "Poem of Dialogue" (*Sajak Dialog*), although written earlier in 1958, illustrates his critical social approach to writing and politics:

Tenteramlah anak
walaupun kebanjiran sawah kita
hujan ini dari Tuhan
yang mencurah-curah rahmatnya.

Ada siang masakan tiada terang
dengarlah
si katak sudah tiada memanggil lagi
besok hari panas
padi kita akan lepas!

Tidurlah ibu
kita manusia kerdil
siang membanting tulang
malam menanggung bimbang.

Ada besok maka pasti ada suria
aku akan pergi
dengan seribu Jebat si anak tani
kian lama kita mati dalam setia
kali ini kita hidup dalam derhaka![41]

---

41   Kassim Ahmad, *Kemarau Di Lembah* (Kuala Lumpur: Teks Publishing, 1985), 48.
         "Be at peace my child / even if our rice fields are flooded / this rain comes from God / pouring blessings. If there is day how can there be no light / listen / the frogs are again no longer calling / tomorrow will be a warm day / and our paddy will live! Sleep my mother / we are common folk / working slavishly during the day / burdened with worries during

The poem tells of the "common folk" (*manusia kerdil*) whose life is disempowered and lives in poverty, although always hard at work and burdened with worries. For that, the narrator promises to fight to attain change and overcome these abject conditions. 'For too long we have died in loyalty, this time we live in disloyal rebellion' is an iconic phrase in the Malay cultural and literary discourse.

Sajak Dialog and the phrase, which have at times courted controversy due to its subversive and anti-feudal tones, nevertheless expressed Kassim's social thought and his emphasis on the three fundamental components of a work. For him, in carrying out socially based commentary and analysis, knowledge and theories to guide social perspectives can be obtained from the fields of the humanities, sociology, politics, and philosophy.

Social criticism constituted a central facet and structure of the works of the writers in Iran. The Iranian writers of the committed literary movement, if not intellectuals themselves, were also part of a broader intellectual discourses and currents. Jalal Al-e Ahmad, for instance, was himself an intellectual and an early ideologue of the 1979 Iranian revolution.[42] He was part of various political and religious and intellectual organizations at different phases of his life. Al-e Ahmad's usage and popularization of the term *gharbzadegi* is an outcome of those different engagements with diverse theories and philosophies.

Others, such as Forough Farrokhzad, Simin Daneshvar, and Mehdi Akhavan Sales, among others, employed means of social critique and analysis in different degrees in their aesthetic expressions. Part of the social analysis discourse then prevailing included the tension between traditional values and modern ideas, changing social and economic structures, the questioning of authority and traditional centers of power, and the construction of the nation. Observations of those conditions and the questioning of their cause and impacts can be found in their works. Consider Farrokhzad's poem, "Someone who is not like Anyone" (*Kasi keh Mesl-e Hich-kas Nist*), written in 1964:

> I have dreamed that someone is coming
> I have dreamed of a red star
> And my eyelids keep fluttering
> And my shoes keep pairing
> And may I be struck blind

---

the night. If there is tomorrow then brightly will the light shine / I will go / with a thousand Jebat the children of peasants / for too long we have died in loyalty / this time we live in defiance!"

42   Ibid., 30, 41; Ibid., 31, 28.

If I am lying
I have dreamed of that red star
While I was not sleeping
Someone is coming
Someone is coming
Someone else
Someone better

...

Someone is coming
Someone is coming
Someone who is with us in his heart, someone who is with us in his
    breath, and in his voice

Someone whom
We cannot stop from coming
Someone who cannot be handcuffed and sent to prison.[43]

Farrokhzad writes of the existing frictions in Iranian society and advocates for the coming change that is about to occur, brought about by a movement and its leader. She also depicts in this poem the poverty of the people, as well as the violence and oppression of the State. In her poem, Farrokhzad poignantly and passionately expresses the troubles and sufferings of society, and the social commitment to movement and change for Iran.

7 Conclusion: The Struggle for "*Cita Sempurna*" and Constructing a Perspective of Politics

A historical basis and memory, the grounding in social reality and the use of social knowledge, constitute the central and fundamental bases of the literary movements in Malaysia and Iran. These currents of culture and protest articulated the political discourses of commitment and change to reform society for the better. In the union of these three features, their writers sought to defend and attain the moral and humanistic values of justice, freedom, liberation, and

---

43   Talattof, "Iranian Women's Literature," 538; Karimi-Hakkak, "Revolutionary Posturing," 512–513.

equality. For writers such as Usman Awang, Keris Mas, and Kassim Ahmad, the establishment of an independent and sovereign nation was a primary vision of literature. The formation of a just and democratic Malaysian society was only possible through political commitment and writing.

That endeavor for a nation free from domination and exploitation was also a key desire of the Iranian writers of the 1950s to the 1970s in the lead up to the 1979 revolution. In these periods, the literary as well as intellectual movements took part in protest and organizing against the ruling regime. Writers such as Jalal Al-e Ahmad, Gholam-Hoseyn Sa'edi, Forough Farrokhzad, Simin Daneshvar, Mehdi Akhavan Sales, and Sadegh Chubak, together with other thinkers including Ali Shariati and Mahmud Taleghani, among others, articulated their opposition to injustice, poverty, and oppression. In its place, they sought to institute the ideals of social justice and emancipation, as well as structures of an egalitarian politics and economy in Iranian society.

The vision and principles that the Malaysian and Iranian writers sought to articulate and establish are no different from the characteristics and meaning of *cita sempurna,* or the "ideal of excellence" that Syed Hussein Alatas elaborated at length in *Cita Sempurna Warisan Sejarah*. As suggested by Alatas, the movements in Malaysia and Iran were guided by a historical ideal, as well as memory, consciousness of realities and problems, and the use and formulation of knowledge for action.

Based on the discussions of the Malaysian and Iranian literary movements, we can similarly identify and derive the outlines and characteristics of perspectives and traditions, if not philosophy, of political thought that is embedded in the social conditions of their societies and directed towards the human aspirations of its people for a better and just nation and future. Alatas' *cita sempurna* provides a framework that enables us to understand and study political ideologies and discourses in Asia in a systematic and critical manner. Further, it guides us to construct and conceptualize autonomous, relevant and humanistic political philosophies for Asian societies and communities. The work of Syed Farid Alatas on the *Taj al-Salatin*, is similarly another guide and instance of this endeavor to build theory, the nation and the world.[44] It reflects the urgency and necessity to defend and uphold values of equality, social justice, democracy, and humanity, that which Syed Hussein Alatas calls *cita sempurna,* or the "ideal of excellence." In a time where a global pandemic, changes in the world economic order and natural climate are rapidly evolving and

---

44 Syed Farid Alatas, "Anti-Feudal Elements in Classical Malay Political Theory: The Taj al-Salatin," *Journal of the Malaysian Branch of the Royal Asiatic Society* 91, no. 314 (June 2018): 29–39.

intensifying, threatening the security and moral and political fabric of nations and societies everywhere, the need for the study and discourse of political philosophy has never been more important for Malaysia and Asia.

Bibliography

Alatas, Syed Farid. "Against the Grain: Malay Studies and the School of Autonomous Knowledge." *The Edge Weekly*. https://www.theedgemarkets.com/article/against-grain-malay-studies-and-school-autonomous-knowledge (accessed June 7, 2021).

Alatas, Syed Farid. "Anti-Feudal Elements in Classical Malay Political Theory: The Taj al-Salatin." *Journal of the Malaysian Branch of the Royal Asiatic Society*, Vol. 91 (2018), No. 314 (June): 29–39.

Alatas, Syed Farid, and Vineeta Sinha. *Sociological Theory Beyond the Cannon*. London: Palgrave Macmillan, 2017.

Alatas, Syed Farid. *Applying Ibn Khaldun: The Recovery of a Lost Tradition in Sociology*. London; New York: Routledge, 2014.

Alatas, Syed Farid. *Alternative Discourses in Asian Social Science: Responses to Eurocentrism*. Thousand Oaks: Sage Publications, 2006.

Alatas, Syed Hussein. "The Autonomous, the Universal and the Future of Sociology." *Current Sociology*, Vol. 54(1) (2006): 7–23.

Alatas, Syed Hussein. *Cita Sempurna Warisan Sejarah*. Bangi: UKM Press, 2000.

Alatas, Syed Hussein. Intellectual Imperialism: Definition, Traits, and Problems. *Southeast Asian Journal of Social Sciences*, Vol. 28 (2000), No. 2: 23–45.

Alatas, Syed Hussein. *Intellectuals in Developing Societies*. London: Cass, 1977.

Alatas, Syed Hussein. "The Captive Mind and Creative Development." *International Social Science Journal*, Vol. 26 (1974), No. 4: 691–700.

Alatas, Syed Hussein. "The Captive Mind in Development Studies: Some Neglected Problems and the Need for An Autonomous Social Science Tradition in Asia." International Social Science Journal, Vol. 24 (1972), No. 1: 9–25.

Alatas, Syed Hussein. "The Prerequisites of Asian Political Philosophy." In *Moral Vision and Social Critique: Selected Essays of Syed Hussein Alatas*, edited by Azhar Ibrahim Alwee, Mohamed Imran Mohamed Taib, 56–62. Singapore: The Reading Group, 2007.

Anderson, Benedict. "Indonesian Nationalism Today and in the Future." *Indonesia*, No. 67 (April) (1999): 1–11.

Dabashi, Hamid. *The Last Muslim Intellectual: The Life and Legacy of Jalal Al-e Ahmad*. Ediburgh: Edinburgh University Press, 2021.

Dabashi, Hamid. *Theology of Discontent: The Ideological Foundation of the Islamic Revolution in Iran*. New York: Routledge, 2017.

Dabashi, Hamid. "The Poetics of Politics: Commitment in Modern Persian Literature." *Iranian Studies*, Vol. 18 (1985), No. 2/4: 147–188.

Daneshvar, Simin. *A Persian Requiem: A Novel*. New York: G. Braziller, 1992.

Farrokhzad, Forough. *Another Birth: Selected Poems*, translated Ismail Salami. Tehran: Zabankadeh Publications, 1386.

Karimi-Hakkak, Ahmad. "Revolutionary Posturing: Iranian Writers and the Iranian Revolution of 1979." *International Journal of Middle East Studies*, Vol. 23, No. 4 (Nov) (1991): 507–531.

Kassim Ahmad. *Kemarau Di Lembah*. Kuala Lumpur: Teks Publishing, 1985.

Kassim Ahmad. *Dialog Dengan Sasterawan*. Kuala Lumpur: Pena, 1979.

Keris Mas. *The Memoirs of Keris Mas: Spanning 30 Years of Literary Development*, translated by Shah Rezad Ibrahim, Nor Azizah Abu Bakar. Kuala Lumpur: Dewan Bahasa dan Pustaka, 2004.

Keris Mas. *Kumpulan Cerpen Sasterawan Negara Keris Mas, 1946–1989*. Kuala Lumpur: Dewan Bahasa dan Pustaka, 1991.

Milani, Farzaneh. *Word not Swords: Iranian Women Writers and the Freedom of Movement*. Syracuse, New York: Syracuse University Press, 2011.

Talattof, Kamran. "Iranian Women's Literature: From Pre-Revolutionary Social Discourse to Post-Revolutionary Feminism." *International Journal of Middle East Studies* (1997): 531–558.

Usman Awang et al. *Peranan Intelektual*. Petaling Jaya: SIRD, 2016.

Usman Awang. *Koleksi Terpilih Sasterawan Negara*. Kuala Lumpur: Dewan Bahasa dan Pustaka, 1995.

Zurinah Hassan. *Sasterawan Negara Usman Awang*. Kuala Lumpur: Dewan Bahasa dan Pustaka, 2006.

CHAPTER 17

Contributions of Syed Hussein Alatas towards Global Sociology

Habibul Haque Khondker

1 Introduction

In certain areas of life, we are justified in acclaiming the possible contributions of the West. The spread of modern education, modern medicine, modern methods of science, modern methods of combatting natural catastrophes, and the elimination of slavery will go down in Asian history as the incontestable contributions of the West. Whatever the balance is when the results of the interaction between Asia and the West are better documented, one thing is certain: The West has given Asia the methods and insights which are indispensable for the uplifting of the Asian masses towards their humanitarian ideal of a perfect society.[1]

This chapter attempts to achieve the following: First, it provides a framework of global sociology by surveying its development and highlighting the tensions between national and global sociology on the one hand and parochial and universal ambitions of sociology on the other. Second, it reexamines the works of Syed Hussein Alatas with special attention to his contributions to the sociology of development and modernization in the context of that tension. To situate his contributions between the West-centric sociology and what is now known as post-colonial, critical studies that decenter and discard the hegemonic West-centered sociology by a process of "delinking" and the mainstream sociology that has become nominally global as a consequence of the diffusion of knowledge. Syed Hussein Alatas was at the same time a critical thinker and a pragmatist. His steadfast search for truth and uncompromising integrity led him to where evidence and his critical mind took him to. He was not a prisoner of preconceived theoretical and ideological scaffolds. The main argument of the chapter is to delineate Alatas' work as ambivalent, original, and innovative

---

1 Syed Hussein Alatas, *Modernization and Social Change* (Sydney: Angus & Robertson, 1972), 137.

© HABIBUL HAQUE KHONDKER, 2023 | DOI:10.1163/9789004521698_019

where he is critical but not dismissive of the so-called Western sociology and does not go to the extent of espousing the idea of delinking or rejecting the very idea of social science. Rather, his work recognizes the contributions of the European and the Asian masters and thus outlines a credible and practical global sociology. Here, a quotation of Michel Foucault, albeit associated to a mundane context, will reflect Alatas' position as well. Foucault claimed: 'I am no prophet. My job is making windows where there were only walls.'[2] So did Alatas, he removed blinders and opened windows so that the true light of knowledge could remove darkness, whether the darkness was created by the dominant ideology of the west-centered discourse or by self-imposed parochialism. Finally, this chapter posits Alatas as a public intellectual, and as an organic intellectual in the Gramscian sense.

2 A Brief Biographical Prologue

It may be useful to begin with some reminiscence, albeit somewhat self-referential. One fine morning in 1987, I got a call from Professor Syed Hussein Alatas, Head of the Malay Studies Department of the National University of Singapore inviting me to his office for a discussion. Earlier, I had sent him a paper that I wrote, entitled: "How to Think About Corruption?" for a conference. I was advised by one of my sociology colleagues to share the paper with Alatas since he was an authority on that subject. As I walked into his office, I was impressed by his appearance and felt that I was in the presence of Fidel Castro. He wore a Blue Jeans Jacket and pipe in hand, he gave me some good advice asking me to do more empirical work on corruption in Bangladesh and elsewhere. The subject of intellectual dependence and hegemony of the West came up in our discussion as he mentioned that his son and daughter were studying in the United States. 'I need to reeducate them a bit when they return.' I remember him telling me that if he or I wrote a book on American society or the problems of their society, they would laugh at our imperviousness, but when after spending three months an American writer writes a book, say, on Malaysia, that becomes an essential reading. This remark, although presented in a light-hearted manner, conveyed some of his concerns about the imbalance of knowledge, intellectual inequities, and the hegemony of the West-centered

---

2 Michel Foucault, "Foucault's Confession" *PostPhilosophy.* April 23, 2020 https://postphiloso phy.medium.com/foucaults-confession-139f10bcb5c5.

social sciences and intellectual dependence that he was engaged with. These are subjects that Alatas thought deeply and critically over for a long time. In that conversation, I understood that he still believed in rigorous research based on empirical data, that's why he asked me to do more empirical work on corruption, not limiting myself to the conceptualization that my paper addressed. His writings on corruption and various commentaries are not mere theoretical exercises, but rather are works that relied on evidence and data. Alatas sought to put knowledge at the service of humanity; he was not squeamish about progress, he believed in the idea of a better society, a more humane and just society based on fairness. And knowledge, according to him, can play a role in creating that desired society.

I also visited Professor Alatas in Kuala Lumpur when he was serving as the Vice-Chancellor of the University of Malaya. At that time, he was in the middle of some controversy for the right reasons. The University of Malaya as other public institutions in Malaysia at that time was engaged in affirmative action programs to redress historical injustices and disadvantages by assisting ethnic Malays – the so-called *bumiputra* – with favorable considerations concerning hiring and promotions. Although Alatas recognized the rationale of affirmative action – a form of positive discrimination – he was in favor of merit-based appointments, at least, in the universities and other institutions of higher learning. His position was rational because he did not want to endorse a policy of short-term political gain, at the expense of the long-term social cost of compromising with the development of knowledge.

My last meetings with him were in Singapore at Syed Farid Alatas' apartment and our apartment when he came for a visit. I remember during our last meeting he was talking about the sociology of the fool, regretting that much attention has been given to the intellectuals and less on the fools. It is heartening to see Syed Farid Alatas has taken up the task here in this volume.

Sociological knowledge – as scientific knowledge in general – is premised on the ambition of the universalist claims to valid knowledge. Knowledge and universality are intertwined. This is what we can distill from Auguste Comte, Karl Marx, or much earlier sociologist Ibn Khaldun. Ibn Khaldun wanted to provide a universal framework to understand history. In the globalized world, knowledge production, whether in natural or social sciences, has been a global endeavor. Globalization as a process of social and cultural interpenetrations must be seen as a basis for a transcultural explanation of commonality and variations at the societal level. Social knowledge, even though it is produced in a national context, becomes de-territorialized as it becomes part of a global fund of knowledge.

3 Working Definitions

At this point, it may be useful to try to achieve some conceptual clarity. What is sociology? Out of literal scores of definitions, we can pick a couple representing different periods. In the words of Morris Ginsberg: 'In the broadest sense, sociology is the study of human interactions and interrelations, their conditions and consequences.'[3] Decades later, Anthony Giddens defines sociology as 'the study of human social life, groups, and societies. It is a dazzling and compelling enterprise, having as its subject matter our behavior as social beings ... The scope of sociology is extremely wide, ranging from the analysis of passing encounters between individuals in the street up to the investigation of worldwide social processes.'[4] The micro and the macro perspectives in sociology were foreseen by Raymond Aron who stated: 'Sociology, the science of the social, may just as well be the science of the microscopic relationships between two people on the street or three dozen people in a military or academic group, as the science of society as a whole.'[5]

To discuss global sociology, we explore the origin and spread of sociology in Europe, starting in France and its dissemination in England and Germany and later in the United States, where it flowered to become a multi-layered discipline. In the late nineteenth century under the colonial project, and especially in the early twentieth century social sciences in general and sociology, in particular, were being embraced by national governments in Japan, China, and Egypt. In the mid-twentieth century under the auspices of the United Nations Educational and Cultural Organization (UNESCO), sociology was promoted in many so-called developing countries.

Following the critique of the hegemonic western knowledge and the attempted indigenization of knowledge, we examine the challenges and promises for the rise and spread of global sociology.

4 Sociology as an Atlantic Project

In the mainstream discussion of the origin of sociology, the 1830s is viewed as the birth decade of sociology more as a title rather than a full-fledged academic field. It was in volume II of Auguste Comte's Positive Philosophy that sociology appears in 1838. Comte having mapped all the fields of knowledge

---

3 Morris Ginsberg, *Sociology* (London: Oxford University Press, 1934/1963), 7.
4 Anthony Giddens, *Sociology* (Cambridge: Polity Press, 1989), 4.
5 Raymond Aron. *Main Currents in Sociological Thought. Vol. 1.* (New York: Pelican, 1965), 15.

and proposing holistic knowledge wanted a science of society that would follow the logic, epistemology, and ambitions of natural science. He wanted a science of society that he initially called "social physics," which would discover the laws of society, as physics discovers the laws of nature of the universe. Comte elevated sociology to the queen of sciences, placing it on a hierarchy of knowledge that begins with biology.

Sociology, in the words of its putative founder, August Comte (1798–1857), is both a science of society and humanity. The other and much older founder of sociology, Ibn Khaldun (1332–1406), also envisioned sociology as a universal social science. Following these leads, it is important to examine its trajectory of development into a global sociology and the challenges it faces around the world. One of the sources of the challenge is that the world is unequal, not only politico-economically but also intellectually. The hegemony of the West in the creation and dissemination of knowledge superimposed on material inequality poses a huge challenge for the creation of a global sociology, a social science that can address the problems of common humanity. This chapter explores the rise of sociological discourse and its spread across societies, first in Western Europe as an academic discipline in the late nineteenth century and its spread to the United States, where it was nurtured since the early twentieth century. Sociology evolved as a discipline in the non-Western world as higher education expanded in the early twentieth century and was promoted by UNESCO to several countries in the South in the middle of the twentieth century. Sociology faced challenges as an academic discipline both as a pedagogical subject in the higher educational institutions as well as a research program in various countries in the global South. The chapter also explores the possibility of bridging the two competing demands as well as movements of universalizing and indigenizing sociology. This chapter argues that "global sociology," which supersedes and synthesizes "national sociologies," provides a framework for incorporating both universal tenets of sociology and the programmatic concerns of indigenized sociology. Global sociology provides a bridge between societies across the globe promising to engage with the growing malaise and despair emanating from a variety of interlinking crises of global scope.

Launching it as a scientific field, Comte ended up with a call for sociology that would be more like a universal religion, a secular religion for modern society. He was a humanist who sought to establish a religion of humanity. Universalism or universal claims to knowledge is the ambition of all the fields of scientific knowledge. Sociology did not want to be an exception.

Comte's program did not take off; his ambiguity towards the end of his life was not helpful either, although his initial program of sociology was sound. Comte sought to see two branches of sociology: social statics, which would examine the structure of society, wherein the main problem would be social stability; and social dynamics, a branch that would explore social transformation. Despite the soundness of the program, the field which eventually emerged as an autonomous field of inquiry and a subject to be taught at the university had to wait for Emile Durkheim, who launched sociology on a firmer scientific program. Durkheim's success owes to his intellectual position. As a specialist of pedagogy and a philosopher, Durkheim laid out not only the program of sociology on the solid scientific ground but also undertook several important sociological studies to show the efficacy of this distinct field. Durkheim, in his *The Division of Labor in Society* (1893), argued that social transformation was not just a materialist economic process, but also a moral process. Terms such as "moral density" were sociological. His sociology was in opposition to economics and psychology. Economics as a field tends to either ignore or subsume sociology in its fold by denying the autonomy of society, a theme clearly stated by late Lady Margaret Thatcher's pronouncement, "there is no society." Durkheim argued that the market or economy was socially embedded. I believe that at Oxford, Mrs. Thatcher skipped her lessons in Durkheim or else she would not have made that statement.

The other discipline that in some sense overlaps with sociology, or an important part of sociology, was psychology, more specifically, social psychology. If sociology is the study of society, and if society, in the final analysis, is composed of people, in some sense psychology can double as sociology. Durkheim showed in his research on suicide that causal relations cannot be simply reduced to psychology. One can find certain important patterns in regard to suicide. Durkheim was not interested in suicide per se, he was more interested in examining the suicide rate, which is a collective phenomenon, not a purely psychological one. His thesis was that psychological explanations can be supplemented by a social explanation of suicide. He related the suicide rate to the degree of social solidarity. In one case, when solidarity is fractured, one type of suicide – egoistic suicide – can rise. In another type, when there is excessive solidarity, people do not see themselves as being separate from society or the collective, leading to suicide on behalf or in the interest of collectivity. In order words, excessive social integration can be a cause of suicide. The third type is anomic suicide, caused by major social disruption.[6] His research put the program of sociology in terms of its contents and methods on a sound basis.

---

6 Emile Durkheim, *Suicide, A Study in Sociology,* ed. J.A. Spaulding and G. Simpson. London: Routledge, 1897.

Sociology emerged first in Europe and then migrated to the United States and other parts of the world. In the late 19th century, it arrived in the US as it also reached China and Japan. India was a late start, wherein political economy dominated thanks to James Mill and his illustrious son John Stuart Mill. British universities were also slow to embrace sociology. The major universities, Oxford and Cambridge, did not have a sociology program until quite late. One historian of British sociology commented: "Before 1950 sociology scarcely existed" in Britain.[7] In the Oxbridge setting, anthropology was solidly entrenched. Anthropology was a handmaiden of colonialism and thus was more acceptable and useful. Sociology, perhaps in the conservative British academe, was seen as an "upstart." An upstart discipline was embraced in an upstart society, like in the US. Again, Harvard was slow to accommodate this field even until the end of the first world war. In the post-war Harvard, Pitirim Sorokin, a Russian émigré in the University of Minnesota, where he taught sociology, moved to Harvard. Talcott Parsons, a doyen of US sociology, was educated at London School of Economics (1924–25) after his undergraduate training at Amherst College in 1924. Then he went to study at Heidelberg, Germany, and received his doctorate in 1927. He became acquainted with the works of Max Weber in Germany, where Weber taught and died just 5 years before the arrival of Parsons. Parsons translated Weber's famous *The Protestant Ethic and the Spirit of Capitalism*. At LSE, Parsons was exposed to the ideas of Durkheim and other social anthropologists such as Bronislaw Malinowski and scholars such as L.T. Hobhouse.

As far as anthropology is concerned, its colonial lineage can be easily established. The anthropological field was a handmaiden of colonialism. For Talal Asad, anthropological knowledge was part of the expansion of Europe's power.[8] The complicity of sociological knowledge with power cannot be ruled out either, but those colonial links are not as evident. There are, at least, three narratives of the origin of sociology in the West.

First, sociology has been viewed as a child of the Enlightenment. The discipline after a prolonged period of gestation in the debates and writings of the Enlightenment philosophers arose in French academia. Hence, the contributions of Voltaire, Montesquieu, and Rousseau are considered precursors to sociology. Sociology in this view emerged as responses to Enlightenment

---

7 A. H. Halsey, *A History of Sociology in Britain: Science, Literature and Society*. Oxford Scholarship Online, 2004.

8 Talal Asad, "Afterword: From the History of Colonial Anthropology to the Anthropology of Western Hegemony," in *Colonial Situation: Essays on the Contextualization of Ethnographic Knowledge*, ed. George Stocking. Madison, WI: University of Wisconsin Press, 1991.

philosophy. This line of argument continued in the presentation of sociology as an attempt to understand modernity.

Second, sociology was viewed as an offspring of the revolutions of the late 18th century: the industrial revolution, the American revolution (1776), and the French revolution (1789). The disruptions of society and the changes that began were unsettling, and thus needed to be understood. The idea of social order came to dominate the thoughts of early sociologists such as Auguste Comte. For Comte, social progress must be based on social order. This view became the dominant discourse since Comte, which often explains a conservative bias in sociology. Additionally, sociology is often viewed as an attempt to deal with the Hobbesian problem of social (dis)order.

The third narrative viewed sociology as a conservative response to nineteenth-century radicalism and a response to Marxism, in the words of Irving Zeitlin (1969). Zeitlin counterposed the two prominent early sociologists, Max Weber and Emile Durkheim, as attempting to respond to Marx's critique of capitalist society. In the words of Albert Salomon, Weber became a sociologist after 'a prolonged and intense debate with the ghost of Karl Marx.'[9]

Sociology has been a discourse riven by competing schools and paradigms. Raymond Aron presented at least three distinct traditions of sociology from the origin of his discipline. A liberal tradition, which treated the political sphere as autonomous and developed political sociology. Here, Aron enlists Montesquieu and Tocqueville. The second school follows from Auguste Comte to Emile Durkheim, who underplayed politics as well as economics in relation to society. In other words, they look at society as being autonomous with an emphasis on consensus. Ginsburg stated in the 1930s that 'Sociology may be said to have arisen as an extension of the field of political inquiry to cover other institutions than the state, for example, the family, or the forms of property and other elements of culture and civilization such as morals, religion art, regarded as social products and seen in their relations to each other.'[10] The third school, according to Aron, was the Marxist school of sociology.[11] Of the three schools, Aron remarked, the 'Comtist school is optimistic, with a tendency to complacency; the political school is cautious, with a tinge of skepticism; and the Marxist school is utopian ...'[12]

---

9 Albert Saloman, quoted in Irving Zietlin, *Ideology and the Development of Sociological Theories.* (Inglewood, NJ: Prentice-Hall, 1968), 111.

10 Ginsberg, *Sociology*, 25.

11 Aron. *Main Currents in Sociological Thought*, 257–258.

12 Ibid., 260.

All these narratives are present today with several offspring of their own. George Ritzer (1980) rightly calls sociology a "multi-paradigm" science.[13] Sociologists today agree that plurality in sociology is a sign of strength rather than weakness. There are several narratives or approaches to the subjects that sociologists are interested in, and no one tries to synthesize all these narratives into a grand narrative. The ambition of a grand theory is absent today. In the post-war development of sociological theories in the US, we saw the last great attempt to produce a synthetic grand theory of social action in the contributions of Talcott Parsons. The grand theory provided an action framework that was criticized by Alvin Gouldner and others. Gouldner's *The Coming Crisis of Western Sociology* (1970) was a critique of Parsonian sociology and its dominance of American sociology. The leftist critique inspired by various strands of Marxism came to hold a strong position in American sociology. Under these onslaughts, the so-called consensus over the structural-functional paradigm came to an end. While the rise of Marxist sociology was one response, the other response was the rise of interpretative sociology. The shift was from an abstracted macro to micro. In the late 1970s and 1980s, a plethora of fashionable sociology – post-modernist sociology – with French connections, won the hearts and minds of many in American sociology and through them other parts of the world as well.

5   Globalization of Sociology

To understand how sociology was transplanted to other parts of the world we need to dwell on the larger political context of that period. During the Cold War, it was a widely shared view that the world was split on an ideological line: Capitalist versus Socialist. The two worlds were different not only as politico-economic systems but also in terms of the production and distribution of systems of knowledge. The Bourgeoisie West had sociology; the socialist world had historical materialism, which allegedly provided a scientific account of society, its historical development, and its future trajectory. For Bukharin and the other Marxist intellectuals, knowledge, especially about society, was not disinterested and was linked to class interests. Such class-specific relativistic understanding of social knowledge production retreated in the post-Cold War world but was replaced by a new form of relativism ushered in by post-modernism. This new genre of relativism offered multiple interpretations of

---

13   George Ritzer, *Sociology: A Multi-Paradigm Science*. Boston: Alyn and Bacon, 1980.

social reality as well as the rise of sociology. The conventional wisdom, it was argued, needed to be dismantled. While postmodernism as an intellectual trend in sociology may be passé, the idea of a plurality of interpretations about the practice of sociology across societies has gained wider acceptance.

Should one look at the practice of sociology within the disciplinary matrix or consider sociology as a mode of examining society as social cognition? In fact, for C. Wright Mills, one need not be a sociologist to be equipped with sociological imagination as the reverse is equally possible. It is thus useful to recognize the multiplicity of approaches and divinations in the ability for societal self-reflection. In Bengal, India, for example, writers such as Sarat Chandra Chattapodhay (1876–1938) had an incisive sociological mind. His novels, mostly "thick descriptions" about the complexities of rural society, the tension between traditionalist and the modernist ideas and views that his characters represented, were sociological in the broad sense of the term. In one of his speeches, he even mentioned sociology. Calcutta University offered sociology as a subject in such departments as philosophy and later economics in the early twentieth century. One of Sarat Chattapodhay's novels is titled *Palli Samaj* (1916) or literally, "Village Society." Such writers and men and women of letters with a sensitive understanding of the affairs of society, I believe, could be found in other societies as well. The sociological imagination was neither restricted to sociologists, as Mills indicated, nor to any geo-cultural region. As an outgrowth of modernity, reflexivity and sociological imagination spread globally.

However, in discussing sociology as a profession we need to limit our attention to institutional sociology as it was developed in the European and North American academia before spreading to the other parts of the world. Sociology as a subject was taught in Calcutta (Kolkata) at the turn of the 20th century, but as a self-conscious intellectual field it flourished only after India's independence in 1947. The first Indian sociologist to get published in the western sociological journals was perhaps, Radhakamal Mukerjee of the University of Lucknow, who published three articles in the *American Journal of Sociology* in the 1930s. Indian sociology since the 1970s has been the site of debates over indigenizing sociology. Indian sociologists did not reject the key concepts such as class and social stratification but sought to ground them in local contexts.[14]

Japanese sociology remained quite faithful to the mainstream European sociological traditions in the 19th century and the American sociological

---

14   Habibul Haque Khondker, "Globalization and Sociological Practice," in *ISA e—Symposium, International Sociological Association* 3 (March 2006): 55–61.

paradigms and personalities in the 20th century. Even American sociology, where as a discipline it developed most comprehensively since the establishment of the first sociology department in 1892 at the University of Chicago, the impact of European sociology was pronounced, albeit selective and serendipitous. American sociologists at the early stage were not influenced so much by Marx, Durkheim, Pareto, or Weber as by Spencer and Simmel. The Spencerian legacy was most visible in the Social Darwinist movement in American sociology. Several American sociologists and other social scientists studied in Berlin, where they came under the spell of Simmel's influence. One of them was Robert Park. Albion Small, who founded the sociology department at the University of Chicago, sent three students to Berlin to study under Simmel. He also translated several of Simmel's articles in the *American Journal of Sociology* which he edited.[15]

In both Japan and China, Sociology began its career in the late 19th century. Japan developed a theoretical tradition reflecting first the European and later the US sociological traditions. The word "society" (*Shakai*) appeared in Japan in 1876 and "sociology" (*Shakaigaka*) in 1878.[16] The works of the British social philosopher Herbert Spencer were translated into Japanese in the early 1880s. Japan's sociology bore the influence of European, especially German and French, influence. As such, there was a greater emphasis on social theory rather than social research.[17] Today there are serious Parsonians in Japan, disciples of Blumer in China, and Foucauldian almost everywhere. Sociology reached China at the end of the 19th century. The first book with sociology in its title was published in 1903 with the translation of Spencer's *Principles of Sociology* by Yen Fuh.[18] Sociology in China became effervescent in the 1930s and 1940s. In the wake of the Communist Revolution, as sociology was banned in 1952, Chinese sociologists of the day had three options: Some fled the country; those who remained either reinvented themselves as historians or demographers or something less controversial; the third option was to be in the good graces of the regime, highlighting the role of sociology in the post-revolutionary society. The reputation of Fei Hsiao Tong became somewhat tarnished for his lending support to the revolution. One of the émigré sociologists from China, C.K.

---

15   Donald Levine, E. B. Carter, and E. M. Gorman. "Simmel's Influence on American sociology." *American Journal of Sociology* 81, no. 4 (1976): 816.

16   Kunio Odaka, "Japanese Sociology: Past and Present," *Social Forces* 28, no. 4. (May 1950): 400–407.

17   Jesse Frederick Steiner. "The Development and Present Status of Sociology in Japanese Universities," *American Journal of Sociology* XLI, no. 6 (1936): 707–722.

18   Pen-Wan Sun, "Sociology in China," *Social Forces* 27, no. 3 (March 1949): 247–251.

Yang, a famed family sociologist took refuge in the University of Pittsburgh. Following the opening of China, especially with Deng Xiao Peng's initiative of reforms, sociology was revived in China in which the University of Pittsburgh played an important role alongside other American institutions. However, China wanted to develop sociology with Chinese characteristics.[19]

Sociology in Egypt was introduced in 1925 at the National University in Cairo, later renamed Egyptian State University and as Foud I University. In 1942, sociology was introduced in Alexandria based in Farouk I University and in Ibrahim Pasha the Great University in Cairo in 1950.[20] The first sociological dissertation was written by Mansur Fahmi at the Sorbonne under the supervision of sociologically inclined philosopher, Lucien Levy Bruhl. Fahmi, a brilliant law lecturer, was sent to study philosophy in Paris. His dissertation entitled, "The Condition of Women in the Tradition and Evolution of Islam," which he defended on December 1, 1913, created some controversy in his native land. Fahmi, upon his return from France, lost his university job and was banned from government services.[21] Another prominent literary intellectual of Egypt, Taha Husayn, wrote his doctoral thesis on the social philosophy of Ibn Khaldun under the renowned sociologist Emile Durkheim in 1917.[22] Apart from Durkheim, the well-known orientalist Paul Casanova was the cosupervisor of Taha's thesis.[23] According to Sharky, the Sorbonne in those days was dominated by the intellectual ideas of Georg Simmel, Auguste Comte, and Emile Durkheim.[24]

Mona Abaza laments that despite such an early start of sociology in Egypt, it did not develop as it did in other contexts. Abaza quotes Saad Ibrahim, 'As a formal academic discipline, sociology was first offered in the newly established (1908) secular Egyptian University in 1913 only 20 years after the University of Chicago (1892), 7 years after the University of Paris (1906), and 6 years after the London School of Economics and Political Science. Indeed, Cairo's Egyptian University introduced sociology ahead of most Western European Universities,

---

19   Khondker, "Globalization and Sociological Practice," 55–61.
20   S.A. Huzayyin and H. El-Saaty. "On the Teaching of Sociology, Social Philosophy and Anthropology in Egypt" *UNESCO Report*. Paris: March 4, 1952.
21   Donald Malcolm Reid, *Cairo University and the Making of Modern Egypt*. Cambridge: Cambridge University Press, 2002.
22   Omina El Sharky, *The Great Social Laboratory: Subjects of Knowledge in Colonial and Post-Colonial Egypt*. Stanford: Stanford University Press, 2007.
23   Reid, *Cairo University and the Making of Modern Egypt*.
24   Sharky, *The Great Social Laboratory*.

which did so only after World War I. Scandinavian universities had no professorships of sociology until after World War II.'[25]

Sociologists on the periphery who were trained in the sociological centers in Europe or North America brought home respective traditions. India's development in social anthropological traditions marked a distinctive English anthropological influence as contemporary Chinese sociology bears an American sociological influence. In some countries, the European heritage gave way to American influences, which by the last quarter of the twentieth century reached various corners of the world. US political hegemony had an ally in her academic preeminence. However, such an equation of military power with intellectual power is neither automatic nor everlasting. Contrary to Wilbert Moore's claim that sociology became remarkably international, Oromaner demonstrated by analyzing citations that the internationalization of sociology was tantamount to the Americanization of sociology.[26] Before accepting the thesis of American hegemony and issuing calls for "provincializing" American sociology, we need to deconstruct, that is, dismantle "American sociology." There is no American sociology; there are multiple tendencies – divergent sociologies – within American sociology. It would be a mistake to equate Immanuel Wallerstein with Charles Murray (co-author of *The Bell Curve*) just because in a spatial sense and by citizenship, both are American sociologists. It would be an ecological fallacy of great proportion. Besides, American mainstream sociology as practiced in the United States today remains largely provincial. The critique of American sociology being not global enough may be seen as a sign of assertiveness in the periphery. This assertiveness is more nuanced and different from the earlier call for indigenization. The indigenization movement of the 1970s and 80s was an early expression of that intellectual nationalism that is now giving way to a call for (genuinely) globalizing sociology.

The ebbing of the national sociology movement and methodological nationalism has ushered in a new possibility of comprehensive and meaningful globalization of sociology and the rise of global sociology. Yet, the new dividing lines are not so much geo-cultural but are based on disciplinary specialisms.

---

25   Mona Abaza. "Social Sciences in Egypt: The Swinging Pendulum between Commodification and Criminalization" Conference on the Council of National Association of International Sociology, ISA, Taipei, 2009.

26   Wilbert E. Moore, "Global Sociology: The World as a Singular System" *American Journal of Sociology* 71, no. 5 (March 1966): 475–482; Mark Jay Oromaner, "Comparison of Influentials in Contemporary American and British Sociology: A Study in the Internationalization of Sociology," *The British Journal of Sociology* 21, no.3 (September 1970): 324–332.

For example, a Singaporean medical sociologist will have more in common with an Australian medical sociologist than with a colleague working in a separate field of specialization next door. Internet and modern telecommunication and frequency of international meetings and conferences have made such interconnected global clusters a reality. Specialism and professionalism have gone hand in hand, which has the potential of undermining the role of sociologists as public intellectuals. The paradox is: to claim intellectual legitimacy one cannot downplay the importance of professionalism and the global connectivity it entails, yet in the short-term, it might lead to the depoliticization of sociology. In the long-term, however, a call for global or transnational public sociology may usher in a new and comprehensive revaluation of the role of sociology and sociologists.

6   Praxis, Practice and Sociological Practice

What does sociological practice mean? How has sociological practice been affected by the forces of globalization? Are sociological practices like sociological theories and concepts in flux as a result of globalization? Praxis as a concept has a strong Marxist flavor. Theory derives from praxis, which is not just practice but a reflexive action. Practice in the sense of Bourdieu has a similar connotation where the subjective and the objective remain intermingled. Such a nuanced understanding is not what we are aiming for here. By sociological practice, we will restrict its meaning to the practice of sociology as an intellectual discipline as well as the practice of sociology as a profession.

The sociological practice involves minimally teaching sociology and conducting research that sociologists would recognize as sociological. The broader meaning, however, refers to the public role of sociology as a discipline and the wider responsibility of sociologists as agents of change in society. Sociologists can be social reformers or at least social critics. The reformist ambition in sociology was pronounced in the writings of Auguste Comte, the putative founder of modern sociology. Comte's call for the religion of humanism was tilted in favor of sociology as a religion. Now with the theological ambition out of the way, sociology continues to cherish the ambition of becoming a moral science and not just a science of morality as Durkheim would like it to be. It is, thus, not surprising that some sociologists tend to identify Adam Smith as one of the founders of sociology. Here, Smith, the author of *The Theory of Moral Sentiments* (1759), not the *Causes of the Wealth of Nations* (1776) gets preeminence.

For sociology to be relevant to the needs of society, it is important to acknowledge the social role of sociology. At the abstract level, both sociology and sociologists can be social commentary or social critics, or at a more mundane level, a sociologist is someone who can be gainfully employed because of the value placed on the discipline. For example, in Bangladesh, with the remarkable proliferation of Non-Governmental Organizations (NGOs) – many with western links – sociology graduates became suddenly employable, which adds to the prestige of sociology as a discipline. The employers in NGOs preferred sociology graduates who with methodological skills were competent in carrying out social research.

In Singapore, sociology graduates found employment in various government departments ranging from housing to community development. Many sociology graduates had better research skills that could be tapped by the employers in carrying out program-specific research. Thus, sociology continues to be a popular subject for students in Singapore. Sociology is thriving in many developing countries when it seems to be in decline in many advanced countries.[27]

Some sociologists accuse sociology, an archetypical social science, as a prisoner of the nation-state. The definitions as well as the boundaries of society, which sociology seeks to study, often overlap with those of the nation-state. The definitions as well as the boundaries of society, which sociology seeks to study, often overlap with those of the nation-state. Anthony Giddens and Immanuel Wallerstein have both lamented that sociology has been the study of modern nation-states.[28] And they have since made bold efforts at rectifying that lacunae. Roland Robertson and other protagonists of globalization discourse since the late 1970s have redefined the scope of sociology as the social scientific study of the global processes.[29] Ulrich Beck has explicitly called for the development of new concepts to capture the new realities of interconnectedness, plurality, multi-locality, and cosmopolitanism.[30]

---

27 Habibul Haque Khondker, "Sociology in Singapore: Global Discourse in Local Context," *Soziologie, Journal of German Sociological Association* 4 (2001): 5–18.

28 Anthony Giddens, *Beyond Left and Right*. Cambridge: Polity Press, 1996; Immanuel Wallerstein, Immanuel. "From Sociology to Historical Science," *The British Journal of Sociology* 51, no. 1 (2000): 25–35.

29 Roland Robertson, *Globalization Theory*. London: Sage, 1992.

30 Ulrich Beck. "The Cosmopolitan Perspective: Sociology of the Second Age of Modernity," *The British Journal of Sociology* 51, no. 1 (2000): 79–105.

7 Sociology and Globalization

Globalization, though it means many things to many people, is one of the master processes of our time. Globalization as a field in sociology is a legatee of the macro-sociological interests and development. The study of globalization addresses the connectivity of broad processes of technological, economic, political, cultural interrelationships. Whether one looks at the economic, cultural, or media connectivity worldwide, one has to take a much broader understanding of society and social institutions. Sociology focuses its analytical lenses on the flows and processes in society whether at the local, national, or global levels. In other words, sociology has a genuine claim over the field of globalization.

Globalization as a phenomenon of societal and cultural interactivity and connectivity, now generally agreed, is an age-old process but as a concept in social science has a relatively short history.[31] The word global has kept cropping up in various social science literature as well as popular books since the 1960s. The clearest exposition was in the writings of Marshall McLuhan who popularized the phrase "global village."[32]

Globalization as a concept in social science has a short history. It was first used as a book title only in 1990 (as far as the US Library of Congress catalog reveals). A book titled *Globalization, Knowledge, and Society* (edited by Martin Albrow and Elizabeth King) was published drawing on the essays published in various issues of International Sociology the journal of International Sociological Association (1986–1990). Some of the journal articles contained globalization as a phrase in the titles in the 1980s and even earlier.[33] One could even claim that the first social science text that dealt with the subject of globalization was *The Communist Manifesto* (1848). One could even argue that Ibn Khaldun (1332–1406), the author of *Prolegomenon to the Universal History* was

---

31 Nayan Chanda. *Bounded Together*. New Haven: Yale University Press, 2008.

32 Marshall McLuhan. *Understanding Media*. London: Routledge and Kegan Paul, 1964.

33 See Wilbert E. Moore, "Global Sociology: The World as a Singular System," *American Journal of Sociology* 71, no. 5 (March 1966): 475–482; John. W. Meyer, "The World Polity and the Authority of the Nation-State," in *Studies of the Modern World System*, ed. A. Bergesen. New York: Academic Press, 1980; Roland Robertson, "Religion, Global Complexity and the Human Condition," in *Absolute Values and the Creation of the New World, Vol. 1.* New York; International Cultural Foundation, 1983; Roland Robertson, "Interpreting Globality," in *World Realities and International Studies Today.* Glenside, PA: Pennsylvania Council on International Education, 1983; Roland Robertson. *Globalization Theory.* London: Sage, 1992.

the real claimant of the credit. Globalization as a social process is old and has a much longer history. Many writers have traced the early globalizing processes in the dissemination of religion and culture, interactions of people, groups, communities through trade and commerce from ancient times.

Sociology has been traditionally defined as the study of society. And as the boundaries of society have expanded from the local community, through states to global society, sociology has become the study of the global society. This is a good illustration of how ideas, knowledge, and (social) sciences expand with the changes and expansion of realities. Sociology, it is often said, deals with social life. All social sciences deal with social life or its various aspects. It is difficult to conceptualize social as a singular or delimited category. In sociology, there are two meanings of the word "social." Social used in the sense of Immanuel Wallerstein or for that matter Karl Marx encompasses technology, economy, politics, and culture. Sociology is interested in the understanding of these broad processes, especially at their interrelatedness.

There is, however, a narrow meaning of social which is often equated with the social system or what some people call societal. Here society is an abstract system of social relations, a web or network of social relations. Following Talcott Parsons (and before him, Durkheim), some social scientists sought to view sociology as the scientific study of society. I put the stress on "scientific" because one of the goals of science is to define one's field narrowly so that specialized and predictable knowledge can be produced and accumulated. Sociologists with a positivistic bent of mind were quite happy with the narrow definition of sociology, hence the delimited conceptualization of society in the sense of the social system. In this formulation, the field of study of economics is the economic system; the field of political science is the political system, and so on. All social sciences could live happily in a world of segregated systems of knowledge. However, a large number of sociologists, having been dissatisfied with this narrow conceptualization of society, sought to view society and the scope of sociology broadly. They also found the earlier compartmentalization unnecessary, unproductive, and overly abstract. All these so-called subsystems interact. Albert Hirschman called for the need to trespass into each other's domains. The rise of macro-sociology is a clear response to the attempt to overcome a delimited view of sociology. Barrington Moore, Immanuel Wallerstein, Charles Tilly, Theda Skocpol, and others have looked at society in the broadest sense of the term. That inspiration came from Marx, Weber, and later Braudel and other social historians. Bryan Turner has argued that sociology has been about the "social," which did not quite equate with national society.[34] The "social" could easily refer to the global society and not be limited to the national society.

If sociology has to forego its claim over globalization as a field of study, it will mean a major capitulation, a truly regressive step towards objectivist, scientistic sociology, and a return to what C. Wright Mills called "abstracted empiricism." Or worse, sociology becomes a residual discipline to pick up areas left unattended by other social sciences. Sociology can then be asked to relinquish its claim to study society because other branches of social sciences do study aspects of society. For example, institutional economists deal with social structure and cultural values to explain economic processes and market behaviors. Political scientists, such as Robert Putnam, have done important sociological studies on political processes. Such fields as political sociology, illustrate the crossover of political science and sociology all the time. Social sciences are tasked to analyze society in all its various aspects and constellations.

Given the long-standing relationship between sociology and globalization, I would submit that sociology as a discipline should be the main discipline for the study of globalization, a master process in human society. This does not preclude the claims of other disciplines to the subject of globalization. Rather, it reminds us of the importance of each field's autonomy to venture out and explore using its traditions and conceptual frameworks.

Globalization impacts sociology and the practice of sociology by presenting new challenges. Globalization created sociology or made sociology globalized. Sociologists as professionals, creatures of globalization, a multifaceted process, stand in opposition to the downside of globalizations. Many sociologists stand up against the adverse effects of neoliberal globalization – the miseries, poverty, and violence – but in their struggle affirm globalization by invoking rationality and a common humanity.

Sociology as the most abstract of social sciences needs to be public philosophy.[35] The moral concerns must be brought back to the center stage of sociologists' concern. A social science concerned with the entire society has to be historical and philosophical. The focus on history will ground social science locally (but not at the expense of the global); while the philosophical orientation will strengthen universality, which is under attack from both religious and neoliberal fundamentalists.

---

34   Bryan Turner, "Classical Sociology and Cosmopolitanism: A Critical Defence of the Social," *The British Journal of Sociology* 57, no. 1 (2006): 133–151.

35   Robert Bellah, R. Madsen, W.M. Sullivan, A. Swidler, and S. Tipton. *Habits of the Heart.* New York: Perennial Library edition, 1986.

It is in this context Syed Hussein Alatas's work can be read as a contribution to both autonomous sociology and global sociology as Maia has argued.[36] Alatas uses the so-called western sociology as a starting point to formulate the problem of the gap between theoretical knowledge and empirical reality. Alatas stood against the dominant western position, prevalent in the academia, which claims that theoretical research is a prerogative of western scholars, and that their theories should be used to understand and explain the empirical realities of the non-western societies. Instead, Alatas argues that non-Western societies should devote themselves to the development of concepts and theories. In his arguments, Alatas does not propose an indigenous epistemology or the epistemology of the South.[37] He does not quarrel with the notion of a universal epistemology that can produce divergent theories. This position is pragmatic and more tenable than a wholesale repudiation of so-called western epistemology.[38] This is not the place for a critical engagement with the contributions of Walter Mignolo or Boaventura de souse Santos except to suggest that ideas such as cognitive empire may be uplifting or attractive to the free-floating intellectual class, but such radical relativism has both serious intended and unintended consequences in the real societies encompassing the Global South and the Global North.[39] How would a protestor in Myanmar or Palestine who is fighting for human rights and risking their lives for democracy, view such ideas? The suggestions that human rights and democracy are "Eurocentric concepts" would be music to the ears of the military junta of Myanmar and the oppressors in occupied Palestine. Similarly, claims such as secularism is a "Western concept" would be appreciated and embraced by the right-wing Hindus in India and the Taliban in Afghanistan.[40] Many of the fashionably critical "post-colonial studies" scholars fail to consider the consequences of their proclamations. The critical discussions on epistemology often limit the discussion to social sciences. However, if broadened to the natural sciences, say, scientific research on vaccine or medicine for coronavirus, the alternatives or rejections will yield to QAnon style interpretations.

---

36   João Marcelo Maia. "History of Sociology and the Quest for Intellectual Autonomy in the Global South: The Cases of Alberto Guerreiro Ramos and Syed Hussein Alatas," *Current Sociology* 62, no.7 (2014): 1097–1115.

37   Boaventura de souse Santos, *Epistemologies of the South*. New York: Routledge, 2016.

38   Walter Mignolo, "The Geopolitics of Knowledge and the Colonial Difference," *The South Atlantic Quarterly* 101, no. 1 (2002): 57–96.

39   Boaventura de souse Santos, *The End of the Cognitive Empire*. Durham and London: Duke University Press, 2018.

40   Nandy quoted in Zaheer Baber, "Orientalism, Occidentalism, Nativism: The Culturalist Quest for Indigenous Science and Knowledge," *The European Legacy* 7, no. 6 (2002): 748.

Alatas makes his stand clear when he argues for an autonomous social science tradition in Asia or Asian social science that can be drawn from the common core of universal social science knowledge. In his own words: 'There already exists an idea of an American or European social science tradition, though both draw upon a common universal fountain of social science knowledge.'[41]

An autonomous, Asian social science need not be delinked from the rest of the world. 'Should Asian social science isolate itself from that of the West and the rest of the world? Definitely not. On the contrary, there should be greater and continuous attention paid to knowledge developed elsewhere, particularly in the West.'[42] Alatas did not endorse theoretical nationalism. He was very much aware that social sciences were needed to be freed from 'the relatively ethnocentric offshoots which have grown around them. They have to be disentangled from the distorting influence of the cultural groups involved in scholarship so that a more profound and objective result can be attained.'[43]

8   Professor Syed Hussein Alatas as a Public Intellectual

> The scholar is a god, seated on a sublime eminence, observing dispassionately the life of society in all its varying forms; they think (and yet more loudly proclaim) that vile "practice" has no relation whatever with pure "theory." This conception is of course a false one; quite the contrary is true: all learning arises from practice.[44]

The above quote from *Historical Materialism: A System of Sociology*, an important yet unacknowledged text of sociology published in 1921, not only outlines in broad terms the relationship between theory and practice, it also provides a point of departure for thinking about public sociology across the globe. Bukharin's thesis is founded on a materialistic theory of knowledge i.e., social existence creates social consciousness or Manheimian society creating knowledge thesis, a view if conceived narrowly opens the possibility of intellectual

---

41 Syed Hussein Alatas, "The Development of an Autonomous Social Science Traditions in Asia: Problems and Prospects," *Asian Journal of Social Science* 30, no. 1 (2002): 151.

42 Alatas, "The Development of an Autonomous Social Science Traditions in Asia," 153.

43 Syed Hussein Alatas, "The Captive Mind in Development Studies," *International Social Science Journal* 24, no. 1 (1972): 25.

44 Nicolai Bukharin, *Historical Materialism: A System of Sociology*. Moscow: Progress Publisher, 1921.

relativism. It also presents, on the positive side, a view of engaged sociology or what is now known as "public sociology". The relativistic view generates some problems. First, it denies the possibility of creating social knowledge that is transcultural, if not transcendental, and lends support to an untenable and highly parochial view that each society (nation-state) will produce its own sociology. The view is untenable because it goes against the grain of scientific status of the truth, which demands trans-valuation to attain its scientific status. Secondly, the definition of society, or the equation of society with a nation-state, is highly problematic. In a multi-national state, what would society be? In India, can sociological knowledge generated based on the experiences and social conditions of Bihar (one of the poorest states) apply to Punjab (one of the richest states)? While accepting the view of engaged sociology, one has to avoid falling into the trap of relativism.

The practice of sociology and the public role of sociology needs to be situated in the broader conceptualization of social. Sociologists have not quite disappeared from the limelight of public office. Fernando Henrique Cardoso is not only one of the leading sociologists but was elected as the President of Brazil for two terms. However, the first sociologist as president of a country credit goes to Thomas G. Masaryk, who was a professor of sociology at the University of Prague at the turn of the twentieth century.[45] In the Netherlands, Pim Fontuyn was a sociologist who met with an assailant's dagger. Saad Ibrahim, the Egyptian sociologist, was sent to prison for criticizing Egypt's sham democracy. He was released after the Egyptian authority yielded to the moral pressure of the international community.

The idea of public sociology is rooted in the Marxist idea of practice – it is the social existence that determines social consciousness. Marx's eleventh thesis on Feuerbach, 'philosophers have so far interpreted the world, the point is to change it,' grounds the very idea of public sociology.

Michael Burawoy has been a leading proponent of public sociology and it is no coincidence that Burawoy has also been recognized as a leading Marxist sociology with important contributions to work and organization. Immanuel Wallerstein, the other prominent late 20th century sociologist was also a Marxist sociologist with a deep commitment to public sociology, as he too thought that a better world was possible and historically minded social scientists can play a role in that transition.

---

45 Earle Edward Eubank, "European and American Sociology: Some Comparisons," *Social Forces* 15, no. 2 (December 1936): 151.

Professor Alatas' works on sociology of development, and corruption and his questioning on history writing are a clear indication of his commitment to putting social knowledge at the service of socio-economic development and for generating social consciousness. Alatas' popular writings in the media and his public speeches reflect his commitment to social causes. He was, in the Gramscian sense, an organic intellectual, who had a deep understanding of the pulse of the society. There are numerous references in his writings about his awareness of challenges that the developing societies were faced with and proposing well-grounded, practical, down-to-earth solutions to those problems. Upon return from the Netherlands to Malaysia, Alatas not only pursued an intellectual career, but he was also involved in politics. He was one of the founders of *Gerakan*, a labor-oriented political party, and won a seat in the parliament. His involvement in direct politics was short-lived. He returned to academia and engaged himself in critical studies of historiography and sociology.

The task ahead for sociologists is to focus more on the production of socially useful knowledge for the benefit of common humanity. Sociology was the child of enlightenment. As such, it has a critical role in society as sociology cannot free itself from the larger public role. It is only when sociology became institutionalized as an academic discipline and nurtured in American academia rather than in Europe, that mainstream sociology lost that critical worldview and became involved in the search for localized social problems. It is time the problem-solving role of sociology be broadened and integrated with a critical stance towards reconstructing global society based on "equality, liberty, and fraternity." Here public sociology becomes salient. Because of the variety of sociology, there are many forms of "engaged sociology"; liberal societies provide one model. Critical sociology may take an autonomous, context-dependent stance as long as it follows the norms of objectivity and universality. In any case, there is no excuse for not putting sociology at the service of society and humanity. Syed Hussein Alatas would surely endorse these propositions.

Bibliography

Abaza, Mona. "Social Sciences in Egypt: The Swinging Pendulum between Commodification and Criminalization." Conference on the Council of National Association of International Sociology, ISA, Taipei, 2009.

Alatas, Syed Farid. "Alatas, Fanon, and Coloniality," in *Frantz Fanon and Emancipatory Social Theory: A View from the Wretched*, edited by Dustin J. Byrd and Seyed Javad Miri. Leiden/Boston: Brill, 2020.

Alatas, Syed Hussein. "The Captive Mind in Development Studies." *International Social Science Journal* 24, no. 1 (1972): 19–25.

Alatas, Syed Hussein. *Modernization and Social Change.* Sydney: Angus & Robertson, 1972.

Alatas, Syed Hussein. "The Development of an Autonomous Social Science Traditions in Asia: Problems and Prospects." *Asian Journal of Social Science* 30, no. 1 (2002): 150–157.

Alatas, Syed Hussein. "The Autonomous, the Universal, and the Future of Sociology." *Current Sociology*, 54 no.1 (2006): 7–23.

Aron, Raymond. *Main Currents in Sociological Thought, Vol. 1.* New York: Pelican, 1965.

Asad, Talal. 1991. "Afterword: From the History of Colonial Anthropology to the Anthropology of Western Hegemony," in *Colonial Situation: Essays on the Contextualization of Ethnographic Knowledge,* edited by George Stocking. Madison, WI: University of Wisconsin Press, 1991.

Azizan, Hariati. "Alatas: The Towering Thinker" *The Star* January 28, 2007. https://www.thestar.com.my/opinion/letters/2007/01/28/alatas-the-towering-thinker.

Baber, Zaheer. "Orientalism, Occidentalism, Nativism: The Culturalist Quest for Indigenous Science and Knowledge." *The European Legacy* 7, no. 6 (2002): 747–758.

Beck, Ulrich. "The Cosmopolitan Perspective: Sociology of the Second Age of Modernity." *The British Journal of Sociology* 51, no. 1 (2002): 79–105.

Bellah, Robert, R. Madsen, W.M. Sullivan, A. Swidler, and S. Tipton. *Habits of the Heart.* New York: Perennial Library edition, 1986.

Bukharin, Nicolai. *Historical Materialism: A System of Sociology.* Moscow: Progress Publisher, 1921.

Chanda, Nayan. *Bounded Together.* New Haven, CT: Yale University Press, 2008.

Durkheim, Emile. *The Division of Labor in Society.* Translated by George Simpson. New York: Macmillan, 1893/1933.

Durkheim, Emile. *Suicide, A Study in Sociology,* edited by J.A. Spaulding and G. Simpson. London: Routledge, 1897.

Eubank, Earle Edward. "European and American Sociology: Some Comparisons." *Social Forces* 15 no. 2 (December 1936):147–154.

Foucault, Michel. "Foucault's Confession" *PostPhilosophy.* April 23, 2020. https://postphilosophy.medium.com/foucaults-confession-139f10bcb5c5.

Giddens, Anthony. *Sociology.* Cambridge: Polity Press, 1989.

Giddens, Anthony. *Beyond Left and Right.* Cambridge: Polity Press, 1996.

Ginsberg, Morris. *Sociology.* London: Oxford University Press, 1934/1963.

Gouldner, Alvin. *The Coming Crisis of Western Sociology.* New York: Basic Books, 1970.

Halsey, A. H. *A History of Sociology in Britain: Science, Literature and Society.* Oxford Scholarship Online, 2004.

Huzayyin, S.A. and H. El-Saaty. "On the Teaching of Sociology, Social Philosophy and Anthropology in Egypt." *UNESCO Report*. Paris: March 4, 1952.

Khondker, Habibul Haque. "Sociology in Singapore: Global Discourse in Local Context." *Soziologie, Journal of German Sociological Association* 4 (2001): 5–18.

Khondker, Habibul Haque. "Globalization and Sociological Practice." *ISA e— Symposium, International Sociological Association* 3 (March 2006): 55–61.

Levine, Donald, E. B. Carter, and E. M. Gorman. "Simmel's Influence on American sociology." *American Journal of Sociology* 81, no. 4 (1976): 813–845.

Maia, João Marcelo. "History of Sociology and the Quest for Intellectual Autonomy in the Global South: The Cases of Alberto Guerreiro Ramos and Syed Hussein Alatas." *Current Sociology* 62, no. 7 (2014): 1097–1115.

McLuhan, Marshall. *Understanding Media*. London: Routledge and Kegan Paul, 1964.

Meyer, John. W. "The World Polity and the Authority of the Nation-State." In *Studies of the Modern World System*, edited by A. Bergesen. New York: Academic Press, 1980.

Mignolo, Walter. "The Geopolitics of Knowledge and the Colonial Difference." *The South Atlantic Quarterly* 101, no.1 (2002): 57–96.

Moore, Wilbert E. "Global Sociology: The World as a Singular System." *American Journal of Sociology* 71, no. 5 (March 1966): 475–482.

Nettl, John Peter, and Roland Robertson. *International Systems and Modernization of Societies*. New York: Basic Books, 1968.

Odaka, Kunio. "Japanese Sociology: Past and Present." *Social Forces* 28, no. 4 (May 1950): 400–407.

Oromaner, Mark Jay. "Comparison of Influentials in Contemporary American and British Sociology: A Study in the Internationalization of Sociology." *The British Journal of Sociology* 21, no. 3 (September 1970): 324–332.

Reid, Donald Malcolm. *Cairo University and the Making of Modern Egypt*. Cambridge: Cambridge University Press, 2002.

Ritzer, George. *Sociology: A Multi-Paradigm Science*. Boston: Alyn and Bacon, 1980.

Robertson, Roland. "Religion, Global Complexity and the Human Condition." In *Absolute Values and the Creation of the New World, Vol. 1*. New York; International Cultural Foundation, 1983.

Robertson, Roland. 1983. "Interpreting Globality." In *World Realities and International Studies Today*. Glenside, PA: Pennsylvania Council on International Education, 1983.

Robertson, Roland. *Globalization Theory*. London: Sage, 1992.

Santos, Boaventura de souse. *Epistemologies of the South*. New York: Routledge, 2016.

Santos, Boaventura de souse. *The End of the Cognitive Empire*. Durham and London: Duke University Press, 2018.

Sharky, Omina El. *The Great Social Laboratory: Subjects of Knowledge in Colonial and Post-Colonial Egypt*. Stanford: Stanford University Press, 2007.

Steiner, Jesse Frederick. "The Development and Present Status of Sociology in Japanese Universities." *American Journal of Sociology* XLI, no. 6 (1936): 707–722.

Stocking, George, ed. *Colonial Situation: Essays on the Contextualization of Ethnographic Knowledge.* Madison, WI: University of Wisconsin Press, 1991.

Sun, Pen-Wan. "Sociology in China." *Social Forces* 27, no. 3 (March 1949): 247–251.

Turner, Bryan. "Classical Sociology and Cosmopolitanism: A Critical Defence of the Social." *The British Journal of Sociology* 57, no. 1 (2006): 133–151.

Wallerstein, Immanuel. "From Sociology to Historical Science." *The British Journal of Sociology* 51, no. 1 (2000): 25–35.

Weber, Max. *The Protestant Ethic and the Spirit of Capitalism.* London and New York: Routledge, 1930/2001.

Zietlin, Irving. *Ideology and the Development of Sociological Theories.* Inglewood, NJ: Prentice-Hall, 1968.

CHAPTER 18

East-West Interactions and Complexities

Syed Hussein Alatas, Willem Wertheim and Edward Said

Victor T. King

1 Introduction

Syed Hussein Alatas spent many years of his higher education at the University of Amsterdam during the 1950s and the early 1960s. There he encountered the work of Willem (Wim) Frederik Wertheim. Alatas had discussions with him and attended his lectures. Wertheim, as Professor of the Modern History and Sociology of Indonesia in the Faculty of Political and Social Sciences, stamped his own research interests and perspectives on the programs that he founded there. He situated himself in the more radical arena of social science in spite of, or perhaps because of, his early experiences as a Dutch colonial civil servant in the 1930s. After his 15-year sojourn in the Netherlands East Indies, and after the Japanese occupation, he returned to his homeland in 1946 and was then appointed to the Chair in the Modern History and Sociology of Indonesia in December 1946. Subsequently, following his increasing interests in Southeast Asia and the wider Asia, and after revisiting Indonesia during his sabbatical in 1956–1957, he developed an expanded program in the history and sociology of Southeast and South Asia. His professorship was later redesignated as non-Western sociology. It was a critical, questioning sociology that reflected the comparative breadth of his work and the specific focus on regions beyond the West.

Wertheim then set about recruiting students from Indonesia, Malaysia, and elsewhere in Southeast Asia.[1] Many of his students came together to honor him in a *Festschrift* in 1971.[2] It was at this time in the late 1950s and early 1960s that Syed Hussein Alatas (born in Buitenzorg [Bogor] in the Dutch East Indies in

---

1 Jan Breman, "W.F. Wertheim: A Sociological Chronicler of Revolutionary Change," *Development and Change* 48, no. 5 (2017): 1132–42; Han F. Vermeulen, "Anthropology in the Netherlands: Past, Present and Future," in *Other People's Anthropologies: Ethnographic Practices on the Margins*, ed. Aleksandar Bošković (New York: Berghahn Books, 2008), 51–52.

2 Cora Vreede-de Stuers, ed., *Buiten de grenzen: Sociologische opstellen aangeboden aan prof. dr. W.F. Wertheim, 25 jaar Amsterdams hoogleraar, 1946–1971* (Meppel: Boom, 1971).

© VICTOR T. KING, 2023 | DOI:10.1163/9789004521698_020

1928 and subsequently moving to colonial Malaya) studied for his Ph.D. under the supervision and guidance of Professors Jan van Baal, Guillaume Frédéric Pijper, and Wim Wertheim. Like Wertheim, van Baal and Pijper had served in the Dutch colonial civil service in the East Indies. Van Baal had also served as the Governor of Dutch New Guinea from 1953 to 1958 before he pursued a senior academic career, from the late 1950s, as Professor of Cultural Anthropology at the University of Amsterdam and the State University of Utrecht, and assumed the directorship of the Royal Tropical Institute in Amsterdam until 1969. At the time Pijper was guiding Alatas in his doctoral work he occupied the Chair of Arabic, Islam, and Semitic Languages; his own early research was on Malay manuscripts, and, as an accomplished linguist, he had studied Malay and several Indonesian and Semitic languages. Van Baal, who had studied Indonesian cultures, law, and languages at Leiden University in the interwar years, developed a particular interest in the anthropology of religion and symbolism and had worked on the ethnology of western New Guinea cultures.[3]

Alatas's Amsterdam experience accustomed him to working in multidisciplinary environments and this provided him with a sound basis for his later research and publications in the Malay studies programs at Universiti Malaya and the National University of Singapore, which embraced the sociology and history of Islam, Malay language and literature, and Southeast Asian cultures and history. He was awarded his doctorate at Amsterdam on "Reflections on the Theories of Religion,"[4] a subject on which he continued to publish on his return to his homeland.[5] Alatas was a pioneer in the study of a range of issues in Southeast Asian sociology at a time when locally generated sociological studies were thin on the ground. In this chapter, the primary focus is the work for which he is best known, *The Myth of the Lazy Native*, as well as the issue of the relations between Western and non-Western social science, drawing on the work of the Dutch historical-sociological school which influenced Alatas in his early scholarly years and which continued as a significant presence in his

---

3   W.E.A. van Beek and J.H. Scherer, eds., *Explorations in the Anthropology of Religion: Essays in Honour of Jan van Baal* (The Hague: Martinus Nijhoff, Verhandelingen van het Koninklijk Instituut voor Taal-, Land- en Volkenkunde, Vol. 74, 1975).

4   Syed Hussein Alatas, "Reflections on the Theories of Religion" (PhD diss., University of Amsterdam. 's-Gravenhage: Drukkerij Pasmans, 1963); Syed Hussein Alatas, "The Autonomous, the Universal and the Future of Sociology," *Current Sociology* 54, no. 1 (2006): 7–23.

5   See, for example, Syed Hussein Alatas, *Modernization and Social Change: Studies in Modernization, Religion, Social Change and Development in South-East Asia* (Sydney: Angus & Robertson, 1972).

422   KING

intellectual life.[6] This chapter also provides a brief discussion of the relationship between Alatas's work and Edward Said's *Orientalism*.[7]

2   Syed Hussein Alatas and a Personal Engagement

I had two encounters with Alatas, one personal and brief, the other intellectual
and extended. Unfortunately, I was only able to meet with him on one occasion in 1991 when he was Vice Chancellor of Universiti Malaya. At that time, I
had recently been promoted to the Chair in South-East Asian Studies at the
University of Hull and to the directorship of the Centre for South-East Asian
Studies there (at that time Hull rendered the name of the region as South-East,
rather than Southeast, Asia). Immediately after the founding of the centre in
1963 an externally funded exchange program had been agreed in which staff
from Universiti Malaya would spend time at Hull studying for their doctorates
while staff from Hull would attach themselves to the partner university for the
purposes of teaching and research. The arrangement proved very successful,
but it was terminated in the early 1970s when the earmarked funding was no
longer available.

We decided to reinstate the exchange program with Universiti Malaya in the
late 1980s, and it was for that reason that I met with Alatas, as the then Vice
Chancellor of the university, to discuss the outlines of an exchange agreement.
His reputation went before him, and I was somewhat daunted in meeting him
and proposing a collaboration with a British university. I had read his work
on East–West relations, the "captive mind," and "academic imperialism," and
his wide-ranging postcolonial critiques.[8] In spite of my anxiety, Alatas turned

---

6   Syed Hussein Alatas, *The Myth of the Lazy Native: A Study of the Image of the Malays,
       Filipinos and Javanese from the 16th to the 20th Century and Its Function in the Ideology of
       Colonial Capitalism* (London: Frank Cass, 1977).
7   Edward W. Said, *Orientalism* (London: Routledge and Kegan Paul, 1978).
8   See, for example, Syed Hussein Alatas, "Academic Imperialism," Lecture delivered to
       the History Society, University of Singapore, September 26, 1969; Syed Hussein Alatas,
       "The Captive Mind in Development Studies," *International Social Science Journal* 34,
       no. 1 (1972): 9–25; Syed Hussein Alatas, "The Captive Mind and Creative Development,"
       International Social Science Journal 36, no. 4 (1974): 691–99; Syed Hussein Alatas, "Towards
       an Asian Social Science Tradition," *New Quest* 17 (1979): 265–69; Syed Hussein Alatas, "Social
       Aspects of Endogenous Intellectual Creativity: The Problem of Obstacles – Guidelines
       for Research," in *Intellectual Creativity in Endogenous Culture*, ed. Anouar Abdel-Malek
       and Amar Nath Pandeya (Tokyo: The United Nations University, 1981), 462–70; Syed
       Hussein Alatas, "Intellectual Imperialism: Definition, Traits and Problems," *Southeast
       Asian Journal of Social Science* 28, no. 1 (2000): 23–45; Syed Hussein Alatas, "Academic

EAST-WEST INTERACTIONS AND COMPLEXITIES 423

out to be most helpful, friendly, and supportive. He was keen to continue to expand his university's international links, which were already substantial, and was doing this on the basis of academic equality. I also knew that he was fully committed to the principle of meritocracy irrespective of ethnic and national identities.[9] It was this principle that unfortunately led to political tension and his departure as Vice Chancellor in 1991 so that the Hull–Malaya plan, which we discussed informally, was not realized. However, the ground had been prepared. Four years later, in 1994–1995, Hull managed to renew its relationship between the Centre for South-East Asian Studies at Hull and Universiti Malaya, specifically with the Departments of South-East Asian Studies and Malay Language there. There was both student exchange and staff collaboration, funded through the universities and the British Council.

On an intellectual level, I had long admired Alatas's published work and the themes which he chose to explore. As a sociologist-anthropologist specializing in Southeast Asia, and trained in a more radical tradition of social science in Britain under such mentors as Talal Asad,[10] I was responsible from the early 1970s for developing undergraduate courses on processes of social change and development in the region. It was this focus that resulted in my encounter with Alatas's thinking. At that time, and aside from the publications of Alatas and a few others, in my view there was generally very little interesting material that could be used for the purposes of teaching.[11]

In this connection, in the 1970s the German sociologist Hans-Dieter Evers could still remark, in his *Sociology of South-East Asia*, that 'relatively little progress has been made in furthering the understanding of changing South-East Asian societies.'[12] In a review article of Evers's book, I too observed that '[u]p

---

Imperialism," in *Reflections on Alternative Discourses from Southeast Asia: Proceedings of the ISA Regional Conference for Southeast Asia, Singapore, 30 May–1 June 1998*, ed. Syed Farid Alatas (Singapore: Centre of Advanced Studies and Pagesetters Services, 2001), 32–46; Syed Hussein Alatas, "The Development of an Autonomous Social Science in Asia: Problems and Prospects," *Asian Journal of Social Science* 30, no. 1 (2002): 150–57.

9   Masturah Alatas, *The Life in the Writing: Syed Hussein Alatas* (Shah Alam: Marshall Cavendish Editions, 2010); Masturah Alatas, "Four Decades of a Malay Myth," *The Malay Mail*, January 24, 2017, https://www.malaymail.com/news/what-you-think/2017/01/24/four-decades-of-a-malay-myth-masturah-alatas/1299401.

10   Talal Asad, ed., *Anthropology and the Colonial Encounter* (London: Ithaca Press, 1973).

11   Victor T. King, "The Sociology of South-East Asia: A Critical Review of Some Concepts and Issues," *Bijdragen tot de Taal-, Land- en Volkenkunde* 150, no. 1 (1994): 172–75.

12   Hans-Dieter Evers, "Editor's Introduction," in *Sociology of South-East Asia: Readings on Social Change and Development*, ed. Hans-Dieter Evers (Kuala Lumpur: Oxford University Press, 1980), ix; Hans-Dieter Evers, ed., *Sociology of South-East Asia: Readings on Social Change and Development* (Kuala Lumpur: Oxford University Press, 1980).

to now any lecturer faced with the task of teaching South-East Asian sociology cannot fail to have noted the piecemeal and often "localized" nature (in content, relevance and orientation) of the sociological literature. With a few notable exceptions ... South-East Asian sociology has not really distinguished itself.'[13] A few years before this, Evers had also co-edited a volume entitled *Studies in ASEAN Sociology* with Peter Chen, the Singapore sociologist. The editors stated then that '[o]ne common problem faced by all sociology lecturers in Southeast Asia is the lack of local teaching materials.' They continued:

> Nearly all university text-books are imported from Britain and the United States. Theoretical frameworks, empirical examples and conceptual illustrations, which may be familiar to most academics who were trained in these countries but in most cases are strange to the students, are taught in the classes and transmitted to the students.[14]

A decade later, in the volume on Southeast Asia in the Macmillan Sociology of "Developing Societies" series, the editors, John Taylor and Andrew Turton, drew attention to the persistence of the problems highlighted in the 1970s. They phrased these in terms of a paradox. They emphasized the crucial importance and social complexity of Southeast Asia as a region within a globalizing world. 'Yet the degree and quality of much of the research on the region often does not enable one to address the most important aspects of its current and future development.'[15] In this regard, they contrasted sociological research on Southeast Asia with the incisive research of Latin American and other scholars on dependency and world systems, East African studies on 'the role of the state and its relation to indigenous classes,' and the analyses of capitalist relations of production in agriculture and the processes of agrarian differentiation in South Asia. Taylor and Turton bemoaned the fact that Southeast Asian scholars had adopted ideas from outside the area 'rather than generating indigenous explanations of the region and its place in the world economy.'[16]

---

13   Victor T. King, "Sociology in South-East Asia: A Personal View," *Cultures et développement* 13, no. 2 (1981): 391.

14   Peter S.J. Chen and Hans-Dieter Evers, "Introduction," in *Studies in ASEAN Sociology: Urban Society and Social Change*, ed. Peter S.J. Chen and Hans-Dieter Evers (Singapore: Chopmen Enterprises, 1978), XIII.

15   John G. Taylor and Andrew Turton, "Introduction," in *Southeast Asia*, ed. John G. Taylor and Andrew Turton (Basingstoke: Macmillan, 1988), 1.

16   Ibid. See also Clark D. Neher, "The Social Sciences," in *Southeast Asian Studies: Options for the Future*, ed. Ronald A. Morse (Lanham, MA: University Press of America, 1984), 130;

EAST-WEST INTERACTIONS AND COMPLEXITIES   425

Given this unpromising situation, as a young lecturer I turned with some relief and gratitude to a range of Alatas's books, particularly *The Myth of the Lazy Native* and *Thomas Stamford Raffles: Schemer or Reformer?*, a study which revealed Raffles as hardly a "benevolent colonialist,"[17] and Alatas's studies from the late 1960s into the 1970s: *The Sociology of Corruption,*[18] a theme on which James Scott subsequently expounded;[19] *Modernization and Social Change,* which I used as one of my textbooks; and *Intellectuals in Developing Societies.*[20] I developed a particular interest in this latter subject, given Alatas's reputation as a prominent public intellectual and a political activist, critical of Malaysia's communal, ethnically divisive national ideology.[21]

3   Syed Hussein Alatas, Willem Wertheim, and Dutch Non-Western Sociology

My interest in Alatas's work was not merely because it was refreshing and that it coincided with some of my emerging interests and perspectives at the time, but also because he had embraced several of the ideas of Wertheim's Amsterdam school of historical sociology.[22] Wearing my other disciplinary hat as an anthropologist, I had undertaken field research in Indonesian Borneo in the early 1970s, spent long periods of time working in the Dutch archives in Amsterdam, Leiden, and The Hague in the 1970s and 1980s, and developed a close affinity with the work of Wertheim, and some of the earlier Dutch socio-historical studies of such writers as Jacob C. van Leur, a pioneer of "domestic" or "autonomous history" or "history from below,"[23] Julius H. Boeke,[24] and Bernard

---

Richard F. Doner, "Approaches to the Politics of Economic Growth in Southeast Asia," *Journal of Asian Studies* 50, no. 4 (1991): 819.

17   Syed Hussein Alatas, *Thomas Stamford Raffles 1781–1826: Schemer or Reformer?* (Sydney: Angus & Robertson, 1971).

18   Syed Hussein Alatas, *The Sociology of Corruption: The Nature, Function, Causes and Prevention of Corruption* (Singapore: Donald Moore, 1968).

19   James C. Scott, *Comparative Political Corruption* (Englewood Cliffs, NJ: Prentice-Hall, 1972).

20   Syed Hussein Alatas, *Intellectuals in Developing Societies* (London: Frank Cass, 1977).

21   Charles Hirschman, "The Making of Race in Colonial Malaya: Political Economy and Racial Ideology," *Sociological Forum* 1, no. 2 (1986): 330–61.

22   See, for example, King, "Sociology in South-East Asia."

23   J.C. van Leur, *Indonesian Trade and Society: Essays in Asian Social and Economic History,* trans. James S. Holmes and A. van Marle (The Hague: W. van Hoeve, 1955). See, for example, John R.W. Smail, "On the Possibility of an Autonomous History of Modern Southeast Asia," *Journal of Southeast Asian History* 2, no. 2 (1961): 72–102.

24   J.H. Boeke, *Economics and Economic Policy of Dual Societies, as Exemplified by Indonesia* (New York: International Secretariat, Institute of Pacific Relations, 1953). See also W.F.

J. O. Schrieke.[25] A comparable example from the English-speaking colonies in Southeast Asia was John S. Furnivall's work on colonial policy and practice in Burma and Netherlands India.[26] Moreover, Alatas, early on, drew our attention to some of the problems raised by colonial historical interpretations and narratives of the Southeast Asian and particularly the Malaysian past.[27]

Wertheim was the main driving force in the development and promotion of this emerging Dutch sociological perspective, which, with qualifications, Alatas also embraced. Wertheim drew substantially on European sociological traditions (Marx, Weber, Mannheim, and Gramsci, among others), as did Alatas, in addressing the issue of whether or not 'we could establish similarities between developments in earlier European history and developments in contemporary Asian societies.'[28] Wertheim accomplished this with sociological perception and historical sensitivity in his *Indonesian Society in Transition*,[29] and then in a collection of comparative essays on Asia, *East–West Parallels*, in which he adapted concepts in the engagement with Western experiences to enable the qualified and conditional analysis of the rapidly changing societies of Asia.[30] He concluded that 'such parallel developments could certainly be revealed; but ... in each instance they only hold to some extent.' This was partly for the reasons that, in general contrast to the West, Asia demonstrates an enhanced role of the state in economic affairs, and that, at the time of writing, he witnessed only the recent emergence of an urban bourgeoisie, which had not had the opportunity 'to play a dynamic, innovative role similar to that played by a

---

Wertheim, ed., *Indonesian Economics: The Concept of Dualism in Theory and Policy* (The Hague: W. van Hoeve, 1961).

25 B.J.O. Schrieke, *Indonesian Sociological Studies: Selected Writings of B. Schrieke* (The Hague: W. van Hoeve, 2 volumes, 1955–1957).

26 J.S. Furnivall, *Colonial Policy and Practice: A Comparative Study of Burma and Netherlands India* (Cambridge: Cambridge University Press, 1948).

27 Syed Hussein Alatas, "Reconstruction of Malaysian History," *Revue du Sud-est Asiatique* 3 (1962): 219–45; Syed Hussein Alatas, "Theoretical Aspects of Southeast Asian History: John Bastin and the Study of Southeast Asian History," *Asian Studies* 2, no. 2 (1964): 247–60.

28 W.F. Wertheim, *Comparative Essays on Asia and the West* (Amsterdam: VU University Press, Comparative Asian Studies, 12, 1993), 2. See also King, "The Sociology of South-East Asia," 184, 190–92; Victor T. King, "Southeast Asia: Personal Reflections on a Region," in *Southeast Asian Studies: Debates and New Directions*, ed. Cynthia Chou and Vincent Houben (Leiden: International Institute for Asian Studies, 2006), 23–44.

29 W.F. Wertheim, *Indonesian Society in Transition: A Study of Social Change* (The Hague: W. van Hoeve, 1956; second edition, 1959; reprint, 1964).

30 W.F. Wertheim, *East–West Parallels: Sociological Approaches to Modern Asia* (The Hague: W. van Hoeve, 1964). See also Wertheim, *Comparative Essays on Asia and the West*.

EAST-WEST INTERACTIONS AND COMPLEXITIES 427

parallel group in the West.'[31] In much of his career Alatas was also exercised by the issue of East–West interactions and complexities.

In *East–West Parallels* Wertheim also began to develop his concept of 'society as a composite of conflicting value systems', and his focus on the principle of emancipation in human history (from "the forces of nature" and from "human domination") as a major driving force in the dynamics of social change.[32] A decade later he deployed these elements in a wide-ranging theory of social change and "progress." He argued against essentialist interpretations of social structure and proposed that, in any given society, there are always "counterpoints" or alternative and opposing views to those which are dominant. Rather than accepting that the structures of society are those imposed by the powerful and wealthy, he argued that we should think of society as contingent and unstable, and as constituted in terms of "conflicting value systems." Moreover, he proposed that conflicts, contradictions, and tensions are not fundamentally Marxist-type class struggles but rather emancipation struggles.[33] The impulse that he detected was "a spiritual motivation" and a "mental urge" for emancipation from domination by others. He therefore criticized orthodox Marxist interpretations which he perceived as materialist, determinist, and reductionist, in favor of an approach closer to Antonio Gramsci in which emphasis is placed on the role of ideas, cultural subjectivism, and probabilism.[34] Over time, Wertheim modified his perspective, especially in response to unanticipated developments in China and his disillusionment with the Chinese Communist state, though he retained the distinction between gradual change and radical change. His major theoretical work, based on his notions of "emancipation" and "conflicting value systems," was *Evolution and Revolution*, first published in a Dutch edition in 1971, and then brought out in English translation in 1974.[35]

---

31   Wertheim, *Comparative Essays on Asia and the West*, 3.

32   W.F. Wertheim, "Society as a Composite of Conflicting Value Systems," in *East–West Parallels: Sociological Approaches to Modern Asia* (The Hague: W. van Hoeve, 1964), 23–38.

33   Jan Nederveen Pieterse, "Counterpoint and Emancipation," *Development and Change* 19, no. 2 (1988): 333.

34   Ibid., 334.

35   W.F. Wertheim, *Evolutie en revolutie: De golfslag der emancipatie* (Amsterdam: Van Gennep, 1971); W.F. Wertheim, *Evolution and Revolution: The Rising Waves of Emancipation* (London: Penguin, 1974). See also W.F. Wertheim, *Emancipation in Asia: Positive and Negative Lessons from China* (Rotterdam: Comparative Asian Studies Programme, Erasmus University, 1983); W.F. Wertheim, *Third World Whence and Whither? Protective State versus Aggressive Market* (Amsterdam: Het Spinhuis, 1997); W.F. Wertheim, "Globalization of the Social Sciences: Non-Western Sociology as a Temporary Panacea," in *Tales from Academia: History of Anthropology in the Netherlands*, ed. Han Vermeulen and Jean Kommers (Saarbrücken: Verlag für Entwicklungspolitik Saarbrücken, 2002), 267–96.

Although Alatas did not adopt Wertheim's grand evolutionary/revolutionary scheme, he did engage thoroughly with the role of ideas and knowledge in human history.

Vermeulen's overall appreciation of Wertheim's project was that the 'fundamental contribution of the historical sociology promoted by Wertheim was to show that the worlds [the West and non-West] are interconnected and interdependent.'[36] Furthermore, building on the work of Schrieke, van Leur, and Boeke, among others, it was Wertheim's task to understand how Indonesian society, and later the wider Southeast Asian region, had been transformed and had responded to external forces.[37] Wertheim also notes that his mentors, Schrieke and van Leur, though they had adopted a Weberian approach to the analysis of Indonesian society, using in particular the concept of an "ideal type," were silent on the colonial relationship.[38] One of Wertheim's major contributions was to fill this gap in Dutch research in adopting a "dissenting perspective," moving away from Dutch Orientalism, and exposing colonial racist ideology.[39] In doing this, he worked within the framework of the sociology of dominance, resistance, conflict, and underdevelopment. These were precisely the perspectives that attracted Alatas in his studies of racist-based colonial myths. Wertheim also came under the influence of the Dutch historian Jan Romein, deploying his concept of the "dialectics of progress" (or "dialectical evolutionism") in that the process, speed, and direction of change, or progress towards emancipation are always uneven (or dialectical).[40] In addition, like Romein, Wertheim searched for "common human patterns" in history with particular reference to the achievements of Asia in the twentieth century.[41]

Wertheim and other European-based social scientists, working in a more radical scholarly tradition than that which was generally being pursued in American social science, focused on structuralism, neo-Marxism, political economy, dynamic and conflictual change, and the marginal, subordinated populations of the region. They offered alternative paradigms to what Ruth McVey referred to, in her comments on American modernization theory of

---

36   Vermeulen, "Anthropology in the Netherlands," 60.

37   Wertheim, *Comparative Essays on Asia and the West*, 1.

38   Ibid., 2.

39   Breman, "W.F. Wertheim," 1132–36.

40   Jan Romein, *The Asian Century: A History of Modern Nationalism in Asia*, trans. R.T. Clark (London: Allen & Unwin, 1962).

41   Wertheim, *East–West Parallels*, 3–20; Otto van den Muijzenberg and Willem Wolters, *Conceptualizing Development: The Historical-Sociological Tradition in Dutch Non-Western Sociology* (Dordrecht: Foris, Centre for Asian Studies Amsterdam, Comparative Asian Studies, 1, 1988), 20–24.

the 1950s and 1960s, as the "regnant paradigm."[42] In part, at least, Wertheim's approach was followed by Alatas, but, in Alatas's case, with decisive reference to Southeast Asian experiences. The Amsterdam school was critical of American-led modernization theory and, to some extent, ran in parallel with other streams of radical scholarship, though in some ways it also predated it.[43]

This tradition, established by Dutch scholars from the early postwar period, had only modest influence on the American modernization-democratization-economic growth paradigm, and received very little attention from neo-Marxists and political economists whose work began to take on a higher profile in the study of Southeast Asia from the late 1970s.[44] In important respects, Wertheim and his followers, including Alatas, presented some of the same messages as the underdevelopment and dependency writers, but they provided an intriguing bridge between neo-Marxist concerns, certain neo-evolutionary ideas, and Weber's sociology. What is more, their contribution to the conceptual understanding and analysis of social change did not receive much attention in general sociological and political economy texts on Southeast Asia which began to emerge in the 1980s.[45] The Dutch contribution was also only mentioned in passing in Richard Higgott and Richard Robison's pioneering book on Southeast Asian political economy, to the effect that the Wertheimian socio-historical approach "sought to integrate political, social and economic approaches" but had been overtaken by other Western writings influenced by "Orientalist" and "empiricist" preoccupations.[46] In fact, after reading my paper published in the Dutch journal *Bijdragen tot de Taal-, Land- en Volkenkunde* in

---

42 Ruth McVey, "Change and Continuity in Southeast Asian Studies," *Journal of Southeast Asian Studies* 26, no. 1 (1995): 1–9. See also Victor T. King, "Southeast Asia: An Anthropological Field of Study?" *Moussons: Recherche en sciences humaines sur l'Asie du Sud-Est* 3 (2001): 19–23; King, "Southeast Asia."

43 Muijzenberg and Wolters, *Conceptualizing Development*.

44 Victor T. King, "Sociology," in *An Introduction to Southeast Asian Studies*, ed. Mohammed Halib and Tim Huxley (London: I.B. Tauris, 1996), 168–73.

45 Evers, "Editor's Introduction"; Evers, *Sociology of South-East Asia*; Hans-Dieter Evers, "The Challenge of Diversity: Basic Concepts and Theories in the Study of South-East Asian Societies," in *Sociology of South-East Asia: Readings on Social Change and Development*, ed. Hans-Dieter Evers (Kuala Lumpur: Oxford University Press, 1980), 2–7; P.W. Preston, *Rethinking Development: Essays on Development and Southeast Asia* (London: Routledge & Kegan Paul, 1987); Taylor and Turton, "Introduction."

46 Richard Higgott and Richard Robison, "Introduction," in *Southeast Asia: Essays in the Political Economy of Structural Change*, ed. Richard Higgott and Richard Robison (London: Routledge and Kegan Paul, 1985), 5; Richard Higgott and Richard Robison, eds. *Southeast Asia: Essays in the Political Economy of Structural Change* (London: Routledge and Kegan Paul, 1985); Victor T. King, "South-East Asia: Essays in the Political Economy of Structural Change (Review Article)," *Journal of Contemporary Asia* 16, no. 4 (1986): 520–33.

which I refer approvingly to Wertheim's work and that of other Dutch sociologists, and that they had not received the attention they deserved,[47] Wertheim wrote to me and sent copies of some of his unpublished work, expressing surprise and some satisfaction that I had given him and his colleagues a prominent place in Southeast Asian sociology whereas others had not.[48]

Wertheim's concept of society and social change, though problematic in some respects, contains elements that have considerable analytical value and some resonance with the approach of political economists.[49] The area of Wertheim's theory which seems questionable is his attempt to reformulate and use evolutionary theory, including the notion of certain societies "skipping stages" and others being overtaken and even regressing, and his development of a grand theory of human history. In my view, his approach to an understanding of the dynamics of social change does not need to be cluttered with a generalizing view of evolution in order to organize societies on a scale or trajectory of progression. His concept of evolution is rescued to some extent by the notion of rapid revolutionary change, but aside from the distraction of evolution what is important is Wertheim's focus on points of strain, tension, contradiction, opposition, antagonism, protest, discontent, and struggle in societies. He says, 'no human society is a completely integrated entity,'[50] and that, although there is a dominant set of values in any given society, there are always undercurrents of protest and competing sets of values.[51] James Scott also comes close to this position, according to Grant Evans, in his "motto" that 'wherever there is domination there is bound to be resistance.'[52]

These undercurrents of protest can be controlled, channeled, and institutionalized so that the appearance of integration and harmony is reinforced, but the "counterpoints" do not disappear. They can resurface and become 'rallying points for opposition to the official hierarchy.'[53] An interesting and contentious position that Wertheim promotes is that value systems are "psychical realities" and 'subjective interpretations of society by different social layers'; they are 'accepted in different shades of intensity among definite segments

---

47   King, "The Sociology of South-East Asia."

48   Willem Wertheim, Personal communication, January 26, 1995.

49   King, "Sociology," 170–71.

50   Wertheim, *Comparative Essays on Asia and the West*, 8.

51   Ibid., 11.

52   Grant Evans, *From Moral Economy to Remembered Village: The Sociology of James C. Scott* (Clayton, Vic.: Monash University, Centre of Southeast Asian Studies, Working Paper No. 40, 1986), 30.

53   Wertheim, *Comparative Essays on Asia and the West*, 11.

of society.'[54] Wertheim argues against the concept of an objectively existing, generally accepted hierarchical social system and against the structural-functionalist position that social structures are "rigid realities."[55] For him societies are about "thinking" and "feeling" and '[t]his conceptualization enabled him to describe and analyze developments in a less deterministic and reified way.'[56] Indeed, in this sense, Wertheim also follows Weber's criticisms of reification in social science, the need to take account of human consciousness, motives, and meanings, and to beware of essentialist tendencies to assume that there are "social facts" which exist beyond the individual.[57] Alatas, too, followed this path of reasoning.

Wertheim's focus on ideas and "mentalities" in human history, and his claim that social institutions are only "images" in the minds of real people, need qualification. This seems too "idealistic," indeed a Hegelian view of social organization. After all there are institutions which we simply cannot "un-think"; they have a presence and a reality above and beyond what we imagine; they direct and constrain us to act and behave in certain ways. It is not merely that they are a product of the value system of those in power. They are supported and enforced by something more than a value system. There are clues to the ways in which those in power defend their position, and which Wertheim does not address sufficiently, in Evans's remark that "hegemony is not simply a matter of high ideals it must have some material reality."[58]

There is also a close interconnection, in their mutual concerns with conflict, struggle, and opposition, between the Dutch historical-sociological perspective and that of the later Australian-based political economists. Garry Rodan proposes that not only institutions but also markets are defined 'within wider and system-level processes of social and political conflict.'[59] The focus, as with Wertheim, is on competing and conflicting interests, but for these political economists, power and economic control are much more substantial. The transitory nature of social formations in Wertheim's theory is translated into something more real in the political economy framework: '[e]xisting regimes, therefore, cannot be dismantled at will because they embody a specific

---

54   Ibid., 13, 14.

55   Ibid., 16.

56   Muijzenberg and Wolters, *Conceptualizing Development*, 23.

57   Pieterse, "Counterpoint and Emancipation," 329–30.

58   Evans, *From Moral Economy to Remembered Village*, 27.

59   Garry Rodan, "Theorising Markets in South-East Asia: Power and Contestation," in *The Political Economy of South-East Asia: Markets, Power and Contestation*, ed. Garry Rodan, Kevin Hewison, and Richard Robison, 3rd ed. (Melbourne: Oxford University Press, 2006), 6.

arrangement of economic, social, and political power.'[60] What is also apparent is that wealth and the control of economic resources (money politics and capitalist accumulation) 'provide mechanisms by which powerful corporate interests directly capture and appropriate state power.'[61]

Alatas demonstrates his engagement with many of the issues raised by the Dutch historical-sociological school in a paper written while he was still undertaking doctoral studies in Amsterdam and then in subsequent publications on religion and modernization.[62] It emerged from the subject of his thesis in the sociology of religion and more broadly in the sociology of knowledge. He addresses Max Weber's thesis on religion and capitalism and some of his more general pronouncements on the importance of examining "psychological attitudes" and the "spirit" and "soul" of capitalism.[63] Alatas also pursues the theme raised by Wertheim in *East–West Parallels* of the applicability (or not) of Western concepts to non-Western contexts; and he displays his knowledge of Dutch historical-sociological scholarship in his overview of the work of D.M.G. Koch, Schrieke, van Leur, and Wertheim himself.[64] Alatas suggests that overall Wertheim, in his study of Islam in Indonesia, appears to be supportive of Weber's thesis on the role of religion in the development of capitalism in Europe, and that differences in religion between Europe and Asia help explain the lack of a locally generated capitalism in Asia. Alatas refutes this argument and comes down on the side of an explanation in terms of the political-economic context of change and development. He proposes that capitalism 'can arise in Asia from within itself,' that 'capitalism in Europe need not have a religious qualification for its uniqueness,' that the "spirit of capitalism" can be detected in certain groups of 'Muslim traders and small industrialists' and there are variations in types of economic engagement among Muslims in Southeast Asia, and that entrepreneurial activities and the "mentality" and spirit that accompany them are much more a product of migrant status (and the freedom of movement and networking that this entails) and the distance from colonial government control and interference.[65] The alternatives to a

---

60   Ibid., 7.

61   Ibid., 25.

62   Syed Hussein Alatas, "The Weber Thesis and South East Asia," *Archives de sociologie des religions* 15 (1963): 21–34; Syed Hussein Alatas, "Religion and Modernization in Southeast Asia," *European Journal of Sociology* 11, no. 2 (1970): 265–96; Alatas, *Modernization and Social Change.*

63   Alatas, "The Weber Thesis," 27.

64   Ibid., 29–30.

65   Ibid., 30–34.

EAST-WEST INTERACTIONS AND COMPLEXITIES   433

politically dominant Muslim Malayness in Malaysia are also captured by Joel
Kahn in his *Other Malays*.[66]

4   Syed Hussein Alatas and Edward Said

After achieving international renown for his study of Orientalism, specifically
with reference to the Middle East, Edward Said drew attention, in a later book
on culture and imperialism, to the importance of Alatas's work.[67] Said refers
approvingly to Alatas's thesis in *The Myth of the Lazy Native* on colonial image-
making and representations which was published prior to his own major publication. Indeed, in the 1960s, Alatas was already presenting some of his ideas
on the European construction of images of the "native" or the "other" and the
ways in which these images have become embedded and internalized in intellectual discourse and in the "captive mind" of local elites in the former colonial
world.[68] In addition, he noted that colonial governments were always dependent on a range of co-opted members from local elites, in that domination was
never absolute. Moreover, in the 1950s he was already engaging with "the world
of thinking" in a colonial context, and the psychological dimensions of intellectual and academic imperialism, which Said was to address two decades later.[69]

Said's general thesis, although based primarily on the part of the world
that he knew best, attracted widespread attention because of the power of
the argument and its general relevance to the colonial world, whereas Alatas's
study, in its title and its focus on three populations in Southeast Asia, did not
achieve the profile, international impact, and level of interest of Said's bold
statements. Nevertheless, Alatas's thinking prefigured the conceptual framework of Orientalism that Said subsequently presented: as a field of intellectual endeavor, as a Nietzschean worldview, and as a Foucauldian-Gramscian
hegemonic discourse and a repressive instrument of domination.[70] This view

---

66   Joel S. Kahn, *Other Malays: Nationalism and Cosmopolitanism in the Modern Malay World*
      (Honolulu: University of Hawai'i Press, 2006).
67   Edward W. Said, *Culture and Imperialism* (New York: Knopf, 1993).
68   Alatas, "Academic Imperialism"; Alatas, "The Captive Mind in Development Studies."
69   Syed Farid Alatas, "Intellectual and Structural Challenge to Academic Dependency,"
      International Sociological Association E-Bulletin 9 (2008), https://www.isa-sociology.org/
      uploads/imgen/328-e-bulletin-9.pdf.
70   Fikret Güven, "Criticism to Edward W. Said's Orientalism," *RumeliDE Journal of Language
      and Literature Studies* 15 (2019): 418–30; David Zarnett, "A Review of *Defending the West: A
      Critique of Edward Said's Orientalism* by Ibn Warraq and *Reading Orientalism: The Said
      and the Unsaid* by Daniel Martin Varisco," *Democratiya* 12 (2008): 50–61.

is widely shared. For example, Arndt Graf states: 'In hindsight, Alatas's book can be considered a major Southeast Asian contribution to the wider discourse on Orientalism.'[71]

Syed Farid Alatas, Syed Hussein's son, has captured the main elements or "traits" of the Saidian concept and operation of Orientalism, which is also revealed in his father's Syed Hussein's work: "Orientals" are treated as the objects of study or as informants and not as the source of ideas; as objects of study they are constructed, as are the categories, concepts, and characteristics used to understand them; 'Europe is the sole origin of modern civilisation in all of its expressions'; questions and issues of a universal nature raised by Western thinkers in understanding the West do not figure in relation to those territories and populations considered to be outside Western civilization; there is a paradox between Western discourse on such matters as freedom, equality, and humanism in the West and those policies and practices pursued outside the West; and there is a tendency toward silence on the part of Western writers on matters which are contrary to the dominant image of "non-Western others."[72]

Said's *Orientalism* was the subject of much praise as well as criticism. The criticisms of Said focused on historical errors; the selectivity of material to substantiate the case being made; de-essentializing the Orient while essentializing the West; that Western writing and thinking on the Orient was not an undifferentiated, homogeneous body of work but rather a set of discourses with divergences and contradictions, among which was the role of rationalism, universalism, and self-criticism in European thought and action; and the problematic West–non-West binary in that it is not as crisply and cleanly defined as Said's mutually exclusive entities tend to suggest.[73] A closer reading of some of these criticisms requires a degree of qualification and elaboration, and Alatas was careful, in his own studies, to avoid some of these criticisms. We now turn to some of these issues in examining Alatas's study of colonial representations and his concept of the "captive mind."

---

71 Arndt Graf, "Electronic Orientalism? The Afterlife of Syed Hussein Alatas' *The Myth of the Lazy Native* in Online Databases," *New Media and Society* 12, no. 5 (2010): 836.

72 Syed Farid Alatas, "Silencing as Method: The Case of Malay Studies," in *Fieldwork and the Self: Changing Research Styles in Southeast Asia*, ed. Jérémy Jammes and Victor T. King (Singapore: Springer, 2021).

73 Bernard Lewis, *Islam and the West* (New York: Oxford University Press, 1993); Fred Halliday, "'Orientalism' and Its Critics," *British Journal of Middle Eastern Studies* 20, no. 2 (1993): 145–63; Fred Halliday, *Islam and the Myth of Confrontation: Religion and Politics in the Middle East* (New York: I.B. Tauris, 1996); Daniel Martin Varisco, *Reading Orientalism: Said and the Unsaid* (Seattle: University of Washington Press, 2007); Ibn Warraq, *Defending the West: A Critique of Edward Said's Orientalism* (Amherst, NY: Prometheus Books, 2007).

5 Syed Hussein Alatas and *The Myth of the Lazy Native*

In an edited collection of essays presented in honor of Syed Hussein Alatas (among them contributions by senior local social scientists including Shamsul A.B., Zawawi Ibrahim, Jomo K.S., Syed Farid Alatas, and Vineeta Sinha), the editor, Riaz Hassan, draws attention to the breadth of Alatas's scholarship in his studies of corruption, religious ideology and values, Islam, intellectuals, academic dependency, development planning and underdevelopment, and colonial myth-making.[74] With direct reference to *The Myth of the Lazy Native*, Riaz states that Alatas was concerned to 'deconstruct and demystify the dominant ideas and myths which have allowed the exploitation of the peoples and societies of Southeast Asia, and which are still used to perpetuate the exploitation by the new national elites in many countries of the developing world.'[75] Zawawi Ibrahim, in particular, has presented an appreciation of Alatas's deconstruction and demystification of the colonial myth in his work on the Malay peasantry, and, following Alatas, has explored the differences and interactions between colonial and indigenous scholarship.[76]

Aside from his connections with Said's work, Alatas's focus on colonial myths (or ideology) puts him firmly within the Dutch school of historical sociology.[77] He focuses on relations of domination between Europeans and those subjugated in the context of colonial capitalism and processes of underdevelopment. He is interested in what Karl Mannheim, in his sociology of knowledge, refers to as "ideology," Gramsci's "cultural hegemony," and Wertheim's "conflicting

---

74 Riaz Hassan, "Introduction," in *Local and Global: Social Transformation in Southeast Asia. Essays in Honour of Professor Syed Hussein Alatas*, ed. Riaz Hassan (Leiden: Brill, 2005), vii–ix. See also Johan Meuleman, "Review: *Local and Global: Social Transformation in Southeast Asia. Essays in Honour of Professor Syed Hussein Alatas (Social Sciences in Asia, 3)* by Riaz Hassan," *Journal of Islamic Studies* 17, no. 3 (2006): 387–91; Abdul Rahman Embong, "Obituary: Professor Datuk Dr. Syed Hussein Alatas (1928–2007)," *Internationales Asienforum* 38, nos. 1–2 (2007): 227–28.

75 Riaz, "Introduction," vii.

76 Zawawi Ibrahim, *The Return of the Lazy Native: Explaining Local/Immigrant Labour Transition in Malaysian Postcolonial Plantation Society* (Universiti Malaysia Sarawak: Institute of East Asian Studies, IEAS Working Papers, 2001); Zawawi Ibrahim, "The Anthropology of the Malay Peasantry: Critical Reflections on Colonial and Indigenous Scholarship," *Asian Journal of Social Science* 38, no. 1 (2010): 5–36; Zawawi Ibrahim. "From a 'World-system' to a Social Science Knowledge 'Scape' Perspective: Anthropological Fieldworking and Transnationalising Theory-making in the 'Periphery'," *Journal of Glocal Studies* 2 (2015): 45–68.

77 Alatas, *The Myth of the Lazy Native*, 1.

value systems."[78] Alatas is also primarily concerned with conflicting interests and image construction; like Wertheim he too had more radical sociological leanings. He says that the concept of ideology 'reflects that segment of the thought world which has characterized the political philosophy of colonialism in the Asian setting.'[79] He then elaborates that this ideology (or set of dominant interests) both justifies a particular system and also counters those values, ideas, images, and interests which contradict or challenge it. It therefore creates "false consciousness" among those who are subject to domination and "distorts" the characteristics which define them and give them identity. In the case of Malays, Javanese, and Filipinos, Alatas demonstrates, with substantial evidence, that they were not "indolent," "dull," and "backward," and in need of support to achieve progress and civilization. Rather they were evaluated by Europeans in terms of their "instrumental functions" in the colonial mode of production and in relation to other Asian immigrant populations, and in that context were subject to an external construction of "racialized" stereotypes.[80] What is also important in Alatas's mode of analysis, and as a critical and qualified observation on Wertheim's conception of society, is that images or representations are situated in a particular political-economic context exercised and controlled by a European colonial power.

Given his politically active stance and his strong opposition to racial images or representations, Alatas was especially critical of Mahathir Mohamad's depiction of the Malays in his *The Malay Dilemma*,[81] prior to his becoming prime minister of Malaysia, in adopting colonial constructions which had been generated in a particular historical context and which were seen to have an overriding and continuing importance following political independence. Alatas argued that Mahathir had uncritically adopted this ideological, racial mode of thinking unsupported by the evidence.

---

78   Karl Mannheim, *Ideology and Utopia: An Introduction to the Sociology of Knowledge* (London: Routledge & Kegan Paul, 1936); Karl Mannheim, *Structures of Thinking*, trans. Jeremy J. Shapiro and Shierry Weber Nicholsen (London: Routledge & Kegan Paul, 1982); Antonio Gramsci, *Prison Notebooks*, ed. Joseph A. Buttigieg, trans. Joseph A. Buttigieg and Antonio Callari (New York: Columbia University Press, 1992); Wertheim, *Evolution and Revolution*.

79   Alatas, *The Myth of the Lazy Native*, 1.

80   Farish A. Noor, "In Memoriam: Prof. Syed Hussein Alatas, Myth-breaker," *Ummahonline*, January 27, 2007, https://ummahonline.wordpress.com/2007/01/27/in-memoriam-prof -syed-hussein-alatas-myth-breaker/.

81   Mahathir Mohamad, *The Malay Dilemma* (Singapore: Donald Moore for Asia Pacific Press, 1970).

In an interesting analysis of the published responses to Alatas's *The Myth of the Lazy Native*, Arndt Graf addresses another major issue raised by Alatas and that is intellectual hegemony and academic imperialism and the dominance of Anglo-American voices as against those of Southeast Asians, which largely "remain unheard."[82] Graf offers critical observations on the inequalities that are manifested in electronic databases, paying detailed attention to 51 reviews and references to Alatas's volume, mainly from the digital library JSTOR, and accessed in the Cornell University Library. He classifies the authors into three categories: those who were trained and worked in the Western academy, including non-Western academic migrants; those from former colonized territories but who studied in the West; and those entirely trained and employed in non-Western academies, and publishing primarily in non-Western languages. He reveals that 'almost all the voices in the discourse' on Alatas's book have been educated in the West, work in developed countries, mainly use English as a medium of communication, and are 'affiliated with well-established universities.'[83] Graf finds that from 1977, the date of the publication of *The Myth of the Lazy Native*, until around 1982 reviews tended to be critical of the volume.[84] But from 1983 up to the early 2000s 'almost all represented articles refer to *The Myth* as an authoritative work, with relevance for various fields of study in different periods.'[85] Alatas's impact was also seen to be greatest in postcolonial and Southeast Asian studies and in the field of Orientalism.[86]

Nevertheless, overall Graf does not detect an undue negative bias in the views of the authors, and even for those who were rather more critical there is a recognition of the importance of the book in emphasizing the role that knowledge, image construction, and representation plays in relations of power and domination. However, with a lack of "local voices" in the digital world, Graf

---

82 Graf, "Electronic Orientalism?" 835–36.

83 Ibid., 839.

84 See, for example, Bruce Cruikshank, "Review: Syed Hussein Alatas, *The Myth of the Lazy Native: A Study of the Image of the Malays, Filipinos and Javanese from the 16th to the 20th Century and Its Function in the Ideology of Colonial Capitalism*," *American Historical Review* 83, no. 1 (1978): 258–59; and Peter Carey, "Review: *The Myth of the Lazy Native* by S.H. Alatas," *English Historical Review* 97, no. 385 (1982): 920–22. Both historians criticize Alatas for historical inaccuracies, the assumed link between myth and colonial capitalism, and of overgeneralization, exaggeration, and speculation in relation to the European discourse.

85 Graf, "Electronic Orientalism?" 835.

86 Ibid., 836.

calls for more "intellectual liberalization" and a "re-negotiation of the internet," a recommendation with which, I feel sure, Alatas would have agreed.[87]

6   Syed Hussein Alatas and the "Captive Mind"

Alatas frequently returned to the issue of Euro/Anglo-American intellectual hegemony, non-Western dependence, and the problem of developing alternative approaches to the study of Asia with the objective of establishing an "autonomous social science." His central concept is the "captive mind" defined as an 'uncritical and imitative mind dominated by an external source [Western thought], whose thinking is deflected from an independent perspective.'[88] These are themes that his son, Syed Farid Alatas, has pursued vigorously since the 1990s.[89] The absence of creativity and separation from indigenous interests and perspectives is among the symptoms of this mental captivity.

The remedy has been sought in what Syed Farid Alatas, building on his father's work, refers to as "alternative discourses."[90] Father and son have not been alone in this exercise of decentering, diversification, and decolonization. Other local powerful and persuasive voices have reinforced this movement toward alternatives, autonomy, and a reorientation to local priorities, interests, and perspectives and away from Euro-Americanism and Orientalism.[91] Other

---

87   Ibid., 848. See also Eric C. Thompson, "Internet-mediated Networking and Academic Dependency in Indonesia, Malaysia, Singapore and the United States," *Current Sociology* 54, no. 1 (2006): 41–61.

88   Alatas, "The Captive Mind and Creative Development," 692; Alatas, "The Captive Mind in Development Studies," 11.

89   See, for example, Syed Farid Alatas, "On the Indigenization of Academic Discourse," *Alternatives* 18, no. 3 (1993): 307–38; Syed Farid Alatas, "An Introduction to the Idea of Alternative Discourses," *Southeast Asian Journal of Social Science* 28, no. 1 (2000): 1–12; Syed Farid Alatas, "Alternative Discourses in Southeast Asia," in *Reflections on Alternative Discourses from Southeast Asia*, ed. Syed Farid Alatas (Singapore: Centre of Advanced Studies and Pagesetters Services, 2001), 13–31; Syed Farid Alatas, "Academic Dependency and the Global Division of Labour in the Social Sciences," *Current Sociology* 51, no. 6 (2003): 599–613; Syed Farid Alatas, *Alternative Discourses in Asian Social Science* (New Delhi: Sage, 2006); Syed Farid Alatas, *Ibn Khaldun* (New Delhi: Oxford University Press, 2013); Alatas, "Silencing as Method"; Syed Farid Alatas and Vineeta Sinha, "Teaching Classical Theory in Singapore: The Context of Eurocentrism," *Teaching Sociology* 29, no. 3 (2001): 316–31; Syed Farid Alatas and Vineeta Sinha, *Sociological Theory beyond the Canon* (London: Palgrave Macmillan, 2017).

90   See especially Alatas, *Alternative Discourses in Asian Social Science*.

91   See, for example, Goh Beng-Lan, "Southeast Asian Perspectives on Area Studies in a Global Age," *Jati: Journal of Southeast Asian Studies* 15 (Special Issue) (2010): 45–61; Goh Beng-Lan, ed., *Decentring and Diversifying Southeast Asian Studies: Perspectives*

EAST-WEST INTERACTIONS AND COMPLEXITIES

terms such as "native" and "indigenous" theories, concepts, and methods have also emerged in the debates about Western dominance and the need for the localization of social science.[92] However, on matters to do with "alternative discourses" and the "captive mind" in the context of local, especially Singapore-based, sociology, Syed Farid Alatas has been critical of a range of publications, including some of those of Goh Beng-Lan and Stella Quah, in regard to what he proposes as their neglect of the contribution to alternative discourses of his father's and his own work and that of others in the Department of Malay Studies at the National University of Singapore. He conceptualizes the neglect in terms of "silencing," "omission," "marginalization," and "dismissal."[93]

---

from the Region (Singapore: Institute of Southeast Asian Studies, 2011); Goh Beng-Lan, "Disciplines and Area Studies in the Global Age: Southeast Asian Reflections," in *Decentring and Diversifying Southeast Asian Studies: Perspectives from the Region*, ed. Goh Beng-Lan (Singapore: Institute of Southeast Asian Studies, 2011), 1–59; Goh Beng-Lan, "Southeast Asian Perspectives on Disciplines and Afterlives of Area Studies in a Global Age," in *Social Science and Knowledge in a Globalising Age*, ed. Zawawi Ibrahim (Petaling Jaya: Strategic Information and Research Development Centre, 2012), 79–102; Goh Beng-Lan, "Moving Theory and Methods in Southeast Asian Studies," in *Methodology and Research Practice in Southeast Asian Studies*, ed. Mikko Huotari, Jürgen Rüland, and Judith Schlehe (London: Palgrave Macmillan, 2014), 27–43; Ignas Kleden, "The Orient and the Occident: From Binary Opposition to Hermeneutic Circle," in *Reflections on Alternative Discourses from Southeast Asia*, ed. Syed Farid Alatas (Singapore: Centre of Advanced Studies and Pagesetters Services, 2001), 104–18; Stella R. Quah, "Of Consensus, Tensions, and Sociology beyond the Western Sphere," in *Reflections on Alternative Discourses from Southeast Asia*, ed. Syed Farid Alatas (Singapore: Centre of Advanced Studies and Pagesetters Services, 2001), 68–77; Shaharuddin Maaruf, "The Social Sciences in Southeast Asia: Sociology of Anti-Sociology and Alienated Social Sciences," in *Reflections on Alternative Discourses from Southeast Asia*, ed. Syed Farid Alatas (Singapore: Centre of Advanced Studies and Pagesetters Services, 2001), 88–103; Vineeta Sinha, "Reconceptualizing the Social Sciences in non-Western Settings: Challenges and Dilemmas," *Southeast Asian Journal of Social Science* 25, no. 1 (1997): 167–81; Vineeta Sinha, "Re-building Institutional Structures in the Social Sciences through Critique," in *Reflections on Alternative Discourses from Southeast Asia*, ed. Syed Farid Alatas (Singapore: Centre of Advanced Studies and Pagesetters Services, 2001), 78–87; Vineeta Sinha, "De-centering Social Sciences in Practice through Individual Acts and Choices," *Current Sociology* 51, no. 1 (2003): 7–26; Wang Gungwu, "Shifting Paradigms and Asian Perspectives: Implications for Research and Teaching," in *Reflections on Alternative Discourses from Southeast Asia*, ed. Syed Farid Alatas (Singapore: Centre of Advanced Studies and Pagesetters Services, 2001), 47–54.

92 Stella R. Quah, "The Native Sociologist and the Challenge of Science: National, Indigenous and Global Sociologists," *Current Sociology* 41, no. 1 (1993): 95–106; Stella R. Quah, "Beyond the Known Terrain: Sociology in Singapore," *American Sociologist* 26, no. 4 (1995): 88–106.

93 Alatas, "Silencing as Method"; Raewyn Connell, "Northern Theory: The Political Geography of General Social Theory," *Theory and Society* 35, no. 2 (2006): 237–64.

Syed Farid Alatas notes that I have acknowledged (and continue to do so) the pioneering contribution that Syed Hussein Alatas has made to the development of sociology in Southeast Asia and to the provision of a range of issues and ideas for contemplation and further research.[94] Nevertheless, I have raised the question of what alternative discourses might comprise in that, following Wertheim, I held to the view that alternative discourses could act to modify, qualify, and set conditions to Western-derived concepts and perspectives.[95] In addition, and in the context of social science methodologies specifically in Southeast Asian studies and area studies more generally (in which the disciplines of sociology and anthropology have played a significant role), I was skeptical that these scholarly projects, in addressing non-Western materials, had developed or were capable of developing innovative and distinctive approaches.[96] Let us leave aside for the moment theories and concepts. I had recognized that Syed Hussein Alatas, while acknowledging the role of Western social science in addressing and understanding non-Western issues, had pushed the boundaries of his mentor's, Wertheim's, position as expressed in *East–West Parallels* in that he was in search of a release from the "captive mind" and the discovery of an autonomous status for locally generated social science. However, he most decidedly did not argue for the rejection, replacement, or the inapplicability of the contributions of Western social science to non-Western contexts. Rather, he encouraged critical engagement and creative application.

Syed Farid Alatas has recently clarified my doubts and uncertainties in proposing that he is pursuing a "universal" and not a "parochial" social science, and arguing for a merger between alternative discourses, rather than simply

---

94 Victor T. King, *The Sociology of Southeast Asia: Transformations in a Developing Region* (Honolulu: University of Hawai'i Press, 2008); Alatas, "Silencing as Method."

95 Victor T. King, "Southeast Asian Studies: Insiders and Outsiders, or is Culture and Identity the Way Forward?" *Suvannabhumi: Multi-disciplinary Journal of Southeast Asian Studies* 8, no. 1 (2016): 21–22, 24.

96 Victor T. King, "Southeast Asian Studies: The Conundrum of Area and Method," in *Methodology and Research Practice in Southeast Asian Studies*, ed. Mikko Huotari, Jürgen Rüland, and Judith Schlehe (London: Palgrave Macmillan, 2014), 44–64; Victor T. King, "Alternative Approaches in Southeast Asian Studies: Compounding Area Studies and Cultural Studies," *Suvannabhumi. Multi-disciplinary Journal of Southeast Asian Studies* 10, no. 2 (2018): 7–27; Victor T. King, "Some Thoughts on Social Science Research: 50 Years of Engagement in Southeast Asia," *Horizon Journal of Humanities and Social Sciences Research* 1, no. 1 (2019): 3–8; Victor T. King, *The Construction of Southeast Asian Studies: Personages, Programmes and Problems*. Gadong: Institute of Asian Studies, Universiti Brunei Darussalam, Working Paper Series, No. 49, 2019; and see King, "Southeast Asia."

replacing (or modifying) one discourse with another.[97] In addition, he refines and amplifies his argument by referring to "various levels" of engagement or interaction between Western and non-Western-local theory/theories: that is, the application of local theory (and methods) to "local reality"; of local and Western theory to "local reality"; of Western and non-Western theory to other "local realities"; and, at the highest level, the realization of "locally generated universal theory."[98] At the highest levels of conceptualization, Syed Farid Alatas refers to the work of the Tunisian-born philosopher Ibn Khaldun in the study of society and history, and that Syed Hussein Alatas, early on in his contribution to the development of "progressive Islam" from the 1950s, had already recognized Ibn Khaldun as a major figure in social and historical philosophy, and bemoaned his omission from serious consideration in Western social science.[99]

Undoubtedly, debates on the interactions between Western and non-Western social science will continue, but clearly Syed Hussein Alatas made a significant and sustained contribution to these exchanges. In my view, we will continue to engage with the conceptualization of the West and the non-West (or, in this case, the East); the foreign and the local; outsider and insider; external and internal; the problems generated by binary categorizations; the nature of the interactions between alternative discourses; and what constitutes theory, concept, paradigm, discourse, tradition, and method. For me, the major issue still stands. Frequently it remains unclear at what level of conceptualization we are operating and whether or not, in certain contexts and in engagement with "local realities" in the Western–non-Western debate, we are referring not to theories or paradigms but to different interests, priorities, perspectives, approaches, and emphases, and to a range of often disconnected "lower-level concepts." Disagreements often turn on our different interpretations of these terms.

7   Syed Hussein Alatas and Borneo?

Borneo is perhaps an unlikely place to find Syed Hussein Alatas. I take examples from the island because it is one of the places that I know best and it provides

---

97   Alatas, "Silencing as Method."

98   Ibid.

99   Alatas, *Ibn Khaldun*; Syed Farid Alatas, *Applying Ibn Khaldun: The Recovery of a Lost Tradition in Sociology* (London: Routledge, 2014).

an occasion for commenting on Alatas's *The Myth of the Lazy Native*.[100] First, it enables us to widen Alatas's use of the concept of myth or ideology and its expression in another part of Southeast Asia. As we have seen, his focus was on the representation of some of the lowland agricultural populations (formerly commonly referred to as "peasantries") of what is now Malaysia, Indonesia, and the Philippines, and their location within a political economy of colonial capitalism. An overriding construction or image was one of "laziness" or "indolence." However, there were other native communities which were perceived in rather different terms, and indeed were also often seen by settled lowland farmers in a somewhat disparaging way. For example, some of the remote interior, non-Malay, non-Muslim populations of Borneo (most of them referred to by the general term "Dayak" and categorized in popular terms as "tribal") had long been characterized by European travelers, explorers, merchants, administrators, and missionaries as violent, dangerous, and untamed, and requiring pacification and the imposition of law and order. This was not indolence in a colonial capitalist context, but aggressiveness, expressed in such institutions as head-hunting, raiding, piracy, and slavery, which threatened the peaceful conduct of European commercial affairs.[101]

Second, the same stereotype did not apply to all upriver populations. From the nineteenth century, when the Dutch began to explore the southern two-thirds of the island, they made a distinction, also found in the Malay language, between those Dayaks who were tied through taxation, tribute, services, and forced trade to Malay states and were seen as docile subjects, sharing some of the features of Alatas's subjugated lowland farmers, and others who lived in remoter regions and were largely free from Malay control and retained their established ways of life.[102] In this connection, Europeans interpreted docility in terms of Malay–Dayak relations, shifting attention away from the effects of European intervention. European categorizations were still within the realm of the increasing desire to pacify and control those who opposed them, and to

---

100   See, for example, Victor T. King, *The Peoples of Borneo* (Oxford: Blackwell, 1993); Victor T. King, ed., *Tourism in Borneo: Issues and Perspectives* (Williamsburg, VA: Proceedings of the Borneo Research Council, No. 4, 1994); Victor T. King, *Convergence and Divergence in Tourism Development: Issues of State and Region in Malaysian Borneo, Brunei Darussalam and Indonesian Kalimantan* (Gadong: Institute of Asian Studies, Universiti Brunei Darussalam, Working Paper series, No. 24, 2016); Victor T. King, "Tourism Development in Borneo: Comparative Excursions 20 Years On," *Asian Journal of Tourism Research* 1, no. 2 (2016): 63–102; Victor T. King, Zawawi Ibrahim, and Noor Hasharina Hassan, eds., *Borneo Studies in History, Society and Culture* (Singapore: Springer, 2017).

101   King, *The Peoples of Borneo*, 8–17.

102   Ibid., 128–29.

divide indigenous populations into those who were potential allies and those who were not. Be that as it may, the construction of images of "other natives" was not the sole preserve of Europeans.

Third, in regard to the concepts of "indolence" and "wildness," I would argue that the latter has a much more complex origin and development in Western thought, and though it was consolidated and elaborated in a colonial capitalist context to justify pacification and control, its history goes back to the first encounters of Europeans with other cultures. Indeed, there is a set of interrelated images of "natives," which even before the period of high capitalism in the nineteenth century was increasingly explained in terms of theories of evolution. In a Borneo context, wildness was concerned with the boundaries between humanity and animality, and between civilization and savagery. It also became entwined with notions of "wild men of the forest," the orangutan, hairy hominids, and humans with tails, and the perception of certain Dayak populations as untamed, violent, and barbaric, even animal-like.[103]

Finally, Alatas considers the persistence of the colonial myth into the post-independence period, and proposes that, in the case of Malaysia, in justifying a particular ideology of plural or racial governance, the European image of the rural Malays was embraced by members of the political elite, including Mahathir Mohamad. This entailed a policy of positive discrimination on the part of government to support the development and progress of its "indigenous" Malay citizens. Furthermore, the myth of wildness in Borneo, and associated ideas of danger, the unknown, and the untamed, has also persisted. But in the post-independence period it is used not as a mode of governance and a means of ordering society, but as a representation of "ancient and exotic tradition," primarily for tourism development purposes. The international and national tourism industry in Malaysia and Indonesia, government tourism agencies, and the people themselves who serve as hosts for visiting tourists (the guests), use the image of "wildness" to market their tourism assets. Moreover, the representation of "wildness" is used in the construction of culture and also nature.[104]

---

103   Robert Cribb, Helen Gilbert, and Helen Tiffin, *Wild Man from Borneo: A Cultural History of the Orangutan* (Honolulu: University of Hawai'i Press, 2014); Gregory Forth, *Images of the Wildman in Southeast Asia: An Anthropological Perspective* (London: Routledge, 2008); King, *The Peoples of Borneo*, 10–16.

104   Norman Backhaus, "'Non-place Jungle': The Construction of Authenticity in National Parks of Malaysia," *Indonesia and the Malay World* 31, no. 89 (2003): 151–60; Kevin Markwell, "'Borneo, Nature's Paradise': Constructions and Representations of Nature within Nature-based Tourism," in *Interconnected Worlds: Tourism in Southeast Asia*, ed. Peggy Teo, T.C. Chang, and K.C. Ho (London: Pergamon, 2001), 248–62.

In his structuralist and post-structuralist analysis of tourism brochures, including some from Borneo, Tom Selwyn argues that promotional materials are now "in the business of selling myths," and they are designed to create "emotional sensation" and "discontinuous intensity."[105] The main elements presented are "rich cultural heritage," "ancient tribes," head-hunting, longhouses, tattooed and loin-clothed warriors, bejeweled and colorfully costumed maidens, "hard travel," adventurous river journeys, jungle-trekking, orangutans, hornbills, proboscis monkeys, crocodiles, and Rafflesia. As Graham Saunders has said, 'there are certain sights which they [tourists] expect to see, certain experiences they expect to enjoy, certain activities they expect to undertake.' This is because '[t]hey carry with them an idea of Borneo, an image which tourist brochures have conveyed and tourist authorities have cultivated.'[106] The image is also reinforced constantly in popular literature, for example in Andro Linklater's *Wild People* and Nick Garbutt and J. Cede Prudente's *Wild Borneo*.[107]

The case above illustrates the ways in which Alatas's seminal study of myth-making might be translated, extended, elaborated, and modified in a range of other cases where relations of inequality operate in historical and current cross-cultural encounters and in certain political-economic contexts.

8 Conclusions

Syed Hussein Alatas pursued a wide range of interests in the fields of social change, modernization, development, and culture. This chapter has focused on two of his pioneering achievements in the sociology of knowledge and specifically in the construction of images or representations of subject populations in Southeast Asia and on intellectual/academic imperialism and mental captivity. In this investigation the relationships between his work and that of Willem Wertheim (in non-Western sociology) and Edward Said (in Orientalism) are explored, as well as the complex interactions between what

---

105   Tom Selwyn, "Peter Pan in South-East Asia: Views from the Brochures," in *Tourism in South-East Asia*, ed Michael Hitchcock, Victor T. King, and Michael J.G. Parnwell (London: Routledge, 1993), 127, 129–33.

106   Graham Saunders, "Early Travellers in Borneo," in *Tourism in South-East Asia*, ed. Michael Hitchcock, Victor T. King, and Michael J.G. Parnwell (London: Routledge, 1993), 271.

107   Andro Linklater, *Wild People: Travels with Borneo's Head-Hunters* (London: John Murray, 1990); Nick Garbutt and J. Cede Prudente, *Wild Borneo: The Wildlife and Scenery of Sabah, Sarawak, Brunei and Kalimantan* (Cambridge, MA: MIT Press, 2006).

has broadly been categorized as Western (or Euro-American) and non-Western (or local/indigenous/Eastern/Asian) social science. Many of his writings have had a lasting influence on sociological research in Southeast Asia, and the chapter also draws attention to the ways in which his thesis on colonial myth-making enables us to extend our analyses into related concerns in cultural construction and representation. Given his training in the Netherlands and, on his return to Southeast Asia, his desire to elaborate a vision for local social science, he continued to be preoccupied with the relations between Western and Eastern scholarship. In this endeavor he began to depart from his mentor, Wertheim, to develop an innovative, locally generated, and autonomous rather than an imitative, dependent social science. His son, Syed Farid Alatas, has continued this mission in his work on alternative discourses.

Aside from his scholarly achievements, Syed Hussein Alatas enjoyed a formidable reputation as a "model public intellectual," a "mentor-figure," and an "activist-oriented" academic.[108] He guided others on the journey upon which he embarked as an intellectual, a teacher, and a progressive Muslim.[109] On a personal note, Mona Abaza, in her comparative study of the work of Syed Hussein Alatas and his brother, Syed Naguib Al-Attas, says of Syed Hussein that he was "most pleasantly approachable" and "very generous towards his students."[110] He was also one of 'the founders of sociological investigation in Southeast Asia' and his works 'are of primary significance for anyone interested in the contemporary sociology of Southeast Asia.'[111]

Let me leave the final words with Farish A. Noor's "In Memoriam," following Syed Hussein Alatas's death on January 27, 2007. He writes:

> Much of his work and the focus of all his energy was towards critically questioning and deconstructing many of the staid comfortable assumptions upon which both the colonial and post-colonial order of knowledge and power were based ... demonstrating that academic work does not

---

108   Farish, "In Memoriam."
109   Abdul Rahman, "Obituary: Professor Datuk Dr. Syed Hussein Alatas."
110   Mona Abaza, *Debates on Islam and Knowledge in Malaysia and Egypt: Shifting Worlds* (London: Routledge, 2002); Mona Abaza, "Some Reflections on the Question of Islam and Social Science in the Contemporary Muslim World," *Social Compass* 40, no. 2 (1993): 301–21. See also Peter L. Burns, "Meeting Hussein – 1958," in *Local and Global: Social Transformation in Southeast Asia. Essays in Honour of Professor Syed Hussein Alatas*, ed. Riaz Hassan (Leiden: Brill, 2005), 331–34; Salil Tripathi, "Putting an End to the Myth of the Lazy Native," *Global Asia* 5, no. 4 (2010): 107–8.
111   Abaza, *Debates on Islam and Knowledge*, 122, 124.

only have social and political relevance but also that such critical think-ing was politically necessary.[112]

Bibliography

Abaza, Mona. "Some Reflections on the Question of Islam and Social Science in the Contemporary Muslim World." *Social Compass* 40, no. 2 (1993): 301–21.

Abaza, Mona. *Debates on Islam and Knowledge in Malaysia and Egypt: Shifting Worlds.* London: Routledge, 2002.

Abdul Rahman Embong. "Obituary: Professor Datuk Dr. Syed Hussein Alatas (1928–2007)." *Internationales Asienforum* 38, nos. 1–2 (2007): 227–28.

Alatas, Masturah. *The Life in the Writing: Syed Hussein Alatas.* Shah Alam: Marshall Cavendish Editions, 2010.

Alatas, Masturah. "Four Decades of a Malay Myth." *The Malay Mail*, January 24, 2017. https://www.malaymail.com/news/what-you-think/2017/01/24/four-decades-of-a -malay-myth-masturah-alatas/1299401.

Alatas, Syed Farid. "On the Indigenization of Academic Discourse." *Alternatives* 18, no. 3 (1993): 307–38.

Alatas, Syed Farid. "An Introduction to the Idea of Alternative Discourses." *Southeast Asian Journal of Social Science* 28, no. 1 (2000): 1–12.

Alatas, Syed Farid. "Alternative Discourses in Southeast Asia." In *Reflections on Alternative Discourses from Southeast Asia*, edited by Syed Farid Alatas, 13–31. Singapore: Centre of Advanced Studies and Pagesetters Services, 2001.

Alatas, Syed Farid. "Academic Dependency and the Global Division of Labour in the Social Sciences." *Current Sociology* 51, no. 6 (2003): 599–613.

Alatas, Syed Farid. *Alternative Discourses in Asian Social Science.* New Delhi: Sage, 2006.

Alatas, Syed Farid. "Intellectual and Structural Challenge to Academic Dependency." *International Sociological Association E-Bulletin* 9 (2008). https://www.isa-sociol ogy.org/uploads/imgen/328-e-bulletin-9.pdf.

Alatas, Syed Farid. *Ibn Khaldun.* New Delhi: Oxford University Press, 2013.

Alatas, Syed Farid. *Applying Ibn Khaldun: The Recovery of a Lost Tradition in Sociology.* London: Routledge, 2014.

Alatas, Syed Farid. "Silencing as Method: The Case of Malay Studies." In *Fieldwork and the Self: Changing Research Styles in Southeast Asia*, edited by Jérémy Jammes and Victor T. King. Singapore: Springer, 2021 (in press).

---

112   Farish, "In Memoriam."

Alatas, Syed Farid, and Vineeta Sinha. "Teaching Classical Theory in Singapore: The Context of Eurocentrism." *Teaching Sociology* 29, no. 3 (2001): 316–31.

Alatas, Syed Farid, and Vineeta Sinha. *Sociological Theory beyond the Canon*. London: Palgrave Macmillan, 2017.

Alatas, Syed Hussein. "Reconstruction of Malaysian History." *Revue du Sud-est Asiatique* 3 (1962): 219–45.

Alatas, Syed Hussein. "Reflections on the Theories of Religion." PhD diss., University of Amsterdam. 's-Gravenhage: Drukkerij Pasmans, 1963.

Alatas, Syed Hussein. "The Weber Thesis and South East Asia." *Archives de sociologie des religions* 15 (1963): 21–34.

Alatas, Syed Hussein. "Theoretical Aspects of Southeast Asian History: John Bastin and the Study of Southeast Asian History." *Asian Studies* 2, no. 2 (1964): 247–60.

Alatas, Syed Hussein. *The Sociology of Corruption: The Nature, Function, Causes and Prevention of Corruption*. Singapore: Donald Moore, 1968.

Alatas, Syed Hussein. "Academic Imperialism." Lecture delivered to the History Society, University of Singapore, September 26, 1969.

Alatas, Syed Hussein. "Religion and Modernization in Southeast Asia." *European Journal of Sociology* 11, no. 2 (1970): 265–96.

Alatas, Syed Hussein. *Thomas Stamford Raffles 1781–1826: Schemer or Reformer?* Sydney: Angus & Robertson, 1971.

Alatas, Syed Hussein. *Modernization and Social Change: Studies in Modernization, Religion, Social Change and Development in South-East Asia*. Sydney: Angus & Robertson, 1972.

Alatas, Syed Hussein. "The Captive Mind in Development Studies." *International Social Science Journal* 34, no. 1 (1972): 9–25.

Alatas, Syed Hussein. "The Captive Mind and Creative Development." *International Social Science Journal* 36, no. 4 (1974): 691–99.

Alatas, Syed Hussein. *The Myth of the Lazy Native: A Study of the Image of the Malays, Filipinos and Javanese from the 16th to the 20th Century and Its Function in the Ideology of Colonial Capitalism*. London: Frank Cass, 1977.

Alatas, Syed Hussein. *Intellectuals in Developing Societies*. London: Frank Cass, 1977.

Alatas, Syed Hussein. "Towards an Asian Social Science Tradition." *New Quest* 17 (1979): 265–69.

Alatas, Syed Hussein. "Social Aspects of Endogenous Intellectual Creativity: The Problem of Obstacles – Guidelines for Research." In *Intellectual Creativity in Endogenous Culture*, edited by Anouar Abdel-Malek and Amar Nath Pandeya, 462–70. Tokyo: The United Nations University, 1981.

Alatas, Syed Hussein. "Intellectual Imperialism: Definition, Traits and Problems." *Southeast Asian Journal of Social Science* 28 no. 1 (2000): 23–45.

Alatas, Syed Hussein. "Academic Imperialism." In *Reflections on Alternative Discourses from Southeast Asia: Proceedings of the ISA Regional Conference for Southeast Asia, Singapore, 30 May–1 June 1998*, edited by Syed Farid Alatas, 32–46. Singapore: Centre of Advanced Studies and Pagesetters Services, 2001.

Alatas, Syed Hussein. "The Development of an Autonomous Social Science in Asia: Problems and Prospects." *Asian Journal of Social Science* 30 no. 1 (2002): 150–57.

Alatas, Syed Hussein. "The Autonomous, the Universal and the Future of Sociology." *Current Sociology* 54, no. 1 (2006): 7–23.

Asad, Talal, ed. *Anthropology and the Colonial Encounter*. London: Ithaca Press, 1973.

Backhaus, Norman. "'Non-place Jungle': The Construction of Authenticity in National Parks of Malaysia." *Indonesia and the Malay World* 31, no. 89 (2003): 151–60.

Beek, W.E.A. van, and J.H. Scherer, eds. *Explorations in the Anthropology of Religion: Essays in Honour of Jan van Baal.* The Hague: Martinus Nijhoff, Verhandelingen van het Koninklijk Instituut voor Taal-, Land- en Volkenkunde, Vol. 74, 1975.

Boeke, J.H. *Economics and Economic Policy of Dual Societies, as Exemplified by Indonesia.* New York: International Secretariat, Institute of Pacific Relations, 1953.

Breman, Jan. "W.F. Wertheim: A Sociological Chronicler of Revolutionary Change." *Development and Change* 48, no. 5 (2017): 1130–53.

Burns, Peter L. "Meeting Hussein – 1958." In *Local and Global: Social Transformation in Southeast Asia. Essays in Honour of Professor Syed Hussein Alatas*, edited by Riaz Hassan, 331–34. Leiden: Brill, 2005.

Carey, Peter. "Review: *The Myth of the Lazy Native* by S.H. Alatas." *English Historical Review* 97, no. 385 (1982): 920–22.

Chen, Peter S.J., and Hans-Dieter Evers. "Introduction." In *Studies in ASEAN Sociology: Urban Society and Social Change*, edited by Peter S.J. Chen and Hans-Dieter Evers, XIII–XX. Singapore: Chopmen Enterprises, 1978.

Connell, Raewyn. "Northern Theory: The Political Geography of General Social Theory." *Theory and Society* 35, no. 2 (2006): 237–64.

Cribb, Robert, Helen Gilbert, and Helen Tiffin. *Wild Man from Borneo: A Cultural History of the Orangutan*. Honolulu: University of Hawai'i Press, 2014.

Cruikshank, Bruce. "Review: Syed Hussein Alatas, *The Myth of the Lazy Native: A Study of the Image of the Malays, Filipinos and Javanese from the 16th to the 20th Century and Its Function in the Ideology of Colonial Capitalism.*" *American Historical Review* 83, no. 1 (1978): 258–59.

Doner, Richard F. "Approaches to the Politics of Economic Growth in Southeast Asia." *Journal of Asian Studies* 50, no. 4 (1991): 818–49.

Evans, Grant. *From Moral Economy to Remembered Village: The Sociology of James C. Scott*. Clayton, Vic.: Monash University, Centre of Southeast Asian Studies, Working Paper No. 40, 1986.

Evers, Hans-Dieter, ed. *Sociology of South-East Asia: Readings on Social Change and Development*. Kuala Lumpur: Oxford University Press, 1980.

Evers, Hans-Dieter. "Editor's Introduction." In *Sociology of South-East Asia: Readings on Social Change and Development*, edited by Hans-Dieter Evers, IX–X. Kuala Lumpur: Oxford University Press, 1980.

Evers, Hans-Dieter. "The Challenge of Diversity: Basic Concepts and Theories in the Study of South-East Asian Societies." In *Sociology of South-East Asia: Readings on Social Change and Development*, edited by Hans-Dieter Evers, 2–7. Kuala Lumpur: Oxford University Press, 1980.

Farish A. Noor. "In Memoriam: Prof. Syed Hussein Alatas, Myth-breaker." *Ummahonline*, January 27, 2007. https://ummahonline.wordpress.com/2007/01/27/in-memoriam -prof-syed-hussein-alatas-myth-breaker/.

Forth, Gregory. *Images of the Wildman in Southeast Asia: An Anthropological Perspective*. London: Routledge, 2008.

Furnivall, J.S. *Colonial Policy and Practice: A Comparative Study of Burma and Netherlands India*. Cambridge: Cambridge University Press, 1948.

Garbutt, Nick, and J. Cede Prudente. *Wild Borneo: The Wildlife and Scenery of Sabah, Sarawak, Brunei and Kalimantan*. Cambridge, MA: MIT Press, 2006.

Goh Beng-Lan. "Southeast Asian Perspectives on Area Studies in a Global Age." *Jati: Journal of Southeast Asian Studies* 15 (Special Issue) (2010): 45–61.

Goh Beng-Lan, ed. *Decentring and Diversifying Southeast Asian Studies: Perspectives from the Region*. Singapore: Institute of Southeast Asian Studies, 2011.

Goh Beng-Lan. "Disciplines and Area Studies in the Global Age: Southeast Asian Reflections." In *Decentring and Diversifying Southeast Asian Studies: Perspectives from the Region*, edited by Goh Beng-Lan, 1–59. Singapore: Institute of Southeast Asian Studies, 2011.

Goh Beng-Lan. "Southeast Asian Perspectives on Disciplines and Afterlives of Area Studies in a Global Age." In *Social Science and Knowledge in a Globalising Age*, edited by Zawawi Ibrahim, 79–102. Petaling Jaya: Strategic Information and Research Development Centre, 2012.

Goh Beng-Lan. "Moving Theory and Methods in Southeast Asian Studies." In *Methodology and Research Practice in Southeast Asian Studies*, edited by Mikko Huotari, Jürgen Rüland, and Judith Schlehe, 27–43. London: Palgrave Macmillan, 2014.

Graf, Arndt. "Electronic Orientalism? The Afterlife of Syed Hussein Alatas' *The Myth of the Lazy Native* in Online Databases." *New Media and Society* 12, no. 5 (2010): 835–54.

Gramsci, Antonio. *Prison Notebooks*, edited by Joseph A. Buttigieg, translated by Joseph A. Buttigieg and Antonio Callari. New York: Columbia University Press, 1992.

Güven, Fikret. "Criticism to Edward W. Said's Orientalism." *RumeliDE Journal of Language and Literature Studies* 15 (2019): 418–30.

Halliday, Fred. "'Orientalism' and Its Critics." *British Journal of Middle Eastern Studies* 20, no. 2 (1993): 145–63.

Halliday, Fred. *Islam and the Myth of Confrontation: Religion and Politics in the Middle East*. New York: I.B. Tauris, 1996.

Higgott, Richard, and Richard Robison, eds. *Southeast Asia: Essays in the Political Economy of Structural Change*. London: Routledge and Kegan Paul, 1985.

Higgott, Richard, and Richard Robison. "Introduction." In *Southeast Asia: Essays in the Political Economy of Structural Change*, edited by Richard Higgott and Richard Robison, 3–15. London: Routledge and Kegan Paul, 1985.

Hirschman, Charles. "The Making of Race in Colonial Malaya: Political Economy and Racial Ideology." *Sociological Forum* 1, no. 2 (1986): 330–61.

Kahn, Joel S. *Other Malays: Nationalism and Cosmopolitanism in the Modern Malay World*. Honolulu: University of Hawai'i Press, 2006.

King, Victor T. "Sociology in South-East Asia: A Personal View." *Cultures et développement* 13, no. 2 (1981): 391–414.

King, Victor T. "South-East Asia: Essays in the Political Economy of Structural Change (Review Article)." *Journal of Contemporary Asia* 16, no. 4 (1986): 520–33.

King, Victor T. *The Peoples of Borneo*. Oxford: Blackwell, 1993.

King, Victor T. "The Sociology of South-East Asia: A Critical Review of Some Concepts and Issues." *Bijdragen tot de Taal-, Land- en Volkenkunde* 150, no. 1 (1994): 171–206.

King, Victor T., ed. *Tourism in Borneo: Issues and Perspectives*. Williamsburg, VA: Proceedings of the Borneo Research Council, No. 4, 1994.

King, Victor T. "Sociology." In *An Introduction to Southeast Asian Studies*, edited by Mohammed Halib and Tim Huxley, 148–88. London: I.B. Tauris, 1996.

King, Victor T. "Southeast Asia: An Anthropological Field of Study?" *Moussons: Recherche en sciences humaines sur l'Asie du Sud-Est* 3 (2001): 3–31.

King, Victor T. "Southeast Asia: Personal Reflections on a Region." In *Southeast Asian Studies: Debates and New Directions*, edited by Cynthia Chou and Vincent Houben, 23–44. Leiden: International Institute for Asian Studies, 2006.

King, Victor T. *The Sociology of Southeast Asia: Transformations in a Developing Region*. Honolulu: University of Hawai'i Press, 2008.

King, Victor T. "Southeast Asian Studies: The Conundrum of Area and Method." In *Methodology and Research Practice in Southeast Asian Studies*, edited by Mikko Huotari, Jürgen Rüland, and Judith Schlehe, 44–64. London: Palgrave Macmillan, 2014.

King, Victor T. "Southeast Asian Studies: Insiders and Outsiders, or is Culture and Identity the Way Forward?" *Suvannabhumi: Multi-disciplinary Journal of Southeast Asian Studies* 8, no. 1 (2016): 17–53.

King, Victor T. *Convergence and Divergence in Tourism Development: Issues of State and Region in Malaysian Borneo, Brunei Darussalam and Indonesian Kalimantan.*

Gadong: Institute of Asian Studies, Universiti Brunei Darussalam, Working Paper Series, No. 24, 2016.

King, Victor T. "Tourism Development in Borneo: Comparative Excursions 20 Years On." *Asian Journal of Tourism Research* 1, no. 2 (2016): 63–102.

King, Victor T. "Alternative Approaches in Southeast Asian Studies: Compounding Area Studies and Cultural Studies." *Suvannabhumi. Multi-disciplinary Journal of Southeast Asian Studies* 10, no. 2 (2018): 7–27.

King, Victor T. "Some Thoughts on Social Science Research: 50 Years of Engagement in Southeast Asia." *Horizon Journal of Humanities and Social Sciences Research* 1, no. 1 (2019): 3–8.

King, Victor T. *The Construction of Southeast Asian Studies: Personages, Programmes and Problems.* Gadong: Institute of Asian Studies, Universiti Brunei Darussalam, Working Paper Series, No. 49, 2019.

King, Victor T., Zawawi Ibrahim, and Noor Hasharina Hassan, eds. *Borneo Studies in History, Society and Culture.* Singapore: Springer, 2017.

Kleden, Ignas. "The Orient and the Occident: From Binary Opposition to Hermeneutic Circle." In *Reflections on Alternative Discourses from Southeast Asia*, edited by Syed Farid Alatas, 104–18. Singapore: Centre of Advanced Studies and Pagesetters Services, 2001.

Leur, J.C. van. *Indonesian Trade and Society: Essays in Asian Social and Economic History.* Translated by James S. Holmes and A. van Marle. The Hague: W. van Hoeve, 1955.

Lewis, Bernard. *Islam and the West.* New York: Oxford University Press, 1993.

Linklater, Andro. *Wild People: Travels with Borneo's Head-Hunters.* London: John Murray, 1990.

Mahathir Mohamad. *The Malay Dilemma.* Singapore: Donald Moore for Asia Pacific Press, 1970.

Mannheim, Karl. *Ideology and Utopia: An Introduction to the Sociology of Knowledge.* London: Routledge & Kegan Paul, 1936.

Mannheim, Karl. *Structures of Thinking.* Translated by Jeremy J. Shapiro and Shierry Weber Nicholsen. London: Routledge & Kegan Paul, 1982.

Markwell, Kevin. "'Borneo, Nature's Paradise': Constructions and Representations of Nature within Nature-based Tourism." In *Interconnected Worlds: Tourism in Southeast Asia*, edited by Peggy Teo, T.C. Chang, and K.C. Ho, 248–62. London: Pergamon, 2001.

McVey, Ruth. "Change and Continuity in Southeast Asian Studies." *Journal of Southeast Asian Studies* 26, no. 1 (1995): 1–9.

Meuleman, Johan. "Review: *Local and Global: Social Transformation in Southeast Asia. Essays in Honour of Professor Syed Hussein Alatas* (*Social Sciences in Asia, 3*) by Riaz Hassan." *Journal of Islamic Studies* 17, no. 3 (2006): 387–91.

Muijzenberg, Otto van den, and Willem Wolters. *Conceptualizing Development: The Historical-Sociological Tradition in Dutch Non-Western Sociology.* Dordrecht: Foris, Centre for Asian Studies Amsterdam, Comparative Asian Studies, 1, 1988.

Neher, Clark D. "The Social Sciences." In *Southeast Asian Studies: Options for the Future*, edited by Ronald A. Morse, 129–36. Lanham, MA: University Press of America, 1984.

Pieterse, Jan Nederveen. "Counterpoint and Emancipation." *Development and Change* 19, no. 2 (1988): 327–41.

Preston, P.W. *Rethinking Development: Essays on Development and Southeast Asia.* London: Routledge & Kegan Paul, 1987.

Quah, Stella R. "The Native Sociologist and the Challenge of Science: National, Indigenous and Global Sociologists." *Current Sociology* 41, no. 1 (1993): 95–106.

Quah, Stella R. "Beyond the Known Terrain: Sociology in Singapore." *American Sociologist* 26, no. 4 (1995): 88–106.

Quah, Stella R. "Of Consensus, Tensions, and Sociology beyond the Western Sphere." In *Reflections on Alternative Discourses from Southeast Asia*, edited by Syed Farid Alatas, 68–77. Singapore: Centre of Advanced Studies and Pagesetters Services, 2001.

Riaz Hassan. "Introduction." In *Local and Global: Social Transformation in Southeast Asia. Essays in Honour of Professor Syed Hussein Alatas*, edited by Riaz Hassan, VII–IX. Leiden: Brill, 2005.

Rodan, Garry. "Theorising Markets in South-East Asia: Power and Contestation." In *The Political Economy of South-East Asia: Markets, Power and Contestation*, edited by Garry Rodan, Kevin Hewison, and Richard Robison, 3rd ed., 1–38. Melbourne: Oxford University Press, 2006.

Romein, Jan. *The Asian Century: A History of Modern Nationalism in Asia.* Translated by R.T. Clark. London: Allen & Unwin, 1962.

Said, Edward W. *Orientalism.* London: Routledge and Kegan Paul, 1978.

Said, Edward W. *Culture and Imperialism.* New York: Knopf, 1993.

Saunders, Graham. "Early Travellers in Borneo." In *Tourism in South-East Asia*, edited by Michael Hitchcock, Victor T. King, and Michael J.G. Parnwell, 271–85. London: Routledge, 1993.

Schrieke, B.J.O. *Indonesian Sociological Studies: Selected Writings of B. Schrieke.* The Hague: W. van Hoeve, 2 volumes, 1955–1957.

Scott, James C. *Comparative Political Corruption.* Englewood Cliffs, NJ: Prentice-Hall, 1972.

Selwyn, Tom. "Peter Pan in South-East Asia: Views from the Brochures." In *Tourism in South-East Asia*, edited by Michael Hitchcock, Victor T. King, and Michael J.G. Parnwell, 117–37. London: Routledge, 1993.

Shaharuddin Maaruf. "The Social Sciences in Southeast Asia: Sociology of Anti-Sociology and Alienated Social Sciences." In *Reflections on Alternative Discourses from Southeast Asia*, edited by Syed Farid Alatas, 88–103. Singapore: Centre of Advanced Studies and Pagesetters Services, 2001.

Sinha, Vineeta. "Reconceptualizing the Social Sciences in non-Western Settings: Challenges and Dilemmas." *Southeast Asian Journal of Social Science* 25, no. 1 (1997): 167–81.

Sinha, Vineeta. "Re-building Institutional Structures in the Social Sciences through Critique." In *Reflections on Alternative Discourses from Southeast Asia*, edited by Syed Farid Alatas, 78–87. Singapore: Centre of Advanced Studies and Pagesetters Services, 2001.

Sinha, Vineeta. "De-centering Social Sciences in Practice through Individual Acts and Choices." *Current Sociology* 51, no. 1 (2003): 7–26.

Smail, John R.W. "On the Possibility of an Autonomous History of Modern Southeast Asia." *Journal of Southeast Asian History* 2, no. 2 (1961): 72–102.

Taylor, John G., and Andrew Turton. "Introduction." In *Southeast Asia*, edited by John G. Taylor and Andrew Turton, 1–13. Basingstoke: Macmillan, 1988.

Thompson, Eric C. "Internet-mediated Networking and Academic Dependency in Indonesia, Malaysia, Singapore and the United States." *Current Sociology* 54, no. 1 (2006): 41–61.

Tripathi, Salil. "Putting an End to the Myth of the Lazy Native." *Global Asia* 5, no. 4 (2010): 107–8.

Varisco, Daniel Martin. *Reading Orientalism: Said and the Unsaid*. Seattle: University of Washington Press, 2007.

Vermeulen, Han F. "Anthropology in the Netherlands: Past, Present and Future." In *Other People's Anthropologies: Ethnographic Practices on the Margins*, edited by Aleksandar Bošković, 44–69. New York: Berghahn Books, 2008.

Vreede-de Stuers, Cora, ed. *Buiten de grenzen: Sociologische opstellen aangeboden aan prof. dr. W.F. Wertheim, 25 jaar Amsterdams hoogleraar, 1946–1971*. Meppel: Boom, 1971.

Wang Gungwu. "Shifting Paradigms and Asian Perspectives: Implications for Research and Teaching." In *Reflections on Alternative Discourses from Southeast Asia*, edited by Syed Farid Alatas, 47–54. Singapore: Centre of Advanced Studies and Pagesetters Services, 2001.

Warraq, Ibn. *Defending the West: A Critique of Edward Said's Orientalism*. Amherst, NY: Prometheus Books, 2007.

Wertheim, W.F. *Indonesian Society in Transition: A Study of Social Change*. The Hague: W. van Hoeve, 1956; second edition, 1959; reprint, 1964.

Wertheim, W.F., ed. *Indonesian Economics: The Concept of Dualism in Theory and Policy*. The Hague: W. van Hoeve, 1961.

Wertheim, W.F. *East–West Parallels: Sociological Approaches to Modern Asia*. The Hague: W. van Hoeve, 1964.

Wertheim, W.F. "Society as a Composite of Conflicting Value Systems." In *East–West Parallels: Sociological Approaches to Modern Asia*, 23–38. The Hague: W. van Hoeve, 1964.

Wertheim, W.F. *Evolutie en revolutie: De golfslag der emancipatie*. Amsterdam: Van Gennep, 1971.

Wertheim, W.F. *Evolution and Revolution: The Rising Waves of Emancipation*. London: Penguin, 1974.

Wertheim, W.F. *Emancipation in Asia: Positive and Negative Lessons from China*. Rotterdam: Comparative Asian Studies Programme, Erasmus University, 1983.

Wertheim, W.F. *Comparative Essays on Asia and the West*. Amsterdam: VU University Press, Comparative Asian Studies, 12, 1993.

Wertheim, W.F. *Third World Whence and Whither? Protective State versus Aggressive Market*. Amsterdam: Het Spinhuis, 1997.

Wertheim, W.F. "Globalization of the Social Sciences: Non-Western Sociology as a Temporary Panacea." In *Tales from Academia: History of Anthropology in the Netherlands*, edited by Han Vermeulen and Jean Kommers, 267–96. Saarbrücken: Verlag für Entwicklungspolitik Saarbrücken, 2002.

Zarnett, David. "A Review of *Defending the West: A Critique of Edward Said's Orientalism* by Ibn Warraq and *Reading Orientalism: The Said and the Unsaid* by Daniel Martin Varisco." *Democratiya* 12 (2008): 50–61.

Zawawi Ibrahim. *The Return of the Lazy Native: Explaining Local/Immigrant Labour Transition in Malaysian Postcolonial Plantation Society*. Universiti Malaysia Sarawak: Institute of East Asian Studies, IEAS Working Papers, 2001.

Zawawi Ibrahim. "The Anthropology of the Malay Peasantry: Critical Reflections on Colonial and Indigenous Scholarship." *Asian Journal of Social Science* 38, no. 1 (2010): 5–36.

Zawawi Ibrahim. "From a 'World-system' to a Social Science Knowledge 'Scape' Perspective: Anthropological Fieldworking and Transnationalising Theory-making in the 'Periphery'." *Journal of Glocal Studies* 2 (2015): 45–68.

CHAPTER 19

Hidden Connections

Syed Hussein Alatas and Latin American Sociology

João Marcelo E. Maia

In the 1970s, Syed Hussein Alatas delivered a powerful critique of Eurocentrism and its effects on colonized societies in three texts that are among his most well-known and quoted works. In 1972, *The Captive Mind in Development Studies: Some Neglected Problems and the Need for an Autonomous Social Science Tradition in Asia* came out in vol. XXIV of International Social Sciences Journal, the flagship journal of UNESCO.[1] Five years later, the English publishing house Frank Cass edited *The Myth of the Lazy Native: A Study of the Image of the Malays, Filipinos and Javanese from the 16th to the 20th century and Its Function in the Ideology of Colonial Capitalism* and *Intellectuals in Developing Societies*.[2]

While *The Captive Mind* examines the imitative thinking that shapes the production of social science knowledge in Southeast Asia, *The Myth of the Lazy Native* exposes the ideologies of colonial capitalism by focusing on the European racist stereotypes of Southeast Asian people, and *Intellectuals in Developing Societies* analyzes the shortcomings of intellectual life in Malaysia through a comparative history of intellectuals in different national contexts. These texts are good samples of Syed Hussein Alatas' ideas and methods, which have been influential in the recent debates on how to build a truly global and non-Eurocentric social science.[3]

---

1 Syed Hussein Alatas, "The Captive Mind in Development Studies (Part 1)," *International Social Science Journal* 24, (1972): 9–25.
2 Syed Hussein Alatas. *The Myth of the Lazy Native: A Study of the Image of the Malays, the Filipinos and the Javanese from the XVI to the XX Century and Its Function in the Ideology of Colonial Capitalism.* London: Frank Cass, 1977a; Syed Hussein Alatas, *Intellectuals in Developing Societies.* London: Frank Cass, 1977b.
3 Syed Farid Alatas "Alatas and Shari'ati on Socialism: Autonomous Social Science and Occidentalism," in *Local and Global: Social Transformation in Southeast Asia*, ed. R. Hassan (Leiden: Brill Academic Publishers, 2004), 161–179; Raewyn Connell, *Southern Theory: The Global Dynamics of Knowledge in Social Sciences.* London: Routledge,1997; João Marcelo E. Maia, "History of Sociology and the Quest for Intellectual Autonomy in the Global South: The Cases of Alberto Guerreiro Ramos and Syed Hussein Alatas." *Current Sociology* 62, no. 7 (2014): 1097–1115.

© JOÃO MARCELO E. MAIA, 2023 | DOI:10.1163/9789004521698_021

Despite renewed interest in the so-called founding father of social science in the Southeast Asia, there is still a lot to understand about the place of his life and works in the development of sociology in peripheral contexts. We still miss more comparative studies that analyze Syed Hussein Alatas in the light of the history of the discipline outside Euro-America, wherein a rich tradition of autonomous social science flourished in the decades after World War II.

My goal in this chapter is to explore intellectual affinities between Syed Hussein Alatas' sociological discourse and the works of two Latin American sociologists between 1950 and 1970. By "affinities" I mean both similarities between concepts and ideas and real intellectual connections that can be traced through quotes and footnote references. My main contention is that both in Asia and Latin America the emergence of critical perspectives on development leads to new forms of conceptualizing sociology that challenged mainstream theories and concepts. The sociologists that put forward these critical perspectives highlighted the effects of colonialism and imperialism in shaping traditional ideas of development and modernity and promoted new concepts based on how underdevelopment capitalism unfolded outside Europe and the United States. Syed Hussein Alatas was thus part of a bigger picture, which encompassed intellectuals, organizations, and journals throughout the so-called Third World in a global search for autonomy and creativity.[4]

This chapter is divided into three sections. In the first, I demonstrate how Alatas' critique of development in Southeast Asia is intricately linked to his interest in the center-periphery dynamics that shaped intellectual life in postcolonial societies. In the following section, I explore the same issue in major works from Latin American sociology from the same period, authored by the Mexican Rodolfo Stavenhagen and the Brazilian Luiz de Aguiar Costa Pinto. Both are representative of the critical sociology of development that flourished in Latin America during the 1960s and 1970s and wrote relevant texts for this debate. Moreover, Stavenhagen and Costa Pinto were key players in the process of institutionalizing social sciences research in Latin America, due to their role in initiatives like Latin American Centre for Social Science Research (CLAPCS). I conclude by pointing out future research subjects that should be pursued for those interested in a history of sociology in the Global South.

---

4 Eduardo Devés-Valdez. *Pensamiento Periférico. Uma tesis interpretativa global.* Santiago: Idea-USACH, 2012; Maia, "History of Autonomy."

1   Development and Knowledge in Hussein Alatas

In *The Captive Mind,* Alatas analyzes how Southeast Asian experts fail to understand the region's problems due to an imitative thinking similar to the demonstration effect that produces underdeveloped economies. His main argument can be summarized in the following quote:

> The main drive in the assimilation of social science knowledge from the West is the belief in its utility and superiority. The assimilation of this knowledge and technique exhibits parallel traits to those of the demonstration effect. They are (a) frequency of contact; (b) weakening or breakdown of previous knowledge or habit; (c) prestige attaching to new knowledge; and (d) that it is not necessarily rational and utilitarian.[5]

"Demonstration effect" was a key concept in economic theories that challenged mainstream liberalism. It was originally coined by Dusenberry and later applied by Nurske to international relations. It means that the rising incomes of elites and middle classes in developing societies allows them to imitate the consumption pattern of their counterparts in the Global North, even in the absence of the same industries and levels of investment. This eventually hindered capital formation in the global peripheries thus impacting saving rates. In Alatas' work, this concept describes how local elites in Southeast Asia introjected theoretical frameworks coined in Europe that lacked utility for solving problems that were particular to the postcolonial nations. Imitative thinking thus precluded autonomous knowledge production in these former colonized nations.

But the "captive mind" that characterized the action of postcolonial elites in Southeast Asia had deep historical roots. *The Myth of the Lazy Native*, perhaps Hussein Alatas' most famous single work, explores how Europeans created a set of images to depict colonized people in an extremely negative fashion. The central concept in this book is "colonial capitalism," which the author details through a number of characteristics such as: foreign control of economy and politics, the presence of a non-free labor force, the lack of organized civil associations and dualism. Regarding this last feature – dualism – Syed Hussein Alatas mentions the debate on J. H. Boeke' thesis on dualistic economies published in the book Indonesian Economics.[6] Boeke was one of the pioneers of the dualist

---

5   Alatas, "The Captive Mind," 10–11.

6   J.H. Boecke, ed., *Indonesian Economics: the concept of dualism in theory and policy.* The Hague: W. van Hoeve, 1961.

thesis, which would become a key issue for Latin American economists and social scientists interested in understanding underdeveloped economies.[7]

But the similarities do not stop at this detail. The concept of colonial capitalism connects Syed Hussein Alatas to one of the main arguments fostered by Latin American scholars who analyzed global capitalism in the 1950s and 1960s. The international division of labor based on massive slavery was a central idea to understand the global formation of capitalism since the XVI century, and this process was also detailed in the works of economists such as Celso Furtado. Besides, the idea that underdevelopment was a historical route peculiar to colonized societies – and not a universal phase of modernization that every nation went through at some point – was a cornerstone of Furtado's analysis.[8] The role of center-periphery dynamics in engendering inequalities in former colonized societies was a key element of Raul Prebisch's classic text on international trade, which targeted the theory of comparative advantages.[9] Both Prebisch and Furtado were among the most influential economists working in the famous Economic Commission for Latin America (ECLA), whose theories about underdevelopment became one of the main intellectual resources available in the 1950s and 1960s for Third World scholars interested in building a counter-theory about development.[10]

Alatas relates his critique of colonial capitalism and development to his own views on knowledge and intellectuals. He explicitly states that "Colonialism, or on a bigger scale, imperialism, was not only an extension of sovereignty and control by one nation and its government over another, but it was also a control of the mind of the conquered or subordinated."[11] Therefore, the "lazy native" was an ideological tool that performed a key function in colonial domination by justifying coercive labor and imperialism. By the same token, one can say that the "captive mind" was a late output of colonialism, playing a similar role in the postcolonial nations where local elites were unable to think of development strategies through local frames of relevance.

Alatas' belief in the role of ideas explains why he wrote extensively on the collective action of intellectuals and their responsibility as an elite group since

---

7   Claudia Sunna. "Dual Development Models in Historical Perspective," in *Development Economics in the Twenty-First Century;* D. Gualerzi, eds. (London: Routledge, 2015).

8   Celso Furtado, *Development and Underdevelopment.* Berkeley, CA: University of California Press, 1964.

9   R. Prebisch and G. M Cabanas. "El desarrollo económico de la América Latina y algunos de sus principales problemas." *El trimestre económico* 16, no. 3 (1949): 347–431.

10 Joseph Love. "Raul Prebisch and the Origins of the Doctrine of the Unequal Exchange." *Latin American Research Review* 15, no. 3 (1980): 47–72.

11 Alatas, *The Myth of Lazy Native,* 17.

HIDDEN CONNECTIONS

his early days as a young Muslim intellectual in the magazine "Progressive Islam." His other 1977 book by Frank Cass – "Intellectuals in the Developing Region" – further explores this classic theme by linking a critique of colonialism to a search for intellectual creativity. The book was sparked by Alatas' engagement with Malaysian politics in the late 1960s and his failed efforts to organize a true modern democratic movement that transcended ethnic cleavages.

One of Alatas' key ideas in this book is that Western colonialism in Southeast Asia created schools, universities, and bureaucracies, but the spirit of science and critical inquiry was not promoted. He draws extensively from the Russian example to explain the divorce between intellectuals and ruling elites in developing societies. He writes that: "The incomplete nature of the modernization process, the substance without the spirit, is the cause of the prevailing backwardness of the developing societies."[12]

Although Alatas' diagnosis is pessimistic, he puts a strong faith in the possible role of intellectuals in the developing societies. He claims that the failures of postcolonial nations must be addressed by a vibrant intellectual community, which is still lacking in these societies. The task of this community is the following:

> ... to help formulate a sociology of elites suitable to their surroundings. The method of the sociology of knowledge should be applied. New concepts should be created. Existing ones like bankrupt elites and decadent elites, should be operationally defined.[13]

At the end of the book, Alatas presents a concept of development based on his intellectual creed. He lists several features of development, such as the prevalence of rational behavior in all dimensions of life; a fair income distribution; good standards of living; lack of foreign control over local society; education and literacy, etc. This political agenda is similar to left-leaning ideas that were popular among Latin American intellectual communities in the post WWII era, from mild reformist programs to more radical utopias, which gained momentum after the Cuban Revolution in 1959.Syed Farid Alatas provides an interesting insight for explaining these similarities, which will be fully explored in the next two sections. While explaining Alatas' relation towards Marxism and socialism, Farid Alatas states that:

---

12   Alatas, *Intellectuals*, 78–79.
13   Alatas, *Intellectuals*, 109.

To my mind, Alatas' relatively positive assessment of socialism and selective approach to Marx can be explained in terms of his overall orientation to the question of the relationship between First World and Third World social science.[14]

Farid stresses the concept of endogenous intellectual creativity as a key to understand his father's sociology. This means that an autonomous tradition of social science must be based on a critical appropriation of the so-called "Western" ideas and on the recognition of the conditions of peripheral societies. That is why the sociology of knowledge was a starting point for almost every analysis put forward by Hussein Alatas.

Alatas maintained a huge interest in the sociology of knowledge for most of his life, particularly in the works of Karl Mannheim. In 1955, Alatas published in the 7–8 edition of "Progressive Islam" a short piece on the famous German sociologist in which he critically engages with relationism and its assertions on truth and knowledge.[15] This analysis is coherent with his intellectual project, which rested on a search for an autonomous social science tradition that preserved the universal features of scientific reasoning while recognizing the historical contexts that shaped its application. In one of his latest texts, Hussein Alatas criticized the indigenization program, claiming that science rests on universal concepts and methods, although the selection of problems and issues must be guided by criteria of relevance.[16] Therefore, his blasting attacks on intellectual imperialism did not target science as such but imitative thinking instead. He believed that regarding science as purely "Western" was a common mistake made by peripheral intellectuals that were unable to differentiate between what is contingent and what is universal.

This also holds true for many critical sociologists in the global periphery, who drew on Mannheim's works and supported ideas of planned development to help their nations to achieve national liberation. The balance between First World and Third World sociology described by Syed Farid Alatas does not apply only to his father; a significant number of Latin American intellectuals also managed to combine professional sociology and critical perspectives on Eurocentric views. In the next section, I shall explore this balance.

---

14   Syed Farid Alatas, "Alatas and Shari'ati on Socialism," 172.

15   Syed Hussein Alatas, "Karl Manheim (1894–1947)," *Progressive Islam*, 7–8 (1955): 4.

16   Syed Hussein Alatas, "Intellectual Imperialism: Definition, Traits, and Problems," *Asian Journal of Social Science* 28, no. 1 (2000): 23–45.

HIDDEN CONNECTIONS   461

2   Development and Knowledge in Latin American Sociology

In the 1960s and 1970s, development and imperialism were crucial issues in
Latin American sociology. Some of the major texts written at that time bear
striking similarities with Hussein Alatas' ideas. I would like to begin this search
for intellectual affinities with a key text by Rodolfo Stavenhagen, entitled "Siete
tesis equivocadas sobre América Latina" (The Seven Erroneous Theses about
Latin America).[17]

This text came out in 1965, in a charged political context in both Mexico and
Latin America. Stavenhagen was trained as an anthropologist at the National
School of Anthropology and History in the 1950s and then joined the National
Indigenist Institute, where he witnessed the contradictions of the policies
of integration that contributed to maintaining indigenous populations in a
subaltern position in Mexican society. After a few years teaching at National
Autonomous University of Mexico (UNAM), he defended his PhD in Paris
under the supervision of the famous colonialist scholar George Balandier.[18]
Stavenhagen also circulated in Latin America, and in 1964 spent a year in
the Latin American Centre for Social Sciences Research (CLAPCS), where he
gained familiarity with the dominant functionalist theories on modernization. CLAPCS was a UNESCO-sponsored institution created in 1957 as part of a
global effort to increase science capabilities in the global periphery. It became
an important hub for the community of social scientists in the region, but the
sequence of military coups that broke democracy in Latin America heavily
affected the resilience of the institution.

The Seven Erroneous These about Latin America condensed this early intellectual trajectory. On the one hand, it was a reaction against modernization
theories that rested on rigid dichotomies between modern and traditional
societies. On the other hand, it took issue with some assumptions associated
with Latin American Marxism that were regarded by the author as deeply
Eurocentric and flawed.

One of the main contentions of Stavenhagen is that the so-called "backward
sectors" of economy in Latin America performed a decisive role in reproduc-
ing global capitalism through the exploitation of cheap labor, particularly of

---

17   Rodolfo Stavenhagen, 1973 (1965) "Siete tesis equivocadas sobre América Latina," in
      Tres ensayos sobre America Latina, ed. R. Stavenhagen, Ernesto Laclau, Ruy M. Marini.
      (Barcelona: Anagrama, 1965/1973): 7–41.
18   E. Rodriguez Domingues, ""Seven Erroneous Theses about Latin America" and the
      Emergence of a New Mexican Anthropology," *Latin American Perspectives* 45 no. 2 (2018):
      85–94.

Indigenous groups. Stavenhagen had been working on the concept of "internal colonialism" with his colleague Pablo González Casanova to explain how modernization in Mexico was based on the subaltern integration of these Indigenous communities. Consequently, there was no single path from "tradition" to "modernity" as Latin American modern societies were based on the unequal relations between classes and ethnical groups.

The seven theses criticized by the Mexican anthropologist derived from this dualist perspectives. For instance, the idea that middle classes were modernizing actors and that national bourgeoisie would be interested in leading a struggle against imperialism was a deeply flawed one, because it was based on an evolutionist perspective that failed to understand the role of backwardness in engendering capital accumulation.

Stavenhagen also targeted the discourse on "mestizaje," which had been influential in the field of *indigenismo* in both Mexico and Latin America. The intellectuals who supported the "mestizaje" thesis claimed that Indigenous people would be acculturated in the modernizing Latin American nation-states, as they would eventually melt together with white groups thus engendering a future "Latin" people who could be bearers of nationality. Stavenhagen criticized this culturalist idea and argued instead that Indigenous in Mexico provided cheap labor for "national" capitalism development and thus remained second-class citizens. Full integration could only be achieved through the demise of internal colonialism.

The concept of "internal colonialism," which would be highly influential in the years to come, is a nice example of the endogenous intellectual creativity supported by Hussein Alatas.[19] Much like his Southeast Asian colleague, Stavenhagen drew on modern social sciences and Marxian concepts, but criticized the naïve application of such theories to non-European realities that required an autonomous intellectual exercise. On the one hand, Stavenhagen pointed out how modernization theories depicted a single path from "tradition" to "modernity" that overlooked the dynamics of underdevelopment and global capitalism. On the other hand, he also targeted the Marxist thesis that believed that capitalism would erase ethnic cleavages and promote a homogenizing process of modernization.

The hidden connections between Syed Hussein Alatas and Latin America do not stop at Mexico. The works of Brazilian Luiz de Aguiar Costa Pinto, who was a key figure in Latin American sociology, provides another good piece of evidence. Costa Pinto was trained as a social scientist at the University of Brazil

---

19   Ibid.

HIDDEN CONNECTIONS

(currently named Federal University of Rio de Janeiro), graduating in 1942, and then took a post as assistant professor in the same institution. During the following years, Costa Pinto gained more recognition and eventually became the first director of CLAPCS (1958–1961).

Costa Pinto's work must be seen in a broader context, shaped by the exportation of modernization theories from the US and its reception in Latin America in the 1960s. Historians of the discipline have already pointed out that these theories were closely linked to the science-military complex that emerged in the late 1940s in the USA, in what is known today as "Cold War social science." Neils Gilman, for instance, argues that modernization theory reflected postwar American liberalism and its mix of optimism about Americanizing the world and insecurity about the global status of the United States in face of Third World uprisings.[20] Mark Solovey calls attention to the nexus between the Ford Foundation and the military system in crafting a social science that promoted scientism and a strong belief in social engineering.[21] Solovey argues that Ford poured hundreds of millions of dollars during the 1960s into international research projects that investigated how to "safely" develop poor countries to avoid the threat of communism. These projects were based on a discourse about the scientific rigor of the "behavioral sciences," which was essential to legitimize modernization theories within the military establishment. These theories were eventually spread throughout the Third World, generating a vast body of scholarship on the paths to development and democracy.

One of Costa Pinto's most famous books is a collection of lectures on development delivered at Brazilian universities in the mid-1960s. The book, *Desenvolvimento Econômico e Transição Social* (Economic Development and Social Transition) sums up the most significant contributions he made to theories of development and modernization.[22]

In the first chapter, Costa Pinto differentiates between modernization and development. While the former means a process of economic growth that increases consumption and changes the mentality of middle and upper strata, development is considered as a global process of change that affects the whole structure of society. In this sense, he regards modernization as an ethnocentric

---

20 Neils Gilman, *Mandarins of the Future: Modernization Theory in Cold War America.* Baltimore: JHU Press, 2003.

21 Mark Solovey, *Shaky Foundations: The Politics-Patronage-Social Science Nexus in Cold War America.* New Brunswick, NJ: Rutgers University Press, 2013.

22 Luiz. de A. Costa Pinto. *Desenvolvimento Econômico e Transição Social.* Rio de Janeiro: Civilização Brasileira, 1970.

project that reinforces the power of traditional elites without raising the general living standards of the entire population.

Costa Pinto also argues that development is a planned process that requires drive and intention. This means that intellectuals and experts play a decisive role in this process, as science becomes a fundamental tool to raise awareness about structural problems and the proper ways for solving them. This faith in the organizing powers of intellectuals bears similarities with Alatas' belief that developing societies could achieve true development only through a rational process based on a solid power of will. Costa Pinto moreover shares with the Malaysian sociologist a positive assessment of planned development close to socialist perspectives (the Brazilian was a former member of the Communist party).

In fact, the role of intellectuals in developing societies was a key topic for Costa Pinto, who writes on the problem of alienation in the fourth chapter of the book. Costa Pinto begins the text drawing on North American scholarship on intellectuals (mainly Shills, Parsons and Hofstader), arguing that the historical situation in Latin America was quite different from the United States due to different levels of professionalization and social differentiation. The Latin American case also differed from other Third World contexts, particularly Asia and Africa, where decolonization was recent and gave intellectuals a leading role they did not have in modern Latin American.

Costa Pinto then introduces a conceptual discussion on alienation, drawing on Marx, Gramsci, Weber, and other Western canonical thinkers. His goal is to demonstrate that a shared experience of disconnection and dissatisfaction is a common thread for intellectual groups on the margins of European civilization – Russia being the paradigmatic case. The alienation of the Russian intelligentsia fed utopian and messianic visions that reflected the lack of place in the social order for such groups – a common topic for the peripheral sociology of knowledge, which is also key in the reflections of Syed Hussein Alatas.

Costa Pinto closes this reflection on intellectuals arguing that alienation could turn into a creative force if intellectuals were able to reconcile their feeling of inadequacy with a reasonable agenda of social change, articulating their ideas to promote coordinated processes of transformation. The way Costa Pinto defines "creative alienation" has strong similarities with Hussein Alatas' views on endogenous intellectual creativity, which could be fostered by intellectuals in developing regions who were able to employ the methods of social science without mimicking the set of problems and values of their European counterparts.

3 Concluding Remarks

The comparisons I traced in this chapter demonstrate how rich and powerful the thought of Hussein Alatas is. While he is mostly remembered for his contribution to postcolonial scholarship, I would argue that we must shed light on his role in the global history of sociology. The Latin American connection I outlined is a first step towards this effort, but much remains to be done.

Firstly, one needs to scrutinize the role of ECLA in shaping concepts and arguments that would later be widely used in sociological discourses in the Third World. If we want to move from simply identifying intellectual affinities to empirically analyzing connections and receptions, we must study the circulation of ECLA's theories and its different outcomes in particular locations. How did economists and sociologists exchange ideas, theories, and frameworks during the 1950s and 1960s? Which were the main events and institutions that contributed to disseminating books, working papers and articles by Prebisch and Furtado?

In a recent text, Edward Baring argues that we need an archival concept of international exchanges to deal with such problems.[23] Baring states that one should not restrict "contexts" to physical locations, because we can think of the former as transnational archives that span nationalities and physical spaces. Following Baring's suggestion, we can think of ECLA's global discursive communities as a kind of transnational intellectual archive for the Third World. Therefore, we must study not only books and journal articles, but syllabi, magazines, convention proceedings, and other textual sources that allow us to infer how ideas and references circulated in the Global South.

Secondly, one needs to seriously study the footnotes and references in the works of Syed Hussein Alatas to demonstrate to what extent he drew on ECLA's transnational intellectual archive. New tools available for Digital Humanities scholars can greatly contribute to expand our knowledge about editions, collections and publishing houses that played a pivotal role in Third World connections.

Finally, new comparative studies are required. Language issues are well known barriers, but we must move from studying just single intellectuals from the South to analyzing larger historical contexts. This current volume on Hussein Alatas is a relevant step in the right direction.

---

23 Edward Baring. "Ideas on the Move: Context in Transnational Intellectual," Journal of the History of Ideas 77, no. 4 (2016): 567–587.

Bibliography

Alatas, Syed Farid. "Alatas and Shari'ati on Socialism: Autonomous Social Science-and Occidentalism." In *Local and Global: Social Transformation in Southeast Asia*, edited by R. Hassan. Leiden: Brill Academic Publishers, 2004.

Alatas, Syed Hussein. "The Captive Mind in Development Studies (Part 1)," *International Social Science Journal* 24, (1972): 9–25.

Alatas, Syed Hussein, "Intellectual Imperialism: Definition, Traits, and Problems." *Asian Journal of Social Science* 28, no. 1 (2000): 23–45.

Alatas, Syed Hussein. *Intellectuals in Developing Societies*. London: Frank Cass, 1977.

Alatas, Syed Hussein, "Karl Manheim (1894–1947)." *Progressive Islam*, 7–8 (1955): 4.

Alatas, Syed Hussein. *The Myth of the Lazy Native: A Study of the Image of the Malays, the Filipinos and the Javanese from the XVI to the XX Century and Its Function in the Ideology of Colonial Capitalism*. London: Frank Cass, 1977.

Baring, Edward. "Ideas on the Move: Context in Transnational Intellectual." *Journal of the History of Ideas* 77, no. 4 (2016): 567–587.

Boecke, J.H. ed., *Indonesian Economics: the concept of dualism in theory and policy*. The Hague: W. van Hoeve, 1961.

Connell, Raewyn. *Southern Theory: The Global Dynamics of Knowledge in Social Sciences*. London: Routledge, 1997.

Costa Pinto, Luiz de A. *Desenvolvimento Econômico e Transição Social*. Rio de Janeiro: Civilização Brasileira, 1970.

Devés-Valdez, Eduardo. *Pensamiento Periférico. Uma tesis interpretativa global*. Santiago: Idea-USACH, 2012.

Furtado, Celso. *Development and Underdevelopment*. Berkeley, CA: University of California Press, 1964.

Gilman, Neils. *Mandarins of the Future: Modernization Theory in Cold War America*. Baltimore: JHU Press, 2003.

Love, Joseph. "Raul Prebisch and the Origins of the Doctrine of the Unequal Exchange." *Latin American Research Review* 15, no. 3 (1980): 47–72.

Marcelo E. Maia, João. "History of Sociology and the Quest for Intellectual Autonomy in the Global South: The Cases of Alberto Guerreiro Ramos and Syed Hussein Alatas." *Current Sociology* 62, no. 7 (2014): 1097–1115.

Prebisch, R. and G.M. Cabanas. "El desarrollo económico de la América Latina y algunos de sus principales problemas." *El trimestre económico* 16, no. 3 (1949): 347–431.

Rodriguez Domingues, E. ""Seven Erroneous Theses about Latin America" and the Emergence of a New Mexican Anthropology". *Latin American Perspectives* 45 no. 2 (2018): 85–94.

Solovey, Mark. *Shaky Foundations: The Politics-Patronage-Social Science Nexus in Cold War America*. New Brunswick, NJ: Rutgers University Press, 2013.

Stavenhagen, Rodolfo. "Siete tesis equivocadas sobre América Latina." In *Tres ensayos sobre America Latina,* edited by R. Stavenhagen, Ernesto Laclau, and Ruy M. Marini. Barcelona: Anagrama, 1965/1973.

Sunna, Claudia. "Dual Development Models in Historical Perspective." In *Development Economics in the Twenty-First Century,* edited by D. Gualerzi. London: Routledge, 2015.

Index

Abaza, Mona 46, 72, 406, 445
Abdulhamid II 284
academic corruption 95–96, 106–111
academic dependency 11, 64–65, 102, 105–106, 109, 435
academic imperialism 63–64, 95, 100, 106–108, 111–112, 335, 422, 433, 437, 444
Adorno, Theodor 78, 89
ahistoricism 345
Alatas, Syed Farid 4, 12, 20, 44, 72, 104, 212, 392, 397, 434–435, 438–441, 445, 459–460
Alexandrowicz, C. H. 277–278
al-Fasi, Muhammad 290
Al-i Ahmad, Jalal 81, 95, 97–100, 102–103, 105, 109, 383–384, 390, 392
alliance 123, 184, 277, 284, 285, 350
al-Rahuni, Ahmad 290
alternative IR discourses 347
American Medical Association 26
amok 32, 226
Amrikazadegi 95–100, 102–103, 105
anarchy 338–348
Angkatan 45 381
Angkatan Sasterawan 50 (ASAS 50') 381–386, 388
Anquetil-Duperron, Abraham Hyacinthe 280
anthropology 117, 119, 149–151, 212, 240–241, 258, 265, 267, 270–271, 401, 421, 440, 461
architecture 28, 31, 181, 280
Arslan, Shakib 290
Asad, Talal 193, 401, 423
assimilation 18, 31, 43, 88, 120, 196, 297, 334, 457
Association of Southeast Asian Nations (ASEAN) 346, 350–351, 424
autonomous history 425
autonomous knowledge 2, 9–21, 53–76, 378, 457

Balafrij, Ahmad 290
bathtub 38
Bebalisma 4, 14–15, 18, 45, 123, 333

Behrangi, Samad 95, 99–100, 102–103, 105, 109, 383
Belinsky, Vissarion Grigoryevich 280
benchmarking 341
Beng-Lan, Goh 438–439
Benjamin, Walter 78, 335
Bentham, Jeremy 278–279
Benumeya, Rodolfo Gil 289
Bhabha, Hommi 252, 254, 259
bias(es) 55, 77–79, 91, 121, 123, 125–126, 147, 152, 170, 229, 238, 256, 262, 266, 278, 285, 293, 336–338, 341, 346, 350, 402, 437
Binnuna, M'hammad 290
Blaut, James Morris 293
Boeke, Julius H. 425, 428, 457
Boestamam 383
Borneo 56, 425, 441–444
Bourdieu, Pierre 272, 408
Buitenzorg (Bogor) 4, 420
Burgess, John William 275–276
Burke, Edmund 280

capitalism 12, 54–55, 58, 60, 62–63, 70, 115, 122–123, 161, 168–169, 173, 194, 199–200, 214, 234, 237–238, 240, 242, 247, 249, 263–267, 270, 293, 296–297, 344, 348, 401, 432, 435, 442–443, 455–458, 461–462
Captivity Narrative 36
Carr, Edward Hallett 293
Catch-22 24
César Pelli 31
Chaudhuri, Amit 29
Chekov 30
Chen, Peter S.J. 424
China 123, 198, 201–204, 218, 263, 297, 327, 340, 346, 350–352, 358, 361, 398, 401, 405–406, 427
Chinese 32–33, 37, 44, 60, 118, 121, 123, 126, 200–201, 212, 217–218, 230, 263, 351, 359, 387, 405–407, 427
Chrisitian 35, 88, 121, 130–131, 146–147, 149, 192, 261, 264, 269, 275, 278–279, 284, 288, 292
Cita Sempurna 15, 376, 378–380, 388–393

colonialism 1–2, 9, 20, 27, 31–32, 36, 39–40, 43–44, 46, 53–54, 57, 62–64, 69–70, 102, 119, 124, 126, 138, 146–149, 153, 158, 161, 170, 176–177, 195, 199, 217, 239, 246–260, 265, 270–273, 276, 282–283, 287, 290–291, 293–296, 298, 337, 344–347, 349, 359, 401, 436, 456, 458–459, 462
colonialist 32, 217, 271, 342–343, 425, 461
colonized mind 39, 77–78, 84, 89
commerce 56, 223, 339–340, 411
communism 17, 36, 128, 130, 139, 143, 463
Confident Mind 38
conflict 60, 80, 139, 157, 175, 195, 197, 216, 266, 285–286, 325, 331, 338–341, 343, 345, 384, 387, 427–427, 431, 435–436
containment 269, 350
creative mind 12, 18–20, 31
creativity 28, 31, 37, 43, 46, 71, 94, 98, 102, 109–110, 119–121, 139, 143, 438, 456, 459–460, 462, 464
critical tradition 19–20, 72
Cromwell, Oliver 286

Dabashi, Hamid 2, 384
Daneshvar, Simin 383, 387–388, 390, 392
Dawud, Muhammad 290
de Certeau, Michel 294
de Gobineau, Joseph Arthur 275
de Vattel, Emmerich 278
decolonial 39, 45, 54, 57, 70, 72, 246–248, 250, 252–253, 255–258, 320, 343
decoloniality 39
decolonization 1, 199, 246, 257–258, 337, 343, 352, 438, 464
Derrida, Jacques 24
developing world 9–12, 189, 344, 435
dialectics of progress 428
double captivity 45–46
double-consciousness 80–81
Du Bois, W.E.B. 80–81
Dudley Seers 22
Dutch East Indies 1, 4, 420
Dutch New Guinea 421

economic development 12, 29, 37, 41, 189, 199–203, 205, 215, 224, 241, 416, 463
engagement 97, 115, 211–212, 241, 247, 249–250, 253, 258, 350–351, 357, 376, 413, 422, 426, 432, 440–441, 459

Engels, Friedrich 61
Enghelabi 108, 110
epistemic 62–63, 213, 242, 336–337, 342–344
epistemiscide 84, 91
epistemology 91, 138, 192, 212, 241, 251, 274, 343, 399, 413
Erasmus students 36
Ethnos 85–88
Eurocentrism 67, 101, 168, 247–248, 250, 253–256, 259, 273, 278, 280, 316, 325–330, 337–338, 342–343, 346, 353, 455
Evans, Grant 430–431
Evers, Hans-Dieter 423–424
evolutionary theory 271, 430

false consciousness 60, 79, 227, 266, 436
Fanon, Frantz 27, 109, 171, 229, 254, 335
Farang Rafteh 100, 103, 107–108, 110
Farhangian 100, 103
feminist 43, 161, 293
Fernando, Lloyd 30
field slave 79
food 26, 28, 45, 218, 263
fool 4, 14–15, 397
Foucault 171, 249, 316, 396
Franco, Francisco 288–290
Frankfurt School 2, 20, 78
Freire, Paulo 27
Freud, Sigmund 85, 128
functioning intellectual 14–15, 310, 322–324, 326–327, 329–330
Furnivall, John S. 426
future proof/proofing 341

Garbutt, Nick 444
gender studies 31
geographical constructs 337
geopolitics 45, 337, 341, 344, 347–351
Gerakan 1, 3, 22, 115, 168, 374, 416
Ghalib, Mirza Asadullah 284
Gharbzadegi 81, 95–100, 102, 105, 109, 383–384, 390
Global South 1, 66, 193, 203, 205, 212, 344–349, 353, 358, 372, 399, 413, 456, 465
globalisation 26
Gonggrijp, George 297
Gorer, Geoffrey 270
Graf, Arndt 437

Gramsci, Antonio   24, 161, 257, 316, 330–331, 335, 396, 416, 426–427, 435, 464
Grosfoguel, Ramon   257
Gungwu, Wang   3

Habermas, Jürgen   86, 193
Hamzah, Tengku Razaleigh   37, 182, 381
Hassan, Riaz   435
Hastings, Warren   146, 280
Hegelian view   431
hegemony   27, 63, 77, 101, 148, 246, 251, 282–283, 296, 316, 342–344, 396, 399, 407, 431, 435, 437–438
Heidegger, Martin   261
Herzen, Alexander   280, 309
Higgott, Richard   429
higher education policy   341
Hirschman, Charles   229, 411
historiography   27, 174, 274, 285, 293, 311, 327, 416
Hobbes, Thomas   338, 402
humanitarian   33, 55, 124, 377, 389, 395
Huntington, Samuel   285
hybridity   252–253, 256, 258–259
hypocognition   89–92

ideals of excellence   15–18
imitation   12, 20, 28, 34–35, 38–39, 45, 53, 65, 98, 101, 103, 109, 112, 130, 138, 149, 155, 218, 254–256, 258, 352, 378, 383
imperialism   1, 19, 27–28, 30–31, 39, 54–55, 60–68, 85, 95, 99–103, 106–109, 111–112, 115, 124, 143, 193, 214, 247, 249–250, 253, 255, 285, 289, 293–295, 297–298, 335, 337, 346, 348–349, 351, 377, 422, 433, 437, 444, 456, 458, 460–462
inauthenticity (uneigentlichkeit)   82, 87
Indians   37, 147–148, 150, 212
Infante, Blas   289
inferiority   28–29, 41, 53, 83–84, 163, 251, 254, 295
integration   196, 279, 400, 430, 461–462
international relations   45, 192, 273, 277–280, 336–356, 457
Iqbal, Muhammad   2, 132, 136, 289–290
Iranian revolution   120–121, 139, 191, 383, 390
Iserloh, Erwin   262
Italian publishers   30
Italy   41, 45, 344

Jadong   377, 379
Japan   28, 44, 120–121, 123, 283, 297, 309, 344, 348, 350, 358–359, 398, 401, 405
Jefferson, Thomas   26
Jews   88, 116, 289, 291

Kahn, Joel S.   433
Kazancigil, Ali   23
Khaldun, Ibn   67–72, 129, 131–132, 171, 255, 347, 397, 399, 406, 410, 441
Khan, Sayyid Ahmad   284
Khomeini, Ruhollah   98, 105
Kidd, Benjamin   296
Kincaid, Jamaica   40
knowledge production   10, 64, 72, 77, 90, 107–108, 256, 337, 343, 345, 397, 403, 457
Koch, D.M.G.   123, 432
Kuala Lumpur   15, 22, 25, 31, 116, 397

Lane, Edward William   282
Latin America   63, 125, 191, 339, 424, 455–467
laziness   31, 58, 68, 82, 219, 224, 235, 323, 442
Leiden University   421
Lengyel, Peter   23–24
Lewis, Bernard   197
LGBT   31
Linklater, Andro   444
literary prize   30
longue durée   345
Luther, Martin   261–262

Maaruf, Shaharuddin   20, 44, 69, 72, 169, 172, 229
Maia, Joao Marcelo   256, 413
Maine, Henry   57, 281
Malaysian publishers   30
Mandeville, John   291
Mannheim, Karl   61–62, 71, 124, 131, 136, 170–171, 265–266, 271, 426, 435, 460
marginalize   213, 315, 349
markets   191, 339–340, 431
Marx, Karl   17, 59–61, 132, 191, 397, 402, 405, 411, 415, 426, 460, 464
May 13 Riots   22–23, 32
McVey, Ruth   428
Melaka   225–227, 229, 382–383
mental captivity   2, 27–28, 29, 65, 77–93, 95, 102, 106–109, 111–113, 115, 254, 438, 444
menticide   81–82

INDEX

Merriam, Charles Edward 275
MeToo 31
Mignolo, Walter 247–248, 255–257, 413
Mill, John Stuart 279, 401
Milosz, Czeslaw 10, 35–36, 94–95
mimicry 254
misogyny 31
Moghuls 339
Mohamad, Mahathir 32, 175, 182, 217, 436, 443
Moosavi, Leon 45, 57, 256
Mosaddegh, Mohmmad 104
multiple modernities 193–194
Myrdal, Gunnar 36, 358

Nair, Devan 36–37
Napoleon 278, 286
narcissism 83–84, 88
nation state 128, 139, 190, 225, 338, 340, 343, 345, 409, 415, 462
National University of Singapore 4, 22, 68, 118, 168, 171–172, 174, 396, 421, 439
nativism 18, 27, 43
negative dialectics 89, 92
neo-colonialism 64, 153, 349
nepotism 56, 107–108
New Delhi 22, 153
New Economic Policy (NEP) 37, 240
New Testament 35
Nobel Prize 36, 38, 146
Noor, Farish A. 20, 44, 72, 445

Oblomovism 24
obscurantism 27
occidentalism 248
occidentosis 81, 95, 103, 107–108
Oedipus complex 26
ontology 80, 274
orientalism 1, 18, 67, 69, 98, 101, 119, 121, 125, 126, 168–169, 171, 195, 211, 213, 219, 246–249, 287, 422, 428, 433–434, 437–438, 444
Orwell, George 261, 274
Ottoman Empire 270, 279, 284, 291, 340

paradigm 29, 160, 192, 240, 258, 263, 268, 325, 330–331, 343, 346–348, 403, 429, 441

peace 19, 33, 66, 134, 214, 268–269, 279, 294, 342–343, 345, 389
Peace of Westphalia 338
periodization 345
Petronas Twin Towers 31
Pijper, Frederic 128, 421
political economy 64, 153, 240, 342, 344, 348, 401, 428–429, 431, 442
political philosophy 2, 54–55, 57, 68, 265, 267, 377–378, 380, 393, 436
Polo, Marco 291
post-colonial 27–28, 31, 36, 64, 161, 212–217, 234–239, 247, 273, 293, 316, 335, 422, 435, 437, 456–459, 465
proteophobia 87–89
Prudente, J. Cede 444

Quadrilateral Security Dialogue (QUAD) 350–351
Quah, Stella R. 439
Queen Victoria 284
Quijano, Aníbal 251
Qutb, Sayyid 17, 280

racism 276, 314, 346, 348
Raffles Must Fall 34
Raffles, Thomas Stamford 1, 31, 33–34, 54–58, 60, 68, 124, 214, 267–269, 425, 444
regnant paradigm 429
religionswissenschaft 90
resistant-consciousness 79, 88
revisionist 55, 350
Revolusi Mental 32, 126, 216–217, 222, 234, 238, 241
Rhodes Must Fall 34
Rodan, Garry 431
Romein, Jan 428
Royal Tropical Institute 421
ruling class 32, 70, 168, 171–180, 184, 220, 226, 228–229, 238–239, 266, 373

sadomasochistic symhedonia 87
Said, Edward W. 1, 9, 30, 55, 109, 126, 171, 211, 248–249, 316, 325, 433–435, 444
Saunders, Graham 444
Savushun 387–388
Scandinavia 28
schadenfreude 87

INDEX 473

Schmitt, Carl   264
Schrieke, Bernard J.O.   123, 426, 428, 432
scientific power   38
Scott, James C.   425, 430
Second Malaysia Plan   31, 33
secularity/secularisation   189, 192, 198
self-loathing   29, 82
Selwyn, Tom   444
Semenya, Caster   267
Shariati, Ali   2, 9, 40, 325, 335, 392
Shumei, Okawa   383
silence   55, 239, 349, 382, 434
Sinha, Vineeta   152, 435
social change   19, 40, 68, 133, 162, 168, 171–172,
   177, 179, 193, 296, 328, 349, 381, 388, 423,
   425, 427, 429–430, 444, 464
socialism   12–14, 19, 22, 119–120, 122, 124, 129,
   160, 170–171, 459–460
Society for International Development   22
sociology of religion   69, 118, 189, 190–193,
   263, 432
sociopathy (sociopath)   83
South Africa   148
South China Sea   346, 350–351
sovereignty   212, 270, 277, 284–285, 340, 343,
   358, 458
spaghetti Westernization   45
stability   147, 269, 294, 338, 343, 400
Stamford Raffles, Thomas   1, 31, 33, 54–55, 57,
   214, 267, 425
State University of Utrecht   421
Stockholm Syndrome   84
subaltern   161, 229, 257, 315–316, 461–462
superiority   11, 28, 33, 53, 58, 61, 83–84, 89,
   107, 146, 205, 215, 254, 270, 280, 295, 457
sustainability   111

Tagore, Rabrindanath   39
Taj al-Salatin   392
Taylor, John G.   424
Thiong'o, Ngugi wa   39, 109
threat   64, 79–80, 88–89, 109, 128, 342, 348,
   350–351, 374, 393, 442, 463
transsexuality   31
Turgenev   30
Turton, Andrew   424

Uncle Tomism   24

UNESCO   23–24, 398–399, 455, 461
United Malays National Organization
   (UMNO)   32, 126, 173, 175, 179, 182–184
United States   28, 119, 143, 146, 151, 264, 267,
   276, 285, 344, 346–349, 352, 358, 396,
   398–399, 401, 407, 424, 456, 463–464
universalism   29, 253, 277–279, 345, 399, 434
University of Amsterdam   1, 53, 61, 118, 135,
   357, 420–421
University of Hull   422–423
University of Macerata   36
University of Malaya   1, 115–116, 118, 128, 397

van Baal, Jan   421
van Leur, Jacob C.   123, 425, 428, 432
Vanmour, Jean-Baptiste   270
Vermeulen, Han F.   428
Volksgemeinschaften   86
Voltaire   286, 340, 401
von Herder, Johann Gottfried   293

Wallerstein, Immanuel   240, 273, 339, 348,
   407, 409, 411, 415
Weber thesis   31, 122–124
Weber, Max   115, 122, 123, 136, 164, 191, 263,
   401–402, 432
Wertheim, Willem (Wim)   128, 420–454
West-bashing   40
West-centrism   337–338, 342
Westernization   9, 26, 40, 45, 95, 97–100, 189,
   193–194, 205, 251
Westoxication   95, 383–384
Westphalian bias   338
Wheaton, Henry   279
Willensgemeinschaften   86
Winkler, Heinrich August   285
Woolf, Virginia   293
world order   280, 283, 342–344, 348, 350
World Systems Theory (WST)   348–349
World War I (WWI)   345–346, 348, 401, 407
World War II (WWII)   94, 112, 123, 143, 151,
   264, 295, 297, 337, 343–344, 348, 357–
   359, 407, 456
writers   9, 29–30, 72, 134, 173, 219, 286, 296,
   315, 323, 346, 378, 381, 385–388, 390–
   392, 404, 411, 425, 429, 434

X, Malcolm   79, 334–335

xenia 81
xenocentrism (xenocentric) 86–87
xenophilia 85–86
xenophobia 43, 85
xenos 85–87

Yew, Lee Kuan 29, 370

Zeitgeist 120, 341